The New International Financial System:
Analyzing the Cumulative Impact
of Regulatory Reform

World Scientific Studies in International Economics
(ISSN: 1793-3641)

The complete list of the published volumes in the series can be found at
http://www.worldscientific.com/series/wssie

48 World Scientific Studies in International Economics

The New International Financial System:
Analyzing the Cumulative Impact of Regulatory Reform

Editors

Douglas D. Evanoff
Federal Reserve Bank of Chicago, USA

Andrew G. Haldane
Bank of England, UK

George G. Kaufman
Loyola University Chicago, USA

World Scientific

NEW JERSEY · LONDON · SINGAPORE · BEIJING · SHANGHAI · HONG KONG · TAIPEI · CHENNAI · TOKYO

Published by

World Scientific Publishing Co. Pte. Ltd.
5 Toh Tuck Link, Singapore 596224
USA office: 27 Warren Street, Suite 401-402, Hackensack, NJ 07601
UK office: 57 Shelton Street, Covent Garden, London WC2H 9HE

Library of Congress Cataloging-in-Publication Data
Annual International Banking Conference (17th : 2014 : Federal Reserve Bank of Chicago)
  The new international financial system : analyzing the cumulative impact of regulatory reform /
edited by Douglas Evanoff, Andrew G Haldane, George Kaufman.
    pages cm. -- (World Scientific studies in international economics)
  "This volume contains the papers and keynote addresses delivered at the [seventeenth Annual
International Banking Conference held at the Federal Reserve Bank of Chicago in November 2014]."
  Includes bibliographical references and index.
  ISBN 978-9814678322 (hardcover) -- ISBN 9814678325 (hardcover)
  1. International finance--Congresses. 2. International finance--Laws and legislation--Congresses.
3. Financial institutions--Congresses. 4. Financial institutions--Law and legislation--Congresses.
5. Banks and banking, International--Congresses. I. Evanoff, Douglas Darrell, 1951–
II. Haldane, Andrew G. III. Kaufman, George G. IV. Title.
  HG3881.A644 2014
  332'.042--dc23

                                                                        2015015476

British Library Cataloguing-in-Publication Data
A catalogue record for this book is available from the British Library.

Cover Illustration by John Dixon

In-house Editor: Philly Lim

Typeset by Stallion Press
Email: enquiries@stallionpress.com

Printed in Singapore by B & Jo Enterprise Pte Ltd

Preface

In response to the Great Financial Crisis of 2007–10, and the perceived failure of market discipline in the financial sector, government regulation of the financial system was greatly expanded and intensified. This process culminated in the United States with the enactment of the Dodd–Frank Wall Street Reform and Consumer Protection Act in July 2010. Many other countries and official international organizations enacted similar measures. What new or modified government regulations were adopted? For what purpose? What impact have they had to date or are expected to have in the near and distant future? Were the regulatory changes 'just right' or did they overshoot or undershoot the optimum target and produce suboptimal results? If suboptimal, what corrective actions may need to be taken in the future?

On November 6–7, 2014, the 17th annual International Banking Conference was held at the Federal Reserve Bank of Chicago, cosponsored by the Chicago Fed and the Bank of England, to analyze and develop answers to these and similar questions. Nearly 200 financial policymakers, regulators, and practitioners, as well as financial researchers, scholars, and academics from some 25 countries attended the two-day conference and engaged in a lively discussion. As a result, the regulatory changes and the remaining issues were clarified.

The papers presented here, as chapters, focused in turn on the near-term effects of the new regulations on financial institutions and markets, the intermediate and mostly transitional effects being observed, and the longer-term potential steady-state outcomes for both the financial and real sectors of the economy. The conference concluded with a discussion of what should be done next.

This volume contains the keynote addresses (in Part I) and the papers (subsequent chapters) delivered at the conference. The volume is intended to bring the analyses and conclusions presented at the conference to a wider audience in order to clarify and improve understanding of the issues and to stimulate further discussion aimed at guiding future financial public policy.

Acknowledgments

Both the conference held at the Federal Reserve Bank of Chicago, November 6–7, 2014, and this book represent a joint effort of the Federal Reserve Bank of Chicago and the Bank of England. Various people at each institution contributed to the effort. The editors served as the principal organizers of the conference and would like to thank all the people from both organizations who contributed their time and energy to the effort. This includes the program committee consisting of Sarah Breeden, Iain de Weymarn, Andrew Haldane and Victoria Saporta from the Bank of England; Douglas Evanoff from the Federal Reserve Bank of Chicago; and George Kaufman from Loyola University Chicago. We would also like to thank Julia Baker, Ella Dukes, Rita Molloy and Sandra Mills for support efforts. Special mention should be accorded Kathryn Moran, who managed the Chicago Fed's web effort; Sandy Schneider, who expertly managed the conference administration; John Dixon who developed the art work for both the conference program and the book cover; as well as Helen O'D. Koshy and Sheila Mangler, who had the responsibility of preparing the manuscripts for the volume.

Contents

About the Editors

Douglas D Evanoff is a vice president and senior research advisor for banking and financial institutions in the economic research department of the Federal Reserve Bank of Chicago. He serves as an advisor to senior management of the Federal Reserve System on regulatory issues and is chairman of the Federal Reserve Bank of Chicago's annual 'International Banking Conference'. Evanoff's current research interests include financial regulation, consumer credit issues, mortgage markets, bank cost and merger analysis, payments system mechanisms and credit accessibility. Prior to joining the Chicago Fed, Evanoff was a lecturer in finance at Southern Illinois University and assistant professor at St. Cloud State University. He currently is an adjunct faculty member in the School of Business at DePaul University and is associate editor of *the Journal of Economics and Business* and the *Journal of Applied Banking and Finance*. He is also an institutional director on the board of the Midwest Finance Association. His research has been published both in academic and practitioner journals including the *American Economic Review, Journal of Financial Economics, Journal of Money, Credit and Banking, Journal of Financial Services Research,* and the *Journal of Banking and Finance,* among others. He has also published in numerous books and has edited a number of books addressing issues associated with financial institutions; most recently, *New Perspectives on Asset Price Bubbles*

(Oxford University Press), and Dodd-Frank Wall Street Reform and Consumer Protection Act (World Scientific Publishing Co Pte Ltd). He holds a PhD in economics from Southern Illinois University.

Andrew G Haldane is the Chief Economist at the Bank of England and Executive Director, Monetary Analysis and Statistics. He is a member of the Bank's Monetary Policy Committee. He also has responsibility for research and statistics across the Bank. In 2014, TIME magazine voted him one of the 100 most influential people in the world. Andrew has written extensively on domestic and international monetary and financial policy issues. He is co-founder of 'Pro Bono Economics', a charity which brokers economists into charitable projects.

George G Kaufman is the John F Smith Professor of Economics and Finance at Loyola University Chicago and a consultant to the Federal Reserve Bank of Chicago. From 1959 to 1970, he was at the Federal Reserve Bank of Chicago, and after teaching for ten years at the University of Oregon, he returned as a consultant to the Bank in 1981. He has also been a visiting professor at Stanford University, the University of California, Berkeley, and the University of Southern California, as well as a visiting scholar at the Reserve Bank of New Zealand, the Federal Reserve Bank of San Francisco, and the Office of the Comptroller of the Currency. He has also served as the deputy to the assistant secretary for economic policy at the US Department of the Treasury. He is co-editor of the Journal of Financial Stability; a founding co-editor of the Journal of Financial Services Research; past president of the Western Finance Association, Midwest Finance Association, and the North American Economics and Finance Association; president-elect of the Western Economic Association; past director of the American Finance Association; and co-chair of the Shadow Financial Regulatory Committee. Kaufman holds a PhD in economics from the University of Iowa.

Part I
Special Addresses

Financial Entropy and the Optimality of Over-regulation

— CHAPTER 1

- Alan S. Blinder
  Princeton University

Preview

One frequently hears, often as a complaint, about the financial regulatory 'pendulum' swinging too far in one direction or the other — from excessively tight regulation to excessively lax, and vice-versa. My concern in this paper is precisely with those swings. I will argue that, in fact, they may be optimal. Rather than searching for some sort of long-run equilibrium in which the marginal costs and marginal benefits of financial regulation are equated, we should expect a never-ending game of cat-and-mouse between the industry and its regulators in which first one side and then the other gains the upper hand — in a kind of cyclical equilibrium.[1]

Alan Blinder is the Gordon S. Rentschler Memorial Professor of Economics and Public Affairs at Princeton University and former Vice Chairman of the Board of Governors of the Federal Reserve System. He is a co-founder and Vice Chairman of Promontory Interfinancial Network and a Senior Advisor to Promontory Financial Group. It should be noted that financial regulation affects the businesses of both of these firms. The views expressed here are his own, however, and are not shared by any institutions with which he is, or has been, affiliated. Helpful comments from a number of conference participants are acknowledged and appreciated.

[1]I am hardly the first person to make such an observation. See, for example, Aizenman (2011) and, in less detail, Tirole (2014).

In true Minskyan fashion,[2] a period of financial tranquility — not to mention an asset price boom — begets regulatory complacency and deregulation as the industry, trumpeting its wondrous successes and ignoring its excesses, makes inroads against supervision and regulation. That regulatory laxity, however, hastens the inevitable crash, which brings harsher regulation in its wake — maybe even *over*-regulation. Both the tighter regulation and market participants' newfound attention to risk combine to create a far safer financial environment in which financial ructions become rare — for a while. Then the whole cycle repeats.

In this sort of world, the conceptual objective of policymakers should not be to move the financial system from a 'bad equilibrium' to a 'good equilibrium,' as economic models often assume, but rather to push the process, on average, in a positive direction. Because of what I will call 'financial entropy,' doing so will require periods of 'over-regulation.'

All this will be made more concrete and specific in III and IV below. Then I will breathe life into the conceptual framework by applying it to several current issues in financial regulation in Section V. But to set the stage, let's briefly consider why we have a financial industry and why we regulate it in the first place.

I. Why Do We Have Finance? Why Do We Regulate It?

While an exhaustive list would be lengthy, I think a financial system should serve four main purposes.

The first, though very important, will play no role here: creating, developing, and running cheap, efficient, and reliable payment mechanisms for financial transactions of all sorts — including, of course, cross-border transactions. The common metaphor 'financial plumbing' offers an appropriate image of how messy things can get if such mechanisms break down.

The other three purposes, which will be my focus, pertain to *mismatches* of some sort.

---

[2] See, for example, Minsky (1986).

Intermediation: Financial markets and financial institutions intermediate between savers and investors or, as I prefer to put it, between lenders and borrowers.[3] Over any period of time, some economic units (households, business firms, governments,...) have more funds coming in than going out; they want to be lenders. Other units have, or want to have, more funds going out than coming in; they may want to be borrowers. Financial markets and institutions help such prospective lenders and borrowers 'meet' to settle on prices, quantities, and other terms.

Maturity transformation: Such intermediation often involves maturity transformation because of mismatch between the two parties' desired contract lengths. The classic example, of course, is a bank, which borrows short from its depositors (the ultimate lenders, who want short-maturity assets) and lends long to its loan customers (the ultimate borrowers, who want longer-maturity liabilities). In such cases, the bank becomes the counterparty to each transaction, e.g., providing borrowers with long-term financing and lenders with short-term saving vehicles. In so doing, it exposes itself to maturity mismatch in the opposite direction. While this observation is trite, I repeat it here because I have often heard it claimed that financial intermediaries should *not* engage in maturity transformation; it's too dangerous. On the contrary, maturity transformation is one of the core functions of finance. The trick is to do it safely, which may involve e.g., moderation and/or hedging.

Stores of value: A third, closely related, mismatch involves moving value through time. The period of time may be short, as when a household wants to smooth consumption relative to a lumpy schedule of paychecks (weekly, monthly,...). Or it may be long, as when a worker wants to save for retirement. Naturally, different sorts of financial institutions and/or financial instruments have arisen to bridge gaps of different length (compare checking accounts with term life insurance). Once again, the financial firm takes the opposite side of each transaction: absorbing funds when customers want to invest them and returning funds when customers want to cash out. Activities like that can pose risks of illiquidity (or even of insolvency) to some financial institutions

---

[3] Not all lenders are savers, and not all borrowers are investors. In the lender-saver classification, equity providers count as 'lenders.'

(e.g., bank runs) but not to others (e.g., withdrawals from a mutual fund). It depends, among other things, on the nature of the instrument.

As long as all parties are well informed and there is sufficient competition — two big and important *ifs* — free markets should be able to handle all three of these mismatches well. So why, then, is finance so heavily regulated in virtually all societies? I group the answers into four broad categories:[4]

1. *To protect borrowers and lenders*: The two big *ifs* mentioned above must be vigorously protected; otherwise sophisticated parties will fleece the unsophisticated and/or monopolists will reap huge rents. This is familiar territory, hardly unique to finance.

2. *To protect taxpayers*: For many reasons, virtually every country provides some sort of government safety net to backstop (parts of) its financial system. Deposit insurance and the lender-of-last-resort function of central banks may be the most familiar examples, but there are others. Such a safety net tacitly turns the taxpayer into the 'counterparty of last resort.' And since most taxpayers have limited means and play no role in financial transactions that go awry, they must be protected by their government — perhaps by regulations that limit their exposure. So, for example, we have safety and soundness regulations designed to limit claims on the deposit insurance fund, orderly resolution procedures (such as least-cost resolution) to minimize taxpayer liability, Bagehot-like principles that take most of the risk out of central bank emergency lending, and various mechanisms designed to limit moral hazard.[5]

3. *To limit financial instability*: Moving closer now to the macroeconomic concerns on which I will concentrate, history amply demonstrates that financial instability can impose substantial spillover costs on third parties. Some of these costs take the form of extreme volatility in asset prices, that is, bubbles and crashes. Other costs

---

[4] Notice that 'to protect banks' does not make the list. The justification of the much-maligned 'too big to fail' doctrine is to protect the financial system and the economy.
[5] Critics will note that there are also rules and regulations that *exacerbate* moral hazard, which is a fair point.

arise when, e.g., the failure of markets and/or institutions threatens the financial plumbing. Perhaps the most worrisome spillovers stem from contagion from one institution (or one market, or one country) to others, whether or not that contagion has a sound, rational basis. Each of these provides a rationale for financial regulation.

4. *To reduce macroeconomic instability:* The spillovers from extremely adverse financial events — crashes, runs, failures, etc. — are rarely if ever confined to the financial sector. They typically infect the real economy, sometimes seriously. Furthermore, financial-sector problems and macroeconomic problems often interact in vicious cycles. For example, when a banking crisis causes a recession, many 'good loans' turn into 'bad loans,' thereby exacerbating the banking crisis — which in turn wreaks further havoc on the real economy.[6] Knowing that these kinds of risks and interactions exist, a government may want to regulate its financial sector to make it safer — even if such regulations cause microeconomic inefficiencies.

II. The Big Tradeoff: Less Mean for Less Variance

That last point is central. It is probably generically true that regulations limiting dangers to taxpayers and to the macroeconomy impose microeconomic costs in terms of both static and dynamic inefficiencies. Put somewhat too simply, financial regulations (a) distort decision making in financial markets, thereby giving rise to conventional deadweight losses, and (b) dull, or some cases eliminate, incentives to innovate, thereby potentially reducing the economy-wide rate of technical progress. Given the wonders of compounding, the dynamic costs are likely to dwarf the static costs — eventually. So the big tradeoff in financial regulation is about how much to limit innovation in order to keep the financial system safer and the economy more stable.

Formally, we can imagine a social planner solving a dynamic optimization problem something like this: Think of real GDP at some future

---

[6]This is the idea behind the 'financial accelerator.' See, for example, Bernanke *et al.* (1999).

date, Y_t, as a stochastic variable from today's viewpoint.[7] Many factors will influence the probability distribution of Y_t. But if the government toughens regulations between now and then, the mean of Y_t will probably be lower (which is bad) while the variance will probably also be lower (which is good). Conversely, if the government is less regulatory, both $E(Y_t)$ and $Var(Y_t)$ will probably be higher. There is in principle an optimal level of — or, more likely, an optimal time path for — financial regulation. That's the *static efficiency* part of the story, which is what most economic models are designed to study.

Here is a prominent recent example. In 2010, the Bank for International Settlements (BIS) established a Model Assessment Group to estimate the effects of higher Basel III bank capital requirements on real GDP in 16 countries plus the Eurozone. The main channel through which higher capital charges reduce GDP in these models runs from higher lending rates to reduced lending volumes to lower economic activity. In total, the group's technicians used nearly 100 models to estimate these effects in different countries. Naturally, the models did not all agree. The BIS (2010b, p. 2) summarized the results as follows:

> "…bringing the global common equity capital ratio to a level that would meet the agreed minimum and the capital conservation buffer [under Basel III] would result in a maximum decline in GDP, relative to baseline forecasts, of 0.22%, which would occur after 35 quarters. This is then followed by a recovery in GDP towards the baseline."[8]

That's about 2.5 basis points off the growth rate for about nine years (the Basel standards are phased in very slowly) before the effects start to dissipate.

To what should that be compared? Measuring the *gains* from greater macroeconomic stability is more elusive, but it is hard to imagine they could be worth *less* than 2.5 basis points of GDP growth per year. Indeed, a wide range of estimates from the BIS expert group (BIS 2010a, pp. 8–20) suggested that they are *far greater* than this — especially if

---

[7] Y_t could easily be a vector.
[8] These estimates include cross-border spillover effects.

some of the crisis-induced output losses are permanent. James Tobin's famous quip that it takes a lot of Harberger triangles to fill an Okun gap is apposite here because the macroeconomic damage from financial instability can be large. For example, by the time the United States returns to full employment, the cumulative effects of the Great Recession could top 50% of a year's GDP; and in many other countries, the ultimate losses will be far larger.[9] Tobin was not thinking about Okun gaps anywhere near that large.

Moving from the macro to the micro, it is worth mentioning that most of the risks from financial instability *to individuals* are undiversifiable and uninsurable. If my bank fails, the FDIC protects me from loss up to an account balance of US$ 250,000; and I may be able to obtain insurance for larger amounts.[10] But if hundreds of banks fail all over the country, and the economy tanks as a result, no insurance policy will protect me or my business from the losses from recession.[11] Such losses are highly correlated across individuals and firms, making it unlikely that there are enough winners from recessions to make a private market in recession insurance viable. (The government might be able to do better, but that's an issue for a different paper.)

Let's now turn from *static* inefficiencies to *dynamic* efficiencies — things that can affect *growth rates*. Total factor productivity (TFP) growth is one main reason why $E(Y_t)$ grows over time, and financial innovation is presumably one of the many factors behind overall TFP growth. If we could parse out the contribution of financial innovation to TFP growth and then estimate the marginal (presumably negative) effects of more regulation on financial innovation — two tall orders — we could estimate the toll financial regulation takes on growth. (The variance-reducing effects of financial regulation would constitute the benefits, as before.) Such dynamic inefficiencies could be much larger — eventually — than the static inefficiencies just discussed.

---

[9] The US figure is based on CBO estimates of potential GDP. Haldane (2010) estimates *a minimum* loss of *global* output of 90% of a year's GDP.

[10] Disclosure: I am a part owner of a company, Promontory Interfinancial Network, involved in such a business.

[11] Despite the best efforts of Bob Shiller. See, for example, Shiller (2012).

Plainly, however, measuring such effects in general is an impossible task owing, among other things, to the huge range and heterogeneity of possible financial innovations — which are limited only by the imaginations of inventors (and financial market participants have proven themselves to be highly imaginative).

At least two other major considerations favor regulation over *laissez faire*. One is the question of whether the innovations stifled by financial regulation are really *valuable*. Economists are accustomed to thinking of *all* innovations as valuable. After all, inventions raise TFP, don't they? Or at least raise people's utility by providing new products. But is that always, or even usually, true of *financial* innovations? You don't have to go all the way to the Volcker extreme to recognize that many financial innovations are designed for regulatory arbitrage (example: off-balance sheet SIVs) or to enable clever financiers to pick the pockets of unwary and unsophisticated customers (example: opaque OTC derivatives).[12] These are social *gains*? If financial regulation succeeds in reducing regulatory arbitrage, deception, and rent-seeking behavior, are we to count the implied 'distortions' of free-market behavior as *costs*? I don't think so.

Second, remember that the bases of all those Harberger triangles are *reductions in quantities*. Are we so sure that shrinking the financial industry is a bad thing *per se*? Thomas Philippon's pathbreaking work on the size of the industry should at least give us pause. Philippon (2012, 2015) estimates that the share of the financial industry in US GDP has risen almost steadily from World War II to 2010, from about 3% to about 8%. Both price and quantity grew, and he estimates that the per-unit cost of financial intermediation did not decline despite impressive innovation, massive investments in IT, and claims of huge economies of scale? It seems odd.

Philippon's research thus paints a picture of (these are *not* his words) a bloated, rent-seeking, inefficient, and overpaid financial industry that is focused much more on churning assets than on any of the important purposes outlined earlier in this chapter. If so, the case that shrinking the industry would be harmful to society seems weak.

---

[12] Paul Volcker (2009) famously quipped that "the most important financial innovation I've seen in the last 25 years is the automatic teller machine."

One final and important point: I have been talking about *shrinking* the financial industry. But is that what tighter regulations really do? Perhaps they do. But some regulations clearly *shift* human resources and assets out of the regulated sector (e.g., banks and broker-dealers) and into the unregulated sector (e.g., hedge funds and other shadow banks). If it's more the latter than the former, there is at least a case that overall financial risk might *increase* when regulations are tightened.[13] But even in that case, *systemic* risk probably decreases because hedge funds are so much smaller than banks.

III. The Financial Entropy Theorem

As if all this weren't complicated enough, I will now explain why even this characterization of the long-run tradeoff between financial innovation and safety is too simple. I begin with a theorem which I will first prove and then elaborate on via a series of examples:

THE FINANCIAL ENTROPY THEOREM: Financial regulations and their effectiveness tend to get weakened over time by (a) industry work-arounds, (b) regulatory changes, and (c) legislative changes. The main exceptions come during and after financial crises or scandals, when public revulsion against financial excesses enables, perhaps even forces, a tightening of regulation.

The premises on which the entropy theorem is based are roughly as follows. I don't think any of them is even modestly controversial, although a few (e.g., the first two) may be truer in the United States and the United Kingdom than elsewhere.

Premise 1: The monetary rewards for successful producer activity in the financial sector are enormous, among the largest society has to offer prospective talent.

---

[13] See, for example, IMF (2014). But this is not so clear to me since, as I have emphasized, hedge funds operate with less leverage and (relatively) much more MOM ('my own money') than OPM ('other people's money'). See Blinder (2013, pp. 81–84). More on this later.

Premise 2: Because of these huge potential payoffs, the financial industry attracts an inordinate share of the nation's top brainpower and most innovative talent. People who pursue careers in finance are not just smarter than the average person; they are also more creative, more avaricious, and less risk-averse — maybe even risk-loving.

Premise 3: Because many financial regulations reduce the (actual or potential) profitability of financial firms, finding ways to innovate around regulatory roadblocks ('regulatory arbitrage') pays off handsomely.

Premise 4: There is at least some truth to the regulatory capture theory, if not indeed to Stockholm syndrome. While the wheels of financial commerce are only rarely greased by bribery, and some regulators are truly tough, financial regulators often share the perspectives of the regulated industries — especially in good times, when nothing seems to be going wrong.[14]

Premise 5: Money talks in politics. Financiers have a lot of it and spend a lot on lobbying both the legislative and executive branches of government.

Premise 6: Major legislation is difficult to pass. So what has been legislated tends to stay on the books.[15]

Premise 7: Financial regulators do not have anything close to the independence that, say, most central banks enjoy in making monetary policy. In worst cases, financial regulators are under direct political control.

Premise 8: In normal times, politicians have little compunction about pressuring financial regulators to bend in the direction of the industry.

Premise 9: The principal exceptions to Premises 4–8 come immediately following a serious financial scandal or catastrophe. Then regulators stiffen their backs, politicians run away from financiers, and tightening regulation becomes much easier — if not obligatory.

---

[14] This is sometimes called cognitive capture.

[15] This is the one premise that is highly American and applies less to other countries. It is not essential to my argument, though it helps. That said, the premise probably applies with even greater force to international agreements, which are extremely difficult to change.

If you grant these nine premises, the proof of the theorem follows easily. Start with any set of financial laws and regulations inherited from the past. Firms in the industry will virtually always perceive some of these regulations as wrong-headed interferences with commerce (Premise 3). Large firms with smart and highly-motivated workforces will rationally assign a cadre of talented and well-paid employees to find legal ways to circumvent such regulations, that is, to avoid the spirit of the law while adhering to its letter (Premises 1–3). Indeed, prodding from the top of the house might not even be necessary, as smart, ambitious employees will see the opportunities and go after them (Premises 2 and 3).

Given the enormous complexities and ambiguities in financial laws and regulations, clever people will be able to find loopholes, gray areas, and other ways to get around regulations. Some of these workarounds may utilize new instruments created by financial engineering. Novel and even unknown risks may inhere in such instruments, but the 'masters of the universe' involved in creating them will probably be long on self-confidence (after all, they are earning a fortune, right? — Premise 1) and short on both judgment and risk aversion (Premise 2). Besides, the rewards for successful regulatory arbitrage are palpable and immediate while the risks are conjectural and delayed. This establishes part (a) of the theorem.

By Premise 6, the governing statutes tend to remain unchanged for long periods of time. To the extent that these laws interfere with profit-making activities by financial firms (Premise 3), smart people working in these firms will have strong incentives to get (i) the laws, (ii) the implementing regulations, and (iii) the enforcement of those laws and regulations altered in their favor (Premises 1–3).

Changing legislation is the more difficult route (Premise 6), but it is certainly possible — except when the industry is held in disrepute (Premise 9). The influence of money will be terribly one-sided in most legislative battles (Premise 5) because of the usual interplay between concentrated gains and diffuse losses.[16] And the natural path for politicians, other than those whose ideological predilections point strongly in

---

[16] See, for example, Olson (1965).

the other direction, will be to 'follow the money' (Premise 8). This establishes part (c) of the theorem.

Typically, however, it is easier to work on regulators than legislators (Premises 4, 7, and 8), so rational financial executives will concentrate on that (Premises 2 and 4), and perhaps enlist politicians to help them (Premises 5 and 8). Such political pressure can be effective (Premise 7), especially when regulators are predisposed toward sympathy with the industry's concerns anyway (Premise 4).[17] In normal times, there is little countervailing force pushing in the opposite direction since the issues tend to be obscure, the general public is rarely engaged with them, and regulators have minimal contacts with the general public, anyway. Hence virtually all the intellectual, financial, and political firepower pushes toward lighter, not heavier, regulation. That establishes part (b) of the theorem.

The big exception, of course, comes in the wake of financial scandals, market crashes, and other serious ructions, when the public, the politicians (perhaps fearing the public wrath), and the regulators (fearing congressional retribution and embarrassed by their recent failures) all turn toward tougher regulation. In such times, the usual barriers to tighter regulation recede or disappear (Premise 9).

Let me illustrate how the financial entropy theorem works with a few examples.

Glass–Steagall

The Glass–Steagall Act (1935) arose out of the carnage of the Great Depression and the resulting anger at the financial industry, whose excesses were publicized by the Pecora hearings. It made many huge changes in law, including separating banking from investment banking.[18] Thus crisis begat regulation.

In the 1960s and especially the 1970s, investment banks and other nonbank institutions started to figure out ways to poach business away

---

[17] This last clause takes no view on whether the industry's desired changes are in the public interest or not.

[18] And also from insurance, but I'll have nothing more to say about that.

from commercial banks. For example, checkable money market funds resembled bank accounts (albeit uninsured ones) and commercial paper substituted for bank loans to major corporations. Some broker-dealers actually opened (or bought) banks. Seeing their franchise values imperiled, commercial banks began to fight back in the 1970s and especially the 1980s, assisted by favorable regulatory rulings from the Federal Reserve and the Office of the Comptroller of the Currency (OCC).

The biggest steps came in 1987, when a series of Federal Reserve rulings allowed several large banks to establish and then expand 'Section 20' subsidiaries to conduct activities normally associated with investment banking, such as underwriting and dealing in certain types of securities — despite the serious reservations of Fed Chairman Paul Volcker. After that, the Glass–Steagall wall began to erode and then eventually crumble via ever-more-permissive regulations. Congress finally repealed the Glass–Steagall separation entirely in 1999.[19] But by then it was close to meaningless anyway.

Thus the Glass–Steagall story illustrates all three parts of the Financial Entropy Theorem: industry workarounds, loosening of regulations, and finally legislative repeal.

Interstate Banking

Restrictions on the ability of banks to branch across state lines — or even to branch *within* states — had a long history in the United States, reflecting America's traditional hostility to concentrated economic power. Two hundred years after Alexander Hamilton started the Bank of New York, even the largest US banks, some of which operated in many countries, were still limited to a single state. In this instance, industry workarounds were ineffective for quite a while. One reason, of course, was that local banks often were happy to keep out potential competitors.

The ban on interstate banking finally began to break down, under both market and lobbying pressure, in the 1980s. In 1980, Maine was

---

[19] This repeal, part of the Gramm–Leach Bliley Act, is often blamed for the financial crisis — falsely in my view. See Blinder (2013, pp. 266–267).

the only state that allowed out-of-state banks to acquire local banks. By 1990, 46 states allowed out-of-state banks into their markets, though a number imposed regional or other restrictions.[20] This unwieldy patchwork of state-by-state regulation was finally ended in 1994, when Congress abolished most restrictions on interstate banking as part of the Riegle–Neal Act.

So in this case, while sympathetic regulatory rulings certainly helped, deregulation was largely accomplished through legislation. But it took a long time.

Derivatives

Derivative instruments are the new guy on the banking block. Financial derivatives did not really blossom until the late 1980s and early 1990s; but then they grew like kudzu. Dealing in derivatives falls more within the natural domain of broker-dealers than of banks; but as noted above, most megabanks had large broker-dealer affiliates by the 1990s. In fact, just prior to the financial crisis, two of the biggest derivatives dealers were JP Morgan Chase and Citigroup.

The history of regulating derivatives, if you want to call it that, is one of malign neglect. The 1990s saw several well-publicized 'accidents' (to use a too-polite term) with derivatives — at Merrill Lynch, Bankers Trust, and Barings — followed by the Long-Term Capital Management calamity that almost brought down the world's financial system in 1998. Yet derivatives remained unregulated despite increasingly desperate pleas from Brooksley Born, who then headed the Commodity Futures Trading Commission (CFTC).

Regulatory capture and extensive industry lobbying, it seems to me, go a long way toward explaining what amounted to a case of regulatory malfeasance. But, as if that weren't enough, Congress chipped in with the odious Commodity Futures Modernization Act of 2000, which actually instructed regulators to keep their hands off derivatives. This horrific gap in the regulatory system was a major contributor to the worldwide financial crisis; and the gap was only partially closed by the Dodd–Frank Act (2010). (See Section V.) International negotiations

---

[20] See Mengle (1990, p. 3).

over regulating derivatives have been going on — but maybe not going far — for years. It remains a struggle.[21]

IV. The Optimality of Over-regulation

In discussing financial regulation, conservative economists, conservative politicians, and industry representatives often make the valid point that it is possible to *over-regulate* as well as to *under-regulate* the industry. And they offer the Dodd–Frank Act as an example of regulatory over-reach. Perhaps the financial system was under-regulated in the years leading up to the crisis, they may (or may not) concede, but it's certainly over-regulated now.

I have my doubts that Dodd–Frank really swung the proverbial pendulum too far in the regulatory direction. But it would have been entirely rational to do so. The reason is an important corollary of the Financial Entropy Theorem:

THE OVER-REGULATION THEOREM: When major financial reforms are made, which is generally in the aftermath of a serious financial crisis, it is rational to make the new laws and corresponding regulations "too tough," that is, to over-regulate the industry.

The proof is almost immediate. Let $B(R_t)$ and $C(R_t)$ be, respectively, the benefits and costs of regulation, R_t, and let $B'(R^*) = C'(R^*)$ define the optimal degree of regulation, R^*.[22] According to the Financial Entropy Theorem, R_t has a *systematic* downward drift. Suppose it also has a random component, e.g., $\Delta R_t = -\beta t + \varepsilon_t$, where ε_t is a zero-mean independent and identically distributed random variable and β is the time trend toward weaker regulation.[23] Over any time period of length T, the *expected* change in regulatory stringency is therefore $-\beta T$.

---

[21] Among the many recent news stories that could be cited, see Miedema (2014) or Ackerman *et al.* (2014).

[22] R can be a vector instead of a scalar, and R^* will change over time if the functions B(.) and C(.) do. These complicate but do not change the argument.

[23] This particular stochastic process is by no means necessary; ΔR just has to have a negative mean. For example, it is plausible that the industry fights harder for deregulation when R is higher.

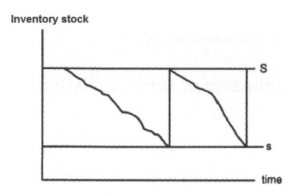

Figure 1. The (S, s) inventory policy.

Regulators know this. So, at the discrete intervals when regulations can be tightened, R should be set *above* R*.

The reasoning here is similar to that behind the well-known (S, s) model of inventory management. In that canonical model, sales in each period (which deplete inventories) are stochastic. But because there is a fixed cost of re-ordering to replenish inventories, it is not optimal to maintain a fixed 'optimal' inventory *stock* (analogous to holding R = R*) at all times. Instead, the optimal inventory *policy* is defined by a lower bound, s, below which the inventory stock is not permitted to fall, and an optimal order size, S-s, which brings inventories back to S after each order (see Figure 1.)[24] In some sense, an inventory stock of S is 'too high' and an inventory stock of s is 'too low.' But as long as the stock remains between S and s, it is optimal for the firm to allow inventories to drift downward stochastically.

In the regulatory application, politics, industry lobbying, and the inertia built into the American system of government combine to create a sizable fixed cost of achieving major regulatory change (Premises 5 and 6). So pro-regulation officials know they will have only sporadic opportunities to tighten regulation. Specifically, crises or scandals — which *do* happen, but at unpredictable moments — temporarily reduce the fixed costs of getting significant legislation passed or major regulations promulgated

---

[24] In reality, R is multi-dimensional. Figure 1 is meant metaphorically.

(Premise 9). They also know that regulation will almost certainly grow lighter during the intervals between such galvanizing events (that's the Financial Entropy Theorem). So when a chance to raise R arises, it should be reset *above* R*. A simple, but not mathematically accurate, way of thinking about the optimality of over-regulation is that it gets the degree of regulation 'right on average' over time.

Two final points about the (S, s) analogy. First, unlike in the inventory case, changing laws and/or regulations imposes adjustment costs on firms in the industry. This fact should moderate regulatory changes.

Second, the standard (S, s) model delivers bounds, S and s, that are *constant* over time. But if the firm has a secular growth (or decline) trend in sales, both S and s will be rising (or falling) over time. One important question in the application of (S, s) reasoning to financial regulation is whether the corridor in which R meanders is tilted upward (toward heavier regulation) or downward (toward lighter) — as indicated by the two panels of Figure 2.

The long-run tilt of the regulatory corridor has several major determinants. One is the pace of financial innovation and whether it produces more or less *complexity* over time. Somehow, the answer always seems to be 'more,' which probably calls for more and more detailed regulations. But *more* regulation might not spell *tighter* regulation.

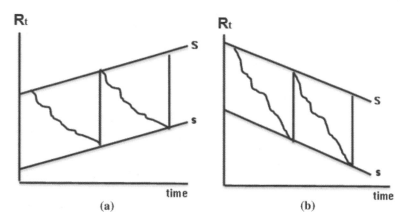

Figure 2. Secularly rising or falling regulation.

Why not? Because financial regulators can never move as quickly as financial markets. When I was a bank regulator, I used to quip that our job was to stay one or two steps behind the markets.[25] We could never hope to be as nimble as the markets. But things got worrisome when we slipped four, five, or six steps behind. When the pace of financial innovation accelerates, for whatever reason, regulators will almost certainly fall further behind fast-moving market developments. So even if they write *more* regulations, or arch their eyebrows more often and more sternly, effective regulatory constraints on financial activity are likely to *loosen*, not tighten. Thus my suspicion — it is not more than that — is that the long-run regulatory corridor has a natural tendency to slope *downward* over time, as in Figure 2(b).

This natural tendency toward lighter regulation may be either mitigated or exacerbated by broad political forces. If a country's politics swings to the right, as in 2000, political and bureaucratic barriers to regulation will rise, thereby strengthening the tendency toward lighter regulation. If a country's politics swings to the left, as during the New Deal, those same barriers will be weakened and regulation will become tougher. Thus there may be political long swings in the degree of effective regulation. But if periods of right-leaning and left-leaning politics roughly balance out, the natural economic tendency toward lighter regulation will eventually win out. One interesting research question in political economy is what sorts of institutional arrangements might counteract this tendency.[26]

V. Appraising the Long-run Effects of Some Recent Reforms[27]

Let me now use the theorizing above to consider some recent financial regulatory reforms and speculate on how they might evolve over time.

---

[25] I was Vice Chairman of the Board of Governors of the Federal Reserve System in 1994–1996.

[26] Aizenman (2011) takes a stab at this.

[27] This section borrows from Blinder (2014).

Systemic Risk Regulation

One of the most shocking inadequacies revealed by the financial crisis was the absence, in most nations, of any regulator responsible for system-wide risk. Instead, the global norm was to confine regulators to 'silos.' In the United States, for example, bank regulators watched over the banks, securities regulators minded the security markets, basically no one monitored the derivatives markets, and so on. Indeed, the regulator for X often encountered a 'stop sign' if it peered too closely into the Y business. Thus the newly-perceived need to control *systemic* risk called for new institutions that cut across regulatory silos.

In the US, the Dodd–Frank Act (2010) established the Financial Stability Oversight Council (FSOC), chaired by the Secretary of the Treasury and including all the financial regulators. Its purview is the entire financial system, and its remit is to focus on *systemic* risks. A new division of the Federal Reserve Board staff in Washington essentially provides staff support for the FSOC via the Chairman of the Fed, as does a new Office of Financial Research in the Treasury. A few months after Dodd–Frank passed, the EU created the European Systemic Risk Board (ESRB), chaired by the President of the European Central Bank and staffed largely by ECB personnel. The UK established a new Financial Policy Committee (FPC) of the Bank of England, patterned on its Monetary Policy Committee (MPC), in 2013. (A predecessor had been in operation since 2011.) These and other agencies around the world are now at work.

Creating an institution with a *single focus* — in this case, systemic risk — is an important counterweight to the Financial Entropy Theorem. If the FSOC, ESRB, FPC, and others don't pay attention to emerging systemic risks, what else will they do? Nonetheless, a Minskyan view of the dynamic process suggests that enthusiasm for systemic regulation will wane over time. Whether support for these new agencies will fade, or even whether they will be weakened by politics, is a major question that only the passage of time will resolve. But there is reason to worry.

One predictable weakness of the FSOC, a committee composed of many regulators with disparate constituencies and interests, is apparent already: a particular industry may be able to use its (partially captured?) regulator to champion its interests against the FSOC. For example, the SEC dragged its feet over changes in the regulation of money market mutual funds that would reduce or eliminate their vulnerability to runs. And this despite the facts that (a) the vulnerability was apparent, (b) the presumably-powerful Federal Reserve was a vocal critic, and (c) such runs had actually happened in September 2008.

Finally, a note of irony here: to the extent that new systemic risk regulators around the world succeed in making major financial blowups less frequent, that will make the sporadic opportunities to strengthen regulation even more rare. The Financial Entropy Theorem and the Over-regulation Theorem will then become even more important.

Too-big-to-fail and Resolution Authority

Perhaps the biggest boost to post-crisis regulation came from the hatred — that is not too strong a word — of bank bailouts in all countries. The bailouts of 2008–2009 created a huge demand for ways to resolve what we now call systemically-important financial institutions (SIFIs) without subjecting taxpayers to potentially huge costs — and without imperiling large parts of the financial system.[28]

Did I say 'resolve'? That's the appropriate word in Europe, where work on the Single Resolution Mechanism (SRM) is progressing, albeit grudgingly. The rules have recently been agreed, but two nagging questions remain: Is the SRM target of a 55 billion euro fund enough? (Answer: No.) And where will the money come from? Given the number of countries involved and the absence of a Rawlsian veil of ignorance to mask their self-interests, it was predictable that funding would be the big stumbling block, Nations like Germany and Finland know they are far more likely to pay into the SRM than draw from it, while nations like Greece, Spain, and Portugal know they are more likely to be

---

[28] The different perspectives of experts versus the broad public on this matter are telling. The public cares (only?) about taxpayer expense; the experts care (mostly) about systemic risk.

recipients than donors. How will German taxpayers like bailing out Greek banks? To ask the question is to answer it.

Since the United States is a single country, everyone knows where any bailout funds will come from. That said, Title II of Dodd–Frank calls for the creation of a new "orderly *liquidation* authority." In 2009, the U.S. Treasury recommended that Congress give the authorities a choice between either *resolving* a sick SIFI or *liquidating* it. But Congress rejected that idea. There would be no more bailouts. Lest anyone miss the point, Section 214 of Dodd–Frank states unequivocally that "Taxpayers shall bear no losses from the exercise of any authority under this title," and goes on to specify that any losses from a liquidation "shall be the responsibility of the financial sector, through assessments." It is hard to imagine any future Congress loosening those strictures. (Imagine the vote!) So I doubt that this particular aspect of regulation will be weakened.

The Federal Deposit Insurance Corporation (FDIC) and the Bank of England have adopted the same concept for how to liquidate a large, complex financial institution.[29] The central idea is the Single Point of Entry (SPOE). Under SPOE, a large financial holding company's liabilities should be structured (e.g., with enough long-term unsecured debt) so the parent can absorb all the losses in a liquidation procedure, leaving the bank subsidiaries to carry on as usual — or as close to 'as usual' as possible. In particular, bank depositors should not be 'bailed in,' which runs counter to some past European practice (e.g., in Cyprus), but perhaps not to *future* practice.

The logic behind SPOE seems sound, even clever. But will it work in practice? Hopefully, we won't get a definitive answer for a while because no SIFI will need to be liquidated. But I am concerned with, among other things, contagion via reputation. Suppose BigBancorp (the holding company) fails, grabbing headlines and imposing highly-publicized losses on its bondholders. Will other counterparties continue to do business-as-usual with BigBank (the banking subsidiary)? I have my doubts.

---

[29] See FDIC and Bank of England (2012). For a good and thorough explanation and evaluation of the US version of SPOE, see Bovenzi *et al.* (2013).

Higher Capital Requirements

When the financial crisis opened the door to stiffer regulations, one crying need was for more bank capital. Basel III came quickly (in 2010) and did improve upon Basel II by raising capital requirements for internationally-active banks and placing more emphasis on tangible common equity — what I like to call 'real capital.' Another welcome change is that capital requirements will now be imposed on certain nonbank SIFIs.

But it's mostly downhill from there. First, giving banks until 2019 to comply with the higher capital standard can only be called embarrassing.[30] Second, and perhaps even more astonishing, Basel III carries over the single worst regulatory innovation from Basel II: Letting banks use their own internal models to measure risk. That this fox-guarding-the-chicken-coop provision survived the debacles of the 2000s is truly amazing. It must be one of the most egregious examples of regulatory capture ever. Third, Basel III continues to give rating agencies a central role in assigning risk weights to assets, despite their abysmal performance in the years leading up to the crisis — something Dodd–Frank banned in the US.[31]

The big non-debate, of course, is whether even Basel III sets banks' capital requirements too low. I call it a 'non-debate' because there is little evidence that officials anywhere have given a second thought to imposing much higher capital requirements, despite academic protestations.[32] The industry, of course, is portraying even the Basel III capital requirements as a threat to the foundations of capitalism.

Two concerns are most frequently raised in this regard. The first is that requiring banks to replace cheaper debt with more expensive equity

---

[30] Fortunately, many banks already exceed Basel III requirements. So this disgraceful error may not cause any problems.

[31] The Basel Committee has approved the US's non-use of the rating agencies.

[32] Most prominently from Admati and Hellwig (2013). That said, in September 2014 the Federal Reserve indicated it would propose capital requirements above Basel III levels on SIFIs. See Eavis (2014).

in their capital structures will force lending rates higher. As noted in Section II, this is the regulatory cost that has garnered the most attention and the most attempts to estimate its magnitude, which looks small.[33]

The second concern is that some financial activities will migrate out of comparatively well-regulated banks and into lightly-regulated or unregulated shadow banks. This worry has the ring of truth. But as counterweights, let's remember that many shadow banks, especially hedge funds, operate with far less leverage than banks — partly because they operate without a safety net and partly because the partners' own money is at risk.[34] Furthermore, if shadow banks grow large enough, they can be designated as SIFIs and subjected to bank-like regulation.

Restricting Proprietary Trading

Rightly or wrongly, many critics viewed proprietary trading by banks as among the leading causes of the financial crisis. So limits on proprietary trading became one focus of financial reform — on both sides of the Atlantic.[35] Three different, though related, approaches have now been adopted.

The United States included the so-called Volcker Rule, which forces proprietary trading out of FDIC-insured banks, in Dodd–Frank (2010). The UK's 2013 banking reform included the Vickers Commission's 2011 recommendation that only normal retail and commercial banking activities should be protected by the official safety net, leaving other financial activities — including trading, but also other things — outside the 'ring fence' that protects the retail bank.[36] In January 2014, the European Union adopted, after some modifications, the recommendation of an international group of experts headed by Bank of Finland

---

[33] According to the Miller–Modigliani theorem, changing the debt-equity mix should not change banks' weighted-average cost of capital at all — a point Admati and Hellwig (2013) emphasize.

[34] See again Blinder (2013, pp. 81–84).

[35] Japan seems not to have moved in this direction.

[36] Independent Commission on Banking (2011).

Governor Erkki Liikanen that most trading be conducted in separate subsidiaries, rather than in the banks themselves.[37]

The three approaches are first cousins, not siblings. All three aim to protect depositors and taxpayers from the consequences of trading losses. While Vickers and Liikanen keep trading under some sort of bank-regulatory regime (in a bank subsidiary), Volcker moves proprietary trading entirely out of banks (though with some exceptions, e.g., dealing in Treasuries and market-making activities). However, it is extremely difficult for regulators to distinguish between market-making and proprietary trading in practice. After all, the same trade could fall in either category depending on the bank's other positions and the trader's intent — which the trader knows, but the regulators don't. This conundrum is one main reason why the UK gave up on the distinction and why it took US regulators four years to agree on detailed regulations to implement Volcker. How they will work in practice remains to be seen.

While Volcker pushes bank holding companies (the American term) out of the trading business, Vickers keeps trading and other activities inside banking groups (the European term), but 'ring fences' them away from core banking activities such as deposit-taking and commercial lending. Once implemented, UK taxpayers will be off the hook for any trading losses but potentially on the hook for, say, the consequences of outsized loan losses.

The Liikanen group also decided that distinguishing between market-making and proprietary trading was too difficult, so almost all trading should be segregated into separately-capitalized subsidiaries.[38] But the key word turned out to be 'almost.' Liikanen made an exception for 'hedged, client driven' transactions, which can remain in the bank. The EU's final proposal (January 2014) defined 'proprietary' as "for the sole purpose of making a profit for own account, and without any connection

---

[37] High-level Expert Group (2012) on reforming the structure of the EU banking sector.

[38] I have long advocated a Liikanen-like approach, but without the 'almost' and with one important proviso: that the parent be prohibited from downstreaming capital to its trading sub to cover losses. See Blinder (2010). I first proposed this idea at a Federal Reserve conference in 2009. It was not popular!

to actual or anticipated client activity or for the purpose of hedging the entity's risk as a result of actual or anticipated client activity."[39] Good luck making those distinctions.

How will these rules evolve over time? The Financial Entropy Theorem makes a clear prediction: more and more trades will become 'market-making' or 'client-driven' or 'hedged,' probably due to both regulatory interpretations and industry ingenuity. This promises to be a bigger problem for Volcker and Liikanen than for Vickers, which eschews such subtle distinctions.

Regulating Derivatives

There is no doubt that wild and wooly derivatives played a major role in bringing on and propagating the financial carnage. The remedies seem clear enough, at least to me: standardize derivatives and trade them on organized exchanges with price transparency, central clearing, and adequate collateral. Dodd–Frank pushes in this direction, but not hard enough. For example, by *volume* (though not by *riskiness*), most OTC derivatives are exempt from Dodd–Frank strictures. This was a clear lobbying victory for the industry.

Besides, Dodd–Frank governs only the United States. Europe in general seems way behind on pushing derivatives into safer trading environments — and more reluctant to do so. Indeed, many European authorities, not to mention the big banks, have been battling America's CFTC, which has taken more aggressive positions for a long time. (More on this shortly.)

About eighteen months before the conference, *The New York Times* entitled an editorial on this subject, "Derivatives reform on the ropes."[40] Since then, reform has taken a few more body blows. While disconcerting, these developments cannot be surprising given the enormous amount of money at stake. After all, banks that now earn a king's ransom on some customized OTC derivatives would earn nickels and dimes

---

[39] Brown (2014, p. 5). The EU provision applies only to large banks and is not quite binding on member states.
[40] May 19, 2013.

on standardized, exchange-traded products. They don't relish the prospect, and they let their regulators and legislators know that it no uncertain terms. Bank lobbying has been pretty successful even while memories were fresh; the Financial Entropy Theorem predicts that lobbyists will succeed even more as memories fade.

Compensation Incentives

In the popular debate, CEO compensation hogs the headlines. The sheer size of the bonuses that pliant corporate boards routinely bestow upon their chief executives seems obscene to many. In my view, however, these excessive pay packages are mainly matters of CEOs extracting rents from powerless shareholders. They rarely if ever pose systemic risks. If so, it's the shareholders who should try to block outrageous pay packages, not the government.[41]

Public policy should worry, instead, about the *incentives* embedded in the way *traders* are compensated. Before the crisis, it was common for banks, investment banks, and hedge funds to give traders what I call 'go-for-broke' incentives. Winning bets made traders fabulously wealthy by awarding them a non-trivial share of the profits. On the other hand, if they lost the firm's money, their bonuses would vanish and they might (or might not) lose their jobs. But such losses were puny compared to the potential gains. Offering young, risk-loving traders such hugely asymmetric incentives was playing with fire. And we were all badly burned by excessive risk taking when the crisis broke — excessive, that is, relative to the best interests of either their superiors or their shareholders.[42]

The post-crisis news here is relatively good, however. Substantial progress seems to have been made without much new regulation.[43]

---

[41] In the United States, Dodd–Frank included the so-called say-on-pay provision, giving shareholders a nonbinding vote on CEO pay. These votes were negative in only about 3% of cases in 2012. See Krueger (2013).

[42] One exception: if CEOs and other top executives share in the trading profits, then they inherit some of the skewed incentives of the traders.

[43] See Financial Stability Board (2011) and Board of Governors of the Federal Reserve System (2011).

Many more businesses now realize that their previous compensation practices exposed them to outsized, even existential, risks. So their compensation packages now adjust for the amount of risk taken, include claw back provisions, make more payments in restricted stock, and embody other features that make traders and executives bear more of the downside risk. That should induce more caution.

The main driver of change here appears to have been the sobriety induced by the crisis, although regulatory authorities in a number of countries have taken useful actions by, for example, treating compensation incentives as part of a bank's risk-management system. Thus we might hope to defeat the Financial Entropy Theorem in this domain. But as a Minskyan, I still worry about what happens as financial activity proceeds without further blowups, as greed displaces fear, and as CEOs and boards forget what happened in 2008. Will the bad old practices return?

The Need for International Harmonization

The main motivation behind most of the activity in Basel since the 1980s is the (sensible) notion that *international* banking needs *international* rules. Uniformity across countries is one way to reduce opportunities for regulatory arbitrage.

But the importance of international harmonization varies greatly from one regulatory issue to another. Consider the issues dealt with in this section. It does *not* seem critical that different countries organize their systemic risk regulation in the same way (just do it!), restrict proprietary trading by banks in the same way (someone will do the trading anyway), or compensate traders in the same way (to each his own, as long as incentives are not crazy). The famous Basel accords, of course, have always concentrated on making capital standards in different countries (sort of) the same. This leaves two other regulatory issues where, it seems to me, the case for international harmonization is strong, but getting it done is difficult.

The first is the resolution of failing SIFIs, as the EU nations so clearly recognize in their Single Resolution Mechanism. Financial giants conduct huge volumes of business across national borders. They may have hundreds of subsidiaries, thousands of counterparties, and millions of existing contracts — perhaps spanning scores of countries. For such a global SIFI, life is international but death (or the prospect of death) is national. Bankruptcy laws and resolution procedures vary enormously across nations. If a global SIFI starts to fail, the resulting scramble for its remaining assets can lead to chaos, paralysis, legal uncertainty, endless lawsuits, and the like. Need I mention that the Lehman Brothers bankruptcy was chaotic — and is still in the courts?

While the *need* for harmonization is clear, how to get from here to there is not. I rather doubt that the rest of the world will adopt Dodd–Frank's "orderly liquidation authority" since so many countries prefer resolution (and continued life) to liquidation.[44] But I also doubt that the United States will change its orderly *liquidation* procedure to make it consistent with the EU's Single *Resolution* Mechanism. Remember, the U.S. Treasury wanted a resolution option, but Congress rejected it. So it appears that, the next time a global financial giant teeters on the brink of failure, world markets will have to deal with different resolution/liquidation regimes in different countries.[45]

The regulation of derivatives also cries out for international homogenization. Unlike most of the instruments that underlie them (e.g., bonds, mortgages, forex,...), derivatives have no well-defined geographical home. A loan is booked in a bank. A bond is the liability of a corporation that is domiciled somewhere. But if an American calls his broker in New York, who trades a derivative in Singapore with a Japanese counterparty, and then debits or credits the funds to the customer's account in London, which country's regulations rule? With geography so arbitrary or even irrelevant, we can confidently predict that trading will migrate to the venues with the most lenient regulations (read: no regulations at all) — unless the major nations homogenize their rules.

---

[44] One of my favorite quotes from the financial crisis is from the anonymous European central banker who told journalist David Wessel (2009, p. 22), "We don't let banks fail. We don't even let dry cleaners fail."

[45] One ray of sunshine: as mentioned, the US and the UK are adopting the same orderly liquidation regime.

So far, that has not happened. On the contrary, US efforts (led by the CFTC) to impose a meaningful regulatory regime on OTC derivatives have run into stiff opposition — not only from the industry (which hears the death knell of capitalism sounding again!), but also from foreign authorities who complain (with some validity) about extraterritoriality. Just a few months before this conference, Bloomberg reported on successful efforts to escape US regulations on derivatives trading in overseas affiliates of US banks.[46]

I am not optimistic about achieving international harmony in derivatives regulation. However, the task might be easier than harmonizing resolution regimes because, while the failure of a global SIFI is a rare event that might not occur again for years, accidents in the unregulated derivatives markets are almost certain to occur much more frequently. At some point, the world's governments might grasp the importance of agreeing on a global regulatory regime. It is even possible that, after suffering through a number of chaotic cross-border derivative disasters, the industry might come to welcome some regulatory clarity. At least we can hope. That said the fact that even the biggest derivatives blowups in history (starting in August 2007) have not been enough to spur countries to act is sobering.

There is, however, one piece of good news about global harmonization: if and when an international agreement is painstakingly reached, it will be very hard to dismantle it via legislation or regulation. In that case, inertia will become regulation's friend.

Summary

Financial markets are regulated for a number of (good) reasons. Chief among them is that financial instabilities spill over into the real economy, causing *macroeconomic* instability. While there are clearly other aspects to financial regulation, I characterize the 'big tradeoff' as balancing the *net* benefits of innovation (netting out, e.g., harmful innovations) against those of living in a safer financial (and hence real) environment.

---

[46] Brush (2014).

But even if such a rump optimum could somehow be achieved, it would not be an equilibrium state because of what I call *financial entropy*, that is, the natural tendency for both the stringency of regulations and enforcement to erode over time. I sketch a Minsky-type cycle of first lighter and then heavier regulation. In relatively placid times, financial entropy derives from industry workarounds (some of which are celebrated as 'financial innovation'), from lighter-touch regulation and supervision, and from legislative changes that make life kinder and gentler for the industry. All these changes make it easier for financial excesses to build up during a boom — and they do. When the 'bubble,' or whatever it is, finally bursts, the government turns in a more regulatory direction and the lobbying power of the industry wanes. So, for a while, regulations tighten and tougher laws are passed. The tighter regulatory corset combines with prudence induced by the recent scare to produce a safer financial environment for a while, few accidents happen, and the whole cycle repeats.

At the critical moments when regulations are tightened, it is rational for regulators and legislators to go 'too far' because they know that whatever they do will be eroded over time. I call this result the *optimality of over-regulation*. But, of course, the over-regulation is transitory. If we imagine a scalar that indicates the tightness of regulation, it follows a path reminiscent of the (S, s) model of inventories — rising abruptly to a ceiling and then gradually sinking toward a floor.

In the regulatory cat-and-mouse game, financial innovation virtually always moves at a speed that regulators cannot match. Thus the regulators' goal should not be keeping up with the industry. Rather, the sensible goal is not falling *too far* behind. This natural lag of regulation behind reality suggests a tendency toward lighter *effective* regulation in the long run.

I use this theoretical framework to speculate on the future prospects of several recent regulatory reforms, including systemic risk regulation, orderly liquidation or resolution, Basel III capital requirements, restrictions on proprietary trading by banks, regulating (or not) derivatives, and adjusting the pay incentives of traders. The news is mixed — after all, regulation has just recently jumped to the upper bound, S. But in every case, the Financial Entropy Theorem is lurking in the background.

References

Ackerman, A., K. Burne, and V. Dendrinou (2014), "Derivatives Rules Have US, EU at Impasse," *Wall Street Journal*, September 26.

Admati, A. and M. Hellwig (2013), *The Bankers' New Clothes: What's Wrong with Banking and What to Do about It* (Princeton, NJ: Princeton University Press).

Aizenman, J. (2011), "Financial Crisis and the Paradox of Under- and Over-Regulation," in J. Y. Lin and B. Pleskovic (eds.), *Lessons from East Asia and the Global Financial Crisis*, ABCDE World Bank conference volume (Annual Bank Conference on Development Economics), pp. 213–234.

Bernanke, B. S., M. Gertler, and S. Gilchrist (1999), "The Financial Accelerator in a Quantitative Business Cycle Framework," in J. B. Taylor and M. Woodford (eds.), *Handbook of Macroeconomics* (Amsterdam: North-Holland), pp. 1341–1393.

Bank for International Settlements [BIS] (2010a), *An Assessment of the Long-Term Economic Impact of Stronger Capital and Liquidity Requirements*, August 2010. Available at: http://www.bis.org/publ/bcbs173.pdf.

Bank for International Settlements [BIS] (2010b), *Final Report: Assessing the macroeconomic impact of the transition to stronger capital and liquidity requirements*, Macroeconomic Assessment Group, December 2010. Available at: http://www.bis.org/publ/othp12.pdf.

Bovenzi, J., R. Guyunn, and T. Jackson (2013), *Too Big to Fail: The path to a solution*, Bipartisan Policy Center, May 2013. Available at: http://bipartisanpolicy.org/wp-content/uploads/sites/default/files/TooBigToFail.pdf.

Blinder, A. S. (2010), "It's Broke, Let's Fix It: Rethinking financial regulation," *International Journal of Central Banking*, 6(4): 277–330.

Blinder, A. S. (2013), *After the Music Stopped: The Financial Crisis, the Response, and the Work Ahead* (New York: The Penguin Press).

Blinder, A. S. (2014), "Guarding against Systemic Risk: The remaining agenda," in E. Jokivuolle and J. Vilmunen (eds.), *Banking After Regulatory Reforms — Business As Usual?* SUERF Studies: 2014/3 (Vienna, Austria: Larcier), pp. 41–49.

Board of Governors of the Federal Reserve System (2011), *Incentive Compensation Practices: A report on the horizontal review of practices at large banking organizations* (Washington, D.C.: Board of Governors of the Federal Reserve System), October 2011.

Brush, S. (2014), "Wall Street Faces Scrutiny of Tactic to Evade Swaps Rules," *Bloomberg News*, July 31, 2014. Available at: http://www.bloomberg.

com/news/2014-07-31/wall-street-faces-new-u-s-scrutiny-of-derivatives-tactic.html.

Brown, M. (2014), "Does Volcker + Vickers = Liikanen? EU proposal for a regulation on structural measures improving the resilience of EU credit institutions," *Legal Update*, February 2014.

Eavis, P. (2014), "Federal Reserve Signals Intent to Pressure Largest Banks to Slim Down," *The New York Times*, September 9, 2014.

Federal Deposit Insurance Corporation [FDIC] and the Bank of England (2012), *Resolving Globally Active, Systemically Important, Financial Institutions,* December 10, 2012. Available at: https://www.fdic.gov/about/srac/2012/gsifi.pdf.

Financial Stability Board (2011), *2011 Thematic Review on Compensation: Peer review report*, Basel, Switzerland, October 7, 2011. Available at: http://www.financialstabilityboard.org/wp-content/uploads/r_111011a.pdf?page_moved=1.

Haldane, A. (2010), *The $100 billion question*, Speech at the Institute of Regulation and Risk, North Asia (IRRNA), Hong Kong, March 30, 2010.

High-level Expert Group (2012), *High-level Expert Group on Reforming the Structure of the EU Banking Sector*, Chaired by Erkki Liikanen, Final Report, Brussels, Belgium, October 2, 2012. Available at: http://ec.europa.eu/internal_market/bank/docs/high-level_expert_group/report_en.pdf.

Independent Commission on Banking (2011), *Final Report Recommendations*, Vickers Commission (London: Domarn Group), September 2011.

International Monetary Fund (2014), *Global Financial Stability Report — Risk Taking, Liquidity, and Shadow Banking: Curbing excess while promoting growth*, Chapter 2, October 2014.

Krueger, A. B. (2013), *Land of Hope and Dreams: Rock and roll, economics and rebuilding the middle class*, Speech delivered at Rock and Roll Hall of Fame, Cleveland, OH, June 12, 2013.

Mengle, D. L. (1990), "The Case for Interstate Branch Banking," *Federal Reserve Bank of Richmond Economic Review*, 76: 3–17.

Miedema, D. (2014), "Exclusive: US, Europe head toward delay in squabble over swaps rules — source," *Reuters*. September 4, 2014. Available at: http://uk.reuters.com/article/2014/09/04/uk-financial-regulations-swaps-exclusive-idUKKBN0GZ0BO20140904.

Minsky, H. P. (1986), *Stabilizing an Unstable Economy* (New Haven, CT: Yale University Press).

The New York Times, "Derivatives reform on the ropes" (Editorial), May 19, 2013. http://www.nytimes.com/2013/05/20/opinion/derivatives-reform-on-the-ropes.html?_r=0.

Olson, M. (1965), *The Logic of Collective Action: Public Goods and the Theory of Groups*, Cambridge, MA: Harvard University Press.

Philippon, T. (2012), "Finance Versus Wal-Mart: Why are financial services so expensive?" in A. Blinder, A. Lo, and R. Solow (eds.), *Rethinking the Financial Crisis* (New York: Russell Sage), pp. 235–246.

Philippon, T. (2015), "Has the US Finance Industry Become Less Efficient? On the theory and measurement of financial intermediation," *American Economic Review*, 105: 1408–1438.

Shiller, R. J. (2012), *Finance and the Good Society* (Princeton, NJ: Princeton University Press).

Tirole, J. (2014), "The Contours of Banking and the Future of Its Regulation," in G. A. Akerlof, O. J. Blanchard, D. Romer and J. E. Stiglitz (eds.), *What Have We Learned? Macroeconomic Policy after the Crisis* (Cambridge, MA: MIT Press), pp. 143–154.

Volcker, P. A. (2009), speech to the *Wall Street Journal*'s Future of Finance Initiative, Horsham, West Sussex, UK, December 8, 2009.

Wessel, D. (2009), *In Fed We Trust: Ben Bernanke's War on the Great Panic* (New York: Crown Publishing).

Implementing the Regulatory Reform Agenda

The Pitfall of Myopia

— CHAPTER 2

- Stefan Ingves
  Sveriges Riksbank

The subject of this conference is indeed very timely — six years after the outbreak of the financial crisis, there has been substantial progress in the post-crisis regulatory reform agenda, with a number of important milestones reached. Therefore, now is a good time to take a step back and ask how the different bits and pieces of the regulatory framework fit together. And, more specifically — have the vulnerabilities revealed in the crisis been adequately addressed? Are additional adjustments still necessary? Or, conversely, have we gone too far and created a regulatory Frankenstein's monster that no-one has full control over and that stifles lending and economic growth?

This latter view is one that I sometimes hear when meeting representatives of the banking industry. The feeling seems to be that we are overwhelming the financial system with a regulation tsunami with too many reforms being implemented too soon. This will lead to unacceptable consequences in the form of higher funding costs, reductions in

---

Stefan Ingves is Governor of Sveriges Riksbank and chairman of the executive board, and is Chairman of the Basel Committee on Banking Supervision.

market liquidity with market-makers pulling out of markets, collateral shortages; and many banking activities simply disappearing, or moving to the so called shadow banking sector.

And indeed, the financial crisis has led to a comprehensive response from regulators and policymakers across the world. Compared to the pre-crisis era, international banks will face:

- substantially higher capital requirements,
- higher demands on the quality of capital,
- a leverage ratio,
- an international liquidity framework, with both short-term and structural liquidity requirements (I am proud to note that the Basel Committee, less than a week ago, published the final standard for the net stable funding ratio, NSFR), and
- a regulatory framework for global systemically important banks (G-SIBs).

When you add to this ongoing work related to reducing RWA variability and disclosure, you end up with a pretty impressive list — a list that represents an unprecedented leap forward in terms of global banking regulation.

So then, how do I see this?

Do I claim to know how all these new rules will play out together? Am I confident that there will be no inconsistencies and contradictions? No, definitely not. We have every reason to be humble in this respect. Monitoring and assessing the effects of reforms will therefore be imperative.

Will the reforms be costly for banks in the short term? Yes, they will.

Will banks have to adjust their activities? Yes, a return to pre-crisis banking behavior is neither appropriate nor viable.

Do I therefore think that regulation has gone too far and that parts should be undone? No, not at all.

In this presentation, I will try to explain why I think this is so. I will also speak about what is still lacking and the regulatory challenges we face ahead.

Why we Shouldn't Back-track on Regulation

There are several reasons why I don't think the regulatory agenda has gone too far. First of all, my experience is that important regulatory and structural reforms are all too often hindered by myopia. People tend to focus on costs and pains in the short run, leaving aside the longer term gains that reforms aim to achieve.

The perceived short-term costs are simply much easier to sell politically, compared to the abstract benefits of lowering the risk of crises. This is especially so, since the benefits may accrue only to future generations — a group that has difficulties making its voice heard in today's policy debate.

This time has been no exception: for years, people shied away from necessary actions to strengthen the financial system. When the crisis hit, perceptions changed, providing a window of opportunity for regulatory reforms that were long overdue. However, we must not begin to close this window and lose sight of why we are undertaking these reforms.

Let me start with a reminder of the regulatory framework before the crisis. Both Basel I and II included a risk-weighted capital adequacy framework. However, for the last 20 years banks' balance sheets ballooned, while their equity failed to take off. For example, from 1993 to 2008 the total assets of a sample of what we call global systemically important banks saw a twelve-fold increase (increasing from US$2.6 trillion to just over US$30 trillion). But the capital funding these assets only increased seven-fold, (from US$125 billion to US$890 billion). Put differently, the average risk weight declined from 70% to below 40%. The problem was that this reduction did not represent a genuine reduction in risk in the banking system.

To take an even more concrete example from my own country: during the past twenty years or so, the risk weights for retail mortgages in the major Swedish banks have decreased from 50% to 35% with the adoption of Basel II (from Basel I) and further, to about 6% when banks themselves were allowed to model risk weights. In equity terms, this means that instead of SEK 17,000 of their own equity to fund a mortgage of 1 million, banks' models implied that SEK 1,200 was enough.[1] In retrospect, it is clear that the decrease in risk weights did not reflect actual risks and banks therefore needed more capital.

Furthermore, although it is a historical fact that banks' problems often start in the form of liquidity constraints, there were no global liquidity regulations for banks prior to the crisis. This meant that banks could rely heavily on very short-term market funding to finance highly illiquid and long-term assets. This worked fine during the Great Moderation, but unfortunately with the collapse of Lehman Brothers another old truism suddenly came to life: "markets function the worst when you need them the most".

Against this background, it is quite embarrassing that so few could see the crisis coming. From a regulatory point of view, all the ingredients were there, or rather they were lacking. And this is the first point I want to make — the regulatory framework was unsatisfactory and becoming more so the more complex the financial system became.

Then, turning to my second point, which is: The costs of financial crises are huge. This is true in general, but especially so for the recent one. For example, according to a recent study by IMF economists, in a sample of countries representing just over 50% of world GDP, the total amount of government recapitalization, asset purchases and guarantees during the period 2007–2011 amounted to nearly US$5 trillion. This is equivalent to 16% of the GDP of these economies, or nearly US$ 5,000 per citizen.[2]

But, this is only a lower bound of the cost of the crisis. If we also include the impact on GDP and the loss of production relative to its pre-crisis trend, the costs rise. This has been showed by several studies, including the one just mentioned by IMF economists, which estimates that banking crises that occurred between 1970 and 2000 are resulting in output losses of more than 20% on average if we look at all

---

[1] The figure SEK 17,000 = 1,000,000*50%*3.4%, where 3.4% is the implied minimum core Tier 1 capital requirement under Basel I. The risk-weight for mortgages was 50% during this period. Under Basel II the implied minimum core Tier 1 capital requirement fell from 3.4% to 2% of risk-weighted assets, and was 2% in 2011–2012 when banks' internal average risk weights for mortgages was 6%. SEK 1,200 SEK = 1,000,000*6%*2%. For more information see Sveriges Riksbank (2013, pp. 21–24).
[2] Calculations of costs are based on Laeven and Valencia (2013). The calculation uses data from the banking crisis database and the methodology of the BIS and the Riksbank.

countries, and more than 30% of GDP in advanced economies.[3] These results are in line with the BIS finding that the median discounted cumulative loss of output over the course of a crisis in the same period was about 19% of pre-crisis GDP.[4]

Now, the question of exactly how much regulation leads to the optimal outcome in terms of long-term growth is, of course, debatable. But let me underline that ambitious attempts have been made by the BIS, but also the OECD and others, to assess the net effect of recent regulatory reform measures, and the results generally point in one direction: that the net effect of reforms is positive.

In addition, let me also underline that the Basel Committee has not been blind and deaf to the worries expressed by the industry about excessive regulation. Many adjustments have been made, not least when it comes to the new liquidity regulation. It is also standard procedure that new regulations are subject to industry consultation and in many cases additional discussions also take place with the industry itself, as well as with investors, to avoid unintended consequences.

In this context, however, let me remind us all that the reactions we get from the banking industry are sometimes slightly biased, if I dare say so.

A telling example is the lobbying effort during the design of the Basel II framework. As part of that work, in 2003 the Committee consulted on a new securitization framework, which, with the benefit of hindsight, turned out to be very weak. Yet the comments from the industry on the proposed securitization framework were in general quite alarming.

Allow me to quote just a couple of the replies to the consultation proposal that the Committee received (all of which are publicly available):

---

[3] See Laeven and Valencia (2013). Output losses are computed as the cumulative sum of the differences between actual and trend real GDP over the crisis period in relation to pre-crisis GDP.

[4] Basel Committee on Banking Supervision (2010). The loss of output referred to represents the median cumulative discounted output loss reported by a number of academic studies assessed in the study, measured over the period from the peak to the end of the crisis. The output loss does not include permanent losses in GDP, i.e., where the GDP trend does not recover to the pre-crisis level.

- One bank wrote: "The prescribed risk weightings for securitisation exposure(s)...result in excessive risk weights compared to the economic risks of securitisation tranches, particularly for retail and mortgage portfolios." — This particular bank happened to incur US$24.7 billion in losses from CDOs during the crisis.[5]
- Another bank wrote: "If adopted, the current proposal for securitisation will materially impair the ability of banks to distribute risk from their own balance sheets into the capital markets." — This bank incurred US$ 13 billion losses in Q1 2008 and US$19 billion in write downs on real estate and related structured credit positions.[6]

Let me emphasize that there is nothing special with these two examples. I can assure you that there are many more similar examples to quote — the message being that the proposed reforms were overly restrictive, would damage the market and reduce activity. This illustrates that we need perspective when assessing the feasibility of reforms.

To sum up so far: yes, there has been a strong regulatory reaction to the crisis, but as I see it, this is appropriate, given:

- the pre-crisis regulatory framework,
- the costs crises give rise to, and
- the efforts that the Basel Committee has made to mitigate risks of unintended consequences.

The problem is that myopic observers tend to forget these aspects.

Are We There Yet? What are the Remaining Challenges?

I would now like to change perspective slightly and ask, are we there yet? Have our efforts done the trick, or are there still challenges to be tackled?

---

[5] The bank stating this was Merrill Lynch. Source: The Financial Crisis Inquiry Report, January 2011.
[6] Source: Shareholder Report on UBS' Write-Downs.

Well, from a Basel Committee perspective I am pleased to be able to say that the Basel III framework is now agreed — in principle. This is a major achievement that all participating parties should be proud of. If I widen the scope, beyond the Basel III framework, and look at other parts of the reform agenda, it is obvious that the work on ending the 'too big to fail' problem has been difficult, and that some work still remains to be done.

However, the reason we have not yet reached our goal is not lack of effort, but simply that the resolution of very large, cross-border banks is not easy. The main remaining issue here concerns how to ensure that global systemically important banks have sufficient capacity to absorb losses in resolution, without having to ask tax-payers to foot the bill. This work goes under the name of T-LAC, or total loss absorbing capacity. I find it reasonable to believe that there will be an agreement on a consultative document to be published in the context of the G20 summit in Brisbane.

So, viewed against the broad regulatory reform agenda put in place as a reaction to the crisis, it is fair to say that we are indeed seeing some light at the end of the tunnel. The main pieces are starting to come in place.

Unfortunately, concluding the post crisis reform agenda does not mean that we can lie down, relax and declare 'mission accomplished'. We need to look closely at the regulatory framework, remind ourselves of the reasons we put these measures in place, and ask whether they are delivering the right outcomes. And here I would like to focus on the interlinked issues of implementation and calibration. Let me start with some reflections on implementation.

For some time now, the Basel Committee has engaged in the process of monitoring and assessing how members implement what has been agreed by the Committee. The assessment work is carried out on a jurisdictional as well as on a thematic basis.

In the jurisdictional assessment we look at how Committee members have implemented the Basel standard — determining whether or not it is a fair reflection of the Basel III requirements. After an assessment has been thoroughly debated in the Committee, the final assessment becomes public.[7]

The assessments, and the publication of the results, have proved to be a powerful tool. To date, more than 200 adjustments have been made by member jurisdictions in response to findings raised by the assessment teams. In addition, the process has also generated a positive feedback loop, meaning that the lessons learnt from assessments are used to improve and clarify the standards. So far, the assessments have concentrated on the capital framework, but from 2015 onwards the scope of this work will widen further to include the implementation of the liquidity coverage ratio and the SIB-requirements.

However, for the new, stricter requirements to bring the benefits we are aiming for, it is important that they be properly reflected, not only in national legislation, but also at the level of individual banks. To use an analogy of car safety, if we are now providing banks with air bags, in the form of higher capital requirements, it is important that those airbags are actually activated in case of an accident. For this to happen, the sensors need to be functioning and well-calibrated. For banks, this means that risk weights need to signal appropriately the risks that individual banks actually face.

This aspect is captured in the Committee's thematic assessments. To put it simply, in these assessments we examined whether the banks' risk-weighted assets could be trusted. The results showed that banks' risk-weighted assets differ to an extent that goes well beyond what can be explained by business models and historical experiences. If we just take the banking-book results, two banks with exactly the same assets could report capital ratios that differ by as much as 4 percentage points.

The potential for differences this wide, particularly as they are derived from only a part of a bank's business, weakens confidence in the measurement of bank capital. Of course, this was not a total surprise. It was a reflection of what I mentioned earlier: that internally-modelled

---

[7]By end-2014 it is expected that all jurisdictions with G-SIBs will have been assessed, in addition to some others (total 17 countries). By 2016, all Basel Committee member jurisdictions are expected to have gone through the assessment of their capital framework.

risk weights lead to capital not keeping pace with asset expansion. This has undermined the confidence in banks and the credibility of the concept of banks' internally-modelled risk weights. Ensuring consistency in the implementation of risk-based capital standards will therefore be a key factor in restoring confidence in banks.

The Committee is thus assessing bank capital ratios with a view to ensuring that they appropriately reflect the risks that banks face. There should be 'truth in advertising' for the regulatory ratios that banks present. To achieve this, the regulatory framework needs to deliver readily comprehensible and comparable outcomes. In my view, these assessments, both the jurisdictional and the thematic that compares risk-weighted assets, are absolutely vital for achieving our goals. This will be an important focus for the Committee in the coming years.

I would now like to take a step further and focus on the link between implementation and how the system should be calibrated. Because my view is that there are a number of trade-offs at play here, which need to be taken into account.

For instance, if we don't implement the necessary changes and succeed in properly restoring the credibility of risk-weighted capital ratios, a more important role will have to be played by other parts of the regulatory system, such as the leverage ratio. For now, our working hypothesis is a regulatory minimum leverage ratio of 3%, but to me this is more of a place-holder. What the final outcome should be will depend on the calibration of the whole regulatory framework, in which the risk weights and leverage ratio are important pieces.

An important element in this calibration will be transparency — the more transparent banks are with methods and models to calculate risk weights, the better it will be for the credibility of the system as such.

If we widen the perspective further, I think there is also an interesting issue of calibration linked to the concept of going-concern capital requirements on the one hand, and gone-concern capital requirements on the other. When we discuss appropriate levels of TLAC we should keep in mind that the less we strengthen the credibility of the system for going concern capital requirements, the higher banks' gone-concern capacity to absorb losses will have to be.

Concluding Remarks

So, to wrap up: I see no reason to pull the brake on regulatory reforms. We must not lose sight of the long-term benefits of limiting the costs to society that financial crises cause.

And, although a lot has been achieved, challenges still remain — especially when it comes to implementation, implementation monitoring and calibration of the whole framework. As I said earlier, I do not know with full certainty how all the different parts of the reforms will play out together. This further underlines the necessity to constantly monitor what is happening, very much in line with what the organizers of this conference are doing. And as financial systems have an amazing ability to reinvent themselves, regulatory reform is a never-ending task. Therefore, we need forums such as this conference to evaluate where we are, and where we should be going — hopefully, then, we won't have to make regulatory leaps quite as far as we were forced to this time.

References

Basel Committee on Banking Supervision (2010), *An Assessment of the Long-Term Economic Impact of the New Regulatory Framework*, August 2010. Available at: http://www.bis.org/publ/bcbs173.pdf.

Laeven, L., and F. Valencia (2013), "Systemic Banking Crises Database," *IMF Economic Review* 61(2), 225–270.

The Financial Crisis Inquiry Report (January 2011), Available at: http://fcic.law.stanford.edu/report.

Shareholder Report on UBS' Write-Downs (April 18, 2008), Available at: http://www.ubs.com/1/ShowMedia/investors/agm?contentId=140333&name=080418ShareholderReport.pdf.

Sveriges Riksbank (2013), *Financial Stability Report 2013:2*, November 2013, Available at: http://www.riksbank.se/Documents/Rapporter/FSR/2013/FSR_2/rap_fsr2_131128_eng.pdf.

A Financial System Perspective on Central Clearing of Derivatives

— CHAPTER 3

- Jerome H. Powell
  Board of Governors of the Federal Reserve System

Thank you for the opportunity to address the important topic of how the financial system and its regulation have evolved in response to the global financial crisis. I will focus my remarks on the global initiative to expand central clearing of over-the-counter (OTC) derivatives. While we have made significant progress in enlisting central clearing to reduce systemic risks, I will argue that there is a good deal more to do to ensure that the reforms achieve their potential and minimize the possibility of unintended and undesirable consequences.

Prior to the crisis, the then highly opaque market for OTC derivatives grew at an astonishing and unsustainable pace of nearly 25% per annum in a context of relatively light regulation and bilateral clearing.[1] With the benefit of hindsight, we know that along with this torrid

---

Jerome Powell is a Member of the Board of Governors of the Federal Reserve System. The views expressed here are the authors and are not necessarily shared by other members of the Federal Reserve Board or the Federal Open Market Committee.
[1] According to the Bank for International Settlements, the notional amount of OTC derivatives outstanding grew from US$80.3 trillion in December 1998 to US$598.1 trillion in December 2008, which corresponds to an annual growth rate of 22.2% per year. For more information, see Bank for International Settlements (2014).

growth came an unmeasured and underappreciated buildup of risk. The spectacular losses suffered by American International Group, Inc., or AIG, on its derivatives positions, and the resulting concerns about the potential effect of AIG's failure on its major derivatives counterparties, serve as particularly apt reminders of the wider failures and weaknesses that were revealed by the crisis.

The threats posed were global, and the response was global as well. In September 2009, the Group of Twenty (G-20) mandated that all sufficiently standardized derivatives should be centrally cleared — a sea change in the functioning and regulation of these markets. And in the five intervening years, substantial progress has been made in the United States and abroad to implement this reform and begin to reduce systemic risk in these markets. According to public data, roughly 20% of all credit derivatives and 45% of all interest rate derivatives are now centrally cleared — amounts that have grown substantially since 2009, when central clearing of credit derivatives began and the amount of cleared interest rate derivatives was at roughly one-half of its current level.[2] These amounts should continue to grow over time as central clearing and, especially, client clearing requirements take effect in more jurisdictions.

Given the global nature of derivatives markets, the success of the reform agenda depends critically on international coo rdination. Thus, to support the move to central clearing and address other lessons from the financial crisis, regulators developed the new *Principles for Financial Market Infrastructures* (PFMIs) for the infrastructures that clear derivatives, securities, and payments.[3] The PFMIs are comprehensive international standards for the governance, risk management, and operation of central counterparties (CCPs) and other financial market infrastructures. Such standards are essential given that, in the interest of transparency and improved risk management, policymakers have encouraged the concentration of activities at these key nodes. And it is particularly important that the standards be promulgated globally, given the potential for OTC derivatives to span multiple jurisdictions and to migrate to jurisdictions where standards and risk management are less robust. Regulators

---

[2] Financial Stability Board (2014a).

[3] See Committee on Payment and Settlement Systems and Technical Committee of the International Organization of Securities Commissions (2012).

are now engaged in the important work of translating these principles into national regulations. Only when these strong international standards have been implemented at CCPs around the world can the risk reduction promised by the global clearing mandate be fully realized.

Further Challenges Facing Central Clearing

The task is far from complete. We must consider how central clearing and CCPs fit into the rest of the financial system. From this systemwide perspective, central clearing raises a number of important issues that should be kept in mind as its use increases. I will now consider several of those issues and associated challenges in some detail.

A number of commentators have argued that the move to central clearing will further concentrate risk in the financial system. There is some truth in that assertion. Moving a significant share of the US$700 trillion OTC derivatives market to central clearing will concentrate risk at CCPs. But the intent is not simply to concentrate risk, but also to reduce it — through netting of positions, greater transparency, better and more uniform risk-management practices, and more comprehensive regulation. This strategy places a heavy burden on CCPs, market participants, and regulators alike to build a strong market and regulatory infrastructure and to get it right the first time.

It has also been frequently observed that central clearing simplifies and makes the financial system more transparent. That, too, has an element of truth to it, but let's take a closer look. Charts similar to the ones shown in Figure 1 are frequently offered to illustrate the point that, as a CCP becomes a buyer to every seller and a seller to every buyer, it causes risks to be netted and simplifies the network of counterparties. The dizzying and opaque constellation of exposures that exists in a purely bilateral market, illustrated in the chart on the left, is replaced by a neat hub-and-spoke network that is both known and more comprehensible, illustrated in the chart on the right. The CCP and its regulators are then in a position to observe the CCP's entire network, which can be important in the event that one or more clearing members become impaired. CCPs may also be able to coordinate a response to problems in their markets in ways that individual clearing members would find very difficult.

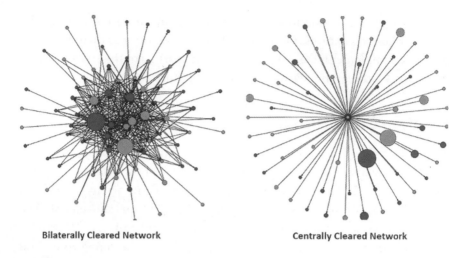

Bilaterally Cleared Network   Centrally Cleared Network

Figure 1. Bilateral and centrally cleared networks.

Note: The figure on the left shows a bilateral network in the credit default swap (CDS) market for a single and highly traded CDS contract. The figure on the right shows the hypothetical network that would exist if the contract were cleared through a single central counterparty. In each figure, a light grey circle denotes a protection seller and a darker grey denotes a protection buyer. The size of the circle represents the amount of protection bought or sold. [Both light grey and dark grey are orange and blue respectively in color.]

Source: Depository Trust & Clearing Corporation.

Figure 2 shows that, at the same time, in the real world CCPs bring with them their own complexities. As the figure shows, we do not live in a simple world with only one CCP. We do not even live in a world with one CCP per product class, since some products are cleared by multiple, large CCPs.[4] Also, significant clearing members are often members of multiple CCPs in different jurisdictions. The disruption of a single member can have far-reaching effects. Accordingly, while CCPs simplify some aspects of the financial system, in reality, the overall system supporting the OTC derivatives markets remains quite complex.

To carry out their critical functions, CCPs rely on a wide variety of financial services from other financial firms, such as custody,

---

[4] As an example, both the Chicago Mercantile Exchange and the Intercontinental Exchange clear credit default swaps.

Figure 2. Direct links between LISCC banks and global CCPs.

Note: The figure illustrates the network between banks in the portfolio of the Large Institution Supervision Coordinating Committee (LISCC), represented by dark grey, and central counterparties (CCPs), represented by lighter grey circles. Each connection indicates the relationship between a member bank and the CCP. [Both light grey and dark grey are orange and blue respectively in color.]
Source: Federal Reserve Board.

clearing, and settlement. Many of these services are provided by the same global financial institutions that are also the largest clearing members of the CCPs. The failure of a large clearing member that is also a key service provider could disrupt the smooth and efficient operation of one or multiple CCPs, and vice versa. In the event of disorderly CCP failures, the netting benefits and other efficiencies that CCPs offer would be lost at a point when the financial system is already under significant stress. Ultimately, the system as a whole is only as strong as its weakest link.

People often think of these relationships between CCPs and clearing members in terms of credit exposures, but there are also important interconnections in the need for and use of liquidity. Historically, some CCPs viewed liquidity in terms of daily operational needs. From a macroprudential perspective, this view of liquidity is far too narrow. If a CCP is to act as a buffer against the transmission of liquidity shocks from a clearing member's default, the CCP itself must have a buffer of liquidity it can draw on to make its payments on time even during periods of market stress. The PFMIs introduced a new liquidity standard that requires CCPs to cover, at a minimum, the liquidity needs of the CCP on the failure of the single clearing member and its affiliates with the largest aggregate position, in extreme but plausible market conditions. Liquidity needs are to be met with a predefined list of liquid resources, starting with cash.

Moreover, the largest clearing members participate in many CCPs around the world. Cash management at these clearing members, particularly intraday cash management, involves interconnected cash flows to and from a clearing member's various CCPs, other market infrastructures, and other financial institutions. If a clearing member were to default, cash flows and needed financial services could be disrupted simultaneously at several CCPs. Failure of one or more CCPs to pay margin or settle obligations as promised could impair the ability of a clearing member to meet other obligations and transmit liquidity risk to others in the financial system. Accordingly, CCPs require a liquidity profile that will allow them to absorb rather than amplify the liquidity shocks that are likely to materialize during a period of financial stress following a member's default.

Of course, clearinghouses have been around for quite some time and have generally stood up well even in severe crises.[5] But let's look a little deeper at the risks. During the global financial crisis, governments around the world took extraordinary actions to shore up many of the large financial institutions that are also large clearing members. While it is not possible to say with confidence what would have happened if these measures had not been taken, it is surely the case that whatever

---

[5] See, for example, Jerome H. Powell (2013); and Ben S. Bernanke (2011) in a speech delivered at the 2011 Financial Markets Conference, a meeting sponsored by the Federal Reserve Bank of Atlanta, held in Stone Mountain, GA, April 4.

pressures CCPs faced would have been many times greater and the potential consequences much greater as well. Moreover, as CCPs grow into their enhanced role in the financial system, they will represent an ever larger locus for systemic risk. It is therefore important not to be lulled into a false sense of security that past performance is a guarantee of future CCP success.

After the crisis, governments firmly resolved that even the largest financial institutions must be allowed to fail and be resolved without taxpayer support and without threatening the broader financial system or the economy. CCPs therefore need to adapt to a world in which their largest clearing members will be allowed to fail and to be resolved without taxpayer support. And, as I will discuss a little later, the same is true of CCPs — they, too, should have no expectation of taxpayer support if they fail. To say it as plainly as possible, the purpose of all of this new infrastructure and regulation is not to facilitate the orderly bailout of a CCP in the next crisis. Quite to the contrary, CCPs and their members must plan to stand on their own and continue to provide critical services to the financial system, without support from the taxpayer.

The Road Ahead: Meeting the Challenges

As you can see, central clearing represents the confluence of critical market infrastructure and systemic financial institutions. As a result, the regulation and supervision of CCPs present particular challenges. What matters most is the stability of the entire system, not that of one sector or another. In the United States, CCPs are primarily regulated by either the Commodity Futures Trading Commission or the Securities and Exchange Commission. Under authority provided by the Dodd–Frank Wall Street Reform and Consumer Protection Act of 2010, the Federal Reserve also plays a role in supervising and regulating systemically important CCPs and other financial market utilities.[6] In addition, the Federal Reserve is the holding company supervisor of a number of the largest clearing members. The challenge is to ensure that regulation and

---

[6] The Federal Reserve Board's authority to supervise systemically important CCPs is provided in title VIII of the Dodd–Frank Act.

supervision take into account the broad implications of derivatives trading for CCPs, their members, and the broader financial system. Close collaboration between regulators — both domestically and internationally — will be necessary to ensure that central clearing can promote the kind of financial system resiliency that will be required when another severe crisis threatens.

While central clearing and CCPs do present a number of complex and unique challenges, these challenges are not insurmountable. Several measures should be considered in the near term to further strengthen the market and regulatory infrastructure relating to liquidity, transparency, stress testing, 'skin in the game,' and recovery and resolution.

Liquidity

The adoption of the PFMIs around the world is driving improvements in CCP liquidity.[7] Ultimately, CCPs and their supervisors will need to maintain vigilance to ensure that liquid resources are sufficient to withstand the kinds of liquidity shocks that would likely accompany a member's default. In addition, it is crucial that liquidity scenario analysis be a regular part of a CCP's stress testing program to help ensure that appropriate liquidity planning does not suffer from a lack of vision or imagination.

Transparency

Enhanced transparency is central to the reform agenda, and there has been some progress in this area. But CCPs need to provide still greater transparency to their clearing members and to the public. The G-20's central clearing mandate shifted a significant amount of activity and control away from dealers to CCPs. With this shift, CCPs took on

---

[7] In the United States, these standards were implemented by the Commodity Futures Trading Commission for derivative-clearing organizations in November 2013 and by the Federal Reserve for certain financial market utilities that are designated as systemically important by the Financial Stability Oversight Council in October 2014.

the responsibility of managing risks in a way that is transparent to the clearing members who are subject to the decisions of the CCP. Clearing members need a full and detailed understanding of their risk exposure to CCPs, which means that clearing members must have detailed and appropriate information on stress test results, the specification and application of margin models, and the sizing of default funds to cover losses. Without a clear picture of a CCP's risk profile, clearing members cannot make informed decisions about whether to clear with a particular CCP or how to judge their exposures to it. All major stakeholders — clearing members, clients, regulators, and the broader market — should be aware of the risks involved so that they can take appropriate steps to mitigate them.

Stress Testing

The disclosure of CCP stress test results to clearing members is important so that clearing members can have a full understanding of a CCP's risk profile. This disclosure, however, would be of little help if the stress tests themselves were insufficiently comprehensive and robust. For example, consider a case in which a bank belongs to two CCPs that clear similar products but the disclosed stress tests for the CCPs are based on materially different scenarios. This state of affairs could easily result in more confusion than clarity.

It is time for domestic and international regulators to consider steps to strengthen credit and liquidity stress testing conducted by CCPs. Currently, most major CCPs engage in some form of stress testing. However, both clearing members and regulators need a more systematic view of what stress tests are performed, at what frequency, with what assumptions, and with what results. Aside from these issues involving individual stress tests, there are also important questions about the comparability of stress scenarios, assumptions, and results across similar and different types of CCPs. A related issue is whether regulators should consider some sort of standardized approach to supervisory stress testing. Not all CCPs are alike. But there may be approaches that could bring some of the benefits of standardization while allowing tailoring of some scenarios to the activities of particular CCPs or groups of CCPs. Clearly, a greater degree of uniformity would be helpful to clearing members that are comparing test results across several CCPs and to regulators that are considering systemwide stability. For example, there are likely some financial market stresses, such as rapid and significant increases in market volatility, that would be expected to have broad effects across financial markets and participants. Coordinated stress tests could also help us better understand the macroprudential risks around liquidity that I discussed earlier. Understanding the effect of such correlated stresses on a wide array of CCPs will be important for ensuring overall system resiliency. Going forward, regulators will need to work collaboratively to ensure that stress tests are robust, informative, and appropriately comparable.

Skin in the Game

A number of commentators have urged US authorities to consider requiring CCPs to place significant amounts of their own loss-absorbing resources in front of the mutualized clearing fund or other financial resources provided by clearing members. These skin-in-the-game requirements are intended to create incentives for the owners of CCPs for careful consideration of new products for clearing, for conservative modeling of risks, and for robust default waterfalls and other resources to meet such risks as may materialize.[8] The issue is a complex one, however, and a number of factors would need to be considered in formulating such a requirement.

Recovery and Resolution

I have focused so far on what we can do to ensure that CCPs do not fail: more transparency, enhanced stress testing, more robust capital and default waterfalls, stronger liquidity, and increased incentives to appropriately manage risks. I will conclude my remarks today by discussing what happens when all of these efforts encounter a severe stress event.

---

[8] See, for example, the related discussion in Committee on Payment and Settlement Systems (2010).

Try as we might to prevent the buildup of excessive risk, we need to be prepared for the possibility that a CCP may fail or approach failure in the future. When and if such a crisis materializes, CCPs will be called on to stand on their own. CCPs and regulators need to develop clear and detailed CCP recovery and resolution strategies that are well designed to minimize transmission of the CCP's distress to its clearing members and beyond.

Recovery and resolution planning is a matter of intense focus among regulators and industry participants. Just last month, the Committee on Payments and Market Infrastructures and the Board of the International Organization of Securities Commissions released their final report on the recovery of financial market infrastructures.[9] The report is part of an ongoing effort to provide guidance on implementing the PFMI requirements for recovery planning. On the same day, the Financial Stability Board released a new report on the resolution of financial market infrastructures and their participants to supplement its earlier work on the report *Key Attributes of Effective Resolution Regimes for Financial Institutions.*[10]

These reports stress that CCPs must adopt plans and tools that will help them recover from financial shocks and continue to provide their critical services without government assistance. It has been a challenge for some market participants to confront the fact that risks and losses, however well managed, do not simply disappear within a CCP but are ultimately allocated in some way to the various stakeholders in the organization — even if the risk of loss is quite remote. This realization has generated a healthy debate among CCPs, members, and members' clients and regulators that has provided fertile ground for new thinking about risk design, risk-management tools, and recovery planning. To ensure that CCPs do not themselves become too-big-to-fail entities, we need transparent, actionable, and effective plans for dealing with financial shocks that do not leave either an explicit or implicit role for the government.

---

[9] See Committee on Payments and Market Infrastructures and Board of the International Organization of Securities Commissions (2014).
[10] See Financial Stability Board (2014b).

Conclusion: Realizing the Promise of Central Clearing

A key question posed at this conference is whether the reforms instituted in response to the crisis have improved the strength and stability of the financial system. In my view, the answer for OTC derivatives reform — and central clearing, in particular — is a positive one. But final pronouncements are premature. Post-crisis reforms and the rise of central clearing have started us down a path toward greater financial stability. At the same time, central clearing brings with it a number of complexities that relate to the interaction between CCPs and the rest of the financial system, especially the global systemically important financial institutions that represent many of their largest clearing members. Given the increasingly prominent role that central clearing will play in the financial system going forward, it is critical that we collectively get central clearing right. To do so, I have argued that it is imperative that we consider central clearing from a system wide perspective, and that regulators will need to continue to work collaboratively with each other, both domestically and internationally.

References

Bank for International Settlements (2014), *Derivatives Statistics*, Nov 6. Available at http://www.bis.org/statistics/derstats.htm.

Bernanke, B. S. (2011), *Clearinghouses, Financial Stability, and Financial Reform*, Speech delivered at the 2011 Financial Markets Conference, Stone Mountain, GA, April 4.

Committee on Payment and Settlement Systems (2010), *Market Structure Developments in the Clearing Industry: Implications for Financial Stability* (Basel, Switzerland: Bank for International Settlements), November 2010. Available at http://www.bis.org/cpmi/publ/d92.pdf.

Committee on Payment and Settlement Systems and Technical Committee of the International Organization of Securities Commissions (2012), *Principles for Financial Market Infrastructures* (Basel, Switzerland: Bank for International Settlements and International Organization of Securities Commissions). Available at http://www.bis.org/cpmi/publ/d101a.pdf.

Committee on Payments and Market Infrastructures and Board of the International Organization of Securities Commissions (2014), *Recovery of Financial Market Infrastructures* (Basel, Switzerland: Bank for International Settlements and International Organization of Securities Commissions), October 2014. Available at http://www.bis.org/cpmi/publ/d121.pdf.

Financial Stability Board (2014a), *OTC Derivatives Market Reforms: Seventh Progress Report on Implementation* (Basel, Switzerland: FSB). Available at http://www.financialstabilityboard.org/wp-content/uploads/r_140408.pdf?page_moved=1.

Financial Stability Board (2014b), *Key Attributes of Effective Resolution Regimes for Financial Institutions.* (Basel, Switzerland: FSB), October 2014. Available at http://www.financialstabilityboard.org/wp-content/uploads/r_141015.pdf?page_moved=1.

Powell, J. H. (2013), *OTC Market Infrastructure Reform: Opportunities and Challenges,* Speech delivered at the Clearing House 2013 annual meeting, New York, November 21.

Part II
Regulatory and Market Response to the Financial Crisis — Banking

Shadow Banking in China
— Chapter 4

- Andrew Sheng
  Fung Global Institute

I want to thank Doug Evanoff for the kind invitation to this Conference, but apologize that I cannot physically attend. As is the usual caveat, all opinions and errors and opinions expressed today are solely my own and not related to any organization that I am affiliated or associated with.

This note supplements the remarks that I have made on tape, with various data analysis/rationale on why I think the shadow banking risks in China are manageable.

Shadow banking (or non-bank financial intermediaries) have been in existence in China, much like elsewhere, and their fast growth in recent years, especially since 2009 when China embarked on a reflation policy and loosened credit to combat the global financial crisis, reflected market needs and responses to funding and investment requirements.

Andrew Sheng is a former central banker and financial regulator in Asia and a commentator on global finance. He is the Chief Adviser to the China Banking Regulatory Commission, a member of the International Advisory Council of the China Investment Corporation, the China Development Bank, the Advisory Council on Shanghai as an International Financial Centre. He is a member of the Board of Khazanah Nasional Berhad, Malaysia and also an Adjunct Professor at the University of Malaya and the Graduate School of Economics and Management, Tsinghua University, Beijing. Sheng would like to thank his colleagues at the Fung Global Institute, especially Ng Chow Soon, Jodie Hu, Wang Yao, Li Sai Yau, Cathleen Tin and Jillian Ng for their helpful research. All errors and omissions are the author's own.

Shadow banking is not some scary phenomenon that should be regulated out of existence. There is global concern that China may experience its own sub-prime crisis through the fast growth in shadow banking credit. This was predicated on Chinese debt/GDP ratio of over 200%, rising more than 70% since 2008. The 2014 Financial Stability Board (FSB) report on shadow banking claimed that China had the fourth largest shadow banking sector in the world after the US, the UK and Japan. The 2013 FSB report indicated that the size was US$2.1 trillion or roughly 25% of GDP at the end of 2012. Private estimates of the size of Chinese shadow banking ranged from 14 to 70% of GDP. Using the FSB Monitoring Universe of Financial Institutions (MUNFI) total size of US$75.2 trillion in 2013, of which China had a 4% share, China's shadow banking size was estimated at US$3 trillion, which is less than 12% of the size of the shadow banking industry in the US and EU.

The Fung Global Institute study *Bringing Shadow Banking into the Light: Opportunity for Financial Reform in China*, which was published in March 2015, found that there is considerable confusion and double-counting in the estimation of shadow banking numbers in China, mainly because wealth management products (WMPs) sold in the banking system (originating from the shadow banks) were erroneously included. This is like adding a liability to an asset. The study found that the non-bank financial intermediaries (NBFIs) fundamentally accessed the funding of the banking sector through WMPs and other securitized means in order to lend at 'market' interest rates to borrowers. They were able to sell these WMPs because these offered higher rates than officially controlled deposit rates.

The best way to think about these WMPs is that they are deposit-substitutes and their rapid growth represented another form of deposit-taking. Some analysts take the view that a rapid growth in shadow banking means that the credit risks would implode. Focusing solely on shadow banking as high risk does not address the more fundamental structural issues concerning the way that the real economy is funded. Shadow banking arose because the official financial sector (dominated by banks) was not able to meet fully the funding needs of the real economy, especially during a period of transition in structural terms.

Our study, using the national balance sheet numbers of China, Li Yang (2013), available for 2011, illustrated the inter-relationships between the different subsectors and showed that the Chinese economy and financial system has strong net wealth that is able to deal with shocks from credit risks from the shadow banking system. Even allowing for data errors and possible adjustments in real estate prices, the broad numbers suggest that the Chinese economy can deal with shadow banking risks because there is sufficient fiscal space and net worth available to cover such risks.

First, even though the size of shadow bank assets has grown very fast since 2011, China's overall debt to GDP ratio in 2013 (262% of GDP) is about the same level as its neighbors such as South Korea, Thailand and Malaysia, but the composition of its debt is very different. By comparison with advanced countries, such as the US (307%), Eurozone (491%) and Japan (567%), China's total debt to GDP ratio remains moderate. Chinese household debt is low at 39% of GDP, but the non-financial corporate debt is high, at 150% of GDP at the end of 2013, compared with only 97% at the end of 1990 (Table 1).

An examination of the China National Balance Sheet (Li Yang 2013), compiled by a team at the Chinese Academy of Social Sciences for 2011, is very revealing (Tables 2 and 3). The data revealed the following:

- China has a high level of national solvency, with net assets of RMB308 trillion or 655% of GDP.
- The bulk of the National Net Wealth comprised nonfinancial or real assets of 606% of GDP, with net financial assets of 51% of GDP. Unless real estate prices decline very substantially, which is unlikely, there is sufficient solvency to take care of internal contingencies.
- Since China is a net lender to the rest of the world, any domestic debt problem is not a global systemic issue. It is an internal debt problem.
- Unlike deficit economies, China had RMB25.2 trillion (nearly US$4 trillion) of net foreign assets or 25.9% of total depository institutions assets (regulated banks + central bank) at the end of 2011 (Table 4). The bulk of this comprised official FX reserves, but this was funded through statutory reserve requirements on banks.

Table 1. Asia debt by sector.

Debt by Sector as a Percentage of GDP

Year End	Household Debt			Non-Financial Corporate Debt			Non-Financial Private Sector Debt			Public Sector Debt			Total Non-Financial Sector Debt			Financial Sector Debt			Total Debt			Foreign Debt 2013		Debt/Equity Ratio[1]	
	1990	1998	2013	1990	1998	2013	1990	1998	2013	1990	1998	2013	1990	1998	2013	1990	1998	2013	1990	1998	2013	Short Term	Long Term	1998	2013
Hong Kong	35	57	62	63	113	211	97	169	273	2	8	41	99	178	315	496	228	226	595	405	541	29	32	0.55	0.19
Taiwan	74	74	86	40	82	74	114	156	160	6	38	101	120	194	261	n/a	15	22	120	208	283	26	3	0.90	0.44
China	n/a	1	39	97	114	150	97	115	188	13	30	55	110	145	244	n/a	22	19	110	167	262	2	13	4.97	3.57
Korea	38	45	86	69	103	88	107	148	174	21	33	73	128	181	247	40	88	98	168	270	345	9	26	3.55	0.98
Japan	67	69	63	121	115	84	188	183	147	60	137	249	247	320	396	n/a	157	171	247	477	567	44	14	2.14	0.86
Singapore	34	70	74	48	64	151	82	134	224	77	100	133	159	234	357	n/a	374	168	159	608	525	3	32	0.34	0.59
Malaysia	22	42	70	87	168	110	109	210	181	91	63	86	200	273	267	n/a	19	22	200	291	289	12	19	1.27	0.64
Thailand	16	34	72	93	166	89	108	200	161	26	59	55	135	259	216	8	34	26	143	292	242	16	20	6.05	0.92
Indonesia	11	8	17	59	99	35	70	107	52	45	66	27	116	173	79	n/a	0	3	116	173	83	13	20	5.38	0.76
Philippines	2	5	7	25	66	33	28	70	40	61	69	54	89	139	93	18	22	12	107	162	105	4	18	1.27	0.32
Vietnam	n/a	n/a	n/a	n/a	n/a	n/a	n/a	10	70	n/a	32	48	n/a	42	119	n/a	n/a	5	n/a	42	124	0	13	n/a	6.24
India	n/a	2	10	40	36	65	n/a	38	75	52	49	65	92	87	140	n/a	1	5	92	88	145	5	18	1.33	0.95
USA	62	67	78	44	44	56	106	111	135	60	56	89	166	167	224	45	72	83	211	239	307	34	62	0.28	0.39
Australia	26	41	118	35	36	70	61	77	188	7	10	16	68	87	204	15	20	50	83	107	254	n/a	n/a	0.65	0.73
Euro area	n/a	45	64	n/a	60	98	n/a	105	161	n/a	78	101	n/a	183	262	n/a	73	229	n/a	256	491	n/a	n/a	n/a	n/a
UK	66	65	91	67	67	93	132	132	185	33	49	94	165	181	278	65	104	588	230	285	866	n/a	n/a	0.42	0.65
EU	n/a	47	68	n/a	62	97	n/a	109	165	n/a	72	94	n/a	181	259	n/a	80	270	n/a	261	530	n/a	n/a	n/a	n/a

Source: Ogus (2014).

Table 2. China net assets by sector (RMB trillion [trn]), 2011.

	RMB trn	% GDP	Nonfinancial assets	Real estate	Financial assets	Total assets	Financial liabilities	Net financial assets	Net assets
China			288	217	258	546	242	16	304
Foreign + E&O			(3)	—	(68)	(71)	75	8	4
National net assets	308	655	285	217	190	475	167	24	308
Households	149	317	104	96	58	162	13	45	149
Nonfinancial enterprises	80	170	126	69	71	197	117	-46	80
Central govt.	18	38	3	3	23	26	8	15	18
Local govt.	61	130	52	49	38	90	29	9	61
GDP	47	100							

Source: Chinese Academy of Social Sciences (2013).

Table 3. China net assets by sector (% GDP), 2011.

	RMB trn	% GDP	Nonfinancial assets	Real estate	Financial assets	Total assets	Financial liabilities	Net financial assets	Net assets
China			613	462	549	1162	515	34	647
Foreign + E&O			(6)	–	(145)	(151)	160	17	9
National net assets	308	655	606	462	404	1011	355	51	655
Households	149	317	221	204	123	345	28	96	317
Nonfinancial enterprises	80	170	268	147	151	419	249	–98	170
Central govt.	18	38	6	6	49	55	17	32	38
Local govt.	61	130	111	104	81	191	62	19	130
GDP	47	100							

Source: Chinese Academy of Social Sciences (2013).

Table 4. Results of China's Depository Corporations Survey (In RMB trillion).

Items	2007	2008	2009	2010	2011	2012	2013	2013 (% of total)
A. Assets								
Net Foreign Assets	13.8	17.9	19.6	22.6	25.2	25.9	28.1	22.1%
Domestic Credits	34.0	37.9	49.5	58.7	68.8	80.6	92.7	73.1%
Claims on Government (net)	2.8	2.9	3.2	3.5	4.2	5.1	4.9	3.9%
Claims on Non-financial Sectors	28.6	32.6	43.4	52.2	60.1	69.4	79.6	62.8%
Claims on Other Financial Sectors	2.6	2.4	2.9	3.1	4.5	6.1	8.1	6.4%
Other Items	-1.1	-0.8	0.6	1.2	3.3	5.7	6.1	4.8%
Total Assets	46.6	55.1	69.7	82.5	97.3	112.2	126.9	100.0%
B. Liabilities								
Money & Quasi Money M2	40.3	47.5	61.0	72.6	85.2	97.4	110.7	87.2%
Money M1	15.3	16.6	22.1	26.7	29.0	30.9	33.7	26.6%
Currency in Circulation M0	3.0	3.4	3.8	4.5	5.1	5.5	5.9	
Demand Deposits	12.2	13.2	18.3	22.2	23.9	25.4	27.9	
Quasi Money M2	25.1	30.9	38.9	45.9	56.2	66.5	76.9	60.6%
Time Deposits	6.4	8.2	11.3	14.3	16.7	19.6	23.3	

(*Continued*)

Table 4. (*Continued*)

Items	2007	2008	2009	2010	2011	2012	2013	2013 (% of total)
Saving Deposits	17.3	21.8	26.0	30.3	35.3	41.1	46.7	
Other Deposits	1.4	0.9	1.5	1.3	4.2	5.8	7.0	
Deposits Excluded from Broad Money	1.0	1.1	1.2	1.4	1.7	2.4	2.6	
Bonds	3.4	4.2	5.2	5.9	7.5	9.2	10.4	8.2%
Paid-in Capital	1.9	2.2	2.3	2.7	2.9	3.1	3.3	2.6%
Total Liabilities	46.6	55.1	69.7	82.5	97.3	112.2	126.9	
WMP (per CBRC)	0.5		1.7	2.8	4.6	6.7	14	
Money + Dep + WMP	41.9		63.9	79.5	91.4	106.6	127.2	
Domestic Credit + WMP	34.5		51.2	61.5	73.4	87.3	106.7	
Credit/Deposit ratio	82.3%		80.1%	77.4%	80.3%	81.9%	83.9%	

Source: People's Bank of China, Depository Corporation Survey (2013).

- With nearly a quarter of assets locked into lending to the foreign sector, domestic credit comprised 70.7% of total financial assets of the depository institutions. Roughly two-thirds of this was lent to state-owned enterprises (SOEs) and the local and central government entities, which meant that private sector enterprises could access less than 24% of total financial resources. Since the household and private corporate sector accounted for substantial private savings and the bulk of growing employment creation, value added and innovation, there was a structural shortage of market funding for these sectors.

- Unlike other economies, the Chinese corporate sector holds a large proportion of deposits due to the lack of alternative financial investment avenues. Out of the deposit base at end 2012, households accounted for RMB41.1 trillion and non-financial corporates accounted for RMB45.9 trillion.[1] Thus, even though the enterprise sector may have high bank debt (118.7% of GDP in 2012), its deposit holdings amounted to 86.8% of GDP, with a net credit exposure of 31.9% of GDP. By way of comparison, the US non-financial corporate net credit exposure in 2013 was 32.8% of GDP.[2]

Risks are in the Corporate Sector

The above data analysis suggested that the vulnerable area of risk is the corporate (or enterprise) sector, because the household, central government and even local government sector had large net assets, equivalent to 317%, 38% and 130% of GDP respectively (Table 3). Although the local governments had financed their large investments in the 2008–2013 period using local government financing platforms (LGFPs), the recent National Audit Commission study had identified the scale of debt, and the IMF Article IV report for 2014 had clarified that the general government debt at the end of 2013 was 39.4% of GDP, low by advanced country standards.

---

[1] National Bureau of Statistics of China (2013), Table 19.1.
[2] Federal Reserve Board Flows of Funds (2014) data, Z.1, Table B.102.

In other words, the central government has the fiscal space to deal with the local government debt issue through the sharing of fiscal revenue with the local governments. Since local governments have accumulated large real assets and also financial assets in the form of equity in local government-owned enterprises, there is significant scope for the sell-down of state assets to pay off debt or the use of debt/equity swaps. In addition, the central government has already decided to share fiscal revenue with local governments and allow them to issue municipal bonds to pay down their debt.

In other words, the shadow banking risks lie mostly in the enterprise sector. Whilst the latest data is not available, the national balance sheet data as of 2011 showed that the enterprise sector borrowed more from inter-enterprise credit than from the formal banking system (Li Yang 2013, Table 5).

Thus, the structural issue in China is how the enterprise sector can be funded on a more stable and sustainable basis, given the fact that it tends to be asset heavy, investing heavily in fixed assets and inventory, including real estate, but funding it largely through debt rather than equity.

There are historical reasons why Chinese enterprises rely more on inter-enterprise or trade credit than bank loans. Firstly, Chinese

Table 5. Balance sheet of China's nonfinancial corporations, 2011.

	RMB trn	% of GDP	% of total assets
Nonfinancial assets	126	268%	64%
Financial assets	71	151%	36%
Total Assets	197	419%	100%
Liabilities	117	249%	59%
Credit mkt instruments	39	83%	20%
Trade credit	51	109%	26%
Other	26	55%	13%
Net financial assets	−46	−98%	
Net assets	80	170%	41%
Net assets as % of liabilities		68%	

Source: Chinese Academy of Social Sciences (2013).

enterprises are part of the global supply chain. Prior to the crisis, they received buyer's credits from their foreign buyers, but this reversed as the buyers now sought credit from Chinese suppliers. In other words, as the GFC hit, Chinese enterprises had to seek not only extra funding to finance their own committed investment expenditure, but also to fund their export buyers. Second, trade credit has traditionally been interest-free, so they rely firstly on trade credit than on bank loans (at official rates) and for temporary funding, on alternative sources at higher interest rates (shadow borrowers).

Shadow banks bridge the gap between enterprises that cannot access bank credit. As they are able to lend at higher than official rates, shadow banks can offer the formal banks and their customers financial products that yield higher returns than official bank deposit rates.

Once we appreciate that WMPs are deposit substitutes, then we can augment the Depository Corporation Survey (the combined balance sheet of the banks and central banks) with the total size of WMPs on both the asset and liability side (Table 4). This demonstrated that a M4 type table would reveal that the banking system is using the shadow banks to lend beyond its loan/deposit ratio limit of 75%, rising steadily to 83.9% in 2013.

The above analysis suggests that we cannot look at shadow banking independently of how the real sector is financed. Table 6 illustrates the core problem of real sector financing by the financial system in China. Using the Total Social Financing (or Aggregate Financing for Real Economy) data published by the People's Bank for the years 2007–2013 (the years of high investments), bank loans funded 60% of total real sector needs, foreign loans 4.9%, net bond funding of 10.2% and IPO proceeds only 3%. This implies a funding structure where the equity capital market has not stepped up to increase the capital base of the corporate sector. Furthermore, whilst superficially the banking system only funded 60%, in reality items like entrusted loans, bankers' acceptances and part of corporate bonds were funded in the banks' balance sheet as securities or inter-bank assets. Hence, ultimately the banking system, being the large custodian of household savings, bore the brunt of risks in the system.

Table 6. Total social financing (aggregate financing for real economy [AFRE]).

	AFRE*	RMB loans	Foreign currency-denominated loans	Entrusted loans	Trust loans	Undiscounted bankers' acceptances	Net financing of corporate bonds	Equity financing from domestic stock market by non-financial enterprises
2007	5.8	3.6	0.4	0.3	0.2	0.7	0.2	0.4
2008	6.8	4.9	0.2	0.4	0.3	0.1	0.6	0.3
2009	13.6	9.6	0.9	0.7	0.4	0.5	1.2	0.3
2010	13.7	7.9	0.5	0.9	0.4	2.3	1.1	0.6
2011	12.4	7.5	0.6	1.3	0.2	1.0	1.4	0.4
2012	15.3	8.2	0.9	1.3	1.3	1.0	2.3	0.3
2013	16.6	8.9	0.6	2.5	1.8	0.8	1.8	0.2
Total	84.2	50.6	4.1	7.4	4.6	6.4	8.6	2.5
% of Total	100.0%	60.0%	4.9%	8.8%	5.5%	7.6%	10.2%	3.0%

Note: *Totals do not necessarily agree with totals per PBC data due to rounding errors in adding up components. Total per PBC for the period is RMB 86.8 trillion

Source: People's Bank of China (2013).

Some Observations

While we are continuing work to zero in on a more accurate assessment of the scale of shadow banking in China and the risks of their non-performing loans, several key observations can be made at this juncture.

First, because the Chinese economy is basically investment driven, the funding model needs to be re-examined. There is a rising maturity mismatch because the system is too reliant on the banking (and increasingly the shadow banking) system. There is no foreign exchange mismatch, because China is a net lender to the world and has sufficient foreign exchange reserves to cushion against external shocks. There is however a major debt/equity mismatch, because the equity capital market has not been sufficiently developed to inject equity capital into leveraged enterprises. There is more than sufficient domestic savings in the household sector, but there is an institutional constraint on how to increase capital for the innovative enterprises.

Second, because of high rates of domestic savings and also investments, China has high national wealth in land and fixed assets (as well as foreign exchange reserves). Given the low debt of the central government and the household sector, it will take very large real estate shocks or another global crisis to hurt China on the solvency side. The central bank has been limiting liquidity for fear of inflation, but there is more than sufficient monetary policy space to provide liquidity for the economy to adjust to a new, slower growth equilibrium.

Third, although investments in real estate are high and prices have risen in many cities, the funding of even real estate companies have been less bank-funded, but more from internal resources.[3] Provincial and local governments also have sufficient net assets on hand (equivalent to 130% of GDP) to sell or privatize for use to reduce their debt. This is not to say that individual real estate companies or some local governments would not have difficulties if land prices were to fall, but for the system as a whole, the risks are manageable.

---

[3] Between 2009–2012, National Bureau of Statistics of China (2013) showed that total funding for real estate companies was bank loans (29.9%), foreign funds (1.4%) and internal sources (68.6%). The internal sources have been high during this period due to high profits from rising land prices.

Fourth, the complexity of risks lie in the enterprise sector, which has relied largely on debt, including inter-enterprise debt, to fund their heavy investments. There are three solutions to an overhang of corporate debt — debt/equity swaps for viable enterprises, raising equity through IPOs and private equity arrangements and exit of failed companies, where losses are recognized and written off. All three solutions are work in progress, because efforts are already underway to restructure state-owned enterprises by reducing excess capacity and at the same time, improve the IPO process at both the main stock exchanges and also in what is called Third New Market, a platform for trading unlisted corporate shares. An exit or resolution mechanism is already on the design agenda. It must also not be forgotten that China still has one of the fastest growth rates at the continental level of around 7% per annum. Growth engenders resources to deal with losses.

Fifth, the Chinese banking system is still strongly capitalized with a capital adequacy ratio of 12.4% as at the end of June 2014, with Tier 1 capital of 10.1%. Chinese banks still earn a healthy net interest margin and even though the non-performing loan ratio was only 1.08% of risk assets, the loan provision was 262% of the NPL levels.[4]

All these factors suggest that China will be able to manage the shadow banking risks. This study has demonstrated that we need to look more carefully at the core way the real sector is funded by equity rather than debt. We can never solve a debt overhang problem with more debt. We can only solve this through structural change, with more equity funding and bringing productivity levels up. The shadow banking issues provide an excellent opportunity for structural reforms in the Chinese financial system, which is already underway.

References

China Banking Regulatory Commission [CBRC] (2014), Official website: http://www.cbrc.gov.cn/index.html.
Federal Reserve Board (2014), *Financial Accounts of the United States: Flows of Funds, Balance Sheets and Integrated Macroeconomic Accounts*,

---

[4] CBRC (2014) data.

Federal Reserve Statistical Release, Z.1. Available at: http://www.federal-reserve.gov/releases/z1/Current/z1.pdf.

Li, Y. (2013), *China National Balance Sheet 2013: Theory, Methods and Risk Assessment* (in Chinese), Beijing, China: Chinese Academy of Social Sciences.

National Bureau of Statistics of China (2013), *China Statistical Yearbook 2013*, Beijing, China: China Statistic Press. Available at: http://www.stats.gov.cn/tjsj/ndsj/2013/indexeh.htm.

Ogus, S. (2014), "February 2014 compilation," *DSG Asia*.

People's Bank of China, (2013), "Depository corporation survey." Data available at: http://www.pbc.gov.cn/publish/diaochatongjisi

Sheng, A. and Ng, C. (2015), *Bringing Shadow Banking into the Light: Opportunity for Financial Reform in China*, Fung Global Institute report.

Fed Liquidity Policy During the Financial Crisis

Playing for Time

— CHAPTER 5

- Robert Eisenbeis and Richard Herring
  Cumberland Advisors and *University of Pennsylvania*

Introduction

This chapter focuses on how the Federal Reserve (Fed) responded to the early stage of the international financial crisis, from 2007 through 2008, which it characterized as a short-term liquidity problem, despite growing evidence of potential insolvencies among some of the largest banks and investment banks.[1] The Fed provided large amounts of liquidity to both domestic and international institutions when credit risk spreads suddenly widened in September of 2007 and still more liquidity when these spreads virtually exploded in September of 2008 in the wake of the collapse of Fannie Mae and Freddie Mac and the bankruptcy of

---

Eisenbeis serves as Cumberland Advisors' Vice Chairman and Chief Monetary Economist. Herring is Jacob Safra Professor of International Banking at the Wharton School, University of Pennsylvania.

[1] The scope of this analysis is limited to US dollar-denominated markets and the actions of the Federal Reserve. Of course, the financial crisis was truly international in scope and foreign central banks adopted many of the same policies implemented by the Federal Reserve. For a comparative analysis of these policies across countries see IMF (2009, Chapter 3).

Lehman Brothers.[2] We argue that signs of increasing financial fragility and potential insolvencies appeared much earlier than fall of 2007. If these had been recognized and acted upon by the regulatory authorities, then it is possible that the most serious financial crisis since the Great Depression might have been substantially mitigated. While it is inherently difficult to disentangle issues of illiquidity from insolvency, the failure to recognize and address the insolvency problems in several major institutions delayed necessary adjustments and undermined confidence in the financial system.

The classical role of the Lender of Last Resort (LLR) is often summarized by a simple set of rules.[3] The LLR should: (1) lend freely, (2) against good collateral, (3) to solvent institutions, (4) at a penalty rate. If the LLR follows these rules strictly, the economy benefits from a virtuous circle. So long as the LLR lends only to solvent institutions, its willingness to lend freely to a particular institution signals that the institution is sound. This will restore market confidence in the institution and enable it to regain access to its creditors and counterparties without borrowing significant amounts from the LLR.

In what follows we briefly describe the events that led up to the crisis, and concentrate on the policies initiated by the Fed to deal with the crisis and minimize systemic contagion.

Causes of the Crisis

In the US Shadow Financial Regulatory Committee's chapter for the book *The World in Crisis* (2011), the authors noted that "The 2007–2009 financial crisis … had its origins in US housing policies, the subprime mortgage market in particular, and the end of the real estate bubble in the US." While the collapse of the housing bubble triggered

---

[2] Note that we do not address the Quantitative Easing Programs or other policies implemented by the Fed to counter the recession.
[3] The role of the LLR has been clearly recognized and analyzed since the days of Henry Thornton (1802) and Walter Bagehot (1873). For a summary and interpretation of these rules see Humphrey (1989); for a contrasting view, see Goodhart (1999).

the crisis, the fragility of the financial system amplified the scope and magnitude of what otherwise might have been a collapse in a relatively small sector of US financial markets. Indeed, the causes reached far beyond housing to include excessively accommodative monetary policy, international capital inflows that kept the risk-free interest rate too low and contributed to the housing bubble, structural defects in the primary dealer system and related tri-party repo market, inadequate risk measurement and monitoring by both institutions and regulators, and relaxed prudential standards. These factors were both domestic and international in scope and origin. They were compounded by US government policies to subsidize homeownership that encouraged over-investment in housing, and contributed to a housing bubble that ultimately collapsed.

These policies and the 'Great Moderation,' the generally benign macroeconomic environment characterized by exceptionally low volatility, led borrowers, lenders, and investors to increase leverage and take riskier positions without necessarily perceiving that they were exposing themselves to a greater risk of insolvency. Borrowers took out mortgages that they could afford only in good times; lenders made loans that fell below traditional underwriting standards; and investors bought what were (and were disclosed to be) illiquid, complex securities in enormous amounts assuming that secondary markets would continue to be highly liquid. The resulting housing bubble first burst in the subprime sector, and then spread to mortgage-backed securities, other asset-backed commercial paper (ABCP), and interbank markets, ultimately damaging the real economy.

No one of these factors was likely to have been sufficient alone to cause the financial crisis, but together they formed what is often characterized as a 'perfect storm' that destroyed several key financial markets, de-capitalized several important financial institutions and helped cause the ensuing recession (see the Financial Crisis Inquiry Commission's (2011) final report). Among these factors were a number of events outside the US — fiscal shocks, current account surpluses and financial market developments — that had important impacts on US financial markets, and arguably played a role in the financial crisis.

The Accumulation of US Dollars Abroad and the Demand for High Quality Safe-Haven Assets

Over most of the period of the Great Moderation, the US. was running persistent fiscal deficits, as entitlement spending expanded without the provision of adequate funding.[4,5] Simply put, the growth in government spending outstripped tax collections.

Three key international developments contributed to the accumulation of dollars abroad. This accumulation helped fuel demand for US Treasury debt, as US fiscal deficits increased the supply. Foreign demand for Treasury debt was so strong that it helped keep both US and foreign interest rates lower than they otherwise would have been (see Figure 1).

First, the rise of oil prices, led by OPEC countries, meant that many oil exporters (including Russia) began to accumulate significant amounts of dollar claims in excess of their expenditures. Oil exports were denominated in dollars (as were many of the goods and services these countries purchased) and so it was natural for oil producers to allocate a substantial amount of their reserves to dollar-denominated US Treasury debt.

Second, beginning in the 1990s, China emerged as a major exporter of consumer goods, with exports greatly exceeding China's purchases from the rest of the world. The resulting large current account surpluses led to rapidly growing accumulations of claims on the rest of the world that were allocated mainly to dollar-denominated assets.[6] China is now

---

[4] For discussions on the fiscal deficit, see Auerbach (1994, 1997, 2000), and Reinhart and Rogoff (2008).

[5] For a brief period during the Clinton administration, the US ran a surplus, and the national debt was cut to the point that the Federal Reserve even became concerned about the availability of sufficient Treasury securities to conduct day-to-day open market operations.

[6] For a discussion of China's exchange-rate policies and global imbalances, see, for example, US Treasury Department (2007). See also, Bernanke (2005, 2007b). Because the markets for US Treasury debt are by the far the broadest, deepest and most resilient in the world, foreign entities that manage large international portfolios will almost inevitably make a significant allocation to US treasury securities to facilitate large transactions. Relative to the alternatives, US Treasury debt is usually regarded as the safest, most reliable source of liquidity (Herring 2012).

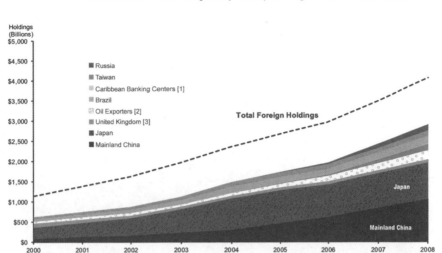

Figure 1. Major foreign holders of treasury securities and US government agency long-term debt, 2000–2008.

Note: Data area annual and represent holdings in June of each year in the period shown.

(1) Caribbean Banking Centers include Bahamas, Bermuda, Cayman Islands, Netherlands, Antilles, and Panama. Beginning in June 2006, Caribbean Banking Centers also includes British Virgin Islands.

(2) Oil Explorers include Ecuador, Venezuala, Indonesia, Bahrain, Iran, Kuwait, Oman, Qatar, Saudi Arabia, the United Arab Emirates, Algeria, Gabon, Libya, and Nigeria.

(3) The United Kingdom includes the Channel Islands and the Isle of Man.

Source: Department of the Treasury.

the largest external holder of US Treasury debt. Indeed, only the holdings of the Federal Reserve exceed those of China (see Figures 1 and 2).

Third, Japanese monetary policy also contributed to the demand for dollar liquidity and enabled the US to fund its fiscal deficit (and current account deficit) on favorable terms. Japan was mired in a protracted slowdown, which led to severe deflationary pressures. Auerback (2006) argued that during this time Japan experienced a deleveraging, which, when combined with the Bank of Japan's extremely expansionary monetary policy, flooded the market with cheap funds which could be borrowed at near-zero interest rates.[7] Arbitragers quickly perceived an opportunity to borrow yen and purchase higher yielding dollar assets,

---

[7] See Auerback (2006).

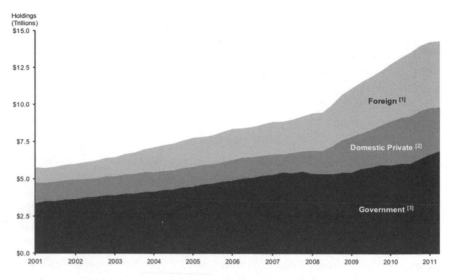

Figure 2. Ownership of federal debt, 2001–2011.

Note: Data are quarterly from Q1 2001 though Q2 2011.

(1) Foreign includes foreign and international investors.

(2) Domestic private includes: depository institutions, US Savings Bond holders, private pensions, insurance companies, mutual funds, and other domestic investors.

(3) Government includes: Federal Reserve holdings, intragovernmental holdings, and state and local pensions.

Source: US Department of Treasury.

including US Treasuries, in what became known as the yen 'carry trade.' This return was perceived to be nearly risk free so long as the yen was not expected to appreciate against the dollar by more than the interest differential. While the size of the yen carry trade was difficult to measure, estimates range from US$400 billion to US$1 trillion.[8]

Foreign central banks accumulated large stocks of US government debt as part of their foreign exchange reserves. Moreover, sovereign wealth funds invested substantial amounts in U.S. Treasury and agency securities, which were viewed as safe and liquid.

In essence, these three factors allowed the U.S. Treasury to finance its debt internationally at low rates. If the same volume of debt were to

---

[8] See Cecchetti *et al.* (2010); Fackler (2008); and, *The Economist* (2007).

have been financed through domestic savings alone, the required interest rates would have risen sharply. The Fed would have had to buy Treasuries in the market to keep its target policy rate at the desired level. This, of course, would have increased the monetary base and the risk of inflation.[9]

The Changing Nature of Real Estate Lending, the Asset-Backed Commercial Paper Market and Its Role in the Crisis

A considerable amount of the interbank funding was related to the growth of the 'originate to distribute' model for mortgages — both prime and sub-prime.[10] Figure 3 shows the rapid growth in the issuance of residential (and commercial) mortgage-backed securities. Note that issuance accelerated during the latter half of 2006 and the first half of 2007, after housing prices had peaked in 2006 and had begun to fall precipitously. While much attention has been paid to the role that commercial banks played in the issuance of subprime related securities, Figure 4 shows that foreign institutions, based in both the UK and Continental Europe each issued a more significant share of residential mortgage backed securities in 2006 that US commercial banks. But, US investment banks accounted for the dominant share.

Not only did the issuance of residential mortgage-backed securities (RMBS) accelerate, but also the market for these instruments became more opaque because these securities were increasingly repackaged and tranched in Collateralized Debt Obligations (CDOs). Figure 5 shows that the issuance of CDOs during the first half of 2007 exceeded the

---

[9] The combination of external demands for US debt from three disparate sources contributed to keeping inflation and interest rates lower than they might otherwise have been and helps to explain Greenspan's 'conundrum.' Indeed, this downward pressure on rates occurred despite the efforts of the FOMC to raise rates in 2004.

[10] Huertas (2011) notes that for some banks a more accurate description of the business model would be 'acquire to arbitrage.' In effect, these banks substituted holdings of securitized debt in the trading books for mortgage loans in their banking book in order to take advantage of the lighter regulatory capital charge against trading book assets.

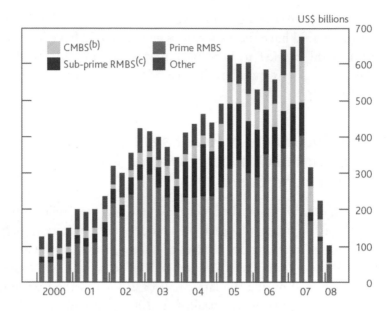

Figure 3. Growth in issuance of mortgage-backed securities.

Notes: (a) Quarterly issuance. 'Other' includes auto, credit card and student loan ABS; (b) commercial mortgage-backed securities; and (c) residential mortgage-backed securities. *Source*: Bank of England Financial Stability Report, May 1, 2008 and Dealogic.

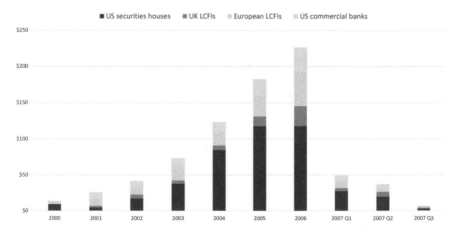

Figure 4. LCFI issuance of RMBS backed by sub-prime lending (US$ billions).

Source: Bank of England Financial Stability Report (2007).

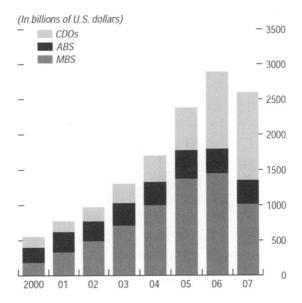

Figure 5. Acceleration in the issuance of CDOs by European and US firms.

Note: Issuance during the second half of 2007 was virtually nil. The primary market had simply disappeared when the secondary market evaporated.

Source: IMF Global Financial Stability Report (IMF 2009, p. 56).

total issuance of CDOs during the entire previous year, which had set a record.

By 2007, issuance of RMBs and CDOs had become a dominant source of revenue for many primary dealers, which included most of the largest banks and investment banks in the United States and Europe. Figure 6 shows the growth in revenue for these banks.[11] The Bank of England (2007, pp. 37–38) observed that both trading profits and fees and commissions were important drivers of growth, which was "… supported by the growth in structured credit markets. The [institutions] have not only generated revenues through their origination and distribution activities, but demand for structured credit products has also

---

[11] The Bank of England measure is for Large Complex Financial Institutions (LCFIs); which in October 2007 included ABN AMRO, Bank of America, Barclays, BNP Paribas, Citi, Credit Suisse, Deutsche Bank, Goldman, HSBC, JPMorgan Chase, Lehman, Merrill, Morgan Stanley, RBS, Société Générale, and UBS.

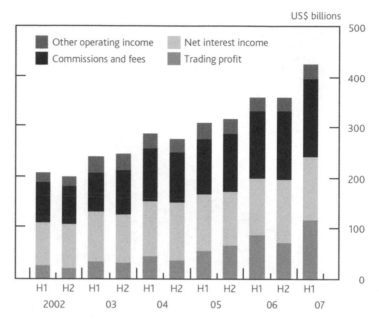

Figure 6. Growing importance of trading profits, commissions and fees for large dealer banks.

Source: Bloomberg and Bank of England calculations (Bank of England Financial Stability Review 2007, p 38).

allowed them to earn fees through the traditional investment banking activity of underwriting new debt issues."

Of course, the issuance of large volumes of MBS could not have been sustained without robust demand for such securities. Sovereign wealth funds had already begun to accumulate the debt of Freddie Mac and Fannie Mae, which was widely perceived to benefit from an implicit US government guarantee. However, demand for high quality assets was also supported by the accumulation of dollars held in large institutional cash pools both in the U.S and abroad. These cash pools, the short-term cash balances of global non-financial corporations and institutional investors, are large and centrally managed. The demand from these cash pools for safe alternatives to insured deposits far exceeded the supply of government guaranteed instruments and so private sector alternatives emerged to fill the gap. According to Pozsar (2011), estimated demand exceeded available supply by some US$1.6 trillion in 2007.

The Unfolding of the Financial Crisis

While the real estate bubble, the surge in lending to the subprime sector, and securitization of low-quality mortgages surely ignited the crisis, they cannot explain the damage to the financial system and the real economy. Subprime mortgages were a relatively small proportion of aggregate financial assets and if the claims on the subprime sector had been held in well-diversified portfolios, the collapse in the value of subprime mortgages (which was less than a standard-deviation fall in the value of the S&P 500) would have resulted in losses that could have been easily absorbed without significant spillover effects on other financial markets and key financial institutions. However, the activity was heavily concentrated in some of the largest financial institutions, many of them foreign institutions.[12] Moreover, many of the significant players were designated as 'primary dealers' in government securities. These institutions held highly leveraged positions funded with very short-term wholesale market liabilities that were subject to substantial rollover risk. Our focus will be on these institutions and the markets on which they relied for short-term funding.

The US Shadow Committee (2012) divided the financial crisis and responses to it into three distinct phases: (1) a Liquidity Phase from mid-summer 2007 to adoption of the Troubled Asset Relief Program (TARP) in October 2008; (2) a Solvency Phase that extended from introduction of TARP; (3) a Recovery Phase that began in January 2009. Our focus is the Liquidity and Solvency Phases, during which the Fed perceived that markets had frozen and several institutions could no longer fund themselves in the short-term money markets. The Fed's response was to

---

[12] The large role played by European institutions helps to explain in part how problems in US markets were transmitted to Europe so rapidly. Indeed, some of the first institutions that received substantial government subsidies were some German Landesbanks and Northern Rock in the UK.

liberalize existing lending facilities and to introduce a number of new liquidity facilities to augment funding for large institutions that experienced difficulty in financing their balance sheets.

Liquidity vs. Solvency?

As with all such spreads, precisely how to separate the credit risk component from the liquidity risk component remains an ongoing challenge for research. If it were possible to make such inferences from the TED spread with a high degree of confidence, then it would be a useful guide to policymakers (and investors). If an increase in spreads were attributable to an increase in liquidity risk, then the appropriate policy response would aim to improve liquidity conditions, but if the increase is attributable to an increase in credit risk, then corrective policy should focus on bolstering solvency.

Unfortunately, it is not yet possible to distinguish these factors in real time and, indeed, the interdependence between liquidity and default risks is so complex that it may always present a challenge. For example, when concerns arise about the liquidity of a financial institution, solvency concerns are sure to follow, particularly if the institution is thinly capitalized. If an institution is obliged to sell assets quickly to meet its cash-flow obligations, it will incur losses that undermine its solvency. But causation may run in the opposite direction. Concerns about an institution's liquidity often arise because of doubts about its solvency. When one adds to that the importance of changes in beliefs about an institution's access to government support, the two factors become almost inextricably intertwined. More importantly, liquidity crises do not last for months. As the duration of liquidity problems increases, it almost always signals growing concerns about solvency. If liquidity problems persist, policy-makers should shift their attention to the possibility of underlying solvency problems if they have not already done so.

Bank managers are sure to argue that their central problem is lack of access to liquidity. Similarly, bank supervisors and central banks tend to support this view, both because they often lack reliable information about an institution's solvency, and because they believe that providing generous liquidity support may forestall the necessity of taking difficult and politically painful choices about resolving an insolvent institution.

The Liquidity Phase

The precise onset of the Liquidity Phase is subject to debate. Those who focus on the emerging weaknesses in the housing market would select a date in 2006, after the housing bubble peaked and older vintages of subprime mortgages (that had readjusted from very low, teaser rates to a much higher floating rates) began to default at an unexpectedly high rate (see Figure 7). Others might identify the profit warning regarding losses on subprime debt issued by HSBC on February 7, 2007, the first such warning in its 142-year history (HSBC 2007), and the illuminating transcript of the conference call with security analysts on February 8 that followed the profit warning (HSBC 2007). HSBC announced that it would need to set aside an additional US$1.8 billion to cover unexpectedly higher default rates in its holdings of subprime loans at its US

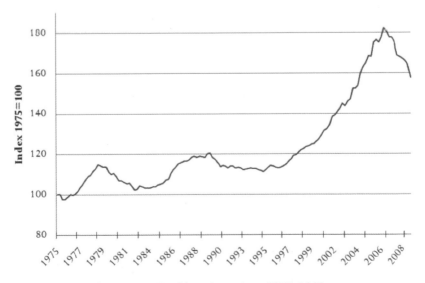

Figure 7. Real housing prices, 1975–2008.

Source: US Office of Housing Enterprise Oversight.

consumer finance subsidiary. This may have been the first clear sign of the implications of the decline in house prices for the financial sector.

The first unambiguous signs of unease in the key interbank markets appeared in early June 2007, after Standard and Poor's, and Moody's Investor Services downgraded over 100 bonds backed by second-line subprime mortgages. A week later Bear Stearns suspended redemptions from its High-Grade Structured Credit Strategies Fund and its Enhanced Leverage Fund because of difficulties in valuing various types of mortgage-backed securities. Bear Stearns liquidated these funds on July 31, 2007.

The stress in interbank markets became highly visible on August 9, 2007, after the announcement by BNP Paribas (Dealbook 2007) that it had suspended redemptions from three of its funds — Parvest Dynamic ABS, BNP Paribas ABS Euribor and BNP Paribas ABS Eonia — because the collapse of liquidity in the US subprime related ABS made it impossible for them to compute reliable net asset values. The bank stated, "The complete evaporation of liquidity in certain market segments of the US securitisation market has made it impossible to value certain assets fairly regardless of their quality or credit rating." This prompted extraordinary actions by the European Central Bank, which on August 9, 2007 injected €95 billion overnight to improve liquidity. On August 17, 2007, the Fed approved a temporary 50-basis point reduction in the discount window borrowing rate, extended term financing, and noted that it would accept 'a broad range of collateral.'[13]

Precisely how the degree of distress should be measured is also open to some debate. The traditional measure has been the difference between the London Interbank Offer Rate (LIBOR)[14] and the Treasury

---

[13] Board of Governors of the Federal Reserve System (2007).

[14] LIBOR is not an actual market rate. Rather, it is the result of a survey of 20 (formerly 15) banks, conducted by the British Bankers Association. Each bank is asked the question: "At what rate could you borrow funds, were you to do so by asking of and then accepting interbank offers in a reasonable market size, just prior to 11:00 GMT." With 20 bank responses, the top five and the bottom five are dropped and the remaining 10 are averaged.

TED Spread %

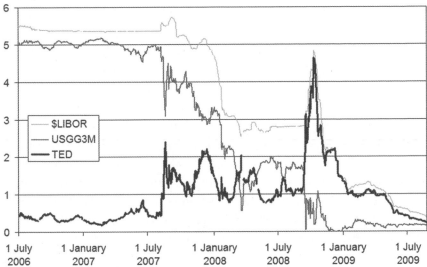

Figure 8.   The LIBOR/Treasury Bill spread.

Bill Rate (the TED spread[15]; see Figure 8[16]). The TED spread (and other similar measures such as the LIBOR/OIS spread) attempt to capture 'funding liquidity risk,' the banks' difficulty in borrowing to meet its cash flow needs. However, 'market liquidity risk' also matters. If a bank

---

[15] But LIBOR is an indicator, not a market rate at which actual transactions take place, and LIBOR deposits are not traded in secondary markets. Moreover, interbank deposits cannot be used as collateral. In contrast, Treasury Bill (T-Bill) rates are actual market rates; indeed, Treasury bills are traded in arguably the most liquid secondary market in the world and they are preferred as collateral in any secured lending. These differences imply that one should be cautious about making inferences from movements in the TED spread. Critics of this measure emphasize that the T-Bill rate may be subject to a variety of influences that have no implication about the fragility of the banking system.

[16] Although in principle a credit default swap contract could be entered into with the issuer's LIBOR rate as the reference rate, in practice the transaction's costs would be prohibitive, and so there is no practical way to insure against the default of an interbank deposit.

experiences difficulty in borrowing to meet its cash flow needs, it will need to sell assets; but if it is unable to sell assets without adversely affecting market prices, it may have to accept fire-sale prices. Unfortunately, transacting at fire-sale prices may trigger further sales if, for example, the firm is obliged to meet margin calls or is required to provide more security on collateralized borrowings. Moreover, the fall in prices will transmit the bank's funding problem to other financial institutions holding the same asset that has fallen in price.

Both measures are broadly consistent with one another in terms of the signals that were sent about financial stress. The behavior of the TED spread is illustrative. For example, before the crisis, the typical TED spread averaged about 25 basis points through April 2007. It then jumped to an average of about 50 basis points in May. This doubling of spreads should have raised questions about the cause of increased anxieties within the interbank market. The TED spread increased sharply from about 50 basis points to 100 basis points on August 10, 2007 (just after the previously mentioned announcement by BNP Paribas), then to 130 basis points on August 15, 2007 before peaking at 237.5 basis points on August 20, 2007. On August 10 the Federal Reserve (2007) issued a press release indicating that it would provide liquidity through open-market operations to ensure that the funds market would trade near its target of 5.25% and that the discount window was open.

By September 2007, the broad outline of the unfolding crisis was clear even though the Fed continued to characterize it as a liquidity crisis. What was initially perceived as a disruption in a relatively minor sector of the debt market had spilled over to damage much of the rest of the financial system. The process began with a drop in demand and a sharp downward revaluation in the price of subprime-related debt, which was attributable to deterioration in the performance of underlying subprime mortgages. This led market participants to realize that (at best) credit ratings indicated the probability of default, not the overall risk of asset price volatility. The virtual evaporation of liquidity in the secondary market for subprime-related debt meant that trading was infrequent (and possibly at fire-sale prices), and so it was very difficult to verify the market value of the outstanding debt. The sharp fall in the prices of these assets undermined confidence in the customary valuation models, which had relied heavily on credit ratings for tranches of particular issues. This undermined confidence in the ability to forecast losses and the correlation of losses in the underlying collateral. Valuations were further complicated by the complexity of asset structures that had previously had been virtually ignored by investors. This concern immediately spread to other complex securities and these market disruptions triggered several knock-on effects. The CDO and Collateralized Loan Markets virtually disappeared (See Figure 9).

The fall in prices had an immediate impact on institutions heavily involved in securitization, which threatened to become self-reinforcing. Collateralized lenders reacted to the drop in prices by demanding larger haircuts to accept ABCP, when they would accept it at all. Demands for more collateral pressured borrowers to sell ABCP in illiquid markets in order to maintain their access to funds. This put additional downward

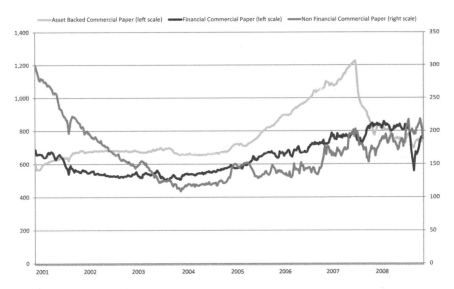

Figure 9. Weekly outstanding volume of asset-backed commercial paper, financial commercial paper and non-financial commercial paper (US$ billions).

Source: Board of Governors of the Federal Reserve System as of November 14, 2008 in Eisenbeis (2009).

pressure on prices, which led to additional demands for more collateral. Borrowers also tried to reduce the size of their balance sheets as funding costs became uneconomic.

These market responses intensified pressures on primary dealers and other participants in the market for subprime mortgages, who were unable to securitize existing warehouses of mortgages and were forced to seek other forms of funding. The rapid contraction of the ABCP market forced banks to honor backstop liquidity facilities or take securitized assets back onto their balances sheets. The emerging pressure on dealer balance sheets and income statements was apparent, even though accounting disclosures failed to reflect the extent of the damage or, importantly, how the losses that had already occurred would be allocated across institutions. Institutions attempted to hoard liquidity to meet contingent commitments and protect against further disruptions. They attempted to reduce the size of their balance sheets and increase their borrowings in interbank markets. This put upward pressure on the cost of term funding. Institutions responded by shifting much of their borrowing to overnight funding markets, but this increased their exposure to the risk they would be unable to roll over their borrowing if they should suffer a loss of market confidence.

The Fed viewed this series of events as a liquidity crisis that required intervention by the central bank to increase bank liquidity. In the August 10, 2007 conference call of the Federal Open Market Committee, Fed Chairman Bernanke provided the rationale for this diagnosis of the problem and the Fed's remedy, emphasizing that the "goal is to provide liquidity support not to support asset prices per se in any way." He added that "[T]he price discovery process was inhibited by the illiquidity of the subprime-related assets that are not trading, and nobody knows what they're worth and so [t]here's a general freeze up. The market is not operating in a normal way. The idea of providing liquidity is essentially to give the market some ability to do the appropriate re-pricing it needs to do. So it's a question of market functioning, not a question of bailing anybody out" (Federal Open Market Committee 2007, p. 8).

The Fed hoped that if it provided more liquidity to banks they would be induced to buy subprime-related assets from other market participants trying to unload them. Even if the underlying diagnosis is accepted, this remedy seems dubious. It ignores the fact that many of the market participants attempting to unload their subprime-related debt were the same banks to which the Fed was providing liquidity. It is unlikely that more liquidity would induce them to shift their portfolio preferences in favor of holding more subprime-related debt (although it might have mitigated pressures to sell into illiquid markets).

More fundamentally, the inability of the market to find a market-clearing price may have had deeper explanations. Normally, when demand shifts downward the market price will fall until supply equals demand. Presumably investors would have been willing to pay some positive price for the distressed debt, and so the underlying problem must have been the unwillingness of holders of the debt to sell at that price. This would certainly make sense if holders of the debt believed the fall in prices were temporary and would be quickly reversed.

The economic fundamentals offered no support for this view, however. Delinquencies on subprime mortgages were rising and housing prices continued to fall. Moreover, structured credit facilities were designed so that losses experienced by the most junior tranches could not be recouped in subsequent recovery operations. Alternatively, holders of the distressed debt may have believed they could delay recognition of the loss (and the unpleasant consequences that might follow, such as increased regulatory capital requirements and heavier margin requirements, or larger haircuts imposed by counterparties).[17] Moreover, some holders of the distressed debt may have believed recognition of losses could be postponed more or less indefinitely if the government could be induced to support the price of the debt. Indeed, the first draft of the Troubled Asset Relief Program (and the name of the proposed legislation itself) aimed to do just that.[18]

---

[17] Some issuers were reportedly subject to contractual provisions that strongly discourage selling at lower prices that might have cleared the market, such as clauses stipulating that if the spread increases beyond some agreed amount the conduit facility would need to be liquidated (Federal Reserve 2007).

[18] Originally the TARP was intended to enable the government to purchase troubled assets from banks and hold them until favorable market conditions returned. This reluctance to recognize losses that had already been incurred meant that doubts

It seems possible that market clearing was inhibited by the possibility of government support and accounting practices and regulations that permitted institutions to avoid marking their positions to market. This illustrates the difficulty in disentangling a credit shock from a liquidity shock. While the institutions experiencing an increased cost and limited access to funds surely perceived these events as a liquidity shock, the underlying cause was a credit shock that raised questions about the value of MBS and, by inference, concerns about the solvency of the thinly capitalized institutions that had played a leading role in these markets.

Although the Fed chose to frame the series of events as a liquidity crisis, the implications for the solvency of institutions heavily involved in the ABS markets were clear. First, these institutions experienced direct losses on their holdings of downgraded securities. Second, banks experienced losses from honoring their implicit (and often explicit) guarantees to back up off-balance sheet vehicles, whether by extensions of liquidity or purchases of securities that the vehicle could no longer finance in capital markets. Third, institutions actively engaged in underwriting securitized debt experienced losses from assets they were holding on their balance sheets in preparation for securitization. Fourth, the collapse of the ABS markets meant not only a loss of current revenue, but also quite possibly the loss of an important continuing source of revenue. Banks also faced a capital challenge. They needed to replace lost capital to meet regulatory requirements and regain market confidence, and they also experienced pressure to stockpile capital as a precaution against loss of access to funding. In addition, they needed to prepare for the possibility that they would be obliged to bring many of their off-balance sheet activities back onto the balance sheet. Credit Default Swap spreads indicated that anxieties focused on particular categories of institutions and specific institutions within these categories. As Figure 10 shows, US investment banks experienced the heaviest pressure.

---

about the solvency of major institutions that were central to the functioning of the international financial system would remain and lead to increasing financial fragility. Moreover, information regarding losses due to securitized assets was sporadic and often incomplete, undermining confidence in the reliability of banks' disclosures.

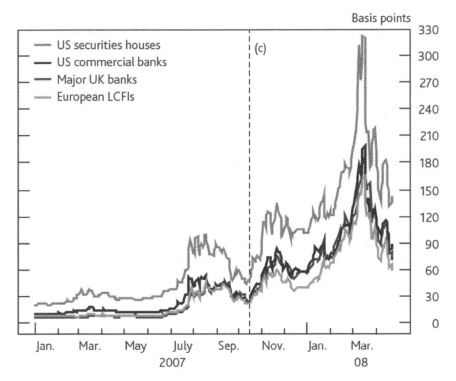

Figure 10. The evolution of credit default swap spreads from January 2007 through May 2008.

Source: Bank of England Financial Stability Report (2008, p. 11).

The Fed's Policy Responses

The Fed devised numerous ways of injecting liquidity into the system without subjecting borrowers to the 'stigma' of being observed to receive funds from the Fed. These programs included expanded discount-window access; emergency lending facilities for both bank and non-bank primary dealers; and lending securities, both short and longer term, from the Fed's portfolio to institutions needing better-quality collateral to pledge in overnight markets to obtain funding on more favorable terms. Calomiris *et al.* (2011) discuss these programs in detail. Table 1 lists the principal Fed liquidity facilities during the crisis along with the maximum outstanding amount under each facility.

Table 1. Federal reserve liquidity facilities during the crisis.

	Facility	Date Announced	Eligible Borrowers	Maximum Amount Outstanding
DW	Discount window	Ongoing	Depository institutions	111
TAF	Term Auction Facility	December 12, 2007	Depository institutions	493
ST OMO	Single-tranche Open Market Operations	March 7, 2008	Primary dealers	80
TSLF	Term Securities Lending Facilities	March 11, 2008	Primary dealers	236
PDCF	Primary Dealer Credit Facility	March 16, 2008	Primary dealers	147
AMLF	Asset-Backed Commercial Paper Money Market Mutual Fund Liquidity Facility	September 18, 2008	Depository institutions	152
CPFF	Commercial Paper Funding Facility	October 7, 2008	Commercial paper issuers	351
Programs for Central Banks and Non-bank, Non-Primary Dealer Borrowers				
CBLS	Central Bank Liquidity Swaps	December 12, 2007	Banks	583
	Money Market Investor Founding Facility	October 21, 2008	Money market investors	0
	Term Asset-backed Securities Loan Facility	November 25, 2008	Asset-backed securities investors	48

Notes: Maximum amounts outstanding in US$ billions based on weekly data as of Wednesday. Primary Dealer Credit Facility includes other broker-dealer credit. Central Bank Liquidity Swaps are conducted with foreign central banks which then lend to banks in their jurisdiction.
Source: Fleming (2012).

Five of the programs including, importantly, the programs available to non-depository primary dealers, were established under the emergency provisions of Section 13(3) of the Federal Reserve Act, which authorizes the Fed to lend to various entities in unusual and exigent circumstances.[19] Because of this, the Fed could not legally extend these programs beyond the period deemed "unusual and exigent" under the terms of the statute.[20]

Discount-window Lending (DW)

The Fed's first response to the crisis was to attempt to make discount-window borrowing more attractive. In a conference call on August 10, 2007 the Fed (Bernanke 2007a) pledged to provide reserves as necessary through open-market operations to promote trading in federal funds at rates close to the Federal Open Market Committee's target rate of 5.25%. In addition, they committed to work against any remaining stigma[21] associated with borrowing at the discount window.[22] New York

---

[19] See Brave and Genay (2011) for a description of these programs.

[20] The prospect that these programs would terminate undoubtedly influenced the decisions of Goldman Sachs and Morgan Stanley to give up their decades-old efforts to resist Fed supervision and apply to become bank holding companies during the fall of 2008. As bank holding companies, they would have access to the full range of liquidity programs established for depository institutions.

[21] Ashcraft et al. (2010) provide a compelling alternative explanation for the relatively limited borrowing from the primary credit discount window. US depository institutions had access to a lower cost government-sponsored liquidity backstop: The Federal Home Loan Bank System (FHLBS). Indeed, the FHLBS remained the largest lender to US depository institutions until the fall of 2008.

[22] The stigma in discount-window borrowing is inconsistent with the Thornton/ Bagehot view that discount-window lending by the central bank should be a positive signal to restore confidence. The reason is that the Fed (and other central banks) have repeatedly used discount-window lending to prop up a failing bank until appropriate arrangements could be made for its resolution. Removing the stigma continued to be one of the Fed's major concerns throughout the crisis. This view did not go unchallenged. Richmond Fed President Lacker, for example, expressed skepticism that discount-window lending presented much of a stigma, noting that "[B]anks in New York were borrowing money to lend to banks in the Fifth District when the Fed funds rate spikes above the discount rate. That suggests that the price

Fed President Geithner (Federal Open Market Committee 2007, p. 8) emphasized that the Fed was sending a "signal that we're prepared to relax or to provide liquidity to help make sure markets come back in some more orderly functioning." The meeting ended with an observation that it might be necessary to lower the discount rate to reduce the 100 basis point spread between the discount rate and the federal funds rate.

Just six days later, another special telephonic meeting of the Open Market Committee was convened to consider lowering the discount rate as well as liberalizing other features of the primary credit discount window lending. The Fed agreed to lower the spread between the primary credit rate[23] and the Federal Open Market Committee's discount rate to 50 basis points. Two important additional features accompanied this reduction in the cost of discount-window borrowing. Banks would be permitted to borrow for as long as 30 days renewable by the borrower, not just the traditional overnight borrowing. The Fed agreed to continue accepting a broad range of collateral (including mortgage-related debt) at the Fed's existing collateral margins even though haircuts in the tri-party repo market had increased substantially, particularly with regard to private MBS. The hope was that (Federal Open Market Committee 2007, p. 10) "[The] signal would help the banks come to the collective judgment [that it's] in everybody's interest to start financing these securities." This proved to be the first in a long series of reductions that brought the discount rate from 6.25% during the summer of 2007 to 0.50% by December 16, 2008.

Despite the Fed's efforts to make discount-window borrowing more attractive, very little lending was done during the fall of 2007. Figure 11 shows that during 2007 lending volumes peaked at US$2.9 billion on September 12, 2007, and then tapered off significantly until

---

for overcoming stigmas might be relatively low" (Federal Open Market Committee 2007, p. 24).

[23] Armantier *et al.* (2011) argue that TAF transactions provide evidence of a significant discount-window stigma. Banks were willing to pay an average premium of 37 basis points at the height of the crisis to borrow from the TAF rather than the discount window. Moreover, they found that banks using the discount window tended to face a rise in borrowing costs and a decrease in stock prices relative to banks that did not use the discount window.

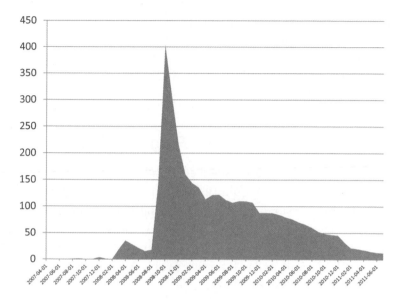

Figure 11. Primary credit extension through the discount window, April 2007–2011.

they began to expand during March 2008, in the wake of the collapse of Bear Stearns.

The Term Auction Facility (TAF)

The Fed introduced TAF in December 2007. The design was motivated by the Fed's frustration that its efforts to promote use of the discount window had yielded only minimal participation (Cecchetti, 2009). The Fed believed that the stigma associated with discount-window borrowing was inhibiting prospective borrowers from making use of liberalized access to the discount-window facility directly.

Wu (2011) and Armantier *et al.* (2008) examine the effectiveness of the TAF. The TAF auctions ranged from US$20 to 50 billion per auction. The first 10 auctions were over-subscribed and all were above the applicable stop-out rate. For five of the first 10 auctions, successful bidders were able to borrow from the TAF at rates that were anywhere from 8 to 42 basis points below rates at which they could have borrowed at the discount window. Thus, for several of the auctions, the TAF provided a subsidy over traditional discount-window borrowing to the successful bidders. Wu (2011) suggests that the introduction of the TAF reduced LIBOR-OIS spreads by 31 basis points, and the three-month LIBOR-OIS spread by about 44 basis points, in the first and into the second quarter of 2008.[24] He finds no effect on counterparty-risk premiums.

Central Bank Liquidity Swaps Program (CBLS)

The TAF was part of a two-pronged effort announced on December 17, 2007. The Central Bank Liquidity Swaps program was introduced to reduce liquidity pressures on major financial institutions operating in US and European money markets. While TAF provided liquidity to US institutions and the US affiliates of foreign depository institutions, CBLS attempted to alleviate dollar-liquidity problems abroad, using foreign central banks as the intermediary. The need for liquidity was forcing institutions based abroad to liquidate dollar-denominated assets. The swap program permitted foreign central banks to draw on predetermined swap lines as needed in order to provide short-term dollar funding to depository institutions in local money markets, mainly in the European Monetary Union, Sweden, Switzerland and the United Kingdom.[25] The program was subsequently widened on at least two occasions, first by upping the size of the lines and then by removing the size caps. The largest amounts extended during any one week under that program were about US$642 billion.

The Fed hoped that by increasing the availability of dollars in foreign markets, financial market stability in the US would be enhanced. To evaluate the effectiveness of the swap program, Fleming and Klagge (2010),

---

[24] Wu's result (2011) differs from that of Taylor and Williams (2008) who use a similar methodology but differ in how the spread effect is measured.

[25] Swaps were arranged with the Reserve Bank of Australia, the Banco Central do Brasil, the Bank of Canada, Danmarks Nationalbank, the Bank of England, the European Central Bank, the Bank of Japan, the Bank of Korea, the Banco de Mexico, the Reserve Bank of New Zealand, Norges Bank, the Monetary Authority of Singapore, Sveriges Riksbank, and the Swiss National Bank. Those arrangements terminated on February 1, 2010, but some were re-established temporarily in May 2010.

examined LIBOR spreads, the comparative cost of borrowing dollars directly from the foreign central bank versus the cost of borrowing in euros, for example, and then buying dollars in the foreign exchange market, and finally, the auction rates for dollars from foreign central banks. Before the crisis, spreads were close to zero; they rose to over 300 basis points in the late fall of 2008 and finally settled in a range of from 2 to 25 basis points by year-end 2008 and thereafter. The relative cost of borrowing in the euro market and purchasing dollars tended to follow the path of the LIBOR spreads, but the cost appears to have risen much more.

Finally, their analysis of the stop-out rates on overnight auctions again followed the pattern of LIBOR spreads more generally and gradually fell to zero, which is consistent with the conclusion that the policy was effective in relieving pressures in the overnight markets. Goldberg *et al.* (2010), who review both the spread studies and event studies of the announcement effects of the swap program, reach similar conclusions about the likely beneficial effects. However, they are careful to point out that because of the close relationship between the TAF and swap program, isolating the impact of the swap program is suggestive at best.

In one of the few studies of the swap program conducted outside the Federal Reserve System, Aizenman and Pasricha (2011) examined the exchange-rate impacts of the swap programs, and found significant short-run positive impacts on the exchange rates for certain emerging markets (those to which US banks had the greatest exposures), but less of an impact on other emerging markets. However, those impacts also appeared to be relatively short lived and may have subsequently been reversed.

Single-tranche Open Market Operations (ST OMO)

Secured lending markets began to show signs of strain early in 2008. Primary dealers rely heavily on this market to fund their positions. As lenders became concerned about the possibility of a decline in the value of collateral, and the credit risk of their counterparties, they responded by demanding larger haircuts and greater compensation for lending against riskier collateral; and by halting lending against certain types of collateral. To ease liquidity pressure on primary dealers, the Fed announced on March 7, 2008 that it would initiate a series of single-tranche open market operations (ST OMOs) directed toward primary dealers. Fleming (2012) offers additional details. Primary dealers could bid to borrow funds through repos for a term of 28 days while providing any collateral that would be eligible in conventional open market operations. Like TAF, this program was designed to provide term funding via an auction format, but it was directed at non-depository primary dealers. These single-tranche open-market operations were structured as an extension of the Fed's regular open-market operations and were thus intended to allocate an amount of funds equal to the full quantity of offered collateral at a market-determined interest rate. The program was relatively small in size, peaking at US$80 billion, and was overshadowed by later programs to provide liquidity assistance to non-depository primary dealers, most notably the PDCF introduced nine days later on March 16, 2007. (See the PDCF section below.)

Term Securities Lending Facility (TSLF)

To further enhance the access of primary dealers to liquidity, the Fed created the Term Securities Lending Program (TSLF) on March 11, 2008. This program broadened the Fed's securities lending program to include all of the primary dealers, not just the depository institutions. It permitted the primary dealers to borrow securities overnight from the System Open Market Account (SOMA) for as long as 28 consecutive days. The dealers could in turn repo these higher-quality, borrowed securities, using them as collateral in the market for overnight funds. This enabled them to avoid liquidating securities at fire-sale prices.

The Fed employed an auction process to allocate securities among bidders. Each morning the securities were taken back into the Fed's portfolio so that the program was off balance sheet. This enabled the Fed to enhance the liquidity of primary dealers without reporting an increase in bank reserves on its own books. Thus the effect of the TSLF was to reallocate bank reserves away from smaller banks or other holders of Fed funds to the primary dealers. While the intent was to make funds available to dealer banks, it is not obvious that the TSLF increased the availability of credit more generally, especially since smaller banks and other holders of Fed funds might have used them to support lending and asset acquisition.

Fleming *et al.* (2009) examined the TSLF and emphasized the difficulty in assessing the effectiveness of the program.[26] Indirect evidence, however, suggests that the program did supply liquidity to institutions experiencing stress, but that demand quickly tailed off. The first four auctions between March 2008 and April 17, 2008 were fully subscribed at stop-out rates above the minimum. But the next six auctions (which cover the period of April 24–May 29) were not fully subscribed and the amounts bid declined; all stopped out at the minimum. This suggested that liquidity conditions had improved. In addition, spreads narrowed in several key markets, such as the agency MBS repo and Treasury repo markets. Similarly, using event-study methodology, Campbell *et al.* (2011) find evidence that the TSLF helped to lower spreads for some classes of asset-backed securities, namely, in the highly rated auto-loan -backed securities and commercial mortgage-backed securities markets, but had only small effects on the pricing of individual securities. The key question not addressed by this research, however, is whether the improvement in liquidity translated into increased credit availability, thus improving the functioning of the credit channel.

Primary Dealer Credit Facility (PDCF)

The rapidity of the collapse of Bear Stearns on March 13, 2007 made clear that Single Tranche Open Market Operations and the TSLF were not sufficiently flexible to meet the emergency liquidity needs of non-depository primary dealer banks. On the day that JP Morgan Chase agreed to take over Bear Stearns (with a US$29 billion subsidy), the Fed announced the creation of the PDCF. The new facility enabled the Fed

---

[26] Specifically, the difficulties they cite are the "broad objectives of the program, the scarcity of detailed financing data, and the wide variety of factors influencing financing markets, including the existence of other liquidity facilities" (Fleming *et al.* 2009, p. 7).

to make overnight loans to primary dealers at the discount window's primary credit rate. In effect, this was an extension of the privilege of discount-window borrowing to non-depository primary dealers at the primary credit rate. The Fed relied on the "unusual and exigent" circumstances clause of the Federal Reserve Act to extend this privilege to non-depository institutions.

The PDCF was more flexible than the Single Purpose Open Market Operations or auction facilities because it was available to non-depository primary dealers at any time and allowed them to borrow against a wider range of eligible collateral. Later the Fed announced liquidity support for certain securities subsidiaries of Goldman Sachs, Morgan Stanley, and Merrill Lynch; and for the London-based broker–dealer of Citigroup under terms parallel to the PDCF (Fleming 2012, p. 7).

Cecchetti (2009) indicates that one of the purposes of the PDCF was to reduce the spreads between the rates on asset-backed securities that served as collateral for interbank borrowing, and the rates on Treasury securities that were regarded as higher-quality collateral in the interbank and repo markets. During the first three weeks of the PDCF outstanding borrowing averaged US$30 billion per day.

Two important features of the PDCF are worthy of note. First, although the PDCF was initially billed as a way of providing liquidity to all primary dealers, Figure 12 shows that the two institutions were the main beneficiaries of the facility from its inception in March 2007 through June of that year: Barclays and Bear Stearns. After the collapse of Lehman Brothers in September 2008, use of the facility expanded greatly, but even then there were only four major beneficiaries: Morgan Stanley, Goldman Sachs, Citigroup and Bank of America. Since none of these institutions was in robust financial condition when it accessed the PDCF, the program had the effect of having provided life support for institutions with questionable economic capital, rather than providing broad liquidity support to the market. Second, while the bulk of the funding support went mainly to four large US institutions, eight of the 17 primary dealers listed in Figure 9 as borrowers were foreign institutions, mainly from Europe and Japan.

The market effects of the program are hard to identify specifically. Cecchetti (2009) provides some evidence that the 90 basis point spread

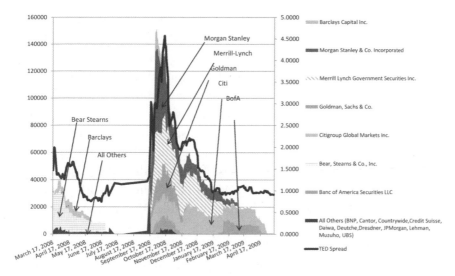

Figure 12. Lending under the primary dealer credit facility vs. TED spread.

between US agency securities and US treasuries fell the day after the program was announced, and declined modestly thereafter to about 50 basis points.[27] But no statistical tests were performed so the spread effect is at best an indirect index of program effectiveness.

Assessing the Effects of Liquidity Facilities

Teasing out the individual effects of the TSLF, TAF and CBLS programs presents a challenge because several other policy changes were made both in the US and abroad at more or less the same time, and the impacts of earlier liquidity programs continued. At root this is an identification problem, a fundamental issue for most empirical research in finance and economics. Aside from examining program usage, studies have focused on the behavior of spreads in various markets that would have been most likely to benefit from the liquidity programs. Those studies have tended to produce more mixed results.

---

[27] Cecchetti (2009) goes on to note other possible explanations for the decline in the spread.

Kwan (2009) notes that LIBOR-OIS spreads narrowed somewhat and that in regressions, variations in perceived credit risk explained only 44% of the variation following the introduction of the liquidity programs in 2007. He hypothesizes that variations in liquidity premiums might also be important, and indirectly may account for the reduction in spreads. However, work by Taylor and Williams (2008) fails to find a significant liquidity effect. This contrasts with McAndrews *et al.* (2008), who estimate that the TAF reduces the LIBOR-OIS spread by some 50 basis points. Cecchetti (2009) notes that the TED spread declined in early December 2007, which corresponded with the introduction of the TAF. However, he also concludes that as the crisis went on, the TAF had a limited impact upon spreads. In a more detailed study, Christensen *et al.* (2009) examine the impact of the TAF on three-month TED spreads. Their model attempts to control for variations in Treasury rates and credit-risk premiums, and when they do, they conclude that spreads after the introduction of the TAF were lower than they would have been had the program not been introduced.[28]

Market Liquidity: The Commercial Paper Funding Facility (CPF)

Although the asset-backed commercial-paper market peaked in the first week of August 2007, the financial commercial-paper segment remained buoyant until a year later in September 2008, after the bankruptcy of Lehman Brothers and rescue of AIG. Remarkably, the volume of commercial paper issued by non-financial firms did not peak until even later, in January of 2009. It should be noted, however, that in 2007 the commercial-paper market as a whole did not suffer from liquidity problems. Liquidity problems centered on the RMBS market, albeit the largest segment of the commercial-paper market at that time (Calomiris *et al.* 2011, Figure 3).

---

[28] Importantly, the authors cannot parse out how much of the reduction in actual relative to predicted spreads may have been due to other concurrent programs that had been put in place.

On October 7, 2008 the Fed addressed the collapse of liquidity in the financial commercial-paper market by establishing a new facility under the "unusual and exigent" circumstances clause. The CPFF was designed to provide temporary liquidity in the form of support to commercial paper issuers and to facilitate the issuance of longer-term commercial paper, which had virtually disappeared. The CPFF operated through a special-purpose vehicle that purchased highly-rated paper from qualified issuers. This effectively gave discount-window access to issuers of commercial paper who were not otherwise eligible for discount-window loans. It was designed as a backstop facility, but because it provided funds directly, it augmented demand for paper that might otherwise have come from money-market mutual funds, which were themselves experiencing liquidity problems due to increasing redemptions by shareholders. The CPFF supplemented the supply of funds to the asset-backed commercial-paper market while also bolstering the money-market mutual funds, which normally purchased commercial paper. The pricing was structured to be attractive when spreads widened, but would not be cost effective when spreads returned to average levels.

The CPFF program enabled both foreign and domestic issuers to obtain short-term funding for their commercial paper. Foreign sponsors, and by inference foreign issuers, were significant beneficiaries of CPFF program. About 125 different issuers received more than US$730 billion in financing; with more than half going to issuers in 16 foreign countries (this credit was not outstanding at any one time). This included financing provided to issuers in China, Japan, Korea, and Germany. Approximately 57% of the sponsoring institutions and entities were European including entities from Scandinavia, UK, France and Germany, in particular.

It is not clear whether the foreign entities that received credit under the CPFF had been significant issuers in the US commercial-paper market, but the Fed published criteria for access to the facility indicating that those receiving credit should have issued paper in the US during at least one period of three consecutive months from January 1 through August 31, 2007.[29] Moreover, it is hard to justify the systemic

---

[29] See http://www.newyorkfed.org/markets/cpff_faq.html.

importance to the US of many of the recipients. Most of the foreign sponsors were banks and some were of questionable credit quality including Dexia, Fortis, RBS and UBS. There were also some puzzling borrowers including Toyota and the Republic of Korea.

The criteria used to allocate funding remain murky. In the case of US participants included not only banks, but also major US companies with recipients as diverse as AIG, Caterpillar, Ford, Chrysler, GE, Genworth, GMAC, Georgia Transmission Corp., Members United Corporate Credit Union, PACCAR, Wisconsin Corporate Credit Union, Verizon and even Harley Davidson. Given the law suit by creditors of AIG against the government for undue taking of funds, it is worth noting that large benefit that AIG reaped by issuing paper through the CPFF at very favorable, rates that constituted a subsidy from the US taxpayer to creditors and shareholders of AIG.

Both the asset-backed and financial segments of the commercial-paper market continued to trend down over the life of the CPFF. Subsequently, the non-financial segment began to pick up, but only after the CPFF program had been terminated.

The CPFF proved to be both large in absolute and relative terms, accounting for over US$175 billion of the commercial paper issued at the end of October 2008. The usage peaked in January 2009 at US$350 billion and accounted for 20% of the outstanding volume (Adrian *et al.* 2011). Federal Reserve economists suggest that CPFF was successful in stabilizing the market in two respects. First, although the outstanding volume of commercial paper declined, the Fed's purchases offset the decline in demand. At its peak, the facility contained about 20% of the volume of outstanding commercial paper, thereby cushioning what would have been a precipitous decline in volume. To be sure, total outstanding volume did decline but the pace and trajectory was much more gradual than it would have otherwise been. As the pricing of the CPFF became less favorable, purchases of non-CPFF paper declined slightly from about US$130 to US$125 billion from the middle of 2009 through the end of 2010. Second, in contrast, the impact on spreads is unmistakable. Adrian *et al.* (2011) note that spreads in the market eligible for CPFF funding declined from 256 to 86 basis points from the inception of the program until year-end 2009, as the markets revived.

In comparison, spreads in the A2/P2 market, which were not eligible for CPFF funding, actually increased from 483 to 503 basis points over the same period.

Which Institutions Received the Largest Amount of Liquidity Assistance?

This question could not be answered until Bloomberg won a suit against the Fed under the Freedom of Information Act, and a team of reporters sifted through the massive amount of data released by court order. Figure 13 shows total peak and average borrowing amount over the period from August 2007 through December 2009 under eight Fed programs: DW, TAF, ST OMO, TSLF, PDCF, AMLF, and CPFF.[30] Institutions that had primary-dealer status are identified by an asterisk.

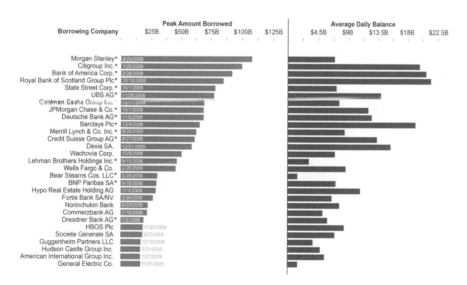

Figure 13. Total peak and average borrowings from fed liquidity facilities from August 2007 through December 2009.

Source: Kuntz and Ivry (2011) for *Bloomberg*.

---

[30] The totals do not include subsidies to Bear Stearns, Citi, Bank of America or AIG.

Note that all 12 of the institutions that drew the peak amounts from the Fed's liquidity programs had primary dealer status. Nine of the 12 also had the largest average daily balance outstanding from August 2007 through December 2009. Five of the 12 were headquartered abroad. These totals reflect the Fed's direct (collateralized) exposure to these banks, but do not include whatever amounts these institutions may also have received indirectly through the Central Bank Liquidity Swap Lines. The important difference between the two channels is that under the CBLS, the Fed's credit exposure is to the counterparty foreign central bank, which is usually considered the highest-quality exposure within any country. The foreign central bank, not the Fed, then assumes the credit risk in loaning the funds to local borrowers.

It is also instructive to examine how much these institutions borrowed under each of the Fed's liquidity programs. Figure 14 disaggregates the total amount borrowed by each of these institutions by each of the seven Fed special liquidity facilities: DW, TAF, ST OMO, TSLF, PDCF, AMLF, and CPFF. Overall DW borrowing was relatively unimportant except in the case of Wachovia, which was forced to merge with Wells Fargo, and Dexia and Hypo Real Estate Holding, two European financial institutions that failed during the crisis. These data raise doubts about whether the Fed was restricting its primary credit lending to solvent institutions. In any event, these discount window loans certainly did not dispel the presumption that borrowing from the Fed through the primary credit window signals impending insolvency, which might have been the best hope of eliminating the 'stigma' that concerned the Fed so greatly during the crisis. The TAF was very important to Bank of America and Wells Fargo; and less so for Citigroup, Royal Bank of Scotland, Deutsche Bank, and Dresdner Kleinwort Securities. For the other banks TAF borrowings were relatively inconsequential.

Single Tranche Open Market Operations accounted for half or more of the outstanding credit at Credit Suisse, Goldman Sachs, BNP Paribas, Countrywide, and Cantor Fitzgerald. Morgan Stanley, Royal Bank of Scotland, UBS, Deutsche Bank, and Barclays also benefited from the ST OMO, but for a much smaller proportion of their outstanding borrowings from the Fed. Apart from these 10 institutions, the ST OMO had negligible impact.

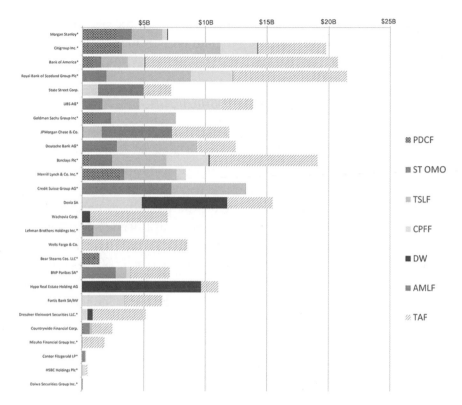

Figure 14. Average borrowing (April 2007–December 2009), disaggregated By facility.

Source: Kuntz and Ivry (2011) for *Bloomberg*.

The TSLF accounted for a third or more of the borrowing at Morgan Stanley, Citigroup, Royal Bank of Scotland, Goldman Sachs, Deutsche Bank, Barclays, and BNP Paribas. It was much less important to Bank of America, UBS, JPMorgan Chase, Merrill Lynch, Credit Suisse, and Countrywide. For the other banks, the TSLF was irrelevant. The impact of the AMLF was even more concentrated. It was hugely important for State Street and JPMorgan Chase, but not for any of the other institutions.

The CPFF produced substantial benefits for UBS, Citigroup, Dexia and Fortis, which all experienced serious financial stress and had questionable solvency. Barclays also benefited while the CPFF accounted for the majority of the borrowing by HSBC, although the overall amount of its borrowing was trivial. The program did not matter for the other institutions.

Special Benefits for Special Institutions

Overall, it is remarkable that the benefits of each of these programs were so narrowly focused. In most cases it appears that the programs were tailored for the needs of a handful of institutions. None of the programs had the wide impact that one might expect to observe if they had been designed to address the liquidity needs of the broader market. In several cases, it appears that the Fed may have been engaged in disguised bailout lending since the institutions that drew heavily from these programs had dubious economic capital. In fact, half of these institutions (listed in Figure 14) failed during the crisis, required a government-assisted merger, or received substantial government subsidies (in addition to access to these liquidity programs).[31]

The prominence of primary dealers on this list — all twenty of the primary dealers in 2007 appear — raises questions about why they appear to have received special treatment. Primary dealers are banks or securities firms that have received authorization to trade directly with the Fed. They must make bids or offers when the Fed conducts open-market operations, provide information to the Fed's open-market trading desk, and participate actively in auctions of US Treasury securities.[32]

The Fed has been conscious of the special status and of the potential implicit subsidy that the primary dealer designation might convey. At the urging of President Corrigan of the Federal Reserve Bank of New York it decided in 1993 to stop surveillance of the primary dealers and, instead, to focus solely on the quality of the collateral they pledged. The

---

[31] This does not take into account the TARP program that required all of the largest US banks to accept an infusion of government equity capital.

[32] The relationship between the Fed and the primary dealers is governed by the Primary Dealers Act of 1988 and the Fed's operating policy, "Administration of Relationships with Primary Dealers."

hope was that this would blunt any perception that these institutions had a privileged position. Yet it did not dispel the belief that such institutions had a special status — at least in part because the Fed does require institutions to meet demanding criteria before being designated as primary dealers. Several central banks, governments and some institutional investors continue to insist on transacting only with primary dealers and, of course, primary dealers benefit from spreads earned in intermediation. Thus, abandoning Fed oversight of primary dealers may have inadvertently exacerbated the problem. It did not eliminate the perception that primary dealers had a special status, yet it surrendered one potentially important constraint over moral hazard — regulatory oversight.

The fact that so many of the designated primary dealers required and received special liquidity assistance during the crisis certainly reinforces the presumption that these institutions may be too important to fail — Lehman Brothers notwithstanding. And it raises the question of whether the special category of firms is still essential to the functioning of debt markets in the United States. Improvements in information and communications technology since the primary dealer system was established surely reduce the need for the Fed to have a 'special relationship' with a handful of institutions. Moreover, it seems likely that more bidders for new issues of government securities would result in more favorable prices for the Treasury. The European Central Bank, for example, is able to conduct transactions with literally hundreds of counterparties without obvious difficulty.

Policy Concerns Shift From Illiquidity to Insolvency

After the horrifying series of events during the fall of 2008 — the placement of Fannie Mae and Freddie Mac in conservatorship, the bankruptcy of Lehman Brothers, the bailout of AIG, the run on institutional money market funds, and the seizing up of much of the commercial paper market — the Fed was obliged to recognize that improvising yet another special liquidity program would not quell the crisis. The Fed and the Treasury confronted the possibility that the fundamental issue was uncertainty about the solvency of many of the largest financial institutions. They appealed to Congress for US$700 billion to fund the Troubled Asset Relieve Program (TARP). The aim was stabilize the financial system by buying troubled assets. After an initial false start, Congress passed the Emergency Economic Stabilization Act of 2008 on October 3, 2009, which authorized the funding of a program to purchase troubled assets in the hope of stabilizing the financial system. Although TARP appeared to be yet another attempt to provide liquidity to the financial system by purchasing 'troubled assets' from the institutions which held them, the Treasury changed course within a few days and used the funds to inject capital into the nation's largest financial institutions (and others on an as-needed basis) through a Capital Purchase Program.

This was a turning point in the crisis. Officials no longer characterized the crisis as a liquidity problem affecting specific markets and a few unlucky institutions that were exposed to these markets. The Treasury was focused on recapitalizing weak financial institutions. The Fed shifted from channeling liquidity to the major primary dealers (while offsetting those efforts with sales of assets from its portfolio) to one of unprecedented monetary expansion.

Once the TARP program was launched, the banking agencies attempted to restore confidence by requiring that the largest banks pass a Supervised Capital Assessment Program. They compelled the nineteen largest banks to demonstrate that they could maintain adequate capital under the most severe of three regulator-specified stress scenarios during the first quarter of 2009. Ten of the 19 largest banks failed the test and were estimated to have a capital gap ranging from US$0.6 billion to US$33.9 billion. They were obligated to fill in the shortfall by drawing on the Capital Purchase Program.[33] This recapitalization succeeded in restoring public confidence in the large financial institutions. In fact, the losses at those institutions were large enough to raise questions about their solvency. From 2007 Q3 to 2009 Q2, losses in the banking system exceeded US$1.6 trillion, with the nineteen largest institutions accounting for more than two thirds of the total.

---

[33] From http://www.newyorkfed.org/research/staff_reports/sr460.pdf.

Why Did the Regulatory Authorities Delay Recognition of the Solvency Problem for So Long?

When so many of the primary dealers experienced financial stress, why did authorities focus mainly on the liquidity symptoms rather than examining the underlying problem of impending insolvencies? It seems clear (albeit with the benefit of hindsight) that the financial disruptions arising in mid-2007 differed from traditional, temporary liquidity crises. They were rooted in three fundamental problems that required a different solution.

First was the reliance of several large institutions on a business model that required the funding of longer-term assets with overnight liabilities. Although maturity mismatches have been a recurrent problem in financial history, this mismatch was different from earlier examples, such as the Savings and Loan (S&L) crisis in which assets with maturities of 20 to 30 years were funded with liabilities of one to two-year duration. In the recent crisis, many institutions were simply warehousing longer-term assets for a short interval before they could be securitized and placed with investors who preferred to hold longer-term assets. The mismatch seemed temporary and, indeed, had been so as long as the securitization process could be completed as expected. When the secondary market dried up, however, institutions found that it was impossible to place new securitizations. The warehousing operations, which most of these institutions expected to be very short-term commitments, needed to be financed for a much longer period. This proved a challenge because many mortgage-related securitizations were no longer acceptable for collateralized loans (or could be pledged only at haircuts that were uneconomic). The potential threat to the solvency of these institutions made it increasingly difficult to renew overnight loans at usual rates. Indeed, the experience suggests that highly leveraged short term-duration mismatches can become very risky positions. The authorities clearly perceived part of the problem and focused on trying to restore liquidity to the secondary market for mortgage-related debt, but given the deterioration in the underlying fundamentals of the housing market, this was impossible without allocating the losses that had already been incurred.

Second, the authorities appear to have underestimated the leverage that some of the largest institutions had achieved. This is highly surprising because in 1998 the Basel Committee had agreed to reduce the minimum required amount of equity to be held against risk-weighted assets from roughly four percent to two percent. In effect the bank regulators were permitting banks to take on leverage ratios of 50:1. Even this understates the magnitude of the policy blunder, because risk-weighted assets tend to be roughly 50% of total assets and so the permissible leverage ratio increased implicitly to 100:1.[34] Interestingly, AIG facilitated regulatory arbitrage with its Regulatory Capital swaps program that shifted credit risk, according to then-current capital adequacy guidelines, from banks to AIG thereby, reducing their regulatory capital requirements (Carney 2009; also Nocera 2009). Certainly, many financial institutions did not take full advantage of the opportunity to increase leverage, but the authorities were simply tracking the wrong capital concept. The new definition of Tier 1 capital provided only half the margin of safety required under the original definition, yet there is no indication that the authorities realized they had authorized a massive expansion of leverage.[35]

Minimum capital ratios based on risk-weighted assets suffered from yet another major defect. The risk-weighted assets were lower than they should have been because the regulators relied heavily on self-reporting and politically motivated risk weights that understated the risks of mortgages, interbank lending, and sovereign debt; and failed to properly consider the interest rate and funding risks inherent in the business models being employed by several major banks.[36] Moreover the regula-

---

[34] This point was made eloquently by Paul Tucker, former Deputy Governor of the Bank of England, in a speech at Yale University on August 1, 2014.

[35] Of course, Tier 2 capital was never relevant as going-concern capital and provided no real constraint on institutions taking greater leverage.

[36] Banks outside the United States and US investment banks may have also understated their risks by crafting internal models that could be used for regulatory purposes. The United States had delayed adoption of Basel II and after the crisis erupted it became irrelevant.

tory ratios fail to reflect market values, which means that regulatory capital is likely to be substantially overstated when market values of assets fall.

The problem of excessive leverage was mitigated to some extent in the United States because the banking regulators maintained a minimum capital-to-asset ratio.[37] But the regulatory measure of leverage was subject to another major flaw: the denominator, total on balance-sheet assets, hugely underestimated the actual scale of banks' risk taking. The measure neglected off-balance sheet positions and off-balance sheet vehicles that might need to be taken onto the balance sheet in times of stress. Moreover, regulators failed to take account of the leverage inherent in collateralized borrowing, which had become a major source of funds for many of the financial institutions most active in capital markets. Given the possibility of re-hypothecating collateral, it was possible to leverage borrowing several times on the basis of the same underlying collateral.

Heightened leverage exacerbated the risk in maturity mismatches and the damage inflicted by any other shock. This feature also served to differentiate the current crisis from the earlier problems with S&Ls. Leverage taken on by some of the largest financial institutions was an order of magnitude greater than that of the earlier S&Ls.

Third was the problem of complexity — with regard to both organizational structures and financial instruments. The complexity of legal structures adopted by many large banks, involving literally a thousand or more subsidiaries, made it difficult for regulators (and, often management) to properly understand an institution's exposure to risks. This may also have discouraged the regulatory authorities from dealing with issues of insolvency, since the complexity of some legal structures that crossed multiple national borders and an even greater number of regulatory jurisdictions defied an orderly resolution. Complexity of legal structures may also have made it difficult for regulators and market participants to understand the fragility of secondary markets in which mortgage-backed securities were traded. For example, regulators

---

[37] This constraint did not apply, however, to investment banks. Moreover, the Fed actively sought to eliminate the leverage ratio.

regarded the special-purpose vehicles established by banks to conduct securitizations as bankruptcy remote and so the required capital for such activities was much lower than if the loans had remained on a bank's balance sheet. This disparity invited regulatory arbitrage by the sponsoring financial institutions.

Complexity of new financial instruments also inhibited regulatory scrutiny and market discipline. Many of the assets that originated in the securitization process were difficult to value. Moreover, it was difficult to anticipate how losses would be allocated if the securities should default. This was particularly a problem in private-label securitizations because many market participants and the regulatory authorities relied primarily on the risk ratings provided by the independent ratings organizations, rather their own independent analysis.

None of these problems — vulnerability to funding, interest-rate risk in the business model underlying the securitization of mortgages, and excessive leverage and complexity in instruments and institutions — could be addressed by the provision of liquidity support. Indeed, the provision of liquidity may have delayed the necessary restructuring process and the allocation of losses already incurred.

Concluding Comments

To date, a certain amount of progress has been made to rectify some of the problems noted above. Accounting standards have been refined, but primary reliance upon book values rather than market prices remains a problem. Regulatory reliance upon ratings issued by the ratings organizations has been written out of banking regulations. Capital requirements have been strengthened and augmented by regular stress tests designed to determine whether an institution can maintain adequate capital in the event regulator-specified macro-shocks. These stress tests should be augmented with an emphasis on shocks likely to affect particular institutions. The Shadow Committee has expressed reservations about the continued reliance upon risk-based capital standards that employ arbitrary weights, and has urged greater emphasis on a simple leverage requirement that would be more transparent and less subject to manipulation (Shadow Financial Regulatory Committee 2012a).

In addition, the Federal Reserve has imposed heavier capital requirements on institutions with assets greater than US$50 billion — a welcome change from the pre-crisis trend of applying differentially lighter capital requirements on the largest institutions. With the FDIC, the Fed is requiring that large institutions submit 'living wills' that will describe how they could be resolved under bankruptcy. The two agencies are also developing procedures that would trigger remediation of financially troubled institutions, including federal intervention to facilitate an orderly resolution when necessary (Shadow Financial Regulatory Committee 2012b). At the same time the Shadow Committee has expressed concerns about the proposed book value measure of capital to trigger the process.

The process would also apply to institutions that the Financial Stability Oversight Council (FSOC) designates as 'systemically important.' Relative to the regulatory framework before the crisis, this is substantial progress. But challenges still remain with regard to the cross-border issues and the possibilities for opaque risk transfers that arise when complex institutions operate in a global financial marketplace. Despite the implementation of the living-will requirement, organizational complexity remains, differential rules and regulations apply, and uncertainty remains about whether and how a large complex financial institution can be resolved in an orderly fashion.

Although changes in regulations and supervisory policies have been made, questions remain about whether the resilience of the financial system will be significantly strengthened by more and higher-quality capital. Will strengthening the leverage ratio provide better shock absorbers? Will the Comprehensive Capital Analysis and Review process, designed to evaluate the capital adequacy of institutions under a severe regulatory-specified stress test, give the regulatory authorities a better sense of emerging problems? Will the overall impact of stronger capital requirements mainly shift risky activities to the shadow banking sector?

Will the new liquidity requirements be effective? Would they have prevented the kind of liquidity crisis that the Fed perceived in 2007? Does the numerator in the Liquidity Coverage Ratio reflect the kind of liquidity that would have been helpful in 2007? Does the denominator in the Liquidity Coverage Ratio reflect the degree of stress experienced by financial institutions in 2007?

Would an earlier focus on solvency issues during the crisis have avoided the massive dislocations and interruption in flows of credit to sound borrowers? Would earlier attention to the solvency problems have restored confidence in the financial system sooner? Clearly the barrage of liquidity programs did not restore confidence. Only full disclosure of stress tests and capital infusions achieved this objective.

With regard to the Bagehot (1873) and Thornton (1802) rules, how do the liquidity programs measure up? Without doubt the Fed lent freely. It did, however, accept some rather dubious collateral at haircuts that were substantially below those determined in the market. Nonetheless, it appears not to have suffered losses as a result. The rate on most Fed facilities was not much of a penalty. It was usually set only slightly above the primary credit discount-window rate. But in most cases it did provide an incentive for institutions to repay as quickly as possible. From the list of the largest recipients of Fed liquidity support during the crisis, it is apparent that the Fed placed little emphasis on solvency. Perhaps, the lack of efficient resolution tools biased the Fed's decision in favor of the generous provision of liquidity. This provision of liquidity to financial institutions with questionable solvency will not diminish the 'stigma' associated with discount-window borrowing from the Fed. But was it costly to the financial system as well?

It is not possible to specify a convincing counterfactual scenario, but it seems possible that delays in addressing the solvency problem may have exacerbated the crisis. Generous provision of liquidity certainly permitted institutions with little or no economic capital to continue operation longer than would otherwise have been possible. This perpetuated a misallocation of financial resources, led some institutions to defer needed recapitalizations and restructurings, and contributed to the perception that some institutions were too big to fail. Moreover, the delay in recognition of losses already incurred undermined confidence in the financial system and exacerbated the deterioration in interbank markets.

The major unknown, however, is whether the resolution tools available to the authorities during the crisis were adequate to address the insolvency issues before the crisis in a relatively small sector of debt markets spilled over. This highlights the importance of completing a set of procedures that will give the regulators and market participants the confidence that an orderly resolution can be achieved for large, complex, international financial institutions. The August 2014 rejection by the Federal Reserve and FDIC of the living wills submitted by 11 of the major institutions, after three rounds of the submissions required by the Dodd–Frank Act, highlights the practical difficulties in unscrambling highly integrated, complex institutions when their operational structures are not aligned with their legal structures.

References

Adrian, T., K. Kimbrough and D. Marchioni (2011), "The Federal Reserve's Commercial Paper Funding Facility," *Economic Policy Review*, Federal Reserve Bank of New York, May 2011.

Aizenman, J. and G. Pasricha (2011), "Net Fiscal Stimulus during the Great Recession," Working Paper 16779, *National Bureau of Economic Research*, February 2011.

Armantier, O., S. Krieger and J. McAndrews (2008), "The Federal Reserve's Term Auction Facility," *Federal Reserve Bank of New York Current Issues in Economics and Finance*, 14(5): 1–10.

Armantier, O., E. Ghysels, A. Sarkar and J. Shrader (2011), "Discount window stigma during the 2007–2008 financial crisis," *Federal Reserve Bank of New York Staff Report*, No. 483, January (revised 2013).

Ashcraft, A., M. Bech and S. Frame (2010), "The Federal Home Loan Bank System: The lender of next-to-last resort?" *Journal of Money Credit and Banking*, 42(4).

Auerbach, A. J. (1994), "The U.S. Fiscal Problem; Where we are, how we got here, and where we're going," *National Bureau of Economic Research*, Vol. 9 (January 1994). Available at http://www.nber.org/chapters/c11009.pdf.

Auerbach, A. J. (1997), "Quantifying the Current US Fiscal Imbalance," Working Paper 6119, *National Bureau of Economic Research* (August 1997). Available at http://www.nber.org/papers/w6119.pdf?new_window=1

Auerbach, A. J. (2000), "Formation of Fiscal Policy: The experience of the past twenty-five years," *Economic Policy Review*, 6(1): 9–23.

Auerback, M. (2006), "The BOJ Talks the Talk (But Will it Walk the Walk?)," Working Paper 109, *Japan Policy Research Institute*, April, 2007.

Bagehot, W. (1873), *Lombard Street: A Description of the Money Market* (New York: Scribner, Armstrong & Co.).

Bank of England (2007), *Financial Stability Report*, Issue No. 22, October 2007.

Bernanke, B. S. (2005), "The Global Saving Glut and the US Current Account Deficit," *The Federal Reserve Board*, March 10, 2005. Available at http://www.federalreserve.gov/boarddocs/speeches/2005/200503102/.

Bernanke, B. S. (2007a), Conference call of the Federal Open Market Committee on August 10, 2007. Available at: www.federalreserve.gov/monetarypolicy/files/FOMC20070810confcall.pdf.

Bernanke, B. S. (2007b), "Global Imbalances: Recent Developments and Prospects," Speech delivered at the Bundesbank Lecture, Berlin, Germany, September 11, 2007. Available at http://www.federalreserve.gov/newsevents/speech/bernanke20070911a.htm.

Board of Governors of the Federal Reserve System (2007), *Press Release*, August 17, 2007. Available at: http://www.federalreserve.gov/newsevents/press/monetary/20070817a.htm.

Brave, S. and H. Genay (2011), "Federal Reserve policies and financial market conditions during the crisis," Working Paper No. 201104, *Federal Reserve Bank of Chicago* (revised in July).

Calomiris, C., R. Eisenbeis and R. Litan (2011), "Financial crisis in the US and beyond," in *Final Report of the National Commission on the Causes of the Financial and Economic Crisis in the United States*, submitted by The Financial Crisis Inquiry Commission, January 2011. Available at: http://fcic-static.law.stanford.edu/cdn_media/fcic-reports/fcic_final_report_full.pdf.

Campbell, S., D. Covitz, W. Nelson and K. Pence (2011), "Securitization Markets and Central Banking: An evaluation of the Term Asset-Backed Securities Loan Facility," *Finance and Economics Discussion Series*, no. 2011-16, Divisions of Research & Statistics and Monetary Affairs, Federal Reserve Board, Washington, DC.

Carney, J. (2009), "How The Banks Used AIG's Swaps to Dodge Banking Rules," *Business Insider*, March 3. Available at: http://www.businessinsider.com/how-the-banks-used-aigs-swaps-to-dodge-banking-rules-2009-3?IR=T&.

Cecchetti, S. (2009), "Crisis and Responses: The Federal Reserve in the early stages of the financial crisis," *Journal of Economic Perspectives*, 23(1): 51–75.

Cecchetti, S. G., I. Fender and P. McGuire (2010), "Toward a Global Risk Map," Working Paper No. 309, *Bank for International Settlements*, May 2010.

Christensen, J., J. Lopez and G. Redebusch (2009), "Do Central Bank Liquidity Facilities Affect Interbank Lending Rates?", Working Paper 2009-13, *Federal Reserve Bank of San Francisco*, June 2009.

Dealbook (2007), "BNP Paribas Suspends Funds Because of Subprime Problems," *New York Times*, August 9. Available at: http://dealbook. nytimes.com/2007 /08/09business/worldbusiness/09iht-09bnp.7054054. html?_r=0.

Eisenbeis, R. (2011), *Limits on Federal Reserve Policies to Sustain the Liquidity of Secondary Markets*, prepared for Wharton Financial Institutions Center Conference, "Strengthening the Liquidity of the Financial System," Wharton Financial Institutions Center Workshop, The Wharton School, University of Pennsylvania, 28 June.

Fackler, M. (2008), "In Japan, a Robust Yen Undermines the Markets," *New York Times*, October 27, 2008. Available at http://www.nytimes. com/2008/10/28/business/worldbusiness/28yen.html.

Federal Open Market Committee (2007), Conference call of the Federal Open Market Committee on 16 August. Available at: www.federalreserve.gov/ monetarypolicy/files/FOMC20070816confcall.pdf.

Federal Reserve (2007), Press Release, August 10. Available at: www.federalreserve.gov/newsevents/press/monetary/20070810a.htm.

Financial Crisis Inquiry Commission (2011), *Final Report of the National Commission on the Causes of the Financial and Economic Crisis in the United States*, submitted by the Financial Crisis Inquiry Commission, January 2011. Available at: http://fcic-static.law.stanford.edu/cdn_media/ fcic-reports/fcic_final_report_full.pdf.

Fleming, M. (2012), "Federal Reserve liquidity provision during the Financial Crisis of 2007–2009," Staff Report No. 563, *Federal Reserve Bank of New York*, July 2012.

Fleming, M. and N. Klagge (2010), "The Federal Reserve's Foreign Exchange Swap Lines," *Federal Reserve Bank of New York Current Issues in Economics and Finance*, 16(4).

Fleming, M., W. Hrung and F. Keane (2009), "The Term Securities Lending Facility: Origin, design, and effects," *Federal Reserve Bank of New York Current Issues in Economics and Finance,* 15(2).

Goldberg, L., C. Kennedy and J. Miu (2010), "Central Bank Dollar Swap Lines and Overseas Dollar Funding Costs," Staff Report No. 429, *Federal Reserve Bank of New York*, February 2010.

Goodhart, C. A. E. (1999), "Myths about the lender of last resort," *International Finance*, 2(3): 339–360.

Hassel, A. and S. Lütz (2012), "Balancing Competition and Cooperation: The state's new power in crisis management," London School of Economics and Political Science (LSE), *Europe in Question,* Discussion Paper Series 50/2012, p. 11.

Herring, R. (2012), "Default and the International Role of the Dollar," in F. Allen, A. Gelpern, C. Mooney and D. Skeele (eds.) *Is US Government Debt Different* (Wharton Financial Institutions Center, PA: FID Press), pp. 21–34.

Huertas, T. (2011), *Crisis: Cause, Containment and Cure* (New York: Palgrave Macmillan).

Humphrey, T. (1989), "Lender of Last Resort: The concept in history," *Federal Reserve Bank of Richmond Economic Review*, 72(2): 8–16.

HSBC (2007), "HSBC Trading Update — US Mortgage Services," *Business Wire*, February 7, Available at: www.businesswire.com/news/home/20070207006360/en/HSBC-Trading-Update — Mortgage-Services#.U_9tBhBAdm0. And the illuminating transcript of the conference call with security analysts that followed the profit warning, on February 8, 2007.

International Monetary Fund [IMF] (2009), "Navigating the Financial Challenges Ahead," *World Economic and Financial Surveys: Global Financial Stability Report*, October 2009. Available at: http://www.imf.org/external/pubs/ft/gfsr/2009/02/.

Kuntz, P. and B. Ivry (2011), "Fed's Once-Secret Data Compiled by Bloomberg Released to Public", *Bloomberg*, December 23. Available at: http://www.bloomberg.com/news/articles/2011-12-23/fed-s-once-secret-data-compiled-by-bloomberg-released-to-public.

Kwan, S. (2009), "Behavior of Libor in the Current Financial Crisis," *FRBSF Economic Letter*, 2009-04, January 23.

McAndrews, J., A. Sarkar and Z. Wang (2008), "The Effect of the Term Auction Facility on the London Inter-Bank Offered Rate," *Federal Reserve Bank of New York Staff Report*, No. 335.

Nocera, J. (2009), "Propping up a House of Cards," *New York Times*, March 2. Available at: http://dealbook.nytimes.com/2009/03/02/propping-up-a-house-of-cards/?_php=true&_type=blogs&_r=0.

Pozsar, Z. (2011), "Institutional Cash Pools and the Triffin Dilemma of the U.S. Banking System," IMF Working Paper, WP/11/190, August.

Reinhart, C. M. and K. S. Rogoff (2008), "This Time is Different: A panoramic view of eight centuries of financial crises," Working Paper No. 13882, *NBER,* April 16. Available at http://www.nber.org/papers/w13882.pdf.

Schwarz, K. (2014), "Mind the Gap: Disentangling credit and liquidity risk spreads," Working Paper, Department of Finance, the Wharton School, May 21. Available at: http://finance.wharton.upenn.edu/~kschwarz/Spreads.pdf.

Shadow Financial Regulatory Committee (2011), "Financial crisis in the US and beyond," in R. Litan (ed.) *World in Crisis: Insights from Six Shadow Financial Regulatory Committees Around the World* (Wharton Financial Institutions Center, PA: FIC Press), pp. 1–60.

Shadow Financial Regulatory Committee (2012a), *Alternatives to the Proposed Risk-Based Bank Capital Standards,* Statement No. 323, February 13.

Shadow Financial Regulatory Committee (2012b), *The Federal Reserve Board Proposal for Enhanced Prudential Standards and Early Remediation Requirements,* Statement No. 322, February 13.

Taylor, J. and J. Williams (2008), "A Black Swan in The Money Market," Working Paper, Stanford University, Stanford, CA. Available at: www.frbsf.org/economic-research/files/Taylor-Williams.pdf.

The Economist (2007), "What Keeps Bankers Awake at Night?" February 1. Available at http://www.economist.com/node/8633485?story_id=8633485.

Thornton, H. (1802/1939), *An Enquiry into the Nature and Effects of the Paper Credit of Great Britain,* edited with an Introduction by F.A. von Hayek (London: George Allen and Unwin).

US Treasury Department (2007), *Report to Congress on International Economic and Exchange Rate Policies,* June 2007. Available at http://www.treasury.gov/resource-center/international/exchange-rate-policies/Documents/2007_FXReport.pdf.

Wallison, P. J. (2011), *Dissent from the Majority Report of the Financial Crisis Commission* (Washington, DC: AEI Press).

Wu, T. (2011), "The US Money Market and the Term Auction Facility in the Financial Crisis of 2007–2009," *Review of Economics and Statistics,* 93(2): 617–631.

Europe's Banking Union
Status and Prospects

— CHAPTER 6

- Nicolas Véron
  Bruegel and Peterson Institute for International Economics

Banking union, or the partly completed shift of authority for banking sector policy from the national to the European level, has been the most far-reaching and structural response to the financial crisis since 2007 in the European Union (EU). When first announced by European policy-makers in mid-2012, banking union was met with a fair amount of skepticism from independent observers and market participants. It is now taken more seriously, since its first step, the transfer of bank supervisory authority from national prudential bodies in the euro area to the European Central Bank (ECB), was completed on November 4, 2014. However, banking union is still incompletely understood by most observers in Europe and internationally, in large part because of the

Nicolas Véron is a Senior Fellow at Bruegel (Brussels) and a Visiting Fellow at the Peterson Institute for International Economics (Washington DC). He is also an independent board member of the global derivatives trade repository arm of the Depositary Trust & Clearing Corporation (DTCC). He was listed on *Bloomberg Markets*' annual 50 Most Influential ranking for 2012, with reference to his early advocacy of European banking union.

inherent complexity of the EU institutional environment. This chapter starts with a brief exposition of the genesis and rationale of Europe's banking union. It then describes and assesses its current status, and outlines prospects for its future development.

The Inception of Europe's Banking Union

The starting point of Europe's banking union was a summit of euro area heads of state and governments, held in Brussels on June 28–29, 2012. At the end of this meeting, the participating leaders issued a joint declaration that started with the words: "We affirm that it is imperative to break the vicious circle between banks and sovereigns" and went on to announce the creation of a Single Supervisory Mechanism (SSM), as well as the possibility of direct bank recapitalizations by the European Stability Mechanism (ESM), a fund whose founding treaty had been signed a few months before. The expression 'banking union' itself had started being widely used in the spring of 2012 in the European public debate, before it was picked up by public policymakers a few weeks before the June 28–29 summit.[1] This expression generally refers, depending on context, either to the process of transfer of authority over banking policy from the national towards the European level, or to the European banking policy framework resulting from that transfer process. In terms of policy decision, Europe's banking union was the direct consequence of the failure of the earlier policy architecture, in which banking policy (including prudential regulation and supervision, crisis management, and deposit insurance) had remained a national responsibility, even as the banking sector was integrated at the European level

---

[1] To the author's knowledge, the public use of the expression 'banking union' in its current sense first appeared in Véron (2011) and was developed in subsequent publications of Bruegel and the Peterson Institute. It further expanded following the reference to it in Barker (2012). The expression's first use in an official document appears to be European Commission (2012).

under several other policy frameworks including the EU Internal Market, EU competition policy, and, in the euro area, Economic and Monetary Union (EMU). As of early 2012, this architecture had signally failed to deliver financial stability, and its flaws appeared increasingly likely to precipitate the breakup of the euro area.

The failure to address Europe's banking crisis from mid-2007 to mid-2012 boils down to a collective action problem, in spite of fleeting moments of co-ordination such as the summits of October 12 and 15, 2008 at the height of the market turmoil following the collapse of Lehman Brothers. For each national banking supervisory authority, the prudential mandate to ensure financial stability collided with the incentives to protect and foster domestically-headquartered banks against their European competitors. In most countries, the domestic banks' interests were widely viewed as aligned with the national interest, under a pervasive mindset of 'banking nationalism' which typically considers banks as instruments or even agents of government for the purpose of industrial policy (directed lending) and/or government financing ('financial repression'), and more generally as 'national champions' that were somehow seen as better contributing to the countries' common good than foreign-owned banking operations.

This legacy of banking nationalism, in combination with uniquely European binding frameworks of cross-border market integration, goes a long way in explaining the build-up of excessive risk in the European banking system in the decade before the crisis, and then the inability to conduct the necessary but painful process of triage, recapitalization and restructuring in most member states during the first five years of crisis. It was also a major contributing factor to the provision by EU member states of excessive guarantees to their domestic banks, their overgenerous use of public money in successive bank bailouts, and their general inability (with the exception of Denmark in 2010) to impose market discipline on bank creditors, even subordinated ones (Véron 2013).

The resulting high level of public support of domestic banks later combined with the simultaneous refusal to extend similar support to fellow member states as sovereign issuers. This latter stance hardened gradually as the Greek sovereign debt crisis unfolded from late 2009 onwards, and was cemented in the French-German declaration in Deauville on October 18, 2010, when President Nicolas Sarkozy and Chancellor Angela Merkel announced that private-sector creditors of Greece would be forced to take a loss as a condition of future assistance by fellow euro area member states, as eventually happened in early 2012. The combination of bank creditor bail-outs and sovereign creditor bail-ins was a core driver of the bank-sovereign vicious circle of market contagion, which became increasingly evident through 2011 and was generally (and rightly) identified by European policymakers as a major source of instability in early 2012.

To break the bank-sovereign vicious circle, policymakers were eventually left with two options, of acting either on the sovereign side or on the banking side. The sovereign-side option would have required 'fiscal union' in the form of a potentially unlimited joint debt issuance capability, which would arguably have required some form of unlimited (if only contingent) joint revenue-raising capacity. This was widely discussed in 2011 but no basis for agreement was found, beyond the imposition of an EU straightjacket on national fiscal decisions whose enforceability remains doubtful. As the bank-sovereign vicious circle intensified in the spring and early summer of 2012, banking union was left as the only remaining strategy to avoid the break-up of the euro area. This option entailed bidding farewell to banking nationalism, through the creation of a joint institutional framework that would dramatically alter policy incentives, and was therefore least favored by most member states and their respective national banking communities. However, euro area break-up appeared as an even less palatable option, which explains the remarkable moment of decision on June 28–29, 2012.

This sequence explains how such a radical shift as the inception of banking became possible, but also why it remained incomplete — what could be termed a 'banking half-union.' The significant pooling of sovereignty that banking union represents was decided under duress, after all alternative options had failed. The ad hoc manner in which it was introduced made it impractical to bind all participants identically on a common vision — by contrast with, say, a treaty revision through an intergovernmental conference. This incompleteness can be observed alongside three dimensions:

- First, not all EU member states are or will be included in the geographical scope of banking union, or banking union area. This limitation was made unavoidable by the stance adopted by the United Kingdom in 2011, reversing earlier policy, and summarized by Chancellor of the Exchequer George Osborne as the 'remorseless logic' of policy integration in the euro area, a process which he suggested the UK would encourage but not participate in (Giles and Parker 2011). Even so, some non-euro-area member states, possibly including Denmark and countries in central Europe, may join the banking union on a voluntary basis in the future. Each of the non-euro member states has to weigh the cost of relinquishing sovereignty over banks against the benefits of banking union in terms of financial stability and market integration (Darvas and Wolff 2013). The political, economic and financial drivers of this assessment are different in each of them. Even in the UK, there is scope for future (if not current) debate. In a committee report, the UK House of Lords wrote that "It would be wise not to close the door on the possibility of some level of [UK] participation in Banking Union in the future, in particular as a means of further promoting and shaping the Single Market in Financial Services and the UK's position within it" (House of Lords 2014).

- Second, even among member states that participate in the banking union, banks are not uniformly covered. At the insistence of the German government, most banks under €30 billion of total assets are not directly supervised by the ECB, even though it is the ECB that ultimately grants their banking license. Together, these small banks represent probably less than 15% of total euro area banking assets, but a much higher share in Germany and Italy (Véron 2014). While they do not appear to represent a systemic risk for Europe in the short term, the regulatory asymmetry could lead to future risk concentrations in them that might be destabilizing for the entire system, as was the case with the US savings and loans in the 1980s, or the Spanish savings banks in the 2000s.

- Third, significant aspects of banking policy remain outside of the functional scope of banking union. Deposit insurance remains a national competence, even though its modalities have been harmonized through successive EU directives in 1994, 2009 and 2014. The insurance of deposits at the national rather than European level is a probable future propagator of the bank-sovereign vicious circle in at least some systemic crisis scenarios, as was illustrated in Cyprus in early 2013. Similarly, any public funding of future cases of bank resolution is mostly backed by national budgets at least until 2024, and the decision-making process on bank resolution is itself a complex hybrid of national and European. Consumer financial protection, the fight against money laundering, and other components of the regulation of bank conduct remain national competencies.

Even incomplete, however, the banking union framework as currently developed represents a radical rather than incremental step for the EU. The SSM in particular is based on a comprehensive pooling of sovereignty conceded by all euro area member states to the ECB. Its legal basis is robust and likely to withstand future court challenges, and the political commitment behind it has been such that the risk of major reversals in its implementation appears low.

Banking Union Legislation, Institutions and Implementation Schedule

The foundation of banking union, as currently framed, is made of two key pieces of EU legislation. First, the SSM Regulation of October 15, 2013 designates the ECB as the licensing authority for all euro area banks, starting from November 4, 2014. Second, the Single Resolution Mechanism (SRM) Regulation of July 15, 2014 creates a Single Resolution Board (SRB) in Brussels and gives it a central role in future bank crisis management. The same Regulation also entrusts the SRB with a Single Resolution Fund (SRF), the modalities of which are specified in a separate intergovernmental agreement that was signed on May 14, 2014 by all EU member states except Sweden and the UK, and is in the process of being ratified by them at the time of writing [early 2015].

Several other pieces of legislation also support the banking union by strengthening the European 'single rulebook' for banks, even though their initial proposals by the European Commission predate the inception of banking union in late June 2012. These include the Capital Requirements Regulation (CRR) and fourth Capital Requirements Directive (CRD4) of June 26, 2013; the Deposit Guarantee Schemes (DGS) Directive of April 16, 2014; and the Bank Recovery & Resolution Directive (BRRD) of May 15, 2014.

Strictly speaking, banking union is neither part of Europe's Economic and Monetary Union (EMU), which is specific to the euro area, nor of its Internal Market policy, which applies to all EU member states. The euro area crisis, and the identification in 2011–12 of the vicious circle between banks and sovereigns, was the trigger for the decisions made by euro area leaders on June 29, 2012. Correspondingly, the SSM Regulation is based on Article 127(6) of the Treaty on the Functioning of the European Union (TFEU), which is part of its chapter on Monetary Policy and EMU. However, the SRM Regulation is based on Article 114 TFEU, which makes it technically part of the Internal Market body of legislation even though some member states are exempted from its scope.[2] Moreover, Article 7 of the SSM Regulation allows non-euro-area member states to join the banking union voluntarily through so-called 'close cooperation' and, as mentioned above, it appears likely that several such member states will do so in the next two years. As a result, the banking union area would be larger than the euro area but smaller than the EU. This geographical aspect echoes the broader hybrid nature of the banking union policy framework, somewhere between EMU and the Internal Market.

Combined with earlier crisis-induced EU reforms enacted in 2010, the banking union legislation results in an entirely new landscape of

---

[2] The legal robustness of this exemption may be tested in court in the future.

European-level financial sector authorities. This inevitably creates uncertainty over their exact respective boundaries of responsibilities, possible areas of overlap or loopholes, and the possibility of turf conflicts, not only between European and national authorities but also among different European authorities, including the European Commission itself. The complexity of this setup results in part from the need to manage several 'concentric circles' of member states which have signed up for different areas of joint policymaking, namely the euro area, banking union area, and European Union (Anderson 2014):

- The European Banking Authority (EBA) started on January 1, 2011 in London. It prepares draft standards on EU banking regulation for adoption by the European Commission; has binding authority to mediate among national banking supervisors of EU member states in specific circumstances; and has additional powers of crisis management in certain emergency situations.
- The European Insurance and Occupational Pensions Authority (EIOPA), in Frankfurt, and European Securities and Markets Authority (ESMA), in Paris, have similar mandates as the EBA in their respective areas of responsibility. They also started on January 1, 2011, and are referred to in the European policy jargon together with the EBA as the three European Supervisory Authorities (ESAs).[3] In addition, ESMA has direct supervisory authority over two categories of regulated financial firms, namely credit ratings agencies and trade repositories, for which no prior supervisory framework existed before the crisis at the national level in the EU.
- The European Systemic Risk Board (ESRB) was established on January 1, 2011 by the same package of EU legislation as the three ESAs.

---

[3] The ESAs themselves build on the previous experience of three so-called Lamfalussy committees created earlier in the 2000s; respectively the Committee of European Banking Supervisors (CEBS), Committee of European Insurance and Occupational Pensions Supervisors (CEIOPS), and Committee of European Securities Regulators (CESR). Unlike the ESAs, however, these committees could have no binding authority under EU law.

It is intended to serve as an umbrella body for macroprudential analysis and policy in the EU, but has no policy instruments of its own except the capacity to issue reports and recommendations to which EU member states must respond. The ESRB is hosted by the ECB in Frankfurt, but its geographical scope is the entire EU of (currently) 28 member states, including the UK.

- The ECB, which had been established in 1998 as the central bank for Europe's EMU and hub of the European System of Central Banks, was conferred direct supervisory tasks by the SSM Regulation. Under that legislation, the ECB's newly created Supervisory Board, whose first members started their terms in the first three months of 2014, has become the central decision-making body for the SSM, which also includes national prudential authorities from all member states of the banking union area. However, in accordance with applicable treaty provisions, the Supervisory Board derives its authority from the ECB's Governing Council, which retains the ability to overrule the Supervisory Board's decisions.

- The Single Resolution Board (SRB) started on January 1, 2015 in Brussels, in accordance with the SRM Regulation. From January 1, 2016, it will become the central decision-making authority for bank resolution procedures in the banking union area. From that date, the European Single Resolution Fund (SRF), also created by the SRM Regulation and whose modalities were further specified by the intergovernmental agreement of May 14, 2014, will be owned and managed by the SRB.

- In addition, the European Stability Mechanism (ESM), which was formally established in Luxembourg late September 2012, may recapitalize banks directly under the decisions made at the Brussels summit in late 2012, even though subsequent developments have made this option increasingly unlikely. For this purpose, the ESM maintains a bank recapitalization program and a team of banking experts, even though it has no actual supervisory authority.

The following table summarizes this new landscape:

Authority	Start date	Seat	Function	Geography
EBA	2011	London	Draft standards, binding mediation, emergency powers on banking policy	European Union
ECB	1998 (monetary); 2014 (supervision)	Frankfurt	Monetary policy; bank supervision	Euro area (monetary); banking union area (supervision)
EIOPA	2011	Frankfurt	Draft standards, binding mediation, emergency powers on insurance & pensions policy	European Union
ESM	2012	Luxembourg	Bank recapitalization program	Euro area
ESMA	2011	Paris	Draft standards, binding mediation, emergency powers on securities & markets policy; supervision of credit ratings agencies and of trade repositories	European Union
ESRB	2011	Frankfurt	Macroprudential analysis and recommendations; hosted by ECB	European Union
SRB	2015	Brussels	Bank resolution procedures; administers Single Resolution Fund	Banking union area

The initial legislative package that underpins Europe's banking union was adopted quickly by EU standards: about a year from the European Commission's proposal to the publication in the *Official Journal of the EU*, for both the SSM and SRM Regulations. However, the SRM will only be substantially in place in early 2016. At that date, the SRF will be established, the SRB will acquire its complete authority over future resolution procedures, and the debt bail-in clauses of the BRRD will become fully operational. By then, the transition period since the initial decision in mid-2012 will have lasted three years and a half. A further transition of eight years then will extend until 2024. Until that date, the SRF will retain 'national compartments' of differentiated funding from each participating member states, and only after 2024 will it become a genuinely European financial resource.

As for the Single Supervisory Mechanism, it is now in place and fully operational since the assumption of supervisory authority by the ECB on November 4, 2014, even though many of its implications will only unfold over time. The key transitional process has been the Comprehensive Assessment of the euro area's 130 largest banks, mandated by the SSM Regulation and which involved the ECB, EBA, national prudential authorities of euro area member states, a project management office run by consultants Oliver Wyman, and additional consultants (mostly from the big four audit networks) hired by national authorities under the control of the ECB. The results of the Comprehensive Assessment, whose components included an Asset Quality Review (AQR) and a stress test (which, under EBA coordination, also included banks from EU member states outside the euro area), were published on October 26, 2014, less than two weeks before the ACB's assumption of authority on November 4. The effectiveness and impact of the Comprehensive Assessment are discussed in the following section.

The structure now in place for banking supervision, in accordance with the SSM Regulation, centralizes a lot of authority at the ECB. On September 4, 2014, the ECB published the list of 120 banks it identifies as 'significant credit institutions' and therefore supervises directly.[4] For

---

[4] This list is similar, though not identical, to the list of 130 banks that were included in the Comprehensive Assessment. The ECB has indicated that the list will be updated regularly in the future, and at least once a year.

each of these, the ECB has established a Joint Supervisory Team (JST) which includes ECB staff in Frankfurt as well as supervisory staff in the respective national prudential authorities of each banking union area member state where the bank has a significant presence. The JSTs prepare draft supervisory decisions for the ECB's Supervisory Board, and the final word on such drafts belongs to the JST head, who is always an ECB agent and never a citizen of the country in which the bank is headquartered in order to avoid national favoritism. If JST members from a national authority disagree with the recommendation from the JST head, their dissenting opinion is also communicated to the Supervisory Board. This procedure ensures ECB control, and prevents the risk of paralysis or erosion of authority that may have arisen if more consensuses among JST members had been required. For the euro area's 3,000-plus 'less significant credit institutions,' all of which are under the threshold of €30 billion in total assets, national authorities remain in charge of 'day-to-day' supervision but under a policy framework set by the Supervisory Board. Even for these, the ECB remains the decision-making authority for key decisions such as the granting or removal of banking licences and the 'fit-and-proper' assessment of the bank's key executives. The ECB also has the discretion to assert direct supervisory authority if it desires so, for example if it does not have enough trust in the quality of 'day-to-day' supervision by the relevant national body.

The ECB supervisory staff is planned to be slightly above 1,000, most of which were recruited in 2014 (a majority from national supervisors, and a minority from the ECB internally and from the broader labor market). In addition to bank examiners in the JSTs, this staff includes support functions as well as inspection staff that may participate in on-site inspections together with staff from national supervisors. Under current rules, such on-site inspections of a bank are conducted by agents who are not members of the bank's JST, in order to minimize the risk of supervisory capture. The ECB will also gradually build joint data systems for supervisory information, and is expected to finalize the establishment of a single Risk Assessment System for all supervised banks in the course of 2015.

Economic Impact

The economic impact of Europe's banking union can be assessed alongside at least four distinct though inter-related dimensions.

First, the inception of banking union in late June 2012 marked a significant change of policy trajectory for the euro area and was the key enabler for ECB President Mario Draghi's subsequent commitment to "do whatever it takes to preserve the euro" in London on July 26, 2012, and the ECB's announcement of its Outright Monetary Transactions (OMT) program in early September 2012.

As an independent institution, the ECB cannot formally acknowledge a causal link between a decision made by national political leaders and its own policy initiatives. Nevertheless, in a speech in Brussels on June 10, 2014, then European Council President (and thus chair of the landmark summit of June 28–29, 2012) Herman Van Rompuy remarked that, "the [European] Central Bank was only able to take this [OMT] decision because of the preliminary political decision, by the EU's Heads of State and Government to build a banking union. This was the famous European Council of June 2012, so just weeks before [Mr] Draghi's statement; he himself said to me, during that Council, that this was exactly the game-changer he needed." In an interview in the Dutch daily *Volkskrant* on April 13, 2014, Mario Monti, who was the Italian Prime Minister at the time of the 2012 summit, similarly noted that "Mr Draghi had been able to say [what he said in London] because he had received the political support of the leaders" on that occasion.

President Draghi himself has hinted more allusively at the same link in several speeches in 2012 and 2013, noting the unique quality of the June 2012 summit in terms of European leaders coming together on a joint constructive vision, and describing OMT as a "bridge" to a destination towards which "the establishment of the SSM is a key step". Not only was the decision to start banking union a show of unity and solidarity; it was also a vote of confidence in favor of the ECB itself, through the choice of Article 127(6) TFEU as the legal basis for the future SSM, for which Mr Draghi had argued personally during the summit.[5]

---

[5] Author's conversations in 2014 with several individuals who had attended the June 2012 meeting.

Mr Draghi's London address of late July 2012, combined with the subsequent OMT program announcement, is widely seen as the key turning point of the crisis from a sovereign debt market perspective. It put an end to the near-panic of the early summer of 2012, and started the phase of 'positive contagion' that has extended until the end of 2014. The inception of banking union in late June 2012 is what made this announcement possible, and can thus be described as the trigger to the resolution of the most acute phase of the euro area crisis.

Second, banking union enabled a shift of Europe from what had been until 2012 a dominant preference for addressing banking crises through nationalizations and creditor bailouts (Goldstein and Véron 2011) towards a system that is expected to rely significantly more on market discipline and the sharing of losses by private-sector creditors. This shift remains subject to many uncertainties, but has already had enough observable consequences to be considered substantial and irreversible, with important economic consequences.

Until the crisis, most EU member states (unlike the US) had no special resolution regime for banks, and most bank failures, except in isolated cases of fraud in relatively small banks, were addressed through government-funded bailouts of all creditors including subordinated ones, often accompanied by partial or complete nationalization. This pattern largely held in the early years of the crisis, the only exceptions in the EU being some instances of bail-in of junior creditors in Ireland, and to a lesser extent in the UK, as well as a more robust experience of resolution involving burden-sharing by senior unsecured creditors and uninsured depositors of two medium-sized Danish banks in 2010. As exposed above, the preference for bailouts was strongly associated with the mindset of banking nationalism that had dominated much of banking policymaking in the EU in the first five years of crisis, and was only eroded in the context that was associated with the inception of banking union.

Specifically, three successive EU policy developments marked the shift of preferences from bank creditors' bail-out to bail-in in the course of 2012. First, in the spring, the European Commission finalized its proposal for the Bank Recovery and Resolution Directive (BRRD), and published it in early June with specific provisions to enable national resolution authorities to bail-in bank creditors, including senior ones, starting from January 2016. Second, in the summer, the 'troika' of the European Commission, ECB and International Monetary Fund (IMF) finalized its targeted assistance to Spain in order to help the restructuring of the Spanish banking system, and thus triggered widespread bailing-in of junior creditors of Spanish banks, in contrast with the Irish program of November 2010 when the protection of bank creditors had been a condition imposed by the troika for its assistance. Third, in December 2012, a European summit confirmed that the SSM would be complemented by a Single Resolution Mechanism, thus reducing the fragmentation of decision-making structures for bank resolution along national lines which had been a key driver of the European preference for bank creditor bail-outs. Following these developments, the European Commission issued new rules on state aid control that entered into force in August 2013 and essentially generalize the stance that had been adopted for Spain to the entire EU, i.e. the bailing-in of junior creditors as a precondition for any use of public funds in bank rescues. In summary, the current applicable framework imposes losses on the subordinated creditors (as well as the shareholders and preferred or hybrid capital holders) of failing banks, and will additionally impose losses on senior unsecured creditors (and in the worst cases, possibly also on uninsured depositors) from 2016 onwards.

Actual practice has broadly followed this evolution of the regulatory framework, with some lags and hiccups. Several member states have effectively transferred public funds to banks through variously stealthy initiatives such as local government guarantees, abandonment of lawsuits or of tax claims, or publicly-triggered revaluation of specific assets held by banks. Conversely, in Cyprus in early 2013, the Troika of the European Commission, ECB and International Monetary Fund imposed a harsh plan that imposed large losses on uninsured depositors of failing banks as a condition for sovereign assistance, following an ill-fated earlier plan that would have imposed losses on all depositors of all banks in the country. In most cases however, including Spanish banks since 2012, SNS Reaal in the Netherlands in 2013, and Banco Espirito Santo in Portugal in mid-2014, the general pattern has been the one in which the bank's shares lose all or almost all their value, subordinated debts are written down or forcibly converted into equity capital, and all senior debts and deposits are protected, in compliance with the 2013 state aid rules. The same pattern is likely to apply to the bank restructurings that may take place until end-2015. The change in expectations about future bank restructuring is also reflected by analysis from the main credit ratings agencies, which have reduced their antici-pations of sovereign support of bank creditors, though only in a partial way that does not apply uniformly to all member states.

Third, the Comprehensive Assessment and subsequent assumption of supervisory authority by the ECB have been expected by many observers and policymakers to lead to a strengthening of trust in the safety and soundness of European banks, which may in turn allow banks to fund themselves on more favorable terms and to lend more freely to the European economy. On this count, it is too early at the time of writing to produce a definitive assessment.

The Comprehensive Assessment was undeniably more robust and demanding than the ill-fated stress tests of July 2010 and July 2011, which gave clean bills of health to groups such as Allied Irish Banks, Bankia or Dexia that collapsed soon afterwards. Those past exercises did not include an AQR, and even more importantly, did not ensure adequate alignment between national supervisors and the EBA (or in 2010, its predecessor the Committee of European Banking Supervisors), in spite of the latter's dedication and efforts. There were strong incen-tives for weaker banks and their national supervisors to hide balance sheet weaknesses from the EBA and the public. By contrast in the 2014 process, the ECB was empowered by the SSM Regulation to have direct and enforceable access to all the information it needed from national supervisors and the banks themselves.

However, there have also been legitimate concerns about the quality and impartiality of the process. The ECB was new to the business of supervision and has had to go through a sharp learning curve. Even though many of its new SSM agents had ample prior professional experi-ence, as an institution it may have shied away from contentious positions on key issues of accounting, recognition and valuation. The audit firms that supported the AQR process had highly skewed incentives, as each of the large audit networks has many statutory audit and consulting clients among the banks that were reviewed, even though it did not have to review its own audit clients. The ECB may also have been understandably wary about creating opportunities for banks or their shareholders to sue it in court for its accounting or valuation judgments, as would transpire in the publication of AQR results. Other possibly skewed incentives in the course of the AQR process may have resulted from the ECB's broader macroeconomic, monetary policy and financial stability responsibilities.

Furthermore, the ECB may have been affected by its own institutional constraints, since national authorities together hold voting majorities in both its Supervisory Board and its Governing Council. The disclosure of hitherto unidentified capital shortfalls in euro area banks, especially if these result from lower asset valuations resulting from the AQR, would inevitably embarrass these banks' national supervisors. This risk materialized in the case of Italy, in which a plurality of the banks identified as undercapitalized in the Comprehensive Assessment were headquartered (Merler 2014). Whether the ECB prevented it to affect a number of other member states at the same time, however, is difficult to assess.

The Comprehensive Assessment process led many European banks to take significant action to strengthen their balance sheet in anticipation of the announcement of its results. The ECB has estimated the positive impact of these 'frontloaded measures' to be more than €200 billion in total, including €60 billion of new capital raising (European Central Bank 2014a). The actual capital shortfalls identified by the Comprehensive Assessment were of limited aggregate size, namely €24.6 billion across 25 banks as of December 31, 2013, reduced to €9.5 billion across 13 banks after taking into account actions taken between January and October 2014 (European Central Bank 2014b). Nevertheless, the AQR also led to uncovering a considerably larger amount of €136 billion in hitherto undisclosed non-performing exposures, some of which may lead to provisions in future financial statements of the banks affected. Overall, even assuming that the ECB has been suitably rigorous, the AQR's consequences can be expected to unfold over a relatively long period of time before a firm judgment can be made about its eventual impact.

Fourth, the advent of banking union may lead to a reversal of the harmful trend of fragmentation of the EU financial system along national boundaries that has been observed during the crisis, particularly inside the euro area. Symptoms of this fragmentation include the divergence of credit conditions across member states; the persistence of high home bias in banks' sovereign debt portfolios; the underdevelopment of cross-border lending, including among entities of the same banking group in different member states; and the sharp deceleration, and occasional reversal, of cross-border bank consolidation since the start of the crisis.

As of early 2015, it is too soon to observe such a 'defragmentation' effect of banking union, which may materialize, perhaps tentatively in 2015 and possibly more strongly in 2016. As with the previous point on the impact of the Comprehensive Assessment, however, this will crucially depend on future policy choices by the ECB. Options for these are outline in the last section of this chapter.

In sum, banking union has already made a massively positive contribution to the European economy by enabling the ECB's OMT program and the ensuing sovereign-debt market reversal and 'positive contagion' since the summer of 2012. It has also enabled a broad shift of approaches to bank restructuring from creditor bail-out to bail-in and corresponding improvement in market discipline, which is already observable as regards junior debt and is expected to extend to senior debt as well from 2016 onwards. It may result in higher trust in the euro area's banks, and thus remove the current tension in credit supply which contributes to the general economic anemia of the euro area, even though such an effect, if it happens, can only be a delayed rather than immediate consequence of the announcement of results of the Comprehensive Assessment. It is also likely to trigger a gradual de-fragmentation of the European financial space, but this will depend on the ECB's specific future actions.

Institutional Implications

Separately from its economic impact, Europe's banking union also leads to significant shifts in the EU institutional landscape. These affect the national, European, and global levels of policymaking.

At the national level, banking union means that bank supervisory authorities in participating member states are no longer autonomous. The larger banks (including, under the SSM Regulation, the three largest ones in each member state) are directly supervised by the ECB through a joint supervisory team; smaller banks are still supervised locally but within the SSM policy framework, and the ECB retains ultimate supervisory responsibility on them as well. Because supervisory frameworks and practices differ widely from one member state to another, though, the consequences are not uniform. In some environments, being part of a European network grants the supervisor additional independence and status; in others, the loss of decision-making autonomy may be felt as a form of institutional downgrading. In some countries (Belgium, Cyprus, France, Greece, Ireland, Italy, Netherlands, Portugal, Slovakia, Slovenia, Spain), the supervisory function is carried out by the central bank or a semi-autonomous body within it, and thus the creation of the SSM adds a major dimension to a pre-existing relationship between the central bank and the ECB within the Eurosystem. In others (Austria, Estonia, Finland, Germany, Latvia, Luxembourg, Malta), a separate agency, e.g., BaFin in Germany, plays a major role in domestic banking supervision, and its participation together with the national central bank in the SSM architecture adds an additional element of complexity.[6] Furthermore, the change remains too recent for all its effects to be already observable, especially as, during most of 2014, most participants' attention has been mobilized on the tight deadline of the Comprehensive Assessment.

One would expect such a transition to be affected by conflicts, particularly over turf and resources. On the face of it, the ECB appears to have been broadly successful in enlisting the cooperation of national bank supervisors for the purposes of the Comprehensive Assessment and the initial setup of the SSM. One indicator of relative harmony is that, contrary to the expectations of many market participants and observers, no early results of the Comprehensive Assessment leaked to the media and the public until the very end of the process. The decision by the ECB not to have its own permanent staff in the participating member states also contributes to the empowerment of national supervisors in the system. SSM Supervisory Board Chair Danièle Nouy has

---

[6] In such cases, both representatives of the national supervisory agency and the national central bank may attend meetings of the ECB's Supervisory Board. In principle, the national supervisory agency holds the country's vote.

argued that the SSM design provides "the best of both worlds: the proximity of [national] supervisors to the banks, and some distance [from local political entanglements] for the [ECB's] decision-making" (Merli 2014). Beyond the rhetoric, this vision appears to have elicited buy-in from many individuals in the participant authorities.

However, the ECB may have had to make compromises to enlist the cooperation of some of the national authorities. Perhaps more consequentially, the ECB may have chosen not to prioritize decisions on issues that could be divisive, but are not urgent, in order to favor an initial cooperative mindset among national participating authorities. For example, the finalization of a centralized Risk Assessment System to score all supervised banks across different categories of risks was announced in 2013 as part of the Comprehensive Assessment and thus to be completed in 2014, but was later delayed to 2015. This delay may be due to technical or operational factors, but also possibly to the fact that different national supervisors defended different methodological choices, which would have had impact on the respective scores of banks from different member states. If a decision had been forced early, the high public visibility of the Comprehensive Assessment could have exposed discrepancies from previous national assessments that might prove unflattering for at least some of the authorities. While such delays appear to have successfully contributed to the avoidance of open conflict between the ECB and national authorities in 2014, it does not result that conflict will be avoided in the future.

At the European level, the addition of supervisory authority considerably reinforces the ECB's heft in the EU's ever-unsettled institutional framework. This is likely to become particularly evident in the area of financial regulatory policy. For example, most of the members of the EBA's supervisory board are also members of the SSM, and it can be expected that over time, the ECB will be increasingly able to shape their positions in EBA decisions. At the UK's insistence, a reform of the EBA's governance in 2014 has introduced a 'double majority' mechanism that creates checks against the possibility of euro area member states dominating the EBA's decision-making, but it remains to be seen how effective and durable this compromise will be, especially as the EBA's governance and funding is due for further reform by the current European Commission (Juncker 2014). More broadly, through its supervisory function, the ECB will gather unparalleled insight into the European financial system which will give it a unique position of influence in the elaboration of EU financial legislation and regulatory policy.

This new position will create opportunities but also challenges for the ECB, especially since the broader EU institutional framework remains in flux and under constant criticism for its lack of both executive decision-making capacity and of democratic accountability. The contrast between the ECB's ability to wield consequential monetary and banking policy instruments at the European level, on the one hand, and the lack of a corresponding executive authority over European economic and financial policy, on the other hand, is likely to foster an ongoing critique of the ECB's unique institutional position. Moreover, the coexistence inside the ECB of authority for both monetary and supervisory policies will give rise to suspicions of conflict of interest, as is already the case among many observers in Germany.

Additional challenges are likely to result from the discrepancies between the concentric circles of the euro area, banking union area (assuming that some non-euro member states join the banking union on a voluntary basis), and European Union. One example is the provision of liquidity to financial infrastructure firms such as clearing houses (or, as they are commonly referred to in the EU, central counterparties). The ECB may adopt a differentiated approach to this question depending on whether a particular clearing house is established inside the euro area (or the banking union area), for reasons of monetary policy, supervisory oversight, and financial stability, but this creates a potential tension with the European Union's internal market policy framework. Similarly, the division of responsibilities for the still-emerging area of macroprudential policy, between national authorities in the euro area, banking union area, and other EU member states, the ECB, and the ESRB, remains a work in progress which may require future adjustments to the policy framework. The development planned by the European Commission in 2015 of a legislative agenda to create a European 'capital markets union,' which appears intended to include all EU member states in its geographical scope, may bring more challenges of jurisdiction and boundaries to the surface.

On the international level beyond the EU, the advent of banking union will inevitably affect the dynamics of decision-making in global bodies, certainly those focused on banking regulation such as the Basel

Committee on Banking Supervision (BCBS), and also possibly broader ones such as the Financial Stability Board (FSB). In October 2014, the ECB and the SSM became full members of the BCBS, in addition to the existing membership of national authorities in six euro area member states (Belgium, France, Germany, Italy, the Netherlands and Spain). While the BCBS's consensus-based culture appears to have prevented the issue of duplication of these countries' representation being raised so far, it is likely to arise in the medium term. In any case, the ECB instantly became the most potentially influential member of the committee, as a plurality of the world's large internationally active banks (those on which the BCBS focuses its work) are under its jurisdiction. These include nine out of the 30 'global systemically important banks' as last listed by the FSB, against eight in the US, four in the UK, three in each of China and Japan, two in Switzerland, and one in Sweden (Financial Stability Board 2014). Similarly, the ECB can be expected to gain significant influence within the FSB itself. Conversely, the inclusion as FSB members (let alone as FSB Steering Committee members) of the central banks of France, Germany, Italy, the Netherlands and Spain may come increasingly into question, especially in the eyes of policymakers from large emerging economies that may be considered comparatively underrepresented.

Prospects for Future Policy Development

This section focuses on possible future developments that are specific to banking policy, leaving aside related ones that may be triggered by other aspects of the unfolding and still unresolved economic condition of the euro area and European Union, including in the area of financial services policy (on these see e.g. Bruegel 2014, and Posen *et al.* 2014). It tentatively reviews policy options at the level of the ECB, as well as possible changes in EU financial legislation.

The ECB's future identity as a supervisor will be primarily shaped by its assessment of supervised banks and supervisory actions on those it deems insufficiently sound. Nevertheless, the ECB also faces significant questions as regards its broader policy framework. As suggested above, the concern to preserve consensus with national supervisors may have led the ECB to err on the side of caution in addressing a number of potentially divisive policy issues during the Comprehensive Assessment, which lasted from late 2013 to end-October 2014. Going forward, the ECB also needs to remain mindful of voting dynamics within its Supervisory Board, in which national representatives held 19 of 25 votes as of early 2015.[7] In voting on policy choices, such representatives may be motivated by their common interest in the success and sustainability of the SSM, but also by their national institutional incentives as well as specific interests. With these constraints in mind, the ECB may consider policy developments in at least six different areas:

1. *A harmonized and rigorous definition of capital.* In principle, the EU Capital Requirements Regulation (CRR) of June 2013 provides a uniform framework for supervisory capital measurement across the EU. In practice, however, there are a number of qualifications. The CRR foresees a long transition to the harmonized standard, and some of the prior practices are grandfathered. Even the steady-state (or, as the jargon has it, 'fully-loaded') capital definitions leave some discretion to national authorities and margins for interpretation. Furthermore, the fully-loaded CRR framework is itself materially non-compliant with the global Basel III standards, as was determined by the Basel Committee's own evaluation process (Basel Committee on Banking Supervision 2014). Under CRD4, the ECB has authority to impose more demanding capital requirements than the minimum defined by the mere application of CRR definitions. Using this so-called Pillar 2 authority as a corrective instrument, the ECB may accelerate the convergence of capital definitions to the fully-loaded CRR standard as early as 2015, and perhaps also impose a common definition that would be more compliant with Basel III, not least in order to maximize its influence within the Basel Committee itself.

---

[7] The number of Supervisory Board members, and among them of representatives from national authorities, may grow further if any non-euro-area member states join the banking union on a voluntary basis.

2. *The removal on current constraints on capital mobility inside the euro area.* The ECB may fight and possibly eliminate widespread practices of ring-fencing of capital and liquidity along national borders, which have been imposed by national supervisors in the euro area over many banks in their jurisdiction, including domestic subsidiaries of non-domestic banking groups. Such geographical ring-fencing is most often not publicly acknowledged by supervisory authorities, but there is ample evidence of its significant extent over the past three or four years. This has been damaging for financial stability in the euro area even though it was understandable (and even defensible) from a national institutional perspective. In some cases, most notably in Germany, such ring-fencing has been occasionally imposed in application of legislation that relates to deposit insurance rather than bank supervision, and thus remains a responsibility of the national competent authority with no transfer to the ECB. However, the compatibility of such legislation with the EU internal market policy framework remains open to discussion.

3. *The reduction of current home bias in banks' sovereign debt portfolios.* It is currently not unusual that banks would hold the equivalent of more than half, and often more, of their core regulatory capital in bonds issued by their home-country government, with the consequence that a weakening of sovereign credit directly triggers a deterioration of the banks' solvency if the bonds' value is marked to market — a key component of the euro area's bank-sovereign vicious circle of 2010–12. The reasons for this home bias have not been analyzed to a point of consensus, but are likely to combine a degree of financial repression (or 'moral suasion' by home-country authorities to support the government's financing by buying its debt), behavioral asymmetries, and anticipation of a positive if small risk of euro area break-up. While domestic national supervisors had incentives to encourage this home bias, the ECB may reduce it by imposing increasingly low limits on such exposures and by encouraging banks to diversify their sovereign-debt portfolios. This stance would have advantages over the oft-discussed option of imposing positive risk weight on sovereign-bond portfolios in regulatory capital calculations, as the latter could reinforce the bank-sovereign

linkage, at least in the current absence of a well-functioning European fiscal union. The transition would need to be managed carefully, because the dismantling of the home bias could result in temporary imbalances between supply and demand in some sovereign debt market segments. But the persistence of benign borrowing conditions for euro area member states since 2013 suggests that such transitional challenges should not be insurmountable.

4. *The removal of national bias in bank restructuring, mergers, and acquisitions.* There have been examples in the past of national supervisors in the EU using their authority to discourage the purchase of banks in their jurisdiction by foreign rivals, even those from fellow European countries. By contrast, the ECB has reasons to encourage cross-border consolidation among European banks. Indeed, several ECB policymakers have indicated that they would view the emergence of genuine pan-European banking groups, beyond existing pioneers such as BNP Paribas, Santander or UniCredit, as a positive contribution to foster broader cross-border financial system integration. Economic benefits may include better resilience against asymmetric risk, more efficient capital allocation, and better transmission of monetary policy through the banking system. Such a development may also gradually result in the formation of a powerful interest group that may call public decision-makers to accelerate the harmonization of regulatory and supervisory frameworks, with mutually reinforcing dynamics of market integration and policy integration. While the banking industry is highly concentrated in several euro area member states, including large ones such as France, it remains fragmented when considered from a European perspective. In terms of systemic risk, the ECB may judge that the drawbacks of creating more systemically important banks would be more than offset by the benefits of cross-border consolidation, especially as many banks simultaneously shed assets and deleverage their balance sheets. Not only may banks from other countries (including, with proper vetting, from outside the EU) be allowed to engage in cross-border acquisitions; private equity firms may also be welcomed to play their part in accelerating the restructuring process, also under the condition of appropriate vetting and oversight. There are past examples of such

a role, both in Europe, e.g., Bawag in Austria and IKB in Germany, and in other parts of the world, e.g., in Japan and Korea.

5. *An increase in supervisory transparency.* In contrast with the United States, bank supervisors in most EU member states only publish limited sets of data about the banks they supervise, with limited comparability across countries (Gandrud and Hallerberg 2014). The ECB may develop its supervisory transparency, and combine it with the imposition of more demanding risk disclosure requirements on the banks it supervises, as an instrument to erode differences in banks' competitive environments across member states and corresponding aspects of financial fragmentation. As an additional incentive, the supervisory practices of the ECB may be increasingly benchmarked by external observers with those of the US Federal Reserve, much more than has been the case until now with national supervisors in euro area member states, because of the sheer size of the banking system that is subject to the ECB's oversight. The Comprehensive Assessment delivered unprecedented such transparency but was only a point-in-time measurement. What is most important to investors and analysts is the availability of regularly disclosed data that allows them to observe time series.

6. *A level playing field between smaller and larger banks.* In some banking union area countries, many local banks participate in mutual support systems that result in linkages between them from a systemic risk perspective, even though they are managed and governed independently from one another. This is specifically the case of savings and cooperative banks in Germany, which represent a large share of all 'less significant credit institutions' that are not directly supervised by the ECB (Véron 2014). The Vice Chair of the ECB's Supervisory Board and member of the ECB's Executive Board, Sabine Lautenschläger, has indicated that such 'virtual groups' might be subjected to specific scrutiny from the SSM (Groendahl and Reicher 2014). This could lead to the erosion of competitive distortions that may be embedded in current policy frameworks that treat such virtual groups in a differentiated way, in particular Germany's so-called three-pillar banking system structure. Conversely, the ECB may opt to be less restrictive in granting new banking licenses than

national authorities have been until now in some of the banking union area's countries. In the US, many recently created 'de novo' banks replace failed or consolidated banks at the local level, and contribute to the country's economic vibrancy. In Europe, by contrast, very few banks have been created de novo during the last hundred years, and those local banks that exist generally trace their roots to the 19th century. The ECB's justifiable calls for consolidation should thus be counterbalanced by policy efforts to facilitate market entry into regional and local banking markets.

In complement with the ECB's policy initiatives to come, the SRB will also face policy choices as it gathers authority over bank crisis management in the banking union area, particularly from 2016 onwards as the SRM Regulation only gradually comes into implementation in 2015. As noted above, the future EU framework for bank resolution and crisis management, which emphasizes market discipline and financial crisis burden-sharing by creditors, is largely untested and thus likely to go through a protracted period of adjustment, the pace of which will obviously depend on the frequency of future financial crises.

Policy choices will also come in the area of EU legislation. The above described initial legislative package, consisting of the SSM and SRM Regulations and key 'single rulebook' texts such as the CRR, CRD4, BRRD, and DGS Directive, appears to provide a workable basis for the initial implementation of banking union. However, it is unlikely to remain unchanged in the medium term. A number of significant further adjustments will be required in the future.

To start with, the 'single rulebook' is currently a misnomer. While some rules are harmonized, much of the legislation that the SSM and the SRB have to enforce differs from one member state to another, and is subject to judicial review by national not European courts. There are also awkward overlaps between the SSM's supervisory mandate and other banking rules enforced by national authorities, e.g., on conduct of business, consumer protection, suitability of bank executives and owners, or the fight against money laundering and the financing of terrorism. In one glaring case of inconsistency, both France and Germany passed new laws in 2013 on bank structure reform, and Belgium did likewise in

2014, in evident neglect of their commitment to a single rulebook and the banking union that had already been initiated at that time. The European Commission in January 2014 put forward a proposal for umbrella EU legislation on this theme, but it still does not guarantee sufficient cross-border consistency, and is unlikely to be adopted in its present form anyway. At a minimum, the issue of separation of activities within banking groups should be dealt with in a manner that enables and ensures full harmonization within the banking union area, and arguably also with all other countries inside the EU to meet the objectives of the internal market.

Accounting and auditing is another area of follow-up legislative work that is likely to be triggered by the early experience of banking union. As things currently stand, the SSM is in the awkward position of relying on different audit firms regulated by different audit authorities for each national component of the cross-border banks it supervises. These audit firms are typically members of a single international network, most often one of the 'big four' (Deloitte, EY, KPMG and PwC), but there are exceptions — for example, the French system of joint audit implies that not all the audit work on a given bank is carried out by one single firm. Even when a single network is involved, practitioners know well how difficult it is for it to enforce strict consistency across national component partnerships, including on critical issues such as the implementation of International Financial Reporting Standards (IFRS). For listed banks, the enforcement of IFRS reporting by securities regulators (or separate ad hoc bodies, like in Germany) is also a national competency which entails some divergence among member states, in spite of the best efforts deployed by ESMA to foster coordination and convergence. Furthermore, IFRS are mandatory in the EU only for consolidated financial statements of issuers of public securities, a category that does not encompass all banks directly supervised by the ECB, let alone all smaller banks over which the ECB has ultimate supervisory authority. Many of these, especially in Germany, only use national accounting standards that differ significantly from IFRS. This raises serious questions about comparability of financial information within the SSM. Further harmonization is likely to be needed in this area. The reform agenda may include the creation of a single European authority for audit regulation; the transfer of responsibility for the enforcement of IFRS from national securities authorities to ESMA; and an obligation for all unlisted banks in the euro area to use IFRS irrespective of size, as is the case in many non-EU jurisdictions.

There is more unfinished legislative business in the area of bank insolvency regimes. Special resolution regimes are defined by the BRRD as an alternative to court-ordered insolvency. The general principle is of 'no creditor worse off' in the resolution scenario than if the bank had gone through ordinary insolvency. Thus, and strictly speaking, there can be no genuine single resolution regime for credit institutions in the banking union area, as long as they are subject to insolvency frameworks that differ widely from one member state to another. As a consequence, the EU may consider introducing a European insolvency regime administered by a European court, whose scope may be limited to the larger credit institutions directly supervised by the ECB. This would be a significant challenge from a legal and political perspective, but a necessary one to complete the banking union and prevent regulatory arbitrage.

Even more tangled from a political standpoint, and significant in terms of European financial integration, is the issue of how banking and other financial activities are being taxed by individual member states. Beyond the highly visible debate on the introduction of a financial transactions tax, this includes, crucially, the taxation of financial investments and savings products as well as other taxes and levies that affect banks and other financial markets participants. This is plainly a matter of national sovereignty, and the EU's subsidiarity principle must apply. Nevertheless, the banking union may highlight various harmful distortions and opportunities for tax evasion that could require corrective action, both at the national level and through EU-level harmonization.

Many of these themes — prudential standards, conduct-of-business regulation and consumer financial protection, accounting and auditing, insolvency reform, and the taxation of financial activities — are prominently on the EU policy agenda under the European Commission's agenda of capital markets union. This agenda provides a welcome opportunity to accelerate reform in areas where it is needed, while putting emphasis on legitimate concerns about the integrity of the single market and the risk of harmful divergence, in particular between the UK and the banking union area (Posen *et al.* 2014). At the time of writing, its exact content and ambition remain to be decided.

Finally, the banking union framework will inevitably be reviewed, and possibly strengthened, whenever the EU treaties are next revised in the future. Issues that would be on the agenda in this context could include the relationship between bank supervision and monetary policy within the ECB, possibly going the full way towards the institutional separation of the SSM from the ECB; the strengthening of the SRB's discretionary authority by giving it a specific basis in the treaty;[8] and the possibility of expansion of SSM authority over areas that may include conduct-of-business regulation and insurance supervision. A future treaty revision agenda may also include broader reform of the fiscal framework in the euro area (or banking union area, or EU), with related challenges of political representation and accountability of EU institutions, which may in turn pave the way for more cross-border integration of resolution funding and deposit insurance. It may be remembered, however, that there is currently no reliable indication of a future timetable for EU treaty revision, and that any such process would be fraught with considerable legal and political uncertainties.

References

Anderson, J. (2014), "A Fragmented, Confused Scramble to Fix Europe's Banking Structure," *New York Times DealBook*, December 2.

Barker, A. (2012), "Eurozone Weighs Union on Bank Regulation," *Financial Times*, April 3.

Basel Committee on Banking Supervision (2014), "Regulatory Consistency Assessment Programme (RCAP) Assessment of Basel III Regulations — European Union," *Bank for International Settlements*, December 2014.

---

[8] This suggestion holds even as the scope for discretionary decision-making by the SRB, an agency established on the basis of Article 114 TFEU, has been effectively widened by the recent decision of the European Court of Justice, Case C-270/12 *UK vs Council and European Parliament*, which updates the Court's earlier *Meroni* doctrine (Repasi 2014).

Bruegel (2014), "EU To Do in 2014–2019: Memos to the new EU leadership," Brussels, September 2014. Available at: http://eu2do.bruegel.org/.

Darvas, Z., and G. B. Wolff (2013), "Should Non-Euro Area Countries Join the Single Supervisory Mechanism?" *Bruegel Policy Contribution* 2013/06, March 2013.

European Central Bank (2014a), "ECB's In-Depth Review Shows Banks Need to Take Further Action," *Press Release*, October 26.

European Central Bank (2014b), *Aggregate Report on the Comprehensive Assessment*, October 2014.

European Commission (2012), *Communication to the European Parliament, the European Council, the Council, the European Central Bank, the European Economic & Social Committee, the Committee of the Regions and the European Investment Bank: Action for stability, growth and jobs*, Brussels, May 30.

Financial Stability Board (2014), *2014 Update of List of Global Systemically Important Banks (G-SIBs)*, November 2014.

Gandrud, C. and M. Hallerberg (2014), "Supervisory Transparency in the European Banking Union," *Bruegel Policy Contribution* 2014/01, January 2014.

Giles, C. and G. Parker (2011), "Osborne Urges Eurozone to 'Get A Grip'," *Financial Times*, July 21.

Goldstein, M. and N. Véron (2011), "Too Big to Fail: The transatlantic debate," *Peterson Institute Working Paper* 11–2, January 2011.

Groendahl, B. and S. Reicher (2014), "ECB Raises Savings Banks Focus on Possible Cluster Risk," *Bloomberg News*, September 30.

House of Lords (2014), "'Genuine Economic and Monetary Union' and the Implications for the UK," *European Union Committee 8th Report of Session 2013–14*, London, February.

Juncker, J.-C. (2014), *Mission Letter to Jonathan Hill, Commissioner for Financial Stability, Financial Services and Capital Markets Union*, Brussels, November 1.

Merler, S. (2014) "Monday Blues for Italian banks," *Bruegel Blog*, October 28.

Merli, A. (2014), "ECB Tells Banks They Should Raise Capital Now," interview of Danièle Nouy, *Il Sole 24 Ore*, July 10.

Posen, A. S., A. Chopra, A. Ubide, P. Mauro, J. F. Kirkegaard, and N. Véron (2014), *Rebuilding Europe's Common Future: Combining Growth and Reform in the Euro Area*, Peterson Institute Briefing 14–5, December 2014.

Repasi, R. (2014), *Assessment of the Judgment of the European Court of Justice in Case C-270/12, United Kingdom vs. Council and European Parliament*, European Parliament Greens/EFA Group, January 2014.

Véron, N. (2011), "Europe Must Change Course on Banks," *Vox EU*, December 22.

Véron, N. (2013), *Banking Nationalism and the European Crisis*, Speech at the European Private Equity and Venture Capital Association Symposium, Istanbul, June.

Véron, N. (2014), "Mapping Europe's Banking System: Most small banks are German," *Peterson Institute Real Time Economic Issues Watch*, September.

Part III
Regulatory and Market Response to the Financial Crisis — Capital Markets

Capital Market Regulation in Japan after the Global Financial Crisis
— CHAPTER 7

- Takeo Hoshi and Ayako Yasuda
  Stanford University and *University of California, Davis*

Introduction

For 40 years between the late 1930s and the late 1970s, capital markets in Japan were heavily regulated and allowed to play limited roles in allocating financial resources. Japan's financial system was dominated by the banks. A large part of household financial assets was held in the form of bank deposits, and most of external funds to corporations came in the form of bank loans. The domination of banks and suppression of capital markets originated from the wartime controls but survived and advanced during the postwar reconstruction and the catch-up economic growth that followed.

Takeo Hoshi is the Henri H. and Tomoye Takahashi Senior Fellow in Japanese Studies at Walter H. Shorenstein Asia Pacific Research Center (APARC) in Freeman Spogli Institute for International Studies (FSI) at Stanford University, Professor of Finance, by courtesy, at Stanford Graduate School of Business, Research Associate at the National Bureau of Economic Research (NBER), and a Senior Fellow at the Asian Bureau of Finance and Economic Research (ABFER). Ayako Yasuda is an Associate Professor of Finance at the Graduate School of Management, University of California, Davis.

Japan's capital markets started to change in the 1980s as various regulations were gradually relaxed. The deregulation took place over a long time and it was lopsided in the sense that deregulation on options for corporate financing moved quicker than those on options for household savers and on the range of businesses that banks can enter. As Hoshi and Kashyap (2000) argued, the lopsided nature of the financial deregulation was a major factor behind Japan's banking crisis in the late 1990s.

The deregulation process continued even during the banking crisis and into the 2000s. By the mid-2000s, major regulatory impediments to growth of capital markets were removed.

This paper examines the evolution of Japan's capital markets and the related regulatory reforms after the Global Financial Crisis. We start by looking at the importance of capital markets in the Japanese financial system. We study how the size of financial flows through capital markets relative to those through the banking sector changed since the 1980s in Section II. Then, in Section III, we look at how Japan's financial system responded to the Global Financial Crisis. We find that the disruption of the financial system in Japan was small. Section IV then surveys the financial regulatory changes in Japan since the Global Financial Crisis. While the Japanese regulators tightened the regulation to improve the financial stability as the regulators in the US and Europe did, they also continued the efforts to develop capital markets in Japan. The efforts continue and receive strong endorsement from Abenomics, which emphasized economic structural reforms to restore growth in Japan. We examine the capital market policies in Abenomics in Section V. The final section concludes.

I. From Banks to Markets

The gradual financial deregulation in Japan started in the late 1970s. During the following 40 years, the importance of securities markets has grown. As Hoshi and Kashyap (2001) showed, the Japanese financial system is in a sense going back the time to resemble what it was like before the World War II. During the pre-war period, Japan had active securities markets that played important roles in corporate financing and governance. Wartime controls were introduced to suppress securities markets. The tight regulation of securities markets and domination of banks in corporate finance and governance continued to characterize the Japanese financial system in the post-war period. As those regulations were gradually removed, the securities markets started to expand again.

The initial phase of deregulation centered on allowing large corporations to use capital markets to raise funds. The size, profitability and collateral requirements that corporations needed to satisfy in order to issue bonds or equities in public markets were gradually relaxed. The result was a dramatic shift from bank financing to market financing by large firms. Figure 1 shows the ratio of total bank loans to total assets for four groups of corporations: large manufacturing firms, large

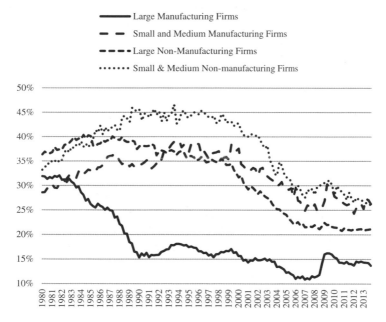

Figure 1. Bank dependence of Japanese firms (bank debt to total assets ratio (%)): 1980–2013.

Notes: The bank debt to total assets ratio is calculated by dividing the total bank borrowings (sum of series #25: Short-term borrowings and #31: Long-term borrowings) by the total assets (series #22: Total assets). Large firms are those with capital of 1 billion yen or more. Small & medium firms are those with capital less than 1 billion yen. Non-manufacturing does not include finance and insurance.

Source: Authors' calculation using *Financial Statements Statistics of Corporations by Industry, Quarterly* (Ministry of Finance Policy Research Institute, accessed on December 9, 2014).

non-manufacturing firms, small and medium manufacturing firms, and small and medium non-manufacturing firms. Large manufacturing firms clearly reduced their dependence on bank financing drastically in the 1980s. Their bank debt to total assets ratio was higher than 30% in the early 1980s, but it fell to 15% by the end of the 1980s. The ratio has moved little around the 15% level since then. For the other groups, the change was not visible in the 1980s, but the bank dependence started to fall in the late 1990s and the 2000s.

Figure 1 indirectly suggests market financing became more important over time, but Figures 2 to 5 show the growth of capital markets in Japan more directly. Figure 2 shows the amount of new corporate bond issues normalized by GDP. Following the financial deregulation of the 1980s, corporate bond issues surged. Especially popular were convertible bonds (CBs) that carried very low coupon rate (sometimes zero) reflecting the expectation of rapid appreciation of the stock prices in the

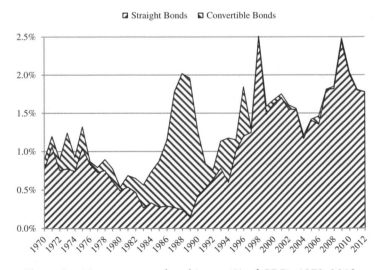

Figure 2. New corporate bond issues (% of GDP): 1970–2012.

Notes: Bond issues from 1998 on are taken from JSDA data. Bond issues before 1998 are taken from a table titled "New Issues of Bonds by Public Offerings" in *TSE Factbook 2002* (p. 99). GDP from 1994 on are based on SNA93, but GDP before 1994 are based on SNA68. *Source*: Authors' calculation using *TSE Factbook 2002*, JSDA's *Issuing, Redemption and Outstanding Amounts of Bonds* and GDP figures from Cabinet Office SNA website (all accessed on December 9, 2014).

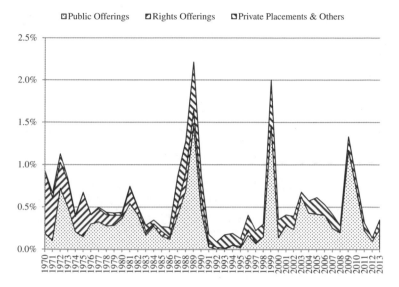

Figure 3. New equity issues (% of GDP): 1970–2013.

Notes: Stock issues data from 1970 to 2011 come from the table "Equity Financing (All Listed Companies" in *TSE Factbook 2012* (p. 107). The data for 2012 and 2013 are taken from "Financing by Listed Companies" Excel file. GDP from 1994 on are based on SNA93, but GDP before 1994 are based on SNA68.

Source: Authors' calculation using *TSE Factbook 2012*, TSE statistics from *Financing by Listed Companies* and GDP figures from Cabinet Office SNA website (all accessed on December 9, 2014).

late 1980s. CBs partially replaced straight bonds, but overall corporate bond issues increased throughout the 1980s. As the stock prices collapsed in 1990, CBs lost the popularity that they enjoyed in the late 1980s, and the bond issues declined substantially. Since then, the corporate bond issues were revived gradually and as of the early 2010s, the amount of new corporate bond issues (relative to GDP) is roughly the same as the peak reached in the late 1980s.

Figure 3 shows new issues of company stocks. New stock issues increased during the stock market boom in the late 1980s, but almost disappeared as the stock prices collapsed in the early 1990s. Except for three spikes (1999, 2003, and 2009), the volume of new stock issues have been very low, perhaps reflecting the stagnation of the stock market (and the economy) in the 1990s and the 2000s.

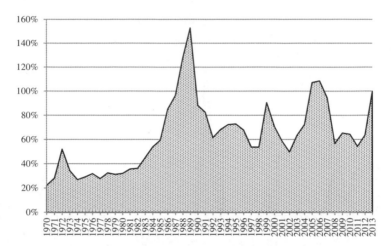

Figure 4. Total market value for the Tokyo Stock Exchange (% of GDP): 1970–2013.

Notes: The market value data from 1970 to 2011 come from the table "Number of Listed Companies, Shares and Market Value" in *TSE Factbook 2012* (p. 106). The data for 2012 and 2013 are taken from *Market Capitalization* Excel file. GDP from 1994 on are based on SNA93, but GDP before 1994 are based on SNA68.

Source: Authors' calculation using *TSE Factbook 2012*, TSE statistics from *Market Capitalization* and GDP figures from Cabinet Office SNA website (all accessed on December 9, 2014).

Looking at the market value of the Tokyo Stock Exchange relative to GDP (Figure 4), the impacts of the stock market boom in the late 1980s and its collapse in the early 1990s again dominate the trend, but even after the collapse, the size of the stock market relative to GDP has been much larger than that before the financial deregulation and the stock market boom.

Although the financial deregulation increased the corporate bond issues, the growth of government bond issues outpaced the growth of corporate bond issues. Indeed, creating the secondary market for Japanese Government Bonds (JGBs) was one of the most important impetuses for the MOF to start the financial deregulation, as Hoshi and Kashyap (2001) pointed out. Figure 5 adds the new issues of JGBs and other government bonds to the corporate bond issues reported in Figure 2. We can see the primary bond market in Japan has been

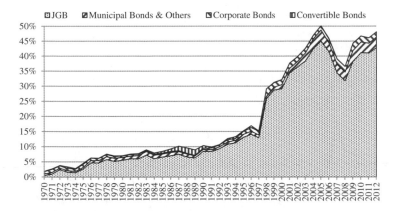

Figure 5. Government bond and corporate bond issues (% of GDP): 1970–2012.

Notes: Bond issues from 1998 on are taken from JSDA data. Bond issues before 1998 are taken from a table titled "New Issues of Bonds by Public Offerings" in *TSE Factbook 2002* (p. 99). GDP from 1994 on are based on SNA93, but GDP before 1994 are based on SNA68. *Source:* Authors' calculation using *TSE Factbook 2002*, JSDA's *Issuing, Redemption and Outstanding Amounts of Bonds* and GDP figures from Cabinet Office SNA website (all accessed on December 9, 2014).

dominated by government bonds, especially after the late 1990s when the budget deficit started to widen.

The financial deregulation that started in the late 1970s continued into the 1990s and the 2000s. Neither the collapse of the asset price bubble (called *baburu keizai,* literally meaning 'bubble economy') in the late 1980s nor the banking crisis in the late 1990s stopped the process of deregulation. Compared to the deregulation on the corporate financing options, the deregulations to expand the options of household savers progressed more slowly. Thus, the proportion of securities in the financial assets of the household sector remained low. Figure 6 shows the proportions of securities and shares in the total household financial assets from 1970 to 2013 calculated from the flow of funds statistics compiled by the Bank of Japan. The classification scheme for the flow of funds statistics changed drastically in the late 1990s, and the current series goes back only to 1997. The old series, on the other hand, was discontinued after 1998. Figure 6 thus reports both old and new series with overlapping observations for 1997 and 1998. The proportion of securities or shares in the total household financial assets shows some

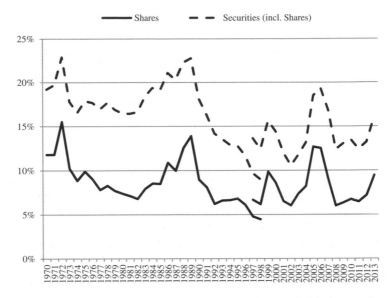

Figure 6. Securities and shares in % of total household financial assets: 1970–2013.

Notes: The data from 1970 to 1998 are taken from the old flow of funds statistics based on SNA68, which was discontinued after 1998. The current statistics are available from 1997. Both old and current flow of funds statistics can be downloaded from Bank of Japan Time Series Data Search (http://www.stat-search.boj.or.jp/index_en.html). For the current statistics, the proportion of shares in the total household financial assets is calculated by dividing the series FF'FOF_FFAS430A330 (Shares and other equities) by the series FF'FOF_FFAS430A900 (Total household assets), and the proportion of securities (including shares) in the total household financial assets is calculated by dividing the sum of the series FF'FOF_FFAS430A300 (Securities other than shares) and the series FF'FOF_FFAS430A330 (Shares and other equities) by the series FF'FOF_FFAS430A900 (Total household assets). For the old statistics, the proportion of shares in the total household financial assets is calculated by dividing the series FF'FFSA270A210 (Stocks) by the series FF'FFSA270A400 (Total personal assets), and the proportion of securities (including shares) in the total household financial assets is calculated by dividing the sum of the series FF'FFSA270A100 (Securities investment trusts) and the series FF'FFSA270A140 (Securities) by the series FF'FFSA270A400 (Total personal assets).
Source: Authors' calculation using the Bank of Japan's *Flow of Funds Statistics* (accessed on December 13, 2014).

fluctuations over time mainly corresponding to the stock prices movements, but overall the proportion has been flat for the last 40 some years.

The Big Bang financial deregulation in the late 1990s marked the final stage of the gradual deregulation process. Almost all the regulations that used to suppress the development of the securities markets were gone.

The household sector, however, did not change the composition of the financial assets very much as we just saw in Figure 6. The investment in securities, such as equities, bonds, and investment trusts, continued to be a small portion of the household financial assets.

To bring in more household financial assets to the securities markets, the government renewed the reform efforts in the 2000s. The policy makers seem to have realized that getting rid of regulations that suppressed the securities markets is not sufficient to increase the household participation in those markets. Active policies that sometimes include new regulations to make the markets more attractive to savers are also important.

Another goal was to expand financing options for startup firms, which were not served well by traditional bank financing. The financial markets, if developed right, were considered to do better in supporting companies with high potential growth but high risk. Yet another motivation for the reform efforts was the proliferation of new financial instrument and services such as financial derivatives, to which the financial regulators were compelled to respond.

Despite the reforms in the 2000s, the Japanese capital markets were still considerably underdeveloped as of the late 2000s. For example, Japan's short-term funding and derivative markets before the GFC were relatively small compared to other development economies such as the U.S. Both commercial paper (CP) and repo markets were relatively small in pre-crisis Japan. The first commercial paper was not issued in Japan until 1987.[1] While the outstanding amount grew from ¥11 trillion in 1997 to ¥20 trillion (about US$200 billion) in 2008, the Japanese CP market was still quite small relative to the US CP market, which had US$1.8 trillion outstanding in 2008. The repo market started in 1996. As of 2008, it had ¥136 trillion (about US$1.3 trillion) in outstanding amount, of which majority were cash-secured bond lending transactions (not repurchase agreements) (Central Tanshi 2014). In contrast, US repo market had US$5 trillion to US$10 trillion in 2008 (Gorton and Metrick 2012).

---

[1] The information on the development of CP market in Japan comes from Inoue (1998) and Bank of Japan (2013b).

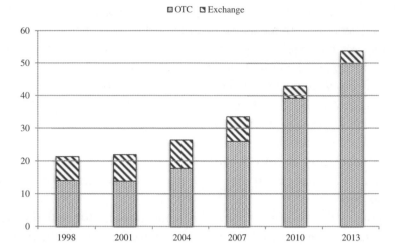

Figure 7. Derivative contracts (notional amount) (US$ trillion).

Notes: Numbers are based on nominal or notional principal amounts outstanding and in US$ trillions. Surveys were conducted as of the end of June each year. For OTC derivatives, data for the following five categories were reported in the survey: Foreign exchange, Interest rate, Equity, Commodity, and credit default swaps (CDS). The amount shown in the chart represents the sum of the five categories. The Bank of Japan started collecting data on CDS in December 2004, and thus the CDS outstanding amounts are reported here only in 2007, 2010, and 2013. For on-the-exchange derivatives, data for the following four categories were reported: Foreign exchange, Interest rate, Equity, and Commodity. The amount shown in the chart represents the sum of the four categories.

Source: OTC data are authors' calculations using the Bank of Japan, *Central Bank Survey of Foreign Exchange and Derivatives Market Activity* (accessed on November 4, 2014). Exchange data are authors' calculations using the Bank of Japan, *Regular Derivatives Market Statistics in Japan* (accessed on November 3, 2014).

Figure 7 shows the expansion of the derivative market in Japan. The outstanding notional amount grew from US$21.4 trillion in 1998 to US$53.8 trillion in 2013. The growth was entirely driven by the rapid growth in the OTC (Over-The-Counter) segment. In contrast, over the exchange outstanding amount actually declined during the period. Among the OTC derivative contracts, interest rate swaps have been the most common transaction type, followed by the foreign exchange-related transactions as Figure 8 shows.

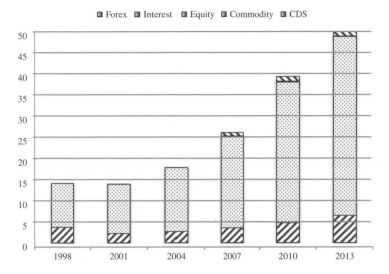

Figure 8. OTC derivative contracts, by type (US$ trillion).

Notes: Numbers are based on nominal or notional principal amounts outstanding and in US$ trillions. Surveys were conducted as of the end of June each year. Data for the following five categories were reported in the survey: Foreign exchange, Interest rate, Equity, Commodity, and credit default swaps (CDS). The Bank of Japan started collecting data on CDS in December 2004, and thus the CDS outstanding amounts are reported here only in 2007, 2010, and 2013. *Source:* Authors' calculations using the Bank of Japan, *Central Bank Survey of Foreign Exchange and Derivatives Market Activity* (accessed on November 4, 2014).

Finally, CDS (credit default swap) and other credit derivative markets were also quite small in Japan compared to the U.S. While Japan had US$800 billion in outstanding notional amount as of June 2007, there was US$62 trillion global notional amount outstanding as of the end of 2007.[2] Thus, Japan accounted for only about 1% of the global CDS market on the eve of the GFC.

---

[2] The information on CDS comes from Bank of Japan, *Central Bank Survey of Foreign Exchange and Derivatives Market Activity* (https://www.boj.or.jp/statistics/bis/deri/index.htm/, accessed on November 4, 2014) and International Swaps and Derivatives Association, Inc., Market Surveys (http://www2.isda.org/functional-areas/research/surveys/market-surveys/, accessed on October 27, 2014).

The renewed reform efforts in Japan in the 2000s led to the fundamental revision of the Securities and Exchange Act to create a comprehensive regulatory framework to cover a wide range of financial instruments and the businesses that handle those instruments. The new law, the Financial Instruments and Exchange Act (FIEA) was promulgated in 2006.

The enactment of the FIEA resulted from amendments, replacements, and consolidation of numerous existing laws, including the Japan Securities and Exchange Act of 1947 that was modeled after the US Securities Act of 1933 and Securities and Exchange Act of 1934. The new act introduced the following key changes:

1. It expanded the range of regulated financial instruments, both by explicitly designating interests in trusts and 'collective investment schemes' (funds) as regulated financial instruments under the Act, and also broadening the scope of the term 'derivative transactions' to include those on interest rate and currency swaps, weather derivatives, and credit derivatives.

2. It redefined categories under which existing and new financial institutions are regulated. In particular, it newly defined Type 1 Financial Instrument Business Operators (FIBOs) as those engaged in sales and solicitation of securities with high liquidity and Type 2 FIBOs as those engaged in sales and solicitation of securities with low liquidity. Type 1 FIBOs are subject to more stringent regulation than Type 2 FIBOs. It also defined professional and general investors. Financial products for general investors face more stringent regulations than those mainly for professional investors.

3. It mandated statutory quarterly financial reporting by issuers of listed equity and bonds and required more stringent disclosure. For example, the management and the external auditor must certify the adequacy of the issuer's internal control on financial reporting. This part of the FIEA was dubbed J-SOX for its similarity to the US Sarbanes–Oxley Act. In contrast, financial instruments with low liquidity (e.g., interests in unlisted trusts and limited partnerships) are exempt from this requirement.

4. It established more explicit rules to be followed by bidders and target company management in public tender offers, and increased penalties for market manipulation. This part of the FIEA was enacted largely in response to the Livedoor and other tender offer attempts that revealed inadequacy of the existing regulation to ensure fairness and transparency in market transactions.[3]

Shortly after the FIEA became effective in September 2007, the Financial Services Agency of Japan (JFSA) started working on amendments, which led to the new FIEA that were enacted and promulgated in June 2008. The key component of the amendments was to allow establishment of a new market similar to the so-called 144A market in the US, where participation was limited to professional investors (*tokutei tōshika*)[4] and securities issued in such a market are exempted from the current disclosure rules intended to protect general investors from frauds.

Thus, on the eve of the Global Financial Crisis, Japan was reaching the end of the long process of financial deregulation. The recovery from the banking crisis that it experienced along the way was also very much complete, and the regulators started to strengthen Japan's capital markets further.

---

[3] The Securities and Exchange Act of 1947 required that the purchase of shares that exceed the one-third of the outstanding amount 'outside stock exchanges' must be done through a public tender offer. In February 2005, the Livedoor Partners (subsidiary of the Livedoor) acquired more than one-third of Nippon Broadcasting shares, to which Fuji Television had already made a public tender offer, through an after-hours transaction in the Tokyo Stock Exchange without making a tender offer. This led to a debate whether the Livedoor violated the 'one-third' rule. The FIEA required that any party who accumulates more than one-third of the outstanding amount 'rapidly' inside or outside stock exchanges must do so through a public tender offer.

[4] 'Professional Investor', as defined by the FIEA, includes Qualified Institutional Investors, the Japanese government, the Bank of Japan and listed stock corporations (*kabushiki kaisha*) and other companies.

II. Japan's Financial Markets after the Global Financial Crisis

The Japanese financial sector experienced smaller disruption in key funding markets compared to the US during the Global Financial Crisis mainly because it had much less exposure to various complex securitized products that were ultimately tied to low quality mortgage loans in the US The Japanese economy, however, was hit hard by the collapse of international trades during the global recession. Consequently, manufacturing sector increased dependence on bank borrowing after the crisis. The Japanese government sharply increased its JGB issues to finance fiscal expansion to combat the recession, and some firms (particularly the large banks and securities houses) were active in the new equity issues market.

Among the segments of short-term funding markets, both the uncollateralized call markets and special collateral repo markets shrank in absolute size and relative importance after the GFC as shown in Figure 9. In contrast, cash secured-repo and collateralized calls stayed active. Japan experienced smaller disruptions in key funding markets compared to the US Japan's repo market, for example, was estimated to have been US$1 trillion to US$1.3 trillion as of 2008, and it was still US$1 trillion as of 2012 (Central Tanshi 2014). Thus, it experienced at most 30% decline in size over the course of the crisis. In contrast, the US repo market was estimated to have been as large as US$5 trillion to US$10 trillion as of 2008 when the crisis began, and it shrank to only US$2 trillion to US$3 trillion by 2012.[5] Not only did the US repo market experience much more dramatic shrinkage (>50%), it also experienced episodic sharp increases in haircuts during the crisis (Gorton and Metrick 2012). In Japan, however, over 99% of the repo contracts were collateralized with the Japanese Government Bonds (JGBs) and thus the haircuts were minimal (Bank of Japan 2013a).

For the CP market in Japan, the estimated shrinkage during the crisis is 30% (US$200 billion in 2008 to US$140 billion in 2012), which is more significant. The CP market, however, represented a fairly small

---

[5] Copeland *et al.* (2012).

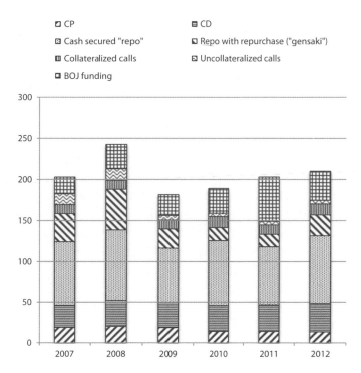

Figure 9. Short-term funding markets in Japan, by type (¥ trillion).

Notes: (1) Interbank market data are based on Central Tanshi's proprietary sources. (2) CP data are based on Japan Securities Depository Center, Inc. (3) Repo with repurchase (*gensaki*) data are based on *Balance of Bond Transactions with Repurchase Agreements* by Japan Securities Dealers Association (JSDA). (4) Cash secured repo market data are based on *Bond Margin Loans* by Japan Securities Dealers Association (JSDA). (5) Excludes Treasury Discount Bills (Treasury Bills and Financing Bills before February 2009) data.
Source: Authors' calculations using Central Tanshi, *Short Term Funding Markets* (accessed on October 21, 2014). Each figure is as of the end of March of each year.

portion of the total funding market in Japan. This contrasts with the US CP market, which was as large as US$1.8 trillion as of 2008 and experienced 40% decline to about US$1 trillion by 2012.

Although the direct impacts on financial markets were small, the Great Recession following the crisis had a negative impact on operational performance of the Japanese firms, especially manufacturing firms that depend highly on exports for their revenues. In terms of corporate financing, Figure 1 shows a sizable increase in manufacturing firms' bank dependence between 2008 and 2010 regardless of firm size. In contrast, there is no discernable pattern among the non-manufacturing firms. The increased bank debt dependence could have been caused simply by operational losses triggering erosion of the assets or by liquidity-constrained corporate bond investors refusing to refinance maturing bonds and firms resorting to more bank debt.

We can revisit Figures 3 and 5 to see what happened to stock issues and bond issues after the global financial crisis. Figure 3 shows that the primary market for shares hit the bottom in 2008, and there was a dramatic increase in 2009. The peak was driven primarily by recapitalization of financial institutions. All the major banks and brokerage firms (Mitsubishi UFJ Bank, Sumitomo Mitsui Bank, Mizuho Bank, Nomura Securities, and Daiwa Securities) issued shares and they accounted for more than 50% of the total stock issues in 2009.

The bond market continued to be dominated by JGB issues after the global financial crisis. The new JGB issues were declining immediately before the GFC, as the Japanese government embarked on the efforts to reduce the budget deficit under the Koizumi administration. Facing the economic downturn following the GFC, however, the administration that followed Koizumi returned to fiscal expansion financed by increasing JGB issues.

III. Regulatory Responses to the Global Financial Crisis

Although the Japanese financial system did not suffer directly from the Global Financial Crisis, it shared some vulnerability with the financial systems in other advanced economies that were directly hit. For example, the majority of growing transactions in financial derivatives were bilateral contracts, which can be subject to large counterparty risks. High degree of interconnection through the complex web of bilateral derivative contracts is often considered to be one of the major factors that made the financial crisis more serious. Thus, the Japanese regulators also started to respond to the Global Financial Crisis by tightening financial regulations, especially in the areas that were lightly regulated such as the OTC derivatives.

At the same time, the Japanese regulators continued the efforts to attract more household financial assets to the capital markets and to expand financing options for startup firms. JFSA seems to have realized that Japan's capital markets were still underdeveloped and just tightening regulation is not a solution.

This section examines the regulatory reforms on Japan's capital markets after the Global Financial Crisis. We do this by mainly tracking the series of amendments to the FIEA and related laws.[6] The FIEA went through significant changes in every year from 2010 to 2013. Rather than looking at the nature of the amendments by year, we divide the regulatory changes into three groups regardless of the year of change and study how the regulatory reforms progressed in each of the three areas.

The first group includes regulatory reforms to improve the stability of financial markets. This is the area where the regulators of the US and many other advanced economies focused on after the global financial crisis. The efforts of Japan's regulators in this area were carried out in coordination with the regulators in other countries.

The second is a series of regulatory reforms to attract more household financial assets to capital markets. The third group is the regulatory changes to enhance the options for users of funds, especially those who traditionally had limited access to capital markets, such as startups. These two types of financial reform were more important to Japan, where the capital markets were still underdeveloped compared with the US.

IV. Reform to Improve the Stability of Financial Markets

An important reform to improve the stability of financial markets was introduction of regulation to the OTC transactions of financial derivatives. Highly interconnected yet opaque nature of the OTC derivative transactions was believed to be an important factor that intensified the

---

[6] These amendments and other important legal changes related to Japan's financial regulation are collected under 'Recent Changes' on the JFSA website http://www.fsa.go.jp/en/laws_regulations/ (accessed on December 21, 2014).

crisis. Japan's regulatory reform in this area has been following the lead of the G-20 (the Group of Twenty). At the Pittsburg Summit, held in September 2009, the G-20 agreed that, by the end of 2012, (i) standardized OTC derivatives should be traded on exchanges or electronic trading platforms, (ii) standardized derivatives transactions should be cleared through central clearing parties (CCPs), and (iii) data relating to OTC derivatives transactions should be reported to trade repositories (TRs).

Following the G-20 agreement, Japan amended the FIEA in May 2010 to address (ii) and (iii) of the agreement. The amended FIEA required (1) clearing of certain standardized OTC derivatives transactions through a CCP and (2) reporting of certain data relating to certain OTC derivatives transactions to the JFSA.

All FIBOs and Registered Financial Institutions (RFIs) registered under the FIEA were required to clear designated OTC derivatives through a CCP. Foreign entities that were not registered in Japan were not covered by this requirement. Just two categories of OTC derivatives transactions were initially covered by the clearing requirement: (1) credit default swap (CDS) transactions on the iTraxx Japan index of which reference entities are 50 or less domestic corporations and (2) yen-denominated plain vanilla interest swaps on 3-month or 6-month Japanese yen LIBOR. No other types of OTC derivatives were included.

CDS transactions on the iTraxx Japan index can only be cleared through licensed Japanese CCPs, whereas interest swap transactions can be cleared through any of licensed Japanese CCPs, licensed foreign CCPs, and foreign CCPs with approved linkage arrangements with licensed domestic CCPs. In November 2012, when the 2010 Amendment went into effect, only one CCP, the Japan Securities Clearing Corporation (JSCC), was in operation as a licensed CCP and no other CCPs, foreign or domestic, had been licensed or approved.

The central clearing of these OTC derivatives was mandated starting in October 2012. Figure 10 shows that the new assumption of obligations (newly contracted OTC derivatives) by JSCC sharply rose from about only ¥20 trillion per month in 2012 to almost ¥60 trillion per month on average in 2014. The open interest amount increased dramatically, from ¥14 trillion in October 2010 to nearly ¥1 quadrillion (or ¥1,000 trillion) in September 2014. The percentage share of centrally cleared

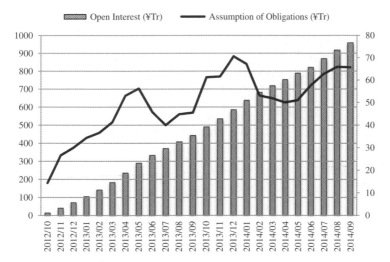

Figure 10. Centrally-cleared OTC derivatives, Open Interest and Assumption of Obligation (¥ trillion).

Notes: The left axis corresponds to the Open Interest amount in ¥ trillions; the right axis corresponds to the Assumption of Obligations in ¥ trillions.

Source: Authors' calculations using Japan Securities Clearing Corporation, *Statistics for Interest Rate Swap* (accessed on November 4, 2014).

OTC derivatives among all OTC derivative transactions in Japan grew from about 20% as of June 2013 to about 40–50% a year later (June 2014).[7] Thus, by this measure the Japanese regulators seem to have been accomplishing one of the main purposes of the OTC derivative reform, namely to reduce systematic risk by subjecting greater portions of OTC derivative contracts to centrally clearing.

---

[7] The comparison is based on notional principal amounts outstanding and assumes that all centrally cleared interest rate swaps are denominated in yen. The total outstanding amounts are based on the Bank of Japan survey of major dealers. The BOJ survey publishes the notional amounts either (i) by currency or (ii) by duration but not by both. Thus, one needs to compare either (i) the centrally cleared swaps (all duration) to the total interest rate swaps (all duration), or (ii) the centrally cleared, short duration swaps to the total short duration swaps multiplied by the proportion of yen-denominated swaps among all. Using the two methods, we obtain that the proportion of centrally cleared interest rate swaps was 18% or 22% as of June 2013 and 40 or 48% as of 2014 respectively.

The amended FIEA also specified a reporting requirement. Information relating to (1) forward transactions and index forward transactions where the settlement date comes three or more business days after the trade date, (2) option transactions and index option transactions where the exercise date comes three or more business days after the trade date, (3) swap (e.g., interest swap and currency swap) transactions, and (4) credit derivatives transactions where the trigger event is in relation to credit condition changes to a reference entity (e.g., CDS) must be reported to the government.

If transactions are cleared through a CCP, the CCP is responsible for keeping the trade information and reporting it to the JFSA. If transactions are not cleared through a CCP, any party to the transactions that is a Type 1 FIBO or RFI must either store and report the trade information to the government itself or provide information to a designated Trade Repository (TR), which in turn must report the information to the government. In March 2013, the JFSA approved DTCC Data Repository Japan (DDRJ) to be the first TR to operate in the Japanese market.

Mandatory use of electronic trading platforms (ETPs), the first point raised by the G20 Pittsburg agreement, was addressed in the 2012 amendment of the FIEA. It is scheduled to take effect within 3 years, i.e., by 2015. In JFSA's implementation proposal as of this writing (December 2014), large FIBOs and RFIs (with derivative contracts exceeding ¥6 trillion or US$59 billion) will be required to use ETPs by September 2015 when they enter into yen-denominated plain vanilla interest swap contracts. This threshold is expected to cover 10 to 20 of the largest dealers. The JFSA will consider expanding this requirement to CDS transactions on the iTraxx Japan index after monitoring the market liquidity of these transactions.

The 2010 amendment of FIEA also introduced two other reforms aimed at improving the financial stability. The first is the reform to strengthen group-wide regulation and supervision of financial companies. The reform expanded the scope of regulation and supervision of securities companies from individual securities companies to the company groups including the subsidiaries and related companies. Large securities companies were now required to report the financial conditions of their subsidiaries and other related companies and those entities became subject to examinations of the JFSA. Regulation at consolidated level was also introduced to groups led by insurance companies. The prudential regulation of insurance companies was expanded to cover their subsidiaries and they now must calculate the solvency ratios on the consolidated basis.

The second is the enhancement of the closure procedures for problem financial institutions. Before the 2010 change, the JFSA was allowed to file a bankruptcy only for securities companies. The JFSA was not allowed to file a petition for the appointment of a new trustee when the license for trust business was rescinded. The enhancement gave the JFSA to power to file a bankruptcy for any FIBO and to file a petition for a new trustee for a deregistered trust business operator. The change also introduced a penal provision for legal persons (in addition to individuals) for violating court injunction orders against unregistered FIBOs.

Another important reform to improve the financial stability was the establishment of orderly resolution mechanism that covers all financial institutions. During the global financial crisis, the failure of Lehman Brothers brought almost entire global financial system to a halt. To avoid repeating such a meltdown, many critics advocated a mechanism to let a large globally connected financial institution fail without bringing down the entire financial system. In October 2011, the Financial Stability Board published *Key Attributes of Effective Resolution Regimes for Financial Institutions*, which was endorsed by the G-20 Summit at Cannes in November 2011 (FSB 2011). Following this G-20 agreement, Japan expanded its resolution mechanism for banks that is specified in Chapter 7 of the Deposit Insurance Act (DIA) to all financial institutions including financial holding companies and securities houses in the 2013 amendment of the FIEA, DIA, and other related laws.

Reform to Attract More Funds to Capital Markets

The 2011 amendment of the FIEA and other related laws included several measures to enhance the asset investment opportunities for savers. For example, the registration requirements and regulations on solicitations for investment management businesses were relaxed. The relaxation was mostly for those businesses that cater to professional investors.

Similarly, the regulation on asset securitization was relaxed by, for example, exempting the special purpose vehicle (SPV) for asset securitization from filing a plan change notice if the change is considered minor.

The 2011 amendment also included some changes to enhance integrity of capital markets, which would encourage more investors to participate in the markets. One such reform was the introduction of the rules that make certain financial transactions (e.g. sales of unlisted stocks by an unregistered FIBO) void. The amendment also strictly prohibited advertising and solicitation by unregistered FIBOs and increased the maximum amount of criminal penalties against an unregistered FIBO.

The efforts to make capital markets more accessible to more investors continued in the reforms in 2012 and 2013. The 2012 amendment of the FIEA introduced measures to further strengthen the regulation against market misconducts. The most important measure was the revision of the Administrative Monetary Penalty (AMP) system for market misconducts. The revision expanded the scope of AMP beyond the entities that commits market misconducts such as falsifying financial statements to include the parties that assist such misconducts by advising on an illegal scheme or knowingly being counterparties to fraudulent transactions. The revision also expanded the authority for the JFSA to investigate market misconducts cases and to make appearance orders to the related parties. Finally, the revision expanded the scope of subjects of AMP beyond FIBOs to include other operators and investors who trade on third party's accounts.

The 2013 amendment again included the tightening of the regulation against market misconducts especially by asset management companies (JFSA 2013). The reform was partially prompted by a large fraud case of the AIJ Investment Advisors, which was revealed in 2012.[8] AIJ managed assets for more than 100 customers, many of whom were corporate pension funds, but ended up losing most of the assets under management. AIJ obtained customers on falsified investment records that showed higher and more stable returns than many other asset management companies. The JFSA forced AIJ to terminate operations in February 2012, at which point most of the assets under management

---

[8] See Maxwell (2012) and Osaki (2013) for more on the AIJ case.

could not be found. The eventual loss amounted to ¥24.8 billion and the top AIJ executives received criminal sentences.

To avoid frauds like the AIJ case, the asset management regulation was strengthened in several aspects. The amounts of criminal penalties for frauds were raised. For example, the fine for making false statements in investment reports was no more than ¥500,000 before the revision. The maximum amount was raised to ¥3 million. Moreover, there were no additional corporate fines before the change. The revision specified additional corporate fines of no more than ¥300 million. Similarly the fines for obtaining investment contracts through fraudulent means were increased (from no more than ¥3 million and additional corporate fines of no more than ¥300 million to no more than ¥5 million and additional corporate fines of no more than ¥500 million). The revision also included stronger requirements to disclose the status of investment assets to customers and clearer obligation for the trust banks that are appointed as custodians for the investment contracts.

The 2012 amendment also clarified the insider trading regulation to allow the transfer of shares of a company by the company's insiders with knowledge of undisclosed material facts in some cases where such trading is not likely to hurt the general investors. Those cases include transfer of equity stakes as part of a business transfer (as long as the equities account for only a part of transferred assets) and use of treasury shares as a compensation for merger.

The insider trading regulation was again revised in the 2013 amendment. The revision was partially motivated by several cases where the lead underwriter of public offering disclosed material facts to asset managers. Although the JFSA imposed financial penalties to those lead underwriters (including major securities companies such as Nomura), the existing insider regulation did not have a clear rule that prohibits disclosure of inside information by lead underwriter. The revision specified that corporate insiders with unpublished material facts cannot disclose such information or recommend trading to the third party. The revision also increased the amount of monetary penalty for insider trading violation by asset managers when they used client accounts to carry out the insider trading. Under the existing rule, the penalty amount was calculated as the amount of management fees for 1 month multiplied by "the ratio of the value of the relevant stocks to the total assets under management." (JFSA 2013, p. 5) The amount was changed to the total management fees for 3 months.

In addition to these changes, the revision expanded the scope of insiders in TOB (Takeover Bid) cases. Under the existing rule, a person who received the information on tender offer facts from the target company before the target company made any agreement with the bidder was considered a secondary recipient of information and excluded from the scope of insider trading regulation. This is because the target company was not considered as a TOB insider before an agreement was made with the bidder. The revised rule expanded the scope of TOB insiders to include the target companies regardless of the existence of agreements with the bidders.

The establishment of a 'comprehensive exchange,' where securities, financial derivatives and commodity derivatives are all traded, in the 2012 reform can also be considered as a part of the efforts to make capital markets available to more investors.

Reforms to Enhance the Options for Users of Funds

The third area of reforms after the global financial crisis aimed at enhancing the options for users of funds. The amendments of the FIEA and other related laws included several reforms in this area.

The 2011 amendment of the FIEA introduced several measures to give diverse alternatives for corporate financing. These included the improvement of legal framework for corporate fund raising through rights offering. The framework allowed a corporation that is raising funds by allocating stock options to simply submit a securities registration statement and post the information on a public website instead of preparing and sending prospectus to every shareholder. How the information on rights offering that shareholders receive is interpreted in the insider trading regulation (it constitutes a material fact) was also clarified.

The 2011 amendment also enhanced the range of borrowers who are allowed to set up commitment lines. Before the change, commitment lines were only available for very large companies. The amendment allowed medium size companies and subsidiaries of large companies to set up commitment lines. Another reform that targeted medium to small companies was the deregulation to allow banks and insurance companies to provide 'financial leases' (non-renegotiable fully amortized loans to purchase equipment) directly to lessees. Even before the change, banks and insurance companies were already able to provide financial leases indirectly through subsidiaries, but now they themselves were allowed to provide financial lease as one of the loan options for their customers.

The 2011 amendment made financing in Japan easier for foreign companies, too. The amendment expanded the type of securities reports that foreign companies listed in Japan can submit in English (instead of Japanese). Before the change, foreign companies listed on a Japanese stock exchange were required to file their financial statements in Japanese. Now the revision allowed them to file the statements and supplementary documents in English.

In the 2013 amendment of FIEA, J-REIT, the Japanese version of REIT (Real Estate Investment Trust) acquired more options for their financing. Introduced in 2001, the market for J-REIT grew steadily and J-REIT became significant users of the Japanese capital markets. The amendment expanded the financing and capital policy choices available for J-REIT including equity repurchase and rights offering. The amendment also allowed J-REIT to acquire overseas real estate indirectly using a Special Purpose Company (SPC) rather than directly owning the real estate.

Improvement of corporate governance of J-REIT was another goal of the reform. To reduce conflicts of interest between J-REIT and the asset management company that sponsors the J-REIT, prior approval from the board of J-REIT was now required for any substantial acquisition of properties from the sponsor company. At the same time, J-REIT was subject to insider trading regulations.

The 2013 amendment also introduced an exception to the restriction on shareholding by a bank, when it is leading restructuring of the corporation. A bank is prohibited from holding more than 5% of voting rights in a non-financial company, but this restriction was relaxed when it is deemed essential for successful corporate restructuring or revitalization of a region.

V. Abenomics and Capital Markets

The global financial crisis and the global recession that followed and affected the Japanese economy were probably important contributing factors for the demise of the Liberal Democratic Party (LDP) in 2009. The LDP failed to get the largest number of seats in the House of Representatives (lower house) Election in August, 2009, and lost power. This was only the second time that LDP was voted out of the power since its inception in 1955. The Democratic Party of Japan (DPJ) instead formed the government, but the financial regulatory policy did not show any drastic changes. As we saw above, the government continued the policy to encourage the development of capital markets to help economic growth while at the same time coordinating with the rest of G-20 to introduce the regulatory reforms to improve the financial stability.

The DPJ government lasted only for a little more than three years (going through three Prime Ministers). The LDP regained the power at the House of Representatives Election in December, 2012, and the Prime Minister Shinzo Abe announced the economic policy package to end the deflation and restore the growth for Japan. The policy package that has come to be known as Abenomics is a combination of expansionary macroeconomic policy (aggressive monetary policy *aka* the first arrow and flexible fiscal policy *aka* the second arrow) and economic structural reform (growth strategy *aka* the third arrow).

Abenomics lists capital market reform as an important part of the growth strategy. Thus, Japan is continuing its efforts to encourage the development of capital markets. Several capital market policies are included in the growth strategy that the Abe administration announced in June 2013. The growth strategy has been revised in June 2014, but the capital market policies are still included as essential measures to stimulate growth. This section reviews the capital market policies in Abenomics.

The revised growth strategy of 2014 identifies ten key reforms, which are (1) enhancing corporate governance, (2) reforming investment of public and quasi-public funds, (3) accelerating industrial restructuring and venture businesses, promoting provision of funds for growth, (4) corporate tax reform, (5) promotion of innovation and a robot revolution, (6) enhancing women's participation and advancement, (7) enable flexible working practices, (8) attracting talent from overseas, (9) aggressive agricultural policy, and (10) vitalizing the healthcare industry and providing high-quality healthcare services. The first three relate to reform of the financial system in general and capital markets in particular.

Of the first three areas, the efforts in the second area (reform of public and quasi-public funds) started by the creation of government panel for "Sophisticating the Management of Public/Quasi-public Funds" in July, 2013. The panel published the recommendations on how to reform management of public and quasi-public funds in November, 2013.

Public pension funds include Government Pension Investment Fund (GPIF), National Public Service Personnel Mutual Aid Fund, Local Public Service Personnel Mutual Aid Fund, and Private School Personnel Mutual Aid Fund, and quasi-public funds include incorporated administrative agencies such as national university corporations. These funds collectively hold more than ¥200 trillion (40% of GDP), so they are huge players in the capital markets. GPIF is by far the largest among these with about ¥114 trillion of assets.

In the recommendation, the panel urged the public funds to adjust their portfolios to increase the returns while keeping the risk at a reasonable level. The panel pointed out that diversifying away from domestic bonds, which constitutes most of the assets of many public funds, is especially important. The funds were encouraged to shift their portfolios into new type of assets including REITs, real estate, infrastructure, venture capital, private equity, and commodities. The panel also endorsed the idea of the public funds become an active investor. To improve returns, the funds were asked to establish close communications with investment targets and exercise voting rights appropriately. The panel also recommended improving governance and risk management structure of the funds. Each fund has a government ministry in charge. For example, the GPIF is under the control of the Ministry of Health, Labor, and Welfare. The panel suggested creation of a governance structure that allows the funds to make investment decisions to maximize the returns within the well-articulated risk tolerance without unnecessary interventions from the ministries in charge.

The government has been acting also on the other two key areas related to capital markets ((1) enhancing corporate governance and (3) accelerating industrial restructuring and venture businesses, promoting provision of funds for growth). Some early reforms have been implemented in the 2014 amendment of the FIEA.

To strengthen the role of the capital market in providing risk money to emerging and growing companies, the 2014 amendment relaxed the entry requirements for FIBOs to engage in equity crowdfunding while introducing new regulation to prevent fraudulent investment solicitation using internet. It also introduced a new trading system for non-listed shares that is less onerous than the one used for listed shares. To encourage foreign providers of risk money to enter the Japanese capital market, the amendment allowed FIBOs to have accounting years different from the standard one (from April 1 to March 31).

The amendment also included some measures to promote new listings and facilitate financing by listed companies. To encourage more new listings, newly listed companies were given three years before they were required to have their internal control report audited. To relieve the regulatory burden of the listed companies, transactions of treasury stock were made exempt from filing large shareholding reports, so that they would not need to submit a report to the regulator each time they acquire or dispose of treasury stocks. The strict liability rule for false statement in the secondary market was replaced by a fault liability rule, so that a listed company is not liable if it proves that it was not at fault.

The emphasis of Abenomics has been the reforms to grow Japan's capital markets, but the 2014 amendment of the FIEA included changes to enhance the stability of capital markets, too. First, regulation on sale of partnership rights was tightened. Type 2 FIBOs (those deal with securities with low liquidity) were prohibited from soliciting investment in a partnership right while knowing that the money invested is used for other purposes. The revision also obligated Type 2 FIBOs to establish at least one office in Japan.

Introduction of regulation of financial benchmarks such as TIBOR was another reform in the 2014 amendment of the FIEA to enhance the financial stability. After the global financial crisis, several incidences of financial benchmark manipulation were discovered, and the G20 advocated for new regulatory framework for financial benchmarks.

Finally, trying to strengthen the regulation against fraudulent conducts, the 2014 amendment established procedures for confiscating electronic share certificates and other intangible property that were acquired through fraudulent transactions, because the old rules did not have procedure to confiscate intangibles.

In the general Election for House of Representatives in December 2014, the ruling coalition led by the LDP has retained two-thirds majority and Shinzo Abe has been reappointed as the prime minister. In the press conference immediately following the formation of the Third Abe Cabinet on December 24, 2014, Prime Minster Abe declared "The foremost issue is making the success of Abenomics a certainty."[9] Thus, the efforts to develop capital markets in Japan are likely to continue.

Conclusion

On the eve of the global financial crisis, Japan's capital markets were underdeveloped compared to more advanced markets in the US Japan had moved significantly away from the bank dominated financial system that characterized Japan until the early 1980s, but the households continued to hold a sizable portion of their financial assets in bank deposits. Corporate financing through bonds and stocks increased, but the corporate bond market was dwarfed by the large and expanding market for JGBs.

The underdevelopment of capital markets meant that the Japanese financial institutions did not have much exposure to the type of securitized products that put many financial institutions in the US and Europe into serious trouble. Thus, Japan experienced smaller disruption in key markets compared to the US during the global financial crisis.

---

[9] From "Inauguration of the Third Abe Cabinet — Press Conference by Prime Minister Abe" available at the website for Prime Minister of Japan: http://japan.kantei.go.jp/97_abe/statement/201412/1224danwa.html, accessed on December 25, 2014.

After the global financial crisis, Japanese regulators adopted two pronged approach. On one hand, they implemented reforms to improve the stability of financial markets in coordination with regulators in other advanced economies. At the same time, Japanese regulators continued their efforts to make capital markets attractive to both investors and borrowers. In Abenomics that aims to restore the growth of the Japanese economy, developing capital markets is one of the most important policy areas. If the policy turns out to be successful, the Japanese financial system will finally complete the transition from the bank dominated system to the system where markets play a central role.

References

Bank of Japan (2013a), Money Market Operations in Fiscal 2012. Available at: https://www.boj.or.jp/en/research/brp/ron_2013/ron130619a.htm/.

Bank of Japan (2013b), *Trends and Issues in the Japanese Short-term Funding Markets*. Available at: https://www.boj.or.jp/research/brp/ron_2013/data/ron130228a.pdf.

Central Tanshi (2014), *Short Term Funding Markets*. Available at: http://www.central-tanshi.com/seminar/1-02.html (accessed on October 21, 2014).

Copeland, A., I. Davis, E. LeSueur, and A. Martin (2012), "Mapping and Sizing the U.S. Repo Market", *Liberty Street Economics*, June 25. Available at: http://libertystreeteconomics.newyorkfed.org/2012/06/mapping-and-sizing-the-us-repo-market.html#.VJ18wLgA8R.

Financial Stability Board (FSB) (2011), *Key Attributes of Effective Resolution Regimes for Financial Institutions*. Available at: http://www.financialstabilityboard.org/2011/11/r_111104cc.

Financial Services Agency, Japan (JFSA) (2013), *2013 Amendment Act of Financial Instrument and Exchange Act, etc. (Act No. 45 of 2013) [Briefing Materials]*, May 2013. Available at: http://www.fsa.go.jp/en/refer/legislation/20130416/02.pdf.

Gorton, G. and A. Metrick (2012), "Securitized Banking and the Run on Repo", *Journal of Financial Economics* 104: 425–451.

Hoshi, T. and A. Kashyap (2000), "The Japanese Banking Crisis: Where did it come from and how will it end?", *NBER Macroeconomics Annual 1999*, 129–201.

Hoshi, T. and A. Kashyap (2001), *Corporate Financing and Governance in Japan: The Road to the Future* (Cambridge, MA: MIT Press).

Inoue, T. (1998), Challenges in Japanese Commercial Paper Market, *Nomura Capital Market Review* 1(1). Available at: http://www.nicmr.com/nicmr/english/report/repo/1998/1998spr03.pdf.

Japan Securities Clearing Corporation (2014), *Statistics for Interest Rate Swap*. Available at: http://www.jscc.co.jp/en/interest_rate_swap.

Maxwell, K. (2012), "Japanese Fund Loses $2.3 Billion," *Wall Street Journal*, February 24. Available at: http://www.wsj.com/articles/SB100014240529 70203918304577242023349153292.

Osaki, T. (2013), "AIJ's Asakawa gets 15 years for huge pension fund fraud," *The Japan Times*, December 18. Available at: http://www.japantimes.co.jp/news/2013/12/18/national/crime-legal/aijs-asakawa-gets-15-years-for-huge-pension-fund-fraud/#.VJh_gP9FFE.

Sources of Data

Bank of Japan, *Central Bank Survey of Foreign Exchange and Derivatives Market Activity*. Available at: https://www.boj.or.jp/statistics/bis/deri/index.htm/ (in Japanese).

Bank of Japan, *Regular Derivatives Market Statistics in Japan*. Available at: https://www.boj.or.jp/statistics/bis/yoshi/index.htm/ (in Japanese).

Bank of Japan, *Flow of Funds Statistics*. Available at: http://www.stat-search.boj.or.jp/index_en.html (in Japanese).

Ministry of Finance Policy Research Institute, *Financial Statements Statistics of Corporations by Industry, Quarterly*. Available at: http://www.mof.go.jp/english/pri/reference/ssc/historical.htm.

Tokyo Stock Exchange [TSE], *TSE Factbook 2002*. Available at: http://www.tsc.or.jp/english/market/data/factbook/.

Tokyo Stock Exchange [TSE], *Financing by Listed Companies*. Available at: http://www.tse.or.jp/english/market/data/financing.

Tokyo Stock Exchange [TSE], *Market Capitalization*. Available at: http://www.tse.or.jp/english/market/data/value/.

Japan Securities Dealers Association [JSDA], *Bonds, Investment Trusts and others*. Available at: http://www.jsda.or.jp/en/statistics/bond-market/index.html. From this page, *Issuing, Redemption and Outstanding Amounts of Bond*; *Balance of Bond Transactions with Repurchase Agreements*; and *Bond Margin Loans* can also be found.

Cabinet Office, SNA (National Accounts of Japan) website. Available at: http://www.esri.cao.go.jp/en/sna/menu.html.

Systemic Risk and Public Institutions

Evolving Perspectives from the Financial Crisis

— CHAPTER 8

- Chester Spatt
  Carnegie Mellon University and National Bureau of Economic Research

Introductory Comments

The Great Recession and Financial Crisis was a monumental event in market history. The near collapse of the financial system and the immediate and longer-term regulatory responses suggest much that we can learn from the extraordinary events that we experienced. While our regulatory system has strongly distinguished between banks and capital markets, the Financial Crisis highlighted the close connections between these different sources of funds, including both banks and shadow banking as well as their regulatory structures. There was considerable learning about the underlying funding mechanisms in the economy and

Chester Spatt is the Pamela R. and Kenneth B. Dunn Professor of Finance at the Tepper School of Business at Carnegie Mellon University and Research Associate at the National Bureau of Economic Research. The author to thank the conference participants and Eli Elias, Mike Piwowar and Neal Stoughton for helpful comments and the Alfred P. Sloan Foundation for financial support.

the regulation of these alternative mechanisms in the aftermath of the Financial Crisis.

In some respects the boundaries between alternative funding sources were not especially sharp. In part, these different funding approaches were actively competing with one another to raise financing and provided financing substitutes — albeit with differences in both access and the underlying regulatory frameworks. At the same time, it is informative to observe that the regulatory treatments themselves were evolving. The treatment of various institutions and transactions themselves changed during the Financial Crisis (e.g., 2007–2009) as various rules and processes were rewritten and adjusted to accommodate the weakness of the financial system and complications associated with specific activities and the resulting import for the financial system.

Indeed, at times the treatment of entire institutions was transformed through a range of techniques for supporting systemic institutions that experienced financial distress.[1] A particularly interesting example that illustrates how the regulatory system responded was the ability of financial institutions that owned banks to obtain bank-holding company (BHC) status, which offered access to the discount window (inexpensive funding) and a degree of protection by the Federal Reserve. In particular, Goldman Sachs and Morgan Stanley, which had not been subject to bank-like supervision during the period of the financial collapse, obtained the protection of the Federal Reserve at its invitation at the height of the Financial Crisis.

The Financial Crisis highlighted the extent and import of systemic risk in the economy. Such a perspective was central to the thinking of key policymakers and their strong desire to avoid the collapse of a significant financial institution during the Financial Crisis. This was reflected in an evolving set of tools and techniques that regulators utilized to fine tune their management of the financial system as well as a renewed appreciation of the potential importance of systemic risk.[2]

---

[1] The impact of the Financial Crisis on a number of regulatory policies is discussed in Bethel and Sirri (2014). *Editor's note*: This is also Chapter 9 in this book.

[2] Hansen (2013) also illustrates that our understanding of the nature of systemic risk, including how to measure and identify it, is far from fully resolved.

This was a perspective that had not been as appreciated in earlier years. For example, in 2006 new Federal Reserve Chairman Ben Bernanke emphasized that much of the systemic risk in the economy (to the extent there was systemic risk) was concentrated in hedge funds — rather than banks.[3] Indeed, a decade ago there was an attitude that risks had substantially declined in the economy from historical levels, which then Federal Reserve Governor Ben Bernanke attributed to much wiser monetary policy. Indeed, implied volatility was at much lower levels than historically. Bernanke used the term 'Great Moderation' to refer to the dramatic reductions in volatility of the economy relative to historical levels.[4] Of course, this philosophy and perspective became much less relevant during and after the Financial Crisis as addressing systemic risk became fundamental to economic policy.

Systemic Institutions

Traditionally, major banks have been viewed as systemically important because of their role in transferring systemic and aggregate risk from one institution to another through their interconnections. The systemic role of banks seems to be widely acknowledged and recognized. Yet in recent years, spurred by powers created under the Dodd–Frank Act, there has been considerable focus upon the designation by the Financial Stability Oversight Council (FSOC) of non-bank systemically important financial institutions (SIFIs). These designations and indeed, even the broader role of the FSOC, which is chaired by the Secretary of the Treasury, have been subject to considerable controversy in the aftermath of the passage of the Dodd–Frank Act. For example, the asset management study undertaken by the Office of Financial Research (OFR) was quite controversial and viewed by some as an attempt to facilitate the designation of large asset management firms as systemically important. Routinely, firms that are on the verge of being designated as systemically important have considered

---

[3] See Bernanke (2006).
[4] See Bernanke (2004).

challenging their designations.[5] As to the FSOC, its role itself has been somewhat controversial — in part because of (a) its authority to designate systemically important financial institutions, (b) its organizational structure, chaired by the senior Treasury official (and so subservient to the Administration) and (c) its members being the leaders of the constituent agencies rather than these agencies themselves.[6] There is a case that the designation decision be independent of other macroeconomic decisions.

The concept of systemic risk refers to the risk associated with the collapse of the financial system rather than the risk confronting an individual firm. Arguably, among the most significant potential causes of systemic risk are decisions that influence the entire economy. It is hard to see what could be more systemic than government and government-like institutions that inherently affect the entire economy and the decisions that these institutions make. For example, actions and decisions by both the government proper and the Federal Reserve would have economy-wide consequences. These could reflect both policy and even supervisory-style decisions that are central to the sources of systemic risk. It is important to recognize that the 'decisions' selected by policy-makers reflect judgment in difficult and challenging circumstances. The notion of 'best decisions' or 'best policies' may not be very clearly defined, particularly in such circumstances. Indeed, in a crisis there might even be considerable learning about the state of nature, which itself may be evolving, or even the strategies considered by decision-makers. Certainly, the optimal decision need not be constant and can be state dependent. An important point to emphasize is that policy decisions during the Financial Crisis had huge systemic consequences. For example, what would be the impact of the decision to 'bail out' the creditors of Bears Stearns by facilitating a merger with JPMorgan Chase or what would have been the impact of the reverse? Analogously, what would be the impact of the decision to not 'bail out' the creditors of Lehman Brothers or the reverse? Similarly, what would be the impact of encouraging Goldman Sachs and Morgan Stanley to apply for bank holding company status and granting that status with unprecedented

---

[5] For example, in January 2015, Metropolitan Life filed a lawsuit challenging its designation as systemically important.
[6] See Piwowar (2014).

speed? Alternatively, what would be the impact of the opposite decision? Surely, these are issues and matters that have system-wide ('systemic') consequences. Yet at a fundamental level the answers to such questions are unknown. Even after the fact, it is very difficult to assess what would have been the impact of different decisions during the Financial Crisis. Indeed, that's a difficult challenge that hasn't attracted much attention, despite the considerable interest in understanding and assessing the impact of policies during the Financial Crisis.

In a broader context (not solely about the Financial Crisis) one should recognize that government and central banks are systemic (as well as systematic) actors. One simple way to illustrate this is to highlight the extent of focus by market participants today about actions of the government and actions of the Federal Reserve. Indeed, on financial networks, such as CNBC, there is tremendous focus on what the central bank will do.[7] Some observers think of Fed policy as a factor driving returns and there is a systematic reaction to the policy through the markets. For example, many policy decisions have important systemic (as well as systematic) consequences, such as capital (equity) requirements for financial institutions which can have a dramatic effect on the risk-taking incentives of the firm. Decisions about bailouts (as illustrated above) and supervision also would have systemic consequences.[8]

Policy, Predictability and Time Consistency

In understanding and evaluating the structure of policy it is very helpful in many contexts if the underlying policy decision is predictable rather than ad hoc. This notion was formally introduced into macroeconomic

---

[7]There are many examples of this in recent years in both the United States and Europe (e.g., the ECB). One recent particularly striking example is the initiative by the Swiss central bank to lift the cap on the exchange rate with the Euro.

[8]Increasingly, there is a recognition of the systemic impact and importance of government and the central bank, as illustrated by the discussions in Acharya (2011), Lucas (2011), Pollock (2012) and Piwowar (2014). Goodfriend (2012) makes a similar point with regard to the Federal Reserve, arguing from Fed history that the independent central bank has contributed to systemic risk via insufficiently circumscribed monetary and credit policies.

policy by Kydland and Prescott (1977), whose Nobel Prize winning work emphasized the virtues of policy makers following time consistent policies. While this theme has had considerable impact on monetary policy, the impact in practice on policies for financial stability and other government policies has been less apparent. It is worth emphasizing, however, that the importance of time consistency as suggesting basic feasibility constraints on a broad set of policy decisions is highly relevant in many contexts, including decisions related to financial stability.[9] Many government policy decisions are being made in settings in which private actors respond (strategically) to policy, so the policy game is not simply the government (or the Federal Reserve) playing against nature, but rather against strategic participants. Yet many of the important decisions during the Financial Crisis did not emphasize this backdrop and may have inadvertently exposed the economy to greater systemic risk due to the lack of emphasis on time consistency.[10] Promoting long-term financial stability could be enhanced potentially by recognizing the linkage from current decisions to future ones.

Decisions about financial stability during a financial crisis are quite difficult.[11] The consequences of these decisions are illustrated by the classic issue of whether to bail out a systemic institution to protect the economy at present and the credibility issues that this would raise regarding future interventions. From a time consistency perspective the difficulty of a bailout is highlighted by the import for ex ante funding costs. To the extent that one anticipates the bailout and protection of

---

[9] A related perspective is provided in Judge (2015), who points to soft constraints, such as the adherence to principled norms and the concerns of the Federal Reserve Chairman about his reputation, as leading to constraints on the behavior of the Federal Reserve that are somewhat related to time consistency.

[10] Of course, it can be challenging to implement time consistent solutions, especially in stochastic dynamic settings due to the complexity of the intertemporal dynamic optimization. I conjecture that time consistent policies will expose the economy to less systemic risk.

[11] The difficulty of the decisions and the potential importance of time consistency also help motivate the idea emphasized by Haldane and Madouros (2012), who suggest that simpler policies would be more effective than complex ones given the complexity of our financial system.

creditors of a systemically important institution, the ex ante cost of the firm's debt would be artificially low and therefore, excess risk-taking would be strongly promoted by the capital markets. This is especially true for banks and other financial institutions, because they are so heavily leveraged. Indeed, in light of this it is not an accident that they are so heavily leveraged as there is a substantial subsidy to debt finance (not only due to the tax deductibility at the corporate level, but also due to the considerable potential for bailouts).[12] This is nicely illustrated by Bear Stearns as the Federal Reserve facilitated the assumption of its debt by JPMorgan Chase, which was an extremely strong credit. While the bailout by the Federal Reserve was indirect, the role of the Fed was apparent in subsidizing the assumption of the debt. In the aftermath of the Bear Stearns intervention, some risky Bear Stearns debt instruments increased in market value by about 50%, highlighting the importance of the federal intervention to the value of the debt.[13] It also is worth noting that the extent of debt is endogenous and increases due to the subsidy. Of course, the consequences of this for financial stability on an ex ante basis are clearly not favorable. Debt is most of the capital structure of 'too big to fail institutions,' so that the cost of the debt is crucial to the financial institution's funding costs given the degree of bank and financial institution leverage. This illustrates that the moral hazard problem, excess risk taking incentives and bail-outs are largely related to the cost of debt rather than the cost of equity.[14] Indeed, significant portions of the Dodd–Frank Act represent an attempt to reduce moral hazard and thereby an attempt to enhance financial stability.[15]

---

[12] See discussion in Admati and Hellwig (2013).

[13] Given the substantial increase in value associated with the intervention, presumably there would have been a substantial decline in value if the Federal Reserve intervention had not occurred.

[14] Yet Secretary of the Treasury Paulson repeatedly referred to whether equity was being supported in the context of moral hazard. For example, he wondered why critics viewed Bear Stearns as enhancing moral hazard as the equity holders did not reap huge payments (though increased from US$2 per share to US$10 per share when the transaction with JPMorgan Chase required restructuring).

[15] As an example, such features as the ability to designate and regulate systemically important financial institutions and the special 'resolution authority' are attempts

The issue of predictability of regulatory and supervisory policies is an important aspect of promoting financial stability, but a difficult challenge given the nuances of what an economy faces during the midst of a crisis. The challenge is illustrated by the events of 2007 through 2009 and the efforts of the financial supervisors and regulators to promote near-term financial stability. The difficult challenge that such an approach leads to is whether promoting near-term financial stability actually undercuts long-term financial stability by promoting moral hazard and excess risk taking. This can be illustrated by a variety of important and creative actions undertaken by regulators and supervisors during the Financial Crisis, which may encourage excess risk-taking in the future. In some of the specific contexts adverse consequences, including systemic costs, would have arisen from the efforts to promote near-term financial stability. These adverse consequences, including moral hazard and excess risk-taking, could occur many years into the future or may have arisen even during the Financial Crisis because of the immediate impact on expectations of future potential interventions.

One of the most important interventions during the Financial Crisis concerned the 'bailout' of Bear Stearns. In particular, the Federal Reserve facilitated its acquisition by JPMorgan Chase by agreeing to essentially purchase about US$30 billion of Bear Stearns assets that JPMorgan Chase was anxious not to acquire. As a result of the transaction the Bear Stearns debt holders exchanged their debt for JPMorgan Chase debt, which was a very strong credit. This essentially eliminated the substantial default risk associated with Bear Stearns debt and the value of the debt rallied by close to 50% to near par. Even though equity holders experienced substantial losses as they received only US$10 per share (originally US$2 per share, but the transaction needed to be restructured to assure the approval of some influential equity holders to guarantee approval of the sale), moral hazard is largely associated with bailout of the debt.

---

to project that financial institutions would not be bailed out and indeed, would be allowed to fail. Ultimately, the credibility of expectations that there would not be a bailout would be crucial to the substantial reduction in moral hazard and the promotion of financial stability.

From the perspective of the Financial Crisis the bailout of Bear Stearns greatly influenced market expectations and made it difficult to forecast the regulatory and supervisory response to the problems at Lehman Brothers. The handling of Bear Stearns encouraged market participants to anticipate the bailout of debt holders of other financial institutions, such as Lehman Brothers. This may have contributed to the failure of the leadership of Lehman to obtain sufficient financing as well as the failure of market participants to adjust and re-price their portfolio holdings to prepare for the possibility of default. In turn the successive handling of Bear Stearns and Lehman Brothers influenced expectations associated with the potential support to other financial institutions. The situation with AIG emerged in the immediate aftermath of Lehman Brothers. Ultimately, the AIG counterparties were handled in a different fashion than the debt holders of Lehman Brothers, as the AIG counterparties were fully paid without any 'haircut' being required. The overall pattern highlights the potential inconsistency in treatment across situations and contexts, making it awkward for market participants to understand and assess the potential response by the authorities to financial difficulties by financial services firms.

Another interesting example of the consequences of lack of clarity in the policy response concerns the case of FNMA and Freddie Mac. During summer 2008 the Treasury indicated that it wanted to provide a US$300 billion credit facility to these Government Sponsored Enterprises (GSEs); when Congress inquired as to how the facility would be used the Treasury indicated that it needed flexibility and a 'big bazooka' to address the potential needs. Of course, without commitment to a particular policy response the capital markets were concerned that new intervening private funding would not be protected and consequently, in early September the GSEs lost their access to private funding. There were a variety of additional innovative approaches to financial stability that arose that could raise questions about intertemporal financial stability, including the surprising and unprecedented approval of banking-holding company (BHC) status for Goldman Sachs and Morgan Stanley, extraordinary guarantees to Citigroup and Bank of America and even the uses of the Troubled Asset Recovery Program (TARP) and the government taking equity stakes after bailouts. This is not to criticize individual aspects of the response to financial instability, but to emphasize that the lack of predictability and potential time inconsistency in the policy response may have amplified financial instability during the Financial Crisis, rather than reducing it.

Systemic Risk Going Forward

One of the important challenges facing bank supervisors and the government with respect to systemic risk is the nature of 'too big to fail' and potential impact of the size of financial institutions. Indeed, mergers that are allowed during a financial crisis may amplify the systemic risk issues subsequent to the crisis (or even during the crisis itself).[16] Perhaps the most visible example along such lines during the Financial Crisis was the acquisition of Merrill Lynch by Bank of America — in this case we had the acquisition of one systemic institution by another.[17] The example illustrates that an important tension in the dynamics of systemic risk is that the acquisition of a failing institution, which seemingly promotes current financial stability, would have adverse consequences for future stability. Certainly moral hazard is especially important in the midst of a crisis, but also potentially relevant afterwards. Mergers by banks that accentuate systemic risk may reflect the deeper recognition by financial institutions of the benefits that they can potentially derive from risk-taking and the possibility of a future bailout. Along related lines the Brown–Vitter bill, which prescribes a higher capital standard for larger institutions, reflects a Congressional response to a combination of both bank mergers in general and bailouts in particular.

The management of systemic risk, particularly for large institutions, is an important feature of the federal regulatory system. Dodd–Frank identified the Federal Reserve as the consolidated supervisor of systemically important financial institutions in the future. This may have reflected the view that the Federal Reserve has more suitable resources

---

[16] Wang (2014) argues that links with a distressed firm can lead to social costs because of the externality associated with the increase in systemic liquidation risk.
[17] Another less stark example was the acquisition of National City Corporation by PNC during late 2008.

for this role and criticism of various other regulators. Of course, even during the Financial Crisis, the Federal Reserve was Citigroup's and Bank of America's consolidated supervisor, while regulatory responsibility for serving as consolidated supervisor was somewhat dispersed for various financial institutions. Institutions that faced systemic difficulty during the Financial Crisis were supervised by a range of regulators. On a going forward basis, there now is more statutory emphasis on the planning for resolution and unwinding of systemic firms ('living wills') in order to encourage regulators to be comfortable in not bailing out financial institutions and make that policy credible to market participants, in which case those funding the firm would internalize the relevant risks. This is an important emphasis in the Dodd–Frank Act.[18]

Systemic Causes of the Financial Crisis

There were a number of factors that contributed to the Financial Crisis; it is important to recognize the systemic nature of these causes and risks. For example, many observers feel that the Federal Reserve maintained artificially low interest rates until 2004, that federal housing policy (including subsidies to the GSEs and the Community Redevelopment Act) further encouraged excess investment in housing, that banking supervisors permitted excessive leverage in the system prior to the Financial Crisis, that risk management oversight was poor (by both the financial institutions and their supervisors as well) and that there were considerable due diligence failures in such domains as mortgage brokers, securitizing firms and credit rating agencies. Many of these were important issues in the policy domain. Indeed, one of the central criticisms of federal regulatory policy in the aftermath of the Financial Crisis has been its failure to seriously address the challenges associated with the GSEs, i.e., Fannie Mae and Freddie Mac. In fact, there appears to be remarkably little interest in designating Fannie Mae and Freddie Mac as systemically important, even at present. This

---

[18] Fischer's (2014) Martin Feldstein Lecture at the National Bureau of Economic Research and Gibson's (2012) House testimony offer updates and overviews of the status of financial reform.

reflects conscious decisions of financial regulators and supervisors, highlighting that the underlying causes of the Financial Crisis were systemic in nature.

Disclosure and Systemic Risks

Two fundamental aspects in setting policy objectives concern a direct focus upon trying to reduce systemic risk and promoting disclosure and fairness in the markets. This cuts in fundamental ways to how we structure financial regulation. At least implicitly, this suggests why multiple perspectives can be useful (that does not necessarily mean that we need to have multiple regulators that are in inherent conflict with one another). To some degree, this suggests a rationale for multiple regulators (though multiple perspectives also could be expressed within a single regulator) in which various functions are separated. Banking regulators, who typically are responsible for managing systemic risk, often are unsympathetic to disclosure (or at least mandatory disclosures) because it interferes with their ability to manage strategically the disclosure.

An interesting example of the conflict concerned the Bank of America acquisition of Merrill Lynch, where there was significant conflict (even between the bank's supervisor and Bank of America) about the potential disclosure of losses at Merrill Lynch, which potentially could have affected the vote on the merger by Bank of America's shareholders. On the one hand, the Federal Reserve and Treasury appear to have discouraged disclosure during the critical period from Bank of America, while on the other hand, the Securities and Exchange Commission (SEC) brought a case against Bank of America (*long after the markets had rebounded*) and achieved a substantial settlement.[19] The difference in regulatory philosophy is conceptually important.[20] The philosophy of a disclosure or fairness oriented regulator is towards protecting investors,

---

[19] This situation and the broader conflict between these underlying regulatory objectives are discussed in more detail in Spatt (2010).

[20] I am not suggesting that the SEC would necessarily have objected in real time during the crisis. Indeed, in the case of short-sale regulation it agreed to follow the request of the President's Working Group and ban short selling in approximately

while a systemic risk regulator focuses upon the financial system. Traditionally, banking supervisors tend to be adverse to disclosures if they assess potential unfavorable systemic risk consequences; indeed, disclosure is not viewed by banking regulators as effective against systemic risk. At the same time, it is important to recognize that disclosures may be appropriate for a number of reasons.[21] The disclosures may be useful from a systemic risk perspective in situations in which the disclosures help the market recognize and manage the risks that are present (systemic or otherwise) and further protect investors against inappropriate exploitation at the hands of systemic risk regulators. Disclosure helps provide discipline and protects against systemic buildup, while the securities law and disclosure framework also protects investors against being 'patsies' that protect the resources of the authorities.

Another interesting example of the conflict between systemic risk regulation and our regulatory disclosure framework concerns whether to disclose stress test results, particularly when they were first introduced by the Federal Reserve in 2009 (subsequently, stress tests were included in the Dodd–Frank framework). Despite comments by the President, Secretary of the Treasury and Chairman of the Federal Reserve then about the introduction and potential importance of stress tests, there was initial ambiguity about whether the results would be disclosed. My view is that was unfortunate because a commitment to disclosure could have been important for the credibility of the tests.[22] Indeed, the securities laws require that the purpose of new funding be disclosed, preventing investors from being 'patsies' and doing the

---

900 financial stocks as the TARP legislation was being debated in September and October 2008.

[21] Even if immediate disclosure were not justified, it may be appropriate for there to be disclosure with a suitable lag. For example, this routinely occurs with the periodic release of the minutes of the Open Market Committee.

[22] It is worth emphasizing, however, that the United States stress tests have been effective and successful. For example, they have examined stress scenarios that were viewed in the market as reasonable ones. In contrast, the European stress tests were less successfully initially, due in significant part to the selection of an awkward stress scenario that was not at the heart of market concerns about sovereign default.

bidding of the bank supervisors. To the extent that a key objective of the stress tests was to assess the extent to which banks require additional funding, disclosure of the results would appear to be crucial in many situations.

One illustration of the potential conflict in principle between securities regulators and bank supervisors is that strict adherence to the securities regulation framework would lead the securities regulators to interview bank supervisors with respect to possible violations of our disclosure framework in such contexts as the Bank of America acquisition of Merrill Lynch or the leakage of stress test results when those results were confidential.

One further aspect of disclosure is the controversy as to whether the supervisor should disclose 'the test.' This was an issue that received considerable public attention during the first round of the Dodd–Frank based stress tests in 2012 — after industry criticism of the lack of disclosure of the framework. This is an interesting conceptual issue in that on the one hand the disclosure would be akin to describing the tradeoffs embodied in stress test standards vs. the potential that detailed disclosure would facilitate gaming the test. It is interesting that the controversy on this front has largely faded, perhaps as a consequence of greater industry understanding of the stress test model approach being undertaken.[23]

Competing Perspectives

In much of this paper I have argued that government and central banks are important sources of systemic risk. To the extent that information production is outsourced to a private firm, such as a credit rating agency, the fundamental systemic difficulty still is present. Even in the case in which there are competing rival firms, but we reduce the reliance upon ratings for regulatory objectives, the systemic concern is not necessarily eased, assuming that the ratings reflect a relatively common underlying point of view. For example, consider the case in which there

---

[23] A recent review of the evolution of stress testing is in Tarullo (2014).

are competing private entities — such as competing credit rating agencies. If these information producers use a similar model and tend to reach similar conclusions — whether or not we rely upon ratings for regulatory goals — the nature of the systemic risk is similar.

With the systemic consequences in mind it also is helpful to focus somewhat on systemic issues and the redesign of derivatives trading and clearing. While netting and transparency can reduce systemic risk, central clearing actually can concentrate risks even further.[24] Indeed, former Federal Reserve Chairman Ben Bernanke quoted the Mark Twain character Pudd'nhead Wilson as stating that "if you put all your eggs in one basket, you better watch that basket."

Concluding Comments

As we conclude it is helpful to reflect upon the lessons and conclusions that we learned from the Financial Crisis and related systemic consequences. It is a challenging subject in part because it is difficult to identify the counterfactual, i.e., what would have happened under alternative policies. Unfortunately, it is not at all clear how to fully evaluate the important consequences from many of the key decisions during the Financial Crisis such as the handling of Bear Stearns, Lehman Brothers, the GSEs, the decisions to grant bank-holding company status to Goldman Sachs and Morgan Stanley, the extraordinary guarantees to Citigroup and Bank of America, etc. Specifically, what would have been the effects on other key firms in the economy of different decisions? What was the impact of the sequence of decisions? Certainly, to the extent that models can be developed that facilitate the analysis of these questions that would be very helpful to understand what happened during the Financial Crisis and to guide decision-making in future crises. It has been seven years since the Financial Crisis, so in light of that and the importance of the Financial Crisis I also would highlight the importance of a broad release of data from that period.

---

[24] A recent discussion of the relationship between the central clearing of derivatives and the financial system is in Powell (2014).

Indeed, understanding the counterfactual is important for monetary policy as well as financial stability policy. In particular, what has been the impact of the various QE policies and what would asset pricing be like otherwise?

One context in which I feel that there was a bit of missed opportunity at the time of the Financial Crisis for learning about the effectiveness of policy responses in crises concerns the Commercial Paper Funding Facility (CPFF) developed then by the Federal Reserve. This would have been a very useful context to undertake a natural experiment with some degree of randomization in the eligibility criteria, which would have been a very helpful design, particularly compared to the actual situation in which eligibility was tied to past usage. This would have facilitated a cleaner approach to identification.[25] My own view is that even in crises it is important to use natural experiments (including some degree of randomization) when feasible. Causality is central to effective empirical analysis, but this can be difficult, even when the eligibility criteria are endogenous. I would encourage the use of randomized design (with differing probabilities across states), even in crises.[26] While crises are very costly to address, information for the next crisis is simply too scarce to forego and very valuable.

A broad theme of this paper is to recognize that even more than private institutions, various publicly-oriented institutions are systemically important including the government, the Federal Reserve, Fannie Mae and Freddie Mac. The decisions of these types of institutions and the policy choices of the government and Federal Reserve have major consequences for the financial system and expose the economy to fundamental systemic risks.

---

[25] Gao and Yun (2012) do study the CPFF and make some headway with respect to identification, but an enhanced program design by the Federal Reserve would have been extremely useful nevertheless.

[26] This was a viewpoint that I developed previously as a byproduct of my 'Discussion' of Gao and Yun (2012) at an academic conference at Wharton.

References

Acharya, V. V. (2011), "Governments as Shadow Banks: The looming threat to financial stability" Federal Reserve Board, Working Paper, September.

Admati, A. and M. Hellwig (2013), *The banker's new clothes: What's wrong with banking and what to do about it* (Princeton, NJ: Princeton University Press).

Bernanke, B. S. (2004), *The Great Moderation*, remarks by Governor Ben S. Bernanke at the meetings of the Eastern Economic Association, Washington, DC, February.

Bernanke, B. S. (2006), *Hedge Funds and Systemic Risk*, speech at the Federal Reserve Bank of Atlanta's 2006 Financial Markets Conference, May.

Bethel, J. E. and E. R. Sirri (2014), "Securities Regulation During and After the 2008 Financial Crisis," Working paper, October 2014, presented at Chicago Federal Reserve Bank Conference. (Or Chapter 9 of this book.)

Fischer, S. (2014), "Financial Sector Reform: How far are we?" Working paper, July.

Gao, P. and H. Yun (2012), "Liquidity Backstop, Corporate Borrowing and Real Effects," Working paper, November.

Gibson, M. S. (2012), Statement before the Subcommittee on Financial Institutions and Consumer Credit of the Committee on Financial Services, US House of Representatives, May.

Goodfriend, M. (2012), "The Elusive Promise of Independent Central Banking," Monetary and Economic Studies, Bank of Japan, November.

Haldane, A. G. and V. Madouros (2012), *The Dog and the Frisbee*, speech at the Federal Reserve Bank of Kansas City, August.

Hansen, L. P. (2013), "Challenges in Identifying and Measuring Systemic Risk," working paper, February.

Judge, K. (2015), "The Federal Reserve: A study in soft constraints," *Law and Contemporary Problems*, forthcoming.

Kydland, F. and E. Prescott (1977), "Rules Rather than Discretion: The inconsistency of optimal plans," *Journal of Political Economy*, 85: 473–492.

Lucas, D. (2011), "Evaluating the Government as a Source of Systemic Risk," working paper, September.

Piwowar, M. S. (2014), *Advancing and Defending the SEC's Core Mission*, speech at the US Chamber of Commerce, January.

Pollock, A. J. (2012), *The Federal Reserve: The biggest systemic risk of all*, American Enterprise Institute.

Powell, J. H. (2014), *A Financial System Perspective on Central Clearing of Derivatives*, speech at the "The New International Financial System:

Analyzing the Cumulative Impact of Regulatory Reform," 17th Annual International Banking Conference, November. (Chapter 3 of this book.)

Spatt, C. (2010), "Regulatory conflict: Market integrity vs. financial stability," *University of Pittsburgh Law Review*, 71: 625–639.

Tarullo, D. K. (2014), *Stress Testing after Five Years*, Federal Reserve Third Annual Stress Test Modeling Symposium, June.

Wang, J. J. (2014), *Distress Dispersion and Systemic Risk in Networks*, unpublished manuscript, Tepper School of Business, Carnegie Mellon University, November.

Securities Regulation During and After the 2008 Financial Crisis

— CHAPTER 9

- Jennifer E. Bethel and Erik R. Sirri
  *Babson College, USA and the US Securities
  and Exchange Commission*

During the 2008 financial crisis, a number of issues surfaced for the SEC, including (1) heavy shareholder redemptions in money market funds that threatened the liquidity of the short-term funding markets, (2) a broad-based mistrust of credit rating agencies and skepticism towards credit ratings based on poor rating performance, especially the ratings of structured products, (3) a falling market amidst heavy short selling, coupled with vocal appeals to impose restrictions and bans on short selling, and (4) failing short- and long-term funding of large broker-dealer holding companies. We examine the regulatory response of

Bethel is a Professor of Finance at Babson College in Wellesley, MA and an Economist in the Division of Economic and Risk Analysis at the US Securities and Exchange Commission. Sirri is a Professor of Finance at Babson College. The Securities and Exchange Commission, as a matter of policy, disclaims responsibility for any private publication or statement by any of its employees. The views expressed herein are those of the author and do not necessarily reflect the views of the Commission or of the author's colleagues on the staff of the Commission.

the SEC during and after the financial crisis. We also discuss the limits of the SEC's regulatory authority and the resulting effectiveness of its regulatory responses.

Introduction

The 2008 financial crisis prompted widespread debate about how the US government should regulate its financial markets. Beyond efforts to resolve the immediate crisis, policymakers have sought to increase the resiliency of the markets and institutions and reduce the likelihood of future similar events. At the heart of these efforts are the initiatives of a number of regulatory agencies that Congress has charged with adopting, implementing, and enforcing rules that regulate the financial markets. Among these agencies is the US Securities and Exchange Commission (SEC).

During the 2008 financial crisis, a number of issues surfaced for the SEC, including (1) heavy shareholder redemptions in money market funds (MMFs) that threatened the liquidity of the short-term funding markets, (2) a broad-based mistrust of credit rating agencies and skepticism towards credit ratings based on poor rating performance, especially the ratings of structured products, (3) a falling market for the shares of financial firms amidst heavy short selling, coupled with vocal appeals to impose restrictions and bans on short selling, and (4) failing short- and long-term funding of large broker-dealer holding companies. In this paper, we examine the regulatory changes undertaken by the SEC during and after the financial crisis to address these issues, including MMFs, credit rating agencies (CRAs), the short selling rules, and the net capital regime for large broker-dealers. We then discuss limits to the SEC's statutory authority and its largely disclosure-focused toolkit and examine the resulting effectiveness of its regulatory responses.

The mission of the SEC, as defined by Congress, is to protect investors, maintain fair, orderly, and efficient markets, and to promote competition, efficiency, and capital formation.[1] Although the SEC oversees

---

[1] See US Securities and Exchange Commission (2014) and Section 106, National Securities Markets Improvement Act of 1996, 110 Stat. 3416, Public Law 104–290, October 11, 1996.

the financial markets, which is where firms whose cash flows are inherently risky raise capital from investors at large, Congress does not provide the SEC with an explicit mandate to manage systemic risk or guarantee the continuing financial viability of issuers or institutions. Instead, Congress passed the Securities Act of 1933 and the Securities Exchange Act of 1934, which require the SEC to promote full public disclosure of company information and to protect the investing public against fraudulent and manipulative practices in the securities markets. In addition, the Securities Exchange Act sets forth a regulatory regime for broker-dealers that has certain prudential aspects.[2] In 1940, Congress passed the Investment Company Act of 1940 to address conflicts of interest that arise in mutual funds. "The focus of this Act is on disclosure to the investing public of information about the fund and its investment objectives, as well as on investment company structure and operations."[3] To fulfill its mission, the SEC often resolves conflicts of interest among market participants and asymmetries in information by requiring "public companies to disclose meaningful financial and other information to the public."[4] It promotes "the disclosure of important market-related information, maintain[s] fair dealing, and protect[s] against fraud."[5]

The 2008 financial crisis highlighted the limits of the SEC's statutory authority and its largely disclosure-focused toolkit as the Federal regulators collectively attempted to stem the crisis. Without an explicit mandate to manage systemic risk, or to guarantee the continuing financial viability of issuers or institutions, the SEC was constrained to consider the economic consequences of its actions in light of their effect on investor protection and efficiency, competition, and capital formation in the markets. In addition, the SEC, by Congressional design, lacked the economic resources necessary to guarantee the financial viability of market participants. The mandates and resources of other financial

---

[2] See, for example, the Net Capital Rule (17 C.F.R. § 240.15c3-1) and the Customer Protection Rule (17 C.F.R. § 240.15c3-3).
[3] See US Securities and Exchange Commission (2014).
[4] See US Securities and Exchange Commission (2014).
[5] See US Securities and Exchange Commission (2014).

regulators, including the Federal Reserve System (Fed),[6] Office of the Comptroller of the Currency (OCC),[7] and Federal Deposit Insurance Corporation (FDIC),[8] provided a broader set of tools with which to work both, during and after the 2008 financial crisis.

Since the 2008 crisis, the SEC has continued to fulfill its mission to protect investors, maintain fair, orderly, and efficient markets, and to promote competition, efficiency, and capital formation. At the same time, the agency has had to adapt and expand its interpretation of what constitutes its mission in light of lessons learned from the financial crisis. It has also found additional non-disclosure-based solutions that are within its authority to meet certain financial market challenges that were highlighted by the financial crisis. In the following sections, we discuss four areas of regulatory reform by the SEC and the limitations presented by its Congressional mandate.

---

[6] The Fed, for example, "was created by the Congress in 1913 to provide the nation with a safer, more flexible, and more stable monetary and financial system." Today, the Fed's responsibilities include supervising and regulating banks and other important financial institutions to ensure the safety and soundness of the nation's banking and financial system and maintaining the stability of the financial system and containing systemic risk that may arise in financial markets. See The Federal Reserve System (2005) and "Current FAQs: Informing the Public about the Federal Reserve," Board of Governors of the Federal Reserve System (2014) at http://www. federalreserve.gov/faqs/about_12594.htm.

[7] Operating in parallel with the Fed, the US Department of the Treasury provides financial regulation of banks and thrifts primarily through the operations of the OCC, which it oversees. The OCC's "primary mission is to charter, regulate, and supervise all national banks and federal savings associations," as well as supervise the federal branches and agencies of foreign banks. One of its four objectives is to "ensure the safety and soundness of the national system of banks and savings associations." See "About the OCC," Office of the Comptroller of the Currency, at http://www.occ.treas.gov/about/what-we-do/mission/index-about.html.

[8] The FDIC, created by Congress in 1933 to maintain stability and public confidence in the nation's financial system, provides deposit insurance that guarantees the safety of depositors' accounts in member banks up to a specified amount for each deposit ownership category in each insured bank. The FDIC also examines and supervises certain financial institutions for safety and soundness, performs certain consumer-protection functions, and manages banks in receiverships. See "FDIC Mission, Vision, and Values," Federal Deposit Insurance Corporation (May 4, 2009) at http://www.fdic.gov/about/mission/.

Regulation of Money Market Funds

In 1983 the SEC adopted rule 2a-7,[9] which allowed MMFs to value portfolio assets using "amortized cost" and "penny round" their prices. These methods allowed MMFs to stabilize their net asset values (NAVs), typically at US$1.00, providing investors with stable principal coupled with same-day liquidity. In exchange for allowing MMFs to use amortized cost to value fund assets, the SEC requires them to meet certain requirements, which included investing in short-term, high credit quality instruments, maintaining a well-diversified portfolio, and other guidelines set forth in rule 2a-7.

Over the next 25 years, MMFs were remarkably successful, both as a financial product and in their regulatory design. From the birth of the MMF industry through summer 2008, only one MMF failed to maintain its stable NAV.[10] The record of funds' success in maintaining stable NAVs, however, belies the financial stress through the years encountered by a number of MMFs when the value of portfolio assets became impaired. In a number of instances, a fund's shadow price, which is the current NAV per share calculated using available market prices or fair value, fell below the fund's stable NAV of US$1.[11] In the late 1980s, for example, several corporate issuers defaulted on their commercial paper (CP), which led to declines in the shadow prices of MMFs that held the instruments. Similarly, the shadow prices of several MMFs that held Orange County's notes fell below US$1 after it defaulted on its obligations in 1994.

If a fund's shadow price falls sufficiently below its stable NAV of US$1 and the fund's board decides to discontinue its use of the

---

[9] See Valuation of Debt Instruments and Computation of Current Price Per Share by Certain Open-End Investment Companies (Money Market Funds), Investment Company Act Release No. 13380 (July 11, 1983) [48 FR 32555 (July 18, 1983)].

[10] In 1994, the Community Bankers US Government MMF broke the buck when Orange County, California filed for Chapter 9 protection, defaulting on its notes (see Fink, 2008, p. 179). The US$100 million fund liquidated at US$0.96 per share. See Crane Data (2007). This event did not receive widespread attention, perhaps because it was a small fund with only institutional investors and its liquidation was based on exposure to targeted securities.

[11] See Fink (2008, p. 177–179).

amortized cost method of valuation to stabilize its price, the fund is said to have 'broken the buck'. Rule 2a-7 requires the MMF's board to then consider whether the deviation creates dilution or unfair treatment of shareholders and what action, including perhaps closing the fund to new investors, suspending redemptions, and liquidating the fund, should be taken to prevent such outcomes.[12] Before the SEC adopted rule 22e-3 in 2010, a fund's board could only suspend redemptions and liquidate a fund pursuant to a Commission order. After the adoption of rule 22e-3, funds that break a buck can suspend redemptions and distribute assets to investors if, among other things, the directors have irrevocably approve the liquidation of the funds.[13] Alternatively, the sponsor of a fund, which can include the fund's adviser or the parent company of the adviser, can provide financial support to the fund to help it maintain a stable NAV of US$1.00. For example, a sponsor can purchase impaired portfolio assets at amortized cost, or directly infuse cash into the fund. In November 2007, Moody's reported there were 145 cases in prior years where money funds received some type of support from sponsors to mitigate losses.[14]

As the 2008 financial crisis unfolded, a number of securities suffered credit rating downgrades and declining prices, which caused some MMFs to no longer meet the credit standards of rule 2a-7 and a number of funds to re-price their portfolio assets.[15] On September 16, 2008, the

---

[12] See Rule 2a-7(g)(1)(i)(C).

[13] See Money Market Fund Reform, Investment Company Act Release No. 28807 (June 30, 2009) [74 FR 32688 (July 8, 2009)] and Money Market Fund Reform, Investment Company Act Release No. 29132 (February 23, 2010) [75 FR 10060 (March 4, 2010)].

[14] See Moody's Investors Service Special Comment (2010), Brady *et al.* (2012) and "Response to Questions Posed by Commissioners Aguilar, Paredes, and Gallagher," in US Securities and Exchange Commission (2014), pp. 15–17.

[15] A number of MMFs received financial support from their sponsors during the 2008 financial crisis. See Money Market Fund Reform; Amendments to Form PF, Release Nos. 33-9408; IA-3616; IC-30551 (June 5, 2013) [78 FR 36834, (June 19, 2013)].

Reserve Primary Fund broke the buck.[16] The Reserve Primary Fund applied to the SEC for an order permitting it to suspend redemptions and postpone payment of shares submitted for redemption, and the fund began a year-long process to liquidate its portfolio.[17]

After the Reserve Primary Fund broke the buck, many investors, especially institutions, began redeeming non-government MMF shares, investing instead in assets offering increased quality, liquidity, transparency, and performance. Investors that held shares of funds whose portfolio holdings' values were impaired redeemed shares to avoid dilution.[18] To meet heightened redemption requests, MMF managers sold fund assets into illiquid asset markets at prices below amortized costs. One fund manager, Putnam, announced that its MMF would liquidate, with shareholders receiving shares on a US$1 per share basis of a Federated fund.[19] To manage portfolio risk and conserve cash, MMF managers dramatically reduced investments in commercial paper, investing instead in government securities. Their withdrawal from the CP market

---

[16] According to *Market Watch*, "Another Reserve fund, International Liquidity Fund, which is only available to offshore investors, also broke the buck. Also Tuesday, Standard & Poor's Ratings Services said that it had downgraded the Colorado Diversified Trust to Dm from AAAm due to exposure to Lehman paper. S&P said the Trust, which had about [US]$260 million in assets, liquidated Wednesday at a net asset value of 98.2 cents. The Trust held money from local schools and governments. Its assets were transferred to the [US]$3.5 billion Colorado Local Government Liquid Asset Trust." See Mamudi (2008).

[17] The Reserve Primary Fund announced on September 16, 2008 that it would reprice its shares at US$0.97, and the SEC issued an order, effective September 17, 2008, allowing the fund to suspend redemptions of shares and liquidate (see http://www.sec.gov/rules/ic/2008/ic-28386.pdf). See also, US Department of Treasury (2010). Ultimately fund investors received more than US$0.99/share (Hurtado and Condon, 2012).

[18] See "Response to Questions Posed by Commissioners Aguilar, Paredes, and Gallagher," in US Securities and Exchange Commission (2014).

[19] See press release by Federated and Putnam Investments, "Federated Investors, Inc. and Putnam Investments Announce Transaction to Benefit Money Market Fund Shareholders" (September 24, 2008), at http://www.federatedinvestors.com/FII/about/pressrelease/detail.do?cid=65207.

dried up critical financing for firms relying on the sale of CP to meet payroll and other short-term expenses.

To help stabilize the financial markets during this period, the Fed and the Treasury took unprecedented actions. On September 19, 2008, the Fed announced the immediate creation of the Asset Backed Commercial Paper Money Market Mutual Fund Liquidity Facility (AMLF) to help guarantee asset market liquidity. The AMLF offered non-recourse loans to US depository institutions and bank holding companies that purchased certain high-quality asset back commercial paper (ABCP) directly from MMFs.[20] On September 29, 2008, the Treasury announced the Temporary Guarantee Program to stem the tide of shareholder redemptions in MMFs.[21] This program insured the September 19, 2008 investments of both retail and institutional investors in funds that chose to participate in the program. The Fed subsequently announced on October 21, 2008 that it would establish the Money Market Investor Funding Facility (MMIFF), effective November 24, 2008.[22] Administered by the Federal Reserve Bank of New York, the MMIFF provided senior secured funding to a series of special purpose vehicles established by the private sector (PSPVs). Each PSPV would purchase eligible money market instruments from MMFs using financing from the MMIFF and from the issuance of ABCP. By facilitating the sale of money market instruments in the secondary market, the Fed hoped the MMIFF would improve the liquidity positions of MMFs, thereby increasing their ability to meet further redemption requests and willingness to invest in money market instruments.[23] The New York Fed engaged in Open Market Operations that indirectly also affected

---

[20] See "Asset-Backed Commercial Paper Money Market Mutual Fund Liquidity Facility," Board of Governors of the Federal Reserve System at http://www.federalreserve.gov/monetarypolicy/abcpmmmf.htm

[21] See US Department of Treasury (2008).

[22] See "Money Market Investor Funding Facility," Board of Governors of the Federal Reserve System, at http://www.federalreserve.gov/monetarypolicy/mmiff.htm.

[23] The Fed created the MMIFF, but no funds were ever used. See "Net Portfolio Holdings of LLCs funded through the Money Market Investor Funding Facility (DISCONTINUED SERIES)," Federal Reserve Bank of St. Louis (September 18, 2014) at http://www.research.stlouisfed.org/fred2/series/WMMIFF.

MMFs. For example, it purchased agency discount notes,[24] commonly held by MMFs, on September 19, 23, and 26, 2008 with the stated purpose of providing liquidity to the market.[25]

Because the markets remained highly illiquid for some time after the initial crisis, the market prices of fund assets diverged from fair fundamental values. In response, the SEC announced on October 10, 2008 that MMFs could shadow price very short-term assets using amortized cost through January 12, 2009, "unless the particular circumstances, i.e., the impairment of the creditworthiness of the issuer, suggest that amortized cost is no longer appropriate."[26]

In response to the MMF issues highlighted by the financial crisis, the SEC adopted amendments to rule 2a-7 of the Investment Company Act in February 2010.[27] These amendments were designed to increase the resiliency of MMFs to losses in portfolio holdings by reducing the interest rate, credit, and liquidity risks of funds and by increasing disclosure of fund portfolios. More specifically, the amendments restricted the maximum 'weighted average life' maturity of MMFs' portfolios and reduced the maximum 'weighted average maturity' of fund portfolios. The rules decreased funds' permissible holdings of instruments with lower credit ratings and increased portfolio diversification requirements. In addition, the rules required that funds hold a minimum percentage of their assets in highly liquid securities so funds could readily

---

[24] These are short-term debt obligations issued by Fannie Mae, Freddie Mac, and the Federal Home Loan Banks.

[25] See press release dated September 19, 2008, by Board of Governors of the Federal Reserve System, at http://www.federalreserve.gov/newsevents/press/monetary/20080919a.htm.

[26] See no-action letter from Robert E. Plaze, Associate Director, Division of Investment Management, SEC to Karrie McMillan, General Counsel, Investment Company Institute (October 10, 2008), at http://www.sec.gov/divisions/investment/noaction/2008/ici101008.htm. The SEC staff's no-action position was "limited to portfolio securities that (i) have a remaining maturity of 60 days or less, (ii) are First Tier Securities as that term is defined in paragraph (a)(12) of rule 2a-7, and (iii) the fund reasonably expects to hold to maturity. For purposes of this letter, the remaining maturity of a security is measured without regard to paragraph (d) of rule2a-7."

[27] See Money Market Fund Reform, Investment Company Act Release No. 29132 (February 23, 2010) [75 FR 10060 (March 4, 2010)].

224 I J. E. Bethel and E. R. Sirri

convert portfolio holdings to cash to pay redeeming shareholders. Finally, the 2010 amendments mandated that MMFs conduct periodic stress tests to assess whether funds could maintain stable NAVs under scenarios involving interest rate, credit, and redemption shocks, and required that funds disclose portfolio holdings monthly.

To explore potential further reforms, the SEC sought comment on a 2010 report on MMF reform prepared by the President's Working Group on Financial Markets,[28] and it hosted a roundtable on May 10, 2011 to discuss MMFs. In November 2012, the Financial Stability Oversight Council (FSOC) recommended the SEC proceed with structural reforms to MMFs,[29] and the SEC staff published an economic study on MMFs addressing a series of questions related to the causes of the fund outflows during the 2008 financial crisis, the effects of the 2010 MMF reforms, and possible effects of further reforms on the short-term funding market.[30] In response to these initiatives, further SEC analyses, and extensive public comment to a June 2013 Proposing

---

[28] See US Department of Treasury (2010). The members of the group included the Secretary of the Treasury Department (as chairman), the Chairman of the Board of Governors of the Federal Reserve System, the Chairman of the SEC, and the Chairman of the CFTC.

[29] See Proposed Recommendations Regarding Money Market Mutual Fund Reform, Financial Stability Oversight Council [77 FR 69455 (Nov. 19, 2012)]. The FSOC has a statutory mandate to identify risks and respond to emerging threats to financial stability and authorities to constrain excessive risk in the financial system. It is chaired by Secretary of Treasury and has ten voting members, which include the heads of the Treasury, Fed, OCC, FDIC, and SEC. Other voting members include the heads of the U.S. Commodity Futures Trading Commission, Federal Housing Finance Agency, National Credit Union Administration, and Bureau of Consumer Financial Protection, as well as an independent member with insurance expertise appointed by the President and confirmed by the Senate. The FSOC also has five non-voting members, including the director of the Office of Financial Research, the director of the Federal Insurance Office, a state insurance commissioner, a state banking supervisor, and a state securities commissioner. See "About FSOC: Frequently Asked Questions," 11 Jul. 2014, Financial Stability Oversight Council (July 11, 2014), at http://www.treasury.gov/initiatives/fsoc/about/Pages/default.aspx.

[30] See "Response to Questions Posed by Commissioners Aguilar, Paredes, and Gallagher," in US Securities and Exchange Commission (2014).

Release,[31] the SEC adopted amendments in July 2014 that require, among other things, (i) institutional prime MMFs to price and transact at a "floating NAV" and (ii) non-government MMFs to impose liquidity fees and redemption gates during times of stress.[32] The 2014 amendments also increase the diversification requirements of MMF portfolios, enhance funds' stress testing requirements, and heighten funds' disclosure requirements to the SEC and the public. Lastly, the amendments enhance the reporting requirements for advisers of large private liquidity funds so that the SEC can monitor the flows and portfolio holdings of these funds.

The 2010 and 2014 MMF reforms addressed many of the issues that arose during the 2008 financial crisis. The reforms enhanced the quality, liquidity, transparency of funds' portfolio holdings, reducing the likelihood that investors choose to redeem shares during times of fund distress. The floating NAV requirement for institutional prime funds addressed the issue of share dilution. The reforms do not, however, eliminate fund risk, and thus do not eradicate the possibility that investors, especially institutions, may want to redeem shares in times of stress. To address this risk, the SEC mandated stress testing to help fund managers and boards better monitor and manage fund risk. The 2014 reforms also require that non-government funds impose liquidity fees and gates in times of fund distress.

Regulation of Credit Rating Agencies

During the decades leading up to the 2008 financial crisis, credit ratings became increasingly important to the US and global financial systems. Investors used credit ratings to inform their investment decisions and some institutional investors were required, either because of their investment strategies, bylaws or statutory requirements, to only hold securities with particular credit ratings in their portfolios. Many lending

---

[31] See Money Market Fund Reform; Amendments to Form PF, Release Nos. 33-9408; IA-3616; IC-30551 (June 5, 2013) [78 FR 36834, (June 19, 2013)].
[32] See Money Market Fund Reform; Amendments to Form PF, Release Nos. 33-9616, IA-3879; IC-31166 (July 23, 2014).

agreements, derivative contracts, and debt securities also tied loan or contract terms to borrowers' or counterparties' credit ratings. CRAs created methodologies to produce ratings and generally used an "issuer pays" business model to collect fees for ratings from issuers. CRAs successfully relied on the free-speech protections afforded by the First Amendment of the US Constitution to defend themselves if and when investors brought legal claims challenging the accuracy or quality of credit ratings.[33]

The use of credit ratings and importance of CRAs in the financial system expanded significantly over time, supported in part by regulatory language in the securities laws.[34] For example, the SEC adopted the term 'nationally recognized statistical rating organization' (NRSRO) in 1975 as part of its reforms to the broker-dealer net capital rule under the Securities Exchange Act of 1934.[35] The net capital rule specifies the amount of net capital that broker-dealers must hold, and it used NRSRO credit ratings to determine the charges to capital that broker-dealers must apply to debt instruments based on their liquidity and volatility. Over time, the SEC incorporated the NRSRO concept into a number of other rules, as well. For example, the SEC adopted Rule 2a-7 under the Investment Company Act of 1940, which prescribed the type of securities that MMFs could hold based on the securities' NRSRO credit ratings.[36] In addition, the SEC adopted regulations under the Securities Act of 1933 that incorporated credit ratings by NRSROs into certain issuer eligibility requirements.[37]

---

[33] See Protess, B. and L. Sebert (2009a; 2009b).

[34] The SEC recently removed references to NRSRO credit ratings from its rules, per the requirements of the Dodd-Frank Act, which requires all federal agencies to remove references to, or requirements of reliance on, credit ratings and instead substitute appropriate standards of credit worthiness in their regulations.

[35] See Adoption of Amendments to Rule 15c3-1 and Adoption of Alternative Net Capital Requirement for Certain Brokers and Dealers, Release No. 34-11497 (June 26, 1975) [40 FR 29795].

[36] Under Rule 2a-7, NRSRO ratings are minimum requirements; fund advisers must also make an independent determination that the security presents 'minimal credit risks'.

[37] See, for example, Adoption of Integrated Disclosure System, Release No. 33-6383 (Mar. 3, 1982) [47 FR 11380] and Shelf Registration, Release No. 33-6499 (Nov.

The SEC did not, however, define 'NRSRO' in 1975, but instead identified NRSROs through staff no-action letters. If a CRA wanted its ratings to be used for regulatory purposes, it requested a no-action letter from the SEC's staff, which would review information about the CRA to determine whether it had the financial and managerial resources and appropriate policies and procedures to consistently issue credible and reliable credit ratings. The SEC's staff also would determine whether the predominant users of credit ratings considered the credit rating agency to be credible and reliable. If these assessments were both affirmative, the SEC's staff would issue a no-action letter stating that regulated entities could treat the CRA as an NRSRO for regulatory purposes; that is, the staff would not recommend an enforcement action against the bank or broker-dealer if it relied upon the CRA's ratings for net capital charges.

Between 1975 and 2006, the SEC's staff identified nine CRAs as NRSROs.[38] As a result of consolidation, however, the number of NRSROs dropped to a low of three during the 1990s. As of 2006, only five CRAs were identified as NRSROs.[39] In September 2006, Congress passed the Credit Rating Agency Reform Act following criticism that the SEC's 'no-action letter' approach lacked transparency and the SEC had too little regulatory oversight of NRSROs.[40] The law required the SEC to establish a process for CRAs to register as NRSROs and gave the SEC the power to regulate NRSRO internal processes regarding, among other things, disclosure, reporting, record-keeping, the handling of material non-public information, and how they guard against conflicts of interest. It also made NRSRO determination a matter of Commission order, rather than staff determination.[41] Notably, however, the law

---

17, 1983) [48 FR 5289], *and* Simplification of Registration Procedures for Primary Securities Offerings, Release No. 336964 (Oct. 22, 1992) [57 FR 32461].

[38] See Definition of Nationally Recognized Statistical Rating Organization, Release Nos. 33-8570; 34-51572; IC-26834 (April 25, 2005) [70 FR 21306].

[39] See Definition of Nationally Recognized Statistical Rating Organization, Release Nos. 33-8570; 34-51572; IC-26834 (April 25, 2005) [70 FR 21306].

[40] See Credit Rating Agency Reform Act of 2006, Pub. L. 109–291, 120 Stat. 1327 (2006).

[41] See "Credit Rating Agencies," US Securities and Exchange Commission (August 6, 2014) at http://www.sec.gov/spotlight/dodd-frank/creditratingagencies.shtml.

specifically prohibited the SEC from regulating either the substance or the methods of an NRSRO's ratings. In 2007, the SEC adopted its first rules to implement the Credit Rating Agency Reform Act.[42]

In 2007 and 2008, the widespread defaults of highly-rated structured finance products raised questions as to the accuracy of credit ratings and the integrity of CRAs' rating processes. Notable was the concern that the 'issuer pays' business model employed by the CRAs led to a conflict of interest with regard to the quality of ratings, especially in the structured finance area. To address these concerns, the SEC adopted amendments in 2009 to its 2007 rules that among other things, improve NRSRO rating transparency and recordkeeping, prohibit NRSROs from engaging in certain practices that create conflicts of interest, and require NRSROs to disclose and provide data on credit ratings history information so that credit rating users and market participants can assess rating performance.[43] The amendments also create a mechanism by which NRSROs not hired to rate structured finance products can nonetheless determine and monitor credit ratings for these instruments.

In 2010 Congress passed the Dodd-Frank Act,[44] which outlines a series of broad reforms to the CRA market, but delegates the responsibility for developing specific rules to the SEC and other federal agencies.[45] First, the Dodd-Frank Act requires all federal agencies to remove references to, or requirements of reliance on, credit ratings and instead substitute appropriate standards of credit worthiness in their regulations. In 2011, the SEC continued the process of amending its rules, which was begun in 2008,[46] to remove references to NRSRO credit

---

[42] See Oversight of Credit Rating Agencies Registered as Nationally Recognized Statistical Rating Organizations, Exchange Act Release No. 34-55857, (June 5, 2007) [72 FR 33564 (June 18, 2007)].

[43] See Amendments to Rules for Nationally Recognized Statistical Rating Organizations, Exchange Act Release No. 59342 (February 2, 2009) [74 FR 6456 (February 9, 2009)] and Amendments to Rules for Nationally Recognized Statistical Rating Organizations, Exchange Act Release No. 34-61050 (November 23, 2009) [74 FR 63832 (December 4, 2009)].

[44] See Dodd-Frank Wall Street Reform and Consumer Protection Act, Pub. L. No. 111-203 (2013).

[45] See Pollard, R. B. and T. Perry (2014).

[46] See Security Ratings, Release No. 33-8940 (July 1, 2008) [73 FR 40106]. In 2009, the SEC re-opened the comment period for the release for an additional 60 days. See

ratings,[47] adopting final rules in 2011 and 2013 and proposing or re-proposing other rules in 2013 and 2014.[48] Second, the Dodd-Frank Act mandates the SEC create an Office of Credit Ratings (OCR) with a director that reports to the Chair of the SEC.[49] The primary purpose of the OCR is to enhance the regulation, accountability, and transparency of NRSROs.[50] The OCR monitors the activities and conducts legislatively mandated annual, risk-based examinations of all registered NRSROs. Third, the Act significantly increases CRAs' liability for issuing inaccurate ratings by lessening the pleading standards for private actions against CRAs under Rule 10b-5 of the Securities and Exchange Act of 1934.[51] In 2014, the SEC also adopted amendments and new rules to enhance its oversight of NRSROs. The changes were designed to enhance the governance of NRSROs in their role as 'gatekeepers' in

---

References to Ratings of Nationally Recognized Statistical Rating Organizations, Release No. 33-9069 (October 5, 2009) [74 FR 52374].

[47] See Security Ratings, Release No. 33-9186 (February 9, 2011) [76 FR 8946 (February 16, 2011)], References to Credit Ratings in Certain Investment Company Act Rules and Forms, Securities Act Release No. 9193 (March 3, 2011) [76 FR 12896 (March 9, 2011)], and Removal of Certain References to Credit Ratings under the Securities Exchange Act of 1934, Exchange Act Release No. 64352 (April 27, 2011), 76 FR 26550 (May 6, 2011).

[48] See, for example, Security Ratings, Securities Act Release No. 9245 (July 27, 2011) [76 FR 46603 (August 3, 2011)], Removal of Certain References to Credit Ratings Under the Securities Exchange Act of 1934 Release No. 34-71194 (December 27, 2013) [79 FR 1521 (January 8, 2014)], Removal of Certain References to Credit Ratings Under the Investment Company Act Release No. 30847 (December 27, 2013) [79 FR 1316 (January 8, 2014)], and Removal of Certain References to Credit Ratings and Amendment to the Issuer Diversification Requirement in the Money Market Fund Rule (July 23, 2014).

[49] Dodd-Frank Wall Street Reform and Consumer Protection Act, Pub. L. No. 111-203, § 931, 124 Stat. 1376, 1872 (2013). §§ 931-939H.

[50] See "About the Office of Credit Ratings," US Securities and Exchange Commission (August 4, 2014) at http://www.sec.gov/about/offices/ocr.shtml.

[51] Imposing greater liability for rating inaccuracies may have some unintended consequences. Using a comprehensive sample of corporate bond credit ratings from 2006 to 2012, Dimitrov, Palia, and Tang find results that suggest CRAs after the passage of the Dodd-Frank Act may be protecting their reputations by lowering their ratings beyond levels justified by issuers' fundamentals. See Dimitrov *et al.* (2015, forthcoming).

the debt issuance process and increase the transparency of the credit rating process as a whole, as well as with respect to structured finance products more specifically.[52]

Since the 2008 financial crisis, a number of investors have brought lawsuits against some of the CRAs,[53] challenging their alleged protection under the First Amendment.[54] In addition, the Department of Justice and a number of states have sued certain CRAs for defrauding investors[55] Some suits have been settled, whereas other suits continue to be litigated, and it will almost certainly take years for all litigation to be resolved.

It is important to note that despite the passage of the Dodd-Frank Act, which mandates sweeping changes to the oversight of CRAs, and the actions of the SEC to enhance CRAs' disclosure of their rating performance and methodologies, the fundamental problem of CRAs remains today. The private sector continues to rely on credit ratings despite understanding the conflicts of interest inherent in the economics of the CRA business model and the limitations of CRAs' methodologies to accurately forecast ratings.

Regulation of Short Selling

The State of Short Selling Regulation Before 2008

A short sale is the sale of a security that the seller does not own or a sale that is consummated by the delivery of a security borrowed by, or for

---

[52] The SEC proposed amendments to existing rules and new rules in 2011. See Nationally Recognized Statistical Rating Organizations, Exchange Act Release No. 64514 (May 18, 2011), 76 FR 33420 (June 8, 2011). The SEC adopted changes in 2014. *See* Nationally Recognized Statistical Rating Organizations, Exchange Act Release No. 72936 (August 27, 2014), 79 FR 55078 (September 15, 2014).

[53] See, for example, Freifeld (2013) and Segal (2009).

[54] Both Standard and Poor's, and Moody's were held liable for 'misleading and deceptive' ratings in litigation in Australia. See Fickling and Robinson (2012).

[55] See "Department of Justice Sues Standard & Poor's for Fraud in Rating Mortgage-Backed Securities in the Years Leading Up to the Financial Crisis," US Department of Justice (February 5, 2013) at http://www.justice.gov/opa/pr/2013/February/13-ag-156.html.

the account of, the seller.[56] Although the process can be complex, there are usually three steps in selling equity securities short. First, the seller must borrow or locate shares for the short sale, though the shares are generally not immediately borrowed. Second, the short sale order is executed. In the last step, delivery and payment occur, generally within three settlement days of the trade date. The seller physically borrows the shares from the lender and delivers them to the broker-dealer to fulfill the settlement obligation. Ultimately the seller must 'cover' the position by purchasing sufficient shares in the open market and returning them to the lender. Alternatively, the lender may demand the return of their borrowed shares by 'calling' the shares in, forcing the short seller either to find another lender for the shares or to purchase new shares in the open market for return to the lender.

Investors may engage in short selling shares for a host of reasons. A short sale may be an expression of a fundamentally negative view about the prospects of an issuer. In such a case, the short seller hopes to replace the borrowed shares sold short with ones purchased at a lower price, pocketing the price difference as a profit. Alternatively, the short sale may be part of a hedging strategy, including a hedge related to a complex security. For example, a buyer of a convertible bond may want to capture the value of a mispriced option embedded in the bond by selling short the stock into which the bonds may be converted.

Regulation of short selling in the United States before 2008 consisted of two distinct strands of regulation. The first strand of regulation focused on the price at which the shorted security was sold, and was commonly known as the 'uptick rule'.[57] Rule 10a-1(a)(1) provided that, subject to certain exceptions, a listed security could be sold short (A) at a price above the price at which the immediately preceding sale was effected (plus tick), or (B) at the last sale price if it was higher than the last different price (zero-plus tick). Short sales were not permitted on minus ticks or zero-minus ticks, subject to narrow exceptions. It was intended to restrict short sales in falling markets, and was in part motivated by a 1937 SEC study of concentrated short selling during the

---

[56] Portions of this section of the paper are adapted from Sirri (2010).
[57] 17 CFR § 240.10a-1

market break of 1937. In part due to a decrease in the tick size from US$0.125 to US$0.01, as well as economic analysis supporting a need to revise the rule,[58] the SEC rescinded the relevant rule in July 2007.

The second strand of the SEC's policy concerning short selling relates to the delivery of shorted shares. The SEC states that 'naked' short selling is "… selling short without having stock available for delivery and intentionally failing to deliver within the standard three day settlement cycle."[59] The SEC historically was concerned naked short selling could result in failures to deliver, which could have harmful effects on the markets and shareholders. Failing to deliver securities on settlement converts a securities contract into a forward contract, causing the buyer (or a clearing agency) to be exposed to the credit risk of the seller. It can also create problems with respect to the voting of shares as a buyer might not be in possession of the security by the record date of the vote and thus would lose the ability to vote. Over the years, the SEC had also become concerned that naked short selling was at times used to facilitate various abusive and manipulative practices.

In response, the SEC adopted new Regulation SHO in August 2004.[60] Among other things, Regulation SHO replaced disparate SRO rules with the requirement that a broker-dealer must either borrow the security, or enter into an arrangement to borrow the security, or have reasonable grounds to believe the security can be borrowed so that it can be delivered on the date delivery is due before it can accept or effect a short sale order in that security.[61] In addition, it established the creation of a 'threshold list' of certain securities for which the aggregate amount of failures to deliver at a registered clearing agency is greater than both 10,000 shares and one-half of one percent of the shares outstanding. If a security is on such a threshold list and the broker-dealer

---

[58] See Office of Economic Analysis (2007).

[59] Short Sales, Exchange Act Release No. 34-48709 (October 28, 2003) [68 FR 62975 (November 6, 2003)].

[60] Short Sales, Exchange Act Release No. 34-50103 (July 28, 2004) [69 FR 48008, (August 6, 2004)].

[61] The locate must occur and be documented prior to the trade.

has a failed to deliver position for 13 consecutive days, the broker must buy shares to 'close-out' this position. The rule originally contained a number of exceptions from these requirements, including a provision for pre-existing fail positions (the 'grandfather' exception) and an exception for options market makers.

Regulation SHO was an attempt to reduce the number of failures to deliver in the settlement system. To promote disclosure, the threshold list made public the names of stocks that had substantial amounts of open failures to deliver for the first time. The SEC gradually moved to reduce the number of securities with substantial fails by tightening and/ or eliminating some of the rule's exceptions. For instance, the SEC eliminated the grandfather exception and proposed to eliminate the options market maker exception in August 2007.[62] In 2008, the SEC eliminated the options market maker exception to the closeout requirement of Regulation SHO.[63]

SEC Actions in 2008–2009

As the large investment banks came under financial pressure in 2008, stories began to circulate about short sellers teaming up to aggressively short the equity of these firms.[64] Heads of major financial firms complained that short sellers were unfairly pressuring their firms' stock prices, driving their companies toward the brink of ruin.[65] Congress became concerned about the effects of short selling as well, questioning SEC

---

[62] See Amendments to Regulation SHO, Exchange Act Release No. 34-56212, (August 7, 2007) [72 FR 45544, (August 14, 2007)] for elimination of the 'grandfather' exception, and Amendments to Regulation SHO, Exchange Act Release No. 34-56213, (August 7, 2007) [72 FR 45558, (August 14, 2007)] for the proposed elimination of the options market maker exception.

[63] See Amendments to Regulation SHO, Exchange Act Release No. 34-58775, (October 14, 2008) [73 FR 61690, (October 17, 2008)].

[64] See Moyer (2008), Burrough (2008), or Saporito (2008).

[65] See The Wall Street Journal's "Mack Blames Short Sellers," dated September 17, 2008 at http://blogs.wsj.com/wallstreetcrisis/2008/09/17/mack-blames-short-sellers/.

Chairman Christopher Cox about these activities and asking the SEC to investigate whether inappropriate trading was occurring.[66] Senator John McCain, who at the time was a candidate for the presidency, said in a portion of a speech that touched upon short selling, "… The Chairman of the SEC serves at the appointment of the President and has betrayed the public's trust. If I were President today, I would fire him."[67]

Beginning in March of 2008, the SEC undertook no less than six regulatory actions targeted at the practice of short selling. While a complete description of each of these actions is beyond the scope of this paper, we highlight the salient points of the key regulatory changes.

Mandatory pre-borrowing to short certain financial firms: Beginning on July 15, 2008, the SEC issued the first of a series of emergency orders to limit short selling.[68] Such orders can be effective for up to 30 calendar days, including extensions. The July 15 order required that for a group of 19 identified financial firms, "… no person may effect a short sale in these securities using the means or instrumentalities of interstate commerce unless such person or its agent has borrowed or arranged to borrow the security or otherwise has the security available to borrow in its inventory prior to effecting such short sale and delivers the security on settlement date."[69] The order essentially required short sellers to pre-borrow shares of those 19 financial firms before selling them short. The 19 firms covered by the order consisted of

---

[66] See *Reuters* (2008).

[67] Sasseen (2009).

[68] Section 12(k)(2) of the 1934 Securities and Exchange Act states that "The Commission, in an emergency, may by order summarily take such action to alter, supplement, suspend, or impose requirements or restrictions with respect to any matter or action subject to regulation by the Commission or a self-regulatory organization under this title, as the Commission determines is necessary in the public interest and for the protection of investors (i) to maintain or restore fair and orderly securities markets (other than markets in exempted securities); or (ii) to ensure prompt, accurate, and safe clearance and settlement of transactions in securities (other than exempted securities)." Such orders can be effective for up to 30 days. 15 U.S.C. §78(l) (2004).

[69] Emergency Order Pursuant To Section 12(k)(2) Of The Securities Exchange Act Of 1934 Taking Temporary Action To Respond To Market Developments, Exchange Act Release 58166, (July 15, 2008) [73 FR 42379 (July 21, 2008)].

Fannie Mae, Freddie Mac, and the seventeen primary dealers in Treasury securities.[70]

The pre-borrow requirement was a significant change from standard industry practice. To comply with the order, a seller had to actually borrow the shares or establish an exclusive arrangement to borrow the shares, known as a 'hard locate,' before the sale was effected. The requirement differed from the usual situation where a short seller could locate the shares before the sale, but not actually take possession of them until settlement date. Pre-borrowing also meant a set of shares could be pledged to only one short seller who ultimately may, or may not actually borrow them, as opposed to being pledged to multiple borrowers.[71]

Tightening Regulation SHO delivery requirements: On September 17, 2008, the SEC enhanced delivery requirements on broker-dealers with respect to the sales of all equity securities.[72] Similar to the previous emergency order, the SEC justified the order by its concern "... about the possible unnecessary or artificial price movements based on unfounded rumors regarding the stability of financial institutions and other issuers exacerbated by 'naked' short selling."[73] The rule penalized a member of any registered clearing agency (any broker-dealer from which it receives trades for clearance and settlement) for having

---

[70] The seventeen dealers were recently given access to the newly created Primary Dealer Credit Facility (PDCF), an overnight facility that makes collateralized loans to insure the liquidity of the dealers (see "Federal Reserve Announces Establishment of Primary Dealer Credit Facility," Board of Governors of the Federal Reserve (March 16, 2008) at http://www.newyorkfed.org/newsevents/news/markets/2008/rp080316.html).

[71] This order was modified three days later by providing a number of exemptions from the order's scope, such as for market makers and block positioners. For example, the order excepted registered market makers, block positioners, and other market makers in certain circumstances, as well short sales effected pursuant to Rule 144 of the Securities Act of 1933. *See* Amendment to Emergency Order Pursuant to Section 12(k)(2), Exchange Act Release 58190, (July 18, 2008) [73 FR 42837 (July 23, 2008)].

[72] Emergency Order Pursuant to Section 12(k)(2), Exchange Act Release 58572 (September 17, 2008) [73 FR 54875 (September 23, 2008)].

[73] *Id.*

a failure to deliver position at a registered clearing agency in any equity security for a long or a short sale transaction in that equity security. The fail had to be closed out by the morning of the day after settlement. If the clearing member or any of its correspondent clients failed to close-out the fail to deliver position, it had to pre-borrow or enter into a bona-fide arrangement to borrow the security before accepting or effecting a short sale in that security, thereby imposing a 'hard locate' requirement.[74] The pre-borrow requirement remained in effect until the fail to deliver position was closed out and the purchased shares settled.

Banning short sales in all financial firms: On September 18, 2008, the SEC issued the most binding of its various emergency orders, banning all short sales in a large group of financial firms, including all banks, insurance companies, and securities firms.[75] The list ultimately contained approximately a thousand financial firms. The SEC's justification for the order was its concern

> "… that short selling in the securities of a wider range of financial institutions may be causing sudden and excessive fluctuations of the prices of such securities in such a manner so as to threaten fair and orderly markets.
>
> Given the importance of confidence in our financial markets as a whole, we have become concerned about recent sudden declines in the prices of a wide range of securities. Such price declines can give rise to questions about the underlying financial condition of an issuer, which in turn can create a crisis of confidence, without a fundamental underlying basis."[76]

---

[74] The order also did two other things. First, it caused Rule 10b-21, the naked short selling anti-fraud rule, to become immediately effective. The rule had been proposed in March 2008 but had not yet adopted. Second, it immediately closed the options market maker exception under Regulation SHO. See Order Extending Emergency Order Pursuant to Section 12(k)(2), Exchange Act Release 58711 (October 3, 2008) [73 FR 58698 (October 7, 2008)].

[75] Emergency Order Pursuant to Section 12(k)(2), Exchange Act Release 58592, [73 FR 55169 (September 18, 2008).

[76] *Id. at 1.*

The order was also remarkable in its implementation in that unlike some of the earlier orders, it went into immediate effect. Market participants had only hours to adjust to the effect of the ban.[77,78]

The return of the price test: The final installment in the SEC's burst of activity with respect to short selling occurred on April 10, 2009 when it proposed four alternative price-driven tests to replace the 10a-1 uptick rule and the bid test that were rescinded in July 2007.[79] The release noted that the extreme market conditions and deterioration in investor confidence had caused many commenters to ask the SEC to reconsider its termination of the old uptick rule, and made it appropriate for the SEC to seek comment on a restriction for short selling. The release asked whether the proposed restriction might help "... to prevent short selling, including potentially abusive or manipulative short selling, from being used as a tool for driving the market down or from being used to accelerate a declining market ..."[80] This justification is notable in the wake of what many regarded as an asset bubble, as well as the generally poor economic condition of a number of large financial firms.[81]

---

[77] *Id.* The order contained a provision that allowed any issuer covered by the ban to opt out of it if they chose to do so. Very few firms took advantage of this opportunity.

[78] This order was subsequently amended to (a) provide an exception from the short sale ban for ETFs and for market makers in derivatives on the covered securities (see Amendment To Emergency Order Pursuant To Section 12(k)(2) Of The Securities Exchange Act Of 1934 Taking Temporary Action To Respond To Market Developments, Exchange Act Release No. 58611, (September 21, 2008) [73 FR 55556 (Septmeber 25, 2008)]), and (b) provide for the order's expiration three business days from the President's signing of the Emergency Economic Stabilization Act, or at the 30-day statutory limit for the Order, whichever came first (see Order Extending Emergency Order Pursuant To Section 12(k)(2) Of The Securities Exchange Act Of 1934 Taking Temporary Action To Respond To Market Developments, Exchange Act Release No. 58723, (October 2, 2008) [73 FR 58994 (October 8, 2008)]).

[79] 74 FR 42033-42037 (August 20, 2009).

[80] *Id.* at 42036.

[81] Omitted from the above discussion is the Naked Short Selling Anti-Fraud Rule, Exchange Act Release No. 34-57511, (March 17, 2008) [73 FR 15376 (March 21, 2008)] and the order requiring public reporting by institutional managers form their daily short positions and trading (Order Extending Emergency Order Pursuant To

Comments on the Effectiveness of the Short Selling Rules

The SEC's 2008–2009 regulatory activities on short selling were remarkable for their direction and motivation. The orders and rules promulgated by the SEC over this period uniformly tightened restrictions on short selling, both on the 'price test' and the 'failure to deliver' branches of regulatory policy. In July 2007, the SEC rescinded the uptick rule and bid test and gradually tightened its grip on the failures to deliver associated with short selling. The SEC tied its position generally to a desire to minimize abusive naked short selling.[82] In 2008 and thereafter, little evidence emerged that naked short selling had increased or was responsible for inaccurate security prices. A review of the September 12, 2008 list of NYSE stocks for which there were a meaningful number of failures to deliver shows neither Lehman, Citigroup, AIG, Morgan Stanley, Goldman Sachs or Wachovia were on the list, nor were any number of other stocks that allegedly were threatened by naked short selling.[83]

The short selling regulations promulgated in 2008 had a notably different stated tone and purpose than preceding rulemakings. The earlier rulemakings expressed concerns about abusive practices, whereas the 2008 orders and rules expressed prudential concerns about issuers, shareholders, and the markets. For example, in the July 15, 2008 order requiring pre-borrowing before shorting the stock of 19 firms, the SEC argued false rumors can cause a lack of confidence, which can lead to panic selling that is exacerbated by naked short selling. The September 18th order banning all short sales makes a similar argument, but goes on to state that ensuing price declines can lead to a loss of confidence. The word 'confidence' appears in a number of the short sale orders and

---

Section 12(k)(2) Of The Securities Exchange Act Of 1934 Taking Temporary Action To Respond To Market Developments, Exchange Act Release No. 58591, (September 18, 2008) [73 FR 55175 (September 24, 2008)]).

[82] See pg. 3, Amendments to Regulation SHO, Exchange Act Release No. 34-54154, (July 14, 2006) [71 FR 41710 (July 21, 2006)].

[83] See Exhibit 2 of Sirri (2010).

rules promulgated during this period, suggesting that the SEC was concerned with boosting market participants' confidence rather than with traditional market quality issues.

Academic evidence has generally not been supportive of efficacy of the 2008 short selling policy changes. While a complete recitation of academic findings related to short selling restrictions is beyond the scope of this paper, a few key results are of note. Using data from 2006 to 2008, Boulton and Braga-Alves (2012) finds no connection between naked short selling activity and future stock price declines.[84] Instead the authors find naked short sellers are contrarians that sell shares short after price increases, and that prices generally rise following public revelations of material fails-to-deliver in issuers' stocks. The authors state their results "... are not consistent with the recent portrayal of naked short sellers as abusive and manipulative, but instead suggest naked short sellers promote efficient markets by providing liquidity, risk-bearing, and selling stocks they view as overpriced."[85] Fotak *et al.* (2014) examines data from before and after the short selling ban. In this paper, the authors conclude the SEC's ban on failures-to-deliver arising from naked short selling "... led to a significant increase in absolute pricing errors, relative bid-ask spreads, and intraday volatility ..." and "... the gently regulated failure-to-deliver regime that existed after Regulation SHO up to mid-2008 was net beneficial for pricing efficiency and market liquidity."[86]

Boehmer *et al.* (2013) looks at the effect of the 2008 short selling bans and finds that although the bans decreased shorting activity, they also decreased market quality, as measured by quoted spread, effective spread, and volatility.[87] The study's results are supported by the findings of Boulton and Braga-Alves (2010), which examines the effects of the July 2008 short sale restriction on the 19 financial firms. The authors

---

[84] See Boulton and Braga-Alves (2012).
[85] See Boulton and Braga-Alves (2012).
[86] Fotak *et al.* (2014).
[87] Boehmer *et al.* (2013).

find that although the prices of the restricted firms reacted positively to the announcement of the ban, the market quality of the subject firms suffered.[88] Although not directly related to the short-sale rules for equity securities in the United States, Arce and Mayerdomo (2014) documents these same negative effects on market quality in a study of the 2011 ban on short selling of Spanish bank stocks.[89] These findings about short selling extend to the fixed income markets as well. A recent paper by Kozhan and Raman (2014) analyzes trading in the corporate bond market and finds evidence that short selling is particularly valuable during a crisis and contributes to price discovery and liquidity.

It is notable that in an interview he gave to *The Washington Post* less than a month before leaving the SEC, Chairman Christopher Cox stated that agreeing to the September 2008 short selling ban on financial firms was the biggest mistake of his tenure.[90] Cox went on to say, "... he had been under intense pressure from Treasury Secretary Henry M. Paulson Jr. and Fed Chairman Ben S. Bernanke to take this action and did so reluctantly."[91]

The SEC and the Consolidated Supervised Entity Program

The United States possesses a complex system for regulating financial firms engaged in the securities business. As a general matter, banks are regulated by one (or more) of several federal banking regulators that include the Fed, the FDIC, and the OCC, in addition to being subject to state banking requirements. The SEC generally regulates activities related to, and entities involved in, securities issuance and trading. Both banking entities and broker-dealers, however, may be part of large firms

---

[88] Boulton and Braga-Alves (2010).
[89] Oscar Arce and Sergio Mayerdomo, "Short Selling Constraints and Financial Stability: Evidence from the Spanish Market," Banco de Espana, Documentos de Trabajo No 1401.
[90] Paley and Hilzenrath (2008).
[91] *Id.*

that are organized in holding company structures. If one of the subsidiaries of a holding company is a banking entity, then the holding company is a "bank holding company" and enterprise oversight falls to the Fed, even if the OCC or FDIC regulates the bank subsidiary. With respect to broker-dealers, if the holding company contains a banking entity, as well as a broker-dealer, then once again enterprise supervision falls to the Fed. If, however, the holding company does not contain a banking entity but does contain a broker-dealer, then there is no federal oversight of the enterprise; that is, although individual subsidiaries, including the broker-dealer, may be functionally regulated by either federal or state regulators, the holding company itself has no overarching supervisor.

With respect to the SEC's regulation of broker-dealers, the basic design of the regulatory framework is to ensure a broker-dealer can unwind itself in the event it becomes insolvent or illiquid in such a way that all customer property is returned and customers suffer no losses due to the impairment of the broker-dealer. Whether the broker-dealer continues as an ongoing entity is less important to the SEC than the broker-dealer's ability to wind down its affairs in an orderly fashion, pay off its liabilities and obligations to counterparties, and return the customer property it carries. Although the regulatory regime of broker-dealers is complex, it revolves around two important core rules, one of which is the broker-dealer net capital rule.[92] The net capital rule basically requires that broker-dealers maintain more actual net capital than required minimum net capital;[93] that is, broker-dealers maintain more than one dollar of highly liquid assets for each dollar of liabilities (other than subordinated liabilities) at all times. Consequently, the net capital rule positions broker-dealers to be able to quickly pay off all liabilities to unsubordinated creditors (subordinated lenders typically are the

---

[92] Net Capital Requirements for Brokers or Dealers, Exchange Act Rule 15c3-1, 17 CFR 240.15c3-1 (1991). The key rule in this area is the Customer Protection Rule, Exchange Act Rule 15c3-3, 17 CFR 240.15c3-3 (2001).

[93] Net capital is defined as net worth plus qualified subordinated loans less illiquid assets such as fixed assets, goodwill, real estate and unsecured receivables, and less the application of rule-based haircut charges associated with the securities positions.

broker-dealer's parent). Because each broker-dealer's actual net capital is adjusted to reflect the riskiness of its assets and operations, the requirement creates a financial cushion that protects creditors and the customer assets held by the broker-dealer.

This regulatory regime has generally worked well for standalone broker-dealers, but may be problematic for broker-dealers that are subsidiaries of large financial firms. In these instances, broker-dealers are exposed to the risk of their parent firms' other subsidiaries, which may include affiliates that engage in derivatives and structured finance trading, as well trading or the holding of illiquid assets that otherwise would receive a 100% capital charge if held by a standalone broker-dealer.[94] The situation was highlighted in the 1980s by the failure of Drexel Burnham Lambert Group. Drexel was an active participant in the market for high yield bonds, and contained one U.S. and one U.K. regulated securities entities. When the holding company came under criminal sanctions due to the actions of Michael Milken and others, and the market liquidity of high-yield bonds fell, the market lost confidence in the holding company's ability to make good on its short-term liabilities. When the holding company suffered a liquidity crisis, its affiliates, including the brokerage entity, suffered as well. Ultimately the holding company was liquidated and the brokerage subsidiaries failed, although no brokerage customers suffered any impairment. This episode caused the SEC to realize that its narrow oversight of broker-dealers within large holding companies was insufficient to guarantee proper functioning.

Congress responded in 1990 by granting additional authority to the SEC,[95] but the SEC's authority was still quite limited. The 1999 Gramm-Leach-Bliley Act, which weakened the line between commercial and investment banking, contained no language to improve the regulatory situation highlighted by Drexel's bankruptcy. The rise of large securities firms, such as Goldman Sachs, Morgan Stanley, Merrill Lynch, Bear

---

[94] Alternative Net Capital Requirements for Broker-Dealers That Are Part of Consolidated Supervised Entities, Exchange Act Release No. 34-48690, (October 24, 2003) [68 FR 62872 (Nov. 6, 2003)].

[95] Section 17(h) of the Securities and Exchange Act of 1934 was added by the Market Reform Act of 1990. See 15 USC 78q(h).

Stearns, and Lehman Brothers, made the disparity between what the SEC regulated on the statutory basis (the broker-dealer) and the far-flung nature of the total enterprise even more stark. In addition, the European Union (EU) instituted a requirement that all financial firms doing business in EU countries must be subject to consolidated supervision. The large U.S. brokerage firms, some of which were holding companies without a consolidated supervisor, needed to either find such a supervisor or else become subject to the EU's requirement to "ring fence" their European operations, a costly and inefficient organizational option.[96]

In response, the SEC created the Consolidated Supervised Entity (CSE) program in 2004.[97] In essence, the SEC tried to do by *rule* what Congress had not done by *statute*. The SEC created an optional regulatory regime for large financial non-bank holding companies in which their broker-dealer subsidiaries would receive more favorable capital treatment in exchange for allowing limited SEC access to, and oversight of, the activities at the holding company and in unregulated subsidiaries. With respect to the regulated broker-dealer entities, the CSE rule allowed the firms to compute capital haircuts not by the standardized method prescribed in the net capital rule, but by using a quantitative VaR-type approach consistent with the then Basel II standards.[98] By doing so, firms would likely get a more efficient use of their regulatory capital. In exchange, the firms consented to enterprise-wide supervision, including (a) providing risk and operational information about the ultimate holding company, (b) implementing an enterprise-wide risk management system for credit, liquidity, legal, and operational risk, (c) consenting to SEC examination on an enterprise-wide basis, and (d) computing enterprise-wide capital and certain risk measures in a

---

[96] Because Lehman Brothers, Merrill Lynch, and Morgan Stanley each owned a thrift, the Office of Thrift Supervision (OTS) was technically the holding company supervisor of these firms. However, the OTS did not take an active rule in supervision of the holding company or other non-thrift subsidiaries.

[97] Alternative Net Capital Requirements for Broker-Dealers That Are Part of Consolidated Supervised Entities, Exchange Act Release No. 34-48690, (June 8, 2004) [69 FR 34428 (June 21, 2004)].

[98] At the same time, the rule required these broker-dealers to maintain substantially higher levels of tentative net capital (i.e., net capital before applying haircuts).

manner consistent with the Basel II standards. Though not part of the original rule, the CSE program later required firms to maintain, and the SEC to be allowed to monitor, a distinct liquidity pool composed of cash and unencumbered assets held for the benefit of the holding company and its unrestricted subsidiaries.[99]

The CSE program was created to overcome a statutory shortcoming with respect to the SEC's supervision of some of the largest financial firms in the world. Although the SEC functionally regulated these firms' U.S. broker-dealers, and certain other functional regulators oversaw other subsidiaries, no single regulator actively exercised oversight or supervision of the entire consolidated firms. By creating this optional regulatory regime, the SEC hoped to entice the firms to exchange limited oversight of the holding company and its unregulated subsidiaries for a more modern treatment of capital — one that was consistent with how the firms' senior managers (and banking regulators) measured, monitored, and managed risk. Ultimately the five firms previously mentioned opted into the CSE program.

As the crisis unfolded in 2008, it became apparent that these firms could not survive without some type of financial support. The SEC had neither the regulatory authority nor the financial resources to guarantee their financial viability, and because the firms were not banks, they lacked direct access to the Fed discount window or Fed 'lender of last resort' facilities. In the end, Bear Stearns was merged into J.P. Morgan, Lehman Brothers was liquidated, Merrill Lynch was merged into Bank of America, and Morgan Stanley and Goldman Sachs' subsidiaries became national and New York state chartered banks, respectively (and thus under the Fed's supervision). It is notable the US broker-dealer

---

[99] "Each CSE firm was expected to maintain a liquidity pool consisting of cash or highly liquid and highly rated unencumbered debt instruments. However, the standards regarding the types of assets that could be included in this liquidity pool, and the manner in which those assets could be held, were not set forth in a Commission regulation ...", Mary L. Schapiro, "Testimony Concerning the Lehman Brothers Examiner's Report," 20 April 2010, before the House Financial Services Committee, at http://www.sec.gov/news/testimony/2010/ts042010mls.htm.

entities of all of these firms remained well-capitalized throughout the financial crisis and made good on their promises to their customers. The same, of course, was not necessarily true of the firms' liability holders and customers of their non-US broker-dealers.[100]

In September 2008, SEC Chairman Christopher Cox announced the termination of the CSE program:

> The last six months have made it abundantly clear that voluntary regulation does not work. When Congress passed the Gramm-Leach-Bliley Act, it created a significant regulatory gap by failing to give to the SEC or any agency the authority to regulate large investment bank holding companies, like Goldman Sachs, Morgan Stanley, Merrill Lynch, Lehman Brothers, and Bear Stearns.
>
> ...As I have reported to the Congress multiple times in recent months, the CSE program was fundamentally flawed from the beginning, because investment banks could opt in or out of supervision voluntarily. The fact that investment bank holding companies could withdraw from this voluntary supervision at their discretion diminished the perceived mandate of the CSE program, and weakened its effectiveness.[101]

In testimony before the House financial services committee, Mary Schapiro, who succeeded Christopher Cox as chairman of the SEC, stated that the CSE program ". . . created classic regulatory arbitrage — a system in which a regulated entity was permitted to select its regulator." She went on to say:

> The SEC believed at the time that it was stepping in to address an existing gap in the oversight of these entities. Once the agency took on that

---

[100] There has been much written about the failure of the SEC's supervision of these five large securities holding companies. Much of this critique is inaccurate, and beyond the space and scope of this paper. A more detailed discussion of these points can be found in a speech by Erik R. Sirri (2009) and in Andrew Lo's working paper (2011).

[101] See US Security and Exchange Commission press release 2008-230, "Chairman Cox Announces End of Consolidated Supervised Entities Program," 26 September 2008, at http://www.sec.gov/news/press/2008/2008-230.htm.

responsibility, however, it had to follow through effectively. Notwithstanding the hard work of its staff, in hindsight it is clear that the program lacked sufficient resources and staffing, was under-managed, and at least in certain respects lacked a clear vision as to its scope and mandate.[102]

It is impossible to know whether the CSE program benefited the US financial system. Such an evaluation would ultimately require knowing how these large firms would have performed in the absence of the limited consolidated supervision of the holding company actually provided by the SEC. Although this counterfactual world cannot, by definition, be observed, it is notable that the grant of regulatory relief to the regulated broker-dealers in terms of net capital treatment caused no impairment to the broker-dealers' liabilities to its customers.

Conclusion

In contrast to many other financial regulators around the world, the SEC's core mandate — to protect investors, maintain fair, orderly, and efficient markets, and to promote competition efficiency, and capital formation — is neither prudential nor merit-based in nature in that Congress does not provide the SEC with an explicit mandate to manage systemic risk or the resources to guarantee the continuing financial viability of issuers or institutions. The SEC's primary tool to regulate the financial markets is disclosure; that is, to ensure market participants are provided accurate and complete information. The four topics discussed in this paper, MMFs, CRAs, short selling, and the regulation of large broker-dealers' net capital, all fall squarely within the ambit of the SEC's core mission. Yet when the 2008 financial crisis hit, it became apparent the mandate and toolkit Congress has provided the SEC were of questionable value to the demands of the moment.

---

[102] See Mary L. Schapiro's testimony before the House of Financial Services Committee, "Testimony Concerning the Lehman Brothers Examiner's Report," 20 Apr. 2010, at http://www.sec.gov/news/testimony/2010/ts042010mls.htm.

For MMFs, the rules in place in 2008 have since been judged inadequate. The chain of events that unfolded during the financial crisis highlighted not only structural weaknesses in the design of certain MMFs, but also the importance of MMFs to the short-term funding markets. SEC rulemaking has since improved certain structural features of funds as well as the quality and diversification of MMF portfolio assets. We note the SEC has continued to focus on its Congressional mandates of investor protection and the promotion of capital formation throughout the post-2008 period rather than attempting to become a prudential regulator. That said, the agency appears to have adapted and expanded its interpretation of what constitutes these mandates in light of lessons it learned from the financial crisis.

In many ways CRAs are the most problematic of the four examples examined in this paper. Throughout the buildup to the crisis, CRAs were largely unregulated. In a rare example of the Congressional intervention before a crisis hits, Congress gave the SEC authority over CRAs in 2006, permitting it to regulate conflicts of interest and increase the transparency of the firms. That said, the changes made by the SEC even to this day are incremental to the core problem of CRAs, which is the continued reliance by the private sector on credit ratings despite understanding the conflicts of interest inherent in the economics of the CRA business model and the limitations of CRAs' methodologies to accurately forecast whether obligors will meet their financial obligations.

With respect to short selling, although the SEC had the tools needed to change the amount and character of short selling, it is impossible to judge whether the SEC's regulatory decisions were correct. The results of empirical academic studies conducted after the crisis strongly suggest the SEC's short selling restrictions harmed customary measures of market quality. Yet we do not know how things would have progressed had the *status quo ante* framework been allowed to continue unaltered. Demagoguery of short sellers was rampant, and the SEC was concerned that the situation, if left unaddressed, could affect investors' perception of the fairness and efficacy of the markets. What does seem clear is that fundamental forces affected the security prices of many financial firms, and that short selling was one of several mechanisms used by traders to express their negative views.

With respect to the CSE program for large broker-dealers embedded within non-bank financial holding companies, it seems clear the primary responsibility for the regulatory shortcomings associated with oversight of these firms should lie on the doorstep of Congress. As discussed above, the SEC attempted to plug the regulatory gap in the oversight of these large holding companies ahead of the crisis. But for the advent of the crisis, its efforts may have been successful for some time. These firms operated for decades without the Fed's guarantee of liquidity, relying instead on the financial markets for both short- and long-term funding needs. What we cannot know is whether things would have been better or worse during the crisis had the SEC not provided limited supervision of the holding companies before the financial crisis.

In terms of future supervision, we note the issues and risks associated with these firms, including daily mark-to-market valuations of trading assets and certain funding models, are now deeply embedded within the banking sector. In recognition of at least some of these risks, the Fed recently expressed concern about the funding stability of broker-dealers that are part of large bank holding companies during times of market stress.[103]

As discussed in the paper, differences in various domestic financial regulators' missions have created inter-agency tensions as each strives to fulfill its congressionally mandated purpose.[104] No other Federal regulators, however, have challenged the SEC's exclusive authority over the securities trading markets or the oversight of CRAs. The same cannot be said of MMFs and large non-bank financial firms. With respect

---

[103] See Tracy (2014), which references a speech by Boston Fed President Eric Rosengren, "Broker-Dealer Finance and Stability," Federal Reserve Bank of Boston (13 August 2014) http://www.bostonfed.org/news/speeches/rosengren/2014/081314/081314text.pdf.

[104] These tensions are nothing new. For example, the SEC and bank regulators disagreed in 1997 about Sun Trust Bank's treatment of certain reserve items (see, for example, Michael Schroeder (1999). More recently, the SEC and the Fed reached a Memorandum of Understanding in 2008 over cooperation with respect to the use of information produced by large bank holding companies that also had significant broker-dealers (see the press release by the Federal Reserve Board of Governors (July 7, 2008), at http://www.federalreserve.gov/newsevents/press/bcreg/20080707a.htm).

to both of these financial institutions, the FSOC, a product of the Dodd-Frank Act, has entered the regulatory fray both directly and indirectly. One can clearly sympathize with the Fed's interest, expressed through the FSOC, in the sound regulation of entities irrespective of the existing regulatory framework and entities' current federal regulators. The Fed serves as a lender of last resort and liquidity provider and has done so to any number of financial institutions, even when the Fed did not directly supervise them. To the extent the Fed is expected to guarantee the performance of the financial system, it is not surprising that it expects to have a hand in all aspects of the financial system's regulation. This view ignores, however, the statutory mandates of the other financial regulators. Let us hope that the toolkit of the respective regulators, as well as the Commissioners and Governors, can work together to find solutions that best meet the needs of taxpayers, investors, and financial market participants.

References

Boehmer, E., C. M. Jones and X. Zhang (2013), "Shackling Short Sellers: The 2008 Shorting Ban," *Review of Financial Studies*, 26: 1363–1400.

Boulton, T. J. and M. V. Braga-Alves (2010), "The Skinny on the 2008 Naked Short-Sale Restrictions," *Journal of Financial Markets*, 13: 397–421.

Boulton, T. J. and M. V. Braga-Alves (2012), "Naked Short Selling and Market Returns," *Journal of Portfolio Management*, 38(3): 133–142.

Brady, S., K. Anadu, and N. Cooper (2012), "The Stability of Prime Money Market Mutual Funds: Sponsor Support from 2007 to 2011," Federal Reserve Bank of Boston No. RPA12-3. Available at: http://www.boston-fed.org/bankinfo/qau/wp/2012/qau1203.pdf.

Burrough, B. (2008), "Bringing Down Bear Stearns," *Vanity Fair*, August.

Crane Data (2007), "A History of Liquidity Incidents Impacting Money Market Funds," Crane Data: Money Fund Intelligence (August 19, 2007). Available at: http://www.cranedata.us/archives/news/2007/8/.

Dimitrov, V., D. Palia and L. Tang (2015, forthcoming), "Impact of the Dodd-Frank Act on Credit Ratings," *Journal of Financial Economics*. Available at: http://ssrn.com/abstract=2444990.

Federated and Putnam Investments (2008), "Federated Investors, Inc. and Putnam Investments Announce Transaction to Benefit Money Market

Fund Shareholders," Press Release (September 24, 2008). Available at: http://www.federatedinvestors.com/FII/about/pressrelease/detail.do?cid=65207.

Fink, M. P. (2008), *The Rise of Mutual Funds: An Insider's View* (Oxford: Oxford University Press).

Fickling, D. and M. Robinson (2012), "McGraw-Hill Plummets after Australian Court Ruling," *Bloomberg.com*, November 5. Available at: http://www.bloomberg.com/news/2012-11-04/s-p-found-liable-by-australian-court-for-misleading-ratings.html.

Fotak, V., V. Raman and P. K. Yadav (2014), "Fails-to-Deliver, Short Selling, and Market Quality," *Journal of Financial Economics*, 114(3): 493–516.

Freifeld, K. (2013), "Moody's, S&P and Fitch Accused of Fraud in Run-Up to Financial Crisis," *Huffington Post*, November 11. Available at: http://www.huffingtonpost.com/2013/11/11/moodys-sp-fitch-sued-_n_4255152.html.

Hurtado, P. and C. Condon (2012), "Reserve Fund Jury Finds One Bent Negligent, Clears Others," *Bloomberg.com*, November 13, 2012. Available at: http://www.bloomberg.com/news/2012-11-12/reserve-fund-jury-finds-one-bent-liable-absolves-another-1-.html.

Kozhan, R. and V. Raman (2014), "Short Selling, Financial Crises and Slow-Moving Capital: Evidence from the Corporate Bond Market," Working Paper, May 31, 2014.

Lo, A. (2011), "Reading about the Financial Crisis: A 21-Book Review," Working Paper, Oct. 24. Available at: http://ssrn.com/abstract=1949908.

Mamudi, S (2008), "Firms Stress Calm as Investors Flee to Safety," *Wall Street Journal: Market Watch*, September 18. Available at: http://www.market-watch.com/story/firms-stress-calm-as-investors-flee-to-safety.

Moody's Investors Service Special Comment (2010), "Sponsor Support Key to Money Market Funds," *Moody's*, August 9.

Moyer, L. (2008), "Get Shorty," *Forbes.com*, April 7. Available at: http://www.forbes.com/2008/04/07/trading-regulation-investing-biz-wall-cx_lm_0407lehman.html.

Office of Economic Analysis (2007), "Economic Analysis of the Short Sale Price Restrictions Under the Regulation SHO Pilot," SEC Office of Economic Analysis, February 6. Available at: https://www.sec.gov/news/studies/2007/regshopilot020607.pdf.

Paley, A. and D. Hizenrath (2008), "SEC Chief Defends His Restraint," *The Washington Post*, December 24. Available at: http://www.washington-post.com/wpdyn/content/article/2008/12/23/AR2008122302765_pf.html.

Protess, B. and L. Sebert (2009a), "Under Attack, Credit Raters Turn to the First Amendment," *Huffington Post: Investigative* Fund, October 28. Available at: http://www.publicintegrity.org/2009/10/28/6995/under-attack-credit-raters-turn-first-amendment.

Protess, B. and L. Sebert (2009b), "How Credit Raters Fended Off Oversight From Congress and SEC," *Huffington Post: Investigative Fund*, November 11. Available at: http://eriewire.wordpress.com/2009/11/16/washington-d-c-the-credit-rating-agency-story/.

Pollard, R. B. and T. Perry (2014), "'Grade Incomplete': Examining the Securities and Exchange Commission's attempt to implement credit rating and certain corporate governance reforms of Dodd–Frank," Kelley School of Business Research Paper No. 2014-21. Available at: http://ssrn.com/abstract=2467590.

Reuters (2008), "Lawmaker urges SEC to broaden short sale probe," April 4. Available at: http://www.reuters.com/article/2008/04/04/us-bearstearns-sec-idUSN0428997820080404.

Saporito, B. (2008), "Are Short Sellers to Blame for the Financial Crisis," *Time*, September 18. Available at: http://content.time.com/time/print-out/0,8816,1842499,00.html.

Sasseen, J. (2009), "McCain to Cox: You're Fired!" *Bloomberg Business Week*, September 18. Available at: http://www.businessweek.com/election/2008/blog/archives/2008/09/mccain_to_cox_y.html.

Schroeder, M. (1999), "Bank Regulators, SEC Jockey to Be the New Securities Czar," *The Wall Street Journal*, February 24. Available at: http://cyber.law.harvard.edu/rfi/press/jockey.htm.

Segal, D. (2009), "Ohio Sues Rating Firms for Losses in Funds," *New York Times,* November 20. Available at: http://www.nytimes.com/2009/11/21/business/21ratings.html.

Sirri, E. R. (2009), "Remarks at the National Economists Club: Securities Markets and Regulatory Reform," Speech presented to the US SEC, Washington, DC, April 9. Available at: http://www.sec.gov/news/speech/2009/spch040909ers.htm.

Sirri, E. R. (2010), "Regulatory Politics and Short Selling," *University of Pittsburgh Law Review*, 71: 517–544.

The Federal Reserve System (2005), *The Federal Reserve System Purposes and Functions*, 9th Edition, Board of Governors of the Federal Reserve System. Available at: http://www.federalreserve.gov/pf/pdf/pf_complete.pdf.

Tracy, R. (2014), "Fed Officials Suggest Limiting Banks' Repo Exposure," *Wall Street Journal*, August 13. Available at: http://online.wsj.com/articles/fed-official-suggests-limiting-banks-repo-exposure-1407936002.

US Department of Treasury (2008), "Treasury Announces Temporary Guarantee Program for Money Market Funds," US Department of the Treasury, September 28. Available at: http://www.treasury.gov/press-center/press-releases/Pages/hp1161.aspx.

US Department of Treasury (2010), "Money Market Fund Reform Options," Report of the President's Working Group on Financial Markets, October. Available at: http://www.treasury.gov/press-center/press-releases/Documents/10.21%20PWG%20Report%20Final.pdf.

Regulatory Reform, its Possible Market Consequences and the Case of Securities Financing
— CHAPTER 10

- David Rule
  Bank of England

The financial crisis revealed fundamental weaknesses in pre-crisis bank regulation. The regulatory response internationally has been broad and deep. Whereas before the crisis, regulators struggled to keep up with financial markets innovation, since the crisis banks have struggled to keep up with regulatory innovation. That may continue for another year or so as reforms are finalized and implemented. But the broad shape of the new bank regulatory regime is now clear.

And, as regulators, we should prepare for a period in which financial markets innovation is likely to increase again — both the good kind that improves services for customers and the more ambiguous kind in which firms adjust their activities in response to regulatory constraints. We need to follow these adjustments closely in order to understand the overall effect of regulatory change on banks and financial stability, and

David Rule is Executive Director, Prudential Policy, at the Bank of England. This article is based on remarks given at the Federal Reserve Bank of Chicago's International Banking Conference. He would like to thank Matthew Willison and Antoine Lallour for their contributions.

to identify, and where appropriate address, any unintended consequences. This article explores some of the possible effects, and focus on securities financing transactions as one area where tougher regulation is both needed but might have wider consequences.

A New Regulatory Framework

The new structure of bank capital regulation will comprise three core elements:

- A foundation of loss absorbing capacity, designed to absorb losses when banks fail so that resolution can take place without taxpayer support or huge damage to financial systems and the wider economy;
- A central structure of going concern capital requirements, with significant reforms to improve quality and quantity of capital; and,
- Capital buffers forming a protective roof against rainy days, with higher buffers for systemically-important firms, whose distress would do the most damage, and macroprudential authorities able to increase buffers counter-cyclically when they see storm clouds gathering.

In the UK, as in other jurisdictions, we will also use more than one approach to assess the robustness of this structure — with different approaches likely to bind on different firms, depending on their business models, at different times.

First, the internationally-harmonized Basel risk-weighted ratio, intended to be risk sensitive and, in our view, with some continuing role for firms' internal models where we can be confident that they make use of firms' internal information to improve risk sensitivity in a robust way. That debate continues internationally.

Second, the leverage ratio, which weights assets equally as a safeguard against errors in *ex ante* estimates of risk and prevents excessive balance sheet stretch. In the UK, the Financial Policy Committee (FPC) has recently announced its plans for leverage ratio requirements and buffers.[1]

---

[1] See Bank of England (2014a).

And third stress testing, to assess capital against the impact of macro-economic scenarios of current concern to policymakers, in the UK modelled partly using firms' internal models and partly our models. The results of our first concurrent stress tests of major UK banks and building societies were announced on December 16.[2]

Adjustments

The new bank capital framework will cause banks to hold significantly more capital than the pre-crisis regime. Major UK bank capital requirements and buffers have increased around seven-fold once you take account of tougher definitions of capital, regulatory adjustments to asset valuations and higher risk weights as well as the more obvious increases in headline ratio requirements and buffers.

But, to use the language of micro-economics, this significant change in regulatory capital requirements — the 'relative prices' of different risks — will lead to substitution as well as income effects. Over time, banks will adjust their portfolios to changed capital requirements. The overall extent to which banks are better capitalized and the financial system is more stable will depend on the scale and nature of these adjustments. Any substitution effects are likely to be stronger if regulation is introduced inconsistently across countries. It is important that we continue to seek consistency in implementing internationally-agreed standards.

One adjustment may be a shift in activity from banks to non-banks. That could be beneficial for financial stability: for example, where long-term market-based finance provides an alternative to bank credit. But we must be alert to the development of new forms of shadow banking, meaning substantial maturity transformation and leverage occurring outside the banking system.

The balance of activities may also shift between banks. The post-crisis reforms include additional capital buffers for global systemically important banks (G-SIBs) as well as a proposal for an international standard on total loss-absorbing capacity (or TLAC) for these banks.[3]

---

[2] See Bank of England (2014b).
[3] See Financial Stability Board (2014b).

These changes are intended to move G-SIBs further away from distress and to make orderly resolution possible if, nonetheless, they do fail.

It is possible that tougher regulation of G-SIBs might also encourage them to become less systemically-important over time, perhaps with some shift of activity to smaller banks. At this stage, it is too early to tell. But, in the other direction, there are some signs that higher regulatory requirements might be leading to greater concentration of activity amongst the largest firms in certain markets: for example long-term derivatives. That might be consistent with micro-economic theory. In a model of oligopolistic competition in which some firms invest in their production capacities before others do, the first-movers use this advantage to invest in larger capacities to force later movers to invest in smaller capacities. This translates into larger market shares and, with that, higher profits for the first-movers. As illustrated in Figure 1, an increase in marginal cost could make those smaller firms unprofitable, leading them to exit, while those larger firms remain profitable, resulting in the market becoming more concentrated. In a banking context, one could think of the G-SIBs as being the firms with the larger capacities/market shares and the increase in marginal cost as being due to the increase in capital requirements. Authorities will need to monitor trends in market concentration closely.

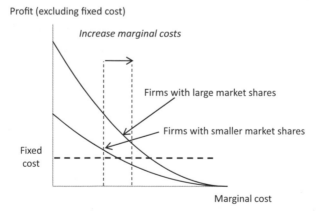

Figure 1. Higher marginal cost and market concentration.

Note: The chart is drawn based on the Stackelberg-Spence-Dixit model described in Chapter 8.2 in Tirole (1988).

Within the scope of their business models, individual banks are also likely to change their mix of activities in response to changing regulatory requirements. Regulators will need to be alert for pure regulatory arbitrage — seeking to change the form but not the economic substance of transactions in order to lower regulatory requirements. We have already seen, for example, transactions seeking to take credit risk in the form of derivatives rather than loans in order to lower the leverage exposure measure.

More legitimately, banks might switch from activities for which risk weights have increased to activities which carry lower risk weights. As illustrated in Figure 2, one might think of a bank choosing an optimal portfolio of assets with different risk-weights subject to the regulatory risk-based capital constraint[4]. An increase in the risk weight on the higher-risk-weighted assets relative to the risk weight on the lower-risk-weighted assets induces a bank to decrease its investment in the higher-risk-weighted assets and increase its investment in the lower-risk-weighted assets. This is analogous to a consumer substituting one good for another when the price of one good increases relative to the price of another.

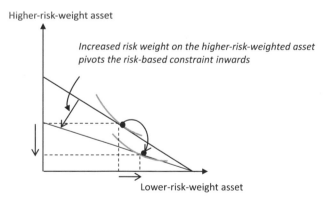

Figure 2. A bank substitutes investment in a lower-risk-weighted asset for investment in a higher-risk-weighted asset when the risk weight for the higher-risk-weighted asset increases.

---

[4] Figures 2 and 3 are based on an approach outlined in Duffie (2013).

The leverage ratio will, however, set an effective floor on the ability of banks to improve their capital position by shifting into low risk-weighted assets, providing a safeguard against uncertainties around our estimates of risk. Conversely, banks for which the leverage ratio is a binding requirement may have incentives to move into higher risk-weighted activities. Figure 3 shows a bank that, if it faced only the risk-based capital constraint, would choose a more highly leveraged portfolio consisting mainly of the lower-risk-weighted asset. The introduction of the leverage constraint — which has a steeper slope than the risk-based constraint because it weights equally assets with different degrees of riskiness — means this portfolio choice is no longer available to the bank. Faced with both constraints, the bank switches to a portfolio with more investment in the higher-risk-weighted asset and less in the low-risk-weighted asset. But the risk-weighted constraint limits the extent of any such risk shifting. In this way, the risk-weighted and leverage ratios should complement one another.

It will be interesting to see how banks allocate capital in a world where they are subject to multiple capital constraints — risk-weighted, leverage and stress test-based. In principle, banks should allocate capital to individual business units based on the marginal capital requirements of those activities to the bank as a whole — so if a bank overall is constrained by risk-weighted capital requirements, it will allocate capital

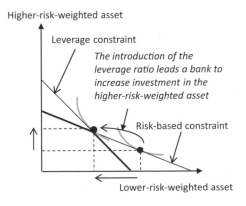

Figure 3. A bank invests more in a higher-risk-weighted asset when facing a binding leverage ratio constraint as well as a risk-weighted capital ratio constraint.

based on risk-weighted assets even to business units for which the leverage ratio or stress test is binding on an individual basis. But as banks move closer to the critical point at which the leverage ratio rather than the risk-weighted ratio becomes binding — an average risk weight of 35% based on a Tier 1 leverage ratio requirement of 3% and risk-weighted requirements and buffers of 8.5%[5] — they will need to be increasingly mindful of both constraints.

The banking system will be substantially better capitalized in future than it was pre-crisis. But regulators will need to follow closely how banks are adapting to tougher bank capital standards and identify any adverse unintended consequences. Those might take the form, for example, of loopholes that provide an opportunity for regulatory arbitrage, an unexpectedly significant impact on financial markets or a conflict with other regulatory priorities, such as shifting derivatives markets towards central clearing. Where appropriate, we will need a snagging process to review and adjust through the international regulatory bodies.

Securities Financing Transactions

One example of a market where tougher regulation was both needed but might have wider consequences is securities financing.

Dealers run large securities financing 'matched books' in which they borrow cash against securities, lend cash against securities, borrow securities against cash, lend securities against cash and borrow securities against other securities. At first hearing, that sounds like a rather point-less daisy chain. But securities financing markets are important (Figure 4). First, reverse repo transactions (short-term cash loans against high-quality bonds) provide money-like assets for risk-averse wholesale investors, like money funds and sovereign reserves managers. As Zoltan Poszar has shown, their demand for money, particularly in US dollars, far outstrips traditional supply in the form of insured bank deposits or Treasury bills (Poszar 2014). Securities financing markets fill the gap. Second, acting as prime brokers, dealers finance the long and short

---

[5] 8.5% is the sum of the 6% minimum Tier 1 to risk-weighted assets ratio plus the 2.5% capital conservation buffer under Basel III.

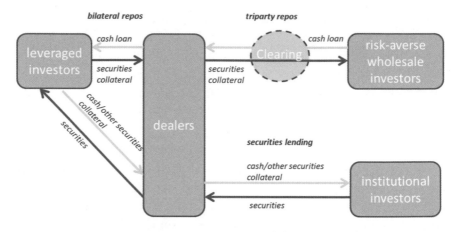

Figure 4. Simplified summary of securities financing market.

positions of leveraged investors such as hedge funds. Third, securities financing markets facilitate the flow of high-quality securities from their underlying beneficial owners, such as pension funds and insurance companies, to banks and dealers which increasingly need to use and reuse them in order to meet regulatory requirements to collateralize their obligations: for example, to other banks and dealers and to central counterparty clearing houses.

Securities financing markets may be important but the financial crisis demonstrated that they can also be fragile. Securities thought to be 'safe' collateral, such as AAA-rated mortgage-backed securities and peripheral European sovereign bonds, became 'risky' collateral. Haircuts on lending against those securities increased (Figure 5). Both the risk-averse money-seeking investors and the leveraged risk-seeking investors on either side of the dealers' balance sheets questioned the liquidity and solvency of many of those dealers. Maturities shortened dramatically until most transactions were at overnight maturities, rolling daily (Gorton *et al.* 2014). Some dealers experienced 'runs'. Financing terms for leveraged investors tightened sharply, causing some to fire sale assets and adding to market instability. In the US, the market infrastructure was flawed, with the daily unwind of tri-party repo transactions relying on massive intra-day financing from private sector clearing banks.

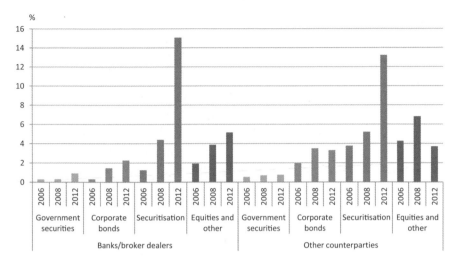

Split by asset class of collateral and by counterparty type.

Figure 5. Average haircuts on securities financing transactions.

Note: Data are based on responses to an FSB quantitative impact study by banks and dealers from a number of countries and uses actual transaction data. Details regarding this dataset are available at http://www.financialstabilityboard.org/wp-content/uploads/r_141013b.pdf.
Source: Financial Stability Board

Since the crisis, regulators have addressed many of the underlying problems of excessive leverage and maturity transformation:

a. Securities financing transactions are included in the internationally-agreed leverage exposure measure adopted by the Basel Committee[6]. Leverage ratio requirements will put prudent limits on the size of dealers' matched books.

b. They are also included in the Basel Committee's measures to address liquidity risks. The recently-announced Net Stable Funding Ratio[7] will require short-term secured loans to financial and non-financial borrowers to be backed by at least 10% stable funding. And supervisors

---

[6] See Bank for International Settlements (2014a).
[7] See Bank for International Settlements (2104b).

can use the Liquidity Coverage Ratio[8], as we have been doing for some time in the UK, to require dealers to hold liquid assets against prime brokerage risks such as withdrawal of cash margin by hedge fund clients.

c. The Financial Stability Board has agreed minimum haircuts[9] in order to limit the leverage that non-banks can obtain through borrowing cash against private sector securities. These haircut floors have deliberately been set at 'backstop' levels designed to prevent excess in times of market exuberance while allowing room for prudent firms to do their own risk management.

d. The US authorities have taken steps to strengthen the tri-party infrastructure.

The reforms are not yet complete. One important missing ingredient is data collection to monitor market trends more closely. For example, the authorities need to understand the composition of the collateral being used across key financial markets in order to identify concentrations. The financial crisis showed the risks associated with a market-wide margin call when widely-used collateral is subject to an unexpected common price shock. Data is also needed to track the terms of transactions, including maturity and haircuts. One interesting idea is for regulators to run exercises in which they ask prime brokers to calculate portfolio haircuts against archetypal leveraged portfolios. The aims would be both to track any loosening in market-wide standards over time and to spot outlier dealers that require lower haircuts than their competitors.

These significant regulatory reforms will have consequences for the behavior of dealers and investors in securities financing markets. Some market participants may seek ways around the new regulations: for example, there has been talking about dealers 'renting' balance sheet from other market participants or establishing off-balance sheet financing vehicles. The flipsides of more resilient dealers and markets in periods of stress may well be less leverage, less maturity transformation

---

[8] See Bank for International Settlements (2013).
[9] See Financial Stability Board (2014a).

and lower dealer inventories in more normal periods. The balance is not easy to strike; we may need to readjust our approach as we learn.

But the goal of these reforms is clear: to make securities financing markets resilient. Robust securities financing markets should help to stabilize rather than destabilize the financial system in the face of shocks. The reduction in dealer inventories has attracted a lot of comment, with questions about whether they will be willing and able to provide liquidity as market makers in falling markets on the same scale as in the past. But the role of dealers in providing stable financing to leveraged investors may be equally important. Those investors may be the most likely to see a market crash as a buying opportunity — but only if they are not over-leveraged and have access to borrowing from financially-sound dealers. Put another way, we want dealers and leveraged investors to be providers not demanders of liquidity in a crisis.

References

Gorton, G B, Metrick, A, and Xie, L. (2014), "The Flight From Maturity". National Bureau of Economic Research Working Paper #20027, 2014.

Poszar, Z. (2014), "Shadow banking: the money view", *Office of Financial Research Working Paper No.14-04*.

Tirole, J. (1988), *The Theory of Industrial Organization* (MIT Press: Cambridge, MA).

Bank of England (2014a), "The Financial Policy Committee's Review of the Leverage Ratio," Financial Policy Committee, October. Available at: http://www.bankofengland.co.uk/financialstability/Documents/fpc/fs_lrr.pdf.

Bank of England (2014b), "Stress testing the UK banking system: 2014 results", Financial Policy Committee, December. Available at: http://www.bankofengland.co.uk/financialstability/Documents/fpc/results161214.pdf.

Financial Stability Board (2014a), *Strengthening Oversight and Regulation of Shadow Banking: Regulatory framework for haircuts on non-centrally cleared securities financing transactions*, October 14. Available at: http://www.financialstabilityboard.org/publications/r_141013a.pdf.

Financial Stability Board (2014b), *Adequacy of Loss-Absorbing Capacity of Global Systemically Important Banks in Resolution*, November 10. Available at: http://www.financialstabilityboard.org/wp-content/uploads/TLAC-Condoc-6-Nov-2014-FINAL.pdf.

Bank for International Settlements (2013), "Basel III: The Liquidity Coverage Ratio and liquidity risk monitoring tools," Basel Committee on Banking Supervision, January. Available at: http://www.bis.org/publ/bcbs238.pdf.

Bank for International Settlements (2014a), "Basel III Leverage Ratio Framework and Disclosure Requirements," Basel Committee on Banking Supervision, January. Available at: http://www.bis.org/publ/bcbs270.pdf.

Bank for International Settlements (2104b), "Basel III: The net stable funding ratio," Basel Committee on Banking Supervision, October. Available at: http://www.bis.org/bcbs/publ/d295.pdf.

Duffie, D (2013), 'Capital requirements with robust risk weights', presentation at the Brookings Institute October 31, 2013.

Part IV
Resolving Systemically Important Financial Institutions and Markets

A Critical Evaluation of Bail-in as a Bank Recapitalization Mechanism
— CHAPTER 11

- Charles Goodhart and Emilios Avgouleas
  London School of Economics and *University of Edinburgh*

Introduction

The scale of losses flowing from bank failures is initially independent of the identity of those upon whom the burden of meeting that loss falls. But, such losses also can then entail critical externalities. These have traditionally justified the public bailouts to avoid the systemic threat that the failure of any bank beyond a certain size carries with it.

Nevertheless, public bailouts of banks are a source of moral hazard and they undermine market discipline. One of the key principles of a free market economy is that owners and creditors are supposed to bear the losses of a failed venture. Bailouts can also have a destabilizing impact on public finances and sovereign debt, with UK and Irish finances being held as illustrative examples of the impact of such costs.[1]

Charles Goodhart is Emeritus Professor of Banking and Finance with the Financial Markets Group at the London School of Economics; Emilios Avgouleas is Professor (Chair) of International Banking Law and Finance at the University of Edinburgh.
[1] This is a nearly undisputable argument against bailouts and it is not contested in this paper. However, bailout costs cannot be accurately measured unless the costs of the alternative: instability, are also counted (Dewatripont 2014).

These concerns have given rise to reforms to internalize the costs of bank failure of which the foremost is the drawing up of bank creditor bail-ins. Essentially, bail-in constitutes a radical rethinking of who bears the ultimate costs of the operation of fractional reserve banking.

A great momentum has built up for basing resolution on bail-in, which sometimes resembles a 'chorus' (wording used in McAndrews et al. 2014, p. 14). The regulatory authorities in most of the world's developed economies have developed, or are in the process of developing, resolution regimes that allow, in principle, banks to fail without resorting to public funding.

The bail-in approach is intended to counter the dual threat of systemic disruption and sovereign over-indebtedness. It is based on the penalty principle, namely, that the costs of bank failures are shifted to where they best belong: bank shareholders and creditors. Namely, bail-in replaces the public subsidy with private penalty (Huertas 2013) or with private insurance (KPMG 2012; Gordon and Ringe 2014) forcing banks to internalize the cost of risks which they assume.

In these new schemes, apart from the shareholders, the losses of bank failure are to be borne by ex-ante (or ex-post) funded resolution funds, financed by industry levies, and certain classes of bank creditors whose fixed debt claims on the bank will be converted to equity, thereby restoring the equity buffer needed for on-going bank operation.

This is an important development, since in the past banks' subordinated debt did not provide any cover when bank liquidation was not an option, which meant that subordinated creditors were bailed out alongside senior creditors by taxpayers (Gleeson 2012). This led to creditor inertia.

Turning unsecured debt into bail-in-able debt should incentivize creditors to resume a monitoring function, thereby helping to restore market discipline. For example, as the potential costs of bank failure would fall on creditors, in addition to shareholders, such creditors should become more alert about the levels of leverage the bank carries (Coffee 2011), limiting one of the most likely causes of bank failures and the governance costs associated with excessive leverage (Admati et al. 2013; Avgouleas and Cullen 2015). Normally, shareholders have every incentive to build leverage to maximize their return on equity (Admati et al. 2012; Avgouleas and Cullen 2014).

Such monitoring might, in turn, reduce the scale of loss in the event of a bank failure: creditors could force the bank to behave more cautiously, especially where the bail-in regime allows for earlier intervention and closure than a bail-out mechanism. It should also, in principle, eliminate the 'too-big-to-fail' subsidy enjoyed by bigger banks.

Essentially, bail-in provisions mean that, to a certain extent, a pre-planned contract replaces the bankruptcy process giving greater certainty (Coffee 2011) as regards the sufficiency of funds to cover bank losses and facilitating early recapitalization. Moreover, the bail-in tool can be used to keep the bank as a going concern and avoid disruptive liquidation or dismembering of the financial institution in distress.

But the idea that the penalty for failure can be shifted onto an institution, such as a bank, is incorrect. Ultimately all penalties, and similarly benefits, have to be absorbed by individuals, not inanimate institutions. When it is said that the bank will pay the penalty of failure, this essentially means that the penalty is paid, in the guise of worsened terms, by bank managers, bank staff, bank creditors or borrowers. The real question is which individuals will be asked to absorb the cost.

The goals of the bail-in process are not the same in every jurisdiction. In the United States the process through which bail-in and subsequent conversion of creditor claims takes place for SIFIs is imbedded in the mechanics and architecture of the resolution process that is applied to systemically important institutions, the so-called Orderly Liquidation Authority (OLA) of Title II of the Dodd–Frank Wall Street Reform and Consumer Protection Act of 2010. This means that triggering the bail-in process under Title II aims at providing with sufficient capital the entities that will emerge following liquidation of the resolved parent institution (see Section I below).

In the European Union, on the other hand, the doom-loop between bank instability and sovereign indebtedness has left Eurozone governments with a major conundrum. The traditional route of a public bail-out is increasingly ruled out, not only due to a principled adherence to the avoidance of moral hazard, but also due to its potential impact on already heavily indebted countries. To answer this challenge, the Eurozone has established the European Stability Mechanism (ESM) to act, amongst other purposes, as an essential component of the European Banking Union (EBU). Both the ESM statute and the new EU

Resolution regime based on the forthcoming EU Bank Recovery and Resolution Directive (BRRD) require the prior participation of bank creditors in meeting the costs of bank resolution. This means that either the bank remains a going concern and the bail-in process is triggered to effect bank recapitalization to restore it to health ('open bank' bail-in process) or in conjunction with the exercise of resolution powers treating the bank as gone concern ('closed bank' bail-in process). This contrasts with DFA's approach to SIFI resolution, further discussed below, where only the second approach is used. This bifurcation is likely to prove problematic.[2]

Similarly, the intention is that intervention will be sooner (forbearance less), so that losses will be less, but whether that hope will be justified is yet to be seen. We discuss this further in Section II below.

The desire to find an effective way to replace the public subsidy and the unpopular bailout process is entirely understandable and can lead to welfare enhancing outcomes. At the same, time, there is a danger of over-reliance on bail-ins, in part owing to the growing momentum for its introduction. One useful role for an academic is to query contemporary enthusiasm for fear of group-think, which the last crisis has shown may prove a dangerous aspect of policy-making in the financial sector. In placing bail-in at the heart of bank resolution regimes, legislators and regulatory authorities ought not to overlook some important shortcomings attached to this approach. This paper sets out to discuss these shortcomings and to explain why, arguably, bail-in regimes will not remove, in the case of resolution of a large complex cross-border bank, (unless the risk is idiosyncratic, for example fraud), or in the event of a systemic crisis, the need for public injection of funds. In our analysis we particularly focus on BRRD's distinction between the resolution

---

[2] Notably, although both the US and the European authorities are moving simultaneously towards reliance on bail-in mechanisms, we are struck by how little attention appears to be paid in each to the detail of what the other is doing. It is instructive that in the FRBNY Special Issue on 'Large and Complex Banks' (2014), the papers by McAndrews *et al.* (2014) and Sommer (2014) hardly mention Basel III, the EU Bank Recovery and Resolution Directive (BRRD) or any European initiative. Equally much of the discussion within Europe on its own resolution mechanisms ignores the DFA, and looks inwards.

of banks that have become bankrupt ('gone concern'), from the recapitalization (also as part of the resolution regime) of banks that have become so fragile as to need intervention and recapitalization, but are not (yet) bankrupt, ('going concern'). Although this distinction is hallowed in the literature, we argue that it may be less clear-cut in practice than is sometimes suggested.

The Architecture of the Bail-in Process

Bank Resolution and Bank Bail-in Under the Dodd Frank Act (DFA)

Overview

Under section 204(a) (1) of the Dodd–Frank Act creditors and shareholders bear all the losses of the financial company that has entered OLA. This is in accord with one of the Act's explicit aims, as stated in its preamble: "to protect the American taxpayer by ending bailouts." To this effect, Title II of the Dodd–Frank Act provides the FDIC with new powers to resolve SIFIs. Under OLA, the FDIC may be appointed receiver for any US financial company that meets specified criteria when resolution under the US Bankruptcy Code (or other relevant insolvency process) would be likely to create systemic instability.

In order to make group resolution effective and to minimize systemic disruption, the FDIC has decided that it will follow the Single Point of Entry approach (SPOE) (FDIC 2013), which is the final step in the implementation of the 'source-of-strength' doctrine (enshrined in section 616(d) of the DFA). In the event of bank failure the top-tier holding company will have to enter into receivership and attendant losses will be borne by the holding company's shareholders and unsecured creditors. Section 210(a)(1)(M) of the Act provides that the FDIC, as the receiver for a covered financial company, succeeds by operation of law to all the rights, titles, powers, and privileges possessed by, inter alia, the creditors of the resolved and all rights and claims that the stockholders and creditors of the resolved institution may have against its assets are terminated, but for their right to receive payment under the provisions of section 210. The FDIC would then form a bridge holding company ('NewCo')[3] and transfer the failed holding company's ownership of healthy operating subsidiaries into it, leaving the holding company shareholders and creditors behind in the estate of the failed holding company. Operating subsidiaries that face no solvency problem will be transferred to the new solvent entity or entities (NewCo).

Section 210 requires the FDIC to conduct a claims process and establish a claims priority pyramid for the satisfaction of claims against the resolved entity without the use of taxpayer funds. At the conclusion of this process claims against the receivership would be satisfied through a debt-for-securities exchange in accordance with their priority under section 210 through the issuance of debt and equity in the new holding company.

Prior to the exchange of securities for claims, the FDIC would determine the value of the bridge financial company based upon a valuation performed by the consultants selected by the board of the bridge financial company. Yet the FDIC has stated that it expects "shareholders' equity, subordinated debt and a substantial portion of the unsecured liabilities of the holding company — with the exception of essential vendors' claims — to remain as claims against the receivership" (FDIC 2013).

This is essentially the bail-in process under Title II, which aims at giving the NewCo what is essentially a clean bill of health rather than turning unsecured creditors into NewCo shareholders. OLA's bail-in process will be utilized to resolve the holding company ('closed bank' process), although the operating subsidiaries remain unaffected, and, thus, it differs from the BRRD approach that provides, in addition, the option to use an 'open bank' bail-in process.

By establishing the bridge financial company with significant assets of the parent holding company and many fewer liabilities, it is hoped that the bridge financial company would have a strong balance sheet that would put it in a good position to borrow money from customary market sources. The FDIC has indicated that contingent value rights,

---

[3] "The term 'bridge financial company' means a new financial company organized by the Corporation in accordance with section 210(h) for the purpose of resolving a covered financial company." (Dodd–Frank, Title II, Section 201 (3)).

such as warrants or options allowing the purchase of equity in the new holding company or other instruments, might be issued to enable funding the transition/resolution (FDIC 2013). If there are shortfalls or these sources of funding are not readily available, the SPOE approach offers the benefit of FDIC's access to the Orderly Liquidation Fund (OLF), provided that borrowings from the fund can be fully secured and repaid. Any costs incurred by the FDIC as the appointed receiver or other public authority which cannot be covered by the above will be recovered from the industry.

The bail-in approach is not new in US bank resolution practice. For example, in 2008, the FDIC exercised its existing powers and resolved the part of the Washington Mutual group that was not sold to JP Morgan Chase, mainly claims by equity holders and creditors, under the least-cost resolution method. It imposed serious losses on the unsecured creditors and uninsured depositors (deposit amount above US$ 100,000).[4] OLA further expands the resolution authority of FDIC, including its power to cherry-pick which assets and liabilities to transfer to a third party, (though these will be subject to strict conditions to be further detailed by the FDIC) and to treat similarly situated creditors differently, e.g., favoring short-term creditors over long-term creditors or favoring operating creditors over lenders or bondholders. This discretion is curbed by the introduction of a safeguard that creditors are entitled to receive at least what they would have received if liquidation had taken place under Chapter 7 of the Bankruptcy Code (comparable to the 'best interests of creditors' test under the Bankruptcy Code).

Evaluation

Although TARP and other forms of direct bank capitalization by the US Treasury during the 2008 crisis did not prove to be loss-making, the issue of moral hazard and principled opposition to a private company receiving public assistance in bankruptcy means that one of DFA's key rationales is exclusion of bailouts. Thus, as mentioned earlier, OLA

---

[4] FDIC Press Release, "Information for Claimants in Washington Mutual Bank" (September 29, 2008), at http://www.fdic.gov/news/news/press/2008/pr08085b.html.

treats the holding company as a bankrupt (gone) concern. There may, however, be some caveats.

First, the dismemberment of the parent holding company, in order to provide the necessary funding for the recapitalization of the operating banking subsidary(ies) may have reputational impact on the entire group, including the (seemingly unaffected) operating subsidiaries.

For example, Bank XYZ Holding Co. liquidation will inevitably be accompanied by round the clock media coverage. It is hard to imagine what that would mean to the ordinary bank depositor and financial consumer. It is very likely that they will assume that Bank XYZ (operational) is also endangered. One reasonable remedy would be to have the names of the holding company, and the operational subsidiary(ies), separated (ring-fenced), but deciding which part of the group gets which (name) will be an issue with potential consequences for franchise value. Also such name separation may not work, as it would not be very hard for the media to explain to ordinary depositors and consumers that it is the parent company of XYZ has entered into liquidation. A further route would be to conduct OLA in utter secrecy and just announce the parent's liquidation once the process has been concluded. But stock exchange rule implications, notices to affected bank creditors, potential litigation, and the structure of OLA itself in DFA, which involves so many stakeholders, makes such a 'secrecy' approach impossible.

Could the subsidiary bank, with help from the authorities, really handle the reputational fall-out?[5] Historical evidence of reputational contagion, e.g. in the case of certain solvent subsidiaries of BCCI, would suggest that this could be a real danger. If such depositor flight should then occur, the Central Bank (or in the USA the Orderly Liquidation Fund) might have to pump in large amounts of liquidity. While this would be protected by seniority and collateral, the previous buffer represented by the holding company's capital would, at least initially, no longer be there. So a large portion of the operating company's continuing liabilities might come either from the Central Bank (or OLF) or be backed by the deposit insurance fund.

---

[5] No doubt the resolution would have to be accompanied by a careful communication strategy, but the example of Northern Rock shows how this can go wrong.

The second question is about the speed of rebuilding the capital structure of the new holding company (HoldCo) after the bankruptcy of the initial holding company. While bail-in is not taken in isolation but is part of a restructuring process under which management is replaced and group business restructured, if the new HoldCo's capital structure is not rapidly rebuilt, one would be left with an initially thinly capitalized operating bank (Sommer 2014) plus large public sector liabilities. The government cannot force private sector buyers to purchase new equity and (subordinated) debt in a new HoldCo, and the prior experience would make private buyers wary. Certainly the authorities could require the operating bank to retain all earnings, (e.g., no dividends, buy-backs, etc.), but in a generalized financial crisis, it could take a long time to regenerate a new holding company by building up retained earnings. Of course, the authorities could massively expedite the process by injecting new capital into a new HoldCo, (with the aim of selling off such equity later back to the private sector), but that would just be another form of bail-out. While the HoldCo proposal has been carefully worked out in its initial stage, what is less clear is what might then happen in the convalescent period.

The third question is about costs to the rest of the sector of rolling over maturing 'bail-inable' debt, once it has been announced that losses have been imposed on XYZ Holdings' creditors (holders of bail-inable debt) in the event of XYZ's failure. The cost of such debt could spike and HoldCos might be tempted to let their own buffers slip below the required level. Of course regulatory authorities could impose sanctions in such cases. But in doing so they will have to consider the impact of rising funding costs to the sector, both in terms of operating costs and in terms of solvency if such intervention takes place, as is likely, in a recessionary economic climate or worse during a generalized bank asset crisis.

The fourth question relates to the interaction between the DFA approach and the Basel III capital requirements, which appear to necessitate an earlier intervention approach than DFA's OLA. Under the latter, the authorities should intervene to resolve a bank whenever its core tier 1 equity falls below 4.5% of Risk Weighted Assets. A bank with CT1E between 0 and 4.5% is not formally insolvent, i.e., it is still 'going', rather than 'gone', concern. It is to be hoped that regulators would intervene in a failing bank before the formal insolvency point is reached. But then they would not be able to bail-in senior unsecured debtors under the 'no creditor worse off' (NCWO) condition. Either all the debt in the HoldCo, comprising subordinated debt or contingent capital instruments (Co-Cos), would have to be designated as bail-in-able, which could have a considerable effect on bank funding costs, or the authorities could just not take pre-emptive action, disregarding the Basel III requirement. Either route might prove problematic.

NY Federal Reserve staff express the opinion that US authorities will disregard the Basel III requirement (of earlier intervention/recapitalization) (McAndrews *et al.* (2014), and go on to state that "[t]he resolution authority in our model is 'slow' in the sense that it will shut down and resolve a firm only once its (book) equity capital is exhausted" (McAndrews *et al.* 2014, p. 5, also p. 15 and footnote 16 therein). Perhaps because the costs of such a slow response are recognized, McAndrews *et al.* express a preference for specially designed 'bail-ina-ble' debt to an equivalent amount of extra equity (McAndrews *et al.* 2014, section 4, pp. 14–23). Subordinated debt issued ex ante and specially designed by contract to absorb losses via conversion or writing down of principal (called hereinafter D bail-inable debt) is essentially a form of pre-paid insurance for bank failure. As such it has specific advantages and costs. Some of the advantages might remain unproven.

McAndrews *et al.* suggest that the existence of sufficient D bail-inable debt would force earlier intervention by the authorities, before all the loss-making buffer had been eaten away. But if the trigger for intervention is to be book value insolvency, it will still be applied far too late to be optimal. If intervention is to be triggered earlier, prior to book value insolvency, the bank is not legally a 'gone concern', making the satisfaction of NCWO principle problematic. At this stage, it remains unclear how US authorities intend to resolve this conundrum.

The FDIC-BoE Approach to Resolving G-SIFIs and Bail-in

Dodd-Frank explicitly authorizes coordination with foreign authorities to take action to resolve those institutions whose collapse threatens financial stability (Title II, section 210, N). A heat-map exercise conducted by US regulators determined that the operations of U.S. SIFIs are concentrated in a relatively small number of jurisdictions, particularly the United Kingdom (UK) — Gruenpeng (Chairman, Federal Deposit Insurance Corporation) 2012. Thus, the US and UK authorities proceeded to examine potential impediments to efficient resolutions and on a cooperative basis explored methods of resolving them.

This culminated in the joint discussion paper published by the Bank of England (BOE) and the Federal Deposit Insurance Corporation (FDIC) titled, *Resolving Globally Active, Systemically Important, Financial Institutions* comparing the resolution regime established by Dodd Frank Act Title II to the resolution powers of the UK's Prudent Regulation Authority (PRA). To this effect the two authorities have proposed that they will adopt the single 'point of entry' (SPOE) approach, when appropriate,[6] in the resolution of G-SIFIs.

The main implication of the SPOE approach to resolution is that G-SIFIs would have to put in place:

- a group structure based on a parent holding company (HoldCo);
- the ring-fencing of (domestic and overseas) subsidiaries that undertake critical economic activities, so that the continuity of these activities can be more easily maintained in a resolution;
- Issuance of bail-inable debt by the holding company to enable the group to be recapitalised in a resolution through the conversion of this debt into equity;
- Holding company debt will be used to make loans to subsidiaries, so that subsidiaries can be supported in a resolution through writing off these loans.

Although initially a group taken into resolution would be 'owned' by the FDIC (in the US) or, perhaps, under a trustee arrangement (in the UK), the intention is that the group would be returned to private ownership, with the creditors whose debt is converted into equity

---

[6] The joint Paper recognizes that multiple point of entry (MPE) may be more appropriate in some cases of complex cross-border banks.

becoming the new owners of the group. Both the BRRD and the UK Financial Services (Banking Reform) Act 2013, implementing government's plans to introduce, with modifications, the Vickers' Report recommendations, include requirements that banks have sufficient capital and debt in issue to make them resolvable using bail-in or other resolution tools.

Under the HoldCo approach the continuity of critical economic activities is preserved because — in most cases — the subsidiaries of the holding company should be able to continue in operation, either because they have remained solvent and viable, or because they can be recapitalized through the writing down of intra-group loans made from the holding company to its subsidiaries. A subsidiary would need to be resolved independently only where it had suffered large losses.

Under the FDIC-BoE joint paper, in the UK the equity and debt of a resolved holding company would be held initially by a trustee, though the BRRD now provides alternative methods as well (Arts 47, 48, 50). The trustee would hold these securities during a valuation period. The valuation is undertaken to assess the extent to which the size of the losses already incurred by the firm or expected to be incurred can be ascertained in order to determine the extent of required recapitalization. Namely, valuation of losses determines the extent to which creditor claims should be written down and converted. During this period, listing of the company's equity securities (and potentially debt securities) would be suspended.

Once the amount of required recapitalization has been determined, an announcement of the final terms of the bail-in would be made to the previous security holders. On completion of the exchange the trustee would transfer the equity to the original creditors. Creditors unable to hold equity securities (e.g. because they cannot legally hold equity shares) will be able to request the trustee to sell the equity securities on their behalf. The trust would then be dissolved and the equity securities of the firm would resume trading.

We discuss the additional questions raised by cross-border banking, which, however, will be the norm for most SIFIs and by definition for GSIFIs, in Appendix A.

The European Approach

Bail-in is a pre-condition for bank resolution in the EU and for (ultimately) ESM implemented bank recapitalization within the Eurozone. In a nutshell before a Member State is allowed to tap ESM resources for direct recapitalization of a failing bank, a round of bail-in and national contributions must have taken place. National regulators must first impose initial losses representing at least 8% of the bank's liabilities on shareholders and creditors (Articles 44(5)&(7), 37(10)(a), Recital 73, BRRD) before they can use the national resolution fund to absorb losses or to inject fresh capital into an institution, and then only up to 5% of the bank's liabilities. In the event that bank losses exceed 13% of its liabilities, a further bail-in round may take place in order for the residual losses to be absorbed by creditors and non-guaranteed and non- preferred depositors before public money and then ESM funds are used. These conditions make ESM assistance an absolute last resort in order both to counter moral hazard and to allay any fears of de facto mutualization of liability for bank rescues in the Eurozone.[7] It is clear that the EU holds high hopes about the effectiveness of this mechanism, an approximation to which has already been tried in Cyprus in March 2013[8] and for the restructuring of the Spanish banking sector.[9] It is also

---

[7] Use of ESM funds when a bank public bail-out proves to be necessary is subject to a number of strict conditions. The ESM may intervene directly only at the request of a Member State stating that it is unable to provide the requisite funds on its own without endangering the sustainability of its public finances or its market access. The relevant institution will also have to be a systemic bank, and the difficulties it faces must threaten the euro zone's financial stability. The ESM takes action only jointly with this Member State, which ensures that countries have an incentive to curb the use of public funds as far as possible. See Arts 1–3 of ESM Guideline on Financial Assistance for the Recapitalisation of Financial Institutions.

[8] While the Cypriot case was very different, given the absence of the resolution tools provided by the BRRD, we feel that its implementation gave important further momentum to the adoption of bail-in processes.

[9] Under the terms of bankruptcy reorganization of Bankia and of four other Spanish banks, and in accordance with the conditions of the July 2012 Memorandum of Understanding between the Troika (EC, ECB, and IMF) and Spain, over 1 million

hoped that bail-in will nullify the need for state aid for the banking sector across the EU and not just within the confines of the Eurozone (Angeloni and Lennihan 2014).

The BRRD allows for group resolution, but resolution at the legal entity level might prove the default position. Yet the legal entity by legal entity approach raises its own set of difficult issues. In the case of non-EBU groups, resolution colleges might smooth co-ordination issues but, a bail-in decision has distributional consequences, potentially with clear losers. So in some cases it might even create a crisis of confidence in a member state's banking system, and strong disagreements are bound to arise as to which subsidiary is bailed-in and which is not. Where there are subsidiaries in non-EBU European countries such disagreements could even go as far as creating serious problems in the relationship of the EBU with non-EBU European countries, especially where losses are bound to fall unevenly.[10]

Another significant challenge that the EU approach to bail-in raises is the aforementioned issue of liquidity support from resolution funds and central banks. This could be provided either to each legal entity, against the collateral available to that entity, or channeled through a parent company. In either case, if that happens within the Eurozone, all liquidity funding from the central banks would eventually have to be booked on the ECB's balance sheet, at least until the bank is successfully restructured.

---

small depositors became Bankia shareholders after they had been sold '*preferentes*' (preferred stock) in exchange for their deposits (FROB, July & Dec. 2012). Following the conversion, the *preferentes* took an initial write-down of 30–70%, which became much wider when the value of Bankia shares eventually collapsed (originally valued at EUR 2 per share, which was further devalued to EUR 0.1 after the March 2013 restructuring of Bankia. Bankia Press Release, "BFA-Bankia expects to culminate recapitalization in May" March 2013, available at http://www.bankia.com/en/communication/in-the-news/news/bfa-bankia-expects-to-culminate-recapitalisation-in-may.html.

[10] See on this point Charles Randell, "The Tale of Two Banks" paper presented in the LSE Conference 'Managing and Financing European Bank Resolution and discussant's comment by Emilios Avgouleas both available at http://www.systemicrisk.ac.uk/sites/default/files/media/%28Final%29-24th%20March%20programme%20-%20Managing%20and%20financing%20European%20bank%20resolution.pdf.

Problems of Bail-in for a "Going Concern" Bank

Effective Liquidation Substitute?

While OLA provides for the liquidation of the bank holding company, it uses bail-in to leave operating subsidiaries unaffected. The EU, on the other hand, has an 'open' bank resolution process that is reliant on the successful bail-in of the ailing bank. So both jurisdictions view the bail-in process as a substitute to liquidation of either the entire group or of parts of the group, combined of course with the use of other resolution tools. This is not an unreasonable approach, especially in the case of a largely idiosyncratic cause of failure, e.g., fraud. But there are four essential conditions that have to be met when using the bail-in process as a resolution substitute: timing, market confidence, the extent of restructuring required, and accurate determination of losses.

First, the issue of when to trigger the bail-in process, taking also into account the requirements of early intervention regimes is matter of cardinal importance. Identification of the right time and conditions to trigger the bail-in tool in a process that extends conversion beyond specially designed bail-able debt will be one of the most important for any bank supervisor. The reasoning leading to supervisors' decision will much resemble first and second order problems in mathematics and logic. If the supervisor triggers bail-in early, then the full measure of losses may not have been fully revealed, risking further rounds of bail-in. But if the supervisor determines to use the bail-in tool at a later stage, when the full scale of losses to be imposed on creditors is revealed, they risk a flight of bank creditors who do not hold D bail-able debt.

Moreover, speed of resolution/recapitalization (albeit at the expense of flexibility) is one of the reasons for the popularity of bail-in among regulators (Sommer 2014). Yet, we doubt whether the adoption of bail-in regimes would lead to earlier regulatory intervention than under the bail-out regimes. The aforementioned paper by McAndrews *et al.* reinforce our view that legal concerns about imposing potentially large losses on private creditors could unduly delay resolution, perhaps until the last possible minute. By then the liabilities needed to be written down could extend beyond HoldCo's specially designated bail-inable debt. Bail-out, being undertaken by the authority of the government, is, we would argue, somewhat less liable to legal suit than bail-in. On the other hand, bail-in of bank liabilities that extends beyond D bail-able debt affects a wider range of creditors; there are more parties to the negotiation, and hence that may be more protracted.

In our view, the more delayed will be the onset of Resolution, the more essential it will be to put more emphasis on an earlier Recovery phase. There are also other concerns. In the absence of a fiscal backstop for other parts of the financial system, if bail-in is triggered before measures have been taken to buttress the rest of the financial system a creditor flight from other banks will be certain, spreading the tremors throughout the financial system, even if those banks retain sufficient amounts of D bail-in able debt. Timothy Geithner (2014, p. 306) has eloquently explained this situation:

> "The overwhelming temptation [in a crisis] is to let the most egregious firms fail, to put them through a bankruptcy-type process like the FDIC had for community banks and then haircut their bondholders. But unless you have the ability to backstop every other systemic firm that's in a similar position, you'll just intensify fears of additional failures and haircuts."

Secondly, market confidence in the bailed-in institution would have to be quickly restored in order to preserve franchise value and repay official liquidity support (Sommer 2014). As mentioned in section B(1)(b) above this is mostly dependent on how fast the capital structure of the requisite bank (or the new bank in the event of a 'closed' bank process) is rebuilt. If the institution has entered into a death spiral with customers, creditors and depositors fast disappearing reversing the trend would doubtlessly prove a task of daunting proportions.

Thirdly, triggering the bail-in process will prove unsuccessful if bank losses are not properly identified in some finite form. The determination of bank losses including unrealized future losses must be accurately determined in order to avoid successive rounds of bail-in losses accruing to bank creditors. This might in fact prove a challenging task. For example, bank losses in the recent crisis have consistently been underestimated.

Normally bank failures occur when macro-economic conditions have worsened, and asset values are falling. Bank failures during boom conditions, e.g., resulting from fraud, such as Barings, are easier to handle with less danger of contagion. In the uncertain conditions of generalized asset value declines, the new (incoming) accountants, employed by the resolution agency, are likely to take a bad scenario (or even a worst case) as their base case for identifying losses, to be borne by the bailed-in creditors, partly also to minimize the above-mentioned danger of underestimation leading to further calls on creditors. Previously the auditors of the failing bank itself will have been encouraged (by management) to take a more positive view of its (going concern) value. Thus the transition to bail-in is likely to lead to a huge discontinuity, a massive drop, in published accounting valuations. This could put into question amongst the general public the existing valuations of other banks, and lead, possibly rapidly, to a contagious crisis, on which we add more below.

Moreover, restructuring should extend to the underlying business model, which led the bank to bankruptcy in the first place, to avoid several bail-in rounds in the future.

Who Meets the Burden?

Overview

In general, banks have three types of creditors:

(1) Banking creditors: including retail and wholesale depositors, needing to use the provision by the bank of payment and custody services;
(2) Investment business creditors: including swap counterparties, trading counterparties, and those with similar claims from trading activity such as exchanges, clearing systems and other investment business counterparties (including repo counterparties);
(3) Financial creditors: comprising long term creditors of the bank, including bondholders and other long-term unsecured finance providers (Clifford Chance 2011).

When banking groups are resolved only the third type of creditors should be affected by bail-in, since banking creditors and investment business creditors will most likely hold claims against unaffected operating subsidiaries. This is, however, not the case where, under the EU approach, resolution is undertaken either at the group land egal entity levels. Under the BRRD business creditors may be exempted, through pre-designed "carve-outs". It is not inconceivable that this exemption may in certain cases result in a disproportionate shift of the burden of bail-in onto other classes of creditors such as bondholders and unprotected depositors.

Arguably, in contrast to bail-outs, where all the taxpayers are, in some sense, domestic constituents, an advantage of bail-in is that some creditors may be foreign, but this is an elusive and possibly false advantage. The aim to penalize Russian creditors of Cypriot banks might have played a significant role in the way that 'rescue' was structured. Similarly the treatment of the creditors of Icelandic banks was organized in such a way as to give preference to domestic depositors over foreign bondholders[11]. But the foreign investors would, of course, realize that they were in effect being targeted, so that they would both require a higher risk premium and flee more quickly at the first sign of potential trouble. The result is likely to be that a larger proportion of bank bondholders will be other (non-bank) financial intermediaries of the same country, providing a further small ratchet to the balkanization and localization of the banking system. In any case, the BRRD disallows discrimination between creditors on the basis of their nationality or domicile, eradicating this mis-conceived advantage of bail-ins over bailouts.

With a purely domestic bank, the effect of shifting from bail-out to bail-in will, therefore, primarily transfer the burden of loss from one set of domestic payers, the taxpayers, to another, the pensioners and savers. It is far from clear whether, and why, the latter have broader backs and are better placed to absorb bank rescue losses than the former. One argument, however, is that savers, and/or their financial agents, have made an ex ante choice to purchase the claim on the bank, whereas the taxpayer had no such option, and that, having done so, they could/

---

[11] See Goodley (2010).

should have played a monitoring role. While this is a valid point, the counter-argument is that charities, small or medium size pension funds, or individual savers, e.g., via pension funds, do not really have the expertise to act as effective bank monitors. Thus, forcing them to pay the penalty of bank failure would hardly improve bank governance. On the contrary it would only give rise to claims that they were 'tricked' into buying bail-in-able debt.[12] Arguably, the BRRD makes provision (Art. 46(3)©) for such concerns by giving resolution authorities the power to exempt (in "exceptional circumstances"), from the application of the bail-in tool, liabilities held by individuals and SMEs beyond the level of insured deposits. The chief rationale for this discretionary exemption is avoidance of contagion (Art. 46(3)(c), (d), BRRD), a very plausible concern. If it is applied in a wider context, this safe harbour could provide adequate protection to vulnerable segments of savers' population. These are, in general, weak bank governance monitors and, at the same time, stable sources of cheap funding. Such wider (albeit ad hoc) protection would reinforce the confidence of these parts of society and economy in the banking system.

Governance

The treatment of bailed-in creditors, especially where creditors will be issued new securities rather than having their claims written-down, is likely to be complex, time-consuming and litigation intensive. Faced with such costs the original creditors are likely to sell out to those inter-mediaries that specialize in such situations, e.g., 'vulture' hedge funds. So, as already seen in the case of the Co-op Bank, ownership may fall into the hands of a group of such hedge funds[13]; the same would

---

[12] Would such bail-in able debt be a suitable investment for pension funds, charities, local authorities and individuals? The Pensions Regulator, the Department for Communities and Local Government, the Charities Commission and the FCA may need to consider whether further rules in this area would be necessary.

[13] Co-op Group, which owned the Co-operative Bank outright, eventually bowed to the demands of a group of bondholders, including U.S. hedge funds Aurelius Capital and Silver Point Capital, and agreed to a restructuring which left them with a 30 percent stake in the bank. See M. Scuffham (2013).

probably have happened had there been creditor bail-in in Iceland and Ireland. In Cyprus creditor bail-in has given a large share of ownership to big Russian depositors.[14] In theory, this problem could be resolved by placing caps on how much bail-inable debt different creditors could hold. In practice, however, such caps would encounter legal constraints, at least, under EU law. In addition, if caps are very strict, they would restrict the liquidity of the market for bail-inable debt and could lead to banks having to hold insufficient amounts of bail-inable debt, increasing the need for a public bail out.

In spite of their numerous disadvantages, bail-outs do give governments the power to direct and specify who is to take over the running of the rescued bank. That is not the case with some versions of the bail-in approach. In the USA the role of the FDIC as 'trustee' of the resulting bridge company should, however, deal with this problem. But elsewhere the resulting governance structure could become unattractive to the authorities and public. While there is a safeguard that the new managers have to be approved by the regulatory authorities, nevertheless the ethos, incentives and culture of a bank, whose ownership is controlled by a group of hedge funds for example, is likely to differ from that of a bank rescued by a bail-out.

Legal Costs

While there might be a few jurisdictions such as the UK where bail-in regimes can be established by contract, elsewhere this route would lead to a stream of litigation (Gleeson 2012). As a result, in most jurisdictions, including the UK, bail-in regimes are given statutory force (e.g., Art. 50(2) of the BRRD). Yet this does not mean that litigation will be avoided when the bail-in process is triggered. Bail-in regimes that extend beyond D bail-inable debt clearly encroach on rights of property, which remain entrenched in countries' constitutions and international treaties. Legal claims will be raised both by shareholders who will see

---

[14] See Illmer (2013).

their stakes wiped out and creditors who will see the value of their claims reduced or diminished[15] and it is unlikely that the 'no creditor worse off' principle, which the DFA (Section 210(a)(7)(B), Title II). and the BRRD (Article 73(b)) have adopted as a creditor safeguard under the bail-in process, will deter the expected stream of litigation. In fact, the principle could make litigation even more likely. Therefore, where the result of government action is that bailed-in creditors receive a demonstrably lower return than they would have done had the bank proceeded to disorderly liquidation, they should be compensated (Gleeson 2012), but by whom and in what form? Would that be in the form of shares in the NewCo or of the recapitalized operating subsidiary? Even so, rapid restoration of public confidence is the only way to make creditors' converted stakes valuable.

Moreover, a significant proportion of the costs of bank resolution could involve settling conflicts of interest among creditors (IMF 2013). This is particularly likely to be so in so far as bail-in will concentrate ownership amongst 'vulture' hedge funds, whose métier is the use of legal means to extract large rents. Shifting the burden of meeting the costs of recapitalization from a small charge (on average) imposed on the generality of taxpayers to a major impost on a small group of creditors, easily capable of acting in unison, is almost bound to multiply the legal costs of such an exercise manifold, however much the legal basis of this process is established beforehand.

This is easily explicable. In the case of taxpayer-funded bail-outs, everyone's tax liabilities go up a little, (and the relative burden has, in a sense, been democratically reviewed and decided); in the case of creditor bail-in, a few will lose a lot, and will, therefore, have stronger incentive to protest and litigate.

Funding Costs

There are two aspects to this, a static and a dynamic one. There have been numerous quantitative studies of the 'subsidy' provided by the

---

[15] For example, see Russia Today (2013).

implicit government bail-out guarantee to the larger banks which are too-big-to-fail (Santos 2014; Morgan and Stiroh 2005; Ueda and Weder-Di Mauro 2011; Li *et al.* 2011). There is sufficient evidence to show that Too-Big-To-Fail banks are prone to take much riskier assets than other banks (Afonso *et al.* 2014; Brandao *et al.* 2013; Gadanetz *et al.* 2012; Gropp *et al.* 2011).

Such a subsidy is also criticized as undesirable and unfair distortion of competition. Taking advantage of lower funding costs, larger banks cut margins aggressively to edge out smaller competitors (Gropp *et al.* 2011). Thus, the subsidy distorts the pattern of intermediation towards larger banks and away from smaller banks and non-bank intermediation, including peer-to-peer channels. But there is a counter-argument. Shifting intermediation to smaller banks or to other parts of the financial system will take it from safer, better regulated and more transparent banks (including bigger banks) to riskier, less regulated, and less understood channels. In addition, dependent on the state of competition between banks, much of that subsidy will have gone to providing better terms, primarily in the shape of lower interest rates, to bank borrowers. Controversially, perhaps, size improves banks operating costs (Kovner *et al.* 2014).

Funding costs may not be a major concern in the case of bail-inable debt but there might be an issue of adverse selection. First, another facet of the same, static question is by how much funding costs of (large) banks have to rise if they have to hold specifically bail-inable debt. There are a range of views about this. As in the case of equity (Miles *et al.* 2011, and Admati *et al.* 2011), if we compare one otherwise identical equilibrium with another, when the sole difference is that some categories of bank debt become bail-inable, it is doubtful whether the overall cost of bank funding would rise by much, say 10–30 bps. Moreover, with a rising proportion of bank creditors at risk from bank failure, there should be a greater benefit, in terms of *lower* funding costs, from a patently safer overall portfolio structure. As explained earlier, one of the fundamental rationales of bail-in, is that creditors at risk will have an incentive to encourage bank managers to pursue prudent policies, a counter-weight to more risk-seeking shareholders.

Secondly, bail-inable debt may affect banks' choice of assets. If institutions are required to issue a minimum amount of bail-inable liabilities expressed as a percentage of total liabilities (rather than as a percentage of risk weighted assets), critically, this will impose higher costs on institutions with large amounts of assets with a low risk weighting (such as mortgages). Such institutions typically hold relatively small amounts of capital as a proportion of their total liabilities. In addition, institutions will face constraints on their funding models and higher costs if they are required to hold bail-inable liabilities in specific locations within a group (for example at group level when their funding is currently undertaken by their subsidiaries).

That bail-in regimes will provide some *ex-ante* incentive to more prudent behavior seems undisputable. Yet market discipline failed to operate effectively ahead of the current financial crisis and holders of bail-inable liabilities will face the same difficulties as other stakeholders in assessing the health and soundness of bank balance sheets (See on complexity as a monitoring barrier Avgouleas and Cullen 2014).

In addition, if bank(s) nevertheless run into trouble, then utilization of the bail-in process will give another twist to pro-cyclicality. With bail-in, the weaker that banks become the harder and more expensive it will be for them to get funding. In this respect high trigger Co-Cos would perform better than bail-in-able bonds. While, in principle, increased creditor monitoring could translate into greater focus on prudence and caution for the individual banker, in the face of a generalized shock, a sizeable proportion of the banks in a given country will seem weaker. Thus a shift away from bail-out towards bail-in is likely to reinforce pro-cyclicality. The ECB has been cautious about bailing-in bank bondholders for such reasons.[16]

Of course, should the sovereign be in a weak fiscal condition, bail-out costs will give another twist to the "doom loop" of bank and

---

[16] In his July 30, 2013 confidential letter to the then competition commissioner Joaquin Almunia, ECB's President Mario Draghi was reported to have expressed key concerns about the EU's bail-in regime under the draft BRRD. In particular Draghi was reported, by Reuters, who saw the letter, to have said that "imposing losses on junior creditors in the context of such 'precautionary recapitalizations' could hurt subordinated bank bonds" and then adding: "… structurally impairing the subordinated debt market […] could lead to a flight of investors out of the European banking market, which would further hamper banks' funding going forward" (*Reuters* 2013).

sovereign indebtedness. But if the costs of recapitalising the banks in a given country are so large, does it help to shift them from the taxpayer to the pension funds, insurance companies and other large domestic investors, and also on the surviving banks? No doubt the crisis would take a different shape, but would it be any less severe? It could be (politically) worse if people began to fear that their pensions were being put at risk?

Liquidity Concerns

Once the bail-in process has been triggered, it is highly likely that the financial institution in question would only be able to continue conducting business with the 'lifeline' of emergency liquidity assistance. But the amount of liquidity support that could be provided by central banks and resolution funds (such as the Orderly Liquidation Fund in the US) may be constrained by a lack of sufficient high quality collateral, and by restrictions on any support that might result in losses falling on taxpayers. This would be accentuated if a number of major financial institutions had to be resolved at the same time. Critically, liquidity could be limited to supporting critical economic functions while other parts of the business are resolved.

Naturally, central banks and resolution funds will be reluctant to pre-commit to provide liquidity support in all circumstances. They will want to ensure that a 'plan B' option is in place, including the immediate winding down of a failing financial institution through rapid sales and transfers, without liquidity support, which again would depend on a resolution plan drawn up in advance (KPMG 2012). However, implementation of such plans would negate one of the biggest advantages of ('open bank') bail-in regimes, namely the continuation of the resolved entity or of operating subsidiaries as a going concern.

Bank Creditors' Flight and Contagion

A desideratum for a revenue raising mechanism is that the taxed cannot easily flee. It is difficult to avoid taxation, except by migration, which has many severe transitional costs. In contrast it is easy to avoid being hit with the costs of creditor bail-in; you just withdraw or sell your claim. Consequently, triggering the bail-in process is likely to generate a capital flight and a sharp rise in funding costs whenever the need for large-scale recapitalizations becomes apparent. Creditors who sense in advance the possibility of a bail-in, or creditors of institutions that are similar in terms of nationality or business models will have a strong incentive to withdraw deposits, sell debt, or hedge their positions through the short-selling of equity or the purchase of credit protection at an ever higher premium disrupting the relevant markets. Such actions could be damaging and disruptive, both to a single institution (Randell 2011). and potentially to wider market confidence, a point that is also highlighted by proponents of the bail-in tool (Micossi *et al.* 2014, p. 9). In our view, market propensity to resort to herding at times of shock means that it is not realistic to believe that generalized adoption of bail-in mechanisms would not trigger contagious consequences that would have a destabilizing effect.

Where the ceiling of guaranteed deposits is set low a significant number of large depositors might migrate to other schemes such as Money Market Funds or even Investment funds that offer higher interest rates, as in the example of contemporary Chinese shadow banks. It would certainly take a lot of explaining to justify why weakening the liquidity of the regulated banking sector and increasing its funding costs in order to boost liquidity levels and lower the funding costs of the unregulated shadow banking sector is a measure to strengthen financial stability. On the contrary, a lack of Lender of Last Resort type of liquidity support in the unregulated sector could make bank-type runs inevitable, increasing the possibility of psychological spillovers into the regulated sector and generalized panic, (as occurred in the USA in 1907).

It is, of course, true that equity holders and bond holders cannot run in the same way that depositors can, but financial counterparties can easily do so and will do so if they do not immediately see a hefty capital cushion in the bailed-in bank (Sommer 2014). If these flee then equity and bond holders would certainly follow and in their attempt to do so they would drive asset values sharply down to an extent that would make the option of raising new money, or rolling over existing maturing bonds, unattractive or virtually impossible. In such circumstances, bank credit extension would stop, amplifying the downturn, lowering asset values yet further and putting the solvency of other banks at risk. Excluding depositors of all brands from bail-in might reduce the danger of contagion but would not remove it.

International Coordination

The resolution of G-SIFIs with bail-in is examined in Appendix A. However, some thoughts are apposite here to provide a fuller evaluation of bail-in advantages and disadvantages. In our view, the top-down SPOE approach adopted by the US regulators is conceptually superior. Assets and liabilities at the operating subsidiary level are not part of the painful debt restructuring bail-in exercise and may continue operations regardless. There are however four clear disadvantages in implementing this approach in the case of G-SIFIs.

First, the (unaffected by resolution) operating subsidiary might, nevertheless, suffer a flight due to reputational contagion, which triggers an irrational but quite likely panic, regardless of parent's ability to sufficiently recapitalize the operating parts of the group through conversion of bail-in-able liabilities. Secondly, apart from closely inter-related banking markets like the UK and the US, where the level of trust between national authorities is high, it is doubtful if non-binding bilateral arrangements, including MOUs, would hold in the event of a cross-border banking crisis, involving a transfer of funds from one jurisdiction to another (Sommer 2014). The gulf between regulators will become even deeper, if the majority of a certain form of group level funding (e.g., tripartite repos) is booked with a specific subsidiary that is not based in the same place as the HoldCo being resolved (Skeel 2014). Thirdly, it is arguable that when the subsidiary is ring-fenced regulators may expect the subsidiary creditors, as well as shareholders like the HoldCo, to bear the cost of bail-in. Fourthly, the top-down approach could increase scope for arbitrage and regulatory forbearance. In most cases it will be the home country regulator that will have the final word as regards the level of D bail-inable debt to be held by the HoldCo. But D bail-inable debt could prove more expensive than other subordinated debt. Thus, a home regulator concerned about the health of banks in its domestic market would be much less keen on increasing the cost of funding of its banks, unless legally bound to do so through bilateral or multilateral arrangements with host authorities. In fact, the absence of such arrangements could trigger multiple races to the bottom meaning that many HoldCos might not have a sufficient level of D bail-able debt to recapitalize the group subsidiaries. In addition, there could also be circumstances where home resolution authorities are reluctant to use the bail-in tool because of its adverse impact on specific groups of creditors.

A host resolution authority might be tempted to trigger its own resolution and bail-in powers if it was concerned that it might not receive sufficient support from the new bridge holding company to meet losses at, and/or to preserve critical economic functions in, its local subsidiary. Art. 87 of the BRRD explicitly extends this power beyond subsidiaries to branches of institutions from outside the EU. By means of this provision, EU member states can apply resolution tools, including bail-in, to such branches to protect local depositors and to preserve financial stability, independent of any third country resolution procedure, if the third country has failed to act. Similarly, subject to a number of conditions and on the basis EU of financial stability concerns, the BRRD (Art. 95) gives the right to European resolution authorities to refuse to enforce third country resolution proceedings over EU-based subsidiaries.

Accordingly the kind of international cooperation required to allow a top-down approach to operate effectively is unprecedented and it might well form the most challenging aspect of cross-border implementation of bail-in recapitalization in the case of G-SIFIs.

Conclusions

"As the emerging-market crises and the entire history of financial crises made clear, imposing haircuts on bank creditors during a systemic panic is a sure way to accelerate the panic"[17]

---

[17] See Geithner (2014, p. 214).

While we fully understand the revulsion from too-big-to-fail banks and the (political) cost of bailouts, we are worried that the development of a bandwagon may conceal from its many proponents some of the disadvantages of the new bail-in regimes. While bail-in may, indeed, be much superior in several contexts, notably in the case of idiosyncratic failure, the resort to bail-in may disappoint unless everyone involved is fully aware of the potential downsides of the new approach.

A bail-in mechanism used for the recapitalization of a bank as going concern has the following advantages, vis-à-vis a bail-out approach:-

- Lower levels of moral hazard
- Better creditor monitoring
- Protects taxpayers
- Places the burden more fairly
- Should improve ex ante behavior of bank management
- Mitigates the Sovereign/bank debt 'doom-loop'

But the bail-in process may also have some important disadvantages over bailouts, as it could prove to be:-

- more contagious and pro-cyclical
- more litigious
- slower and more expensive as a process
- requiring greater subsequent liquidity injections
- leading to deterioration of governance
- requiring higher funding costs to banks
- providing a worse outlook for bank borrowers
- worsening ex post outcomes

That the second list is longer than the first is no indication of which approach should be favored. This paper is not intended to claim that the proposed reforms will make the process of dealing with failing banks necessarily worse. Its purpose is, instead, to warn that the exercise may have costs and disadvantages, which, unless fully appreciated, could make the outcome less successful than hoped. The authorities will no doubt claim that they have already, and fully, appreciated all such points, as and where relevant. But we would contend that many advocates of moving to the latter do not mention such disadvantages at all, or only partially. Perhaps the choice should depend on context.

The bail-in process seems, in principle, a suitable substitute to resolution (whether liquidation of a gone concern, or some other form of resolution in a going concern bank) in the case of smaller domestic financial institutions. It could also be used successfully to recapitalize domestic SIFIs, but only if the institution has failed due to its own actions and omissions and not due to a generalized systemic crisis. Otherwise, a flight of creditors from other institutions, i.e., contagion, may be uncontainable. Even so, successful bail-in recapitalization would require rapid restoration of market confidence (Sommer 2014), accurate evaluation of losses, and successful restructuring of the bailed in bank's operations to give it a sound business model to avoid successive rounds of bail-in rescues. It could, of course, prove very hard for regulators to secure all those pre-requisites of a successful bail-in recapitalization in the event of a systemic crisis.

Moreover, generic structural, governance, legal and other risks and costs associated with a cross-border resolution of a G-SIFI (discussed in Appendix A) make the use of the process highly uncertain in its outcome, unless failure was clearly idiosyncratic, for example, as a result of fraud.

Given these shortcomings and costs of bail-in bank recapitalization, orderly and timely resolution of a G-SIFI would still require fiscal commitments. These could be established by means of ex ante burden sharing agreements, concluded either independently or by means of commitments entrenched in G-SIFI living wills (Avgouleas *et al.* 2013). Moreover, over-reliance on bail-in could deepen the trend towards disintegration of the internal market in the EU (CEPS 2014), while providing uncertain benefits. So, effective recapitalization of ailing banks may still require a credible fiscal backstop. In addition, a fiscal backstop may be essential to avert, in the case of deposits held in the same currency across a common currency area, a flight of deposits from member states with weaker sovereigns to the member states with solvent sovereigns (Schoenmaker 2014). This is more or less a Eurozone specific risk, unless the current structures on the use of ESM funds are gradually loosened. EU policy-makers ought to continue their efforts to build one instead of relying on the unproven thesis that the bail-in process can resolve the recapitalization challenges facing the Eurozone banking sector.

Finally, achieving the goal of making private institutions responsible for their actions would be the best policy in an ideal world where financial "polluters" would be held responsible for their actions. But, in practice, it might prove an unattainable goal. Some of the aforementioned obstacles to effective bail-in, especially in the case of cross-border groups, could prove insurmountable. If this turns out to be the case then developed societies might have to accept that granting some form of public insurance is an inevitable tax for having a well-functioning banking sector. At the same time, other forms of regulation like structural reform and cycle adjustable leverage ratios (plus more emphasis on the prior Recovery stage), if they prove to make banks more stable, should come to the forefront with renewed force.

The SPOE Approach with Bail-in: Important Challenges

1. The Cross-border Dimension

Cross-border Coordination

While the SPOE approach in the event of a cross-border resolution involving jurisdictions with long history of cooperation like the US and the UK makes good sense, especially from the resolution effectiveness viewpoint — UK authorities have stated that they are ready to step aside and give the FDIC a free hand in the event of resolution of a G-SIFI with UK subsidiaries (Tucker 2014) — there is little assurance that other overseas authorities will feel the same. In order to avoid the possibility of home authorities interfering with transfers to, or from, foreign subsidiaries of the resolved group in the course of resolution, host regulators may force foreign subsidiaries to operate as ring-fenced entities increasing the trend towards disintegration of global banking markets. While this might sound like a reasonable strategy it gives rise to two undesirable consequences. First, capital and other resources within the banking group are not employed efficiently. Worse, during bad times the group is not able to shift resources from a healthy subsidiary to a troubled subsidiary. The latter may be located in a country that is in trouble itself and would greatly welcome an injection of capital and liquidity by the parent to the troubled subsidiary (Baer 2014, p. 15). Secondly, recent data shows that localization has serious consequences for cross-border capital flows and investment and levels of global growth.[18]

---

[18] 'The flow of money through the global financial system is still stuck at the same level as a decade ago, raising fresh concerns about the strength of the economic recovery following six years of financial crisis ...' These findings were based on research carried by the McKinsey Global Institute for the *Financial Times* and was published as Atkins and Fray (2014).

Liquidity Provision as Part of the Resolution Funding Framework

Meeting the liquidity requirements of the operating subsidiaries of the resolved group could be a challenging task, given also that access to market-based liquidity might be severely restricted for the resolved group. In the US, in the event of resolution of a SIFI under OLA, the bridge holding company will downstream liquidity, as necessary, to subsidiaries through intra-company advances. When this is not sufficient the FDIC will act as provider of liquidity through loans to the bridge company or any covered subsidiaries that enjoy super-seniority, or by granting of guarantees (section 204 of the Dodd–Frank Act). Yet the issue is far from resolved as such loans and guarantees might not prove sufficient, especially if the quality of the collateral is not of a very high grade and the FDIC has not concealed that fact (FDIC 2013). Normally, a G-SIFI is funded mostly through retail, and other short-term, deposits, which in the event of a bail-in could either dry up or even be withdrawn. So, as commonly recognized, a group in resolution may require considerable official liquidity support. This should only be provided on a fully collateralized basis, with appropriate haircuts applied to the collateral, to reduce further the risk of loss, but this depends on the adequacy of the available collateral.

In the UK, the policy for liquidity provision in resolution follows the provisions of the BRRD, which provides that resolution will primarily be financed by national resolution funds that can also borrow from each other (Art. 99 et seq.). The BRRD does not rule out provision of liquidity, in the event of resolution by the central bank.

The BRRD treats the Deposit Guarantee Scheme (DGS) as a creditor that can be bailed-in, with the costs of this falling on other firms, which have to fund the Scheme. Thus, the requisite DGS will have to contribute for the purpose of ensuring continuous access to covered deposits and relevant contributions will be *in cash* for an amount equivalent to the losses that the DGS would have had to bear in normal insolvency proceedings. Namely, the DGS contribution is made in cash in order to absorb the losses from the covered deposits. In order to provide for sufficient funding, the DGS will rank *pari passu* with unsecured non-preferred claims.

Under the BRRD menber states are allowed to merge the administrative strutures of the DGS with the Resolution Fund. But, even if Member states implement shared administrative structures, the sources of financing of DGS and the Resolution Fund must remain separate, The DGS is solely liable for the protection of covered depositors. If following a contribution by the DGS, the institution under resolution fails at a later stage and the DGS does not have sufficient funds to repay depositors, the DGS must have arrangements in place in order to raise the corresponding amounts as soon as possible from its members. Otherwise, treating the DGS as an unsecured depositor in the event of a systemic crisis might raise doubt about the sufficiency of funds available to it.

Location of Bail-inable Debt and of Bank Deposits

Another important issue is where the debt is located, namely, which entity within the group holds the debt. The joint FDIC-BoE paper envisages that, at least for UK groups, bail-able debt will be issued by the top operating companies within a group, which, however, may operate in different jurisdictions. This means that the SPOE approach might prove elusive for non-US G-SIFIs. For G-SIFIs with substantial operations in the US, the Federal Reserve has introduced a final rule, implementing its Dodd-Frank mandate, requiring these operations to be held through a US holding company (FRB 2014).[19] In the absence of MOUs similar to the one signed between the FDIC and the BoE (2012), it is not clear whether the US authorities would seek to resolve the US operations on a stand-alone basis (by applying the SPOE approach within the US), or would stand back and allow the overseas parent to be resolved without the US authorities taking action.

---

[19] In a substantial break with past practice FRB's final rule requires large Foreign Banking Organisations with US$50 billion or more of (non-branch) assets in US-chartered subsidiaries and all foreign SIFIs to place all their U.S. operations in a US-based intermediate holding company ('IHC') on which the FRB will impose enhanced capital, liquidity and other prudential requirements on those IHCs, separate from and in addition to the requirements of the parent company's home country supervisor. See Federal Reserve System (2014).

The proportion of foreign creditors can go up dramatically when we move from purely domestic banks to cross-border banks with numerous foreign branches or subsidiaries. Most SIFIs, and all G-SIFIs, are cross-border. Indeed, the thrust of many recent proposals for bank resolution, for example those of the UK Independent Commission on Banking (Vickers Report) as incorporated with amendments in the Financial Services (Banking Reform) Act 2013 and some earlier Swiss measures, has been to limit taxpayer contingent liability to the local, domestic part of the bank. But not only will this lead towards further balkanization and localization of banking systems, it also raises the question of how far bail-in of only ring-fenced entities is consistent with a Single Point of Entry (SPOE) resolution mechanisms.

Moreover, legal disputes, and shareholder and creditor objections, will become even more acute where a subsidiary of the holding company is on the verge of failure, while the holding company has other viable and valuable subsidiaries. In such a case it could be perceived as disproportionate to cancel the claims of existing shareholders in the holding company since these retain significant value by virtue of the value of the non-failing group subsidiaries. Even if a value is placed on solvent subsidiaries, so that holding group shareholders are issued new shares of reduced value rather than being wiped out, the bail-in process will be protracted. This development could potentially have a seriously destabilizing impact on the institution that is being resolved, since only speedy resolution can prevent a creditor run on the institution.

Resolving Systemic Subsidiaries

Equally challenging would be the application of SPOE to bail-in when overseas subsidiaries need to be resolved because they are both loss-making and are undertaking critical economic functions (KPMG 2012; Gleeson 2012). It may not be possible, or efficient, to resolve them through an injection of capital from the parent holding company. Overseas resolution authorities may choose to exercise their own national resolution powers to intervene in the overseas subsidiaries — or even branches — of US and UK G-SIFIs. This would be consistent with the "multiple points of entry" (MPE) approach that underpins the EU BRRD, and with the growing trend towards "localisation" under which overseas host authorities seek to protect their national positions through the ring-fencing of the operations of foreign firms in their countries.

2. The EU Approach

By contrast to the FDIC-BoE approach, the EU will operate the bail-in regime on a legal entity basis (with the option of group level resolution also available subject to conditions set in BRRD). The consolidated group approach is based on close cooperation and coordination through resolution colleges and on group level resolution plans agreed in advance. So, in the event of a group resolution, each national authority would apply bail-in (and other resolution tools) to each entity based in its jurisdiction.

This reflects the different legal and operating structures across Europe and the fact that each member state operates, for now, its own Deposit Guarantee Scheme. But once the new Single Resolution Mechanism comes into force, Euro-wide resolution would be conducted by a single authority and SPOE could become an option, but MPE will still be the adopted route for subsidiaries located in the UK and other EU member states that are not part of the European Banking Union.

References

Admati, A., P. M. DeMarzo, M. F. Hellwig and P. Pfleiderer (2011), "Fallacies, Irrelevant Facts, and Myths in the Discussion of Capital Regulation: Why bank equity is *not* expensive." Mimeo, Stanford Business School, April. Available at https://gsbapps.stanford.edu/researchpapers/library/rp2065r1&86.pdf.

Admati, A., P. M. DeMarzo, M. F. Hellwig and P. Pfleiderer (2012), "Debt Overhang and Capital Regulation," Rock Center for Corporate Governance at Stanford University Working Paper No. 114, MPI Collective Goods Preprint, No. 2012/5, 23 March.

Admati, A. R., P. M. DeMarzo, M. F. Hellwig, P. Pfleiderer (2013), "The Leverage Ratchet Effect," Working Paper Series of the Max Planck Institute for Research on Collective Goods 2013/13, Max Planck Institute for Research on Collective Goods.

Afonso, G., J. Santos and J. Traina (2014), "Do 'Too Big To Fail' Banks Take on More Risk?" *Economic Policy Review*, 29(2): 41–58.

Angeloni, I. and N. Lenihan (2014), "Competition and State Aid Rules in the Time of Banking Union", prepared for the Conference, Financial Regulation: A Transatlantic Perspective, June 6–7, Goethe University Frankfurt.

Atkins, R. and K. Fray (2014). "Dramatic Fall in Cross-border Capital Flows Threatens Recovery." *Financial Times*, January 7.

Avgouleas, E., C. Goodhart and D. Schoenmaker (2013). "Recovery and Resolution Plans as a Catalyst of Global Reform," *Journal of Financial Stability*, 9: 210–218.

Avgouleas, E. and J. Cullen (2014), "Market Discipline and EU Corporate Governance Reform in the Banking Sector: Merits, Fallacies, and Cognitive Boundaries," *Journal of Law and Society*, 41: 28–50.

Avgouleas, E. and J. Cullen (2015), "Excessive Leverage and Bankers' Pay: Governance and financial stability costs of a symbiotic relationship," *Columbia Journal of European Law*, 21(1). Forthcoming.

Baer, G. (2014), "Regulation and Resolution: Toward a Unified Theory". Banking Perspective, The Clearing House, 12–21.

Brandao, M., L. R. Correa and H. Sapriza (2013), "International Evidence on Government Support and Risk Taking in the Banking Sector," IMF, Working Paper, 13/94.

Clifford Chance (2011), *Legal Aspects of Bank Bail-ins*. Available at http://www.cliffordchance.com/publicationviews/publications/2011/05/legal_aspects_ofbankbail-ins.html.

Center for European Policy Studies [CEPS] (2014), *Framing Banking Union in the Euro Area: Some empirical evidence*, February. Available at http://www.ceps.eu/book/framing-banking-union-euro-area-some-empirical-evidence.

Coffee, J. C. (2011), "Systemic Risk after Dodd-Frank: Contingent Capital and the Need for Strategies Beyond Oversight," *Columbia Law Review*, 111: 795–847.

Dewatripont, M. (2014), "European Banking: Bail-out, Bail-in and State Aid Control," *International Journal of Industrial Organization*, 34: 37–43.

FDIC and BoE (2012), "Resolving Globally Active, Systemically Important, Financial Institutions," joint paper by the Federal Deposit Insurance Corporation and the Bank of England, December 10.

FDIC (2013), "Resolution of Systemically Import Financial Institutions: The single point of entry strategy," December 18, pp. 76614–76624. Available at: http://www.bde.es/f/webbde/GAP/prensa/info_interes/ficheros/frob 261212en.pdf.

Federal Reserve System (2013), "Enhanced Prudential Standards for Bank Holding Companies and Foreign Banking," February 18. Final Rule, 12 CFR Part 252 Regulation YY; Docket No. 1438 RIN 7100-AD-86.

Gadanetz, B., K. Tsatsaronis and Altunbas, Y. (2012), "Spoilt and Lazy: The impact of state support on bank behavior in the international loan market," *International Journal of Central Banking*, 8(4): 121–173.

Geithner, T. F. (2014), *Stress Test: Reflections on Financial Crises* (New York: Random House).

Gleeson, S. (2012), "Legal Aspects of Bank Bail-Ins," Special Paper 205, LSE Financial Markets Group Series.

Goodley, S. (2010), "Bondholders may take legal action against Iceland over failed banks Bondholders may take legal action against Iceland over failed banks", *The Guardian*, November 7. Available at: http://www.theguardian.com/business/2010/nov/07/iceland-banks-bondholders-legal-action.

Gordon, J. N. and W.-G. Ringe (2014), "Resolution in the European Banking Union: A transatlantic perspective on what it would take," Oxford Legal Research Paper Series No 18/2014 (April).

Gropp, R., H. Hakenes and I. Schnabel (2011), "Competition, Risk-shifting, and Public Bail-Out Policies," *Review of Financial Studies*. 24(6): 2084–2120.

Huertas, T. F. (2013), "The Case for Bail-ins," In P. S. Kenadjian (ed.) *The Bank Recovery and Resolution Directive* (Berlin: De Gruyter), pp. 167–188.

Illmer, A. (2013), "Russia's rich dominate Cyprus' largest bank," *Deutsche Welle*, October 18. Available at: http://www.dw.de/russias-rich-dominate-cyprus-largest-bank/a-17146540.

Kovner, A., J. Vickery and L. Zhou (2014), "Do Big Banks Have Lower Operating Costs?" *Economic Policy Review*, 20(2): 1–27.

KPMG (2012), "Bail-in Liabilities: Replacing public subsidy with private insurance." Available at: http://www.kpmg.com/Global/en/IssuesAndInsights/ArticlesPublications/Documents/bail-in-debt-practical-implications.pdf.

Li, Z., S. Qu and J. Zhang (2011), *Quantifying the Value of Implicit Government Guarantees for Large Financial Institutions*, Moody's Analytics Quantitative Research Group (January).

McAndrews, J., D. P. Morgan, J. Santos and T. Yorulmazer (2014), "What Makes Large Bank Failures so Messy and What to Do about It," *Economic Policy Review*, 20(2): 229–244.

Micossi, S., G. Bruzzone and M. Casella (2014), "Bail-in Provisions in State Aid and Resolution Procedures: Are they consistent with systemic stability?" CEPS Policy Brief, No. 318, May.

Miles, D., J. Yang and G. Marcheggiano (2011). "Optimal Bank Capital," Bank of England, External MPC Unit, Discussion Paper 31. Available at http://www.econstor.eu/obitstream/10419/50643/1/656641770.pdf

Morgan, D. P. and K. J. Stiroh (2005), "Too Big To Fail After All These Years," Federal Reserve Bank of New York Staff Reports, No. 220 (September).

PWC (2013), "US Moving Faster than World," PwC's Financial Services Regulatory Brief, August. Available at: http://www.pwc.com/en_US/us/financial-services/regulatory-services/publications/assets/fs-reg-brief-basel-prudential-standards.pdf.

Randell, C. (2011), "The Great British Banking Experiment: Will the restructuring of UK banking shows us how to resolve G-SIFIS?" Paper prepared for the LSE Financial Markets Group Conference on Banking Structure, Regulation and Competition, November.

Santos, J. (2014), "Evidence from the Bond Market on Banks' 'Too-Big-To-Fail'" Subsidy. *Economic Policy Review*, 20(2): 29–39.

Reuters (2013), "Draghi asked EU to Keep State Aid Rules for Banks Flexible," October 19. Available at http://www.reuters.com/article/2013/10/19/us-banks-bondholders-draghi-idUSBRE99I03B20131019.

Russia Today (2013), "Russian Depositors Begin Seizing Property of Cypriot Banks, "April 12. Available at: http://www.rt.com/business/laiki-cyprus-banks-arrest-765/.

Schoenmaker, D. (2014), "On the Need for a Fiscal Backstop to the Banking System," DSF Policy Paper Series No. 44, July. Available at: http://www.dsf.nl/wp-content/uploads/2014/10/DSF-Policy-Paper-No-44-On-the-need-for-a-fiscal-backstop-to-the-banking-system.pdf.

Scuffham, M. (2013), "Co-op to Cede Control of Bank to Bondholders," *Reuters*, October 21. Available at http://uk.reuters.com/article/2013/10/21/uk-coop-bank-bondholders-idUKBRE99K05O20131021.

Skeel, D. A. (2014), "Single Point of Entry and the Bankruptcy Alternative," University of Pennsylvania, Institute for Law and Econ Research Paper No. 14–10, February.

Sommer, J. H. (2014), "Why Bail-In? And How!" *Economic Policy Review*, 20(2): 207–228.

Tucker, P. (2014), "Regulatory Reform, Stability and Central Banking," Hutchins Center on Fiscal and Monetary Policy, Brookings, January 18. Available at www.brookings.edu/~/media/research/files/papers/2014/01/16% 20regulatory%20reform%20stability%20central%20banking%20 tucker/16%20regulatory%20reform%20stability%20central%20bank- ing%20tucker.pdf.

Ueda, K. and B. Weder-Di Mauro (2011), "Quantifying the Value of the Subsidy for systemically Important Financial Institutions," IMF Working Paper 12/128.

Resolving Systemically Important Financial Institutions and Markets
— CHAPTER 12

- Adam Ketessidis
  BaFin

In a free market economy, no one should be too big, too interconnected or too systemically important to fail. Nevertheless, as we saw the global financial crisis has demonstrated that some banks seem to escape from this concept. Though banks were in the center of the financial crisis, they are not the only species of systemically important financial institutions — the so called SIFIs — with the potential to create chaos in case of their distress or failure. SIFIs also comprise financial market infrastructures and insurers. What all SIFIs have in common is that under a worst-case-scenario, their threatened failure may leave public authorities with no option but to bail them out. This 'de facto insolvency protection' results in lower costs of capital for these SIFIs and may encourage them to take excessive risks.

With the determination to end this situation, the G-20 leaders stated in 2009 at their Pittsburgh Summit inter alia: "We should develop resolution tools and frameworks for the effective resolution of financial groups to help mitigate the disruption of financial institution failures

---

Adam Ketessidis is Head of Group Restructuring at BaFin.

and reduce moral hazard in the future." The Financial Stability Board (FSB) took up the task and in 2011, the G-20 endorsed the FSB's Key Attributes of Effective Resolution Regimes for Financial Institutions ('Key Attributes') as a new international standard. At the St. Petersburg Summit in September 2013, the G-20 committed again to make any necessary reforms to implement fully the Key Attributes for all parts of the financial sector. The G-20 called on the FSB to address the remaining impediments to resolvability, with the aim to establish confidence that resolution strategies can be implemented in practice.

So where do we stand today, on the verge of the next G-20 summit in Brisbane mid-November? To put it briefly, the FSB is pushing international reform efforts forward. Rightly so! Of course, some progress has been made since 2009, in particular regarding the banking sector. However, several crucial steps must still be taken.

Before I will tell you more about current FSB initiatives, let me put things into perspective and recap what has already been achieved with respect to banks, specifically in Europe. The European Union has created a recovery and resolution regime with its Bank Recovery and Resolution Directive (BRRD). The Single Resolution Mechanism is also making good progress. We need both not least for the Banking Union, the new European system of banking supervision, which started a few days ago. The fact that we will in the future have a clear sequence of liability is one of our successes in the negotiations in Brussels. The first to be called upon will be owners and creditors. They will have to be liable for losses of their bank and be responsible for its recapitalization before the Resolution Fund has to bear the cost or — and only as the last possible resort — the taxpayer. If we now succeed in making large systemically important banks 'resolvable', then we in Europe will have taken a crucial step forward. We have already taken this step in Germany: with the Restructuring Law in 2011 and the Act on Ring-fencing and Recovery and Resolution Planning for Credit Institutions and Financial Groups, in force since January 2014 which introduced major structural reforms.

But what do we do with banking groups that operate world-wide? We must design a resolution regime that is effective globally and across borders. On our way there, a major challenge is to identify and remove obstacles resulting from the cross-border activities of these banks. Here is where the FSB's most recent and imminent initiatives come into play.

The most sophisticated resolution concept will not work unless resolution measures can be given prompt effect in relation to assets that are located in, or liabilities or contracts that are governed by the law of other jurisdictions. For this reason, the FSB's Key Attributes require jurisdictions to establish transparent and expedited processes that would enable resolution measures taken by a foreign resolution authority to have cross-border effect. As you may guess, workable processes to that effect are not yet in place in all jurisdictions. Therefore, the FSB has launched on September 29 a public consultation on a set of proposals to achieve the cross-border recognition of resolution actions and to remove impediments to a cross-border resolution.

The FSB proposals comprise on the one hand elements that jurisdictions should consider including in their cross-border recognition frameworks to facilitate an effective cross-border resolution. On the other hand, the FSB suggests the swift adoption of contractual approaches to cross-border recognition that focus on two cases of particular importance. The aim is to accelerate the progress as statutory changes are often complex and time-consuming, though — on the long term — the preferable solution, as contractual solutions have certain limitations. But, on our way towards cross-borders resolvability — they may offer a workable interim solution.

Regarding statutory recognition processes — also my preferred solution — the European Union is again in the forefront with its Recovery and Resolution Directive (BRRD). It provides a framework for the recognition and enforcement of resolution decisions within the EU and between EU member states and third countries.

As I said, the FSB has identified two particular areas where cross-border recognition is a critical prerequisite for an orderly resolution, justifying the swift adoption of contractual approaches to cross-border recognition. On the one hand, we talk about temporary restrictions or stays on early termination rights (including with respect to cross-defaults) in financial contracts. The FSB's Key Attributes state that counterparties should be restricted from exercising early termination rights that arise only by reason of or in connection with a firm's entry into resolution, and, where such rights exists, resolution authorities should have the power to stay counterparties temporarily from exercising them. Effective stays on such termination rights are important to prevent the close out of financial contracts — potentially in significant volumes — of the firm entering resolution. It is crucial that resolution authorities have tools to suspend such early termination rights at least temporarily in order to arrange for an orderly resolution.

However, if the counterparties to the contract are established in different jurisdictions, there is a risk that national courts may not enforce a temporary stay or restriction imposed under a foreign resolution regime, where the contract is governed by their domestic law in the absence of appropriate contractual clauses. Contractual recognition clauses can facilitate the cross-border enforceability of such stays.

In this context, the International Swaps and Derivatives Association [ISDA] is to launch a protocol to supplement its standard documentation concerning bilateral OTC derivative contracts, the ISDA Master Agreement. Adopted — in a first step — by the major global systemically important banks (G-SIB), the protocol supports the cross-border enforcement of a temporary stay of early termination rights with respect to OTC-derivatives governed by the Master Agreement in relation to resolution-based defaults. Reaching out in the near future for even broader adoption of the ISDA protocol will be a major step forward.

The second area where the absence of processes to give prompt effect to foreign resolution measures is a particular concern relates to the write-down and conversion of debt instruments governed by foreign law. Where an entity has issued debt governed by the law of a foreign jurisdiction, there is uncertainty whether the exercise of statutory bail-in powers, i.e. the write down or conversion of debt by the resolution authority of the issuing entity, will be recognized in the foreign jurisdiction. Here again, contractual recognition clauses can help to support the cross-border enforceability of such actions. In its consultation report, the FSB has identified a set of key principles for recognition clauses in debt instruments that should facilitate the exercise of bail-in powers across borders.

The inclusion of appropriate terms could also be a condition for a debt instrument to satisfy a requirement for loss-absorbing capacity in resolution. If we want to avoid that taxpayers bear the costs for resolving a global systemically important bank, we need certainty that sufficient funds are at hand at the moment such firm would enter resolution. A firm's loss absorbing capacity should enable us to implement an orderly resolution that minimizes any impacts on financial stability and keeps public funds out of the equation.

For this purpose, each global systemically important bank should be required to maintain a (firm specific) minimum of total loss absorbing capacity — we called it TLAC. What we need is a common minimum (Pillar I) and an institute specific Pillar II that ensures an international level playing. Of course, there are a lot of other aspects to be considered — let me illustrate just a few.

When we imagine the resolution of cross-border groups, it is important that host jurisdictions and authorities, for example jurisdictions where the firm maintains a subsidiary, have confidence that there will be sufficient loss-absorbing and recapitalization capacity at hand for subsidiaries in their jurisdictions. In the absence of such confidence, host authorities might ask for extra funds to be ring-fenced in their own jurisdictions. This might compromise an orderly resolution and would lead to global fragmentation of the financial system. To avoid this, there need to be mechanisms to facilitate the passing of losses incurred by material subsidiaries up to the parent entity, and to facilitate the write-down and conversion of liabilities at the parent entity in order to generate the funds needed to recapitalize its material subsidiaries.

Another important question is what kind of liabilities and instruments should be eligible for the minimum total loss absorbing capacity. TLAC should for example not include liabilities on which the performance of critical functions depends. To find appropriate answers to these and other questions, the FSB has developed a set of draft principles on loss-absorbing and recapitalization capacity of global systemically important banks in resolution as well as a proposal how these principles can be implemented as an international agreed standard.

Now, given all the due attention we pay to the banks, we must not forget that banks are not the only potential source of systemic and moral hazard risk. The universe of SIFIs is vaster, comprising insurers and financial market infrastructures — FMIs — like Payment Systems,

Central securities depositories, Securities Settlement Systems, Central Counterparties and Trade repositories. All of them should be resolvable in an orderly manner.

Concerning FMIs, let me focus here on Central Counterparties (CCPs), due to their increasing importance since the European Union launched the European Market Infrastructure Regulation (EMIR) — with a clearing obligation for standardised OTC-derivatives at the heart of it. The European Union did so in an effort to make the financial world a somewhat safer place after the outbreak of the global crisis. Similarly, the Dodd Franck Act introduces a clearing obligation for the United States. Under the terms of EMIR, standardised OTC derivatives are to be cleared through CCPs. CCPs reduce the number of bilateral business relationships and make the financial market more transparent. As a result, we gain greater security, but at the cost of new uncertainty: systemic risks can accumulate in CCPs, and we must take care that we do not get caught in a government bail-out and moral hazard trap, as we did with the banks.

The EU Commission is well aware of this danger. A legislative initiative for the resolution of CCPs and other FMIs is already on the stocks. The Financial Stability Board (FSB) also has this item high on its agenda, as CCPs typically do not serve just their home countries. Let me illustrate some aspects we need to consider when it comes to resolve an ailing CCP.

First, it would have to be done rapidly — overnight or over the weekend if we want to prevent chaos. CCPs are closely interlinked with a multitude of other market participants — often across national borders. And the CCPs themselves are linked with each other. Although central clearing reduces the *direct* inter-linkage of financial market participants (for clearing purposes) with each other, all operators are linked with the CCP — and also, therefore, *indirectly* with each other through the CCP. If you now consider that a CCP's clearing members are mainly systemically important banks and their clients are smaller financial institutions, then you can surely imagine what devastating domino effects the uncontrolled demise of a CCP could unleash.

Another important point: we would have to resolve CCPs — like other FMIs as well — in such a way that the financial market as a whole does not suffer too much damage. Some of their functions are vital for the financial market. They *must* be maintained.

If a CCP were to come to grief, then more often than not its international clearing members would also be affected. All resolution measures would therefore have to be effective in all legal jurisdictions in which the clearing members are based. Furthermore, there are CCPs that clear a number of markets in several jurisdictions. And there are CCPs that clear products that are denominated not in their own home-country currency but in other currencies. In the event of a resolution we might therefore also need liquidity in the form of foreign currencies.

If we transfer the functions that we want and have to maintain from one CCP to another CCP or to a bridge CCP, we would have to ensure that this CCP has the necessary authorisations, that it has the operational capacity to take on the business and that it is able to integrate this business into its risk management. If the resolution requires capital, taxpayers' money must not be used unless and until *all* possible sources of private funding have really been exhausted. Business — and not the State — should put up the funds — and if at all possible, in advance.

Ladies and Gentlemen, we also need to think about who should be in charge as the resolution authority. I think that whoever decides must have all the information it needs for a resolution; it must know the FMI. There is quite a lot to suggest that the authority that supervises the FMI should also take the decision on its resolution. The main reason for this is because the supervisor will closely monitor the FMI's recovery planning. Recovery planning and resolution planning go hand in hand and a rapid transition from recovery to resolution might be needed. In that case it would be good if both were under the same roof. But there should be a clear demarcation line separating supervision and resolution, because the resolution agency must act independently. One possible answer would be a resolution unit within the supervisory authority — a solution that I favour.

I'd like to conclude with a few words on global systemically important insurers. The FSB's Key Attributes (of Effective Resolution Regimes for Financial Institutions) also apply to them. However, their business models differ from those of other financial market infrastructures. A key component of recovery and resolution planning for global systemically important insurers is an analysis that identifies the firm's critical economic functions and critical shared services. Such an analysis will facilitate the development of resolution strategies that help to maintain these critical functions. The FSB has issued draft guidance for public consultation to assist authorities in their evaluation of the criticality of such functions.

You see, though banks might be served in the first place this does surely not mean that others would be omitted. Many thanks for your attention.

The Role of Bankruptcy in Resolutions
— CHAPTER 13

- Kenneth E. Scott
  Stanford University

Introduction

This session of the Conference is devoted to resolving the failure of systemically important financial institutions, but why? Is it a moot issue, at least for the US, having been solved by the Dodd–Frank Act of 2010? The two authors of the Act, who ironically were also two of the major Congressional supporters of the housing policies largely responsible for the crisis, assured us that they were making sure that it would never happen again. To that end, the Act vastly increased the powers of financial supervisors, called for almost 400 new regulations aimed at restrictions on risk-taking by financial institutions, launched a wave of increases in their required capital and liquidity, and mandated an unceasing series of stress tests. How could the failure of such institutions still occur?

For an answer, we might look at recent history. The 2008 financial crisis was based on the creation of around US$5 trillion in high-risk ('subprime' and 'Alt-A') mortgages, characterized by insignificant down-payments and modest initial interest rates, made to borrowers

Kenneth Scott is the Ralph M. Parsons Professor of Law and Business, Emeritus, and a senior research fellow at the Hoover Institution, Standford University.

with poor credit histories and often unverified income statements. But, aided by the Fed's very low interest rate policy, housing prices had been increasing at from 6% to 8% per annum for a number of years, so the collateral could repay the lender even if the borrower didn't. As long as the house-price appreciation bubble continued, there was no problem — but that came to an end in December 2006, and was replaced by rising delinquencies and defaults and foreclosure losses.

Ex post, of course, it all is clear. But at the time, as often noted, "they didn't see it coming", and 'they' included most Wall Street managers, financial regulators, politicians, and economists; people in general have found it difficult to accurately forecast the future. And unfortunately, the problems with political and managerial incentives to indulge in risk-taking are not much changed. Congress remains biased toward devising off-budget subsidies for constituents because they bypass the appropriations process; measures to facilitate underpriced mortgage loans for 'under-served' borrowers were at the core of the 2008 debacle. Management compensation in financial firms was, and is, often based on achieving short term targets that were not matched to longer term risk exposures. It is only prudent to think that the promise of 'never again' may not be fulfilled.

Official Resolution Regimes and the Resolution Project

There has quite appropriately, therefore, been considerable governmental activity directed at better ways to handle the failure of large financial firms. In the US, Title II of the Dodd–Frank Act authorized the Treasury Secretary to seize those financial companies whose impending default could threaten financial stability ('SIFIs') and to appoint the FDIC as a receiver. The FDIC has proposed a 'single point of entry' (SPOE) strategy of taking over the parent company and trying to keep operating subsidiaries in business.

The UK has adopted the Banking Act of 2009, and the Bank of England published this year its Approach to Resolution. The Financial

Stability Board issued in 2011 an initial paper on the Key Attributes of Effective Resolution Regimes for Financial Institutions, which was implemented in the EU in 2014 by adoption of the Bank Recovery and Resolution Directive. All of these are discussed by other authors in this volume.

In what has become a crowded field, is there need (so far as the US is concerned) for another entrant? We believe there is. Title II applies only to financial companies whose distress could pose a threat to US financial stability — at present only 12 firms have been so identified (and subjected to enhanced supervision by the Fed) though more could be added. And §203(b) of the Act makes bankruptcy code resolution if viable the necessary first choice even for them. The experience with the Lehman Brothers failure, however, pointed to areas for possible improvements in bankruptcy law that have yet to occur.

The Resolution Project at Stanford began with a 2009 Hoover Institution conference led by George Shultz and John Taylor, with contributions from Paul Volcker, Nicholas Brady and others, on making failure tolerable; the proceedings were published in 2010 as *Ending Government Bailouts as We Know Them*. The group is now composed of nine economists, lawyers and practitioners from the US and UK, and published a proposal (Chapter 14) for bankruptcy reform in 2012, *Bankruptcy Not Bailout: A Special Chapter 14*. Our revised proposal (Chapter 14 2.0) is largely completed, and should be published the first part of next year.

What is Different about Chapter 14?

Compared to Dodd-Frank Title II and FDIC's SPOE

Initially, there is a major difference in coverage. Title II, as noted, applies only to those financial companies whose failure could seriously threaten US financial stability. Chapter 14 is designed to handle all financial companies, not just a dozen or so giants seen as sources of systemic risk, on the premise that their activities have in common features warranting a special procedure.

Both the SPOE proposal and Chapter 14 do make a similar assumption: there will be a bail-in debt requirement in effect for some firms. If such a bail-in debt requirement is adopted, there will be two possible paths to resolution, and the bail-in debt should function in both:

(1) A new 'bridge' company is formed, to which are transferred assets and liabilities (other than the bail-in debt) from the failed firm. With the bail-in debt left behind, the new financial company is to that extent recapitalized.

   Under SPOE, the receiver has discretion to choose some liabilities to transfer to the new company, where they may expect to be paid in full, and to not transfer others, who can expect losses. That discretion is exercised in a closed administrative process, perhaps affected by considerations of systemic risk but also subject to political pressures, and not subject to any judicial oversight.

   Under Chapter 14, there is a set rule that *all* assets and liabilities (except bail-in and subordinated debt) go over to the bridge, enhancing transparency and predictability.

(2) The debtor firm itself, under Chapter 14, may be reorganized in the familiar Chapter 11 process, while continuing to conduct business. Creditors participate, in an open judicial process, to allocate losses and develop a final plan for operation. This seems likely to be the path chosen by smaller firms posing no systemic risk.

Commencing the Resolution Process

The petition may be filed either by the firm's management or by its supervisor, rather than the Treasury Secretary in the manner prescribed by Title II. Management may choose to make a voluntary filing (as is often done in Chapter 11 reorganizations) in order to preserve the firm and its operations (and possibly their jobs and some shareholder value). The Fed as primary supervisor may file (a) for a SIFI with a certification that it is necessary to avoid systemic consequences, or (b) for a non-SIFI financial company with a certification that it has substantial impairment of required regulatory capital.

Judicial Role

The Resolution Project takes the position that judicial oversight affords essential protection from abuse of power or political favoritism, as well as a remedy for gross error. That is lacking in Title II of Dodd–Frank. Section 202 affords the firm about to be seized a token hearing in the federal district court and the judge 24 hours to both conduct the hearing and render a written reasoned decision if negative, or the Treasury Secretary's petition is automatically granted by operation of law. Any appeal is under the high burden of meeting an 'arbitrary and capricious' standard, and any effective remedy is dubious since the receiver's actions to transfer or dismantle the firm cannot be stayed.

Chapter 14, in the case of a supervisory filing for a transfer to a bridge, requires only a certification of the necessary financial stability basis, and would permit the Treasury Secretary to transfer the case to a Title II proceeding with a certification of the inadequacy of a bankruptcy proceeding. This accommodates the severe time constraints for a 'resolution weekend' response to a perceived emergency, but does not pretend to give the debtor firm an ex ante opportunity to challenge the regulatory decisions. Instead, if the firm believes those actions unjustified, it can pursue an explicit ex post damage remedy against the government, testing whether there was at least "substantial evidence" to support the certifications and actions taken.

How Does Chapter 14 Differ from the Present Bankruptcy Code?

A number of provisions have been added to facilitate smooth continuity of operations by SIFIs to lessen spillover consequences. The expedited procedure for transfer motions, while not trampling on due process standards, is one example. Another is provision for DIP-type financing by the bridge, to address possible liquidity concerns. For firms in traditional bankruptcy reorganization, new financing can be given the top priority status of 'administrative expense', but the new bridge company is not in bankruptcy, so the existing provision does not apply. Chapter 14 would extend DIP priority to lenders to the bridge in the event of its subsequent failure within a year.

The automatic stay exemptions for QFCs and derivatives counterparties were cut back to allow time for a transfer to be effected — that is, exercise of any termination, close-out and cross-default rights would be stayed for two days. This is somewhat similar to the new ISDA Resolution Stay Protocol's effort at a contractual solution, but does not depend on voluntary adherence.

To facilitate attainment of international coordination and cooperation, provisions were added to Chapter 15 to allow the bankruptcy court to honor host country stay orders and prevent domestic ring-fencing of assets — if the host country gave similar treatment to US proceedings. Unlike joint supervisory agreements and understandings, court orders would be legally binding and enforceable, and thus more reliable.

What's Not Different?

Context

The functioning and effectiveness of all resolution regimes will depend significantly on the initial condition of the failed firm, as determined in part by regulatory mandates on organizational structure, capital, bail-in debt, liquidity, concentration of risk, and so on. There are still a lot of possible variables.

To take bail-in debt (or Total Loss Absorbing Capacity) as one example: how much was required, and how is it calculated? Is the denominator risk-weighted assets (using what model), total assets, off-balance-sheet assets? How much is left, using what valuations? How is it positioned in the firm's organizational structure?

Does it operate in both a one-firm reorganization through conversion (to what, in what ratio), and in a two-firm recapitalization through being left behind in the debtor estate? What triggers those actions?

Systemic Risk

Both Dodd–Frank Title II and Chapter 14 really address only one model of systemic risk: knock-on losses from the initial failure of a large firm

(Lehman Brothers), which cause other firms to become insolvent in turn and also fail, in a domino chain. That is what seems to have become the standard view of what caused the 2008 crisis, even if it lacks convincing support (e.g., no other firm promptly followed Lehman into insolvency because of large losses on Lehman debt).

A second model of systemic risk is based on a common shock affecting many firms at the same time: for example, the collapse in value of a very widely held asset — in this case, subprime US mortgages and their securitization tranches. Many institutions had large subprime exposures that were opaque to the market and of uncertain value, causing counterparties to lose confidence in their solvency and credit flows to dry up. What might it be next time? Maybe the leveraged loans regulators are now worrying about, maybe something not now visible at all.

So while designing a better resolution regime for a troubled financial institution is still a worthwhile objective, it should not be thought of (or judged) as a cure-all for all situations.

The Single Point of Entry Resolution Strategy and Market Incentives

— CHAPTER 14

■ James R. Wigand
Millstein & Company

Resolving systemically important financial companies without providing public assistance has been an elusive objective. Although popularly characterized as 'too big to fail', in reality these companies are systemically important due to being too connected or integrated into the financial system to fail without causing harm to the broader economy. During the 2008 financial crisis policy makers opted to provide public support to systemically important firms rather than allowing them to fail and further destabilize an already distressed financial system. To address the immediate need to minimize economic fall-out, governments increased moral hazard and the market distortions resulting from 'too connected to fail'.

The topic of this session, "Resolving Systemically Important Financial Institutions and Markets," was a major underlying consideration, if not the principal one, driving public policy responses to the most recent financial crisis. The tools available to policy makers in 2008 either

James R. Wigand is a partner at Millstein & Company and was the former Director of the Office of Complex Financial Institutions, Federal Deposit and Insurance Corporation.

provided public support for the failing firm, thereby increasing moral hazard, or resulted in financial instability. After the crisis, policy makers' attention focused on improving the set of options available to handle the failure of failing systemically important companies and whether a resolution strategy could be developed that imposes market discipline in a manner that mitigates moral hazard and yet avoids financial destabilization. This begs a question: Can a resolution strategy achieve a balance between these outcomes or are they mutually exclusive?

Before this question can be answered, one needs to understand some basic characteristics about systemically important financial companies, why market participants and counterparties react the way they do upon a financial firm's failure, and consider the Single Point of Entry (SPOE) strategy for resolving systemically important bank holding companies.

Systemically important bank holding companies in the United States can be categorized into four business models: universal banks; broker-dealers; processing/custodian banks; and super-regionals. Although within these broad categories each firm is unique, it is the direct and indirect connections with the broader financial system that determines a firm's systemic importance. Generally, these connections arise from a firm providing services critical to the functioning of the financial system or that have significant market share and lack short-term substitutability. Clearing and settlement of certain types of financial transactions or being among the largest providers of certain types of loans to businesses or consumers would be examples. Should these services cease or be interrupted, customers dependent on the service would be unable to transact business, resulting in consequences to the real economy.

However, the systemically important connections to financial system participants may be indirect. Systemically important broker-dealers perform services that are can be found in many non-systemically important broker-dealers. The services are essentially substitutable. In this case the problem that arises is, when a systemically important broker-dealer fails, counterparties have rights to accelerate and terminate their contracts with the failed firm, resulting in massive collateral sales. These fire-sales, in turn, cause collateral asset prices to fall and force other firms holding similar collateral to mark-down the value of similar assets. Consequently, even though a financial firm may not have any direct business with the failing financial company, it could see its capital position erode and become subject to collateral calls due to the re-pricing of its book.

It is because of these direct and indirect effects that systemically important universal banks pose the greatest resolution challenges.

The largest and most complex universal banks conduct their operations by business line, not by legal entity. Those business lines, retail banking for example, perform services through dozens, if not hundreds of subsidiaries chartered in multiple domestic and foreign jurisdictions. The transactions may or may not be booked at the subsidiary from which a customer or counterparty obtained the service. And, although the risk associated with the transaction may be hedged at the enterprise level through off-setting transactions in different subsidiaries, the transaction may remain fully exposed within a single subsidiary. At any moment in time it may not be readily apparent to a counterparty (or to regulators) exactly which legal entity within the banking enterprise is the party to its contract and what the financial condition is of that legal entity. Even though thousands of legal entities comprise the banking enterprise, it operates as a single firm, allocating capital and liquidity by business line, and collectively managing the risks among its many operating subsidiaries.

In other words, systemically important financial companies are directly and indirectly interconnected with other players in the financial system. Some of those connections are known and observable to certain participants prior to failure and others are not.

The failure of Lehman Brothers in September 2008 provides insights to real-world market behavior upon the failure of a systemically important financial company. Among the first 'market' responses upon Lehman Brothers' holding company's bankruptcy filing, was the Lehman Brothers United Kingdom subsidiary board's filing for administrative protection due to the prospect of having insufficient liquidity to meet its obligations, immediately establishing cross-border competing insolvencies among the Lehman enterprise's companies. A Lehman servicing subsidiary in India, its management not knowing which entities had legal rights to the information it produced, ceased the transmission of reports to affiliates. Repo counterparties quickly terminated their contracts and sold posted collateral. As the volume of collateral sales increased, the prices of similar assets decreased, resulting in other financial firms revaluing their holdings and being subjected to collateral calls. One money market fund holding Lehman bonds 'broke the buck', resulting in a run on money market funds not holding any Lehman investments. Banks heavily invested in mortgage related products similar to Lehman's, such as Washington Mutual Bank, experienced increasing deposit withdraws. The direct and indirect connections were clearly observable, but often with unanticipated outcomes.

It is fair to say that the underlying common thread among these observable 'market' reactions is that fear of the unknown and uncertainty of outcome incent counterparties to pull-back and stop transacting business. Any resolution approach that does not provide predictable outcomes for market participants likely will result in disorderly markets and financial instability.

The Single Point of Entry strategy is an approach that has considerable promise for resolving systemically important bank holding companies in a manner that addresses moral hazard and minimizes financial instability. Although commonly associated with its potential application under the Title II set of authorities of the Dodd–Frank Act in the United States, the SPOE strategy could be implemented under other insolvency regimes, including the United States Bankruptcy Code and public agency or judicial insolvency frameworks in other jurisdictions. It is a strategy that requires a set of conditions regarding the capital structure, intra-company relationships, and counterparty contracts of a bank holding company to be met prior to the company's entry into resolution. The combination of the SPOE strategic approach and structural pre-positioning appears to address the key impediments to an orderly resolution.

Under the SPOE strategy the top-tier holding company is the only legal entity within the systemically important enterprise that is placed into resolution. The hundreds, or thousands, of downstream subsidiaries remain open, operating, and outside of insolvency proceedings. In the first step of the resolution process after failure, as quickly as permissible under the applicable insolvency regime, the failed company's insolvency estate conveys the assets of the top-tier holding company, essentially cash and investments (stock) in subsidiaries, to a newly created financial holding company in exchange for all of the equity in the

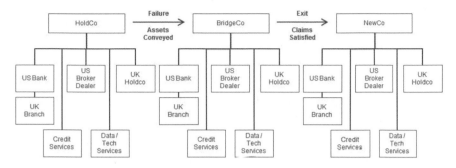

Figure 1. Resolution/Recapitalization process.

new company. Previous examples of the type of conveyance include the establishment of 'bridge banks' under the Federal Deposit Insurance Act and the '363 sale' (named after the relevant provision in the US Bankruptcy Code) of the going-concern assets of General Motors in its bankruptcy proceeding. See Figure 1.

Shareholder equity and liabilities of the former top-tier holding company are now claims in its insolvency estate and the equity of the new financial holding company is the principal asset of the estate available to satisfy those claims.

In contrast, the new financial holding company initially has no liabilities: on the left side of its balance sheet are the assets of cash and investments (stock) in subsidiaries and on the right side of its balance sheet, equity. Until the new financial company issues new debt, it has no liabilities. All of the former top-tier holding company's debts remain as claims in the insolvency estate.

An important feature of this structure from a financial stability perspective is that the operating companies of the financial firm remain open and operating. They continue to provide the critical services and maintain the connectivity that caused the financial enterprise to be considered systemically important. Also, since the operating companies themselves are not in resolution, contracts between these companies and counterparties would remain in place and stand in the normal course of business. Access to customary sources of funding should be available. Bank branches and subsidiaries hosted in foreign jurisdictions now have a top-tier parent with a stronger balance sheet than prior to resolution and would not likely require placement into the jurisdiction's insolvency regime to protect creditors.

However, counterparties and regulators of the operating companies will need to be confident that they will be able to perform in accordance with the terms of contractual agreements. For this reason, mechanisms must exist for ensuring adequate capital and liquidity at the operating subsidiary company level.

Adequate capital can be maintained at the operating subsidiaries either through intra-company capital maintenance agreements or through intra-company subordinated convertible debt instruments. In either approach, upon reaching a threshold trigger, contractual agreements between the operating company and, most likely, the top-tier holding company, would cause the capital level of the operating company to increase and effectively transfer its losses to the parent holding company. These contractual agreements would need to be in place and pre-positioned among the domestic and foreign subsidiaries before the financial holding company goes into resolution.

Although capital support covers actual or perceived capital impairment, a credible back-up source of liquidity must be available directly or indirectly to the operating companies to provide confidence that their obligations can be paid when due. In the Title II set of authorities, the US Treasury can extend a line of credit to the Federal Deposit Insurance Corporation for this purpose.

What has occurred in this first step of the post-failure resolution process is the separation of the going-concern operations of the financial enterprise from the process of adjudicating claims against the failed financial company's estate and the allocation of the value of the failed firm's assets to satisfy those claims. Additionally, the failed firm's businesses have been stabilized to allow for the continuity of services.

The second and third steps of the post-failure process, depending on the jurisdiction and insolvency regime applying the SPOE strategy, envision the so called 'bail-in' of creditors of the failed holding company and restructuring of the failed enterprise's businesses. One can think of these two steps running concurrently, but not necessarily on the same timelines.

'Bail-in' in the context of SPOE is, in essence, the exchange of certain creditor claims in the old financial holding company, such as those held by the failed company's subordinated or senior debt investors, for common or preferred equity, debt, or contingent value instruments in the new financial holding company. The amount of 'bail-in-able' instruments needed for 'bail-in' will depend on the amount of inherent economic loss in the failed financial company's assets and businesses, and the capitalization requirements of the new financial company (or companies) after it exits the process, since these instruments are the source of its capital. The types of financial instruments eligible for 'bail-in' and the calibration of the amount of those instruments that global systemically important financial companies may be required to hold are discussed in the Financial Stability Board's consultative document on Total Loss Absorbing Capital (TLAC). Long term subordinated and senior bonds are among the eligible instruments.[1] See Figure 2.

Given that the financial company failed, neither market participants nor regulators would view a financial enterprise emerging from the resolution process that was essentially the same as the one entering resolution, only with a restructured capital stack, as a practical outcome. The causes of failure will have to be addressed, evolving market conditions taken into account, and all statutory and regulatory requirements for the businesses that survive will have to be met. Market pressures leading up to and through the resolution process almost guaranty that the businesses that emerge will be smaller, in some cases substantially so, than the ones that existed before the company became distressed.

Ultimately, the process results in a new set of owners of the failed financial company's assets and businesses, and a company (or companies) that is smaller and less complex than the failed enterprise.[2]

With the conclusion of this brief overview of the SPOE concept, I would like to return to the question I posed earlier regarding moral hazard and financial instability.

---

[1] See Financial Stability Board (2014).
[2] For a more detailed explanation on how the FDIC proposes to use the SPOE approach under Title II of the Dodd–Frank Act, see *Federal Register* (2013).

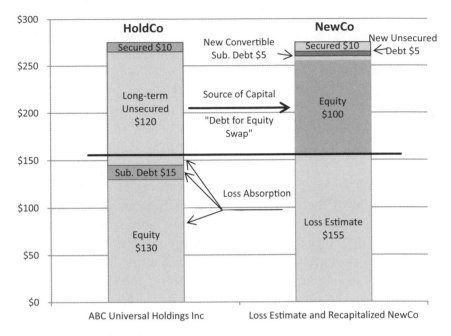

Figure 2. Resolution process: Capitalization of NewCo and distribution of losses claims waterfall (US$ billion).

As noted earlier, uncertainty is the driving force of market participant behavior that ultimately results in financial instability arising from a systemically important financial company's failure. Reducing uncertainty will reduce financial instability. History has repeatedly demonstrated that this premise is true. In fact, the most common approach used to reduce uncertainty has been the direct provision of sovereign support and assurances.

By its very design, the SPOE strategy provides greater certainty of outcome than alternative resolution approaches without the benefit of public support.

The structural subordination established from the pre-positioning of contractual obligations, both internally and to third parties, establishes a clear hierarchy of loss absorption. The failed enterprise's holding company's equity holders are first in line to absorb loss. Then the holding company's long-term debt holders are next, subordinated and senior, in the applicable insolvency framework's order of priority. Only upon the improbable exhaustion of loss absorbing and recapitalization capacity at the holding company level would the stakeholders of a subsidiary within the enterprise be subject to loss. I should note that the SPOE strategy presumes that if a subsidiary within the enterprise could have failed without causing the failure of its holding company and affiliates, both regulators and the enterprise's board would have permitted the subsidiary to fail to preserve the economic and going concern value of the rest of the enterprise.

Being at risk of loss is not the same as being at risk of conversion of a financial interest. In the former case, the claim holder has suffered some degree of economic loss. In the latter case, the claim holder may not have suffered any economic loss, but experienced a change in the characteristics of the economic interest held in the firm's assets and businesses. Those changes, nonetheless, could affect the claimant's liquidity and risk profiles. The calibration of the amount and types of 'bail-in-able' instruments must factor these differing risks.

Under SPOE those impacted at the holding company level by either of these risks are relatively few, compared to all of the enterprise's other stakeholders and counterparties, and should be well aware of being subject to loss and conversion risks at the time of making their investment.

Conversely, the counterparties to the enterprise's subsidiaries are at low risk of default on their contractual obligations and should expect to transact business in the normal course. This is critical to minimizing financial instability associated with resolution, since for the typical post-crisis bank holding company, short term liabilities reside at the subsidiary operating company level and not at the top-tier holding company. Accordingly, the short-term creditor counterparty, such as a repo lender or depositor, is at very low risk of loss and is not incented to run. Market participants, recognizing that other systemically important financial institutions would be resolved through a SPOE approach, also would have less incentive to run from their counterparties, thereby minimizing contagion effects.

The effect of the structural subordination within the systemically important enterprise is that creditors of the subsidiary operating companies become 'senior' to the shareholders and creditors of the top-tier holding company. Rather than a sovereign reducing uncertainty by providing credit support (historically through capital injections to the company or assurances) to the operating companies' creditors, the top-tier holding company's shareholders and creditors do so under SPOE.

But, by providing greater certainty and therefore reducing the likelihood of financial instability, does the SPOE strategy mitigate the moral hazard problem or make it worse?

There are two sub-components to solving the moral hazard question: where within the enterprise should market discipline be imposed, and the agency issue as to whom, among stakeholders, is best positioned to evaluate, price and be at risk of loss.

To address the moral hazard issue, alignment of return and risk with the ability to control is essential. Clearly, the enterprise's owners should be at risk. They benefit from the risk-taking that generates earnings and profits from the holding company's subsidiaries and should incur the losses those risks entail as well. They also elect the board which controls the key business and policy decisions of the enterprise and appoints the management that runs the day-to-day operations of the company. The enterprise's board decided to have the enterprise operate as an integrated whole with businesses crossing multiple subsidiaries and not as a set of independent companies that could individually fail without bringing down the entire enterprise. Control of the enterprise flows from the holding company. Accordingly, proper alignment suggests the answer for 'where' is the holding company.

Given that every risky investment has a probability distribution of possible positive and negative outcomes, an investor reserving onto one's self the upside and being able to exercise a free or inefficiently priced put option for the downside risk is a very appealing situation. Academics for years have asserted that the provision of deposit insurance results in moral hazard, especially when a bank's capital level approaches zero, since at that point the bank's owners have nothing to lose. The depositor insurer absorbs the losses if investments go bad, and the owners gain equity if the investments perform well. Although this issue is most apparent when a bank's capital is near zero, in a highly leveraged firm the amount of equity only serves as a marginal buffer: creditors, not equity holders, will always hold the downside-risk distribution tail. The equity owners effectively exercise a put option for the tail risk to the bank's creditors. Company owners believing, *ex ante*, that gains or profits from business decisions can be privatized and that losses can be mutualized incents excessive risk taking.

As stated earlier, in the United States, all large banks, as well as most small banks, are owned by bank holding companies. These, in turn, are owned by investors. When a bank fails, it is the bank holding company as owner of the bank that exercises the put option, leaving creditors of the bank to bear the consequences of management's decisions. Typically, the FDIC, as deposit insurer, becomes the principal creditor. Very infrequently do other parties become principal creditors. Yet, for non-depository financial firms, that is always the case. The losses are mutualized to the subsidiary's creditors once the holding company's equity is depleted.

Without the adoption of the SPOE strategy and structural prepositioning, creditors of a financial holding company's highly leveraged subsidiaries will continue to hold the downside risk distribution tail. Most of the creditors at the subsidiary level hold short term obligations. In the vast majority of cases, the only control these creditors can exercise is the contractually provided withdrawal or non-renewal of their investment. Rather than exercising any control through covenants or incurring the cost of robust research to decide to invest, short term creditors can terminate their contracts and business relationship at almost any time. For having this option, short term creditors accept a lower yield on their investment than long term creditors.

Short term creditors exercise this option by ending their investment with the counterparty upon the learning of negative news that might impact their counterparty's ability to repay. They become senior to other creditors by being paid earlier, when the distressed firm still has sufficient funds to pay obligations in full when due. This behavior is very apparent in the attrition of uninsured deposits at problem banks. Short term creditors may react to the outcomes of investment decisions, but they have little ability to exert any influence beforehand.

For financial companies, in many respects, short term liabilities are analogous to trade payables in other industries.

Alternatively, long term creditors, by having a long term investment horizon, are better incented to incur the cost of researching a company and its investment practices, thereby pricing the cost of credit to that firm, than are short term creditors. They can exit, but with consequence. The investment portfolio manager at an insurance company, pension fund, or bond mutual fund has both the incentive and skill to better understand the financial information and price risk regarding a systemically important financial firm than does a retail depositor or trader at a repo desk who typically depend on rating agency ratings to assess risk.[3]

This suggests that the answer to 'who' should be the equity holders and long-term creditors. The SPOE strategic approach does appear to mitigate moral hazard by having losses first absorbed at the holding company level by its equity holders and then long term creditors.

However, for the insolvency to be focused at the holding company, a mechanism must be in place to keep the integrated operating companies from failing. Losses occur at the operating company or subsidiary level and flow up to the holding company through accounting consolidation. The resulting capital depletion at the operating company level may cause its creditors or regulators to place the subsidiary into an insolvency process, even if that action would cause affiliates to fail and a loss of value to creditors. To avoid this scenario, SPOE requires a mechanism within the enterprise for down-streaming capital from the holding company to its operating subsidiaries — internal bail-in.

The concept of bank holding companies providing support to their bank depository subsidiaries has been a policy in the United States for over fifty years. However, this "source of strength" doctrine has been challenging to implement in practice, with courts requiring a clear contractual obligation by the holding company to provide that support and

---

[3] For a discussion of short-term vs long-term creditor incentives, see Huang and Ratnovski (2011). Published earlier as: Lev Ratnovski and Rocco Huang (2010), "The Dark Side of Bank Wholesale Funding," IMF Working Papers 10/170, International Monetary Fund.

not recognizing general regulatory directives or policy. Furthermore, the 'source of strength' doctrine extends only to the bank depository and not to other subsidiaries of the holding company, such as a broker dealer.[4]

The solution under SPOE for down-streaming capital from the holding company to its inadequately capitalized subsidiaries is to require the holding company to have a contractual obligation in place before the capital is needed. The contractual obligation could take a variety of forms, although an instrument familiar with the market that would be effective is a convertible bond issued by the subsidiary and owned by the holding company that converts to equity upon the subsidiary's capital level reaching a certain threshold. The automatic conversion may need to be supplemented with an optional call feature that the subsidiary's regulator could exercise to ensure the subsidiary continues to meet all supervisory capital requirements. This feature should mitigate the risk that a host country supervisor will need to ring-fence the financial company's domestic assets and operations.

In summary, the SPOE strategy with the proper structural pre-positioning of the enterprise establishes a hierarchy of loss absorption through the structural subordination of the holding company to its operating companies. This hierarchy better aligns the risk of loss with control of the enterprise than previous resolution approaches. Additionally, the strategic approach puts at greater risk stakeholders of the enterprise who are better positioned to price risk, incur loss, and minimize the systemic consequences of a systemically important company's failure.

References

Financial Stability Board (2014), "Adequacy of Loss-absorbing Capacity of Global Systemically Important Banks in Resolution," Consultative Document, November 10.

Federal Register (1987), "Policy Statement on the Responsibility of Bank Holding Companies to Act as Sources of Strength to Their Subsidiary Banks." *Federal Register*, 52: 15707 (April 30, 1987).

---

[4] See *Federal Register* (1987).

Federal Register (2013), "Resolution of Systemically Important Financial Institutions: The Single Point of Entry Strategy." *Federal Register*, 78: 76614–76624 (December 18, 2013).

Huang, R. and L. Ratnovski (2011), "The dark side of bank wholesale funding," *Journal of Financial Intermediation*, 20(2): 248–263.

Part V
Transitional Impact of the Reforms on the Financial Sector

Model Risk and the Great Financial Crisis

The Rise of Modern Model Risk Management

— CHAPTER 15

- Jeffrey A. Brown, Brad McGourty and Til Schuermann
  Oliver Wyman

Introduction

Banking is not simple, even if we want it to be. Banks intermediate between clients displaying a broad set of needs living in a global and interconnected economy. It is naïve to think that bankers can manage by gut feel and 'expert judgment' alone. Models are critical to help bankers and their clients and customers to make sense of the complexities of their needs and the product and service offerings.

But with complex models comes model risk, and as with any risk, model risk needs to be managed. The professionalization of model risk management is arguably one of the more significant, and welcome, developments since the recent great financial crisis. There are good

Brown and Schuermann are Partners and McGourty is a Principal in New York. They thank Michael Duane and Peter Reynolds, the participants of the Federal Reserve Bank of Chicago's 17th Annual Conference on International Banking, and especially its organizer Doug Evanoff. All remaining errors are the authors.

reasons for this development: models, or rather the blind faith in poorly specified models, were a significant contributor to the financial crisis itself. Examples abound, but perhaps the poster child examples are the alphabet soup of structured credit products such as CDOs, ABS, CPDOs, and so on. These products require estimation of a complex joint return and loss distribution across the hundreds and often thousands of underlying exposure return and loss distributions. The Gaussian copula — essentially a multivariate normal distribution which 'couples' together the underlying possibly heterogeneous distributions — was the model of choice for a very wide range of credit products. The blind faith in this model, and its consequences, is dramatically described in a February 23, 2009 *Wired* Magazine cover page article titled "Recipe for Disaster: the Formula that Killed Wall Street" (Salmon 2009).

In this paper we give a thumbnail history of model risk management (MRM) over the past two decades to help explain the recent sharpened focus on this discipline. As is, alas, often the case, that focus and corresponding resource expenditure has been driven in part by regulatory pressure, and that pressure has increased dramatically in the post crisis years. We present some examples of model risk management failures, trace regulatory developments in MRM requirements and expectations, and end with a cautionary note given the explosion of models that has come with the CCAR (Comprehensive Capital Analysis and Review) program. Importantly, not only has this dramatic growth in the number and use of models occurred at the banks but also at the regulatory agencies, the Federal Reserve in particular which now relies heavily on models to assess bank safety in the face of stress tests through its CCAR program.[1] Proper model risk management is perhaps especially important for regulators since those models, by design, affect not just individual banks but the entire banking system (or at least the roughly 80% subject to the CCAR program), and are thus a nontrivial source of systemic risk.

---

[1] We will use the term 'regulator' and 'supervisor' somewhat interchangeably, erring to the more commonly understood 'regulator' while recognizing that the use of models by banks is touched by both regulatory and supervisory activities. The distinction between regulation and supervision is subtle, but regulation tends to be prescriptive and formal while supervision is more qualitative and informal. Refer to Federal Reserve Board of Governors (2005, pp. 59–60).

To be sure, we are not advocates of making decisions without the use of models. Quite the contrary: we strongly believe that the discipline and empirical rigor that come with formal modeling provide a strong basis for less biased and all around better (e.g. less risky) decision making in banking narrowly and financial services more broadly. We remain suspicious of casual use of so-called expert judgment. However, as long-time model builders (and validators) ourselves, we have built up a healthy skepticism for models and view them strictly as decision aids, not decision makers. The crisis has taught us the dangers of "model on, brain off", and as with any powerful tool, it is needs to be accompanied by a tight control structure, i.e. with proper model risk management.

The Rise of Model Risk Management in Banking

Formal models have long been in use in trading rooms at capital markets intensive firms such as the large investment banks, or those divisions at the large global banks. Jorion (2006) describes a short history of the use of models and, more to the point here, their use in the risk management of trading. Typically, the more complex the product, the more important is a formal model for its risk management.

The regulatory response came with the 1996 Market Risk Amendment of the first Basel Capital Accord (BCBS 1996) which allowed for the use of models to assess and determine the amount of capital needed to support market risk from trading. However, the term 'model risk' does not appear in this regulatory document.[2] Thankfully, many of those banks affected (and likely some that were not) already had a healthy respect for model risk. Much of the work on derivatives modeling was done by modelers trained in the physical sciences, some of whom were aware of the differences between those models and the primarily statistical models used in finance; see for instance Derman (1996).

A rather dramatic example of poor model risk management can be traced to the demise of the hedge fund LTCM (Long-Term Capital

---

[2] By contrast, the most recent version of the Basel Capital Accord, Basel III, makes explicit mention of the importance of model risk; BCBS (2011).

Management) in 1998. LTCM's overly optimistic assumptions of market liquidity needed for seamless hedging are well known. Jorion (2000) presents a rich picture of simple failures in their risk measurement and management framework of value-at-risk (VaR). The firm used VaR results to assess its level of riskiness, and thus required capital, analogous to the Basel Market Risk Amendment of 1996. The VaR approach, which continues to be used in risk management to assess market risk, relies on several key inputs that will impact the level of conservatism (or lack thereof) in the modeled results. Jorion identifies several inputs and assumptions used by LTCM that contributed to a significant underestimation of risk.

Jorion (2000) provides a nice example of a typical LTCM trade. One of LTCM's strategies was to go long corporate debt and short U.S. Treasuries (as a hedge). This strategy works well so long as the correlation between the two positions is sufficiently high. The assumed correlation was around 96%. The implied monthly volatility for this position was around 8.1%. But if the correlation were to drop to 90%, that volatility would go up to 13.6%, and if it dropped further to 85%, the monthly volatility would increase to 19.2%, now more than double the assumed position volatility. Jorion (2000) points out that the empirical correlation was as low as 75% just six years earlier in 1992!

More broadly, model related lessons from LTCM include:

- Volatility was assumed to be constant; in reality, one could expect volatility to increase significantly during periods of market instability, as demonstrated clearly by the development of dynamic volatility models like ARCH (Engle 1982) and GARCH (Bollerslev 1986)[3]
- Returns were assumed to be normally distributed (i.e., symmetric and with well-behaved tails), though it is well-known that asset returns are fat-tailed and often skewed (see Diebold (2012) for a recent survey)
- The time period used to establish model parameters was relatively short and did not give sufficient consideration to historical market downturn events (e.g., the crash of 1987)

---

[3] The assumption of static volatilities has been a common source of series model risk. Another example is the bankruptcy of Orange County due to the long duration strategy by its investment manager, Robert Citron.

- The 10-day horizon prescribed in regulatory guidance may not be adequate for a hedge fund, where investments may become illiquid and the time to raise new equity may be substantially longer, particular during times of stress

Danielsson *et al.* (2014) provide powerful evidence showing how hard it is to find a convincing specification for market risk models like VaR and expected shortfall. They focus on one aspect of model risk: "the potential for different models to provide inconsistent outcomes." They find that model disagreement, i.e. model risk, is higher in periods of market uncertainty than in periods of calm. Model risk thus goes up exactly when you need accurate risk forecasts the most.

In we provide a simple illustration of the rise of model risk management over the last two decades. We divide this time span into three periods. The first is pre-2000 which saw an expansion of model use and a gradual recognition of the corresponding need for model risk management. This period saw a proliferation of model use in banking (valuation, credit evaluation, risk measurement), and an increasing complexity of models generally.

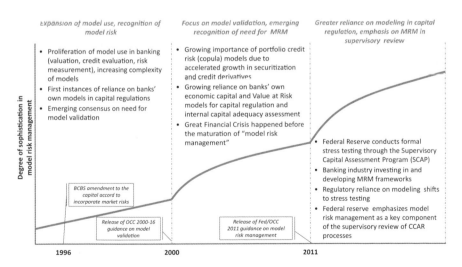

Figure 1. Evolution of model risk management (MRM) in US banking.

An important step in model risk management is independent model validation, and by the mid to late 1990s we saw the birth of independent model validation functions within banks. In 2000, the OCC issued its seminal guidance ('OCC 2000-16') to banks on model validation:[4]

"Model development is a complex and error-prone process."
"Fortunately, model risk can be considerably reduced. Sound modeling includes rigorous procedures for 'model validation.'"

The key insights of OCC 2000-16 were that all financial models are subject to errors, that certain key procedural activities need to be followed to attempt to identify and eliminate those errors, and that those activities need to be executed by qualified and independent parties. Those activities were then largely adopted by the Basel Committee in the requirements for model validation of the internal models that were the centerpiece of the 'Basel II' risk-based capital regime, an early draft of which appeared in 2001. And indeed the US capital regulation implementing Basel II (the Advanced Approaches) requires validation of the advanced systems on an ongoing basis.[5]

The rise of formal regulatory pressure on firms to conduct model validation is a key development of the second phase illustrated above. This period — roughly 2000 through the end of the financial crisis — also marked the rapid development and adoption of complex credit instruments through securitization. In the years prior to the financial crisis, securitization was a powerful tool for banks to manage their credit exposure by tapping new investors hungry for highly rated, yet higher yielding, fixed income assets. This allowed banks to free up capital in order to originate more credit (e.g. make more loans such as mortgages). However, the complex structure of those securitizations, including MBS, was not fully understood by banks or investors, or by the rating agencies. Indeed, the models used to value these products and

---

[4] Office of the Comptroller of the Currency, OCC Bulletin, *Model Validation*, OCC 2000–16 (May 30, 2000)
[5] 12 CFR, Part 225, appendix G, Section 22, (j)(4).

assess their riskiness relied on key assumptions that, if even moderately incorrect, would produce dramatically different results.

Using an example of a relatively simple subprime RMBS (simple because the underlying asset pool was quite homogeneous), Ashcraft and Schuermann (2008) show the confidence of the structurers, and the rating agencies, in being able to accurately determine the riskiness of different tranches of the return and loss distribution. One of those tranches was only 70 basis points wide (at issuance it was rated BB+ and Ba1 by S&P and Moody's respectively), presuming an astounding degree of model accuracy.

Return and loss correlation, or dependence more broadly, is a core modeling feature of all credit securitizations and, of course, re-securitizations like CDOs. Models commonly used in the years prior to the crisis to value securitizations relied upon a 'Gaussian copula function', an approach widely attributed to financial engineer David Li. The approach was attractive in that it offered a simple solution to analyze very complicated securities using data observed from credit default swap transactions. For example, the Gaussian copula is a default choice in the popular FinCAD software. Felix Salmon (2009) described the breathtaking speed and impact of this model in his *Wired* Magazine article. It is worth quoting from this article: "During the boom years, everybody could reel off reasons why the Gaussian copula function wasn't perfect. Li's approach made no allowance for unpredictability: it assumed that correlation was a constant rather than something mercurial. Investment banks would regularly phone Stanford's Duffie and ask him to come in and talk to them about exactly what Li's copula was. Every time, he would warn them that it was not suitable for use in risk management or valuation."

Elsewhere Duffie (2007) has demonstrated that the Gaussian copula model was generating results that should have revealed that model to be invalid for pricing and hedging and, indeed, generated inconsistent pricing across tranches of a given securitization. "If the pool correlation parameter necessary to price one set of tranches is not close to the pool correlation parameter necessary to price another set of tranches then the model is not appropriate" (p. 41). Duffie (2007) illustrates this inconsistency with the hedging failures stemming from a May 2005 GM downgrade and its impact on the CDX, an index of credit derivatives, pointing out that the pricing reaction for the desired hedging position had the wrong sign. "Rather than reducing their losses, hedgers following this approach slightly *increased* their losses!" (p. 42).

Credit derivatives are an easy target for model bashers, but the salient point is that the models featured recognized risks that were not managed. In a cleverly titled paper, "Credit Models and the Crisis, or: How I learned to stop worrying and love the CDOs," Brigo *et al.* (2010) respond to the "hysteria that has often characterized accounts of modeling and mathematical finance in part of the press and media, and the demonization of part of the market products related to the crisis, such as CDOs and derivatives more generally" (p. 1). They argue that model limitations were actually more widely known than often attributed before the crisis, even if not always formally implemented into a given firm's risk management program via formalized model risk management. For example, the model was typically calibrated on the loss of a pool of loans as an aggregate which is not useful for creating hedges for single names. Models designed to address known weaknesses are slow to be adopted because it takes time to test them and overcome the systems issues required to deploy them, and because they frequently end up requiring a net increase in the number of models rather than the replacement of the old model. Despite the known limitations and weakness of the Gaussian copula model, it was widely used without appropriate governance.

Another example of widespread model failures pre-crisis was the disappointing performance of economic capital models used by most large banks in the U.S. and Europe to assess their required capital needs. These models were based on detailed bespoke approaches to assess risks across all activities, on and off balance sheet, of large complex banks, primarily for capital adequacy purposes. Such models were (and still are) typically calibrated to a very low one-year probability of default for the bank, on the order of 0.05%.[6] They became common tools across large complex banks in the 1990s and were widely used in banks' internal

---

[6] For a discussion of economic capital models and their use, see Dev (2004).

**16 INSTITUTIONS WITH PUBLICLY
STATED ECONOMIC CAPITAL**

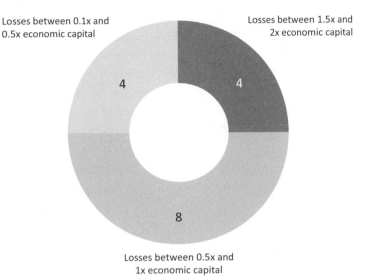

Losses between 0.1x and
0.5x economic capital

Losses between 1.5x and
2x economic capital

4

4

8

Losses between 0.5x and
1x economic capital

Figure 2. Ratio of crisis losses to declared pre-crisis economic capital.[7]

assessment of capital adequacy. However, the use of those models emerged just as model validation standards were emerging and since they were viewed as a contributor to 'internal' assessments of capital adequacy, they were not subject to standardized, formal supervisory review.

Oliver Wyman (2012) provides a comparison of one-year economic capital estimates from the mid-2000s vs. realized one-year losses in the crisis to demonstrate the inadequacy of the modeled results. Of 16 financial institutions with publicly reported economic capital results, 25% experienced losses of at least 150% of their economic capital estimates.

In the US, the worst of the financial crisis came to an end with the 2009 bank stress test, the SCAP (Supervisory Capital Assessment Program) which spawned the post-crisis regulatory stress testing program, now

---

[7] Analysis is based on publicly reported economic capital results within 3 years prior to the start of the crisis and the maximum losses over the worst one-year period, as defined by Bloomberg.

mandated by the Dodd–Frank Act. A key component of the SCAP was the use of supervisory models based on detailed bank data, as described in Hirtle *et al.* (2009). This event marks the beginning of the modern approach to capital regulation, which is characterized by the approval of target capital levels informed by stress test modeling. With the SCAP and subsequent CCAR program which commenced in 2011, risk modeling expanded from just balance sheet exposures to also take into account, formally, income statement dynamics, and did so by explicitly conditioning on economic and market risk factors such as unemployment, GDP, home prices, interest rates and equity indices. All US banks >US$10 billion in assets are required to run such stress tests using three provided supervisory scenarios at least once a year, and banks >US$50 billion in assets that are part of the Fed's CCAR program, are also required to design their own stress scenarios suitable for their particular business and risk profile (which may be different from a more generic profile to which the common supervisory scenarios are tailored).

There are over 200 line items in the CCAR forms, the FR Y-14A, which require some type of modeled output. That requires a lot of models! It is not uncommon for a CCAR bank to have developed 50–150 models specifically for their CCAR submissions. These models are now expected to be subjected to a rigorous and formal model risk management program, including but no longer limited to, model validation. All of this is quite resource intensive. Models can take several months to build, and 4–8 weeks to validate. We see the staffing of model risk management groups approaching the size of the modeling groups themselves.

Model Risk Management Today ... and Going Forward

Over the decade following the issuance of the OCC's Model Validation Guidance in 2000, supervisory attention was broadened from model validation to the more general concept of model risk management. That evolution was reflected in a joint Supervisory Guidance on Model Risk Management issued by the Federal Reserve and the OCC in 2011, which marks the beginning of the phase three in the evolution of model risk management.[8] This modern view of model risk management, articulated in the guidance, recognizes that risk is inherent in model use and calls for a risk management framework that is similar to the frameworks used to manage other important risks to the firm.

A sound model risk management framework is predicated on the notion that modeling is a process as opposed to a discrete, one-time activity. Consequently, model risk management reflects the 'life-cycle' view of the modeling process, from the initial business or risk management need to development, testing and validation, implementation, monitoring and updating, to its ultimate retirement.

As with all risk management activities, model risk management requires a framework that comprises appropriate infrastructure, management attention and board oversight.[9] The key elements of that framework are:

- An expression of an acceptable degree of model risk as part of the firm's risk appetite statement, and a general level of awareness of and respect for model risk within the firm
- Policy and procedures that assign clear responsibilities, accountabilities and controls
- Senior management demonstration of responsibility and accountability for the framework through the devotion of appropriate resources and attention to model risk and its management
- Board of Directors demonstration of oversight over this risk management framework, commensurate with its importance to the institution.

In summary, the modern view of MRM is much broader than the act of model validation, requiring the recognition that model risk is inherent to the use of models and that the proper management of model risk requires a formal program with numerous potential elements that can be used to minimize or respond to the risk. As an indicator of the professionalization of MRM, a casual survey among our clients in the US (in this case about two dozen large banks from

---

[8] Federal Reserve Board and Office of the Comptroller of the Currency, *Supervisory Guidance on Model Risk Management* (April 4, 2011).

[9] For a discussion of the Board's responsibilities, see Yoost (2013).

the CCAR program plus some large foreign banks active in the US) indicates that about half of the heads of model risk management are now direct reports to the Chief Risk Officer, making them peers of heads of market and credit risk management and business risk heads. Chief model risk managers now provide regular reports and direct presentations to the risk committee of Boards of Directors of banks, further evidence of the much elevated stature of MRM following the financial crisis.

This modern view of model risk management, however, is not a completely new invention; instead it reflects the culmination of a view developed over decades. Returning to the 1996 Goldman Sachs Research Note on model risk, for example, Derman noted that there are many types of model risk with an array of appropriate responses. An interesting example was the risk of having the correct model, used inappropriately: "There are always implicit assumptions behind a model and its solution method. But human beings have limited foresight and great imagination, so that, inevitably, a model will be used in ways its creator never intended.... The **only practical defense is to have informed and patient users** who clearly comprehend both the model and the method of solution and even more important, understand what can go wrong" (emphasis added; Derman 1996, p. 7).

As we noted above, an important innovation since the financial crisis has been the development and use of supervisory models, in other words, models developed by regulators, using detailed proprietary bank data (but also public data), whose purpose is to assess capital adequacy of banks. These types of stress testing models have been used as a crisis response tool both in the U.S. and in Europe, but are now being used as a tool for ongoing bank supervision, most especially through the CCAR program (Tarullo 2014). While the Federal Reserve does not provide any detail of its models, some description is given in Board of Governors (2014) and by Hirtle *et al.* (2014) for a complementary set of models based on publicly available bank regulatory reports (the FR Y-9C reports).

With the growing use of models comes the need for model risk management, arguably especially important for regulators since those models, by design, affect not just individual banks but the entire banking system (or at least the roughly 80% subject to the CCAR program), and are thus a nontrivial source of systemic risk. Recognizing this need, the Federal Reserve created a Model Validation Council in 2012, comprised of academics to "provide expert and independent advice on its process to rigorously assess the models used in stress tests of banking institutions."[10]

To summarize, the management of model risk in US banks has improved since it first became a point of emphasis to the industry and to bank regulators two decades ago. Sufficient progress had not been made, however, to avoid being a significant contributor to the Great Financial Crisis. While the attention paid to the management of model risk has accelerated since the crisis, modelling has continued to change, including significant new stress testing modelling efforts by both the banks and the regulators. It is far from clear whether the enhanced model risk management environment is sufficient to control the new risks.

References

Ashcraft, A. and T. Schuermann (2008), "Understanding the Securitization of Subprime Mortgage Credit," *Foundations and Trends in Finance* 2(3): 191–309. A pre-publication version is available as Federal Reserve Bank of New York Staff Report #318.

Basel Committee on Banking Supervision [BCBS] (1996), "Amendment to the Capital Accord to Incorporate Market Risks (No. 24)," January. Available at http://www.bis.org/publ/bcbs24.htm.

Basel Committee on Banking Supervision [BCBS] (2011), "Basel III: A global regulatory framework for more resilient banks and banking systems," June. Available at http://www.bis.org/publ/bcbs189.htm.

Board of Governors of the Federal Reserve System (2014), "Comprehensive Capital Analysis and Review 2014: Assessment framework and results," March. Available at http://www.federalreserve.gov/newsevents/press/bcreg/ccar_20140326.pdf.

Bollerslev, T. (1986), "Generalized Autoregressive Conditional Heteroskedasticity," *Journal of Econometrics*, 31: 307–327.

---

[10] See "Model Validation Council" by Board of Governors of the Federal Reserve System (April 1, 2015), at http://www.federalreserve.gov/aboutthefed/mvc.htm

Brigo, D., A. Pallavicini, and R. Torresetti (2010), "Credit Models and the Crisis, or: How I learned to stop worrying and love the CDOs," working paper. An expanded version appeared as *Credit Models and the Crisis: A journey into CDOs, Copulas, Correlations and Dynamic Models* (Chichester: Wiley), 2010.

Danielsson, J., K. James, M. Valenzuela and I. Zer (2014), "Model Risk of Risk Models," *FEDS Working Papers* 2014-31. Available at http://www.federalreserve.gov/pubs/feds/2014/201434/201434abs.html.

Derman, E. (1996), "Model Risk," Goldman Sachs Quantitative Strategies Research Notes, April.

Diebold, F.X. (2012), "100+ Years of Financial Risk Measurement and Management," in F.X. Diebold (ed.), *Financial Risk Measurement and Management* (Cheltenham, U.K. and Northampton, Mass.: Edward Elgar Publishing Ltd.), Introduction.

Duffie, D. (2007), "Innovations in Credit Risk Transfer: Implications for financial stability," July. Available at http://www.darrellduffie.com/uploads/working/DuffieInnovationsCreditRiskTransfer2007.pdf.

Engle, R. (1982), "Autoregressive Conditional Heteroscedasticity with Estimates of the Variance of United Kingdom Inflation," *Econometrica,* 50(4): 987–1007.

Federal Reserve Board of Governors (2005), *The Federal Reserve System Purposes and Functions,* Ninth Edition, June. Available at http://www.federalreserve.gov/pf/pdf/pf_complete.pdf.

Hirtle, B. J., T. Schuermann and K. J. Stiroh (2009), "Macroprudential Supervision of Financial Institutions: Lessons from the SCAP," Federal Reserve Bank of New York Staff Report #409.

Hirtle, B. J, A. Kovner, J. Vickery and M. Bhanot (2014), "Assessing Financial Stability: The Capital and Loss Assessment under Stress Scenarios (CLASS) Model," Federal Reserve Bank of New York Staff Report #663.

Jorion, P. (2000), "Risk Management Lessons from Long-Term Capital Management". *European Financial Management,* 6(September): 277–300.

Jorion, P. (2006), *Value at Risk* (New York: McGraw Hill).

Wyman, O. (2012), "Strategic Capital: Defining an Effective Real-World View of Capital." Available at http://www.oliverwyman.com/insights/publications/2012/aug/strategic-capital--defining-an-effective-real-world-view-of-capi.html.

Salmon, F. (2009), "Recipe for Disaster: The Formula That Killed Wall Street," *Wired* 17.03, February 23.

Tarullo, D. K. (2014), "Stress Testing after Five Years," speech given at the Federal Reserve Third Annual Stress Test Modeling Symposium, Boston, MA. Available at http://www.federalreserve.gov/newsevents/speech/tarullo20140625a.htm.

Yoost, D. (2013), "Board Oversight of Model Risk Is a Challenging Imperative," *The RMA Journal*, November: 24–30.

Banking in a Re-regulated World

— CHAPTER 16

- Luc Laeven
  IMF and CEPR

The 2008 global financial crisis has triggered large-scale financial regulatory reform with the aim to make banks safer and the financial system more stable. Much of the emphasis has been on raising the capital banks to raise their buffers to withstand shocks and on implementing a more macroprudential regulatory framework that devotes more attention to the stability of the system as a whole rather than that of individual banks per se

In this chapter, I will review the ongoing regulatory changes with the aim before turning to the question how much capital is enough. I will also discuss some shortcomings of the regulatory reform agenda and areas that in my view deserve further attention, including potential unintended consequences of the new capital regulations for systemic risk and the too big to fail problem. To keep the discussion focused,

Luc Laeven is Lead Economist in the Research Department of the International Monetary Fund. This was prepared for the Federal Reserve Bank of Chicago's 17th Annual International Banking Conference on November 7, 2014. It draws partly on joint work with Jihad Dagher, Giovanni Dell'Ariccia, Lev Ratnovski, and Hui Tong. Laeven would like to thank Michaela Erbenova for useful discussions, conference participants for useful comments, and Yangfan Sun for excellent research assistance. The views expressed here are the author's own and should not be attributed to the IMF or IMF Board.

I abstract from alternatives to raising equity capital such as contingent capital and 'bail-inable' instruments that if well designed could also make banks safer. Another important caveat is that much of the discussion on desirable capital ratios is based on partial equilibrium analysis. More work is needed to arrive at more precise estimates. Such work would have to account for country circumstances and general equilibrium effects.

The paper proceeds as follows. Section I will briefly review the main financial regulatory reforms since the crisis. Section II will offer a rationale for (higher) bank capital and present some back-of-the-envelope estimates of 'optimal' bank capital. Section III will discuss costs and adverse consequences of raising bank capital. Section IV concludes.

I. Financial Regulatory Reform Since the Financial Crisis

The regulatory reforms since the recent crisis can broadly be grouped into five categories:

1. Building resilience: In light of the losses experienced by major financial institutions that were threatening the stability of the global financial system and the real economy, there has been a concerted effort and emphasis on raising both the level and the quality of bank capital to allow banks to better absorb shocks in the future and avoid negative spillovers onto the real economy. These improvements in capital are accomplished through the raising of the level of minimum capital adequacy ratios and the part that should consist of high quality capital, i.e., tangible common equity, as well as through the introduction of discretionary counter-cyclical buffers, G-SIB surcharges, and a leverage ratio. In addition, liquidity standards are being introduced to ensure minimum levels of liquidity, including through the introduction of liquidity coverage and net stable funding ratios. The latter is important because the crisis showed that liquidity shortages can quickly spillover into capital deficiency, and the line between the two is often blurred.

2. Structural measures: There have also been growing concerns that banks have become too complex to manage, and that the combination of market-based activities with more traditional banking activities can pose threats to the stability of the core functions of the bank, including payment systems, store of value, and maturity transformation. In response to these concerns, a number of countries have proposed or introduced rules to limit the activities of banks, although there is agreement yet on how best to tackle this problem. For instance, the US Volcker rule imposes restrictions on proprietary trading and ownership of hedge funds; and the UK and EU are introducing structural measures on the basis of the Vickers and Liikanen reports.

3. Ending too-big-to-fail: The crisis has made evidently clear that large banks are different in that they are often deemed too big to fail. These concerns are legitimate because their failure could be disorderly with severe implications for financial stability and the real economy. But these concerns also lead to pressures on the regulators not to act and to regulatory inaction. This is a complex problem that is hard to solve. A number of regulatory changes have been made to reduce the too big to fail problem. In the US, these include limits on the use of taxpayer money to bailout failing banks, the requirement for banks to have resolution plans ('living wills'), and the creation of an Orderly Liquidation Authority with single point of entry to resolve ailing financial institutions. The EU has followed with the Bank Recovery and Resolution Directive which contains a bail-in principle, allowing for the bail in of creditors in case of bank failures.

4. Stability of OTC derivatives markets: There has been a concerted effort to make OTC derivatives markets safer, including through increased margin and transparency requirements, and the requirement of central clearing.

5. Stability of shadow banking: There has also been much emphasis on making shadow banks safer as the crisis made evidently clear that interlinkages with nonbanks had made traditional banks much riskier than they appeared to be. Important changes in this area are

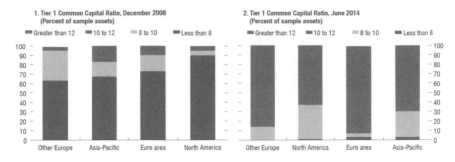

Figure 1. Bank capital ratios in 2008 and 2014.

Source: IMF Global Financial Stability Report, October 2014.

the G-SIFI designation that extends beyond banks, and the minimum 'haircuts' on the value of collateral to back securities lending. However, progress in this area has been more limited and the question about where to draw the regulatory perimeter for nonbanks has still not been settled.

In anticipation of these changes, banks have substantially increased their capital ratios since the crisis, in large part through raising new capital. Market pressures have also led most banks to achieve capital levels in excess of the new regulatory minima, holding safety buffers against adverse shocks. The increase in capital since the crisis is evident from Figure 1 which shows that by the middle of 2014 the majority of banks in all parts of the world had a Tier 1 common capital ratio in excess of 10 percent while this was the case for only a minority of banks in 2008.

II. The Rational for Bank Capital

We have seen that banks have increased their capital positions markedly since the crisis. But what is the economic rationale for higher capital?

First, by contributing more capital, shareholders that are protected on the downside by limited liability have more skin-in-the-game, which lowers their incentives to take risk (Myers and Majluf 1984; Marcus 1984; Keeley 1990).

Second, higher capital increases the bank's buffer to absorb shocks/ losses and avoids bankruptcy costs and spillovers of bank distress onto rest of financial system and real economy (Gale and Ozgur 2005; Admati *et al.* 2010).

There is a growing consensus that the capital levels of banks prior to the crisis were not only insufficient to absorb the shocks from the crisis, as evidenced in the need for public intervention to recapitalize banks, but were also insufficiently high to lower incentives for risk taking. The new Basel III (BIS 2011) capital requirements will increase minimum total capital ratios from 8% to 10.5–15.5%, including conservation buffer, countercyclical buffer, and systemic risk charge. But some economists have suggested that much higher capital ratios of up to 30% are needed (e.g. Admati and Hellwig 2014). But much capital is needed to ensure financial stability without damaging the real economy through more expensive bank lending?

One approach is to calculate what buffer is needed to absorb loan losses from a major financial crisis, using historical experience of non-performing loans during banking crises as a guide to determine loss absorption capacity. An illustrative example that can be fit to country circumstance is shown in Table 1.

According to Laeven and Valencia (2013), the median value of the peak nonperforming loan ratio during banking crises since the 1970s is

Table 1. Loss provisioning approach to bank capital needs.

	Capital ratio
1. Peak NPLs during banking crises	24%
2. Loss given default	50%
3. Loan losses (1 * 2)	12%
4. Absorbed by prior provisioning	1.5%
5. Loan losses net of provisions (3 – 4)	10.5%
6. Margin of safety	0.5%
7. Capital to assets ratio (5 + 6)	11%
8. Total assets / RWA	1.4
9. Capital ratio (% of RWA) (7 * 8)	15.4%

Source: Laeven and Valencia (2013); Authors' calculations.

about 24%. To obtain loan losses, the non-performing loan ratio should be adjusted for loss given default. There is little systematic data on loss given default. We use the estimate of Schuermann (2004) that the mean loss given default on senior secured debt in US over 1970–2003 was on the order of 50%. This means that a 24% non-performing loan ratio corresponds to 12% loan losses. Part of these losses can be absorbed by prior provisioning. Loan loss reserves in the US averaged about 1.5% historically. This leaves loan losses net of provisions of 10.5% of total assets. We add a margin of safety of 0.5% of total assets because system-wide average losses may be distributed unevenly among banks, or because some banks need extra capital to continue operating after absorbing the losses. Using the average risk-weighted assets to total assets ratio for US banks of about 1.4, the resulting 11% equity-to-assets ratio corresponds roughly to a 15% equity-to-risk-weighted-assets ratio (risk-weighted capital).

In practice, these estimates need to be adjusted to bank and country specific circumstances. For instance, to keep the analysis general, we derived median loan losses from as wide a sample of countries as possible. In practice, loan losses are likely to be smaller in advanced economies where asset risks tends to be smaller and recovery rates tend to be higher. Also, the estimate is based on losses on loans, not on the rest of bank balance sheet, including trading assets. One could refine the analysis to arrive at a more precise estimate of capital needs by modeling bank asset structure with associated crisis losses and risk weights in more detail using country specific information.

The next approach considers how much capital banks would need to hold to avoid the need for public recapitalizations of banks during crises. The assumption is that shocks to bank capital are first absorbed by existing capital and then by public recapitalization. Equity raising and asset sales are ruled out since banks typically have limited access to capital markets during crises. Also it is assumed that recapitalizations will bring banks back to the minimum level of capital needed to restore viability.

To arrive at an estimate of capital needs using this approach, we combine data from Bankscope on the average capital ratios in 2007 in banking systems of countries that experienced a crisis over the period 2007–2013 with data on the fiscal outlays associated with bank recapitalizations in these countries obtained from Laeven and Valencia

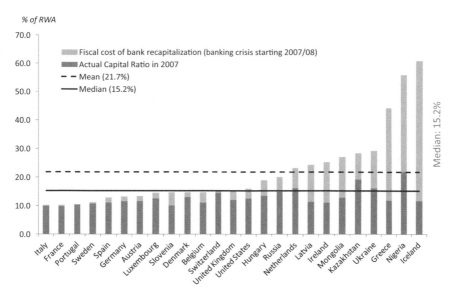

Figure 2. Public recapitalization approach to bank capital needs.

Source: Bankscope; Laeven and Valencia (2013), and authors' calculations.

(2013), both expressed as a percentage of total risk weighted assets of the banking system in each country. The median value of the sum of the pre-crisis capital ratio and fiscal costs is about 15% of risk-weighted bank assets, suggesting that a 15% capital ratio in 2007 would have been sufficient to avoid bank recapitalizations for the median of banks during the crisis (see Figure 2).

III. Real Costs of Raising Capital

While raising capital will boost financial stability, there are also real costs associated with raising capital to high levels. First there are direct costs for the banks and their shareholders. These direct costs consist of:

1. Signaling costs: Placing equity requires discounts when incumbent investors and managers have information about the firm that new equity investors do not have (Myers and Majluf 1982).
2. Underwriting fees: Fees to investments banks and lawyers to underwrite securities average about 5–7% of the value of equity raised for US listed companies.

3. Taxes: Interest payments on debt are tax deductible while dividend payments on equity are not, making equity relatively costly (Modigliani and Miller 1958)

The first of these two costs are transitional, while taxes are costly also in steady state. Then there are also potential costs for borrowers and society at large. These indirect costs include:

1. Increased costs for borrowers: a higher cost of bank capital, by increasing the funding costs for bank loans, will increase the cost of bank borrowing for private sector. The magnitude of this effect will depend on the relevance of financial frictions that may bank equity costlier than bank debt.
2. Liquidity provision of debt: 'cash investors' may value bank debt for its high liquidity and safety (i.e., liquidity insurance) (e.g. Gennaioli *et al.* 2013). If this is the case, then banks may destroy value when they replace debt liabilities with equity (Song and Thakor 2007; DeAngelo and Stulz 2013; Allen *et al.* 2014). The relevance of this channel will depend on the extent to which these cash investors can substitute bank deposits for other financial instruments that provide the same degree of liquidity and safety.
3. Risk migration: higher capital requirements may trigger a migration of activities from banks to the less-regulated and thus potentially riskier non-bank sector, amplifying the boundary problem in financial regulation (Goodhart 2010; Martin and Parigi 2013; Plantin 2015).

An understanding of the potential adverse effects of raising capital requirements on the real economy, including through their impact on borrowing costs, is critically important to determine their optimal level. Yet the empirical evidence on the impact of higher capital on lending rates is scarce, in part because unexpected shocks to bank capital that are actually binding are rarely observed.[1]

---

[1] A recent study by Carlson *et al.* (2013) finds muted effects of higher capital on bank lending.

Table 2. Pass-through of higher capital on loan rates: Evidence from US C&I loans.

	(1)	(2)
Tier 1 capital ratio	2.399*	4.646**
	[1.270]	[2.258]
Tier 1 capital ratio × target federal funds rate		−1.392***
		[0.223]
Target federal funds rate	0.969***	1.096***
	[0.014]	[0.026]
GDP growth	0.006	0.006
	[0.006]	[0.005]
NBER recession dummy	−0.171***	−0.154**
	[0.060]	[0.061]
State personal income	−0.000**	−0.000***
	[0.000]	[0.000]
Change in region CPI	−0.037**	−0.038**
	[0.015]	[0.014]
State unemployment rate	0.104***	0.101***
	[0.013]	[0.013]
Change in state housing prices	−0.007	−0.008
	[0.006]	[0.006]
Bank and loan controls	Y	Y
Bank and state fixed effects	Y	Y
Observations	1,045,153	1,045,153
Number of banks	0.740	0.741
R^2	639	639

Notes: This table reports the results of estimating panel regressions of loan interest rates from the first quarter of 1996 to the fourth quarter of 2011. The dependent variable is the effective interest rate on a given loan, as reported in the Federal Reserve's Survey of Terms of Business Lending (STBL). Loans extended under commitment established prior to the current quarter are excluded from the sample. All regressions include state- and bank-fixed effects. Standard errors clustered by quarter are reported in brackets.
Source: Dell'Ariccia *et al.* (2014)
*** indicates statistical significance at the 1% level, ** at the 5% level, and * at the 10% level.

Under Modigliani–Miller conditions, the loan rate should be independent of the bank's capital ratio. Using US historical, loan-level data, Dell'Ariccia *et al.* (2014) find that a 2% points increase in Tier 1 capital ratio is associated with a 5bp increase in loan rates, which is a small effect: even a 10 percentage points increase in capital requirements would boost loan rates by only 25bp, still a small effect (cf. Hanson *et al.* 2010).

Some have raised concerns that banks will no longer be able to compete with markets at substantially higher capital requirements. They argue that nonbanks are increasingly playing an important role in loan intermediation and take this as evidence that bank lending is being displaced by lending by nonbanks. For instance, mutual funds that traditionally would be extended by banks have been growing in the United States and the Euro area (IMF Global Financial Stability Report, October 2014). However, it could also be that both markets are growing in size. Indeed, at least in the US, there is little evidence that bank lending is being systematically displaced by market financing. Of course some banks have been hit hard during the crisis and have shrunk in size, but on the whole banking assets have continued to grow since the crisis, albeit at lower pace than equity and before the crisis.

At the same time there is evidence that many banks are changing their business models, moving out of certain trading assets. But loans as a fraction of total assets has not fallen in most parts of the world (see Figure 4).

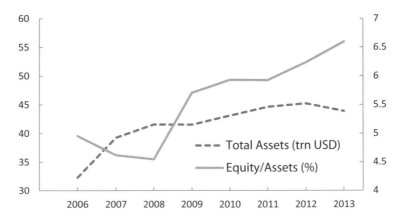

Figure 3.   Total assets and capital ratio of global banks, 2006–2013.
Note: Global top-50 banks with data for 2006–2013.
Source: Bankscope.

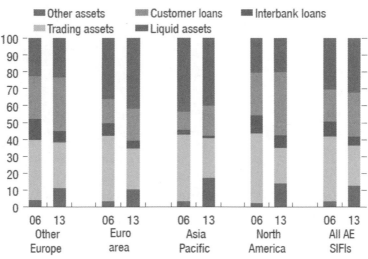

Figure 4. Changing business model of banks.

Source: Global Financial Stability Report, October 2014.

Banks have already responded to the prospects of substantially higher capital requirements by raising capital and most banks today operate at levels of capital ratios that are close to the 15% estimate. The immediate impact of higher capital seems to have been positive overall. Banks have become more highly capitalized since the global financial crisis, and have thus increased buffers. At the same time, banks seem to have been able to adjust to higher funding costs in ways that do not impair the intermediation process, as banks continue to grow and lend (with some exceptions especially in Europe). Yet it is hard to disentangle the impact of regulations from the effects of deleveraging and the low interest rate environment, and the long run impact of higher capital requirements has to be reassessed when interest rates have moved back to more normal levels.

At the same time, systemic risk in the financial system remains elevated (see Figure 5). While systemic risk has decreased somewhat because of increased capital, it remains elevated because of high asset price uncertainty and banks growing bigger.

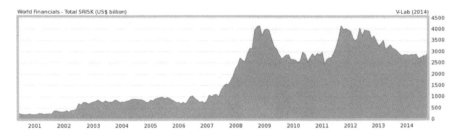

Figure 5. Systemic risk remains high despite capital raising.

Note: Aggregate SRISK (US$ billion) for global sample of financials.
Source: NYU Stern V-Lab.

Laeven *et al.* (2014), using alternative measures of systemic risk, have shown that large banks are riskier and create more to systemic risk than smaller banks, and that low capital in large banks is a key driver of systemic risk. These findings support the Basel III approach to capital surcharges on systemically important banks. Importantly, they show that higher capital reduces systemic risk over and above its impact on standalone risk, lending support to a macroprudential approach to banking regulation.

G-SIB capital surcharges are also desirable because the too big to fail problem is likely to remain, despite concerted efforts by lawmakers to reduce this problem. The reality is that at times of a systemic crisis the largest financial institution in the country will bound to be deemed too big to fail rendering commitments not to bail out time inconsistent. And the too big to fail problem also applies to the shadow banking sector (nonbanks), especially if institutions are leveraged, receive their funding from retail investors, and have large exposures to banks. In this regard, the G-SIFI designation that extends beyond banks and minimum 'hair-cuts' on the value of collateral to back securities lending both constitute important progress. Moreover higher capital surcharges, by acting as a buffer to prevent collapse, will also contribute to reducing systemic risk (cf. Kashyap *et al.* 2008). However, more needs to be done in this area. A key concern is new risks emerging in the shadows, including the risk of fire sales in a downturn by institutions holding illiquid assets, such as loan mutual funds.

Conclusions

Higher capital requirements are needed to make the financial system more stable. They will increase buffers to absorb losses and reduce incentives for risk taking. Back of the envelope calculations using alternative approaches give us an estimate for the desirable minimum capital ratio of roughly 15%. This is in line with the existing Basel III framework, once we account for capital conservation buffers, counter-cyclical buffers, and capital surcharges. Indeed, most banks today have already achieved capital ratios that are broadly in line with this estimate.

Banking will survive higher capital requirements. The impact of higher capital on lending rates is likely to be modest. But some activity may flow to the shadows (i.e., nonbanks) and require additional regulation to ensure systemic risk does not increase as a result.

References

Admati, A., P. DeMarzo, M. Hellwig and P. Pfleiderer (2010), "Fallacies, Irrelevant Facts, and Myths in the Discussion of Capital Regulation: Why bank equity is not expensive," MPI Collective Goods Preprint No. 42.

Admati, A. and M. Hellwig (2014), *The Bankers' New Clothes: What's Wrong with Banking and What to Do about It* (New Jersey: Princeton University Press).

Allen, F., E. Carletti and R. Marquez (2014), "Deposits and Bank Capital Structure," *Journal of Financial Economics*, forthcoming.

BIS (2011), "Basel III: A global regulatory framework for more resilient banks and banking systems," June. Available at: http://www.bis.org/publ/bcbs189.pdf.

Carlson, M., H. Shan and M. Warusawitharana (2013), "Capital Ratios and Bank Lending: A Matched Bank Approach," *Journal of Financial Intermediation*, 22(4): 663–687.

DeAngelo, H. and R. Stulz (2013), "Why High Leverage is Optimal for Banks," National Bureau of Economic Research Working Paper No. 19139, June.

Dell'Ariccia, G., L. Laeven and G. Suarez (2014), *Bank Leverage and Monetary Policy's Risk-Taking Channel: Evidence from the United States* (Mimeo: International Monetary Fund).

Gale, D. and O. Özgür (2005), "Are bank capital ratios too high or too low? Incomplete markets and optimal capital structure," *Journal of the European Economic Association*, 3(2–3): 690–700.

Gennaioli, N., A. Shleifer and R. Vishny (2013), "A Model of Shadow Banking," *The Journal of Finance*, 68(4): 1331–1363.

Goodhart, C. (2010), "How should we regulate bank capital and financial products? What role for 'living wills'?" (Cómo Deberíamos Regular el Capital Bancario y los Productos Financieros? Cuál es el Papel de los 'Testamentos en Vida?') (Spanish) (December 1, 2010). *Revista de Economía Institucional*, 12(23): 85. Available at: Available at SSRN: http://ssrn.com/abstract=1724757.

Hanson, S., A. Kashyap and J. Stein (2010), "An Analysis of the Impact of Substantially Heightened Capital Requirements on Large Financial Institutions," Working Paper, Harvard University. Available at: http://www.hbs.edu/faculty/Pages/item.aspx?num=41199.

IMF Global Financial Stability Report (2014), "Risk Taking, Liquidity, and Shadow Banking: Curbing Excess While Promoting Growth," October. Available at: http://www.imf.org/external/pubs/ft/gfsr/2014/02/.

Kashyap, A., R. Rajan and J. Stein (2008), "Rethinking capital regulation," In *Proceedings Economic Policy Symposium-Jackson Hole*, Federal Reserve Bank of Kansas City, pp. 431–471.

Keeley, M. (1990), "Deposit Insurance, Risk, and Market Power in Banking," *American Economic Review*, 80(5): 1183–1200.

Laeven, L. and F.Valencia (2013), "Systemic Banking Crises Database," *IMF Economic Review*, 61: 225–270.

Laeven, L., L. Ratnovski and H. Tong (2014), "Bank size and systemic risk," IMF Staff Discussion Note 14/04.

Marcus, A. J. (1984), "Deregulation and Bank Financial Policy," *Journal of Banking and Finance*, 8(4): 557–565.

Martin, A. and B. Parigi (2013), "Bank Capital Regulation and Structured Finance," *Journal of Money, Credit and Banking*, 45(1): 87–119.

Modigliani, F. and M. Miller (1958), "The Cost of Capital, Corporation Finance and The Theory of Investment," *American Economic Review*, 48(3): 261–297.

Myers, S. and N. Majluf (1984), "Corporate Financing and Investment Decisions When Firms Have Information That Investors Do Not Have," *Journal of Financial Economics*, 13(2): 187–221.

Plantin, G. (2015), "Shadow banking and bank capital regulation," *Review of Financial Studies*, 28(1): 146–175.

Schuermann, T. (2004), *What Do We Know About Loss Given Default?* (Mimeo: Federal Reserve Bank of New York).

Song, F. and A. Thakor (2007), "Relationship Banking, Fragility, and the Asset-Liability Matching Problem," *Review of Financial Studies*, 20(6): 2129–2177.

Financial Reform in Transition
— CHAPTER 17

- Philipp Hartmann
  European Central Bank

Once the full dimension of the financial crisis became clear in the last quarter of 2008 it became also clear to many that a difficult broad and protracted process of reregulating financial activities would follow. The list of 67 measures proposed by the Financial Stability Forum in its report on "Enhancing market and institutional resilience" (FSF 2008) ranging from bank capital requirements and liquidity management to credit ratings and from accounting standards to international supervisory cooperation, which was endorsed by G7 Finance Ministers and central bank Governors in their meeting in Washington, DC, on April 11, 2008, already foreshadowed this. More than seven years after the first

Philipp Hartmann is Acting Director General Research, European Central Bank, chaired part-time professor for macro-financial economics, Erasmus University Rotterdam, and a CEPR fellow. Any view expressed are solely his own and should not be regarded as views of the ECB or the Eurosystem. He would like to thank Adonis Antoniadis, Martin Bijsterbosch, Magdalena Ignatowski and Paolo Mistrulli for comments, Magnus Andersson, Nicola Doyle, Michael Grill, Luis Gutierrez de Rozas, Paul Hiebert, Alexander Hodbod, Agnese Leonello, Laurent Maurin, Csaba More, Alex Popov, Anton van der Kraaij and Michael Wedow for providing background reading materials and Francesca Barbiero and Elisa Reinhold for research assistance.

material market turbulences emerged in the summer of 2007 the process is advanced but by no means finished.

Therefore it makes sense to look at the transitional effects of financial reforms. In this chapter I first try to assess them in general terms along three lines, the level and structure of financial intermediation, financial stability and the standing of finance business in society at large. Then I consider some specific evidence about the transitional effects of reforms related to bank resolution. In my view, efforts to make banks more resolvable are — together with enhancing their capital and developing a macroprudential approach — among the most important items on the reform agenda.

The discussion suggests that reregulation is weighing on financial intermediation and economic activity in the transition, but this may be a necessary cost for a healthier financial system in the future. At the same time reregulation is particularly concentrated in the banking sector, which will contribute to risks migrating from that sector to less regulated financial sectors. Stress test-based bank recapitalizations and progress in implementing Basel reforms enhancing the quantity and quality of capital probably contributed to significantly greater financial stability today than a few years ago. A process that is perhaps less well advanced is to 'reintegrate finance' in society. It seems to remain a common feature that a good share of the population tends to see 'bankers' and finance business with suspicion and distrust. In order to 're-normalize' the role of the sector financial reform in a broad sense should not only increase the stability of financial institutions but also help 'cleanse' the sector of the practices and individuals responsible for the adverse business culture that prevailed in the past. This, in turn, will allow direct clients and other citizens to regain trust and remove one obstacle to financial intermediation activity. In my view this point about the business culture in the financial sector is often underrated.

The two research examples presented relating to resolution reforms suggest that subjecting banks to a special resolution regime and introducing provisions for bailing in investors in bank debt tend to have some disciplinary effects on risk taking. This alone, however, does not seem to go far enough for solving the 'too-big-to-fail' problem.

General Effects of Financial Reforms During the Transition

In many industrial countries the traumatic experiences with the financial crisis that started with increasing delinquencies in the US sub-prime mortgage market and the subsequent international market turbulences during the summer of 2007 led to comprehensive overhauls of their regulatory and supervisory setups for the financial sector. Moreover, the Financial Stability Forum (FSF) — as of 2009 Financial Stability Board (FSB) — assumed a leading role in the common parts and coordination at the international level. The breadth of the reform efforts were already well reflected in the April 2008 FSF report on "Enhancing market and institutional resilience" (mentioned previously), which was prepared well before the demise of Lehman Brothers and the full breakout of the crisis. Recent detailed summaries of the broad and evolving reform agenda as well as its status of completion and implementation are, for example, in IMF (2012), FSB (2014a) or Basel Committee (2014b) and for the European Union (EU) in European Commission (2014a and b).

Here, I do not try to provide a quantitative assessment of joint effect of all the reforms. This is much too complex a task. The relevant reforms and regulations concern items as diverse as (the quality and quantity of) capital of banks and insurers (plus other loss absorbing capacity), bank leverage and liquidity, bank resolution (including bail-in rules and living wills), structural regulation (requiring specific financial activities to be separated from banks), compensation practices, governance of risk management, credit rating agencies, securitization practices, over-the-counter derivatives market trading and settlement, haircuts for securities financing transactions, accounting rules and financial reporting as well as the characterization of financial fraud and consumer protection. Some of the changes still have to be agreed, others contain long implementation lags, again others differ across countries. It would be preposterous to claim that we have the analytical tools, data or experience for a comprehensive quantitative assessment of all these elements together, including associated uncertainties.

Level and Structure of Financial Intermediation

A number of studies have tried to quantify the financial and macroeconomic effects of specific reforms. Particular attention is paid to the new Basel III bank capital (and liquidity) rules. The broad argument is that increasing capital (and liquidity) buffers will be costly. Banks will pass these costs on through higher loan rates and/or reduce risk-weighted assets. In other words, credit intermediation will become more costly and/or reduce its level, with a corresponding slowdown in economic growth. These costs have to be held against the benefits of the reduced frequency and/or costs of crises through safer banks.

Kashyap *et al.* (2010) argue that large banks operating with substantially higher capital requirements imply relatively limited ongoing costs for the financial sector and the economy at large. But since the frictions of raising new equity are relatively more important it is advisable to make the transition period for moving to the new regime rather long. Comparing the pre-Basel III 'steady state' with the post-reform 'steady state', Basel Committee (2010) finds that substantially higher capital and liquidity requirements can be expected to have distinct net benefits in terms of long-term economic growth. Much like in Yan *et al.* (2012) and Miles *et al.* (2013) for the United Kingdom it is estimated empirically that the growth benefits of decreasing the likelihood and severity of financial crises exceed the additional funding costs through higher capital.[1] Macroeconomic Assessment Group (2010) suggests that the extended 8-year transition period to the full implementation of Basel III is likely to feature only very moderate interest rate increases and associated growth losses. Slovik and Cournède (2011) argue that the growth losses would be a little bit higher if banks continued the pre-crisis/pre-Basel III practice of maintaining capital above the

---

[1] Similar results emerge from a new generation of calibrated macroeconomic models incorporating banks and financial instability, such as Martinez-Miera and Suarez (2012) or Clerc *et al.* (2014). Switzerland adopted tougher banking regulatory reforms than Basel III. Considering capital requirements and the leverage ratio Rochet (2014) reckons that their benefits are also likely to outweigh their costs.

regulatory limit.[2] Institute of International Finance (2011) claims that the costs of Basel III for external finance could be substantially higher than estimated in other studies. Moreover, pointing to the broad range of different regulatory changes in individual countries and of coordinated regulatory changes among G-20 countries beyond Basel III bank capital and liquidity reforms, it estimates higher interest rate increases and growth effects. Most of these studies also acknowledge great uncertainties around the core estimates presented.

Validating such pre-transition assessments in the light of incoming data and the experience over the last five years is a significant challenge, because there are very substantial confounding factors. For example, the incoming interest rate, credit or growth data may overstate or may be erroneously associated with the transitional effects of financial reforms since already the market-driven normalization process from pre-crisis excesses requires substantial deleveraging and increases in capital or because of the sovereign debt and competitiveness crises of some euro area countries. Conversely, the incoming data of the last five years may understate the transitional impact of regulatory reforms because of the unprecedented expansionary monetary policies conducted by most central banks.

To all these arguments further qualitative considerations need to be added in order to assess the transitional impact of regulatory reforms on the level of financial intermediation. First, the number of regulatory and supervisory changes to be accommodated by financial institutions is very large. And the process of change takes a long time, 7 years by now, and it is by no means finished at the time of writing. This imposes a continuous burden on financial institutions to deal with ongoing change in the regulatory framework (e.g. Hetzer 2014). Second, in the transition there is a lot of uncertainty about the end points of the various reforms. For example, various components of the reforms are revised repeatedly over time or are of a discretionary (rather than a rules-based) nature. Therefore, Taylor (2014a and b) includes financial regulation, alongside

---

[2] Elliott *et al.* (2012) find a bit lower effects on lending rates than these studies, considering also derivative reforms, higher taxes and fees.

monetary and fiscal policy, in his list of policies whose discretionary changes and uncertainty are currently weighing on the US economy, for example.

Third, since the height of the financial crisis bank supervision has become much more intrusive than previously the case (e.g. Tan 2014a). One example referred to by industry representatives is for example the March 2013 guidance on leveraged lending by the Federal Reserve Board, the Federal Deposit Insurance Corporation and the Office of the Comptroller of the Currency (2013) in the US and its enforcement. Industry representatives remark that, upon pressure of the supervisory authorities, some large banks abstain from profitable loans (Tan 2014a and b). The limiting effect that this has on some private equity deals, for example, seems to be a consequence intended by supervisors.

Despite the expectation that the stabilizing features of reforms are materializing over time, compensating for the costs of re-regulation, to me it is without any doubt the case that such a slow, broad, deep, complex and uncertain process of financial re-regulation and strengthened supervision is weighing on financial intermediation activity in the transition.

It should be no surprise that the activities of financial intermediaries most affected by regulatory reforms, strengthened supervision and related uncertainties could migrate to intermediaries less or not affected by the reforms. For example, Kashyap *et al.* (2010) suggest that the main competitive advantage of banks in credit business is their access to relatively inexpensive funding sources. Even small increases in banks' funding costs through tightened regulation could, in principle, lead to material regulatory arbitrage in that credit business migrates from banks to so-called shadow banks, i.e. outside the current regulatory perimeter. For example, Tan (2014a) argues that the US leveraged lending guidance already referred to above could make broker-dealers or the capital markets and credit arms of private equity groups gain market share relative to banks. IMF (2014) lists tightened banking regulation as one of the key drivers of the growth of shadow banking, in particular if it is accompanied by ample liquidity and strong demand from institutional investors, as the case over the last few years. It concludes that many indicators for industrial countries point to the migration of intermediation activities, such as corporate lending, from the traditional to the shadow banking sector.[3]

The financial stability risks that this form of regulatory arbitrage may imply are well acknowledged by policy makers, such as the former European Commissioner for the Internal Market, Michel Barnier (2014), the Chairman of the Financial Stability Board, Mark Cearney, and the Chairman of the FSB Standing Committee on the Assessment of Vulnerabilities (FSB 2014c). For this reason the FSB has started to publish an annual monitoring report about developments in shadow banking (FSB 2014b). At the same time it needs to be noted that in countries and regions where the post-crisis bank deleveraging process has not been completed, such as Europe, shadow banks taking over part of the missing credit to finance a stronger recovery may also be desirable from a conjunctural perspective and also as step towards a financial system that is more diversified between banks and capital markets.

From this discussion two broad policy implications stand out for me at the current juncture. First, financial regulation and supervision is an area where there will always be some change, mostly in the form of adjustments to new financial instruments, market practices and risks. At the same time the financial industry needs some clarity about the future 'steady state' of regulation to fulfil its function in the intermediation process. In this regard, it is important that the major reforms target an end point not too far in the future that allows financial intermediaries to fix the business models with which they plan to operate in the medium term. Second, something that has not been properly developed as yet in most countries is macroprudential regulation and supervision. While the need for this approach was widely agreed as a lesson from the crisis progress with establishing it has been generally slow.[4] For example, a truly macroprudential approach to financial regulation and supervision would cover all important elements of a financial system

---

[3] IMF (2012) discusses potential impacts of the regulatory reforms on a broader range of structural features of financial systems that have been associated with financial instability in the past.

[4] For a major effort that aimed at improving the analytical foundations for macroprudential policies, see ECB (2014a).

and treat it in proportion to its contribution to systemic risk. Therefore, a fully macroprudential approach would not allow the important credit intermediation activities of shadow banks to be outside the regulatory and supervisory perimeter as it is still the case.

Financial Stability

Bank restructuring and recapitalization efforts in the countries most affected by the financial crisis that started in summer 2007 went a long way in stabilizing the major banks by now. Particularly important in this regard were a series of stress tests that required banks (and some other financial institutions) to cover capital shortfalls soon. In the US, the 2009 Supervisory Capital Assessment Program (SCAP) and later the yearly Comprehensive Capital Analysis and Reviews (CCARs), in conjunction with a number of public support programs, were instrumental in re-establishing confidence in the US banking system. For example, Neretina et al. (2014) find that individual banks' credit risk, systematic risk and cross-bank equity return correlation as a measure of systemic risk typically declined after the release of the results. In the euro area the Comprehensive Assessment carried out by the European Central Bank in cooperation with national supervisory authorities between November 2013 and October 2014 also seems to have led to such a stabilizing effect. The comprehensive assessment joined up an asset quality review and a stress test (ECB 2014b).

Figure 1 shows the evolution of a contemporaneous indicator of systemic financial instability in the euro area that we developed here in the ECB (see Holló et al. 2012). This Composite Indicator of Systemic Stress ('CISS') not only captures instability in the banking sector but also in financial markets emphasizing the degree of system-wide problems. The figure suggests that since early 2013 systemic financial instability in the euro area has returned to 'normal' levels, i.e. levels observed in the decade before the Great Financial Crisis. Moreover, the release of the information from the ECB's comprehensive assessment seems to have had a further reductionary effect on financial instability, until this effect was compensated by the announcement of a Greek snap election which brought a government in power that had campaigned on questioning the Greek stabilization program.

(a) January 1999 – January 2015

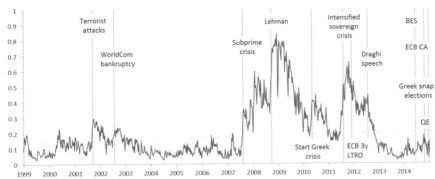

Notes: Composite Indicator of Systemic Stress ('CISS'). ECB 3y LTRO = First 3-year long-term refinancing operation conducted, BES = Banco Espirito Santo fails, ECB CA = Comprehensive Assessment results announced, QE = ECB quantitative easing program announced.

(b) March 2011 – January 2015

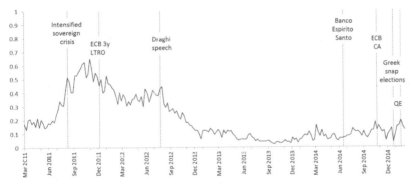

Notes: Composite Indicator of Systemic Stress ('CISS'). ECB 3y LTRO = First 3-year long-term refinancing operation conducted, ECB CA = Comprehensive Assessment results announced, QE = ECB quantitative easing program announced.

Figure 1. Systemic financial instability in the euro area.

Sources: ECB staff calculations based on Holló *et al.* (2012).

Apart from the fact that the benchmark capital levels they use move increasingly towards the ones prescribed by Basel III, bank stress tests and subsequent recapitalizations cannot be used as proof that the regulatory reforms lead to the desired benefits in terms of greater financial stability. The main intended benefits of regulatory reforms lie in the reduced probability and severity of financial crises (Basel Committee 2010, Yan *et al.* 2012 or Miles *et al.* 2013). But these benefits cannot be ascertained at the present juncture. As a first step, instead, it can be tracked to which extent banks or banking systems move towards or beyond the strengthened regulations prescribed by the Basel III rules of December 2010 (revised in June 2011). The Basel Committee (2014a) tracks this for its constituency of 27 countries around the globe and the European Banking Authority (2014a) for 16 European Union countries, both broadly applying the same methodology. The Basel Committee sample covers overall 227 banks and the EBA sample 151 banks. Both authorities distinguish two groups of banks, one with international activities and tier 1 capital in excess of €3 billion (group 1: Basel Committee 102 banks, including 29 global systemically important ones (G-SIBs), and EBA 42 banks) and another for other banks (group 2: Basel Committee 125 banks and EBA 109 banks). Both track the relevant capital, leverage and liquidity ratios and show how they consistently increase over time (latest data end 2013).

Starting with capital requirements, the Basel Committee finds that already 99% of group 1 banks and 98% of group 2 banks met the minimum common equity tier 1 (CET1) ratio of 4.5% in December 2013. The equivalent figures for the EU banks are 98% and 97%, respectively. (According to the Basel time table this minimum requirement is to be met as of January 2015.) As regards the target CET1 ratio of 7% under Basel III, 98% (group 1 and 2) of the global sample met it, including all G-SIBs, and 84% (group 1) and 88% (group 2) of the European sample.[5]

Against the background that the capital conservation buffer that defines the difference of 2.5 percentage points between the minimum and target CET1 ratios is supposed to be fully phased in only in 2019, the continuously increasing capital levels already immediately after the adoption of Basel III suggests that many banks are frontloading substantially. Banks' motivations for frontloading may be to show strength, reduce debt funding costs and in 2013 also the ECB's comprehensive assessment

---

[5] For further information about the evolution of bank capital levels and dispersion in Europe over time, updated until June 2014, see also EBA (2014b).

of euro area banks. While this will be weighing temporarily on credit intermediation activity and short-term economic growth, as already suggested in the previous sub-section, it will also be associated with faster establishment of bank stability (except, of course, for the weaker players that cannot frontload) which is needed for the materialisation of the long-term growth and welfare benefits of regulatory reforms.

As regards the Basel III leverage ratio of 3%, 91% (group 1) and 86% (group 2) of the banks in the global sample already met it in December 2013 and 85% (group 1) and 84% (group 2) of the European sample. (Banks have to report their leverage ratio to supervisors since January 2013, publish it as of January 2015 and full implementation is planned by 2018.) As regards the global liquidity standard of Basel III, the minimum liquidity coverage ratio (LCR) is set to 60% in 2015 and rises every year by 10 percentage points until 2019. At the end of 2013 already 76% of the global bank sample met the 100% threshold and 71% of the European sample (figures for groups 1 and 2 together).

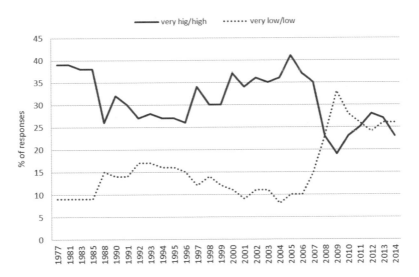

Figure 2. Honesty and ethical standards in banking.

Notes: Share of answers by 800 citizens from all US states to the question "Please tell me how you would rate the honesty and ethical standards of people in these different fields" for the banking industry.

Source: Gallup, Inc., and ECB staff calculations.

The second element of the global liquidity standard, the net stable funding ratio of 100%, is planned to become a minimum requirement in 2018. In both the global and the European sample reported by the Basel Committee (2014a) and the EBA (2014a), respectively, 78% of the banks that provided the relevant information fulfilled it already at the end of 2013.

Also in the area of the financial stability effects in the transition to the full implementation of regulatory reforms there are confounding factors for which it is hard to control. For example, in many constituencies there remain public policies that directly or as a side effect support the financial sector. Certainly, current highly expansionary monetary policies, standard and unconventional, have broad stabilizing effects on financial intermediaries and markets in the short term.[6] Some banks in different countries also still benefit from emergency liquidity assistance by central banks as part of a recovery or resolution strategy.[7] Last, some governments still maintain equity stakes in important banks, which at some point in the future would have to become able again to finance themselves in the stock market.[8] While I believe that the gradually stabilizing effects of regulatory reforms are materializing it should not be forgotten that the real test comes when no public support is granted any longer.

Second, there may be latent risks that are not (yet) visible in contemporaneous measures of financial instability. For example, the very low interest rates and the ample liquidity conditions that are prevalent in

---

[6] Ultra-low interest, for example, are, however, not necessarily stabilising for all financial intermediaries as the case of pension funds illustrates.

[7] Cœuré (2013) reports that the aggregate amount of emergency liquidity assistance that euro area national central banks granted to individual credit institutions in the summer of 2012 was about one seventh of the total amount of liquidity the Eurosystem provided to its counterparties for monetary policy purposes at the same time. At the time of writing this number is much lower and relates only to very few countries.

[8] For an excellent overview of public support measures to the financial sector in Europe and the United States, ranging from unconventional monetary policy to government bank capital injections (but excluding emergency liquidity assistance), see Stolz and Wedow (2010).

major industrial countries since an extended period of time through expansionary, standard and unconventional, monetary policies in conjunction with large savings from some emerging market economies may give rise to search for yield behavior of investors that may lead to the build-up of new financial imbalances that could endanger financial stability in the long term. Based on the historical experience, including the recent financial crisis, a matter of concern may be particularly imbalances in real estate markets. But in what concerns the euro area and contrary to the clear picture of property market overvaluations in the years before 2007, until recently one cannot identify widespread misalignments of real estate prices or generally strong growth in mortgage credit (Hartmann 2015). Other risks that need to be monitored carefully are, for example, related to internationally strong investment in risky corporate debt (after bouts of volatility recently migrating from high-yield bonds to long-duration investment-grade bonds) and, particularly in the US, a post crisis revival of collateralized loan obligations (CLOs) and leveraged lending (IMF 2014 or ECB 2014c). This is setting an interesting counterpoint to the claims mentioned above that the US regulatory leveraged lending guidance could suppress valuable credit. Moreover, the weak and fragile European recovery and potential downward surprises in economic growth going forward could imply risks to banks' loan books.

This discussion leads me to three policy considerations to assure and complete the progress towards financial stability in the time ahead. First, still ongoing initiatives for maintaining stability need to be completed diligently. For example, capital shortfalls detected in the ECB's comprehensive assessment of euro area banks need to be replenished over the agreed time horizons (within six or nine months after their announcement in October last year). Second, exit strategies from ongoing public support schemes need to be planned; be it the phasing out of emergency liquidity assistance, lifting remaining public guarantees, bringing public equity stakes to the market or other measures. This needs to take the individual situations of specific intermediaries or countries into account and be timed carefully. For example, whereas the United States and the United Kingdom are in the beginning of exiting from ultra-expansionary monetary policies, the feeble growth and protracted low inflation or deflation risks in the euro area or Japan do not allow for this step as yet. Third, micro and macroprudential authorities need to monitor carefully whether new financial imbalances are building up and to which extent they imply systemic risks. In those constituencies in which systemically relevant financial imbalances build up notably macroprudential policies need to be bold enough to effectively lean against the wind. This holds irrespective of where the imbalances build up in the financial system (including the shadow banking sector).

Role of Finance in Society

In order to fulfil their role in a market economy financial institutions and professionals need to possess the trust of their customers and of people in society more generally. As the history and theory of banking suggest, trust is a particularly important factor in the money business. But the experiences of the financial crisis, both its macroeconomic consequences in terms of a deep and protracted recession characterized by high unemployment rates and the light it sheds on fraudulent practices and an unhealthy business culture, have eroded trust in banks and other financial service businesses.

For example, the Edelman Trust Barometer shows for at least four years in a row that banking and financial services are the least trusted among 15 industries covered (Harper 2013, Edelman 2014). This barometer is derived from a survey of people described as belonging to the 'informed public' in 20 countries, who are asked how much they trust businesses in different industries. Only half of the respondents trust banks or financial services companies, which is the lowest among all industries covered. In contrast, between 70% and 80% of respondents trust technology or consumer electronics manufacturing companies, the two highest of the industries covered. Wood and Berg (2011) report the results of a Gallup survey asking US citizens how much confidence they have in banks. The share of respondents answering that they had 'a great deal' or 'quite a lot' of confidence in US banks declined from around 50% between 2003 and 2006 to around 20% or below between 2009 and 2011.

Gallup also runs a regular survey about 'honesty and ethics in professions' (Gallup 2014). About 800 adults from all US states are asked in a telephone interview about how they would rate the honesty and ethical standards of people working in different fields. 23% of respondents in the December 2014 survey rated bankers as having 'very high' or 'high' standards. For nurses the equivalent figure was 80% and for members of the US Congress or for car salespeople 7 and 8%, respectively. Figure 2 shows the rating for bankers over time. Around 2005/2006 their rating started to deteriorate materially and stayed relatively low ever since. It is plausible that such important reputation problems also weigh on financial intermediation activity.

Recent research also asks the question whether there may also be, or have emerged over time, some adverse elements in the business culture of finance. Ernst Fehr, one of the leading behavioral economists, together with Alain Cohn and Michel Maréchal (2014) very recently published an experiment in *Nature* that was designed to detect whether the 'honesty norms' in banking business are in line with the permissible behaviors in society at large. The authors let 128 employees from different business lines of a large international bank perform a coin tossing task (remunerated in money) in which cheating can only be detected in the average but individuals cheating cannot be identified in person. Right before performing the task, however, a randomly selected share of the employees (the treatment group) had to answer a set of questions that rendered their professional identity as bankers salient, whereas the other share of employees (the control group) were asked questions unrelated to their professional identity as bankers. Interestingly, the treatment group behaved dishonestly in an economically and statistically significant way, whereas the reporting of coin tosses of the control group was statistically indistinguishable from honest behavior.

Moreover, additional analysis of the results suggests that the bank employees in the treatment group who worked in core business units behaved more dishonestly than the ones employed in support units. In addition, the bank employees in the treatment group seemed to be more driven by 'materialistic values' in that they endorsed more strongly than the control group the statement that social status is primarily determined by financial success. When the authors repeated the experiment with 133 employees from non-financial industries their professional identity had no significant effect on how honestly the participants reported their coin tosses. Last, Cohn *et al.* (2014) asked people from the general population about how they would expect bank employees, physicians, prison inmates and other normal people to report in the coin tossing task. In line with the other surveys on trust and ethics discussed above it turns out that bank employees are expected to be the least honest among the four groups.

More than three years ago another experiment received attention in the media. For their MBA thesis at the University of St. Gallen, Noll and Scherrer (2013) repeated an experiment by Mokros *et al.* (2008), who had let 24 criminal psychopaths and 24 people of the normal population perform 40 iterations of a prisoner's dilemma game against a computer. Noll and Scherrer added a third group of 28 traders (equity, fixed income, derivatives, commodities etc.), most employed at large Swiss banks. The game is embedded in a story of a village with a shortage of water in which inhabitants can get most water if they cooperate in each round and fetch water in pairs of two. But if one of the two defects and fetches water alone, claiming it is for both, he or she can keep in this round almost as much as both portions. On one side of a pair is always the computer, which is programmed to play mechanically a 'tit-for-two-tat' strategy, i.e. it cooperates unless its partner defects two rounds in a row (without the other player knowing this fixed strategy). On the other side is always a human player choosing her own preferred strategy for the 40 rounds.

The result that drew most of the public attention is that among the three groups the traders defect significantly more often than the criminal psychopaths (who also defect more often than 'normal' people). The total amount of water that traders or psychopaths got on average was not significantly different from the amount implied if everybody always cooperated. The computer got the least water when playing against the traders, the second least water when playing against the psychopaths and most water when playing against 'normal' people. Although some of the authors' interpretations of the results are controversial (see e.g. Kirchgässner and Habermacher 2011), they seem at least to be indicative of particularly aggressive and little cooperative behavior of traders even when not 'justified' by a better overall outcome for themselves and irrespective of the side effects on others.

The third and last study on the business culture in finance I would like to mention in this paper is a survey on 'mental models' sponsored by the Aspen Institute (Ochs 2014). Mental models are defined as the powerful non-financial incentives that drive practitioner thought processes and ultimately govern their behavior in the financial industry. The results of the study are derived from the answers of 700 financial services professionals in the United States.

Ochs detects five mental models (in the order of importance): complexity bias; desire for financial success; self-interest; recognition of intelligence; and short-term outlook. From this the author concludes, inter alia, that complex solutions or products are probably taken too much as a sign of intelligence and many financial services professionals are driven by receiving recognition for their intelligence. Moreover, she identifies reserves of empathy, in particular among high-level professionals and experts. Empathy, however, is important to mitigate some harmful mental models. Finally, the author sees a need for closing the gap between inflated self-perception of financial services professionals and reality.

It is plausible that some of these elements of the business culture in financial services have contributed to the excesses and abuses that have led to the crisis. The question that arises then is what could generate change. Since the above three examples are based on relatively recent data, self-correcting forces resulting from the crisis experience do not seem to operate effectively, at least not yet several years after the peak of the crisis. Traditional financial regulation and supervision may contribute to limiting the effects of such a culture. One issue is whether when peoples' behavior exceeds certain limits they risk being penalized.

In the last few years many of the most important international banks received unprecedentedly large fines for some of their employees having engaged in manipulating important financial market reference rates, e.g. for interest rates, exchange rates or commodity prices, inappropriate mortgage practices, money laundering, assisting tax evasion or breaking political sanctions (recent overviews are in Kollewe *et al.* 2014 or Ralph 2014). The banks usually sanctioned or fired the individuals that had engaged in these activities. Many were also (temporarily or permanently) banned from the industry or face also criminal charges in the courts. In my view, an important issue that goes hand in hand with the success of the transition to a new regulatory regime is whether the combination of new rules, better supervisory interventions, bank-internal sanctions, legal penalties on financial institutions and their misbehaving employees and a reaction in society at large have a favorable effect on business culture, over time 'cleansing' the financial services industry from the mentioned adverse practices, attitudes and individuals prone to them.

This needs to work not only at the 'grass roots' but also at the leadership level, because leadership by definition sets the overall tone for a corporate culture. And, indeed, many Chief Executive (CEOs), Chief Financial Officers (CFOs) or Chief Risk Officers (CROs) lost their jobs when their institutions got in trouble during the crisis. But there is a debate about whether the penalties were severe enough to deter executives from letting such an adverse business culture emerge again in the future. On the one hand, there were the 'golden handshakes' (generous exit packages) that tended to sweeten executives' departures until some years ago. On the other hand, some observers criticize that —— contrary to managers and staff — top executives are rarely subjected to criminal charges.

In the United States the issue received attention when Senator Charles Grassley asked the Department of Justice about the numbers how many Wall Street executives were prosecuted for wrongdoing in relation to the financial crisis. The answer first suggested that such numbers had not been calculated systematically and once this was done turned out to be minimal or rather low (e.g. Eaglesham 2012). William Black, a law professor at the University of Missouri at Kansas City and former US banking supervisor, contrasts this 'too big to jail' problem with the very substantial prosecution and convictions of executives related to the US savings and loans crisis of the 1980s (Holland 2013).

The picture is, however, not so one sided. Whilst there have hardly been any high-level cases in the UK and the US so far, there have already been a number of convictions and there are ongoing trials in Europe (see overviews in *The Economist* 2013 and White 2013, for example). These concern, *inter alia*, the CEOs or CROs of Bayerische Landesbank,

Westdeutsche Landesbank or IKB Deutsche Industriebank in Germany. The CEO and entire board of HSH Nordbank were cleared in a 2014 case. In Iceland the CEOs of Glitnir, Kaupthing or Landsbanki went on trial, with the first two being convicted. The CEO of Anglo Irish Bank was found not guilty in a 2014 case. It has to be seen whether this difference between some European countries on the one hand and the UK and the US on the other hand is confirmed over time. One source of the difference may be the legal traditions in the two sets of countries. In the Anglo-Saxon legal tradition there is a tendency not to criminalize negligent mistakes or bad business decisions that are regarded as having been done in good faith. The German legal tradition (including Austria and Switzerland) knows a widely interpretable concept of breach of fiduciary trust ('Untreue'), which broadly refers to neglecting duties and thereby causing real harm to the wealth of others. Whereas the Anglosaxon tradition may be regarded as more business friendly, the German one probably makes it easier to sanction misbehaviour of top executives of financial institutions.

The discussion leads me to two policy considerations. First, I wonder whether micro-prudential supervisory authorities in collaboration with attorneys in major constituencies still need to check whether the approach of 'cleansing' the financial sector from individuals and practices at the border of immorality and crime is systematic enough. And where the legal and regulatory basis for criminal charges or supervisory interventions against the relevant behaviors and practices is not strong enough, I wonder whether legislation or regulation does not need to be strengthened. Also a variety of observers have made alternative or complementary proposals how banks can influence their employees' mental models or the norms associated with their professional identity. This includes, for example, feedback loops checking self-perception and client orientation (Ochs 2014), ethics training and ethics reminders that render normative demands salient in key situations (Cohn *et al.* 2014) up to the swearing of a professional oath (analogous to the Hippocratic oath for physicians; Boatright 2013 or Quinn 2012).

Second, individuals who are prone to the described behaviors and practices are likely to evade greater scrutiny and move outside its perimeter. Therefore financial sub-sectors that turn out to be at the receiving end need to be monitored carefully, both in terms of potential criminal activities and in terms of whether risk-taking develops a dimension that can imply dangers for the wider financial system.

All in all, it is key that the issues of business culture in the financial industry are addressed at all relevant levels. It is my impression that they do not receive as much or as systematic attention as they should. As a consequence, it is not clear whether we are on a path to something much better. Addressing these issues more forcefully would contribute to a 'renormalization' in many areas of the industry, relating to hard features such as profits, remuneration and risk taking or soft features such as client orientation, empathic or cooperative behavior and honesty. The renormalization would allow financial intermediaries and their employees to regain the trust of their clients and of society at large. And it would allow the financial sector and its professionals to 'reintegrate' in society and better play their important role for individuals and the economy as a whole. I believe this is at least as important an area as the traditional regulatory reforms.

Finally, before leaving this part of the paper addressing issues charged with value judgments a strong word of caution is needed. In this sub-section surveys and research have been reported that reflect a very critical attitude towards bankers and other financial services professionals. This resonates with the ongoing popular resentment against this industry and people working in it, as also reflected in the surveys reported at the start. But I tried to base my arguments on available research and analysis. Addressing the issues highlighted in this research should not be interpreted as judging everybody working in this industry. There will be many financial services executives and employees with impeccable ethical standards, cooperative attitudes and prudent risk taking behavior whose stigmatization would be unjustified and counterproductive.

Incentive Effects of Selected Resolution Reforms During the Transition

One part of financial reforms around the globe that I regard as particularly important and that also many others see at the center of better aligning incentives in the financial sector and addressing key financial stability issues is the area of resolution. It refers to how a bank (or another type of financial intermediary) is treated once the supervisory assessment questions its viability. Should it be closed and liquidated, can it come back on its feet through a recapitalizations and restructuring, does it need to be taken over by another bank or should it be (temporarily) nationalized? Bank resolution is often organized differently from regular company insolvency procedures, because problems of viability are often detected relatively late, it is hard to make a clear distinction between illiquidity and insolvency, reimbursing retail depositors is costly and may exceed the money available in the deposit insurance fund, one bank's problems may spill over to other banks and therefore resolution decisions have often to be taken relatively fast (such as over a weekend before financial markets open on Monday). Before the ongoing financial reforms it was widely perceived that there was a bias towards public bail-outs of banks, which in turn distort risk-taking incentives of banks and their creditors.[9]

In this section, I would like to present two early analyses of the effects of different resolution reforms in which we in the Directorate General Research of the ECB have been indirectly or directly involved. The first is a research project that we sponsored under our Lamfalussy Research Fellowship program.[10] It studies the effects of the extension of resolution authority over more financial intermediaries under the Dodd–Frank Act in the United States on risk-taking by banks. We believe that the results are valuable for Europe as well, not the least because they were produced at a time when the Single Resolution Mechanism (SRM)

---

[9] See Glaessner and Mas (1995), Dewatripont and Freixas (2011) or Gimbel (2012) for discussions of main issues around bank resolution.

[10] We introduced this program in 2002 in order to promote young scholars (usually assistant professors or advanced Ph.D. students) and their research on the functioning of the European financial system or its linkages with outside financial systems. Key areas covered over the years include financial integration, capital market development, financial stability and systemic risk as well as public policies associated with them. The program is named after the late Alexandre Lamfalussy, the first President of the European Monetary Institute (which had prepared for the euro before the ECB's existence) who has also made great contributions to developing the internal market for financial services in Europe.

of the European banking union was still being designed.[11] The second analysis concerns some internal, so far unpublished, work from DG Research on how bail-ins — creditor funded loss absorption or recapitalizations — change the pricing of bank debt securities and thereby may discipline bank risk taking. The reason for specifically focusing on resolution and these two examples is not only because of the importance of resolution reforms in overall financial reforms, but also because it is an area that has not been researched very much in the past and deserves greater attention and analytical support.

Resolution Regime and Bank Risk Taking

The ECB Lamfalussy Fellowship paper by Ignatowski and Korte (2014) studies the effects of the recent introduction of the Orderly Liquidation Authority (OLA) in the United States on the riskiness of banks. Being part of the Dodd–Frank Act of July 2010, which introduced a host of financial regulatory reforms in the US, the OLA extended the resolution authority of the Federal Deposit Insurance Corporation (FDIC) to many more financial intermediaries than previously the case. Originally, the FDIC had only resolution authority for deposit-taking institutions. But with the OLA this was extended also to bank holding companies (BHCs) and their subsidiaries as well as to non-bank financial companies. These intermediaries, which include some of the most important banks in the US, were previously not subject to a specific resolution regime, except for the regular corporate bankruptcy codes.

The theoretical hypothesis tested is inspired by the theory of DeYoung *et al.* (2013). By putting banks under clear and specific legal rules how they would be liquidated, restructured or otherwise be dealt with when their viability cannot be ensured any longer, rather than leaving this to the general corporate bankruptcy law and courts, constitutes an improvement in 'resolution technology' and diminishes or removes public bail-out expectations. So, the immediate impact one could expect to see with the introduction of the OLA is that the affected banks become more disciplined in their behavior and reduce risk taking.

---

[11] The SRM is planned to be fully operational in January 2016.

This hypothesis is tested by conducting a difference-in-difference estimation of the riskiness of US bank holding companies, controlling for bank characteristics, time and individual fixed effects. The authors use several risk measures as left-hand side variables, but in presenting the results focus particularly on the Z-score metric (originally put forward by Altman (1968)). This metric is related to the distance to default and therefore a higher Z-score describes less risk and a lower z-score more risk of a BHC. The effect of the OLA is identified with the help of two dummy variables, one marking the periods after and before its introduction and the other marking the BHCs affected and not affected by it. The estimated parameter of the interaction between these two variables describes the 'treatment effect', the change in the Z-scores of bank holding companies that became subject to the new regime compared to those which had no change in the resolution regime (control group). This treatment effect is net of a range of other variables that also influence bank risk, namely the control variables referred to above.

The main result is illustrated in Figure 3 (reproduced from Figure 1 in Ignatowski and Korte (2014)), which for ease of exposition is based on unconditional averages rather than the precise results from the estimations. The figure shows the evolution of average Z-scores over time for BHCs that were affected by the OLA (solid line) and those that were not (dashed line). Three time periods are distinguished: 'after OLA' runs from Q3 2010 to the end of the sample in Q2 2012; 'before OLA' runs from Q3 2007 to Q2 2010; and 'before OLA-1' runs from Q3 2005 to Q2 2007. As one would expect, Z-scores fluctuate over time. But in the pre-treatment periods 'before OLA-1' and 'before OLA' these fluctuations run quite parallel between the two groups of BHCs. But after the resolution reform the Z-scores of the affected banks strongly increase on average, whereas the Z-scores of the unaffected ones increase only mildly. In other words, the 'treated' BHCs' risk decreases by much more than the risk of the others.

The regressions described above and explained in detail in Ignatowski and Korte's paper confirm that the risk reducing effect of the OLA is robust and statistically significant. The reduction is quantified at around 7% of the Z-score. Moreover, additional analysis with loan-level data suggests that affected BHCs' newly originated mortgage loans after the

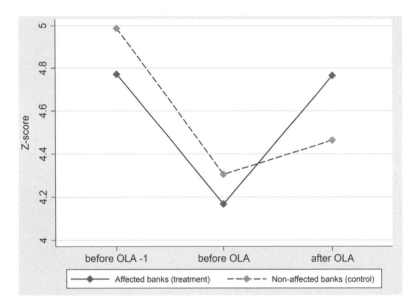

Figure 3. Riskiness of US bank holding companies before and after the introduction of the Orderly Liquidation Authority (OLA) in July 2010.

Notes: Z-score is defined as the return on assets plus the capital ratio divided by the standard deviation of return on assets and computed over 8-quarter periods. Before OLA-1: 2005Q3–2007Q2; before OLA: 2007Q3–2009Q2; after OLA: 2010Q3–2012Q2.
Source: Reproduced from Ignatowski and Korte (2014, Figure 1) with permission from Elsevier.

regime change were also less risky. When breaking the sample of BHCs up in size classes, however, it turns out that the risk reducing effect of the OLA vanishes for the largest banks.

In terms of prudential policy, the results suggest that the introduction of an explicit resolution regime for banks is helpful in that it has a disciplining effect leading banks to reduce their risk. This is consistent with the hypothesis that special resolution regimes for banks at least diminish adverse incentive effects related to bail-out expectations. The bad news for policy, however, is that this does not apply to the largest banks. So, one can agree with the authors that resolution reforms alone may not solve the too-big-to-fail problem, which would have to be addressed through complementary measures.

Bail-in Provisions and Bank Debt Valuation

In so far unpublished work, staff of the Financial Research Division in DG Research of the ECB examined the effects of the Cypriot bail-in of March 2013 on the valuation of European banks' debt securities. When Cyprus needed international financial assistance, inter alia, as a consequence of a banking sector collapse compounded by the Greek sovereign debt crisis, its financing needs were not only covered by official funding from European partners and the IMF (totaling EUR10 billion, i.e. 60% of Cyprus's GDP), but also via a bail-in of bank creditors. The bail-in was needed because covering the country's funding needs fully via official financing would have made the Cypriot government's debt position unsustainable. The bail-in affected both bank bond holders and, unusually, large uninsured depositors (i.e. deposits above EUR 100,000). Since the outstanding amounts of bonds issued by Cypriot banks were very small, depositors had even to cover a much larger part of the burden.

At around the same time drafts of the Bank Resolution and Recovery Directive (BRRD) as an important element of the European banking union were discussed in the EU, even though the final political agreement about the BRRD was only reached in December 2013. The BRRD contains a precisely defined 'pecking order' in which sequence holders of liabilities would have to be bailed in, if a bank becomes non-viable. The list goes down until senior debt securities and the large deposits not covered by deposit insurance (as bailed in the Cypriot crisis). The BRRD requires EU countries to implement it by January 2015, with its bail-in system starting in January 2016.

The internal research conducted by Adonis Antoniadis and Paolo Mistrulli of the Financial Research Division considers the following hypothesis.[12] The Cypriot bail-in at a time at which also the BRRD was negotiated provided a strong signal to investors that even low ranked bank liabilities are now at risk of not being bailed out in the future. Not only was this emerging in the draft BRRD but also the Cypriot

---

[12] Antoniadis is now on the staff of the Bank for International Settlements and Mistrulli returned to the Banca d'Italia.

precedent implied that it would be exceedingly difficult to treat other European countries' banks differently in the future. As a consequence, lower ranked bank liabilities that had not been subject to bail-ins in the past should become more risky for investors who would require a higher yield. If such higher yields emerged, then it would first imply that the new regime of bail-ins was credible. Second, it would also be consistent with the hypothesis that banks' increased funding costs exercise discipline on them, i.e. incentives against taking too much risk.

Our researchers tested this hypothesis by conducting a difference-in-difference estimation of French, German, Italian and Spanish bank bond yields, controlling for bond attributes and issuer-time effects. The data used run from three months before until three months after the March 2013 bail-in. The spreads between three types of senior debt yields (secured debt, senior unsecured debt and unsecured debt) and subordinated debt yields (which are negative) were regressed on dummies for each type of senior yield, on these dummies interacted with time dummies — one for each month starting in March — and the control variables. The parameters of the interacted dummy variables describe the 'treatment effect', the change in senior yields associated with the Cypriot bail-in over and above of what is implied by the typical spread between them and subordinated debt and what changes in bond and issuer characteristics imply for them. If the above hypothesis is correct, then the negative spread should decrease in absolute value because yields on senior debt (which are new to be bailed in) become more similar to subordinated debt yields (sub-debt has already been bailed in in the past).

The main result is illustrated in Figure 4, which for ease of exposition displays unconditional average spreads between the three senior debt categories and subordinated debt pooled for the four countries, over time. In line with the theoretical hypothesis the negative spreads diminish in absolute value and this effect remains valid until the end of the sample.

The difference-in-difference regressions undertaken by Antoniadis and Mistrulli confirm this picture. The result is economically and statistically significant for the pooled data and each country individually,

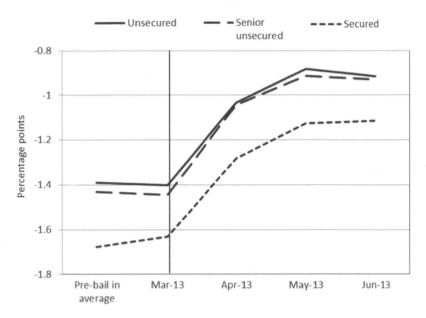

Figure 4. Spreads between senior and subordinated debt yields of French, German, Italian and Spanish bank bonds.

Notes: Monthly averages of bank bond yield spreads, calculated as the difference between three types of senior debt (unsecured, senior unsecured and secured) and subordinated debt. The vertical line marks the month in which creditors of Cypriot banks were bailed in.

Source: Bloomberg and ECB staff calculations

except for the case of Italy. The reason why the effect of the Cypriot bail-in on Italian yields is statistically insignificant likely has to do with the peculiar investor structure of Italian debt. A relatively large portion of Italian bank bonds is held by domestic households, which can be expected to have a relatively inelastic demand. In terms of quantification, the estimations suggest that the bail-in effect shelves around 30 to 60 basis points off the senior-sub-debt yield spread, which amounts to about a fifth of its original size.

In sum, the results of my colleagues suggest that the Cypriot case may have rendered the European bail-in provisions credible for investors. As a consequence, as part of a new resolution regime they may increase investors' sensitivity to bank risk taking and thereby exercise some discipline on bank managements. As a word of caution, however, one could point out — based on past experience — that it is important that investors remain attentive, even when there have not been bank failures for a longer period of time. Not only could the disciplining effects fade in protracted good times when investor inattention creeps in, but also when the 'wake-up call' of a first bail-in happens in a context of financial imbalances discipline could re-emerge violently in the form of contagion and contribute to a destabilization. It is therefore of utmost importance that investor attention is kept alive and not just a transitional phenomenon. Finally, higher funding costs are only one channel for discipline, which likely needs to be complemented by others. These could include measures enhancing the resolvability of banks, such as living wills or even structural regulation (such as Volcker, Vickers or Liikanen type of rules).

Concluding Remarks

The financial crisis has triggered a broad and protracted process of financial reforms in industrial countries. While more than seven years after the start of the crisis this process is still not finished and in some respects in different stages in different countries, the transition to the new regulatory and supervisory landscape has a variety of effects. Broadly speaking, the tightening regulation and supervision is weighing on financial intermediation activity (partly also due to frontloading behavior), as it is probably unavoidable temporarily, and on the contribution of the financial sector to the economic recovery. In terms of the structure of intermediation the somewhat uneven focus on banks drives business and risk taking to other, less regulated financial intermediaries, notably to so-called shadow banks. The wide set of reforms have, ceteris paribus, stabilizing effects on financial systems at this stage of the transition, although in a context of loose monetary policies, limited investment opportunities and search for yield it needs to be monitored carefully whether new financial imbalances emerge. Arguably less advanced so far is the 'reintegration' of finance in society in that large parts of populations remain suspicious of the activities of financial intermediaries and their employees, which may be an additional factor constraining intermediation activity. In what concerns the specific and important reform area of bank resolution, there is evidence that some key elements of it had immediately the desirable effects on incentives. For example, the introduction of an explicit bank resolution regime tended to enhance bank stability and the inclusion of bail-in provisions seemed to be priced in the debt instruments concerned, which show higher yields. Unfortunately, however, there are also signs that resolution mechanisms do not have the same disciplining effects on the largest banks, compared to small and medium-sized banks.

The discussion suggests, inter alia, that the reform process needs to start targeting an end point, which removes uncertainties and allows the financial sector to operate again in a reasonably stable regulatory environment. There are at least two (related) exceptions to this. For the shadow banking sector one should consider whether the migration of risks is of systemic importance, so that it also needs to be subjected to regulatory reform. Second, the macroprudential elements of financial supervision and regulation have not been developed enough. Concerning financial stability, unfinished initiatives such as the recapitalizations from the last round of European stress tests need to be completed. Moreover, the withdrawal of remaining support measures, such as expansionary monetary policies, public stakes in or central bank liquidity assistance to banks needs to be timed well. In my view the steps necessary to 'reintegrate' finance in society is not receiving enough attention. It remains a question whether the financial sector has been 'cleansed' systematically enough of people prone to and incentives leading to misconduct and excessive risk taking. It might be necessary that supervisors and attorneys collaborate more intensively to correct the adverse business culture that seems to have prevailed until quite recently, if the financial industry does not come up forcefully enough itself with trainings and self-correction mechanisms. A follow-up issue may then become that the individuals and practices simply migrate from the traditional banking sector to shadow banking, outside the present supervisory and regulatory perimeter. Concerning bank resolution, continued efforts are needed to make it also credible for the largest financial institutions or complement it with measures that would constrain enough the risk taking of those.

References

Altman, E. I. (1968), "Financial Ratios, Discriminant Analysis and the Prediction of Corporate Bankruptcy," *Journal of Finance*, 23(4): 589–609.

Barnier, M. (2014), "Attack to Win Games and Defend to Win Trophies: safeguarding financial stability in the EU single market," speech at the Worshipful Company of World Traders, September 29.

Basel Committee on Banking Supervision (2010), "An Assessment of The Long-Term Impact of Stronger Capital and Liquidity Requirements," Bank for International Settlements, August.

Basel Committee on Banking Supervision (2014a), "Basel III Monitoring Report," Basel, September.

Basel Committee on Banking Supervision (2014b), "Seventh Progress Report on Adoption of the Basel Regulatory Framework," Bank for International Settlements, October.

Board of Governors of the Federal Reserve System, Federal Deposit Insurance Corporation and Office of the Controller of the Currency (2013), "Agencies Issue Updated Leveraged Lending Guidance," joint press release, March 21.

Boatright, J. R. (2013), "Swearing to be virtuous: The prospects of a banker's oath," *Review of Social Economics*, 71(2): 140–165.

Clerc, L., A. Derviz, C. Mendicino, S. Moyen, K. Nikolov, L. Stracca, J. Suarez and A. Vardoulakis (2014), "Capital Regulation in a Macroeconomic Model with Three Layers of Default," European Central Bank, Mimeo, June, forthcoming *International Journal of Central Banking*.

Cœuré, B. (2013), "Monetary Policy and Banking Supervision," speech at the Institute for Monetary and Financial Stability Symposium on "Central Banking: Where Are We Headed?" Frankfurt am Main, February 7.

Cohn, A., E. Fehr and M. A. Maréchal (2014), "Business Culture and Dishonesty in the Banking Industry," *Nature*, 516(December): 86–89.

Dewatripont, M. and X. Freixas (2011), "Bank Resolution: A framework for the assessment of regulatory interventions," *Oxford Review of Economic Policy*, 27(3): 411–436.

DeYoung, R., M. Kowalik and J. Reidhill (2013), "A Theory of Failed Bank Resolution: Technological change and political economics," *Journal of Financial Stability*, 9(4): 612–627.

Eaglesham, J. (2012), "Missing: Stats on crisis convictions," *Wall Street Journal*, May 13.

Economist, The (2013), "Prosecuting Banks: Blind justice," May 4.

Edelman (2014), "2014 Edelman Trust Barometer — Financial Services Industry Results," Annual Global Study.

Elliott, D., S. Salloy and A. O. Santos (2012), "Assessing the Cost of Financial Regulation," IMF Working Paper No. WP/12/233, September.

European Banking Authority (2014a), "Basel III Monitoring Exercise," London, September 11.

European Banking Authority (2014b), "Risk Assessment of the European Banking System," London, December.

European Central Bank (2014a), "Report on the Macroprudential Research Network (MaRs)," Frankfurt am Main, June 20.

European Central Bank (2014b), "ECB's In-Depth Review Shows Banks Need to Take Further Action," Press Release, October 26.

European Central Bank (2014c), "Financial Stability Review," Frankfurt am Main, November.

European Commission (2014a), "Communication from the Commission to the European Parliament, the Council, the European Economic and Social Committee and the Committee of the Regions: A reformed financial sector for Europe," COM(2014) 279 final, Brussels, May 15.

European Commission (2014b), "Progress of financial reforms," June 27. Available at: http://ec.europa.eu/finance/general-policy/policy/map_reform_en.htm.

Financial Stability Board (2014a), "Financial Reforms — Completing the Job and Looking Ahead," September 15.

Financial Stability Board (2014b), "Global Shadow Banking Monitoring Report 2014," October 30.

Financial Stability Board (2014c), "FSB Publishes Global Shadow Banking Monitoring Report 2014," Press Release, September 30.

Financial Stability Forum (2008), "Report of the Financial Stability Forum on Enhancing Market and Institutional Resilience," April 7.

Gallup (2014), "Honesty/ethics in Professions," 8–11 December. Available at: http://www.gallup.com/poll/1654/honesty-ethics-professions.aspx.

Gimbel, A. (2012), *Bank Resolution, Bailouts, and the Time Inconsistency Problem* (Mimeo: European University Institut).

Glaessner, T. and I. Mas (1995), "Incentives and the Resolution of Bank Distress," *World Bank Research Observer*, 10(1): 53–73.

Harper, C. (2013), "Finanzbranche ist nicht vertrauenswürdig," *Die Welt*, January 21.

Hartmann, P. (2015), "Real Estate Markets and Macroprudential Policy in Europe," *Journal of Money, Credit and Banking*, 47(S1): 69–80.

Hetzer, J. (2014), "Commerzbank-Vorstand Beumer übt scharfe Kritik an Bankenregulierung," *Impulse*, May 29.

Holland, J. (2013), "Hundreds of Wall Street Execs Went to Prison during the Last Fraud-Fuelled Bank Crisis," *BillMoyers.com*.

Holló, D., M. Kremer and Marco Lo Duca, 2012, "CISS — A composite indicator of systemic stress in the financial system," ECB Working Paper No. 1426, March.

Ignatowski, M. and J. Korte (2014), "Wishful Thinking or Effective Threat? Tightening bank resolution regimes and bank risk-taking," *Journal of Financial Stability*, 15(December): 264–281.

Institute of International Finance (2011), "The Cumulative Impact on the Global Economy of Changes in the Financial Regulatory Framework," Washington, DC, September.

International Monetary Fund (2012), "The Reform Agenda: An interim report on progress toward a safer financial system," in IMF's *2012 Global Financial Stability Report*, Washington, DC, October, pp. 75–140.

International Monetary Fund (2014), "Global Financial Stability Report," Washington, DC, October.

Kashyap, A., J. Stein and S. Hanson (2010), "An Analysis of the Impact of 'Substantially Heightened' Capital Requirements on Large Financial Institutions," University of Chicago, May.

Kirchgässner, G. and F. Habermacher (2011), "Sind Aktienhändler wirklich schlimmer als Psychopathen," *Neue Zürcher Zeitung*, November 21.

Kollewe, J., J. Treanor and S. Hickey (2014), "Banks Pay Out £166 Billion Over Six Years: A history of banking misdeeds and fines," *The Guardian*, November 12.

Macroeconomic Assessment Group (2010), "Final report — Assessing the macroeconomic impact of the transition to stronger capital and liquidity requirements," Financial Stability Board and Basel Committee on Banking Supervision at the Bank for International Settlements, Basel, December.

Martinez-Miera, D., and J. Suarez (2012), "A Macroeconomic Model of Endogenous Systemic Risk Taking," CEPR Discussion Paper, No. 9,134, September.

Miles, D., Y. Jing and G. Marcheggiano (2013), "Optimal Bank Capital," *Economic Journal*, 123(567): 1–37.

Mokros, A., B. Menner, H. Eisenbarth, G. W. Alpers, K. W. Lange and M. Osterheider (2008), "Diminished Cooperativeness of Psychopaths in a Prisoner's Dilemma Game Yields Higher Rewards," *Journal of Abnormal Psychology*, 117: 406–413.

Neretina, E., C. Sahin and J. de Haan (2014), "Banking Stress Test Effects on Returns and Risks," DNB Working Paper No. 419, April.

Noll, T. and P. Scherrer (2013), "Professionelle Trader in Einer Gefangenendilemma Situation," In H.-W. Jackmuth, C. de Lamboy and P. Zawilla (eds.) *Fraud Management in Kreditinstituten — Praktiken, Verhinderung, Aufdeckung* (Verlag: Frankfurt School), pp. 257–279.

Ochs, S. M. (2014), "Inside the Banker's Brain: Mental models in the financial services industry and implications for consumers, practitioners and regulators," Aspen Institute, Initiative on Financial Security, Washington (DC).

Quinn, J. (2012), "HSBC Chairman Urges Bankers to Swear an Oath," *The Telegraph*, November 25.

Ralph, O. (2014), "Bank Fines — A World of Pain," *Financial Times*, Lex Live, September 23.

Rochet, J. C. (2014), "The Extra Cost of Swiss Banking Regulation," White Paper, Swiss Finance Institute, Zurich, January.

Slovik, P. and B. Cournède (2011), "Macroeconomic impact of Basel III," OECD Economics Department Working Paper No. 844, February 14.

Stolz, S. M. and M. Wedow (2010), "Extraordinary Measures in Extraordinary Times: Public measures in support of the financial sector in the EU and the United States," ECB Occasional Paper No. 117, July.

Tan, G. (2014a), "Banks Sit Out Riskier Deals — Regulatory Pressure Push Some Lenders to Let Lucrative Deals Go," *Wall Street Journal*, Money Beat, January 21.

Tan, G. (2014b), "Can Banks Lend For Risky Deals? Depends Who You Ask," *Wall Street Journal*, Money Beat, November 19.

Taylor, J. B. (2014a), "An Economic Hokum of 'Secular Stagnation'," *Wall Street Journal*, January 1.

Taylor, J. B. (2014b), "Rapid growth or stagnation: an economic policy choice," *Journal of Policy Modelling*, 36(4): 641–648.

White, S. (2013), "Not one top Wall Street executive has been convicted of criminal charges related to 2008 crisis," *Reuters*, November 13.

Wood, J. and P. Berg (2011), "Rebuilding Trust in Banks," *Gallup Business Journal*, August 8.

Yan, M., M. J. B. Hall and P. Turner (2012), "A Cost-Benefit Analysis of Basel III: Some evidence from the UK," *International Review of Financial Analysis*, 25: 73–82.

Part VI
Transitional Impact of the
Reforms on the Real Sector

The Jury Is In

— CHAPTER 18

- Stephen G. Cecchetti
  Brandeis International Business School

In June 2010, the Institute of International Finance (IIF) warned that the new Basel III capital and liquidity standards would be catastrophic for the global economy. After examining the impact of implementation over a five-year horizon, the IIF concluded that banks would need to increase capital levels dramatically and that this would drive lending rates up, loan volumes down and result in an annual 0.6-percentage-point hit to GDP growth in the United States, the euro area and Japan.[1]

Two months later, the group formulating the new international financial regulatory standards published their report. The Macroeconomic Assessment Group (MAG), a joint creation of the Financial Stability Board and Basel Committee on Banking Supervision composed of nearly 100 macroeconomic modeling experts from around the world, concluded that things were hardly dire.[2] The implied increase in capital would drive lending rates up only modestly, loans volumes down a bit,

Professor of International Economics, Brandeis International Business School; Research Associate National Bureau of Economic Research; Research Fellow, Centre for Economic Policy Research; and Chairman of the Macroeconomic Assessment Group. I would like to thank Ben Cohen for his years of collaboration and support in the work of the Macroeconomic Assessment Group, Michela Scatigna for discussions and assistance with the data, Paul Tucker for many illuminating conversations, and Kim Schoenholtz (for forcing me to sharpen my arguments). All errors are author's own.

[1] See Institute of International Finance (2010).
[2] See Macroeconomic Assessment Group (2010a and 2010b).

and result in a decline in growth of only 0.05 percentage point per year for five years — one-twelfth the IIF's estimate.

You might argue that both of these groups suffer from hopelessly irresolvable conflicts of interest. After all, the IIF is an association of the world's largest private global banks trying desperately to find a way to maintain the implicit government guarantees that have made them so profitable for decades. And the MAG is a group composed of the world's largest central bankers, supervisory authorities and international institutions who were being blamed for letting the crisis happen in the first place. The incentives of each were pretty clear: the IIF would claim the world is coming to an end in an effort to push the regulators to remain lax; and the MAG would minimize the possibility of any negative effects in an effort to support the imposition of stringent requirements.

This natural skepticism is confirmed by the fact that, among the group of studies examining the macroeconomic impact of the transition to strong capital and liquidity requirements, the IIF and MAG are at opposite ends of the spectrum. That said, the broader consensus outside of these two groups was that, as higher capital and liquidity requirements were put into effect, they would put some drag on real activity, but the impact would be relatively small. In other words, those with less personally on the line were closer to the MAG than the IIF.[3]

Well, the jury is in and my reading of the evidence is that the optimists were not optimistic enough. Capital requirements have gone up dramatically, and bank capital levels have gone up with them. In the meantime, lending spreads have barely moved, bank interest margins are down, and loan volumes are up. To the extent that more demanding capital regulations had any macroeconomic impact, they would appear to have been offset by accommodative monetary policy. So, if Basel III pushed up lending costs and discouraged lending, the combination of low policy rates and unconventional monetary policy was sufficient to mitigate the impact on growth.[4]

---

[3] Cohen and Scatigna (2014) Tables 1 and 2 summarize results in range of studies.

[4] The MAG's (2010a) primary headline estimate of decline in growth of 0.05 percentage points per year for five years assumes no monetary policy response. The group's estimate with endogenous monetary policy is slightly smaller.

Before getting to the details, I should note a number of difficulties in coming to any definitive conclusions. First and foremost, at this writing, the implementation of financial reforms is incomplete. In the case of the liquidity requirement, the international standards are not yet final. And, full implementation of the new Basel III requirements will only be complete at the beginning of 2019. That said, banks have generally frontloaded their capital increases. Most large, internationally active banks already meet the 2019 requirements by 2014.

Second, changes in financial regulation are far from the only influence on macroeconomic outcomes over the past few years. For example, as the EU was in the process of adopting the new capital regulation directive (CRD IV), the euro area experienced a set of sovereign debt crises. As the Japanese Financial Service Authority (JFSA) adopted new capital adequacy rules for internationally active banks, the Bank of Japan engaged in Quantitative and Qualitative Monetary Easing (QQE) that has nearly doubled the Japanese monetary base. And as the US authorities were implementing Dodd–Frank, the Federal Reserve has maintained exceptionally accommodative policy with continued low short-term interest rates and a relatively steep yield curve. But even so, as I will explain, the evidence for the optimistic interpretation is reasonably compelling.

In the remainder of this essay, I seek to substantiate my conclusion that the macroeconomic impact of the increases in capital requirements was either imperceptibly small or was neutralized by monetary policy actions. I start with a very brief description of the increase in capital requirements themselves, followed by examination of the sizable increase in bank capital (4.5 percentage points for the largest global banks) and the sources of the increase (two-thirds retained earnings and one-third capital issuance). Next, I examine standard bank performance indicators, and conclude that bank profitability is down, as are net interest margins and operating costs. This is followed by a discussion of lending spreads and loan volumes — the former are largely unchanged, while the latter are up nearly everywhere outside of Europe.

After a brief discussion of why lending is depressed in Europe, I turn to policy implications. Recall that by reducing or removing government subsidies, the changes in capital and liquidity regulation are intended to increase lending costs and reduce credit supply. In the absence of any policy reaction, this would raise the interest rates borrowers face and reduce the level of debt in equilibrium. The evidence that the impact has been small thus far suggests that, in normal times, by lowering the risk-free rate, monetary policy will be able to offset this, mitigating the impact on growth.

And, for policies like the countercyclical capital buffer, one of several time-varying discretionary macroprudential tools, the implication is that these may not be the silver bullet that their designers hoped they could use to combat unwanted credit booms. That is, raising capital standards during a period of euphoria will improve resilience to the eventual bust, but may not do much to reduce the rate of credit growth itself.

Capital Requirements and the Level of Bank Capital

I start with a quantitative examination of changes in capital require-ments and the level of bank capital. It is important to understand that Basel III increased capital requirements considerably — but from a negligible level. While the headline requirement ratio for Basel II was 4%, the reality is that banks were required to hold virtually no capital whatsoever. The reason is that Basel II allowed a range of hybrid instru-ments and intangibles to count as capital, and there were gaps in the coverage of risks in the computation of risk-weighted assets. On the hybrids — things that most people would agree look more like debt than equity — these arose from the arbitrage created by the fact that interest payments are deductible from profits before taxes, while divi-dends are not. On intangibles, things like good will, deferred tax assets and mortgage servicing rights could count, even though they might have little or no value when a bank fails.[5]

In constructing Basel III, authorities took the view that capital should be loss absorbing in resolution and that the computation of

---

[5] Cecchetti and Schoenholtz (2014c) discuss some of the conceptual issues associated with the measurement of capital.

Table 1. Comparing Basel III and Basel II capital requirements (share of risk-weighted assets) for the largest systemic banks: Impact of Basel III capital definition.

Basel III range	8% to 10%
Basel II Baseline	4%
Adjustment for hybrid capital	–2%
Adjustment for goodwill, intangibles, deferred tax assets, etc.	–1%
Adjustment for changes in risk weights	–0.25%
Effective Basel II converted to a Basel III basis	**<0.75%**

Source: Basel Committee on Banking Supervision (2010) and authors' calculations.

risk-weighted assets should be comprehensive, including both on- and off-balance sheet exposures.[6] This more rigorous view led to a dramatic increase in effective capital requirements. While the actual change depends on the exact nature of a bank's activities, Table 1 provides a sense of the size of the adjustments. Using the tighter Basel III definition of capital and risk coverage, the effective pre-crisis Basel II requirement was less than 0.75% of risk-weighted assets. By contrast, standards agreed in 2010 require capital of 8% to 10% of risk-weighted assets for the largest systemic banks.

To address concerns about transition costs, the international agreement specifies that the new standards are to be phased in over several years.[7] But since capital requirements are minima, not maxima, there is nothing to stop banks from raising their capital adequacy ahead of the Basel III timetable. And, they have.

As a part of its implementation monitoring program, the Basel Committee performs periodic quantitative impact studies (QIS). Typically, these have included the 200 or so largest banks in the world (as measured by assets). The results of each QIS include the level of

---

[6] See Basel Committee on Banking Supervision (2011) for details.
[7] See Box IV.A of BIS (2014) for details.

Table 2. Bank's common equity tier 1 relative to risk-weighted assets: Fully phased-in Basel III ratios.

	2009	2011		2012		2013	
	31 Dec	30 Jun	31 Dec	30 Jun	31 Dec	30 Jun	31 Dec
Large internationally active banks	5.7	7.8	7.7	8.5	9.2	9.5	10.2
Other Banks	7.8	8.8	8.7	8.8	9.4	9.5	10.5

Notes: 'Large international active banks' are the 102 global banks with capital in excess of €3 billion. 'Other banks' is a sample of 125 smaller banks.
Source: Basel Committee on Banking Supervision (various years).

capital computed on the fully phased-in Basel III definitions of capital and risk-weighted assets. Table 2 reports the numbers from end-2009 to end-2013.

I take two important points away from the results in Table 2. First, since end-2009, capital (as measured by common equity tier 1) has risen by a total of 4.5 percentage points of risk-weighted assets for the 102 largest banks in the world, and 2.7 percentage points for the smaller banks in the Basel Committee's sample. Second, while there are surely differences across banks and regions, end-2013 capital levels exceed those that Basel III requires for 2019.[8]

These numbers are averages. Some banks remain below the 2019 standard. While they do not report results for individual banks (or single countries or even regions), the Basel Committee does publish information on the capital shortfall for banks that do not currently meet the fully-phased in Basel III requirements. Here, if we accept that the definition of capital is truly harmonized and that all banks are being treated with equal rigor, the numbers are very modest: the December 2013 total was roughly EUR25 billion for all 227 banks included.

In assessing these speedy increases in capital ratios, it is useful to ask how the banks did it. Did they increase the level of capital or reduce assets? If it was the former, was it through retained earnings or new

---

[8] One explanation for this is that regulations only bind in good times; markets bind in bad times. In order to demonstrate their strength to investors, banks have been in a race to meet future requirements early.

issuance. And, if it was the latter, did they reduce total assets, or simply reduce the riskiness of what they were holding?

Cohen and Scatigna (2014) have done these computations. In Figure 1, I reproduce an updated graphic for their sample of 94 banks.[9] Starting with the left-hand panel, note that with the exception of European banks, banks' total assets increased, contributing to bringing the ratio down not up (the dark solid portion of the bar in the graph). The impact of changes in the composition of assets varied across regions. In the United States and the Euro Area, banks reduced riskiness, raising their capital ratios (that's the gray solid portion of the bar). In the rest of the world, it went the other way.

This brings us to increases in capital, the diagonal-patterned portion of each bar in the left-hand panel of Figure 1 and the subject of the right-hand panel. The primary driver of the increase in banks' capital ratio was an increase in capital itself. The right-hand panel shows that the increase in capital largely reflected gains in net income (the light solid portion of each bar in the right-hand panel). Looking more closely at the result for the entire sample, capital increased by 4.13 percentage points (slightly less than for the Basel Committee's sample of banks), two thirds of which, or 2.76 percentage points, is from retained earnings and the remainder from other sources (primarily net capital issuance).[10]

Bank Performance

Next, I turn to bank performance. In Table 3, reproduced from BIS (2014), I report pre-tax profits, net-interest margin and operating costs, all as a fraction of total assets for 11 advanced and 4 emerging

---

[9] This version of Cohen and Scatigna's graphs appear in BIS (2014). As Cohen and Scatigna note, the sample of banks accounts for roughly two-thirds of the assets of the largest 1000 banks in the world, and includes all 29 institutions on the Financial Stability Board's list of systemically important institutions.

[10] Retained earnings is computed as the difference between net income and dividends. The 'Other' category in Figure 1 includes some smaller items such as the revaluation of assets classified as available for sale, but is mostly net equity issuance.

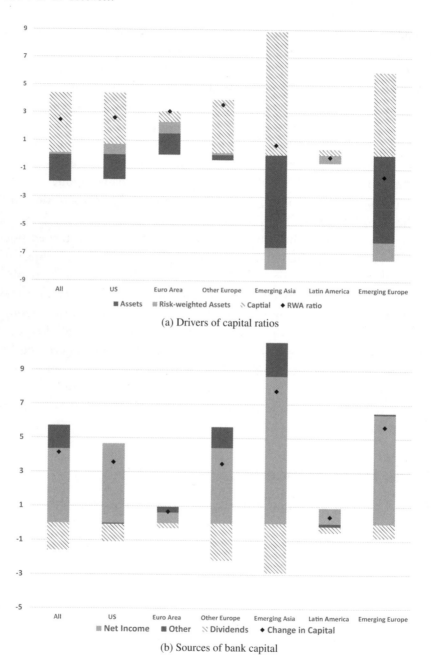

(a) Drivers of capital ratios

(b) Sources of bank capital

Figure 1. Capital accumulation boosts banks' regulatory ratios, changes between end-2009 and end-2013 (in percentage).

Figure 1. (*figure on facing page*).   *Notes*: The graph decomposes the change in the ratio of common equity capital to risk-weighted assets (left-hand panel) and the percentage change in common equity capital (right-hand panel) into additive components. Overall changes are shown by diamonds. The contribution of a particular component is denoted by the height of the corresponding segment. A negative contribution indicates that the component had a depressive effect. All figures are weighted averages using end-2013 total assets as weights. *Source*: Cohen and Scatigna (2014); Bankscope; and, Bloomberg.

Table 3.   Profitability of major global banks.

	Pre-tax profits		Net-interest margin		Operating Costs	
	2000–07	2013	2000–07	2013	2000–07	2013
Australia	1.58	1.28	1.96	1.79	1.99	1.11
Brazil	2.23	1.62	6.56	3.55	6.21	3.28
Canada	1.03	1.06	1.74	1.65	2.73	1.78
China	1.62	1.86	2.74	2.38	1.12	1.01
France	0.66	0.32	0.81	0.92	1.60	1.16
Germany	0.26	0.10	0.68	0.99	1.38	1.55
India	1.26	1.41	2.67	2.82	2.48	2.36
Italy	0.83	–1.22	1.69	1.58	2.27	1.84
Japan	0.21	0.68	1.03	0.77	0.99	0.60
Russia	3.03	2.04	4.86	4.15	4.95	2.68
Spain	1.29	0.50	2.04	2.32	2.29	1.75
Sweden	0.92	0.77	1.25	0.98	1.34	0.84
Switzerland	0.52	0.36	0.64	0.61	2.39	1.90
United Kingdom	1.09	0.23	1.75	1.12	2.02	1.55
United States	1.74	1.24	2.71	2.32	3.58	3.03

Source: BIS 2014, Table VI.2.

market economies. Taking these as a whole, I conclude that profitability is down, net-interest margins are down and operating costs are down. Putting this together with the previous observations, we can conclude that, to the extent that increases in capital were costly and reduced the value of the government subsidies, these costs were borne by the equity holders in the form of lower dividends and the managers in the form of lower compensation (included in operating costs). Most importantly, and contrary to what pessimists predicted, net interest margins did not balloon.

Lending Spreads and Credit Volumes

Macroeconomic indicators reinforce the conclusions from the bank performance data. Figures 2, 3 and 4 report lending spreads, lending standards and bank credit, respectively. With the exception of the euro area, lending spreads are down, lending standards have eased and the ratio of bank credit to GDP is up.

Bringing this all together, the consensus was too cautious and the pessimists were wrong. While weak demand by potential borrowers can

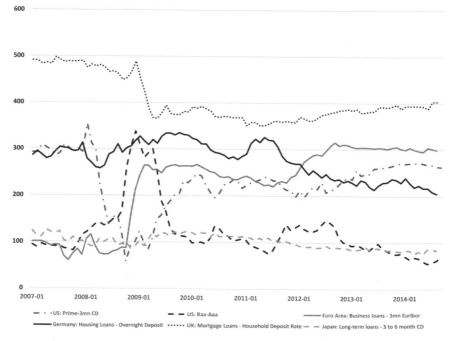

Figure 2. Lending spreads in selected economies, in basis points.

Notes: [1]One to five year business loans. [2]Variable rate mortgages. [3] One to five years housing loans. [4]Deposits of non-financial corporates.
Source: National data.

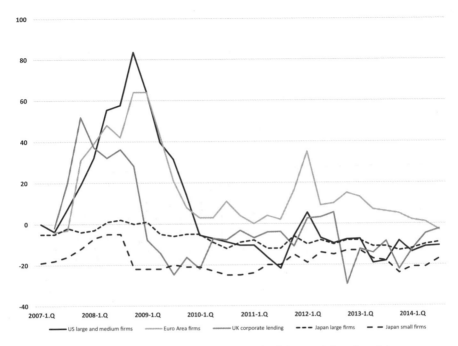

Figure 3. Survey responses on banking standards*, net tightening, in percentage points.

Note:*Difference between banks reporting tighter lending conditions during the previous quarter and those reporting looser conditions.

Source: Bank of England; Bank of Japan; European Central Bank; and, Federal Reserve Board.

explain the reduced spreads and is consistent with easing of lending standards, it is not consistent with the generally higher levels of bank credit. So, while there were lots of other things going on for which these informal methods do not control, the story seems compelling. The sizable increase in capital requirements led to a rapid rise in bank capitalization with very little in the way of macroeconomic impact. And, returning to the debate between the IIF and the MAG, even the optimists appear to have been insufficiently optimistic.

Why is Lending Still Depressed in Europe?

Looking at the data I have presented thus far, Europe stands out. Net interest margins are up in most of continental Europe (Table 2), lending

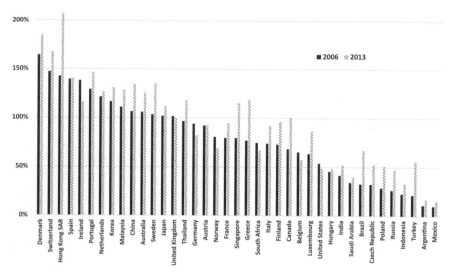

Figure 4. Ratio of bank credit to GDP.

Source: BIS and IMF.

spreads are up and standards tighter in the euro area (Figures 3 and 4), and private credit is down in a number of countries (Figure 5). Furthermore, using bank-level data to examine the impact on lending volumes of the unannounced 2011–12 EBA capital exercise, Mésonnier and Monks (2014) conclude that for each percentage point increase in the ratio of capital to risk-weighted assets, loan growth fell by 1.2 and 1.6 percentage points (over a 9-month period).

The explanation, I believe, is two-fold. First, there is the way in which the sequence of European stress tests and capital assessment exercises were conducted. Instead of requiring banks to raise additional capital to offset a shortfall — as the 2009 US stress test did — authorities allowed them to meet capital ratios by shedding assets.[11] As the left-hand panel of Figure 1 shows, euro area banks did not raise capital. Instead, they reduced both their total assets and their risk-weighted

---

[11] For a discussion of the stress tests, see Greenlaw *et al.* (2011).

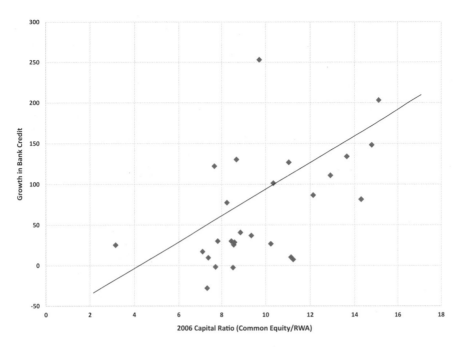

Figure 5. Growth in nominal bank credit and 2006 capital ratio.

Source: BIS and Bankscope.

assets. Second, a number of continental European banks remain under pressure to further raise their levels of capitalization.

We can get some sense of the relationship between capital and lending by looking across countries. With this in mind, in Figure 5, I plot the ratio of bank capital to risk-weighted assets in 2006 (using national definitions) on the horizontal axis against the percentage change in nominal bank credit over the following seven years (through 2013) on the vertical axis for a total of 30 advanced and emerging market countries.[12] The message of this graph is that the higher the 2006 capital ratios were, the larger the increase in bank lending going forward.

---

[12] The countries are Australia, Austria, Belgium, Brazil, Canada, Chile, China, France, Germany, Greece, Hong Kong, Ireland, Italy, Japan, Singapore, South Africa, Spain, Sweden, Switzerland, Thailand, Turkey, the United Kingdom, and the United States.

In fact, a simple cross-sectional regression of bank credit growth on the capital ratio yields a slope coefficient of 16.3. Given that the standard deviation of the initial capital ratio is 2.7, this means that a one-standard deviation increase in the capital ratio is consistent with credit growing by an additional 44% cumulatively over 7 years.[13]

To put it bluntly, banks with a debt overhang do not lend. And, Europe's banks still need capital to reduce the extent of the overhang.

Implications for Policy

The muted impact of increases in capital has implications both for how we set the baseline ratio of required capital — the level in normal times — and for the usefulness of time-varying, discretionary capital requirements — tools like the countercyclical capital buffer envisioned in Basel III.

Starting with the level of capital requirements in normal times, in Cecchetti and Schoenholtz (2014b), Kim Schoenholtz and I describe why this is a difficult problem. In the end, one needs to balance the social costs of imposing higher capital requirements against the social benefits of preventing or mitigating a future costly financial crisis. The uncertainties inherent in this cost-benefit calculus lead us to make a pragmatic proposal: regulators should continue to ratchet up bank capital requirements until the tradeoff between banking efficiency and financial safety shifts appreciably in favor of the latter. Importantly, as capital levels rise, we will become more certain of the costs in terms of increased lending spreads, reduced loan volumes, and shifts of activity to less-regulated intermediaries. The results that I have described from implementing Basel III suggests that, as Admati and Hellwig (2013) forcefully argue, the social costs of higher capital requirements are small.

One of the innovative features of Basel III is its inclusion of a countercyclical capital buffer intended to provide authorities with a tool to combat credit booms (which are inevitably followed by damaging busts). The idea of the buffer is that, when credit is growing relatively

---

[13] Cohen and Scatigna (2014) analysis of individual bank data confirms this result. Better capitalized banks make more loans.

quickly, officials should raise the level of required capital by as much as 2.5 percentage points of risk-weighted assets. The big question is whether this will work to limit a credit expansion, or just provide an extra buffer against the eventual bust. As Aiyar *et al.* (2014) note, there are three preconditions for the capital buffer to work: capital requirements have to bind before they are raised, equity has to be costly and difficult to raise in the short term, and alternatives to bank credit have to be relatively unavailable and costly.

Recent experience is not very encouraging for the efficacy of the countercyclical buffer as envisioned in Basel III. The difficulty is at least three fold. First, lending spreads do not look like the first-order response to higher capital requirements. Second, loan volumes do not look sensitive to changes in capital so long as banks are well capitalized. And finally, at the stage in the business cycle when the countercyclical buffer would be needed, banks' business is likely to be booming and profitable, making it cheaper and easier to raise equity.[14]

Conclusions

In 2010, private banks and the authorities engaged in a heated argument over the likely impact of increasing capital requirements.[15] The industry claimed it would be calamitous, while the official community believed it would be modestly painful. With the benefit of hindsight, even the optimists were too cautious. Capital has increased rapidly with very little impact on anything but bank profitability (and possibly managers' compensation). Lending spreads and interest margins are nearly unchanged, while (outside Europe) loan volumes and credit growth have remained robust. So, in the end, the macroeconomic impact appears to have been small.

---

[14] Kim Schoenholtz and I also argue in Cecchetti and Schoenholtz (2014a) that discretionary prudential policy is impractical for all the reasons that associated with the debate of rules versus discretion. These included information and recognition lags, response and decision lags, and implementation and transmission lags, as well as governance and political resistance.

[15] Giles (2010) provides an example of how heated things were.

While we need to continue to study this episode, performing a proper statistical analysis that controls for macroeconomic conditions and policy responses, I come to two tentative conclusions. First, given that social costs of raising bank capital appear to have been small thus far, we should increase them further, while being wary of a further shift of intermediation to shadow banks. And second, the efficacy of time-varying capital requirements is questionable.

References

Admati, A.R. and M. F. Hellwig (2013), *The Bankers' New Clothes: What's Wrong With Banking and What to do About It* (Princeton, N.J.: Princeton University Press).

Aiyar, S., C. W. Calomiris and R. Wieladak (2014), "Identifying Channels of Credits Substitution When Bank Capital Requirements are Varied," Bank of England Working Paper No 485, January.

Bank for International Settlements (2014), "84th Annual Report," June. Available at: http://www.bis.org/publ/arpdf/ar2014e.htm.

Basel Committee on Banking Supervisions (2011), "Basel III: A global regulatory framework for more resilient banks and banking systems," June. Available at: http://www.bis.org/publ/bcbs189.pdf.

Basel Committee on Banking Supervision (various years), "Results of Basel III Monitoring Exercise." Available at: http://www.bis.org/bcbs/implementation/bprl1.htm.

Cecchetti, S. G. and K. L. Schoenholtz (2014a), "Time-Varying Capital Requirements: Rules vs. discretion (again)," *www.moneyandbanking.com*, June 16. Available at: http://www.moneyandbanking.com/commentary/2014/6/16/time-varying-capital-requirements-rules-vs-discretion-again.

Cecchetti, S. G. and K. L. Schoenholtz (2014b), "Making Finance Safe," *www.moneyandbanking.com*, October 6. Available at: http://www.moneyandbanking.com/commentary/2014/10/6/making-finance-safe.

Cecchetti, S. G. and K. L. Schoenholtz (2014c), "A Primer on Bank Capital," *www.moneyandbanking.com*, November 3. Available at: http://www.moneyandbanking.com/commentary/2014/11/3/a-primer-on-bank-capital.

Cohen, B. H. and M. Scatigna (2014), "Banks and Capital Requirements: Channels of adjustment," BIS Working Paper No. 443, March. Available at: http://www.bis.org/publ/work443.htm.

Giles, C. (2010), "Bankers' 'Doomsday Scenarios' Under Fire from Basel Study Chief," *Financial Times*, May 31.

Greenlaw, D., A.K Kashyap, K. L. Schoenholtz and H. S. Shin (2012), "Stressed Out: Macroprudential principles for stress testing," US Monetary Policy Forum, February.

Institute of International Finance (2010), "Interim Report on the Cumulative Impact on the Global Economy of Proposed Changes in the Banking Regulatory Framework," June. Available at: https://www.iif.com/file/7097/download?token=sNl6fvgy.

Macroeconomic Assessment Group (2010a), "Assessing the Macroeconomic Impact of the Transition to Stronger Capital and Liquidity Requirements: Interim report," August. Available at: http://www.bis.org/publ/othp10.pdf.

Macroeconomic Assessment Group (2010b), Assessing the Macroeconomic Impact of the Transition to Stronger Capital and Liquidity Requirements: Final report," December. Available at: http://www.bis.org/publ/othp12.htm.

Mésonnier, J.-S. and A. Monks (2014), "Did the EBA Capital Exercise Cause a Credit Crunch in the Euro Area?" Working Paper 491, Banque de France. Available at: https://www.banque-france.fr/en/economics-statistics/research/working-paper-series/document/491-1.html.

Regulations, Reforms, and the Real Sector
— CHAPTER 19

■ Martin Čihák
International Monetary Fund

Introduction

Debates about post-crisis regulatory reforms and their real-sector effects have mostly focused on global initiatives, such as Basel III (see for example, Cecchetti 2014). Those discussions are very important and useful, but they overlook that regulation, supervision, and resolution is implemented largely at individual country level.[1] Despite progress on global standards, actual regulation is done by countries and still very much varies across country borders.

This chapter highlights the importance of examining regulation — and its real sector effects — at the country level. An analysis of data on country-by-country regulation underscores that countries had very different starting points before the global financial crisis, and that despite

Martin Čihák is an Advisor at the International Monetary Fund (IMF) in Washington, DC. This chapter builds and expands on previous work with World Bank colleagues — particularly Aslı Demirgüç-Kunt and María Soledad Martínez Pería — and work underlying the IMF's October 2014 *Global Financial Stability Report*. The views expressed here are those of the author and not necessarily those of the IMF or the World Bank.
[1] For brevity, I will use 'regulation' as shorthand for regulation, supervision, and resolution.

changes there are still significant cross-country regulatory differences. In particular, there were and still are significant differences between regulation in countries that were hit by a banking crisis since 2007 and those that did not. During the global financial crisis, regulations have changed: capital ratios increased, bank governance and resolution regimes were strengthened, but regulatory complexity has increased, and private sector incentives to monitor banks deteriorated. Overall, even after the crisis, regulation is differentiated across countries.

What are the financial and real sector effects of the regulatory changes? Measuring the regulatory effects is challenging, not only because the regulatory starting points were different in different countries, but also because there are many other factors to consider, such the massive monetary policy actions. Nonetheless, the analysis suggests that the tightening of regulation in banks has contributed to a shift of credit and risks to nonbanks. This raises concerns about a new imbalance: while financial risk-taking may be too high for stability, economic risk-taking may be too low for growth. It is unclear whether banks can support the real sector's recovery through lending, while risks are moving to shadow banks. Financial policies are in an uncharted territory.

The rest of the chapter is organized as follows. The next section reviews the country-by-country changes in bank regulation. The following section examines the link between bank regulation, bank business models and bank lending to the real economy. The subsequent section studies the nonbanks and their role in funding the real economy. The final section concludes.

Country-by-country Regulation

One of the few publicly available world-wide sources of consistent data on country-by-country regulation is the World Bank's Bank Regulation and Supervision Survey (see Čihák et al. 2012). The most recent edition of the survey, carried out in 2012, follows up and expands on earlier editions, published in 2001, 2003, and 2007.[2] The 2012 edition was the

---

[2] Detailed methodology and results of the survey are at http://go.worldbank.org/WFIEF81AP0. For previous iterations of the survey see http://go.worldbank.org/SNUSW978P0. See Barth et al. (2001), Barth et al. (2004), Beck et al. (2006) and

first to provide comprehensive information on bank regulation after the global financial crisis. The survey covers 37 advanced economies and 106 emerging market and developing economies, for a total of 143 jurisdictions.[3] The sample provides a broadly balanced representation of countries in terms of income level, geographical region, and population size. The survey covers 630 features relating to: (1) entry into banking, (2) ownership, (3) capital, (4) activities, (5) external auditing requirements, (6) bank governance, (7) liquidity and diversification requirements, (8) depositor (savings) protection schemes, (9) asset classification, provisioning, and write-offs, (10) accounting and information disclosure, (11) discipline/problem institutions/exit, (12) supervision, (13) banking sector characteristics, and (14) consumer protection.

A review of the cross-country data suggests two key takeaways. First, countries had rather different starting points in terms of regulation. Second, the cross-country differences have remained sizeable even after the crisis. Figure 1 illustrates this for the capital stringency index, measured on a scale from 0 to 10 (following the methodology of Barth *et al.* 2001). In 2007, the overall capital stringency index was 5.8 on average, with a cross-country standard deviation of 2.0. In 2012, the index increased to 7.2 on average, with a cross-country standard deviation of 1.7. In other words, the increase in the global average between 2007 and 2012 was smaller than one standard deviation. A similar picture emerges also for other aspects of the regulatory framework, such as supervisory power and independence.

The differences were the most pronounced when juxtaposing countries that were directly hit by the recent global crisis and those that were not.[4]

Kim *et al.* (2012), for studies analyzing the previous rounds of the survey. As a robustness check for the results presented here, the same set of analysis was run using the data in Barth *et al.* (2013).

[3] See http://go.worldbank.org/WFIEF81AP0 for a country list. The distinction between 'advanced economies' and 'emerging market/developing/economies' follows IMF's *World Economic Outlook*.

[4] This is in line with studies that have pointed to weaknesses in regulation and supervision as one of the factors leading to the crisis (Dan 2010; Lau 2010; Levine 2010; and Merrouche and Nier, 2010; Caprio *et al.* 2010; Claessens *et al.* 2010; Demirgüç-Kunt and Serven 2010; Rajan 2010; and, Barth *et al.* 2012).

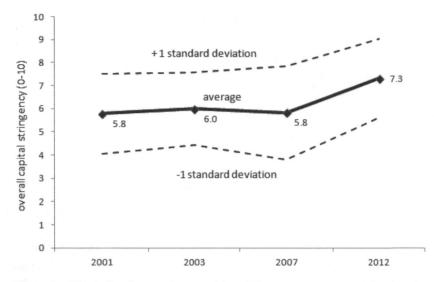

Figure 1. Capital stringency increased but differences across countries remain.

Notes: Capital stringency index has values from 0 (least stringent) to 10 (most stringent) and follows the definition from Barth *et al.* (2013).

For the purpose of these calculations, crisis countries are identified using the often used Laeven and Valencia (2012) crisis database.[5]

An examination of the differences in regulation between crisis versus non-crisis countries (Table 1) shows that crisis countries had less stringent definitions of capital, gave banks more discretion in calculating capital requirements, and exhibited lower actual capital ratios than the rest of the world. Both the 2007 and 2012 rounds of the Bank

---

[5] Specifically, crisis countries consist of two groups identified in Laeven and Valencia (2012): 16 countries that experienced a systemic banking crisis since 2007 (Austria, Belgium, Denmark, Germany, Greece, Iceland, Ireland, Kazakhstan, Latvia, Luxembourg, Netherlands, Nigeria, Spain, Ukraine, United Kingdom, and United States) plus 7 countries that experienced a borderline systemic crisis in the same period (France, Hungary, Italy, Portugal, the Russian Federation, Slovenia, Sweden, and Switzerland). Other countries are treated as non-crisis countries. As a robustness check, we have also run all the calculations based on an alternative classification, defining 'crisis' countries as those that experienced a systemic or borderline systemic crisis in 2007–09 as identified in Laeven and Valencia (2010).

Table 1. Significant differences between 'crisis' and 'non-crisis' countries.

	Question		Crisis	Non-crisis	p-value
Capital regim and actual capital levels	Can the initial disbursement or subsequent injections of capital be done with assets other than cash or government securities? (% Yes)				
		2007	57	37	0.08*
		2012	68	27	0.00***
	Is Tier 2 allowed in regulatory capital? (% Yes)				
		2012	100	86	0.07*
	Is Tier 3 allowed in regulatory capital? (% Yes)				
		2012	81	27	0.00***
	Are hybrid debt capital instruments allowed as part of Tier 1? (% Yes)				
		2012	76	29	0.00***
	Was the so-called advanced internal ratings-based approach (A-IRB) offered to banks in calculating capital requirements for credit risk? (% Yes)				
		2007	78	42	0.00***
		2012	95	44	0.00***
	What was the actual risk based capital ratio of the banking system as of end of: (Average %)				
		2007	12.3	16.5	0.00***
		2012	14.8	18.0	0.03**
	What was the actual Tier 1 capital ratio of the banking system as of end of: (Average %)				
		2007	9.8	14.3	0.00***
		2012	11.8	17.7	0.03**

(Continued)

Table 1. (*Continued*)

Question		Crisis	Non-crisis	p-value
Restrictions on bank activities	Securities activities (Average Index)			
	2007	1.4	2.0	0.02**
	2012	1.2	1.9	0.00***
	Insurance activities (Average Index)			
	2007	2.8	3.3	0.01**
	2012	2.2	2.6	0.07*
	Real estate activities (Average Index)			
	2007	2.5	3.3	0.00***
	2012	2.1	3.0	0.00***
Asset classification mechanisms	Do you have an asset classification system under which banks have to report the quality of their loans and advances using a common regulatory scale? (% Yes)			
	2007	61	88	0.00***
	2012	68	83	0.10*
	Does accrued, though unpaid, interest/ principal enter the bank's income statement while the loan is classified as non-performing? (% Yes)			
	2007	24	12	0.15
	2012	50	22	0.01**
	Do you require banks to write off non-performing loans after a specific time period? (% Yes)			
	2012	5	44	0.00***
	Are there minimum levels of specific provisions for loans and advances that are set by the regulator? (% Yes)			
	2012	32	81	0.00***
	Is there a regulatory requirement for general provisions on loans and advances? (% Yes)			
	2012	27	72	0.00***

(*Continued*)

Table 1. (*Continued*)

	Question	Crisis	Non-crisis	p-value
Supervisory powers in cases of bank losses	Can the supervisory agency require commitment/action from controlling shareholder(s) to support the bank with new equity (e.g. capital restoration plan)? (% Yes)			
	2012	68	84	0.08*
	Can the supervisory agency order the bank's directors or management to constitute provisions to cover actual or potential losses? (% Yes)			
	2007	86	96	0.06*
	2012	91	98	0.06*
	Can the supervisory agency suspend the directors' decision to distribute: Bonuses? (% Yes)			
	2007	33	69	0.00***
	Can the supervisory agency suspend the directors' decision to distribute: Management fees? (% Yes)			
	2007	38	69	0.01***
Incentives and information for markets to monitor banks	Is there an explicit deposit insurance protection system? (% Yes)			
	2007	100	47	0.00***
	2012	100	71	0.00***
	Does the deposit insurance agency have the power to insure liabilities beyond any explicit deposit insurance scheme? (% Yes)			
	2007	10	2	0.09*
	Must banks disclose to public: (% Yes) Risk management procedures?			
	2007	70	40	0.01***
	Regulatory capital and capital adequacy ratio?			
	2012	95	76	0.04**

(*Continued*)

Table 1. (*Continued*)

Question		Crisis	Non-crisis	p-value
Transactions with related parties?				
	2012	91	68	0.02**
Scope of consolidation?				
	2012	91	74	0.08*
Which bank activities are rated: (% Yes)				
Bonds issuance?				
	2007	90	47	0.00***
Commercial paper issuance?				
	2007	76	31	0.00***
Are financial institutions required to produce consolidated accounts covering all bank and any non-bank financial subsidiaries (including affiliates of common holding companies)? (% Yes)				
	2007	100	83	0.03**
	2012	100	97	0.39

Notes: The table shows questions for which there are statistically significant differences between 'crisis' and 'non-crisis' countries. Following Laeven and Valencia (2012), the 'crisis' countries are Austria, Belgium, Denmark, Germany, Greece, Iceland, Ireland, Kazakhstan, Latvia, Luxembourg, Netherlands, Nigeria, Spain, Ukraine, United Kingdom, and United States (systemic banking crises); France, Hungary, Italy, Portugal, the Russian Federation, Slovenia, Sweden, and Switzerland (borderline cases). The securities, insurance and real estate restrictions indexes take values from 1 to 4 where higher values denote stronger restrictions. T-tests are used to test for the equality of the means between crisis and non-crisis samples. *, **, *** denote significance at 10%, 5% and 1% significance, respectively.

Regulation and Supervision Survey show that crisis countries were more likely to allow the initial disbursement or subsequent injections of capital to be done with assets other than cash or government securities. At the same time, while 81% of crisis countries allowed Tier 3 in regulatory capital, only 27% of non-crisis countries did so. Crisis countries were also significantly more likely to allow hybrid debt instruments to be part of Tier 1. Moreover, the share of crisis countries that allowed banks to calculate their capital requirement for credit risk based on banks' internal ratings models was 95%, more than twice as large as in the rest of the world. Finally, while in 2007 the average level of the actual risk based capital ratio (Tier 1 capital to assets) of the banking system prior to the crisis was 16.5% (14.3) among non-crisis countries, this number was 12.3% (9.8) among crisis countries. The same pattern is uncovered when we examine the statistics gathered in the 2012 Bank Regulation and Supervision Survey.

Second, banks in crisis countries faced fewer restrictions to engage in non-bank activities such as insurance, investment banking, real estate, as well as in non-financial activities. Using an index of 1 to 4 to measure restrictions imposed on bank activities (following Barth, Caprio, and Levine, 2001), where higher values denote greater restrictions, we find that non-crisis countries were less likely to allow for a full range of non-bank activities to be conducted directly by banks.

Third, crisis countries were less likely to have in place provisioning requirements and were more lax in the treatment of bad loans and loan losses. Between 80 to 90 percent of non-crisis countries had an asset classification system under which banks had to report the quality of their loans using a common regulatory scale, while 61% and 68% of crisis countries had such systems in place according to the 2007 and the 2012 surveys, respectively. Also, half of the crisis countries allowed accrued though unpaid interest/principal to enter the bank income statement when loans are non-performing, but only 22% of non-crisis countries allowed this by 2012. The comparison with the 2007 survey suggests that the practice of overestimating loan interest and principal payments got significantly worse as the crisis unfolded and as banks tried to prop up their balance sheets. According to the 2012 Bank Regulation and Supervision Survey, while 72% of non-crisis countries had a regulatory requirement for general provisions on loans and advances, only 27% of crisis countries had such provisions in place. The 2012 survey also shows that only 32% of crisis countries had minimum levels of specific provisions for loans and advances set by the regulator. Almost 81% of non-crisis countries had such requirements in place.

Fourth, regulators in crisis countries were less able to demand banks to put up more equity, to constitute greater provisions or to suspend bonus and management fee payments. Based on the 2012 Bank

Regulation and Supervision Survey, in 84% of non-crisis countries the regulator had the power to request banks to put up new equity. This was true in 68% of crisis countries. Similarly, according to the 2012 survey, in 98% of non-crisis countries, the regulator could request banks to constitute provisions to cover actual or potential losses. This was true in 91% of crisis countries. Finally, according to the 2007 survey, in almost 70% of non-crisis countries regulators could suspend banks' decision to pay certain bonuses or management fees. This was true in only 33% and 38% of crisis countries, respectively.

Fifth, even though crisis countries had stronger information disclosure requirements, the incentives for the private sector to monitor banks' risks were weaker in these countries. At the start of the crisis, all crisis countries required banks to produce consolidated accounts covering all bank and any non-bank financial subsidiaries. Crisis countries were more likely to require banks to disclose risk management procedures, capital ratios, transactions with related parties, and scope of consolidation. In 90% (76) of crisis countries, issuance of bonds (commercial paper) received a credit rating, whereas this happened in 47% (31) of non-crisis countries. While all crisis countries had an explicit deposit insurance scheme before the crisis erupted, this was in effect in about 50% of the non-crisis countries before the crisis and in 71% by the 2012 Bank Regulation and Supervision Survey. According to the 2007 survey, in a larger share of crisis countries (10% in crisis versus 2% in non-crisis), the deposit insurance agency had the power to insure liabilities beyond any explicit deposit insurance scheme.

As an alternative approach to analyzing differences in regulation and supervision between crisis and non-crisis countries, Čihák *et al.* (2013) conduct probit estimations where they regress a dummy for all jurisdictions identified as crisis countries against each of the questions/variables considered in Table 1 (i.e., we include each question in a separate regression), while controlling for GDP per capita and the growth in the private credit to GDP ratio. GDP per capita is included to separate differences in crisis classification that come from income differences from other regulation and supervision issues that we are interested in. The growth of the private credit to GDP ratio is included because the literature has shown that financial crises are often preceded by fast growth of bank lending to the private sector (Demirguc-Kunt and Detragiache 2005). This approach yields results that largely confirm those from the mean tests shown in Table 1. In particular, countries that had less stringent definitions of capital, faced fewer restrictions on non-bank activities, were less strict in the regulatory treatment of bad loans, were less able to modify banks' compensation schemes, and had weaker incentives for the private sector to monitor banks had a lower probability of experiencing the recent crisis.

To address possible questions about reverse causality and omitted variables, Čihák *et al.* (2013) also present instrumental variable estimations, using legal origin, pre-crisis religious composition, and distance from the equator as instruments for each of the regulation and supervision variables. For most of the questions, the instrumental variables are jointly statistically significant. Furthermore, the main results are consistent between the probit and the instrumental variable regressions. Overall, the results provide suggestive evidence that crisis countries suffered from greater weaknesses in their bank regulation and supervision frameworks.

An analysis of responses to the 2012 and 2007 surveys provides an insight into the regulatory changes in the global financial crisis. Overall, the survey responses underscore the evolutionary, slow nature of regulatory and supervisory changes. It does not appear that the recent global financial crisis caused a major change in regulatory frameworks around the world. For example, 85% of 'yes' or 'no' responses remained unchanged between the 2007 and 2012 surveys (i.e., 'no' remained 'no', 'yes' remained 'yes'). Similarly, most of the quantitative indicators showed relatively little overall movement throughout the crisis. Notwithstanding this gradual evolution of regulatory frameworks, there have been some notable changes in some areas of regulation and supervision.

One of the visible changes was an increase in regulatory complexity. Figure 2 illustrates that this increase (by 16% according to the proxy used in the chart) is a continuation of a previous trend. This growth in complexity partly reflects an increased granularity of the micro-prudential framework. It also partly reflects increased focus on 'new' areas, such

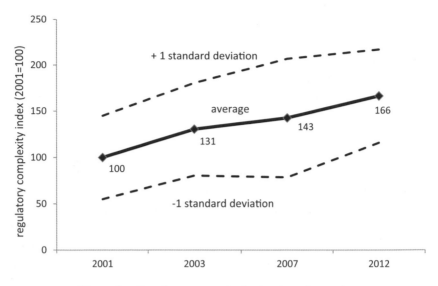

Figure 2. Regulatory complexity has kept increasing.

Notes: Regulatory complexity is approximated by the kilobytes of information per country in the Bank Regulation and Supervision Survey.

as macroprudential policy and consumer protection. Finally, it also reflects the increased complexity of the international standards.[6]

Table 2 shows questions for which there are statistically significant changes between the 2007 and 2012 surveys. The table presents responses from the 2007 and 2012 surveys, highlighting the breakdown between crisis and non-crisis countries. For each question, the table shows p-values from t-tests of differences in average responses across the two surveys. The table only shows the questions for which we found significant differences across surveys.

---

[6] For example, the latest key international standards for banking, insurance, and securities regulation (Basel Core Principles, Insurance Core Principles, and IOSCO Principles) contained 93 individual 'principles' in total as of 2015, a 30% increase from the 1999 total of 72 principles. The average number of pages per assessment of compliance with these standards has increased from 29 to 163 in the same period (see https://www.imf.org/external/NP/fsap/fsap.aspx for the published assessments).

Table 2. Changes in regulation and supervision across countries during 2007–2012.

Section	Question		All	Crisis	Non-Crisis
Capital regime and actual capital levels	What was the actual risk based capital ratio of the banking system? (Average %)	2007	15.5	12.3	16.3
		2012	17.5	14.3	18.3
		p-value	0.00***	0.13	0.01**
	What was the actual Tier 1 capital ratio of the banking system? (Average %)	2007	13.4	9.8	14.5
		2012	15.9	12.0	17.2
		p-value	0.01**	0.10*	0.04**
Governance	Is there a regulatory limit on related party exposures? (% Yes)	2007	13	0	15
		2012	95	80	98
		p-value	0.00***	0.00***	0.00***
Restrictions on activities	What are the conditions under which banks can engage in securities activities? (Index takes values from 1 to 4 where higher values denote stronger restrictions.)	2007	2.0	1.5	2.1
		2012	1.7	1.2	1.8
		p-value	0.01**	0.06*	0.04**
	What are the conditions under which banks can engage in insurance activities? (Index takes values from 1 to 4 where higher values denote stronger restrictions.)	2007	3.1	2.8	3.1
		2012	2.5	2.3	2.5
		p-value	0.00***	0.02**	0.00***
	What are the conditions under which banks can engage in real estate activities? (Index takes values from 1 to 4 where higher values denote stronger restrictions.)	2007	3.1	2.4	3.3
		2012	2.8	2.2	3.0
		p-value	0.01***	0.20	0.02**

(Continued)

Table 2. (*Continued*)

Section	Question		All	Crisis	Non-Crisis
Asset diversification	Are there any regulatory rules or supervisory guidelines regarding asset diversification? (% Yes)	2007	46	43	46
		2012	59	52	60
		p-value	0.03**	0.49	0.03**
	Are banks prohibited from making loans abroad? (% Yes)	2007	9	10	9
		2012	18	0	22
		p-value	0.02**	0.16	0.00***
Deposit insurance	Is there an explicit deposit insurance protection system for commercial banks? (% Yes)	2007	66	100	58
		2012	77	100	71
		p-value	0.00***	—	0.00***
	Were any deposits not explicitly covered by the deposit insurance scheme at the time of failure compensated the last time a bank failed (excluding funds later paid out in liquidation procedures)? (% Yes)	2007	38	12	53
		2012	21	12	27
		p-value	0.03**	—	0.02**

Auditing

Are banks required to prepare consolidated accounts for accounting purposes? (% Yes)	2007	91	100	89
	2012	97	100	97
	p-value	0.02**	.	0.02**
Is it required by the regulators that bank audits be publicly disclosed? (% Yes)	2007	77	75	77
	2012	90	95	89
	p-value	0.01**	0.10*	0.04**
Must banks disclose their risk management procedures to the public? (% Yes)	2007	49	68	44
	2012	82	95	78
	p-value	0.00***	0.03**	0.00***

Notes: This table shows responses to questions for which we found statistically significant differences between the 2007 and 2012 surveys. Following Laeven and Valencia (2012), the "crisis" countries are Austria, Belgium, Denmark, Germany, Greece, Iceland, Ireland, Kazakhstan, Latvia, Luxembourg, Netherlands, Nigeria, Spain, Ukraine, United Kingdom, and United States (cases of systemic banking crises); France, Hungary, Italy, Portugal, the Russian Federation, Slovenia, Sweden, and Switzerland (borderline cases). T-tests are used to test for the equality of the means between responses to the 2007 and 2012 surveys. *, **, *** denote significance at 10, 5 and 1 percent significance, respectively.

Overall, significant changes took place in bank capitalization, governance, activities, diversification, auditing, and deposit insurance. First, countries and especially non-crisis countries exhibited an increase in their risk based and Tier 1 capital ratios. Second, we observe a substantial increase in the share of countries that set regulatory limits on related party exposures. Third, there was an increase in the percentage of countries that impose regulatory rules or supervisory guidelines regarding asset diversification. Fourth, most countries exhibited a relaxation of restrictions on bank activities between 2007 and 2012. Fifth, the share of countries requiring audits and risk management procedures to be disclosed increased significantly across all countries. Sixth, the share of countries with explicit deposit insurance increased among non-crisis countries.[7]

Table 3 shows questions that specifically asked regulators to identify reforms introduced in response to the crisis. The table shows responses provided by crisis and non-crisis countries, and the p-values from tests of the null that the changes observed across countries are not significant. The responses confirm the changes in regulations pertaining to bank governance and deposit insurance highlighted above. Furthermore, Table 3 suggests that bank resolution was an important area of reform after the crisis.

Interestingly, it was only in a few areas that regulatory changes during the global financial crisis differed significantly between countries that were directly hit during the global financial crisis and those that avoided the direct impact of the crisis (Table 3). In the area of bank

---

[7] The findings from the means tests shown here are consistent with the findings of regression models presented by Čihák *et al.* (2013). Specifically, they report the results from regressing responses for each of the survey questions on a dummy variable that takes the value of 1 for the 2012 survey and zero otherwise. A positive coefficient reflects an increase in the dependent variable *vis-a-vis* the pre-crisis, 2007, survey. They also regress each of the same dependent variables on a 2012 survey dummy, a dummy for countries classified as crisis countries based on Laeven and Valencia (2012), and the interaction between the 2012 survey dummy and the crisis country dummy. The purpose of this last interaction is to determine whether changes were smaller or larger for the crisis countries. The results confirm most of the estimations in Table 2.

Table 3. Regulatory changes introduced in response to the global crisis.

Have you introduced changes to the bank governance framework in your country as a result of the global financial crisis?	Crisis	Non-Crisis	p-value
a. New requirements on executive compensation? (% Yes)	68	27	0.00***
b. Independence of the Board? (% Yes)	0	13	0.09*
c. Chief risk officer direct reporting line to the Board or Board Committee? (% Yes)	0	12	0.11
d. Existence of a Board risk committee? (% Yes)	0	20	0.04**
e. Other? (% Yes)	32	59	0.03**

Have you introduced changes to your deposit protection system as a result of the global financial crisis?	Crisis	Non-Crisis	p-value
a. Expansion of coverage (types of exposures, nature of depositors etc.)? (% Yes)	20	16	0.67
b. Increase in amount covered? (% Yes)	70	60	0.45
c. Temporary inclusion of guarantees on bank debt? (% Yes)	0	0	—
d. Government guarantee of deposits and bank debts? (% Yes)	20	2	0.01**
e. Other? (% Yes)	20	33	0.28

Have you introduced significant changes to the bank resolution framework in your country as a result of the global financial crisis?	Crisis	Non-Crisis	p-value
a. Introduce a separate bank insolvency framework? (% Yes)	11	8	0.77
b. Implement coordination arrangements among domestic authorities? (% Yes)	32	42	0.43
c. Other? (% Yes)	74	56	0.16

Notes: Following Laeven and Valencia (2012), the 'crisis' countries are Austria, Belgium, Denmark, Germany, Greece, Iceland, Ireland, Kazakhstan, Latvia, Luxembourg, Netherlands, Nigeria, Spain, Ukraine, United Kingdom, and United States (cases of systemic banking crises); France, Hungary, Italy, Portugal, the Russian Federation, Slovenia, Sweden, and Switzerland (borderline cases). T-tests are used to test for the equality of the means (percentage of 'Yes' responses) between crisis and non-crisis samples. *, **, *** denote significance at 10%, 5% and 1% significance, respectively.

governance, crisis-hit countries were more than twice as likely as non-crisis countries to introduce new requirements on executive compensation, while new requirements for independence of the Board, Board risk committee, and other bank governance regulations were adopted relatively more by non-crisis countries.[8] In deposit protection, there is significant difference between crisis and non-crisis countries when it comes to government guarantee of deposits and bank debts. But in bank resolution framework and other areas, the differences between crisis and non-crisis countries have not been strong.

The data highlight the significant and persistent cross-country variation in regulatory practices. There are particularly stark differences in regulatory frameworks between countries that were directly hit by the crisis and those that avoided a direct hit. First, crisis countries had less stringent and more complex definitions of capital and lower actual capital ratios. Second, banks in crisis countries faced fewer restrictions on non-bank activities such as insurance, investment banking, and real estate. Third, regulations concerning the treatment of bad loans and loan losses were less strict in crisis countries. Fourth, regulators in crisis countries were less able to demand banks to adjust their equity, provisions or compensation schemes. Finally, in crisis countries, there were greater disclosure requirements but weaker incentives for the private sector to monitor banks' risks.

Comparing regulation before and after the global crisis, responses to the crisis have been evolutionary at best, with most features of regulation and supervision unchanged relative to the pre-crisis period. Changes are nonetheless evident in some areas. In particular, perhaps most visible was an increase in regulatory complexity, by 16% or more

---

[8] This result largely reflects regulatory developments in the European Union (EU). Within the EU, 63% of respondents introduced new requirements on executive compensation, compared to 16 percent of non-EU respondents. The respondents from EU member countries explained the new remuneration policies as an effort to bring their national regulations in line with new EU rules, in particular Directive 2010/76/EU. A majority of the crisis observations are within the EU (EU countries account for 17% of the whole sample while including 65% of the crisis observations), which helps explain the observed differences in changes in bank governance regulations between crisis and non-crisis countries.

according to some measures. This reflects more granular micro-pruden-tial framework; it also reflects increased focus on 'new' areas, such as macroprudential policy and consumer protection, as well as an increased complexity of the international standards. Capital ratios increased, reforms were introduced pertaining to bank governance and bank resolution, and deposit insurance schemes became more prevalent. This last change suggests that private sector incentives for monitoring banks' risks have deteriorated.

Bank Regulation and Business Model Challenges

Let us now turn to the effect of regulations on bank business models and bank lending to the real economy.

Across countries, tighter regulation and supervision pushed banks to repair balance sheets and adjust strategies. On average, banks now hold significantly more capital than at the height of the global financial crisis and are less leveraged than before the crisis. However, progress has been uneven across countries and across banks (Figure 3).

The cross-country regulatory data provide a bird's eye view on the relationship between regulatory tightness and credit. Figure 4 illustrates that in 2007–2012, a majority of countries increased capital stringency (those on the right side of the chart), but some loosened. The figure also shows that, overall, the relationship between changes in bank credit and regulatory tightness is weak. However, for advanced economies, there is a negative relationship between capital stringency and change in bank credit relative to output.

Underlying these aggregate developments are banks' struggles to adapt to new business and regulatory realities. Most banks have become stronger and are emerging from post-crisis balance sheet repair, but are in need of adjusting their business models to new economic realities. Overall, their much-strengthened capital base carries higher costs, with the return on equity at historically low levels, excluding the financial crisis period (Figure 5). Low profitability partly reflects cyclical factors — a sluggish economy, the burden of non-performing loans,

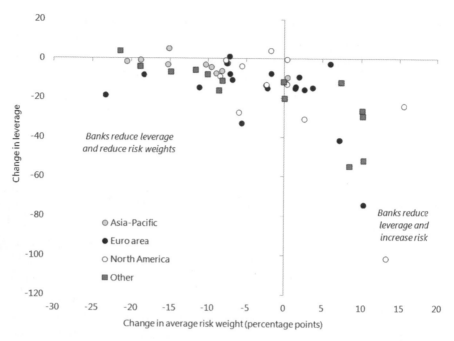

Figure 3. Change in bank leverage and average risk weight, 2008–14.

Notes: The points are for individual banks. 2014 data or latest available.
Source: SNL Financial; BankScope; and, IMF staff calculations.

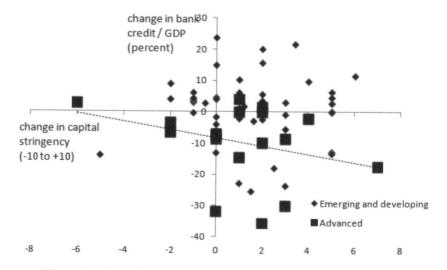

Figure 4. Capital stringency vs. changes in bank credit, 2007–2012.

Notes: The capital stringency measure follows the definition of Barth *et al.* (2013); change between the 2007 and he 2012 surveys. Credit/GDP change in % between 2007 and 2012.

litigation costs from past misdeeds and low interest margins from near-zero policy rates — but also structural market changes resulting from regulatory reforms and acute competition in the context of excess capacity. Banks must regain sustainable profits to ensure that they can build and maintain buffers without taking excessive risk and meet credit demand.

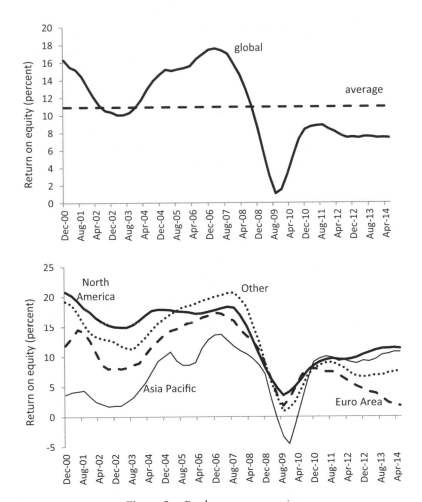

Figure 5. Bank return on equity.

Notes: Shows four-quarter asset-weighted averages.
Source: Bloomberg L.P. and IMF staff estimates.

Banks continue to adapt to new regulations, which act as a further drag on profitability, at least in the adjustment phase. Until now, capital-constrained banks have focused on 'de-risking' their balance sheets to meet risk-based requirements. That has now, however, broadened to include other elements of the Basel III regime, often ahead of the mandated schedule. For example, the leverage ratio and the supplementary leverage ratio in the United States (both mandatory from January 2018), which penalize size, will make it more costly for banks to hold lower-risk assets. New liquidity requirements, such as the liquidity coverage ratio and the net stable funding ratio, will induce banks to hold more liquid (low-risk) assets and to rely more on stable funding sources. And the recent stress test related exercises (for example, the Comprehensive Capital Analysis and Review in the United States and the ECB Comprehensive Assessment in the euro area), which emphasize 'stressed capital', are inducing banks to ask for more high quality collateralization of loans to help absorb losses under stress scenarios, creating non-price constrictions on lending.

At the same time, the cost of equity has risen since pre-crisis, reflecting shareholders' uncertainty about bank earnings. After a spike in 2010, the cost of equity in banks has been slowly trending downwards but is still 5 percentage points above its 2000–05 historical average. This higher cost reflects market concerns about the financial strength of banks, including due to weak and opaque balance sheets, possible litigation costs, and the uncertain impact of regulatory reforms. As a result, banks accounting for 80% of total assets of the largest institutions currently have a 'return on equity gap', where their return on equity is lower than the cost of capital demanded by shareholders (IMF 2014).

In this new environment, in which banks are facing a combination of low profitability and new regulatory requirements, they need to change the way they operate. This is likely to entail a combination of re-pricing current business lines, re-allocating capital away from low-risk assets, and — in some cases — selective retrenchment from certain activities and from the sector altogether. Over the last few years, banks have undertaken measures to address these challenges, including running off portfolios, selling non-core businesses, and cutting operating costs. But there may be only limited room left for further gains in these areas.[9]

As banks adjust to the new environment, they are likely to reallocate capital across activities. Banks with low risk-weights are likely to shift to higher-risk activities, as they start lending. For example, some banks, particularly in the euro area, exhibit close to record low risk-weighted assets and will increase their risk-weighted assets naturally as they shift from zero-risk-weighted bonds to higher risk-weighted loans. Other banks, such as US banks, have already strengthened and re-risked their balance sheets to pre-crisis levels, including by expanding their loan portfolios.

New regulatory requirements may induce banks to retrench from some activities. For example, the leverage ratio could make it uneconomical to hold lower risk assets. This is shown in Figure 6, where the supplementary leverage ratio, applicable to large US banks, introduces a spread floor of 50 basis points (gray bars) on top of the standard risk-based capital charges (black bars) needed to meet a 10% target return on equity. In this example, it becomes uneconomical to hold AAA- and AA-rated U.S. corporate loans. Most affected activities include treasuries and other fixed-income trading, general collateral repo markets, and hedging activities. This has a potentially adverse impact on the corpo rate sector, which may no longer be able to access critical services, such as financial commitments or derivative instruments to hedge their long-term investments.

Re-pricing is likely to occur in asset classes where banks have greater market pricing power and with bank-dependent borrowers, such as in SME and consumer credit. In contrast, re-pricing will be more difficult in investment grade corporate segments, where margins are tight and borrowers have access to capital market funding. In terms of specific products, the cost of mortgage loans and other lower-risk longer-term loans, such as infrastructure finance, is likely to rise as banks

---

[9] Substantial cost-cutting efforts have taken place, with the average cost to income ratio of the sample banks having fallen by seven percentage points to 66% since 2008, in line with the 1995–2005 historical average of 65%.

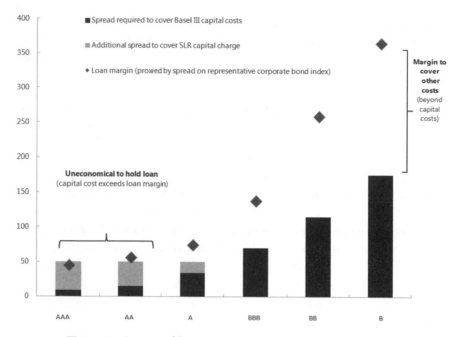

Figure 6. Impact of leverage ratio on corporate loan holdings.

Notes: The blue bars measure the minimum return over US dollar Libor (London Interbank Offered Rate) necessary to cover the Basel III capital costs associated with a U.S. corporate loan for a representative large bank under the Internal Ratings Based model. In this stylized example, the capital cost for an A-rated loan is about 33 basis points (bps) (assuming a 35% risk weight × 9.5% Tier 1 ratio × 10% return on equity target). The gray bars measure the additional spread (over US dollar Libor) to cover the Supplementary Leverage Ratio capital costs. The 50 bps floor is equal to 100 percent leverage exposure × 5% supplementary leverage ratio × 10% return on equity target. The diamonds represent the current loan margin approximated by a representative US corporate bond index spread (over US dollar Libor). The difference between the loan margin (diamonds) and the bars must be sufficient to cover operating expenses, other regulatory costs, and expected losses.
Source: Bloomberg L.P.; European Central Bank; and IMF staff calculations.

adjust to the liquidity coverage ratio, the net stable funding ratio, and the higher regulatory cost of holding long-dated derivatives used for hedging purposes.

Since the onset of the global financial crisis, banks have already increased loan margins, but more may be needed. Banks' ability to re-price may be limited if they are surrounded by stronger competitors that do not need re-pricing or in the context of excess capacity, where weaker banks underprice risk to maintain market share, distorting what sounder banks can charge.

Major banks have already begun their transition to new business models. First, many are shrinking or exiting from capital market activities, especially in fixed income, currencies, and commodities. Only a few large investment banks are expected to maintain a strong presence in these activities. Second, most global banks are also rebalancing their business models away from capital-intensive activities to more fee-based activities, such as mergers and acquisitions and securities underwriting activities, as well as asset management and private wealth management. Third, a large number of global banks are retrenching selectively from international markets and refocusing onto commercial banking activities in home markets and regional markets where they enjoy a leading presence. A notable exception is infrastructure finance, where many banks are reducing their presence or exiting (see Figure 7).

Retrenchment and re-pricing from activities could add to headwinds to the recovery. The transition to new business models could have important implications for the capacity and willingness of banks to

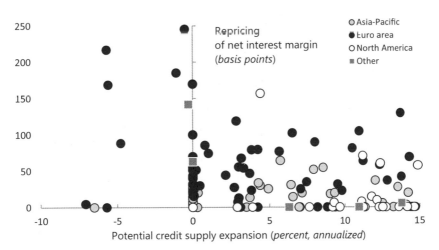

Figure 7. Adjustments in bank business models.

Notes: The return on equity gap is return on equity minus a cost of capital of 10%. The chart is based on simulations.
Source: Bloomberg L.P.; SNL Financial; and, IMF staff estimates.

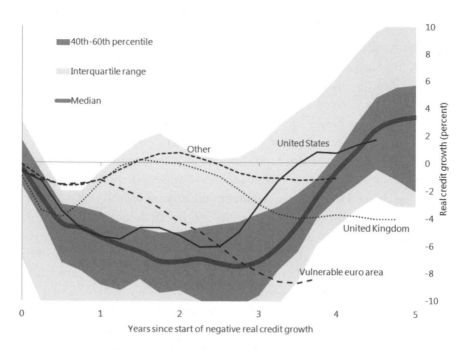

Figure 8. Bank lending relative to past crises.

Notes: Shaded area is for past crisis periods in advanced and emerging economies from the late 1980s to the period before the global financial crisis. Vulnerable euro area countries are those that have faced a sharp fall in bank lending. In this chart, the group includes Greece, Ireland, Italy, Portugal, and Spain. Other euro area comprises Austria, Belgium, Finland, France, Germany, Luxembourg, and Netherlands.

Source: Haver Analytics; IMF; World Economic Outlook database; and, IMF staff calculations.

supply credit to the real economy, potentially creating a headwind against the recovery. This transition is likely to be uneven across banks, and those with a greater return on equity gap, which includes some of the largest banks, will have a greater transition to make. These transition challenges are illustrated through a balance sheet simulation (Figure 8), which is a slightly updated and expanded version of an analysis done for the October 2014 *Global Financial Stability Report* (IMF 2014). The simulation, which is based on a sample of 600 advanced economy and emerging market banks, explores the extent to which banks have made progress in their transition to new business models. The simulation has two stages. In the first stage, the potential size and profitability of balance sheets is estimated at end-2015, not to estimate how much balance sheets are expected to grow, but to assess the capacity of banks to adapt balance sheets, generate earnings and supply credit. The second stage assesses how much interest margins would need to rise to close remaining return on equity gaps in 2015. The idea is not to predict how much margins will actually rise, but to use the implied increase in margins as a gauge of how far banks still have to go in their transition to new business models.

The simulation offers key insights into the transition of bank business models. It suggests that many banks have the capacity to supply more credit, given their increased levels of capitalization. But there are institutions where this capacity is limited by their buffers and expected profitability. For example, about a third of the sample, by assets, cannot deliver more than 5% annual credit growth. There are also a few weak institutions that may need to deleverage — or shrink balance sheets and cut back lending — in order to meet the capital targets.

Some banks can increase lending margins or use other measures to close their return on equity gaps and generate sustainable profits.[10] But for a number of banks in the simulation, the re-pricing needed is very large and not realistic, particularly if done on a stand alone basis and not followed by other market participants. For example, banks with an implied increase in margins of 100 basis points — in addition to the re-pricing already envisaged in analysts' profit forecasts — account for one third of assets in the sample (Figure 8).

At the country level, the largest transition needs are in euro area countries and, to a lesser extent, in the United Kingdom and Japan. In terms of type of banks, the largest transition needs are concentrated among domestic systemically important banks and other large banks, although a number of global investment banks and global systemically important banks have large implied re-pricing needs to close their return on equity gaps.

---

[10] Further cost cutting would also help banks to reduce their return on equity gap, although room for maneuver may be limited given cost cuts achieved in recent years and already factored in the financial plans for the coming years.

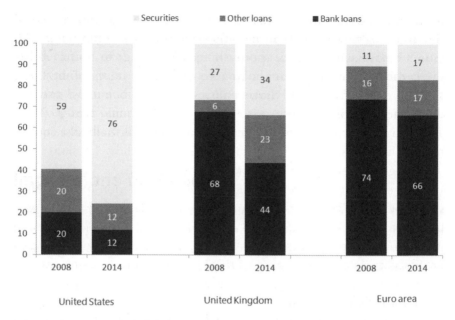

Figure 9. Corporate liabilities by counterparty (% of total corporate liabilities).

Notes: Excludes estimated value of intercompany loans. Rest of World bank loans are "other loans" in the euro area; they are included in bank loans for the other jurisdictions.

Sources: National central banks; Datastream; and IMF staff estimates.

The simulation exercise thus suggests risks to the recovery in bank credit. Indeed, real credit growth is already lagging behind the average recovery path in past banking crises in the euro area and United Kingdom (Figure 9). While bank credit growth should accelerate over time, the recovery could be modest in some economies and continue to be a headwind for the economic recovery.

Nonbank Credit is Important, but does not Compensate for Sluggish Bank Credit

Nonbanks have been increasingly able to compete with banks and have raised their share in credit intermediation. Lending services are provided by a wide and rapidly growing range of nonbank entities, which include asset managers, business development companies, private equity firms, and brokerage firms. Levered private debt funds are investing in loan portfolios and are providing co-financing. Balance sheet constrained banks are partnering with nonbanks — such as insurance companies and pension funds, asset managers, private equity and credit funds — in new intermediation models that allow banks to provide their origination capacity and credit-related expertise, while nonbanks provide the capital needed to warehouse credit risk. A shift towards more non-bank financial intermediation will require strengthening the regulatory framework for non-banks, while ensuring that supervisors can monitor credit developments, assess the build-up of risks, and have the authority and the tools to address the attendant risks.

It remains unclear, however, whether nonbanks can provide sufficient financing to counteract the retrenchment by banks. While bank loans account for only 12% of corporate credit in the United States, they represent 42% of corporate borrowing in the United Kingdom and 68% in the euro area. In the euro area, the steady rise in securities issued by nonfinancial companies since 2008, partly as a result of the falling cost of issuing bonds relative to bank loans, has not been sufficient to offset the sharp fall in bank lending (Figure 10).

Furthermore, the substitution from bank to nonbank credit will take time. So far only banks have financed greenfield projects given their complex construction-period risks, and refinancing by nonbanks has been slow, including due to insurers' risk policies and solvency requirements. Nonbank appetite for SME lending is mixed due to unfamiliarity with the risks, and joint ventures between banks and insurers are developing slowly.

Regulatory frameworks explain some of the regional differences in the use of nonbank credit. In the United States and in Japan, insurance companies and pension funds are directly lending to borrowers, as reflected by their large commercial real estate loan portfolios, while insurers in some European countries are prevented from extending credit. Likewise, mutual funds can purchase loans in the United States, while this is not allowed in Europe. Nonbank lending in Europe is generally done by private equity firms, which focus mostly on real estate. As a result, there is a greater risk in Europe that nonbanks may not be able

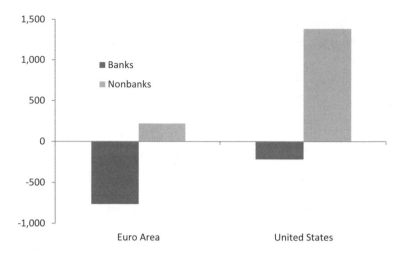

Figure 10. Change in corporate credit by counterparty (EUR and US$ billion, since 2008).

Notes: Nonbanks are insurance companies, pension funds, and mutual funds.
Source: National central banks; Datastream; and, IMF staff estimates.

to compensate for the retrenchment of bank credit, particularly for customers without alternative funding sources.

This could lead to an increased use of securitization or other forms of fee-based originate-to distribute models. Since the global financial crisis, securitization issuance has been declining sharply in Europe — to around one-eighth of the issuance in 2008 — in contrast to the fairly stable volumes in the United States. Kick-starting safe securitization could help diversify funding sources for the real economy and help reinvigorate credit supply. Trade finance, for example, as a short-dated and low-risk asset, may be well suited to this shift towards an originate-to-distribute model.

Expanding securitization markets, however, faces a number of challenges. Structural market factors (high cost of issuance, heterogeneity of loan portfolios across countries), adverse cyclical factors (sluggish economic recovery), and impediments to effective debt restructuring, reduce the incentives for issuance. Regulatory requirement in Basel III (for banks) and Solvency II (for insurance companies) should not disincentives these institutions to buy high-quality securitization instruments.

Conclusions

The statistical analysis presented in this chapter provides interesting insights into regulatory and supervisory practices around the world against the background of the global financial crisis. While these tests do not prove causality, they provide suggestive evidence that crisis-hit countries had significantly weaker regulatory and supervisory frameworks compared to those countries that fared better during the global financial crisis.

The findings suggest that less can sometimes mean more in regulation and supervision. Specifically, simpler but better enforced capital regulation is associated with a lower crisis probability relative to more complex regulations. We find that crisis countries tended to allow for more complex but less stringent definitions of capital, giving banks more discretion in how they calculated capital requirements. This allowed banks in crisis countries to hold lower actual capital ratios.

The analysis is a confirmation of the benefits of stricter, better enforced regulations. In particular, crisis–hit countries were significantly more lax in the treatment of bad loans and loan losses than those that managed to avoid the crisis. Similarly, regulators in crisis countries were less able to demand banks to recapitalize banks, to constitute greater provisions or to suspend bonuses or management fees. The analysis also revealed that banks in crisis countries faced fewer restrictions to engage in non-bank activities such as insurance, investment banking and real estate activities.

Our results reaffirm the important role of market incentives to monitor banks. Publishing more information about banks does not necessarily mean more stability if banks' private sector counterparts do not have incentives to use that information for monitoring. We find that even though crisis countries had stronger information disclosure requirements, the incentives for the private sector to monitor banks' risks were weaker in crisis countries, given the greater prevalence of deposit insurance, which in turn reflected crisis-related increases in both the incidence of deposit insurance and in the amounts covered. These changes may weaken the incentives in the system to monitor banks, since they reduce the pool of market participants that have an interest in monitoring banks.

The survey results underscore the evolutionary nature of the regulatory and supervisory changes at the national level. The recent financial crisis did not trigger a major and sudden revamping of national regulatory and supervisory frameworks around the world. The change was slow and gradual at best, with most of the observed regulatory and supervisory features remaining unchanged. Nonetheless, there have been notable developments in some areas: Perhaps most visible was an increase in regulatory complexity, which reflects a more granular microprudential framework, increased focus on 'new' areas, such as macroprudential policy, consumer protection, and more complex international standards. Also, capital ratios increased, reforms were introduced in bank governance and bank resolution, and deposit insurance schemes became more prevalent. Some of these reforms (e.g., increasing the actual capital ratios, introducing special regimes for bank resolution) are going in the right direction, moving regulatory and supervisory frameworks towards the setup prevalent in non-crisis countries. At the same time, some steps and measures introduced during the crisis (such as the extension of deposit protection and other guarantees) have weakened private sector incentives for monitoring. Overall, our findings suggest that there is significant room for improving regulation and supervision as well as private incentives to monitor risk-taking.

At the same time, the shift to nonbanks raises new questions about the balance between economic and financial risk-taking. The imbalance means that economic risk-taking is too low for growth, while financial risk-taking may be too high for stability? It is unclear whether banks can support the recovery through lending, while risks are moving to shadow banks. Financial policies are in uncharted territory, and a rebalancing may be needed.

For stability, it is important to address excessive financial risk-taking. This means further strengthening of prudential policies. It also means addressing the rising market liquidity risks in shadow banking (which in turn means preventing market runs and preparing contingency measures). For growth, it is key to support economic risk-taking and improve flow of credit to the economy. It is also crucial to facilitate banks' transition to new business models, particularly in Europe, and to encourage safe non-bank credit.

References

Barth, J., G. Caprio and R. Levine (2001), "The Regulation and Supervision of Banks around the World: A new database." In R. E. Litan and R. Herring (eds.) *Brookings-Wharton Papers on Financial Services*, Washington, DC: Brookings Institution Press, pp. 183–240.

Barth, J., G. Caprio and R. Levine (2004), "Bank Regulation and Supervision: What works best?" *Journal of Financial Intermediation*, 13(2): 205–248.

Barth, J., G. Caprio and R. Levine (2012), *Guardians of Finance: Making Regulators Work for US* (Cambridge, MA: MIT Press).

Barth, J., G. Caprio and R. Levine (2013), "Bank Regulation and Supervision in 180 Countries from 1999 to 2011," National Bureau of Economic Research Working Paper 18733.

Beck, T., A. Demirgüc-Kunt, and R. Levine (2006), "Bank Concentration, Competition, and Crises: First results," *Journal of Banking and Finance*, 30: 1581–1603.

Caprio, G., A. Demirguc-Kunt and E. Kane (2010), "The 2007 Meltdown in Structured Securitization: Searching for lessons not scapegoats," *World Bank Research Observer*, 5: 125–55.

Čihák, M., A. Demirgüç-Kunt, M. S. M. Peria and A. Mohseni-Cheraghlou (2012), "Bank Regulation and Supervision around the World: A crisis update," World Bank Policy Research Working Paper No. 6286.

Čihák, M., A. Demirgüç-Kunt, M. S. M. Peria and A. Mohseni-Cheraghlou (2013), "Bank regulation and supervision in the context of the global crisis," *Journal of Financial Stability*, 9(4): 733–746.

Claessens, S., G. Dell'Ariccia, D. Igan and L. Laeven (2010), "Lessons and Policy Implications from the Global Financial Crisis," IMF Working Paper 10/44.

Dan, K. (2010). "The Subprime Crisis and Financial Regulation: International and comparative perspectives," John M. Olin Law and Economics Working Paper No. 517.

Demirgüç-Kunt, A. and D. Enrica (2005), "Cross-Country Empirical Studies of Systemic Bank Distress: A survey," World Bank Policy Research Working Paper No. 3719.

Demirgüç-Kunt, A. and L. Serven (2010), "Are All the Sacred Cows Dead? Implications of the Financial Crisis for Macro- and Financial Policies," *World Bank Research Observer*, 25(1): 91–124.

International Monetary Fund [IMF] (2014), *Global Financial Development Report*, Washington, DC, October.

Kim, T., B. Koo and M. Park (2012), "Role of Financial Regulation and Innovation in the Financial Crisis," *Journal of Financial Stability*, 9(4): 662–672.

Laeven, L. and F. Valencia (2010), "Resolution of Banking Crises: The good, the bad, and the ugly," IMF Working Paper 10/146.

Laeven, L. and F. Valencia (2012), "Systemic Banking Crisis Database: An update," IMF Working Paper 08/224.

Lau, L. (2010), "Financial Regulation and Supervision Post the Global Financial Crisis," Institute of Global Economics and Finance, The Chinese University of Hong Kong, Working Paper No. 2.

Levine, R. (2010), "An Autopsy of the U.S. Financial System: Accident, suicide, or negligent homicide," *Journal of Financial Economic Policy*, 2(3): 196–213.

Merrouche, O. and E. Nier (2010), "What Caused the Global Financial Crisis? Evidence on the drivers of financial imbalances 1999–2007," IMF Working Paper 10/265.

Rajan, R. (2010), *Fault Lines: How Hidden Fractures Still Threaten the World Economy* (Princeton, NJ: Princeton University Press).

Financial Fragmentation, Real-sector Lending, and the European Banking Union

— CHAPTER 20

- Giovanni Dell'Ariccia
  International Monetary Fund and CEPR

Introduction

This note discusses the evolution of bank lending in the euro zone in the wake of the sovereign bond crisis. In that context, it presents several stylized facts on the continued credit stagnation in southern Europe and proposes an empirical strategy to identify its sources. The note also focuses on the effects of the increased fragmentation of credit markets and their implications for the conduct and effectiveness of monetary policy. And it discusses the potential role the nascent banking union may play to ease credit conditions in the South of the euro zone.

Before the crisis, the common currency and single market promoted financial integration in the euro area and EU. Banks and other financial institutions progressively established affiliates and operated with relative ease across borders; credit flows allowed savings to be reallocated across countries; and financial portfolios became increasingly more

Giovanni Dell'Ariccia is Assistant Director in the Research Department at the IMF. The views expressed herein are those of the authors and should not be attributed to the IMF, its Executive Board, or its management. The author would like to thank Ali Al-Eyd, Pelin Berkmen, and John Bluedorn.

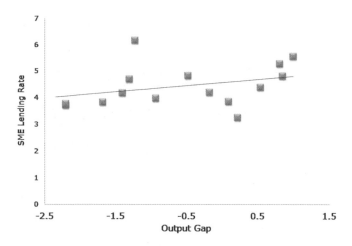

Figure 1. Lending rates and the output gap 2003.

Source: ECB, IMF.

diversified. The interbank market functioned smoothly, with relatively uniform interest rates across the euro zone. And policy rate movements quickly translated into changes in bank lending rates. Pre-crisis, the estimated pass-through from Euribor to corporate lending rates averaged over 0.8 for the euro area and it was generally higher in the South than in the rest of the euro zone (Al-Eyd and Berkmen 2013).

A well-functioning monetary policy transmission mechanism meant that lending conditions were relatively uniform and discrepancies were largely driven by local demand. This reflected in a cross-sectional distribution of lending rates that was negatively correlated with domestic demand across countries. Loosely speaking, local monetary policy conditions were anti-cyclical (Figure 1).

This growth in financial integration had also a darker side, as large capital flows across euro area countries allowed for the buildup of sovereign and private sector imbalances. In several countries, these imbalances manifested in credit booms (mostly funded through capital inflows) which fueled and were supported by booming house prices and buoyant real estate activity (these would later contribute greatly to the cost of the crisis). But, at the time, the "incomplete" financial architecture based on a single currency and common market, but national-based financial safety nets, bank supervision and regulation seemed to serve the euro zone well.

The crisis laid bare the tensions inherent in this institutional design. A host of challenges associated with fragmented bank jurisdictions came to the surface. Some of these (such as the lack of a common safety net) were particularly evident within the common currency area. But others (such as limited cooperation in cross-border supervision and resolution) had broader reach (IMF 2010; Obstfeld 2014; Schoenmaker 2011). This note focuses primarily on the effects of fragmentation on the development of sovereign-bank spirals (for a discussion, see Bolton and Jeanne 2011, Acharya *et al.* 2014, and Farhi and Tirole 2014). It then turns the attention to the potential sources of continued credit stagnation in southern Europe and to the role of the nascent banking union.

Vicious Spirals and the Monetary Policy Transmission Mechanism

Sovereign/bank/real sector vicious spirals emerged that imparted procyclicality to local lending conditions and impaired the monetary policy transmission mechanism (Figures 2 and 3 respectively). Even within a single monetary and fiscal jurisdiction, local conditions will have a tendency to exhibit procyclicality during distressed times, to the extent that bank portfolios are regionally specialized. A negative regional

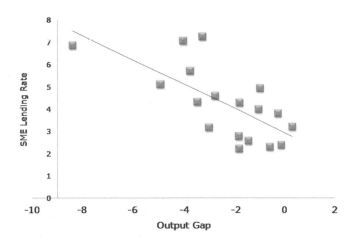

Figure 2.   Lending rates and the output gap 2012.

Source: ECB, IMF.

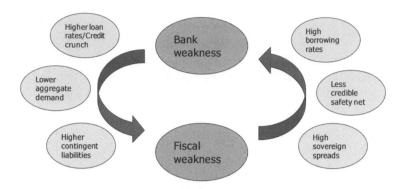

Figure 3. Sovereign/bank/real-sector spirals.

shock to the real sector will reduce borrowers' creditworthiness and increase the risk of local lending. Banks with portfolios concentrated in the region will becomes riskier and their cost of funds will increase. The subsequent increase in local rates will further hinder real activity and so on. However, in a single country setting, two elements intervene to stop or at least contain this spiral. First, a nationwide safety net will assuage the concern for regional bank stability (think about what would have happened during the crisis if the State of California or New York had had to be fiscally responsible for bank stability). Second, should the crisis be broader than regional, and potentially bring the public sector into the spiral, monetary policy can intervene (at least to some extent) to control interest rate conditions.

In contrast, the pre-crisis euro area's financial architecture strengthened the link between a country's banking and real sectors and the health of its public finances; in particular for countries with weak fiscal positions and/or very large banking systems (relative to GDP). In fiscally weak countries, the soundness of national-based bank backstops came into question. Banks became increasingly perceived as vulnerable which led to rising bank funding costs and lending rates. This, in turn, hindered real activity, further damaging public finances. In countries with large banking systems, bank distress overwhelmed national fiscal resources (again the effect of national-based fiscal backstops) directly, through explicit and implicit public guarantees, and indirectly, through its effect on real activity.

The inability to control local interest rate conditions, because of centralized monetary policy exacerbated the problem. The interaction of bank and sovereign weakness described above led to increasingly fragmented financial markets. In certain countries, banks and at times the sovereign found themselves rationed out of lending markets. The result was an inversion of the pre-crisis trend of increasing financial integration. Financial intermediaries retrenched in their home markets (in some cases partly responding to regulatory pressures — ring fencing) and bank spreads started to differ markedly across borders.

Bank lending rates (which until mid-2010 had co-moved closely across euro area countries started to differ. And notwithstanding the ECB's aggressive policy easing, monetary conditions in economies such as Italy and Spain remained relatively tight (and actually moved in the opposite direction for a while). Indeed, there is evidence that the pass-through of the policy rate onto bank lending rates (especially for small business lending) dropped dramatically in the countries hardest hit by the crisis, while remained roughly stable in others (Al-Eyd and Berkmen 2013) (Figure 4).

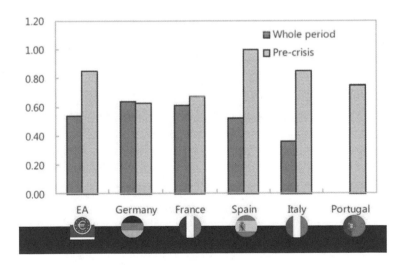

Figure 4. Interest rate pass-through (Small loans, LT coefficient, not controlling for other factors).

Source: Fragmentation and monetary policy in the Euro area, Al Eyd and Berkmen (2013).

The dynamics of banks costs and lending rates can be roughly divided into two phases. The first starts with Greece's request for financial supports in May–June 2010 (which marks the beginning of the sovereign debt crisis). And it ends in July 2012 with ECB president Draghi's *'whatever it takes'* speech.[1] During this phase, bank funding costs in distressed countries increased sharply relative to the rest of the euro zone. The average spread between bank funding costs in Italy/Spain and France/Germany (which before the crisis had been close to zero) peaked at right below 400bp. These diverging conditions reflected on credit markets, with widening cross-country spreads in lending rates (Figure 5).

The second phase starts with Draghi's speech and continues to the present time. In this phase, bank funding conditions gradually normalized (funding costs in the South dropped sharply after Draghi's speech and again after the approval of the baking union) with spreads returning to close to pre-crisis levels, as sovereign spreads declined; although, fragmentation on interbank markets continued at least until early fall 2013 (Garcia de Andoain *et al.* 2014). But the decline in bank funding cost did not translate in a similar drop on loan markets, with the spread in lending rates between Italy/Spain and France/Germany countries remaining well above pre-crisis levels. Consistently, aggregate credit

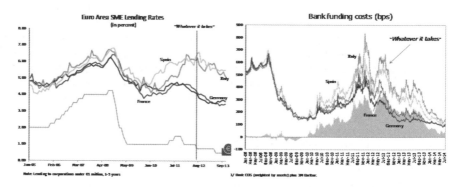

Figure 5. (a) Euro area SME Lending Rules (in %) and (b) Bank funding costs (bps).

---

[1] The transcription of the speech delivered at the Global Investment Conference in London on 26 July 2012 is available at http://www.ecb.europa.eu/press/key/date/2012/html/sp120726.en.html.

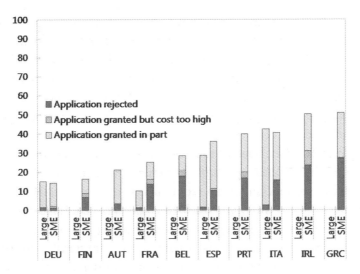

Figure 6. Outcome of loan application by EA firms, 2013H2 2/.

Source: ECB SAFE Survey data.

was stagnant or falling in all 5 countries hardest hit by the crisis (Greece, Italy, Ireland, Portugal and Spain). And credit standards were typically tighter in these countries than in the rest of the euro zone. In what follows, we explore potential explanations for these patterns (Figure 6).

Sources of Credit Contraction: An Identification Strategy

Alternative stories with different implications for policy making may be behind continued tight credit conditions in Southern Europe.

Credit stagnation (our outright contraction in some countries) in the South of the euro zone may stem from disruptions in financial intermediation resulting from banks distress. Banks in these countries have suffered from rising funding costs and losses associated with increased country risk and sovereign spreads. Increased market sensitivity to bank balance-sheet health may have forced them to seek higher capital ratios. This, in turn, in an environment in which raising equity was relatively costly, may have led to a contraction in bank balance sheets and, hence, aggregate credit.

Under the hypothesis that the credit contraction in the South is purely a supply-side story, banks from distressed countries (in this scenario these are the banks with weakened balance sheets) would be expected to contract credit in both distressed and not-distressed countries in an attempt to reduce their leverage and increase capital ratios. In contrast, healthier banks could take advantage of this retrenchment to expand credit in both markets and increase their market share (black arrows in the matrix above); although, barriers to entry (informational asymmetries, regulatory obstacles, etc.) may prevent them to fully offset the credit contraction by distressed banks.

On the opposite side is the view that the decline in credit aggregates is simply the reflection of stagnant economic activity. Under this assumption, banks are able and willing to lend, but the demand for loans is weak as a result of limited investment opportunities, low consumption growth etc. In the 'purest' version of this scenario, lending rates would tend to be low, as a result of weak loan demand. In a more realistic version, weak economic activity leads to an increase in credit risk and the decline in credit occurs without a drop in lending rates.

Under this assumption, banks from both groups of countries would reduce their exposure to the distressed economies. But they would both expand their portfolio in countries with stronger economic activity (grey arrows in the Figure 7).

Finally, there is a 'mixed' story in which financial sector weakness in distressed countries interacts with domestic economic activity generating conditions under which even healthy lenders are unwilling to

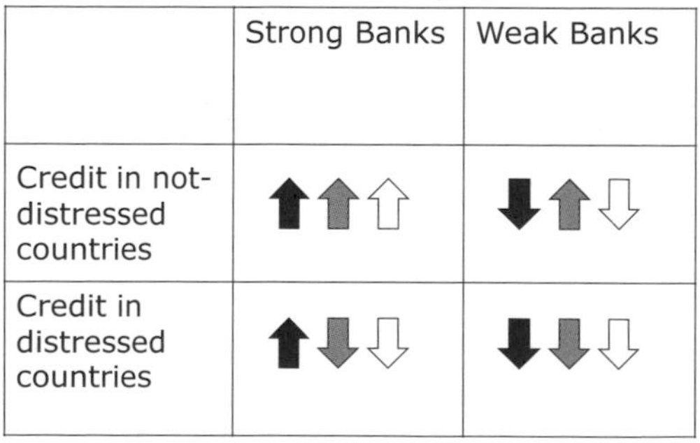

	Strong Banks	Weak Banks
Credit in not-distressed countries	⬆⬆⇧	⬇⬆⇩
Credit in distressed countries	⬆⬇⇩	⬇⬇⇩

Figure 7.   Banks in not-distressed countries vs those in distressed countries.

extend credit. Under this scenario, balance-sheet weakness at domestic banks leads to the expectation of an aggregate credit contraction. This in turn damages the prospects of otherwise profitable potential borrowers (think about a car manufacturer facing a market with very limited availability of consumer credit). And, thus, prevents healthier (foreign) banks from extending credit. This is to some extent a coordination failure story. Individual banks may be reluctant to lend to nonfinancial firms in distressed economies on the assumption that local banks (which provide the bulk of credit to the economy) will curtail lending, and other foreign banks will not come in. These beliefs are validated in equilibrium, as these borrowers would not be able to succeed in an environment with rationed aggregate credit (Bebchuk and Goldstein 2011).

Under this hypothesis, like in the 'pure' supply-side story, under balance-sheet weakness pressures, banks from distressed countries would cut credit across the board. Unlike in that scenario, however, banks from core countries will also curtail lending to distressed economies, while continuing to extend it domestically (white arrows in Figure 7).

Identifying the sources behind aggregate credit decline is critical from a policy standpoint. Under the 'pure' supply-side scenario, the financial sector acts as a constraint on economic activity. The equilibrium is an inefficient one in which profitable opportunities remain unfunded. Policies aimed at restoring bank health and financial intermediation would, in principle, lead to a better outcome. The policy prescription is broadly similar under the more complex coordination failure scenario. Under the demand scenario, however, the decline in credit is simply mirroring aggregate economic weakness. The equilibrium might be an inefficient one, but the inefficiency does not stem from financial constraints. Policies aimed at the financial sector will not improve the situation. Rather, support to aggregate demand and/or structural reforms aimed at easing whatever constraints are at the source of the inefficiency should be the focus of the policy effort (Figure 8).

Comparing the behavior of aggregate credit and cross-border banking statistics in different countries in the euro area sheds some light on the sources behind the tight credit condition in the South. Over the crisis period, domestic credit was essentially flat in Germany and slightly increasing in France. It experienced a mild decrease in Italy and sharp

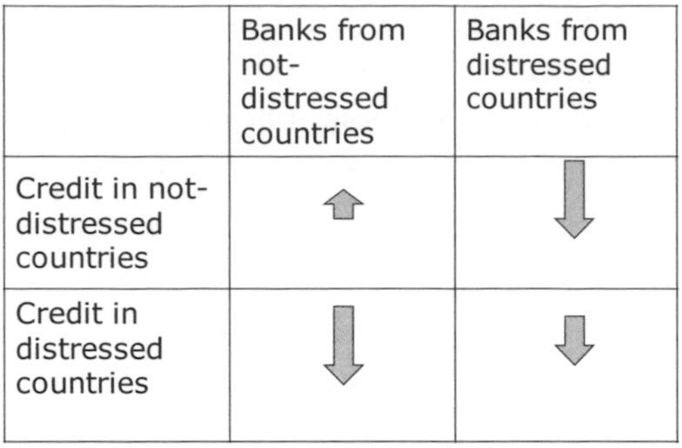

	Banks from not-distressed countries	Banks from distressed countries
Credit in not-distressed countries	⬆	⬇
Credit in distressed countries	⬇	⬇

Figure 8. The 'mixed' scenario.

declines in Spain, Portugal, and Greece. Over the same period, there was substantial financial retrenching, with banks cutting aggressively their cross-country exposures. If taken at face value, this picture lends support to the 'mixed' scenario hypothesized (shown in Figure 8), with banks from stronger countries cutting credit to weaker ones, but maintaining their domestic exposures; and banks from the weak economies curtailing their portfolios across the board. That said, potential, although likely limited, double counting when putting together domestic and cross-border credit statistics, and the inability to control for bank specific factors suggest caution in the interpretation of this data. An examination of credit at the bank affiliate level along with the identification strategy sketched in this note may provide more convincing evidence of the sources of credit stagnation in the South.

Indeed, other stylized facts are less supportive of the 'mixed' story. For instance, there appears to be a strong relationship between NPLs and bank lending rates. Countries with high NPLs tend to experience higher interest rates on loans to small and medium enterprises. This is consistent with the "mixed" view to the extent that higher NPLs reflect in a lower ability to lend on the part of banks. But it could also lend support to the demand story: banks in the South are reluctant to lend because borrowers have become riskier. Consistently, the relationship between bank lending rates and bank capital is unclear, at least at the country level (with its slope depending critically on the inclusion/exclusion of outliers).

How can the Nascent Banking Union Help?

A well-designed banking union can help address the tensions discussed in the previous sections. In particular, by mutualizing (at least to some extent) fiscal backstops for bank safety nets it will weaken the sovereign/bank spirals that have contributed to the re-fragmentation of the euro area banking markets. This will help contain the supply-side factors behind the current tight credit conditions in distressed countries and strengthen the monetary policy transmission mechanism. Obviously, a banking union would do little (beyond perhaps a confidence effect) if the main sources of credit stagnation were on the demand side.

To be effective the new institutional framework has to comprise three elements: a single regulatory and supervisory framework, a single resolution mechanism, and a common safety net. In this context, Europe is moving in the right direction and (given the institutional constraints) at a commendable speed. There are of course implementation challenges related to putting into practice effective common supervision and resolution. It is essential also to avoid stalling on reforms. In this regard, agreeing on a framework and timetable for common safety nets and backstops is critical (Goyal *et al.* 2012).

Indeed, all three elements are necessary (at least for countries belonging to the common currency area). A single supervisory agency without a common safety net framework may help with regulatory externalities (Dell'Ariccia and Marquez 2006; Calzolari and Loranth 2011) and reduce the risk of regulatory capture (Agarwal *et al.* 2014), but will do little to break the vicious circle between banks and sovereigns and reestablish a properly functioning monetary transmission mechanism. And supervision requires a credible resolution framework to be effective (not only to allow for timely decision-making during crises, but also to provide supervision with 'teeth' during tranquil times). In turn, bank recapitalization as well as resolution and deposit insurance mechanisms would lack credibility without the assurance of fiscal backstops and burden sharing arrangements. Finally, common safety nets and backstops without effective supervision and resolution would break sovereign-bank links, but risk distorting incentives, reinforcing tendencies for regulatory forbearance, and shifting losses to the euro area level. In short, power and resources have to go hand in hand.

For countries that retain an independent monetary policy (those outside the euro zone which are not pegging to the euro) sovereign-bank spirals are a less pressing concern (although, they come back to center stage for systems with a high degree of liability dollarization). And, while other shortcomings of uncoordinated regulation and supervision policies remain, for these countries the choice between independent and centralized regulators is less clear cut. Indeed, a centralized supervision, resolution, and safety net framework also entails costs and challenges. An important one: A common agency will find it more difficult to tailor policies to individual countries under its jurisdiction. In this regard the current European design attempts to strike a balance between common supervision and local flexibility by leaving smaller banks under the responsibility of national authorities and allowing some leeway in the use of certain regulatory tools (see, for instance, the treatment of macroprudential measures).

Another important implementation challenge relates to the internal governance of a centralized agency; especially one organized around a hub-and-spokes model. Internal mechanisms will have to be devised to guarantee that the spokes, which (at least in a transition period) may have different objective functions from the hub, act accordingly to the centralized mandate, including with regard to information collection and exchange (Holthausen and Rønde 2004). Finally, there can be unwanted side effects. Financial institutions and their relationship with the real sector will evolve with the new regulatory structure. This may lead to even greater imbalances. For instance, countries may be able to run even larger current account deficits once banks are protected by a common fiscal backstop; or banks may grow even larger in the attempt to become too-big-to-fail at the supra-national level. Vigilance and new policy tools (such as those classified as macroprudential) may be required to limit these risks.

References

Acharya, V., I. Drechsler and P. Schnabl (2014), "A Pyrrhic Victory? Bank Bailouts and Sovereign Credit Risk," *Journal of Finance*, 69(6): 2689–2739.

Agarwal, S., D. Lucca, A. Seru and F. Trebbi (2014), "Inconsistent Regulators: Evidence from banking," *Quarterly Journal of Economics*, 129(2): 889–938.

Al-Eyd, A. and S. P. Berkmen (2013), "Fragmentation and Monetary Policy in the Euro Area," IMF Working Paper No. 13/208.

Bebchuk, L. and I. Goldstein (2011), "Self-Fulfilling Credit Market Freezes," *Review of Financial Studies*, 24(11): 3519–3555.

Bolton, P. and O. Jeanne (2011), "Sovereign Default Risk and Bank Fragility in Financially Integrated Economies," *IMF Economic Review*, 59: 162–194.

Calzolari, G. and G. Loranth (2011), "Regulation of Multinational Banks: A theoretical inquiry," *Journal of Financial Intermediation*, 20(2): 178–198.

Dell'Ariccia, G. and R. Marquez (2006), "Competition among Regulators and Credit Market Integration," *Journal of Financial Economics*, 79: 401–430.

Farhi, E. and J. Tirole (2014), "Deadly Embrace: Sovereign and financial balance sheets doom loops," mimeo, Harvard University. Available at: http://scholar.harvard.edu/farhi/publications/deadly-embrace-sovereign-and-financial-balance-sheets-doom-loops.

Garcia de Andoain, C., P. Hoffmann and S. Manganelli (2014), "Fragmentation in the Euro Overnight Unsecured Money Market," European Central Bank Working Paper No. 1755.

Goyal, R., P. K. Brooks, M. Pradhan, T. Tressel, G. Dell'Ariccia and C. Pazarbasioglu (2013), "A Banking Union for the Euro Area," IMF Staff Discussion Notes No. 13/1.

Holthausen, C. and T. Rønde (2004), "Cooperation in International Banking Supervision," European Central Bank Working Paper No. 316.

International Monetary Fund [IMF] (2010), "Resolution of Cross-Border Banks — A Proposed Framework for Enhanced Coordination," June 11. Available at: https://www.imf.org/external/np/pp/eng/2010/061110.pdf.

Obstfeld, M. (2014), "Trilemmas and Tradeoffs: Living with Financial Globalization," UC Berkeley, working paper. Available at: http://eml.berkeley.edu/~obstfeld/Trilemmas_last%20draft.pdf.

Schoenmaker, D. (2011), "The Financial Trilemma," *Economic Letters*, 111: 57–59.

New Capital and Liquidity Requirements
Transitional Effects on the Economy
— CHAPTER 21

■ Douglas J. Elliott
Brookings Institution

Bank regulation has important economic effects and the round of major financial reforms in response to the great financial crisis of 2007–9 will certainly have impacts on the wider economy. Judging what those will be is complex and difficult. Quantifying them is even harder, but it is important to form some judgments regardless, since regulation is a balancing act. Occasionally we can achieve greater safety for free, principally by insisting on intelligent risk management to block the kind of stupid actions that seem appealing in the middle of a bubble. However, in the great majority of cases safety comes at a cost to efficiency and economic growth in normal years, which must be balanced against the large benefits of reducing the frequency and severity of financial crises. Most financial regulation is effectively a purchase of insurance against crises and we need to judge whether the annual premiums are worth the protection against infrequent, but devastating, events.

Elliott is a Fellow in the Economic Studies program at the Brookings Institution. The views expressed here are solely his own and do not represent those of the Brookings Institution.

My assigned topic is the measurement of the transitional effects of the new financial regulations on the wider economy. My short answer is that I do not think anyone knows the answer to this question and by the time we figure it out, if we ever do, the transition will long be over. There are some serious attempts to measure the impacts, most notably by a 'Macroeconomic Assessment Group' (MAG) established by the Basel Committee for Banking Supervision (Basel Committee) and the Financial Stability Board (FSB). The MAG evaluated the likely impact of the Basel III Accords. These comprise the latest version of global standards on capital, developed by the Basel Committee, plus new standards for liquidity.

The MAG worked with many official and private experts globally and developed a consensus projection of the potential range of effects. However, they necessarily used rough estimates and implicitly or explicitly excluded some important variables. For example, it matters whether equity investors choose to alter their required returns from banks based on the presumed greater safety resulting from the reforms, but the MAG explicitly assumed no such impact. I do not fault the study; it is a sound attempt to do an extremely difficult analytical task while trying to create a consensus within a large international body. However, it cannot be taken as definitive.

Despite my skepticism about our ability to be very precise or accurate in judging the transitional effects, I do not dispute the MAG's overall conclusion that the benefits of the revisions to the capital and liquidity requirements outweigh the costs.

This chapter will begin with a qualitative discussion of the first order effects one would expect from two of the most critical regulatory reforms, the enhanced capital requirements under Basel III compared to the previous Basel Accords and the liquidity and asset-liability management requirements created for the first time by Basel III. It will then review previous analysis by the author of the likely long-term effects of the major global regulatory reforms, principally Basel III. This will be followed by an extensive discussion of the key questions to be answered when trying to quantify those impacts, ending with a further extensive discussion of how the transition period may differ from the long term.

That review of the difficult analytical issues will hopefully explain why the author believes that only the roughest conclusions are feasible about the transitional effects on the wider economy of these regulatory reforms.

Basel III

The latest version of the Basel Capital Accords is almost universally known as Basel III. It very substantially revised the global standards for bank capital requirements and introduced new quantitative requirements for liquidity and for asset-liability management.

On capital regulation, Basel III significantly raises the total required capital levels and, equally importantly, forces that capital to be in stronger forms, principally by requiring that much more of it be in the form of common equity than was previously required. The combined impact of the quality and quantity revisions is to force common equity levels to be three or four times the previous minimums, when all the changes are taken into account.

Basel III also introduces, for the first time, complex, quantitative requirements for bank liquidity. The intent is to ensure that each bank can handle a broad liquidity crisis for at least thirty days, giving authorities time to intervene as necessary. This is done through the Liquidity Coverage Ratio (LCR). Further, the new Net Stable Funding Ratio (NSFR) is intended to ensure that banks do not rely excessively on short-term and/or unstable sources of funding for long-term loans and investments.

It is important to bear in mind that the private sector would have moved a long way in these directions even without new regulation, as all the significant players in the financial sector learned, or re-learned, valuable lessons from the global financial crisis. So, to the extent that one is trying to measure the impact of *regulation*, rather than of the overall changes regardless of their source, it is necessary to make a judgment as to what would have happened voluntarily in the markets. My own, very rough, judgment is that perhaps two-thirds of the movement in capital and liquidity levels would have occurred without official prompting. One could easily reach different conclusions about the proportion, but it is clear that substantial movement would have occurred voluntarily.

At the same time, it is also clear that banks and their funders would not have chosen to move all the way to the levels now being required and would not have used the same methods to calculate the exact quantities as regulators are mandating. This is a crucial point, because it explains why the financial sector is likely to evolve to where banks play a smaller role due to regulatory arbitrage. Markets are willing to support lower-cost business models that are deemed too risky by the regulators, leading to economic pressure for banks to work around the rules and for business to move to shadow banking.

First Order Impacts of Basel III

The first order effects of Basel III are pretty clear, directionally. It is the knock-on effects that are hardest to judge.

Banks, and the overall financial system, should be safer. Capital and liquidity are very important safety buffers and having higher levels of them should, in the first instance, make financial crisis much less likely.

Bank loans and other products should be more expensive. These safety buffers come at a cost to the banks and some of this cost, probably most of it, will be passed through to customers. Improving liquidity means giving up yield by holding shorter-term and higher quality assets, and paying more for funding by increasing the average maturity and locking in funders more firmly. On the capital side, equity, which is the most expensive security to issue, replaces other funding, raising the average cost of funding. There are offsets to this, as famously shown by Modigliani and Miller, but they are far from complete offsets in the real world, especially when looking at the private position of the bank, rather than the overall effects on society (Elliott 2013).

Bank credit volumes, and their provision of other services, should be reduced. Part of this is simple supply and demand. More expensive bank loans will be in less demand. In addition, especially in the short-run, there could be inefficiencies in the ability to raise or allocate capital that creates rationing effects. Beyond that, competitive dynamics make it difficult to force customers to take all the pain up-front, meaning that some products will be temporarily underpriced and therefore rationed to at least some extent.

Non-bank financial institutions should gain market share. As noted, the markets would be content to support business models that are less well-capitalized and less liquid than banks have to be under Basel III. This improves the competitive position of most non-banks.

Business may shift to capital markets. At first blush, capital markets should gain for the same reasons as non-bank financials, as a result of reduced competitiveness for banks. However, new regulations are producing many disincentives for activity by bank groups in the markets, including sharply higher capital requirements under Basel III for much trading activity. Since banks and their affiliates are key supports for most financial markets, there is some level of offset here that will slow down market growth.

Tax revenue should rise. One of the reasons equity is more expensive than debt for banks is that governments provide a tax benefit to interest payments on debt that is not available to the firm paying equity dividends. This relative advantage is only partially offset by other tax advantages for equity holders. Therefore, funding more through equity will, in the first instance, increase tax payments.

Product mixes at banks should also shift. Tougher capital requirements and the new LCR and NSFR mandates will push banks to adapt their business models. This should shift business as follows, in the first instance:

- Away from trading and some investment and securities activities
- Away from derivatives, especially customized or long-term ones
- Away from longer-term lending
- Towards plain vanilla lending
- Away from short-term wholesale funding
- Towards deposits

Cumulative Impact Assessment

A substantial portion of my analytical work over time has been focused on cost-benefit analysis of financial regulation, particularly in regard to capital and liquidity requirements. The most comprehensive explanation of my views on the cumulative impact of the major reforms is contained in two related papers I co-authored as a consultant to the International Monetary Fund (Elliott *et al.* 2012 (hereafter 'ESS'); and Santos and Elliott 2012).

Box 1 contains of summary from one of them.

Box 1: Assessing the Cost of Financial Regulation

Reforming the regulation of financial institutions and markets is critically important and should provide large benefits to society. The recent financial crisis underlined the huge economic costs produced by recessions associated with severe financial crises. However, adding safety margins in the financial system comes at a price. Most notably, the substantially stronger capital and liquidity requirements created under the new Basel III accord have economic costs during the good years, analogous to insurance payments.

There is serious disagreement about how much the additional safety margins will cost. The Institute of International Finance (IIF, 2011) projected that the proposed reforms will reduce annual output in the advanced economies by approximately 3 percent by 2015. Official estimates, particularly those from the Bank for International Settlements (BIS), suggest a far smaller reduction.

Finding an intellectually sound consensus on the costs of reform is critical. If the true price is too high, reforms must be reassessed to improve the cost-benefit ratio. But, if the reforms are economically sound, they should be pursued to increase safety and reduce the uncertainty about rules that creates inefficiencies and makes long-term planning difficult.

This study assesses the overall impact on credit of the global financial regulatory initiatives in, Europe, Japan, and the United States.

(*Continued*)

Box 1: (*Continued*)

It focuses on the long-term outcomes, rather than transitional costs, and does not attempt to measure the economic benefits of reforms. Academic theory is combined with empirical analyses from industry and official sources, plus financial disclosures by the major financial firms, to reach specific cost estimates. The analysis here does not address the significant adjustments triggered by the financial and Eurozone crises and the potential transitional effects of adjusting to the new regulations.

The study focuses principally on the effects of regulatory changes on banks and their lending. This is for three reasons: banks dominate finance; the reforms are heavily focused on them; and it is harder to estimate the effects on other parts of the system, such as capital markets. Loans, in particular, are a major part of overall credit provision and there is substantially greater data available on lending activities. Where possible, the study also looks at the effects of new regulations on securities holdings by banks and on securities markets.

Measuring the cost of financial reform requires careful consideration of the baselines for comparisons. They should incorporate the higher safety margins that would have been demanded by markets, customers, and managements after the financial crisis, even in the absence of new regulation. Some studies take the approach of assuming all the increases in safety margins are due to regulatory changes, exaggerating the cost of reforms.

A simple model is used to estimate the increase in lending rates required to accommodate the various reforms. The model assumes credit providers need to charge for the combination of: the cost of allocated capital; the cost of other funding; credit losses; administrative costs, and certain miscellaneous factors. The study establishes initial values for these key variables, determines how they would change under regulatory reform, and evaluates the changes in credit pricing and other variables needed to rebalance the equation.

Cost estimates are provided for capital and liquidity requirements, derivatives reforms, and the effects of higher taxes and fees.

(*Continued*)

Box 1: (*Continued*)

These categories were chosen after a detailed qualitative assessment of the relative impact of different reforms on credit costs. Securitization reform was initially chosen as well, but proved impossible to quantify.

Finally, an overall, integrated cost estimate is developed. This involves examining the interactions between these categories and including the effects of mitigating actions likely to be taken by the financial institutions as a result of the reforms in totality. This includes, for example, the room for expense cuts to counteract the need for price increases, to the extent that such cuts were not already included in stand-alone impact estimates.

Lending rates in the base case rise by 18 bps in Europe, 8 bps in Japan, and 28 bps in the United States, in the long run. There is considerable uncertainty about the true cost levels, but a sensitivity analysis shows reasonable changes in assumptions do not alter the conclusions dramatically. The results are broadly in line with previous studies from the official sector, partially because similar methodologies are employed. This paper finds similar first-order effects to the official BIS assessments of Basel III (BCBS (2010) and MAG (2010)) and the analysis at the OECD by Slovik and Cournède (2010). The cost estimates here are, however, markedly lower than those of the IIF.

Three extensions of the methodologies from the official studies, though, lead to substantially lower net costs. The base case shows increases in lending rates of roughly a third to a half of those found in the BIS and OECD studies, despite important commonalities in the core modeling approaches with these studies. First, the baselines chosen here assume a greater hike in safety margins due to market forces, and therefore less of a regulatory effect, than the OECD and IIF studies. (The BIS studies do not reach firm conclusions on the additional capital needs). Industry actions through end-2010 suggest that market forces alone would have produced reactions similar to

(*Continued*)

Box 1: (*Continued*)

what was witnessed to that point, even if no regulatory changes were contemplated.

Second, this paper assumes that banks will also react by reducing costs and taking certain other measures that have little effect on credit prices and availability, in addition to the actions assumed in the other studies. The official studies do not do so and the IIF study assumes a fairly low level of change. This accounts for 13 bps of cost reduction in Europe, 10 bps in Japan, and 20 bps in the United States. Third, this paper assumes that equity investors will reduce their required rate of return on bank equity as a result of the safety improvements. Debt investors are assumed to follow suit, although to a much lesser extent. The official studies assume no benefit from investor reactions, for conservatism, and the IIF assumes the benefits, although real, will arise over a longer time-frame than is covered by their projections.

There are important limitations to the analysis presented here. Transition costs are not examined, a number of regulatory reforms are not modeled, judgment has been required in making many of the estimates, the overall modeling approach is relatively simple, and regulatory implementation is assumed to be appropriate, therefore not adding unnecessary costs. Despite these limitations, the results appear to be a balanced, albeit rough, assessment of the likely effects on credit. Further research would be useful to translate the credit impacts into effects on economic output.

Again, all of the analysis is based on the long-run outcome, not taking account of a transition being made in today's troubled circumstances. To the extent that bank capital or liquidity is difficult or very expensive to raise during the transition period — as they are currently in Europe, a reduction in credit supply would be expected and any increase in lending rates would be magnified, perhaps substantially. Deleveraging is clearly occurring at European banks under today's conditions in response to financial market, economic, regulatory, and

(*Continued*)

Box 1: (*Continued*)

political factors. It is impossible to tell whether any appreciable portion of this reaction is due to anticipation of the Basel III rules. Regardless of the transitional effects, it will be possible, over time, for banks to find the necessary capital and liquidity to provide credit, as long as the pricing is appropriate. Capital and liquidity will flow to banks from other sectors if the price of credit rises more than is justified by the fundamental underlying factors.

The relatively small effects found here strongly suggest that the benefits would indeed outweigh the costs of regulatory reforms in the long run. Banks have a great ability to adapt over time to the reforms without radical actions harming the wider economy.

The key conclusions of the quantitative analysis can be seen in Table 1, taken from ESS.

ESS did not undertake an analysis of the stability benefits of the regulatory reforms, but the quite small projected changes in the cost of credit and the even smaller likely effects on credit supply[1] strongly suggested to the authors that the benefits would far outweigh these costs, in the long term.

Key Questions on Long-Term Impacts

The impacts of the regulatory changes can be divided into two parts, those that will be true in both the long-term and the transition and those that apply only during the transition. It is easiest to consider the underlying effects first and then to examine what would be different over the shorter-run.

Assessing the impacts starts with the directional effects described earlier and then requires answers to a series of questions.

---

[1] ESS did not attempt to quantify the effects on credit supply, but argued that banks would prefer, in the long run, to make price adjustments rather than use credit rationing and that, barring special circumstances, the price changes were in a range that would likely not create significant rationing.

Table 1. Cumulative impact of regulatory reforms on lending rates (in basis points).

	Europe	Japan	US
Capital	19	13	40
Modigliani-Miller pass-through	−9	−7	−20
Liquidity Coverage Ratio (LCR)	8	1	11
Net Stable Funding Ratio (NSFR)	10	11	16
Overlap of LCR and NSFR actions (half of smallest)	−4	0	−5
Derivatives	1	N.A	3
Taxes and fees	6	0	4
Total gross effects	31	18	48
Expense cuts (at 5% for Europe, 10% for US)	8	8	15
Other aggregate adjustments	5	3	5
of which: Planned capital mitigating actions	3	N.A.	2
Total Adjustments	13	10	20
Net cost	18	8	28

Source: Elliott *et al.* (2012)

What would markets have done anyway? This is only relevant if one is trying to extract the pure regulatory effects. As noted, I believe that much of the movement towards higher capital and better liquidity would have happened anyway, so it is inappropriate to ascribe the costs and benefits solely to regulation. In FSS, we assumed that the capital levels as of the end of 2010 reflected market pressures without yet reflecting Basel III. (This seemed particularly apt in Europe, since market pressure subsequent to that date forced the authorities to effectively bring Basel III's higher capital requirements forward via the first round of EBA stress tests in order to reassure markets of the soundness of the banks. This strongly suggests that markets on their own would have required at least the end-2010 levels of capital.)

Similarly, and with stronger logic, liquidity levels at that point were assumed to reflect solely market forces and not Basel III, since the LCR and NSFR: would not take effect for several more years; were in flux to some extent; and bank funding methods could be changed relatively quickly, so there was no reason to jump the gun.

What additional buffers will banks choose to hold? Banks will not wish to operate at the exact minimum capital and liquidity requirements, since any adverse developments would trigger regulatory demands and the prospect of this would also unsettle funders and counterparties. Therefore, one must make a judgment as to what the *effective* regulatory requirements are, which will be over and above the stated ones.

How will the multiple capital and liquidity requirements interact and how will banks respond in practice? In ESS, we had the luxury of assuming that the revised Basel risk-weighted capital requirements would be the binding requirements. Since then, the situation has become considerably more complicated. In the US, the largest banks, which collectively control about half the assets of the industry, face three capital requirements, each of which is potentially binding. In addition to risk-weighted assets, there is a new supplementary leverage ratio (SLR) of 5% for consolidated banking groups and 6% for their depository institutions. This is measured as a percentage of total on-balance sheet assets, plus an imputed asset equivalent for derivatives and certain other instruments. Beyond that, the Federal Reserve's Comprehensive Capital Analysis and Review (CCAR) stress tests also create new capital requirements that vary each year.

In practice, the total capital requirements demanded by these three alternative measures are broadly similar for most of the largest banks at the moment. However, the levels from each will ebb and flow and which of them is the most binding constraint can easily change over time. This presents two important complications.

First, it makes it difficult to judge what the relative attractiveness of different product offerings will be for the banks, since capital is a significant cost component and the different measures produce quite different capital requirements at the product level. (For example, risk-weights and stress tests will not demand much, if any, capital for Treasury Bills or repos of Treasuries, but the SLR will demand substantial capital, as it does for all assets.) To the extent that economic effects will depend on the product mixes offered by banks and by non-banks and the pricing of those products, this adds significant analytical uncertainty.

Second, banks will react in part by holding yet another buffer of capital to protect against an unexpected swing from one capital regime to another, since any such shift imposes significant business costs. It is not practical to periodically force line managers to switch from pushing one type of loan to a different type based on migrating capital requirements. Banks will instead choose to hold at least somewhat more capital to give them time and flexibility to respond. This additional practical capital 'requirement' needs to be factored in.

Liquidity requirements will also interact with the capital requirements. For example, if the SLR becomes binding, it would tend to push up banks' risk appetites, since the capital requirements are the same for low-risk and high-risk products, while expected margins, even on a risk-adjusted basis, tend to be higher for high-risk products. However, the LCR and NSFR push in the opposite direction, since the most liquid assets under these tests are high-quality, shorter-term ones. In terms of product mix, this is likely to penalize non-securitized mortgages, since they do not have good liquidity characteristics, but they are low-risk and therefore relatively low-return.

How much will funders reduce their required returns? In theory, most, if not all, of the costs of increased safety margins of capital and liquidity could be offset by a reduction in the returns demanded by the providers of capital and other funds to the banks. Modigliani and Miller showed that, under idealized conditions, there should be an exact offset to the cost of shifting to funding with more equity and less debt. The offset would come from a lowered cost of obtaining each *unit* of equity and debt. That is, there would be more of the expensive source, but the average cost of *each* source of funds would go down. As already noted, some of this offset does not exist in the real world, but much of it does. One needs to make a judgment as to the proportion of any offsets. In ESS, we examined studies that suggested to us that the Modigliani-Miller offset in practice ranged from 25–75% of the effect on funding costs that would occur if there were no offset and we choose to use 50% as our base case.

The equivalent effects from the liquidity requirements have an additional factor, which is that the regulations are intended to shift banks away from liquidity support from authorities in a crisis. Effectively, banks and their funders are being deprived of an element of implicit, free, liquidity insurance. To the extent this is true, there *should* be an increase in costs for the banks. The same would actually be true for capital, if one believes that significant implicit subsidies still exist from a potential rescue of 'Too Big to Fail' banks. Higher capital lowers the chance of needing such a rescue, reducing an externality and increasing the costs borne by the bank itself.

How much do safety margins overlap? As discussed in ESS, actions that banks take to meet Basel III capital requirements generally also help with liquidity requirements and actions taken to meet the LCR mandate also generally help with the NSFR, and vice versa. Therefore, it is important not to double or triple count the costs of meeting regulatory requirements. Instead, one must make a judgment about the degree of overlap. In ESS, we tried to make an approximate direct estimate of the effect of shifting to equity on the LCR and NSFR costs. We further assumed, as a very rough cut, that banks first bore the costs of the LCR or NSFR adjustments, whichever was higher, and then absorbed only half the cost of the other stand-alone adjustment, due to overlaps.

What portion of the costs will pass through to customers? There is plenty of anecdotal evidence that banks had room to cut costs substantially as compared to the pre-crisis period, if only through reduced compensation. Investors themselves may or may not have been willing to lower their return targets, even independent of increases in safety margins. (One could argue that they had inflated return expectations and are now more realistic *or* one could argue that they were actually insufficiently averse to risk and were charging too low a return.) Therefore, judgments need to be made about the extent to which particular costs borne by the banks due to tougher regulation get passed on to customers. In ESS, we made explicit assumptions about expense cuts and other offsets.

How much room is there for gaming and regulatory arbitrage? Analysts virtually always assume, as we did in ESS, that the rules work as intended. In practice, banks will find ways to lower their cost of responding to regulations through what regulators may view as loopholes. Further, some of the business will shift within banks to business that is less harmed by new regulation and, of course, business will shift away from banks. We explicitly did not try to measure this in ESS, although I believe it to be significant. As a general matter, such moves will reduce both the costs and the safety benefits of financial reform.

How efficiently are the rules written and enforced? Again, the intent of the rules and how they are implemented may be two different things. Part of this is reflected in gaming and arbitrage, but part of it relates more to unintended harm that may be done by writing rules in inappropriate ways that are too broad or choose the wrong instruments to effect change. In ESS, we explicitly assumed there would be no negative consequences of this, although there surely will be. If I were writing the paper over, I would emphasize this point more.

What will non-banks and financial markets do? This runs much broader than the simple question of regulatory arbitrage described above. For example, if non-banks choose to take the pricing shelter provided by bank price increases, then overall customer costs will rise more than if non-banks choose market share over profit margins. (This particular example should be a transition issue, rather than a permanent one, assuming markets are not oligopolistic.) We did not address this in ESS.

What is the marginal effect of higher credit spreads on the economy as a whole? Some studies have attempted to estimate the total impact on the economy, rather than stopping as ESS did at the effects on credit pricing and availability.

How much will central bank actions counteract increases in credit spreads? One of the critical questions is whether aggregate credit costs will remain stable because the central bank chooses, and is able, to counteract higher credit spreads by reducing base borrowing costs. In any event, there would still be substantial allocational effects, as credit spreads for different products are affected to quite different extents by Basel III and other regulations, even if the overall impact is offset.

What is the marginal effect of greater stability in the financial system on the economy as a whole? In the first instance, this is the question of measuring the benefits of tougher regulation that reduces the frequency and severity of financial crises. However, there is the question of the knock-on effects of greater stability. At the extreme, one might argue that the Great Moderation produced a similar volatility reduction and that this led to excessive risk taking and ultimately the financial crisis.

Additional Transition Effects

The transition period has quite a number of further impacts that are captured in the following analytical questions. None of these are addressed in ESS, which only looked at the long-term effects.

What are the effects of transition arrangements embedded in the new rules? Basel III and many of the other regulations were set to come into force beginning several years after agreement on their terms and often phased in over a number of subsequent years. The real world impacts lie between two extremes. At one end, banks and funding markets might take the transition arrangements as the be all and end all with reactions spread over the phase-in period. At the other end, banks and funding markets may react instantly to the full rigor of the eventual rules. In practice, US banks in particular tried to move fairly quickly to meet the full Basel III capital standards, in order to reassure markets about their ability to do so. European banks faced too many hurdles to do that, but still moved faster on average than was legally required. Anticipating the eventual rules tends to increase transitional effects, which is exactly why regulators tried to provide the fuller flexibility.

How do we separate out the effects of other regulatory changes? Any measurement of the impact of Basel III, or another subset of the regulatory reforms, faces the difficulty of untangling the effects of that action versus the myriad of other regulatory reforms undertaken over the same period.

What are the effects of uncertainty about the rules? The financial sector has experienced a great deal of uncertainty about what the rules will be. Some claim the uncertainty itself has reduced lending and other financial activities and there is likely some truth to this. Judging the extent is difficult, though. Further, it may be that uncertainty has other effects on the actions of banks, their customers, and their competitors that complicate analysis. For instance, it seems pretty clear that pricing of loans and other bank services has not gone up as much as it will need to do, in part because banks are reluctant to take strong action until they can see what the longer-term landscape will look like. So, uncertainty could have required a pricing buffer to be built in, adding to customer costs, or uncertainty could have caused banks to hold off on price increases, reducing initial customer costs relative to ultimate outcomes.

What are the effects of uncertainty about client and competitor responses? More broadly, banks are holding back to a considerable extent out of uncertainty as to how their customers and competitors will respond to actions they take. Further, it seems likely that some banks will pull out, or back, from some product lines and customer bases. But, none of the banks want to be the first mover in walking away from customers, in case it will turn out that they could have profitably retained them in the long run. This is causing prices and capital allocation moves to be spread out over several years, even once it is clear that regulatory changes will require action.

Is it difficult or unappealing to raise new capital in the short run? One of the worst arguments industry advocates sometimes make is that banks cannot ever raise capital levels sufficiently to provide the full level of credit that authorities want and therefore higher capital requirements will reduce lending sharply. In the long run, this is nonsense. Higher capital costs may shift the competitive dynamic of who provides credit. Further, higher overall credit pricing in the financial sector, for banks and non-banks, may reduce borrowing demand. However, there is plenty of room for capital to be re-allocated to and within the financial sector if it can be profitably employed, so price adjustment should be much more important, in the long run, than changes in availability.

However, this argument is much more convincing in the transition period. Even in the short run, considerable capital could be raised if it were economic to employ it. But, it takes time to re-deploy funds to the banking sector, given the opacity of banks, the problems they are still working through, and the many short-term risks of litigation, fines, regulatory changes, political risks, etc. Adding to this the inertia in bank and investor views about acceptable pricing of bank stocks makes it all the harder.

It appears that profitability of US banks is high enough, and there are sufficient alternatives from non-banks and markets, that the regulatory reforms are not dramatically reducing credit availability during the transition period. (There may well be effects, but they are not dramatic and obvious.) Europe may be a different story. There is a lot else going on there, economically and politically, to hold down credit growth, but it also appears that the need to adjust capital ratios is a significant factor in the short run.

Are there difficulties in shifting funding among liabilities in the short run? This is something of an open question, especially in Europe. It may be that there are insufficient sources of long-term funding for banks and that this will create transitional issues until markets adjust.

Are return expectations of funders rigid in the short run? I strongly believe that equity and debt investors in the long run will lower their return requirements for banks as it becomes clear that they are safer and their earnings less volatile. It is less clear how much inertia there is in these requirements and at what pace the reduction will occur. This is further confused by many short-term risks faced by banks (litigation, fines, etc.) that should temporarily raise return requirements, and hurt stock prices.

What are the effects of the macro-environment, including monetary policy? These regulatory changes are occurring at the same time as we have highly unusual monetary policy conditions and have had unusual fiscal policies. In Europe, there are also many political and economic factors confusing things. To take one fairly specific example of the interaction of the larger environment and Basel III, liquidity is so cheaply and easily available from central banks that it certainly alters the response of banks to the new liquidity and asset-liability management rules. This makes it harder to tell what the effects of those rules will become.

Do low policy interest rates reduce the ability of central banks to offset increases in credit spreads? Even if one accepts that central banks can normally offset higher credit spreads by reducing base interest rates, this is impossible if the rates are already zero. Thus, one enters into a whole realm of discussion about unconventional monetary policies when considering the transition period.

Conclusions

In sum, it is a very difficult task to estimate the economic effects of the new financial reforms. Judgments must be made anyway, since cost-benefit analysis is critical, but those judgments will necessarily have a substantial subjective element.

Nonetheless, we can draw some broad conclusions, which are supported by the best quantitative analyses that have been done. First, the reforms almost certainly slow down the economy at least slightly in normal years, serving as a kind of insurance payment for protection against severely bad outcomes in crisis years. Second, the first-order costs of the reforms should be far outweighed by the financial stability benefits. What is harder to tell is whether there are insidious second- and third-order effects that more than offset these. I do not believe so, but it is possible to construct a scenario in which, for example, the bulk of banking business moves over time into the shadow banking sector and the aggregate financial stability risks in this sector turn out to be larger than the risks that would have existed in the banking sector absent the reforms. In my view, the reforms are intelligently constructed and sufficiently moderate to avoid such an outcome, but one cannot be totally sure. Luckily, it will be possible to moderate or add to the recent reforms if signs develop of such a bad outcome.

My own rough quantifications, shown in most detail in ESS, suggest that the *long-term* costs of financial reform are relatively small in terms of the economy as a whole and are far outweighed by the benefits.

I have not attempted to quantify the *transition* costs and do not believe it can be done with much accuracy *a priori*. However, the good news is that it appears that financial reform is not substantially slowing down the overall economy during the transition period, which we are well into already. I am certain there are *some* negative effects on economic growth, but my judgment is that these are not large once they are separated out from changes to the financial sector that would have occurred regardless of new regulation. Further, the effects would appear to be largest in Europe, but much of that probably results from the Euro Crisis, on top of the market-driven changes to capital levels and business models that would have been more severe in Europe anyway. (I do not personally believe that the pre-crisis European banking model of carrying very large balance sheets balanced by perceived very low asset risks can work now that we understand how difficult it is to be sure that the assets carry that little risk.)

References

Elliott, D. J. (2013), "Higher Bank Capital Requirements Would Come at a Price," The Brookings Institution, February 20. Available at: http://www.brookings.edu/research/papers/2013/02/20-bank-capital-requirements-elliott.

Elliott, D. J., S. Salloy and A. O. Santos (2012), "Assessing the Cost of Financial Regulation," IMF Working Paper 12/233.

Santos, A. Oliveira and D. J. Elliott (2012), "Estimating the Cost of Financial Regulation," IMF Staff Discussion Note 12/11.

Part VII
Long-term Cumulative Steady State Outcome of Reforms — Future Concerns?

Some Effects of Capital Regulation When There are Competing, Nonbank Lenders
— CHAPTER 22

■ Mark J. Flannery
US Securities and Exchange Commission and the University of Florida

Bank regulations introduced in response to the 2008–9 financial crisis have increasingly constrained banking firms' ability to keep risks on their balance sheets. The increase in minimum capital requirements (Basel III) has attracted much of the attention. The US Comprehensive Capital Analysis and Review (CCAR) intensifies the impact of higher minimum capital ratios by predicating capital assessments on the anticipated future losses from a bank's book of business. Beyond capital regulation, bank funding costs have risen due to higher FDIC premium rates for deposit insurance and an expanded assessment base. Most recently,

Mark J. Flannery is Chief Economist and Director of the Division of Economic and Risk Analysis at the US Securities and Exchange Commission, and the Bank of America Eminent Scholar in Finance at the University of Florida. The Securities and Exchange Commission, as a matter of policy, disclaims responsibility for any private publication or statement by any of its employees. The views expressed herein are those of the author and do not necessarily reflect the views of the Commission or of the author's colleagues upon the staff of the Commission. The author would like to thank Tanju Yoralmazer for many constructive suggestions about the model underlying this paper's discussion.

minimum liquidity requirements is intended to reduce the banking system's ability to provide liquidity to the nonfinancial sector. The net effect of these changes will be to drive some lending and liquidity provision outside the traditional banking system. Higher liquidity and capital requirements have the immediate effect of transferring risk from taxpayers to bank shareholders, but they will also affect shareholders' risk-taking incentives. It therefore remains uncertain whether the banks' ensuing portfolio changes leave them more or less prone to default.

This paper considers the extent to which restrictive regulations will transfer traditional bank risks to other lending venues. Many evaluations of new regulatory restrictions ignore the fact that most banking services can be provided via alternative institutional mechanisms, of which regulated banks constitute only one possibility (Merton 1995). To the extent that the bank intermediation channel becomes more expensive, less regulated institutional arrangements will expand at the expense of traditional banks.

'Shadow' banking commonly refers to loan channels that do not directly involve financing by regulated banks. Alternatively, we could contrast 'nonbank' lending with regulated banks' lending. Nonbank institutions include ongoing firms with no access to the federal safety net and no (little) capital regulation (e.g. Blackrock or GE Capital). Special purpose vehicles (SPV) also substitute for bank credit by securitizing portfolios of loans underwritten by a variety of entities, both regulated and unregulated. Where underwriting can rely entirely on hard information, scale economies encourage specialized underwriters to sell loans to SPVs. In other words, the underwriting process can be 'commoditized'. Conventional banks have little comparative advantage in making these 'hard information' loans, as evidenced by the prominence of SPVs in financing (among other things) home mortgages, credit cards, and auto loans. These consumer loans constitute a large component of the banks' historical lending. Bond market competition drove most high-quality corporate borrowers out of the banks in the 1980s. Recently, nonbanks have increasingly financed lower-quality borrowers as well: syndicated bank loans find increasing acceptance in

SPVs selling collateralized loan obligations (CLOs) and in specialized mutual funds.

Looking forward, minimum bank liquidity requirements will enhance the ability of SPVs to fund their portfolios with short-maturity liabilities. Because the banks will curtail their liquidity provision to the nonfinancial sector, investors will be more interested in buying 'quasi liquid', short-term liabilities offered by SPVs. These liabilities are relatively cheap because they compensate investors partly with (promised) ready access to their funds. In other words, tighter bank regulations simultaneously push loan business out of the regulated sector and increase the unregulated sector's ability to finance itself with cheap, short-term liabilities.[1]

Few authors have fully recognized that the competition between regulated banks and unregulated (or less regulated) nonbank lenders importantly affects the impact of bank regulatory changes on the financial system. The effect of tighter bank restrictions on the financial system's stability depends how such restrictions affect the displacement of bank lending into nonbank channels. Despite operating without formal safety net support, shadow banking institutions' actions might have detrimental effects on regulated banks and/or the overall financial system, particularly in a crisis.

This paper is organized as follows. Section I derives a competitive, 'free market' cost of funding a portfolio of homogeneous loans. The next section combines these funding costs with regulatory capital requirements and evaluates the effects of higher bank capital requirements on bank risk and on the financial sector's composition of regulated vs. unregulated lending. Section III discusses the implications of a large nonbank financing sector for financial stability. The paper concludes with a brief summary of the main implications of including nonbank competitors in a model of bank regulation.

---

[1] Perotti (2015) describes the economic forces underlying the emergence of shadow banking in general, while Maes (2015) describes the sector as it has evolved in Europe.

I. A Model of Loan Rate Determination

I present a 'functional' model of lending that can be applied to either banks or nonbanks.[2] In the interests of brevity, I make some simplifying assumptions. First, lenders compete to make two types of loans. Loan defaults are somewhat correlated within each type, giving each loan portfolio an irreducible uncertainty about its ultimate payoff. One loan type has a 'low' portfolio variance; the other loan type has a 'high' variance. Second, lenders finance themselves (only) with a combination of equity and debt. Third, operational lending costs are zero for both types of lenders. Fourth, I measure loan pricing as the expected net return on a portfolio of homogeneous loans. (Lenders can estimate an expected portfolio return from the loans' contract rates.) Fifth, each loan type's portfolio uncertainty is uncorrelated with the other types and with overall market returns. A lender therefore requires only that the loan portfolio's expected return at least equal its cost of funds. Finally, I assume perfect competition in the market for each type of loan. One might change any of these simplifying assumptions without compromising the model's basic implications.

The Modigliani–Miller (MM) Propositions describe the terms on which an unregulated nonbank can lend when it is subject only to market constraints on its funding and underwriting decisions. If corporate interest payments are not tax deductible, a firm's combination of debt and equity financing does not affect its overall cost of funds (WACC). Regulatory capital requirements would therefore have no effect on a bank's loan pricing. However, with tax-deductible corporate interest payments, the lower line in Figure 1 indicates that a lender's WACC falls continuously as leverage rises.[3] The probability of default (PD) also rises with leverage but MM assumes that debt investors will always accept a higher promised payment in return for a higher default probability. In other words, investors holding diversified portfolios are

---

[2] Merton (1995, pg. 23) states that "The functional perspective takes as given the economic functions performed by financial intermediaries and asks what is the best institutional structure to perform those functions."

[3] Some might argue that debt interest payments should not be deductible. But they are. In addition, financial costs can generate an interior leverage ratio at which the firm's WACC is minimized.

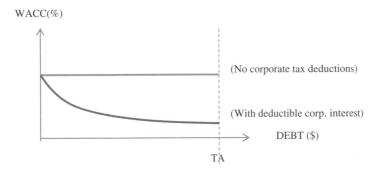

WACC(%)

(No corporate tax deductions)

(With deductible corp. interest)

DEBT ($)

TA

Figure 1. Modigliani-Miller implications for an unregulated firm's financing costs.

relatively indifferent to the failure of any specific obligor. Finance theory does not predict which leverage ratio in Figure 1 will be chosen, but all nonbank lenders will operate with the same leverage because they can survive only if their funding costs are no higher than that of their competitors.

During the financial crisis, short-term liability investors failed to behave according to the theoretical irrelevance of bond default risk. Rather, there were many circumstances in which firms could not roll over debt – particularly short-term debt. Some of these cases involved a substantial chance that the borrowing firm was insolvent. In other cases, the short-term market's alleged 'illiquidity' or 'frozenness' reflected investors' unwillingness to bear more than minimal default risk. In other words, short-term liability-holders behaved more like Merton's (1995) 'customers' than 'investors'.[4] For example, repo investors during the crisis generally sought some return on their funds, but repayment of principal was preeminent. Higher expected interest payments had very little effect on their willingness to accept default risk exposure. At the same time, nonbanks wished to fund themselves with

---

[4] In Merton's framework, investors are willing to accept properly-compensated default risks because they hold diversified portfolios, while a financial firm's customers must accept default risk exposure in order to obtain a financial service (e.g. insurance or a checking account). Undiversified customers are much more averse to default risk than investors are.

substantial amounts of short-term liabilities because their expected liquidity reduced the required explicit interest rate.

This 'disconnect' between traditional corporate finance and our financing experience during the crisis can be modeled as short-term investors tolerating no more than a small (α) probability of default. In other words, investors know the risk characteristics of a firm's asset portfolio and they will lend at the riskless rate only if its PD < α.[5] Holding constant the asset portfolio, a nonbank's default probability rises with its leverage:

$$PD = f(lev, \sigma), f_1 > 0 \text{ and } f_2 > 0. \tag{1}$$

where lev = that ratio of debt to total assets, and
 σ is the loan portfolio's return standard deviation (volatility).

Assume that short-term investors refuse to purchase liabilities from an overly levered borrower whose liabilities are not insured. That is, investors require that leverage be low enough that

$$PD = f(lev, \sigma) < \alpha. \tag{2}$$

Invert (2) to get an expression for the maximum leverage at which a nonbank can finance itself:[6]

$$lev^{max} = \alpha(\sigma), \alpha' < 0. \tag{3}$$

Figure 2 illustrates how a portfolio's aggregate volatility determines how much leverage a nonbank can use to finance itself with short-term, quasi-liquid liabilities. The higher-volatility portfolio permits a lower maximum leverage, which corresponds to a higher minimum funding cost. These leverage limits directly imply the minimum rate a lender must charge on loans of each risk. In an unregulated market, therefore,

---

[5] This behavior resembles the 'neglected risk' model in Gennaoili et al. (2012), which assumes that investors demanding certain repayment overlook some crucial risk that can subsequently turn out badly enough to trigger a financial crisis.

[6] In a multi-period context, the SPV's preferred leverage ratio would reflect not only the current asset volatility, but also possible future changes in the asset portfolio's value or return volatility.

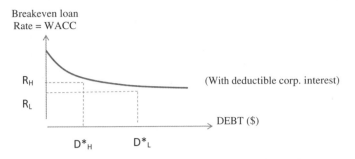

Breakeven loan
Rate = WACC

R_H

R_L

(With deductible corp. interest)

DEBT ($)

D^*_H D^*_L

Figure 2. Unique leverage limits imposed by short-term investors seeking liquidity.

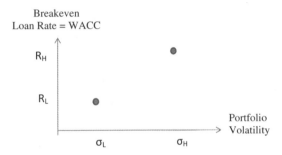

Breakeven
Loan Rate = WACC

R_H

R_L

Portfolio
Volatility

σ_L σ_H

Figure 3. Market-determined loan rates vary with irreducible portfolio risk.

lenders operate with the breakeven loan rates shown in Figure 3. The WACC for a portfolio composed of both low- and high-risk loans will be a linear combination of the two indicated loan rates because the two portfolios' returns are assumed to be uncorrelated.

II. Minimum Capital Requirements and Bank Lending

In order to study the interactions between regulated bank lenders and their nonbank competitors, I have assumed that the risk features of nonbank portfolios are known to potential investors, and that non-banks and regulated banks can underwrite and collect loan proceeds equally well. Both banks and nonbanks finance themselves largely with short-term, money-like debt, reflecting investors' willingness to pay

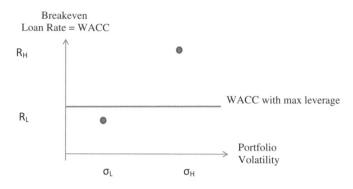

Figure 4. Regulated banks' funding costs vary less with portfolio risk.

a premium for such obligations. Regulated banks confront no leverage constraint like (3) on account of actual or conjectured liability insurance. Therefore, a regulated bank's WACC is determined by the minimum required amount of capital (maximum permissible leverage) set by regulators, as shown by the horizontal line in Figure 4.[7] Competition from unregulated nonbanks means that the maximum feasible loan rates on low-risk and high-risk loans are determined by nonbanks subject to a PD < α restriction.

Some commenters have derived or imagined a situation like Figure 4 and concluded that banks cannot profitably finance low-risk loans or that an increase in a bank's WACC implies that bank loan rates must rise.[8] This is not necessarily correct. The bank's capital ratio determines the required breakeven rate on the *average* loan. Bank shareholders can profitably finance a portfolio of low- and high-risk loans for which its total revenue at least covers its cost of funds. That is, if

$$w_L R_L + \left(1 - w_L\right) R_H \geq WACC_{RB} \tag{4}$$

[7] Absent perfect and comprehensive liability insurance, the WACC line for a regulated bank would increase with portfolio risk. The requirement for my story to go through is that the bank's slope is flatter than that of the unregulated nonbanks' slope.

[8] Some analysts (Hanson *et al.* 2010; Elliott 2009) ignore the potential for outside competition in pricing loans. A higher capital requirement therefore leaves the banks' loan portfolio unchanged and loan rates must rise to cover the banks' increased WACC.

where w_i is the portfolio weight invested in high-risk ($i = H$) or low-risk ($i = L$) loans, R_i is the breakeven loan rate on loans of risk i for non-banks, from Figure 3, and $WACC_{RB}$ is the minimum attainable WACC for a regulated bank (given its minimum capital ratio).

Re-arranging (4), we get the maximum amount of low-risk loans a regulated bank can afford to hold in its portfolio

$$w_L \leq \frac{R_H - WACC_{RB}}{R_H - R_L} \geq 0 \qquad (5)$$

Equation (5) indicates that banks with a relatively high equity requirement ($WACC_{RB}$) can still profitably fund some low-risk loans, but a higher capital requirement reduces the proportion of low-risk loans it can profitably finance. (That is, $\frac{\partial w_L}{\partial WACC_{RB}} < 0$.) Figure 5 illustrates this effect.

Although (5) indicates that an insured and regulated bank could hold some low-risk loans in its portfolio, would it choose to do so? The usual moral hazard story suggests not. In a single-period model, bankers would choose the highest attainable portfolio risk, which here implies a concentration in high-risk loans. But risk-maximization may not be optimal in a multi-period setting (Marcus 1984). Uninsured bank liability-holders could also discourage risk-taking by demanding higher

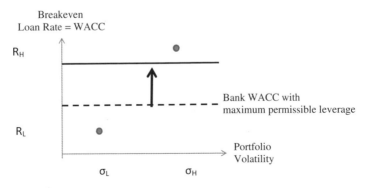

Figure 5. Higher capital requirement reduces a bank's ability to fund low-risk loans.

promised rates to compensate for higher default risk. If a bank finds it optimal to hold some low-risk loans, its required capital ratio determines the banks' portfolio composition, but <u>not</u> the pricing of low-risk loans — which is set by unregulated nonbanks. The combination of higher portfolio risk and higher capital affects the bank's default probability ambiguously.[9]

The banks' shift away from low-risk loans increases their collective demand for high-risk loans, for which there is no competitive demand from nonbanks in Figure 4. Increased competition among regulated banks would tend to push down R_H when bank capital ratios rise. The banks might also adjust loan terms (removing covenants or lower down payment requirements) to shift σ_H to the right.

III. Financial Stability Effects

The nonbanks modelled here accept maturity transformation risk that creates a potential for subsequent fire sales. This possibility is most readily illustrated with SPV financing (Covitz *et al.* 2013). The pressure to shift some loan funding into the nonbank sector will be more intense when private investors view those loans as having particularly low risk. If short-term investors believe that σ_L is cyclically low, they will lend even to highly-levered nonbanks, and nonbank shareholders will have the highest expected returns if they operate with maximum permissible leverage.[10] High nonbank leverage means a low competitive loan rate, and regulated banks' can afford to hold fewer low-risk loans.

If the loan portfolio's perceived volatility of returns (σ) subsequently rises enough or the perceived value of loans subsequently falls enough, the SPV's capital will become insufficient to roll over short-term funding.

---

[9] Kahane (1977) and Kim and Santomero (1988) also conclude that the effect of capital on PD is ambiguous.

[10] I am not suggesting that short-term investors consider only the current σ_L value when evaluating equation (2). With multi-period loans, an SPV's organizer would choose an initial leverage that is likely to withstand some increase (decrease) in asset volatility (loan values), but the pressure to minimize equity in the capital structure would assure that some extreme parameter changes would make short-term debtholders run.

Through equation (1), a sufficient fall in portfolio value or an increase in return volatility would raise the PD above α for the nonbanks' senior claims. While a regular firm (such as GE Capital) might hope to retain earnings, issue additional equity or cover its liability outflow with principal repayments, an SPV's only option will be to sell assets (Covitz *et al.* 2013). If only a few SPVs are affected, their asset sales should have little effect on market prices. But if the portfolio deterioration is widespread (across many nonbanks simultaneously), forced asset sales carry the potential for fire-sale losses and their attendant deadweight costs.[11] Fire sale losses require large aggregate SPV liquidations, although each individual SPV could be quite small.

A purchaser of liquidated assets must have both funding and underwriting expertise. Strahan and Gatev (2006), and Gatev *et al.* (2009) have shown that funds tend to flow into large banks when uncertainty increases in the financial markets. If the regulated banks were then operating with a capital buffer (Flannery and Rangan 2008), they could accept the new deposits and use them to finance the SPVs' assets. (The banks' government guarantees make it easier for them to continue operating even with a reduced capital ratio.) However, this solution will be infeasible if the banking sector's size has been severely diminished by high minimum required capital ratios. In other words, the imposition of higher capital ratios might make the banking system safer, but it can simultaneously increase the overall financial system's exposure to large asset price disturbances. Luck and Schempp (2014) also conclude that financial stability decreases with the relative size of the nonbank lending sector.

A competitive nonbank lending sector also affects the cyclicality of bank capital standards. When the outlook is sunny, loan portfolio risk looks low and nonbanks underprice regulated banks in the new loan market. But when loan portfolio risk looks high, the regulated banking system originates more new loans and the nonbank sector shrinks.

Finally, note that the competitiveness of nonbank lenders can be affected through regulators' control over the banks. Cetorelli and

---

[11] In some models of asset fire sales, the deadweight cost comes from a limited supply of asset management expertise elsewhere in the economy (Acharya and Yorulmazer 2008; Acharya *et al.* 2010; and, Hanson *et al.* 2014).

Peristiani (2012) show that many nonbank activities are directly supported by regulated banks, through loan originations, SPV portfolio selection, and (probably most important) liquidity guarantees that support the SPVs' quasi-liquid liabilities. Imposing a high capital requirement on such lines of credit would severely constrain the nonbanks' ability to finance themselves with short-term funding. To the extent that regulators wish to limit nonbanks' absolute or cyclical importance, they presently have the required tools in hand.

Summary and Conclusions

Enhanced post-crisis bank regulations have raised the cost of providing credit through the regulated banking channel. Banks can now hold less risk on their balance sheets, and they can provide less liquidity to the nonfinancial sector. Substitutes for both of these services are available from the nonbank sector, which operates with less regulation but also less of a federal safety net. Recognizing the competitive effects of nonbank lenders enriches our understanding of how tighter bank restrictions affect bank and financial sector stability.

I present a simple model in which both banks and nonbanks issue liquid, short-term liabilities to finance longer term loans. Formal deposit insurance permits regulated banks to borrow at the riskless rate regardless of their failure probabilities. However, capital requirements determine the regulated banks' minimum feasible cost of funds (WACC). Nonbanks can issue cheap, quasi-liquid liabilities only if their equity ratio and asset return volatility produce a sufficiently low default probability. The requirement that PD < α fixes the nonbanks' maximum leverage for any given portfolio volatility, and hence determines the cost of funding those loans.

The allocation of new loans between the regulated and the unregulated sectors depends on their relative funding costs, which in turn depend on bank capital standards and the public's perception of loan risks. An increase in bank capital forces some lower-risk loans out of the banking system, leaving an ambiguous effect of the higher capital ratios on bank default probabilities. Regardless of the relative importance of bank vs. nonbank lending, the rate on low-risk loans will be determined in the unregulated sector; in particular, a higher capital requirement does not affect the rate banks will charge on low-risk loans.

Within the regulated banking system, higher required capital causes a shift toward making riskier loans. If loan terms were exogenous, risky loan rates might fall in response to higher capital requirements. Alternatively, the banks' need to hold a higher proportion of high-yielding loans may lead them to increase loan risks, for example by lending with fewer covenants, lower FICO scores, or lower mortgage down-payments.

Finally, the existence of a competitive nonbank lending channel affects the cyclical availability of credit. If investors perceive low loan risks, the nonbanks' funding costs will be low and the banks will move into riskier assets. Low perceived risks, however, permit a large increase in highly-levered, nonbank loans. By contrast, when investors perceive higher risks (loan portfolio volatility), lending moves back into the banking system but the effect on credit is muted by the banks' risk-insensitive funding costs. In short, the competition between bank and nonbank lenders expands credit during 'good' times and limits the fall in credit during 'bad' times, relative to what we would see with only a bank lending channel.

The model underlying these conclusions relies on a number of simpli fying assumptions. It would be worthwhile to examine the effect of generalizing the model. For example, how would the implications of tighter capital regulation differ if new equity could enter the lending industry and investors could choose between financing bank vs. nonbank lending channels? Another interesting question is how higher capital requirements would affect bank default probabilities if there were a continuum of asset risks, instead of the two discrete risks assumed here.

References

Acharya, V. V. and T. Yorulmazer (2008), "Cash-in-the-market Pricing and Optimal Resolution Of Bank Failures," *Review of Financial Studies*, 21(6): 2705–2742.

Acharya, V. V., H. S. Shin and T. Yorulmazer (2010), "Crisis Resolution and Bank Liquidity," *Review of Financial Studies*, 24(6): 2166–2205.

Cetorelli, N. and S. Peristiani (2012), "The Role of Banks in Asset Securitization, Federal Reserve Bank of New York," *Federal Reserve Bank of New York Economic Policy Review*, July: 47–63.

Covitz, D., N. Liang and G. A. Suarez (2013), "The Evolution of a Financial Crisis: Collapse of the asset-backed commercial paper market," *The Journal of Finance*, 68(3): 815–848.

Elliott, D. (2009), "Quantifying the Effects on Lending of Increased Capital Requirements," The Pew Financial Reform Project as Briefing Paper #7.

Flannery, M. J. and K. Rangan (2008), "What Caused the Bank Capital Build-up of the 1990s?" *Review of Finance*, 12: 391–429.

Gatev, E., T. Schuermann and P. E. Strahan (2009), "Managing Bank Liquidity Risk: How Deposit-Loan Synergies Vary with Market Conditions," *Review of Financial Studies*, 22(3): 995–1020.

Gennaiolia, N., A. Shleifer and R. Vishny (2012), "Neglected Risks, Financial Innovation, and Financial Fragility," *Journal of Financial Economics*, 104(3): 452–468.

Hanson, S., A. Kashyap and J. Stein (2010), "An Analysis of the Impact of 'Substantially Heightened' Capital Requirements on Large Financial Institutions," The Clearing House Association Unpublished Paper.

Hanson, S. G., A. Shleifer, J. C. Stein and R. W. Vishny (2014), "Banks as Patient Fixed-Income Investors," Harvard University working paper, August.

Kahane, Y. (1977), "Capital Adequacy and the Regulation of Financial Intermediaries," *Journal of Banking and Finance*, 1(2): 207–218.

Kim, D. S. and A. M. Santomero (1988), "Risk in Banking and Capital Regulation," *Journal of Finance*, 43(5): 1219–1233.

Luck, S. and P. Schempp (2014), Banks, Shadow Banking, and Fragility, ECB Working Paper Series No. 1726.

Maes, S. (2015), "Shadow Banking: An European perspective." In S. Claessens, D. Evanoff, G. Kaufman and L. Laeven (eds.) *Shadow Banking Within and Across National Borders*, Singapore: World Scientific, pp. 347–372.

Marcus, A. J. (1984), "Deregulation and Bank Financial Policy," *Journal of Banking and Finance*, 8(4): 557–565.

Merton, R. C. (1995), "A Functional Perspective of Financial Intermediation," *Financial Management*, 24(2): 23–41.

Perotti, E. (2015), "The Roots of Shadow Banking," In S. Claessens, D. Evanoff, G. Kaufman and L. Laeven (eds.) *Shadow Banking Within and Across National Borders*, Singapore: World Scientific, pp. 249–264.

Strahan, P. and E. Gatev (2006), "Banks' Advantage in Hedging Liquidity Risk: Theory and evidence from the commercial paper market," *The Journal of Finance*, 61(2): 867–892.

The Steady State of the Banking Union

— CHAPTER 23

■ Dirk Schoenmaker

VU University Amsterdam and Duisenberg School of Finance

Introduction

The 4th of November 2014 is a memorable day with the start of the Banking Union (BU). It is a milestone in European financial integration after the establishment of the Economic and Monetary Union (EMU) on the 1st of January 1999. Next milestones may be a Capital Markets Union and an Insurance Union.

The establishment of the BU creates a large sub-market within the European Union (EU), comparable to the US banking market. It is expected that the BU will become an integrated market, where banks can manage their balance sheet at the aggregate BU level and the ECB conducts supervision with a European perspective. But national supervisors may still prevent European banks to operate on a European scale, as they informally request banks to lend or invest in the same country as where deposits are collected.

Dirk Schoenmaker is Dean of the Duisenberg School of Finance, Professor of Finance and Banking at the VU University Amsterdam, and a member of the Advisory Scientific Committee of the European Systemic Risk Board at the ECB. He is grateful to Floris van Ham for research assistance on mergers & acquisitions and to Louis Pauly for valuable discussions on the future of the Banking Union.

Moving to the demand side, it may take some time before consumers regard a bank from elsewhere in the BU as a 'domestic' bank to which they can entrust their money. When that happens, a truly integrated retail banking market will emerge. Corporates, especially the larger ones, are expected to adapt faster and select their main banks from across the BU.

Banking Systems at Country Level

The EU banking system can be split into the BU and the non-BU countries. Table 1 indicates that the BU covers about 75% of total EU banking assets.[1] The BU countries have relatively closed banking markets, with assets of banks from other EU countries at 14% and from third countries at 3%. The overall cross-border penetration for the EU is higher, due to the UK with business from third countries at 28% (see Table A.1 in Annex 1). This highlights the current status of London as

Table 1. Banking systems across three regions: BU, EU and US; 2013.

	Number of banks	Total assets in € billion	Home (in %)	Of which: Other EU (in %)	Third country (in %)
BU	5,999	30,035	83	14	3
Non-BU	1,724	12,008	60	19	21
EU	7,723	42,043	77	15	8
US	6,813	11,862	86	—	14

Note: Total banking assets come from the home country, other EU countries, and third countries (i.e. outside the EU or the US). The three components add up to 100%.
Source: Author calculations based on ECB for European banks and Federal Reserve, FDIC and Flow of Funds for US banks.

---

[1] In this chapter, we use country data from the Monetary Financial Institutions (MFIs) of the ECB, which can be split into credit institutions and money market mutual funds. These country data on credit institutions can be combined with the Structural Financial Indicators of the ECB to calculate the geographical segmentation over domestic, other EU and third country. The ECB (2014) uses the Consolidated Banking Statics in its Banking Structures Report, but this dataset is not complete (some small banks are lacking) and does not allow for geographical segmentation of all EU countries.

international financial centre. Will London continue to service the BU, or will Frankfurt emerge as the financial centre of the BU?

The BU banking system is comparable to that of the US in several ways. The number of banks is about 6,000 (see Table 1). The system has a strong domestic orientation with 84% of all assets, while 16% of assets come from other EU and third countries. Foreign bank affiliates account for 14% of the US banking system. But there is an important difference. The US banking system has fewer assets, €12 trillion (amounting to 97% of US GDP) compared to the BU with €30 trillion (amounting to 313% of euro area GDP). The US financial system depends less on bank intermediation and more on capital markets and non-bank financial institutions.

Major Banks

The major banks in the BU and the US are also comparable. Figure 1 shows the geographical segmentation of the top 20 banks in the three

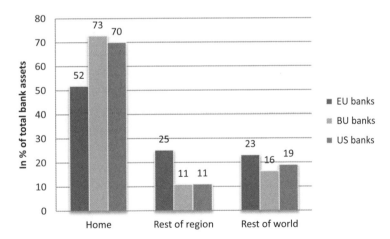

Figure 1. Geographic segmentation of top 20 banks in the EU, BU, and US (in %), 2013.

Note: Total assets of the top 20 banks are segmented into domestic, rest of the region and rest of the world.
Source: Assets are taken from The Banker (July 2014). The segmentation of assets is calculated by the author based on annual reports.

regions (EU, BU and US). The large BU and US banks have just over 70 per cent of their assets at home (i.e. the BU and the US, respectively). The rest of the region (i.e. the rest of Europe — the non-BU part — and the rest of North and South America) counts for 11%, while the rest of the world amounts to about 18%. The large EU banks are more international. They have not only a smaller home base (one country), but they have also more business in the rest of the world. Examples of major global banks outside the BU are HSBC, Barclays and Standard Chartered from the UK.

The picture emerging from our analysis at country and bank level is that the BU, just like the US, is a relatively closed banking system with limited inward and outward expansion.

The European Union Banking Landscape

Zooming in on the European banking landscape, banks can be divided into four categories depending on the international composition of their assets (Schoenmaker 2013). Table A.2 (in Annex 1) shows the biggest 30 banks in Europe before the start of the BU. A global bank has less than 50% of its assets in the home country and the majority of its international assets in the rest of the world. These banks include HSBC, Barclays and Standard Chartered from the UK, Deutsche Bank from Germany, and Credit Suisse and UBS from Switzerland.

A European bank has less than 50% of its assets in the home country and the majority of its international assets in the rest of Europe. Some European banks focus on a specific region in the EU. The Nordea Group, for example, primarily operates in the Nordic countries. Other European banks operate Europe-wide; examples include BNP Paribas, UniCredit, and ING.

A semi-international bank has between 50% and 75% of its assets in the home country. Examples are RBS from the UK, BBVA from Spain, Commerzbank from Germany and KBC from Belgium. Finally, a domestic bank has more than 75% of its assets in the home country. These banks include Crédit Agricole, Lloyds Banking Group, Rabobank and Intesa Sanpaolo.

The New Landscape

The start of the BU entails a paradigm shift for banks and policymakers. The home market expands for banks from their country to the wider BU. This paper presents new data on the top 20 banks in the emerging BU market. Table 2 contains the geographic segmentation, splitting a bank's business in the BU, the rest of Europe (i.e. business in the non-BU member states), and the rest of the world.

Some of the European banks operating on a regional basis (the second group in Table A.2) have now become pan-Banking Union banks. BNP Paribas, UniCredit and ING Bank operate throughout the BU, with 65% to 80% of their assets in the BU. These banks are comparable with the super-regional banks in the US, such as Bank of America (see below), with a large presence across the whole region. Also the semi-international and domestic banks (the third and fourth group in Table A.2) have become large players in the BU.

The market share of the biggest banks in the BU lingers around 2% to 5%, which is low (see the second column in Table 2). The top 5 banks by market share are four French banks (i.e. Crédit Agricole, BNP Paribas, Société Générale and Groupe BPCE) and a German bank (i.e. Deutsche Bank). The market share of the 20 biggest banks amounts to 37%. The prominent position of the French banks is due to their large presence across the BU, ranging from 66 to 89 per cent. By contrast, Deutsche Bank is more international with a strong presence in London and the US, but only 46% in BU. Furthermore, the major Spanish banks, Banco Santander and BBVA, have a strong presence in London (for Santander), the US and South America.

Consolidation Ahead?

Further consolidation within the BU can be expected. The market share of the five biggest banks (CR5) in the BU is 18% (see Table 2). To compare, the CR5 is 47% for the EU-15 countries and 48% for the US. Even in a large country with a dispersed banking system, like Germany, the CR5 is over 30%. The major US banks were formed after the lifting

Table 2.   Top 20 banks in BU, 2013.

Banking Group	Market share in Banking Union in %	Total assets in € bn	Of which Banking Union in %	Of which Rest of Europe in %	Of which Rest of world in %
1. Crédit Agricole	5.0	1,707	89	3	8
2. BNP Paribas	4.0	1,800	66	12	22
3. Société Générale	3.4	1,235	82	7	11
4. Groupe BPCE	3.1	1,124	84	4	12
5. Deutsche Bank	2.5	1,612	46	12	42
6. UniCredit	2.3	846	82	17	1
7. Crédit Mutuel	2.1	659	94	1	5
8. ING Bank	2.0	788	76	10	14
9. Intesa Sanpaolo	1.9	626	92	6	2
10. Rabobank	1.8	674	80	2	18
11. Banco Santander	1.3	1,116	34	37	30
12. Commerzbank	1.1	550	63	21	16
13. DZ Bank	1.1	387	87	7	6
14. La Caixa Group	1.1	351	96	2	2
15. ABN AMRO	1.1	372	90	3	7
16. BBVA	1.1	583	57	3	40
17. Landesbank Baden-Würt.	0.8	274	85	8	7
18. Bayerische Landesbank	0.7	256	83	10	7
19. KBC Group	0.6	241	72	26	3
20. Erste Group	0.4	200	56	41	3
Top 20 banks	37.3	15,400	73	11	16

Note: A bank's market share in BU is calculated as a bank's assets in the BU divided by total banking assets in BU (€ 30,035 bn from Table 1). A bank's total assets are divided into assets in the BU, in the rest of Europe, and the rest of the world. The top 20 is ranked by market share.

Source: Assets are taken from The Banker (July 2014). The segmentation of assets is calculated by the author based on annual reports.

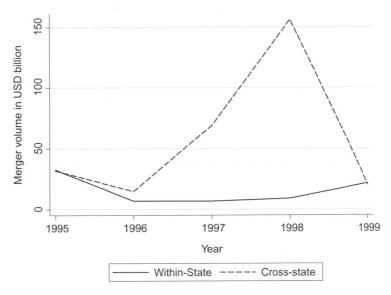

Figure 2. US merger volumes after the Riegle–Neal deregulation (in US$ bn).
Source: Van Ham (2014).

of restrictions on interstate banking by the Riegle-Neal Interstate Banking and Branching Efficiency Act of 1994 (Brook *et al.* 1998). Through several mergers and acquisitions, super-regional banks, such as JPMorgan Chase and Bank of America, emerged with a market share of 13% and 11%, respectively.[2] Stiroh and Strahan (2003) provide interesting evidence on consolidation after the deregulation. They show a competitive reallocation of assets to better performers. Better banks did grow, while the poorly performing banks shrank as well, and those with the worst performance shrank the most. Figure 2 illustrates the cross-state merger wave after the Riegle-Neal Act (see Annex 2 on the bank merger data). A large increase in cross-state mergers is observed, while the volume of within state mergers is relatively flat.

Similarly, the BU may act as a catalyst for change. While there is not much scope for domestic consolidation in most European countries,

---

[2] Federal law prevents any bank from gaining more than 10% of national deposits in the US through acquisition.

there is plenty scope for cross-border consolidation, as the BU market shares are relatively low.

The Single Market in 1993 and the start of EMU in 1999 did not lead to the — at the time — widely expected European consolidation, several domestic mergers in anticipation of the new setting. Examples are the merger of ABN and AMRO in 1991 and the creation of the BNP Paribas Group from the merger of BNP and Paribas in 1999. To analyse the impact of these events, we use data for the original 11 members of the Eurozone. Figure 3 displays Eurozone merger volumes around the start of the Single Market in 1993. No large cross-border mergers with the Eurozone targets took place in the entire 5-year window around the Single Market. From 1994 onwards, however, increased domestic merger volume is observed. Figure 4 shows Eurozone merger volumes around the introduction of the euro in 1999. Large domestic merger volumes are observed in the year before and the year following the introduction of the euro. Only a small increase in cross-border merger volume is observed.

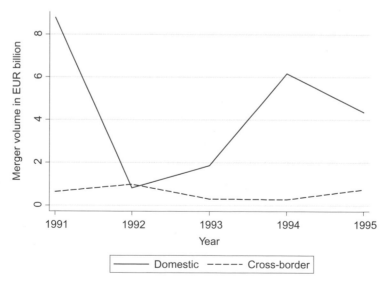

Figure 3. Eurozone merger volumes around the Single Market (in € bn).
Source: Van Ham (2014).

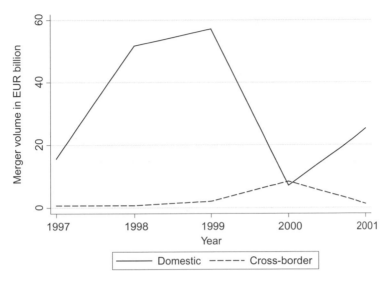

Figure 4. Eurozone merger volumes around the euro introduction (in € bn). *Source*: Van Ham (2014).

Around all three events, it seems that domestic banks acquired attractive targets before the new situation, while foreign and out-of-state targets waited until the new situation actually came into being. In part, this can be explained by the simple fact that foreign and out-of-state ownership was complicated or not allowed at all. The introduction of the euro however did not lift any formal restrictions. Rather, it seems, foreign banks waited until the new currency was actually introduced. This begs the question if the new Banking Union will have similar consequences for the economic environment of banks and similar patterns of bank takeovers may be expected.

There are diverging forces at work. On the one hand, the centralisation of supervision at the ECB as well as the harmonisation of banking regulations in the Single Rule Book may lift the final barriers to a truly integrated banking market and unleash a cross-border merger wave in European banking. On the other hand, company law, insolvency law and taxation are still organised at the national level and thus remain different. More fundamentally, crisis management arrangements are still largely organised at the national level (Schoenmaker 2015). At the time of writing (December 2014), the lender of last resort (so-called emergency liquidity assistance) and deposit insurance functions are organised at the national level. The use of the European Stability Mechanism, the ultimate fiscal backstop, for direct recapitalisation is only available when the country cannot provide the financial assistance itself (ESM 2014).[3] Just the Single Resolution Board is centralised. Political economy suggests that another banking crisis may be needed before all functions, from supervision to crisis management, are aligned at the Banking Union level.

Finally, cross-border expansion may happen in different ways. One approach would be a full merger between banks from different countries. Another approach would be a cross-border acquisition. An expanding bank may first acquire a local bank in a neighbouring BU country and then push more business through this local entity. A case in point is the acquisition of the German Direktbank by the Dutch ING bank. The renamed bank, ING DiBa, is now the third largest retail bank in Germany. A third way would be the cross-border supply of banking services, which can be easily done through Internet. An example is Wells Fargo, a US bank, which entered the Canadian market with small business loans based on credit scoring models. Wells Fargo subsequently established branches in Canada to support its business there.

The International Landscape

An international perspective can be sketched. The Financial Stability Board (FSB 2013) has produced a list of global systemically important banks, the so-called G-SIBs. These banks are the large financial players, which can pose a systemic threat to the global financial system (Bertay *et al.* 2013). Table 3 provides an overview of these G-SIBs, which have assets up to €2 trillion. Remarkably, the BU encompasses most of the G-SIBs with nine out of 29, followed by the US with eight and the UK with four. The ECB, as supervisor of the G-SIBs from the BU, will thus

---

[3] The official condition is that the country would have to be unable to provide financial assistance to the beneficiary bank without very serious effects on its own fiscal sustainability (ESM 2014).

Table 3. Global systemically important banks (G-SIBs), 2013.

Banking groups	Total assets	World assets rank	Capital surcharge	Home country	Rest of region	Rest of world
	in € bn		in %	% of total assets	% of total assets	% of total assets
Global banks						
1. HSBC (UK)	1,937	2	2.5	37	11	52
2. Deutsche Bank (BU)	1,612	10	2.0	46	12	42
3. Barclays (UK)	1,568	11	2.0	36	26	38
4. Citigroup (US)	1,364	13	2.0	43	12	45
5. UBS (Switzerland)	821	23	1,5	33	25	42
6. Credit Suisse (Switzerland)	710	25	1.5	23	22	55
7. Standard Chartered (UK)	489	42	1.0	16	5	79
Regional banks						
1. Banco Santander (BU)	1,116	18	1.0	34	37	30
2. Nordea (Sweden)	631	31	1.0	24	75	1
Semi-international banks						
1. BNP Paribas (BU)	1,800	4	2.0	66	12	22
2. Mitsubishi UFJ Financial Group (Japan)	1,778	5	1.5	66	8	26
3. JPMorgan Chase (US)	1,752	6	2.5	71	2	27
4. Bank of China (China)	1,649	9	1.0	74	16	10
5. Royal Bank of Scotland (UK)	1,228	15	1.5	61	16	23
6. Mizuho Financial Group (Japan)	1,211	16	1.0	75	5	20
7. ING Bank (BU)	788	24	1.0	75	11	14
8. Goldman Sachs (US)	661	29	1.5	53	5	42

(*Continued*)

Table 3. (*Continued*)

Banking groups	Total assets in € bn	World assets rank	Capital surcharge in %	Home country % of total assets	Rest of region % of total assets	Rest of world % of total assets
9. Morgan Stanley (US)	604	35	1.5	69	7	24
10. BBVA (BU)	583	36	1.0	57	3	40
11. Bank of New York Mellon (US)	271	68	1.0	75	1	24
Domestic banks						
1. ICBC (China)	2,248	1	1.0	94	4	2
2. Crédit Agricole (BU)	1,707	8	1.5	89	3	8
3. Bank of America (US)	1,526	12	1.5	86	2	12
4. Société Générale (BU)	1,235	14	1.0	82	7	11
5. Groupe BPCE (BU)	1,124	17	1.0	84	4	12
6. Sumitomo Mitsui Financial Group (Japan)	1,112	19	1.0	78	7	15
7. Wells Fargo & Co (US)	1,107	20	1.0	95	2	3
8. UniCredit (BU)	846	22	1.0	82	17	1
9. State Street (US)	176	96	1.0	79	9	12
Total G-SIBS	1,160			64	12	24

Notes: The second column presents the assets rank on the basis of the Top 1000 World Banks, as published in The Banker (2014). Total assets are segmented over the home country, the rest of region, and the rest of world. Total of G-SIBs is calculated as a weighted average (weighted according to assets).

Source: Schoenmaker (2013).

become a major player together with the Federal Reserve and the Bank of England in international policymaking and supervision.

References

Bertay, A. C., A. Demirguç-Kunt and H. Huizinga (2013), "Do We Need Big Banks? Evidence on Performance, Strategy and Market Discipline," *Journal of Financial Intermediation,* 22: 532–558.

Brook, Y., R. Hendershott, and D. Lee (1998), "The Gains from Takeover Deregulation: Evidence from the End Of Interstate Banking Restrictions," *Journal of Finance,* 53: 2185–2204.

European Central Bank [ECB] (2014), *Banking Structures Report,* Frankfurt am Main.

European Stability Mechanism (2014), "FAQ on the Preliminary Agreement on the Future ESM Direct Bank Recapitalization Instrument," Luxembourg: ESM, June 20.

Financial Stability Board (2013), *2013 Update of Group of Global Systemically Important Banks (G-SIBs),* Basel: FSB.

Schoenmaker, D. (2013), *Governance of International Banking: The Financial Trilemma* (New York: Oxford University Press).

Schoenmaker, D. (2015), "On the Need for a Fiscal Backstop to the Banking System," In M. Haentjes and B. Wessels (eds), *Research Handbook on Crisis Management in the Banking Sector,* Cheltenham: Edward Elgar Publishing.

Stiroh, K. and P. Strahan (2003), "Competitive Dynamics of Deregulation: Evidence from US banking," *Journal of Money, Credit, and Banking,* 35: 801–828.

The Banker (2014), *Top 1,000 World Banks,* London, July.

Van Ham, F. (2014), "Patterns of US and EU Banking Mergers around Three Deregulatory Events," MSc Thesis, Duisenberg School of Finance, Amsterdam.

Annex 1. Before the Banking Union

The Annex provides data at country and bank level before the start of the Banking Union. The geographical segmentation of assets is divided in assets from the home country, other EU countries and third countries. The three categories add up to 100%.

Table A.1. Cross-border banking penetration in EU Member States, 2013.

	Number of banks	Total assets (€ billion)	Of which		
			Home (%)	Other EU (%)	Third country (%)
Austria	731	915	76	17	7
Belgium	103	1,021	34	51	15
Bulgaria	30	47	28	69	3
Croatia	32	57	n.a.	n.a.	n.a.
Cyprus	101	90	71	13	16
Czech Republic	56	191	6	93	1
Denmark	161	1,047	81	18	1
Estonia	31	20	2	92	6
Finland	303	522	34	65	1
France	623	7,565	91	8	1
Germany	1,842	7,525	89	10	1
Greece	40	407	97	3	0
Hungary	189	111	48	48	4
Ireland	458	972	61	29	10
Italy	694	4,039	87	12	1
Latvia	63	29	40	45	15
Lithuania	91	24	27	73	0
Luxembourg	147	843	22	63	15
Malta	27	50	62	25	13
Netherlands	253	2,250	92	6	2

(Continued)

Table A.1. (*Continued*)

	Number of banks	Total assets (€ billion)	Of which		
			Home (%)	Other EU (%)	Third country (%)
Poland	691	362	34	59	7
Portugal	151	513	80	19	1
Romania	39	91	30	70	0
Slovakia	28	61	4	96	0
Slovenia	23	46	69	31	0
Spain	290	3,143	92	7	1
Sweden	168	1,212	91	8	1
United Kingdom	358	8,889	56	16	28
Euro area	**5,999**	**30,035**	**83**	**14**	**3**
Non-euro area	**1,724**	**12,008**	**60**	**19**	**21**
EU-28	**7,723**	**42,043**	**77**	**15**	**8**

Notes: Share of business from domestic banks, share of business of banks from other EU countries, and share of business of banks from third countries are measured as a percentage of the total banking assets in a country. Figures are for 2013. Euro area, non-euro area, and EU-28 are calculated as a weighted average (weighted according to assets).

Source: Author calculations based on ECB Structural Financial Indicators.

Table A.2. Top 30 banks in Europe in 2013.

Banking groups	Capital (in € billion)	Total assets (in € billion)	Home (%)	Other EU (%)	Third country (%)
Global banks					
1. HSBC (UK)	115	1,937	37	11	52
2. Barclays (UK)	67	1,568	36	26	38
3. Deutsche Bank (Germany)	51	1,612	28	30	42
4. Credit Suisse (Switzerland)	37	710	23	22	55
5. UBS (Switzerland)	35	821	33	25	42
6. Standard Chartered (UK)	31	489	16	5	79
European banks					
1. BNP Paribas (France)	72	1,800	34	44	22
2. Santander (Spain)	61	1,116	29	41	30
3. UniCredit (Italy)	43	846	40	59	1
4. ING (Netherlands)	38	788	38	48	14
5. Nordea (Sweden)	24	631	24	75	1
6. Danske Bank (Denmark)	22	432	48	51	1
Semi-international banks					
1. Royal Bank of Scotland (UK)	60	1,228	61	16	23
2. BBVA (Spain)	40	583	51	9	40
3. Commerzbank (Germany)	26	550	51	33	16
4. DNB Group (Norway)	16	285	74	18	8
5. KBC (Belgium)	14	241	53	45	3
6. SEB Bank (Sweden)	12	280	63	34	3

(Continued)

Table A.2. *(Continued)*

				Of which	
Banking groups	Capital (in € billion)	Total assets (in € billion)	Home (%)	Other EU (%)	Third country (%)
Domestic banks					
1. Crédit Agricole (France)	63	1,707	81	11	8
2. Groupe BPCE (France)	47	1,124	77	11	12
3. Lloyds Banking Group (UK)	46	1,012	82	12	6
4. Société Générale (France)	41	1,235	76	13	11
5. Rabobank (Netherlands)	35	674	76	6	18
6. Intesa Sanpaolo (Italy)	34	626	86	12	2
7. Crédit Mutuel (France)	30	659	84	11	5
8. La Caixa Group (Spain)	18	351	91	7	2
9. ABN AMRO (Netherlands)	17	372	80	13	7
10. Landesbank Baden-Würt (Germany)	15	274	75	18	7
11. DZ Bank (Germany)	14	387	75	19	6
12. Bayerische Landesbank (Germany)	14	256	75	18	7
Top 30 European banks	**1,135**	**24,592**	**53**	**24**	**23**

Notes: Top 30 banks a reselected on the basis of capital strength (Tier 1 capital as published in The Banker). Assets are divided over the home country, the rest of Europe and the rest of the world. Banks are divided in four categories. Global banks: less than 50% of assets in the home country and the majority of their international assets in the rest of the world. European banks: less than 50% of assets in the home country and the majority of their international assets in the rest of Europe. Semi-international banks: between 50 and 75% of assets in the home country. Domestic banks: 75% or more of assets in the home country.
Source: Schoenmaker (2013).

Annex 2. Bank Merger Data

Identification Strategy

In the fourth section, bank merger data for the eurozone and the US are used. The following criteria were used to identify bank mergers.

1. Both target and acquirer are a bank or a bank holding company (SIC codes 6000, 6021, 6022, 6712).
2. Both target and acquirer are from one of the eleven countries that introduced the Euro in 1999 for the Eurozone sample, and both target and acquirer are from the US for the US sample.
3. The acquirer holds less than 50% of the shares of the target before the merger and more than 50% of the shares after the merger.

The value of these mergers is aggregated by year, and type of merger (domestic or cross-border). This enables plotting of the domestic and cross-border merger volumes by year for the Eurozone and the US.

Data sources

The data is obtained from Thomson's SDC Platinum database. Merger volume is defined as the total value of all mergers announced in the year of interest. Data is aggregated on the year-country level.

Resolving Systemically Important Entities

Lessons from the Government Sponsored Enterprises

— CHAPTER 24

■ Mark Calabria
CATO Institute

There was perhaps no issue of greater importance to the financial regulatory reforms of 2010 than the resolution, without taxpayer assistance, of large financial institutions. The rescue of firms such as AIG shocked the public conscience and provided the political force behind the passage of the Dodd–Frank Act. Such is reflected in the fact that Titles I and II of Dodd–Frank relate to the identification and resolution of large financial entities. How the tools established in Titles I and II are implemented are paramount to the success of Dodd–Frank. This chapter attempts to gauge the likely success of these tools via the lens of similar tools created for the resolution of the housing government sponsored enterprises (GSEs), Fannie Mae and Freddie Mac.

An additional purpose of this paper is to provide some additional 'legislative history' to the resolution mechanisms contained in the Housing and Economic Recover Act of 2008 (HERA), which established a resolution framework for the GSEs similar to that ultimately created

Mark Calabria is the Director of Financial Regulation Studies, the CATO Institute.

in Title II of Dodd–Frank. The intent is to inform current debates over the resolution of systemically important financial institutions by revisiting how such issues were debated and agreed upon in HERA.

The author served as senior professional staff on the United States Senate Committee on Banking, Housing and Urban Affairs from April 2003 to April 2009. In his capacity on the Banking Committee staff, he served as one of the primary drafters and negotiators of the Housing Economic and Recovery Act of 2008, as well as the Banking Committee's GSE reform bills of 2004 and 2005.[1] It is in that capacity which the following 'legislative history' is recalled. Accordingly emphasis will be on Senate proceeding. As the conservator and receiver provisions ultimately included in HERA are those devised by the Senate, omitting coverage of House proceedings does not diminish the arguments advanced here.

Purposes of a Resolution Authority

To gauge the effectiveness of a resolution regime, it helps to have a clearly defined set of goals or purposes. In the area of bank resolution, there is considerable consensus as to those goals (generally, see White and Yorulmazer (2014)). Many of these goals were explicated debated and examined by members of Congress and their staffs during the drafting of GSE reform.

Foremost among the purposes of a resolution regime, including a court-supervised bankruptcy, is to decide upon the allocation of losses. In most circumstances, and definitely the case for a GSE resolution, the book value of liabilities will exceed the book value of assets. Given that book value can lag market value, the fair value of this difference can be quite substantial in a resolution. In the simplest terms, someone is not getting 100 cents on the dollar.

---

[1] Senator Shelby staff primary responsible for the drafting of 2004, 2005 Shelby GSE reform bills, later incorporated into HERA include, in addition to myself, Peggy Kuhn and Bryan Corbett, under the general supervision of Chief Counsel Doug Nappi and Staff Director Kathy Casey; 2008 efforts also included staff supervision from then Chief Counsel Mark Oesterle and Staff Direct William Duhnke. For particular assistance on development of HERA's resolution mechanism was the counsel provided by Michael Krimminger, then at the FDIC.

A resolution regime determines the process, the priorities and even the 'hair-cuts' imposed on creditors. Such a process was absent for the GSE before the passage of HERA. For instance prior to HERA, holders of agency mortgage-backed securities, a secured asset, had no guarantee that they would receive a greater priority than holders of unsecured GSE debt. In part this was due to the fact that the GSE did not organize their MBS pools as bankruptcy–remote trusts, as had been the case with private MBS pools. Specifying *ex ante* a chain of priorities can give market participants greater certainty as to their potential recovery in insolvency. Such also assists market participants in the pricing of differing tranches of debt. As the largest cost in a corporate bankruptcy is generally the operation of a creditor committee, a resolution regime that specifies creditor priorities *ex ante* can reduce the administrative costs of a resolution considerably.

A resolution regime can also explicitly favor certain creditors over others, even if such creditors would be otherwise *pari passu*. For instance the FDIC has generally treated foreign depositors differently than US domestic depositors (Curtis 2000). Of course the very structure of the FDIC treats depositors as a class separate from unsecured creditors as a general class. As witnessed in a variety of instances during the recent crisis, policy-makers may also choose to treat certain creditors more favorably than others *ex post* and in the absence of statutory authority to do so.

Administrative resolutions are occasionally claimed to be superior to a court-supervised bankruptcy due to concerns over potential 'contagion' or panics (Federal Deposit Insurance Corporation 2011). During the financial crisis it was often claimed that firms could not be allowed to enter bankruptcy without causing a broader panic. The failure of Lehman Brothers is pointed to as evidence of this concern. While there is no debate over the ability of bankruptcy courts to resolve financial firms and allocate losses, the question is one of speed. The FDIC, for instance, allows insured depositors, and occasionally other creditors, to be paid immediately. While such is allowable under the bankruptcy code, it is not usual practice. Title II of Dodd–Frank is essentially a mechanism for quickly resolving non-bank financials in a manner similar to that for banks, with the exception that Title II appears on its surface to only allow for liquidation. It also allows for the protection of certain creditors if such would forestall a panic. Accordingly an administrative resolution regime is presented as an avenue for containing financial market contagion.

Whether an administrative resolution is quicker than a court-supervised bankruptcy is an empirical question. Both an administrative agency and court face similar tasks, such as judging the validity of claims. For most, if not all, of these tasks there is no "special sauce" that agencies have which courts lack. While there is only limited data, with important limitations, what data that does exist, suggests that FDIC receiverships are no faster than the typical Chapter 11 proceeding (Calabria 2010). Both have a median time to resolution of 28 months. Since the FDIC is generally the largest creditor in the resolution of a depository, having FDIC manage the failure of a depository may indeed offer some cost savings. In case where the FDIC is not the largest creditor, for instance with an insurance company, it is far from obvious that having the FDIC manage such a process is cost effective.

A related, but separate, issue to contagion is the importance of maintaining 'critical facilities'. A rationale for deposit insurance is protecting the payments system. Given the important role of certain banks in the tri-party repo market, one could also imagine assistance being provided for those entities based on such a role. If the resolution process for an entity administering critical facilities is uncertain, the ability of those facilities to access credit and basic services may indeed be hindered. For such a reason, both the bankruptcy code and FDIC administrative proceedings allow for operating to be continued during the resolution process. The central role of the GSEs in the U.S. mortgage market also demanded that a continuing operation of core facilities be possible should a GSE become insolvent.

All of the preceding rationales for a resolution framework were debated, either at the staff or member level, during the drafting of GSE reform. The included legislative history[2] is intended to shed some light

---

[2] Of course one person's faulty recollection of events, sometimes a decade previous, does not officially constitute 'legislative history' in any legal sense. The recollections provided here are meant to inform on-going and future debates as to the resolution of large financial companies.

on the substance and conclusion of those debates. The following is also meant to illustrate that regulators were not simply left helpless and without appropriate 'tools' by Congress.

Comparing Bank and GSE Resolution[3]

The resolution framework for the GSEs is explicitly modeled upon the Federal Deposit Insurance Act, as is the orderly resolution authority established in Title II of Dodd-Frank. There are a number of important differences between GSEs and depositories that require some modifications to the traditional FDIC approach.

There are also a number of differences in the GSEs model that make resolution relatively simpler than similarly sized bank (bear in mind that by level of assets, Freddie Mac is close in size to Citibank). One difference that has vexed policy-makers is the issue of cross-border resolution. Given the many foreign subsidiaries of large U.S. banks and the difference in national resolution regimes, handling the failure of a large internationally active entity remains an important public policy issue. Fortunately that is not an issue with Fannie Mae or Freddie Mac. Neither have foreign subsidiaries. There is no need to for Washington (or New York) to coordinate with London (or elsewhere) in the resolution of a GSEs.

Relatedly, the GSEs are relatively 'simple' organizations when compared to similarly-sized financial companies. Their legal structures are not particularly complex. Questions as to the relationship between subsidiaries and a holding company are not relevant. Questions as to the relationship between affiliates, such as those raised under Sections 23A and 23B of the Federal Reserve Act, are not relevant. The GSE engage in a relatively small number of activities and ones that are transparent and easily understood. Their core business is not a mystery. Such should make a GSE far easier to re-organize or resolve than a comparably sized bank.

The GSEs also lack debt that could be described as 'demandable'. Almost all their debt issuance is relatively long-term, with only about

---

[3] For a fuller comparison, see Wall *et al.* (2004), and Carpenter and Murphy (2008).

half coming due within a year. Text book style bank runs simply are not an issue with the GSEs; although roll-over risk may be a (small) concern.[4] About half of GSE debt is in the form of mortgage-backed securities, which offer the security of the underlying mortgages as collateral.

Contrary to popular perceptions, the FDIC generally avoids liquidating a failed bank. The preferred strategy is to sell the bank 'whole' in a 'purchase and assumption' transaction to another bank. Under such circumstances, there is no liquidation. The purchasing bank takes both the assets and liabilities of the failed bank, occasionally with some assistance from the FDIC. It was recognized that such a strategy would be both politically and administratively difficult for a failed GSE. Obviously the size of either Fannie Mae or Freddie Mac would make a direct purchase unlikely. And even if such a purchase could be arranged, Congress wanted ultimate say over such a transaction. Accordingly HERA explicitly relies on a 'bridge bank' structure under which an insolvent GSE continues its operations and the existing charter is retained. As with the FDIC, conservatorship was not viewed as a likely option for an insolvent entity. Conservatorship was largely perceived as a 'holding tank' for an illiquid GSE. Conservatorship for a GSE was envision lasting no more than six months, after which a GSE would be expected to either leave conservatorship or enter receivership.

The Road to GSE Resolution Authority

Chairman Richard Shelby: "There is a perception by some people that some of the largest banks are too big to fail.

... In that context, do we need to give the new proposed GSE regulator the same type of systemic risk powers that FDIC has?

Chairman Alan Greenspan: "I would certainly think so, sir."
(Hearing before the Senate Committee on Banking, Housing and Urban Affairs, February 24, 2004.)

---

[4] For Fannie Mae's outstanding debt, due within one year, the effective term to re-pricing generally runs between four and five months. For Fannie Mae's longer term outstanding debt, the typical effective term to re-pricing is generally around 60 months.

On June 9, 2003, Freddie Mac dismissed its three most senior executives, including its CEO (Atkinson 2003). It was later revealed that Freddie Mac had been engaged in manipulating its earnings; a finding applied to Fannie Mae almost a year later. Of additional concern is that its then regulator, the Office Of Federal Housing Enterprise Oversight (OFHEO), in its annual Report to Congress, also released in June 2003, praised Freddie Mac's audit and accounting functions as 'independent and effective', as well as claiming that Freddie Mac's internal audit function "appropriately identifies and communicates control deficiencies to management and the Board of Directors" (OFHEO 2003, pp. 36–37). These observations on the part of OFHEO proved stunningly wide of the mark.

Public and Congressional concerns as to the potential systemic risk of the GSEs were nothing new. What gave much needed energy to the debate was the sudden loss of confidence in not only their accounting but also in the competence of their regulator. The events of June 2003, and subsequent Congressional hearings that fall, led many in Congress to believe that no one was 'watching the store'. Not the management, not the board and unfortunately not the regulator. What was needed, at a minimum, was a new regulator with enhanced powers. At no time during the 2003 to 2008 Congressional debates was serious consideration given to eliminating the GSEs. Such was simply believed to be politically impossible. As a participant in those debates, I can attest that just imposing 'bank-like' prudential standards on the GSEs was hard enough politically. Reform was almost exclusively focused upon the powers of the regulator.

During the 108th and 109th Congresses, Senator Richard Shelby chaired the Senate Banking Committee and led the Senate efforts to reform the regulatory structure of the GSEs. The author served on Chairman Shelby's staff during that time. Senator Shelby's instructions to staff were to create a GSE regulator that was as 'bank-like' as possible. While the 2003 Shelby bill used as a base text the bill (H.R. 2575) introduced by Congressman Richard Baker in the House of Representatives, it was immediately felt that the receivership provisions (section 134 of H.R. 2575) of the Baker bill did not sufficiently mirror the existing framework for depository institutions.

The 2004 Shelby bill was considered by the Banking Committee on April 1, 2004, using Senator Hagel's bill (S.1508) as the base text for the mark-up. Essentially the entire text of S.1508, as introduced, was struck and replaced by a Chairman's 'mark' drafted by Chairman Shelby's staff. S.1508 was reported out of Committee with receivership provisions that more closely mirrored the Federal Deposit Insurance Act. These provisions were later modified and included in the 2005 Senate consideration of GSE reform, where the base text was S.190, marked-up by the Banking Committee on July 28, 2005.

In crafting the conservator and receivership provisions that eventually comprised Section 1145 of HERA, the Committee staff, under the direction of Chairman Shelby, quite literally 'marked-up' Sections 11 and 13 of the Federal Deposit Insurance Act (FDIA). Every line of those sections were examined and debated over whether they would be appropriate for GSEs. The presumption was that FDIA powers would apply to a GSE resolution, unless there was a compelling reason otherwise. By that time the Committee also had little faith in the ability of the GSE regulator. It was anticipated that OFHEO or any successor organization would not implement regulations surrounding a GSE conservator or receivership before such was needed. The authorities contained in statute would have to suffice on their own. It was also intended that the existing body of law, including court decisions, surrounding the FDIC's exercise of its conservator and receivership powers be incorporated into that governing the GSEs.

It was recognized that such would give the new GSE regulator considerable power. Some would say extraordinary. This was intentional. By placing the GSEs within the body of law governing bank receivership the Committee intended to create additional certainty over how a GSE would be resolved in the case of insolvency. It was also the understanding and intent of the drafters that such powers would be used. The receivership provisions contained in HERA were never intended to be a 'dead letter'. They were meant to be used.

The Banking Committee considered the approach of placing the GSEs within the bankruptcy code. Contributing to the uncertainty of how a failed GSE would be handled is that prior to 2008, the GSEs were understood by many to be exempt from the bankruptcy code, although such is not explicit. In the absence of either explicit court or administrative powers, the failure of a GSE could well force a congressional rescue and at a minimum would entail significant uncertainty. During the Committee mark-up of S.1508 in 2004 Senator Sununu offered amendments (#16 and #17) that would have allowed the regulator to file a bankruptcy petition in the case of GSE insolvency. The Sununu amendments also clarified that a GSE would not be treated as a 'governmental unit' for the purposes of a bankruptcy. The Sununu amendments were withdrawn and never voted upon. The primary concern was that by including these amendments jurisdiction over the proposed legislation might be extended to the Senate Committee on the Judiciary, which has jurisdiction over the bankruptcy code. Given the existing complexity of reform, involving negotiations with another Committee were viewed as an unsurmountable obstacle to reform. These provisions were not rejected because any perceived inadequacies in the bankruptcy process.

The conservator and receivership provisions in HERA were largely taken from the 2005 Shelby bill. Little debate in 2008 occurred around these provisions, despite the change in control of the Senate (control flipped from Republicans to Democrats with the 2006 Mid-term elections). The following are a number of specific issues debated within the Senate Banking Committee in the years leading up to the passage of HERA.

The Role of Treasury

A crucial question during GSE reform was where to house the new regulator. The Bush Administration initially proposed to model the new regulator on the Office of the Comptroller (OCC) and place within the Department of the Treasury. A bill (H.R. 2803) was introduced in the House by Congressman Royce in July 2003 that followed this suggestion. By the time the Senate began its deliberations and in response to Congressional objections, the Bush Administration soften its preferences for Treasury control, only stimulating certain conditions that should apply and expressing some preference for those conditions.[5]

Regardless of the preferences of the Bush Administration, momentum in Congress quickly built against a policy or supervisory role for the Treasury Department. Generally Democrats did not trust the Bush Treasury, fearing a too aggressive regulator, while Republicans feared that housing the regulator within Treasury would 'harden' the implied guarantee, as market participants might perceive such as bringing the GSEs ever closer to having their debt viewed as equivalent to treasuries.

Treasury, or its related agencies (OCC), are often given important roles in the supervision and resolution of depositories. The OCC, as the primary regulator of national banks, can appoint the FDIC as receiver of a national bank. The Treasury also has a critical role to play when the systemic risk exceptions to the least-cost resolution requirements of Section 13G of the Federal Deposit Insurance Act are invoked. Congress specifically and intentionally gave FHFA sole authority over a GSE conservatorship or receivership. Only FHFA can decide when a GSE enters or leaves. No other entity has legal authority to appoint FHFA as conservator or receiver. Nor is there any systemic risk exception contained in HERA.

The sole authority granted to Treasury under the GSE provisions of HERA is in the exercise of its rights as a creditor, should it provide assistance to the GSEs. While a creditor can, of course, negotiate certain provisions as a condition of providing credit, under no circumstances can those conditions supersede other provisions of law. Treasury has no authority to assume the powers of a conservator via its rights as a creditor. Treasury can no more, as a creditor, bind FHFA's authorities, than could a holder of bank debt bind the powers of FDIC. As importantly, FHFA, as an independent regulator, has no ability to delegate its powers as a conservator/receiver to Treasury or any other government agency.

The role of Treasury was viewed under HERA as that of a creditor. The Treasury was directed to consider issues of priority and protection

---

[5] See Statement of John W. Snow, Secretary, US Department of the Treasury, before the United States Senate, Committee on Banking, Housing and Urban Affairs, October 16, 2003.

of the taxpayer. In addition, such assistance was intended to be temporary, as is the nature of credit, rather than perpetual, as is the nature of equity. Put simply Treasury assistance to the GSEs was envisioned to take the form of a senior debt, something like debtor-in-possession financing. Such assistance was not intended to keep the GSEs out of receivership or to transfer losses from creditors to the taxpayer.

Avoiding 'Takings' Claims

Ours is litigious society. The design of any resolution framework must take such into consideration. Such was explicitly examined during the construction of a resolution framework for the GSEs. In order to obtain federal deposit insurance, bank owners agree to accept the terms of the bank charter and the legal framework surrounding those terms. As such their ownership in a bank can have considerable value. That value can be lost in a resolution. In fact one of the objectives of a resolution may well be to impose losses on equity.

The FDIC has authority to invoke a receivership when a depository still has some positive book value. Committee staff were concerned that if FHFA could invoke a receivership while a GSE still had a positive book value, then shareholders could make a 'takings' claim. For this reason, a mandatory receivership is not invoked until a GSE has a book value of zero or less. Furthermore shareholders would also receive any excess value obtained from the performance of a failed GSE's assets. HERA establishes a 'good bank/bad bank' or bridge bank model to allow a failed GSE to be quickly reorganized. In such reorganization, shareholders are left with the 'bad' bank, but could receive any excess value should assets end up being worth more than liabilities.

Treatment of Favored Creditors

A resolution mechanism can explicitly prefer some creditors over others, regardless of what place in line those creditors have contracted for. A variety of entities are significant holders of GSE debt. Insured depositories have large holdings of GSE debt, as do other financial market participants, such as insurance companies and pension funds. Of particular importance are the large holdings of GSE debt by foreign governments, especially foreign banks. Some of these central banks, such as the Chinese and Russian, have unique and critical relationships with the United States. These central banks are also large purchasers of US Treasury debt. The Banking Committee was not unaware of these relationships. In fact concerns were repeatedly voiced that if left to Treasury, credit losses on GSE debt holders by foreign central banks would transferred to the American taxpayer. This was viewed as an unacceptable outcome. The lack of an explicit creditor preference for foreign agencies is not due to Congress having overlooked the issue, but to Congress having rejected such a preference.

Conservatorship Versus Receivership

As a rough approximation, about ninety percent of the energy and thinking of Congress, in relation to resolution, were devoted to receivership, as opposed to conservatorship. Similar to bank conditions under the FDIC, it was assumed that conservatorship would rarely be used and if it was used, it would be brief. As it clear under HERA, any reorganization or wind-down would occur under a receivership, which itself had explicit time limits, albeit measured in years. The receivership framework created in HERA was established both because the existing conservatorship framework was inadequate but also because conservatorship itself was believed inadequate. The limbo currently being experienced by the GSEs was never intended by Congress and is quite contrary to the framework established in HERA.

The Path not Taken

The preceding demonstrates that most, if not all, the rationales asserted commonly for the rescue of large financial entities were contemplated and addressed in regards to the GSEs in HERA. The tools to resolve a failed GSE, without cost to the taxpayer, were created and in place by September of 2008. Those tools closely mirror both the Federal Deposit Insurance Act and those created in Title II of Dodd–Frank. Yet, those tools where not used.

As FHFA and Treasury only offer vague generalities at the commencement of the conservatorships of Fannie Mae and Freddie Mac, one can only parse their statements and actions for the actual intent. Certainly the primary objective of Treasury and FHFA was to guarantee that GSE creditors did not take losses, despite clear statutory intent otherwise. As Dodd–Frank's Title II is presented as a way to impose losses on creditors, this issue is of paramount importance if Dodd–Frank is to have any credibility.

There are at least three reasons that Treasury and FHFA may have wanted to protect GSE creditors. The first is foreign policy concerns. Foreign governmental entities, including central banks, were large holders of GSE debt. Despite Congress having contemplated and rejected treating foreign governmental entities as favored creditors, Treasury, in particular, may have felt that allowing a default on GSE debt would be viewed internationally as the equivalent of a default by the US government. As many large holders of GSE debt were also holders of U.S. treasury debt, this concern was likely foremost on the minds of policymakers. Although a GSE default could well have triggered a 'flight to quality' driving down the yield on US treasuries.

The GSEs were not alone in receiving an implied guarantee, even if they represented an extreme version of such. As their failure came at a time of particular stress in the US financial markets, Treasury officials may have felt that imposing losses on GSE creditors would have called into question any implied guarantee among other troubles institutions. If Fannie Mae and Freddie Mac were allowed to fail, then would not the same be possible for Citibank or Bank of America? If Treasury desired to maintain an implied guarantee behind the largest banks, then protecting Fannie Mae and Freddie Mac would have been necessary.

GSE securities were also held across the US financial markets. At the time of the crisis, GSE securities held by depositories was well over 150% of Tier 1 capital levels for the banking system as a whole. About 3% of insured depositories held GSE securities at levels in excess of 500% of their Tier 1 capital (Federal Deposit Insurance Corporation. 2004). GSE securities were also broadly used as collateral in the repo market. Allowing even minor haircuts on GSE debt could have contributed to the failure of hundreds of (mostly small) banks. The GSEs also held large derivative positions with a small number of commercial and investment banks. To some extent the rescue of Fannie Mae and Freddie Mac was a rescue of the banking system. While most of these holdings were known, in some cases publicly, Treasury may have felt that allowing losses, even small ones, on such a large number of institutions would undermine confidence in U.S. financial markets.

Lessons for the Future of Too-Big-To-Fail

There are perhaps no companies considered more 'too big to fail' than Fannie Mae and Freddie Mac. Recognizing the harm a disorderly failure of a GSE could cause, Congress established in law in the summer of 2008 a resolution mechanism that would allow an insolvent GSE to fail without cost to the taxpayer and in an orderly manner. Despite those tools being in place, they were not used. Such raises the distinct possibility that even though Dodd–Frank creates similar tools for other large complex financial organizations those tools will simply be ignored. How can policy-makers increase the likelihood that such tools will be used?

Both Dodd–Frank and HERA leave regulators with considerable discretion. As long as regulators have such discretion, the choice of personnel also becomes one of policy. One avenue for reducing 'too big to fail' is to only appoint as regulators individuals who place a larger weight on ending bailouts than does the public. Something along the lines of Rogoff's (1985) 'conservative banker' except for rescues rather than monetary policy. The appointment of Thomas Hoenig to Vice-Chairman of the FDIC can be viewed in such a light. His selection was a conscious strategy by the Senate Republican leader along these very lines.

Congress may also choose to limit the discretion of regulators. In a few instances, Dodd–Frank attempts to limit regulatory discretion, such as the Federal Reserve's use of its 13-3 authorities. In establishing a mandatory receivership mechanism for the GSEs, HERA also attempted to limit regulatory discretion. What HERA missed was that regulators would simply ignore those limitations. This is perhaps the hardest question in ending bailouts. Regulators rarely suffer when they violate legal restrictions on their ability to assist failing firms. For instance FDIC's broad guarantee of bank debt during the crisis lacked any basis in law, but no one at the FDIC has paid any penalty for such. The general public lacks any standing to sue regulators for statutory violations. Until a better solution is found, efforts must be made to change the culture of bank regulators. Instead of a 'whatever it takes' mentality, regulators should be encouraged to embrace a 'whatever the law directs' mentality.[6] Regulators should also not simply assume that if they lack tools which they'd like to have that somehow Congress simply forgot to give them such tools. In many instances Congress did indeed debate giving regulators certain tools and then rejected such. A number of regulators have expressed dismay at being 'second guessed' post-crisis, especially by Congress (Geithner 2014). Such regulators may well keep in mind that Congress doesn't usually enjoy being 'second guessed' by regulators on what powers said regulators were given.

The regulatory culture around financial rescues is also driven by how those rescues are portrayed. A number of commentators, including some regulators, have argued that if Lehman Brothers was assisted, much of the financial crisis would have been avoided. Such sends a signal to market participants that regulators are comfortable with rescues. Regardless of one's views on the effectiveness of rescues, the need to avoid the appearance of 'victory laps' should be obvious. A better trend would be for rescues to be accompanied by the resignation of the responsible regulators (along with the responsible management).

A difficult policy question is how to handle foreign governments as creditors (Patalon III 2008). Congress did examine the issue of foreign governments as large holders of GSE debt. Congress made the choice not to treat such creditors as favored. But Treasury Secretary Hank Paulson apparently did not agree with Congress and during the crisis assured Chinese officials that their holdings would be protected, despite Secretary Paulson lacking any legal authority to make such assurances. Given that the role of sovereign wealth funds as investors in many large US financials, the significance of foreign policy considerations is not limited to Fannie Mae and Freddie Mac. Should Congress accept that

---

[6] For an up close picture of 'whatever it takes' see Wessel (2010).

Treasury (and the White House) will occasionally treat some foreign investments as 'favored' despite statutory provisions otherwise? Should such creditors be given an express preference? Such could allow haircuts to be imposed upon other creditors, while also forcing these favored foreign creditors to receive lower yields.

Conclusion

Dodd–Frank's efforts to create an orderly resolution framework closely mirror similar attempts at ending the "too-big-to-fail" status of the housing enterprises, Fannie Mae and Freddie Mac. Title II's orderly liquidation authority mirrors the receivership provisions created for the GSEs in HERA. These provisions were operational by September of 2008, yet were not used. Several of the reasons they were not used are applicable to Dodd–Frank's Title II, suggesting that its tools will also be ignored by policy-makers and the comfortable and familiar route of taxpayer rescue will again be taken.

The neglect of HERA's tools and the likely similar neglect of Dodd–Frank's suggest a much deeper reform of our financial regulatory system is in order. The regulatory culture of 'whatever it takes' must be abandoned. A respect for the rule of law and obedience to the letter of the law must be instilled in our regulatory culture. More importantly the incentives facing regulators must be dramatically changed. If we hope to end 'too-big-to-fail' and to curtail moral hazard more generally, significant penalties must be created for rescues as well as deviations from statute. A very difficult question is that lack of standing for any party to litigate to enforce statutory prohibitions against rescues.

Of course all of these objectives are more difficult to obtain under a regulatory environment that lacks transparency. While Dodd–Frank has made modest advances in forcing financial regulators to become more transparent, it falls short in relation to future regulatory actions. A policy audit of the Federal Reserve would be a useful starting place. Any exercise of the Federal Reserve's 13-3 powers should be subjected to an immediate independent audit.

Policy-makers must also review regulatory decisions that create systemic risk. For instance, despite a the lack of a explicit guarantee and statutory language to the contrary, bank regulators have treated, for regulatory purposes, the debt of Fannie Mae and Freddie Mac as 'risk-free'. Obvious such debt is not risk-free. As a Banking Committee staffer in 2004, I queried senior FDIC staff on this issue and received little more than a shrug. The fact is that a rescue of GSE creditors was made more likely because bank regulators treated it as such. Similar issues have arisen in the Euro area with the regulatory treatment of sovereign debt. It is reckless enough when legislators choose to treat risky debt as risk-free, it is puzzling when prudential regulators choose to do so.

My experience attempting to avoid a taxpayer assisted rescue of Fannie Mae and Freddie Mac leaves me pessimistic as to avoiding such for other large financial institutions. My skepticism of Dodd–Frank's resolutions powers derives from the experience of having tried such for the GSEs and watching it fail. To guarantee the success of Dodd–Frank's efforts to end taxpayer-assisted rescues, we learn from the failure of similar efforts.

References

Atkinson, B. (2003), "Freddie Mac fires president: CEO leaves, Audit woes spur shake-up regulator notes laws," *Baltimore Sun*, June 10, Available at: http://articles.baltimoresun.com/2003-06-10/news/0306100348_1_freddie-mac-weakness-chief-financial-officer.

Calabria, M. (2010), "Failing Banks: Bankruptcy or receivership?" *CATO-At-Liberty*, May 3. Available at: http://www.cato.org/blog/failing-banks-bankruptcy-or-receivership

Carpenter, D. and M. M. Murphy (2008), "Financial Institution Insolvency: Federal authority over Fannie Mae, Freddie Mac, and depository institutions," CRS Report for Congress. Congressional Research Service. September 10.

Curtis, C. (2000), "The Status of Foreign Deposits under the Federal Depositor-Preference Law," *University of Pennsylvania Journal of International Economic Law*, 21(Summer): 237–271.

Federal Deposit Insurance Corporation (2004), *"An Update on Emerging Issues in Banking: Assessing the banking industry's exposure to an implicit government guarantee of GSEs,"* Federal Deposit Insurance Corporation. Available at: https://www.fdic.gov/bank/analytical/fyi/2004/030104fyi.html.

Federal Deposit Insurance Corporation (2011), "The Orderly Liquidation of Lehman Brothers Holdings Inc. under the Dodd-Frank Act," *FDIC Quarterly*, 5(2). Available at: https://www.fdic.gov/bank/analytical/quarterly/2011_vol52.html.

Geithner, T. (2014), *Stress Test: Reflections on Financial Crises* (New York: Crown Business).

Office of Federal Housing Enterprise Oversight [OFHEO] (2003), *Report to Congress*, Federal Housing Finance Agency, June.

Patalon III, W. (2008), "Foreign Bondholders — and not the US Mortgage Market — Drove the Fannie/Freddie Bailout," *Morning Money*, September 11. Available at: http://moneymorning.com/2008/09/11/fnm/.

Rogoff, K. (1985), "The Optimal Degree of Commitment to an Intermediate Monetary Target," *The Quarterly Journal of Economics,* 100(4): 1169–1189.

Wall, L., W. S. Frame and R. Eisenbeis (2004), "Resolving Large Financial Intermediaries: Banks versus housing enterprises," Federal Reserve Bank of Atlanta Working Paper No. 2004-23a.

Wessel, D. (2010), *In FED We Trust: Ben Bernanke's War on the Great Panic* (New York: Crown Business).

White, P. and T. Yorulmazer (2014), "Bank Resolution Concepts, Trade-offs, and Changes in Practices," *Federal Reserve Bank of New York Economic Policy Review*, 20(2). Available at: http://www.newyorkfed.org/research/epr/2014/1403whit.html.

Part VIII
Policy Panel — Where to from Here?

Assessing the Overall Impact of Financial Reforms

— CHAPTER 25

■ Svein Andresen
Financial Stability Board

The following describes what has been done to address the fault lines in the global financial system revealed by the Great Financial Crisis and to make that system more resilient. Policy development to address those fault lines is now substantially complete. The focus has shifted to achieving effective implementation of reforms, assessing impacts and addressing material unintended consequences where they appear. Alongside this, authorities are seeking to manage the system better than they have in the past through better system-wide oversight and use of the tools that reforms have generated to identify and address vulnerabilities. At the end I set out some areas where I believe we need to ask if enough has been done to give the system the resilience needed.

What has the Global Reform Program Achieved?

Although preoccupied by crisis management and local reform debates, the capitals of the world's major economies confronted common issues

---

Svein Andresen is the Secretary General of the Financial Stability Board.

in redrawing the rules of the road for finance. Combined with a shared desire to preserve open, global financial markets, this has meant the main reforms have been international.

Those core reform areas are set out in below. Their overall objectives have been to strengthen the resilience of the system as a whole, reduce contagion when trouble hits, mitigate the pro-cyclicality of financial conditions, and improve system wide oversight and co-operation arrangements.

Building Resilient Financial Institutions

The focus has naturally been on banks, where the Basel III agreement reached in 2011 materially strengthens the quantity and quality that banks will hold. Where Basel II allowed banks to operate with as little common equity as 2% of risk weighted assets (RWA), Basel III sets the common equity requirement at around 10% of RWA for the biggest international banks and 7% for other banks.

Further, Basel III raises the quality of capital by deducting from common equity holdings of assets such as goodwill, stakes in other institutions, and deferred tax assets that cannot absorb losses on a going concern basis.

And to guard against capital compression for holdings of large volumes of low risk weighted assets, Basel III introduces a common leverage ratio as a backstop to the risk weighted assets regime. Supplements to Basel III are also coming that will reduce unwarranted variations in firms' risk models.

Large banks are on course to meet the new capital standards in 2015, four years ahead of the end of the implementation period. The core of the banking system is therefore already now substantially strengthened. And that resilience will grow as the leverage and liquidity standards come on stream in the years ahead.

Basel III also introduces for the first time bank liquidity standards. The Liquidity Coverage and the Net Stable Funding Ratios require banks to maintain a minimum stock of liquid assets and a more stable funding profile in relation to on- and off-balance sheet liabilities, reducing the system's reliance on central bank liquidity support.

A Macroprudential Capital Regime

Besides substantially raising minimum capital requirements, Basel III introduces a richer macroprudential capital regime. This has elements designed to reduce structural and conjunctural systemic risks. The former include common equity surcharges ranging from 1–3.5% of RWA for global systemically important banks (G-SIBs), as well as higher risk weights to discourage intra-G-SIB counterparty exposures. These measures are designed to further reduce the probability of default where the systemic losses given default are the greatest.

In addition, Basel III introduces a countercyclical capital buffer that enables authorities to require banks to increase capital by up to 2.5% of RWA in periods when credit growth is exceptionally strong. Complementing this is a capital conservation buffer above the minimum capital requirement, the breach of which triggers restrictions on dividend payments and share buy backs. These are not tools to constrain the upswing of the credit cycle, but to sustain the resilience of the financial system when that cycle turns.

Operating these buffers well will require that supervisors can judge how robust or vulnerable the system is in the face of gathering threats. The systematic macro stress testing of capital adequacy — such as introduced in the US and now much more widely — is an instrument for that assessment.

Work is also underway to build greater resilience in insurance, including through international capital standards. This has come about in part as a result of AIG's failure. As with G-SIBs, globally systemic insurance companies (G-SII) will be required to meet higher loss absorbency, resolution planning and tighter supervisory requirements. The capital framework being developed will be first group-wide capital requirement for insurance companies, comprising their traditional insurance as well as their non-insurance activities.

Effective Resolution Regimes for Systemic Institutions

Improvements in resiliency levels will not banish financial distress and defaults. And this crisis revealed long-known shortcomings in authorities' ability to handle failures of systemic institutions, with deleterious consequences for public finances. A large effort has therefore gone into the development of effective resolution regimes for systemic entities, whether banks, insurance or financial market infrastructures.

All the major G-SIB home countries are now close to having resolution regimes in place that match the powers and tools of the Key Attributes of Effective Resolution Regimes set out by the FSB in 2012. And cross-border resolution planning has come far from the 'no strategy, no plan' state that existed in 2008/9.

A necessary condition for these new resolution tools to work is that systemic entities maintain a critical mass of liabilities that can be bailed-in to cover losses and recapitalize that systemic firm's critical functions to a level that enables that entity to be re-authorized and sustain those critical functions.

The FSB has proposed that G-SIBs should be subject to minimum total loss absorption capacity (TLAC) requirement of 16–20% of RWAs, or 2 times the Basel leverage ratio, whichever is greater. TLAC will cover the Basel III capital instrument described above, as well as well as longer-dated subordinated liabilities that can be bailed in in resolution.

A part of TLAC will be prepositioned in material overseas subsidiaries of G-SIBs and can be triggered by host authorities. This will provide incentives for co-operation amongst home and host authorities and increase prospects for orderly resolution of cross border banking groups.

A long-standing obstacle to orderly resolution of internationally operating banks is that the resolution actions of home authorities only bind counterparties or contracts operating under that country's laws. Critically, this has meant that the stays on the rights to trigger cross-default and early termination clauses do not bind the foreign counterparties of the bank entering resolution. The effect is an immediate drain of resources from that bank. The long-term solution to this problem is statutory cross border recognition regimes in all countries. In the meantime, authorities have worked with the International Swaps and Derivatives Association on a protocol to ISDA's Master Agreement under which cross-border counterparties will contractually agree to recognize statutory stays in home jurisdictions. The G-SIBs have all signed this protocol, and authorities will this year develop regulatory and supervisory measures to ensure the protocol is widely adopted.

So, good progress has been made towards making orderly resolution of globally operating banks without putting tax payer funds at risk a reality. But G-SIB resolution planning and resolvability assessments need to run their full course and conclusions be drawn for individual G-SIBs.

Addressing Risk from Shadow Banking

If resilient core institutions and ending TBTF are great challenges for financial stability, close behind is endemic regulatory arbitrage. As reformed banking rules come into place, some of the substance of banking will inevitably re-merge elsewhere.

Part of the answer to that should be simple — make sure all bank-like activity (viz. credit intermediation involving leverage and maturity transformation) is subject to bank-like regulation. But such an approach might not be efficient, and it does not address fire sale risks associated with unlevered capital markets activity. Hence, the program to reduce risk from shadow banking has had the five objectives set out below:

- Mitigating risk in banks' interaction with shadow banking
- Reducing run risk in MMFs
- Improving transparency and incentives in securitization
- Reducing leverage and pro-cyclicality in securities financing transactions

Promoting a regulatory framework based on economic functions over form, and regular review of the regulatory perimeter Policy development in the first three areas is largely concluded and implementation is underway. The regulatory framework applying minimum hair cut floors to securities financing transactions will come into effect in 2017.

This will apply initially to banks' lending to non-banks against non-governmental collateral, but we are consulting on its application on a market-wide basis to avoid arbitrage.

The final leg to this work is a framework to assess whether the policies that apply to entities involved in shadow banking are appropriate to their contribution to financial stability risks. The framework categorizes shadow banking activities by economic functions and sets out activity-based policies that should apply to those functions regardless of the legal form or regulatory category carrying them out. The framework requires that authorities obtain information to make these assessments and to adjust regulatory policies or the regulatory perimeter as needed. Implementation of this framework in FSB member jurisdictions is underway.

Reducing the Network on Credit Exposures Amongst Market Participants

The fourth objective of policy has been to reduce the network of credit exposures amongst banks and dealers to mitigate the problem of 'too interconnected to fail'.

The focus here has been on OTC derivatives, where in 2009 the G-20 decided that all 'standard OTC derivatives' must be cleared by CCPs. Simultaneously, they called for minimum margin requirements for remaining bilateral transactions.

Progress has been made on both fronts, and central clearing of derivatives is expanding rapidly. Central clearing has several advantages from a financial stability perspective. It reduces the scope and volume of asset and liabilities that need to be addressed in a bank resolution; it improves information about exposures and concentration of risks, including at unregulated firms whose failure could have system-wide consequences; and it enables the central counterparty to limit those risks. Markets with credible central counterparties are less likely to freeze up, providing greater continuity in their primary function to trade and hedge risks.

CCPs of course become TBTF institutions in their own right, calling for robust standards for their recovery and resolution. Although principles for recovery and resolution of systemic financial market infrastructure have been developed, these need further granularity to generate confidence that the critical functions of CCPs can be maintained under severe stress and when default funds have been exhausted.

Improving System-wide Oversight Capacity

A lesson of the crisis was that countries need to improve their capacity to assess risks to the system and to respond to them. Better system-wide oversight arrangements have come into place in most major jurisdictions, bringing relevant authorities together. The mandates and composition of these bodies differ and there are lively debates about what they should be. Their test of effectiveness will be in whether the collection of policies applied form a more effective and coherent whole, and are more responsive to evolving risks, than before the crisis. Indeed, at a broader level, this test applies to the FSB as well.

As a necessary part of this, considerable effort is going into improving the information used for risk assessments. The crisis revealed large gaps between the data gathered and those needed, including in firms' ability to aggregate internal exposure date and in authorities ability to share data amongst national regulators and to combine and share data across jurisdictions. Progress is being made on these fronts, with a unique global LEI coming into place as a touchstone for better counterparty risk data, as well as a multilateral agreement providing for a data hub at the BIS that receives and makes available to supervisors data on the characteristics and network of G-SIB counterparty and funding exposures.

Assessing the Overall Impact of Reforms

The global financial reform program has been broad and encompassing. And it has been complemented by additional national and regional measures. As a result, financial institutions and the public are right to ask if it all hangs together and whether it will work as intended. And can authorities assess the overall impact of the reforms?

In thinking about the costs of reforms, I'd like to paraphrase something that Randy Krozner said in 2002 with reference to the Sarbanes Oxley Act: "The relevant benchmark for measuring the cost and impact of global reforms is not business as usual as of 2007, but what the market would have demanded anyway in terms of change." In terms of the adequacy of capital and liquidity requirements under Basel II, the market voted with its feet in 2008/9, and again in Europe in 2011/12. We are comfortable that Basel III is not far from what markets would themselves have demanded. TLAC will go beyond that. But reforms that remove public subsidies for TBTF firms are not economic costs of reforms.

All of the major pieces of reform that I have described have been subject to rigorous economic impact assessments, and implementation periods have been set taking the unusual strains on the financial sector and real economy into account. And each of these impact assessments have found that the long term benefits in terms of future crisis avoided or reduced far exceed the economic costs of the reforms.

However, the question that should always be asked is whether authorities have achieved the desired degree of resilience as efficiently as possible.

Some other issues — aside from the resolvability of CCPs already mentioned — that I think merit attention from authorities ahead include:

- Have the policy reforms adequately addressed the vulnerabilities associated with the large dependence on short term wholesale funding in the financial system? There is less such dependence today than before the crisis, but it still very large and likely to grow again when yield curves steepen.
- What can be done to improve the resilience of the liquidity of systemically relevant markets, especially the bond markets? Bond issuance and holdings in open-ended mutual funds have grown very significantly in recent years, far out-stripping the bond markets' underlying market making capacity.
- Last, do the new oversight structures that have come into place give confidence that supervisory and regulatory policies will be more coherent and able to respond to regulatory arbitrage, structural

transformations and cyclical developments than in the past? Regulatory agencies and structures are diverse and individual agencies have different goals. But they are collectively responsible for systemic stability. The differences between them that have prevented timely action in the past need to be confronted so that the relevant regulators understand how they need to act and co-act in the interest of financial stability.

Financial Regulation

Where to From Here?

— CHAPTER 26

- Vítor Constâncio
  European Central Bank

Seven years after the beginning of the crisis, much has been achieved to improve the regulatory framework of the financial system. After the scare of a possible financial meltdown, authorities around the world wanted a simpler system that would be less leveraged, more resilient, transparent and efficient. Nevertheless, several measures are not finalised, implementation of others has been slow and some others will enter into force only in a few years. Referring to the title of this panel "Where to From Here?", I would say that we are not yet 'here'. In my remarks, I will start by highlighting some of the achievements and then move on to comment on what, in my view, is still missing.

In broad terms, the first area where major improvements were achieved concerns capital and liquidity regulation: the increase in capital requirements, the introduction of a (still-to-be- calibrated) leverage ratio and the introduction of the two liquidity ratios. These apply to the regulated part of the system, mostly banks. In the US, the banking sector increased by the consolidation or transformation of major broker-dealers into banks. This was not the case for the European banking sector, which actually shrank in the aftermath of the crisis.

Vítor Constâncio is Vice President of the European Central Bank. He previously served as governor of the Banco de Portugal.

It became apparent that what had emerged in the run-up to the crisis was a new market-based credit system funded by short-term secured transactions, protected by risk transfer operations in the over-the-counter (OTC) derivatives market (IRS, CDS, FXS). This new system had split traditional credit intermediation into separate transactions and was not captured by the statistical system, be it flow of funds accounts or monetary statistics. It was indeed a 'shadow banking' sector that was not fully on the radar of regulators. As a result, 'shadow banking' is a second area where important measures have been taken and a number of others are under way for adoption in the course of next year. Securitisation, repos and OTC derivatives operationally underpin the development of this new credit system. Securitisation standards have been improved by the application of new regulations and the market has abandoned many unsound practices. The definition of standards for high-quality securitisations has continued and a revision of capital charges is being prepared to re-launch the market on a healthier basis.

Some measures are still to be completed, e.g. on shadow banking or OTC derivatives. The implementation of several others has either been delayed or will take some time to be finalised.

Regarding the repo and securities lending markets, a major step forward was the Financial Stability Board's (FSB) recent publication of rules for the introduction of minimum haircuts on transactions basically involving corporate securities that are not centrally cleared. This work stream will be concluded early next year.

Concerning institutions belonging to the 'shadow banking' sector, new recommendations were issued by IOSCO and, in 2015, an assessment will be made of the implementation of new regulations in different jurisdictions. Progress has been uneven and in several cases insufficient, in my view. Other types of institution will also be reviewed next year by the FSB.

Still in the field of 'shadow banking', regarding the OTC derivatives markets, efforts have been concentrated on transferring the settlement of transactions to central clearing institutions and on stimulating the use of trade repositories to gather and disseminate post-trade information on the transactions. However, implementation was not made mandatory in many cases and implementation of the new standards is well behind schedule. The announced transfer of standardised transactions to organised multilateral platforms is even more delayed as only three jurisdictions have introduced trading transfer requirements for a limited type of derivatives.

A third domain of regulatory reform concerns the overcoming of the too-big-to-fail problem. Significant steps forward have been: the increase in capital reinforced by the G-SIB surcharge; the harmonisation of key attributes for resolution already legislated in many jurisdictions; the formalisation of resolution plans that have to be approved by the authorities; the forthcoming introduction of a total loss-absorbing capacity (TLAC) that includes equity and a layer of 'bail-in-able debt'; and finally, the adherence of all the major players in the derivatives market to a new ISDA agreement to forgo the termination of cross-border contracts in the event of a globally systemic bank entering resolution.

This was the maximum that could be achieved to address the risks of ring-fencing. But many other aspects will have to remain open, since the harmonisation of national bankruptcy laws is admittedly unrealistic in the near term. The success of the new approach in moving from a culture of bail-outs to a culture of private bail-in depends also on the credibility of the implementation in the eyes of market participants. Another word of caution against over optimism refers to the possibility that problems may not only relate to one institution being 'too-big-to-fail' but also possible instances where there are to 'too-many-to-fail'.

Another important change in the framework to deal with systemic risk has been the establishment of macroprudential authorities endowed with a set of instruments to counter risks of financial imbalances, triggering asset price boom/bust cycles.

The range of views about what has been achieved is broad: some say that we are close to overregulation, while others will maintain that nothing fundamental has changed. They are both wrong. It has to be acknowledged that there are important delays in the implementation of some measures, while several others are not yet finalised. This is particularly true of 'shadow banking' entities and activities. The recent evolution of the financial system confirms that after an initial decline after 2008, the expanding role of the market-based credit system called 'shadow banking' is progressing. In Europe, the banking sector's total assets have decreased by 11% since 2012, whereas the total assets of investment funds have increased by 30%. A broad concept of 'shadow banking' now represents 63% of bank assets in the euro area and more than 100% in the US.

Entities like special investment vehicles (SIVs) or conduits have receded while new forms of funds have flourished, such as: REITs, ETFs, leveraged loans, some CDO structures, and 'covenant-lite' loans.

This brings me to the core part of my intervention: what, in my view, is still missing or 'where to from here?' for financial regulation. I will concentrate on five key points: 'shadow banking'; OTC derivatives; liquidity mismatches; the macroprudential toolkit; and incentives in financial institutions.

Shadow Banking

The first point to consider concerns the insufficient information about the new market-based credit system I just described. These are non-bank institutions that, in a broad sense, perform credit intermediation. This is not bad *per se*, but the transfer of activity to the 'shadow banking' sector entails new risks that are not being monitored. Therefore, it is unclear whether the impact on the overall risk of the system is positive or negative. Even if overall leverage can become less of an issue, liquidity risks stemming from the maturity transformation may considerably increase. Take the case of investment funds, the overwhelming majority of which is of the open-ended type. As investors incur possible losses, there are as such no issues with excessive leverage. There is, however, a significant question of liquidity risk as investment funds' units are redeemable in the short term and their assets have much longer maturity. The same applies to money-market funds or ETFs. Redemption risk has to be better addressed.

'Shadow banking' is more than just non-bank entities. Shadow banking activities encompass activities often carried out by banks. These include repos and securities financing transactions and the use of different types of derivative. Part of these activities is not covered by existing statistics, justifying the designation of 'shadow banking'.

Flow-of-funds accounts record exposures but not the risk transfer generated by derivatives and become therefore misleading. At the same time, forms of quasi-money, such as secured short-term instruments that now represent and act as money in the 'shadow banking' sector, are not included in monetary statistics.

We need to create a new statistical apparatus and extend our knowledge of this new sector.

A second point: I would highlight the management of the boundary problems between regulated and less regulated sectors. Even before the crisis, the general mantra was that non-banks did not require any regulation because it was enough, from the regulated side, to supervise banks' exposures to non-banks. This was not effectively done before the crisis. And at present, the two Basel decisions, namely on the equity investments of banks in non-bank financial institutions and on the limits to large credit exposures of banks, still do not fully acknowledge the existence of 'shadow banking'. Large exposure limits relate to exposures to individual clients and not to any particular sector, notably the shadow banking sector. The Dodd-Frank Act however imposes specific quantitative limitations.

Furthermore, the FSOC in the US has the competence, which has already been activated, to declare any institution as financially systemic and therefore subject to close surveillance by the Federal Reserve. This is a powerful tool to apply to the regulated side, light- or non-regulated entities, which does not exist in other jurisdictions, notably in Europe. In my view, the question of managing the boundary problems has to be appropriately addressed through financial regulation.

The third point I want to make concerns the regulation of money market funds (MMFs), an important component of the 'shadow banking' sector. Some recommendations on MMFs have been issued by international bodies, particularly IOSCO. There is however still no clarity about what to do in terms of international standards. In the US, the approach taken was to move to variable net asset value (NAV) MMFs. In my view this is an inadequate solution. If Gary Gorton is right in his recent book (2012), variable NAVs can more easily trigger runs. David Scharfstein has also criticised this approach, which I hope will not be followed in Europe.

The fourth aspect relates to the repo market, which is an essential component of the new market-based credit system. A change in the bankruptcy laws exempting repos from automatic stays in default cases (safe harbour clause) triggered the large increase in the repo market's size. The regulation of minimum haircuts on such transactions when not centrally cleared addresses an important issue. The issue of re-hypothecation and re-use of securities in securities financing and repos that create chains of inside (or endogenous) liquidity and facilitate rises in leverage is also being examined by a new FSB work stream. Such inside liquidity creates an illusion of liquidity that disappears in stressed times. The excessive reliance on repos and the subsequent 'run on repo' were important aspects of the financial crisis. Limitations to re-hypothecation were introduced in the US to respond to this problem. This has however not been done in other jurisdictions, notably Europe. It is expected that the FSB work under way will come up with appropriate recommendations.

OTC Derivatives

OTC derivatives play an important role in the new credit system by helping to create 'relatively safe' assets by transferring or hedging risk. The move to central clearing and to trade repositories, which has been mostly voluntary, has improved transparency and safety in a significant way.

The implementation of the intended transfer of transactions to organised markets of sufficiently standardised derivatives however, has been modest. Very little has been done outside the US, where only a segment of the interest swap market has been affected. Obvious candidates to such transfers to organised markets would be certain types of standardised CDS. The present market is dominated by half a dozen institutions and what is known about transaction prices is based on quotes provided by the major players. In 2009, Myron Scholes said in a conference: "We should blow up or burn CDSs [...] and start all over again." The move to multilateral organised platforms would provide price transparency, reduce transaction costs and increase competition. It should therefore be kept on the regulatory agenda.

Liquidity Mismatches

An important regulatory change introduced after the crisis was the liquidity regulation with the two new liquidity ratios: the LCR and the

NSFR. Both ratios have been watered down since the original proposals, and the LCR, in particular, might have become too lax.

Another relevant aspect is that both ratios are static in nature and not sufficiently granular to facilitate liquidity stress testing or to constitute an overall measure of an institution's liquidity position. Brunnermeier *et al.* (2014) have proposed a new liquidity mismatch indicator (LMI) that would attribute liquidity weights to the relevant items of assets and liabilities. It would provide a sector-wide LMI and enable liquidity stress testing. It goes without saying that more information would have to be collected from the banks and non-banks, but that goes along with the necessary enhanced monitoring of liquidity in the system.

Macroprudential Policies

The regulatory reform brought to the forefront macroprudential policy as a set of regulatory instruments focused on the overall situation of the financial system. Most of the instruments are of micro-prudential nature, but applied at system-wide level, which lends them a different dimension. Macroprudential tools are now part of the ECB's policy toolkit since it was entrusted with supervisory tasks.

The objectives of the new policy include both the improvement of the financial system's resilience and the smoothing of the financial cycle, as measured by credit and asset prices developments. Empirically, it has been demonstrated that the financial cycle is normally longer than the business cycle, which implies that they evolve differently during certain periods. Testimony to this is the 'Great Moderation' period before the crisis, or the present situation. Monetary policy is directed to deal primarily with the business cycle and thus to variables like inflation and output. The general environment of low inflation and low growth which, particularly in Europe, has been recently associated with the hypothesis of secular stagnation, requires an accommodative monetary policy. At the same time, the resulting regime of low interest rates may contribute to fostering a search for yield and creating froth in some asset prices.

This requires central banks which are entrusted with safeguarding the stability of the financial system to be provided with an effective set of macroprudential policy tools. The ECB has at its disposal the instruments foreseen in the Capital Requirements Directive and Regulation

(CRD IV/CRR). These are concentrated on the banking sector. However, any froth that may exist in some European asset markets is, this time, not fuelled by bank credit, which continues to decline. The reduction in bank credit is being offset by the expansion of capital market-based financing or the enhanced role of non-bank institutions. The ECB does not have macroprudential instruments to deal with the new market-based credit system. The incoming review of CRD IV/CRR may offer an opportunity to reinforce the toolkit by including other instruments such as loan-to-value (LTV) or debt-to-income (DTI) limits, for instance, addressing risks stemming from real estate, or a more extensive use of large exposure regimes (targeting exposures to sectors rather than individual borrowers). The reality is that without more instruments, including those that the Federal Reserve already has, the ECB can hardly be made fully accountable for financial stability in the euro area.

Remuneration Incentives in Financial Institutions

The recent distressing revelation of malfeasance in several financial institutions is the most deplorable consequence of the wrong set of incentives that has prevailed in the system. Already in 2005, Raghuram Rajan in his Jackson Hole paper (2005) pointed to the destabilising role played by the bad incentives that fostered excessive search for yield and leverage. The aforementioned regulatory changes introduced since 2008 are clearly not enough. I agree with the New York Fed President's recent proposals to introduce deferred compensation (up to ten years) in the form of performance bonds subject to bail-in measures in case of the institution having to pay fines for misbehaviour or having to go into resolution.

Addressing an audience of top managers, Dudley ended with a harsh warning in case incentives did not change in financial institutions: "If that were to occur, the inevitable conclusion will be reached that your firms are too big and complex to manage effectively. In that case, financial stability concerns would dictate that your firms need to be dramatically downsized and simplified so that they can be managed effectively."

This statement illustrates the multiple dimensions that restoring confidence in finance implies. It is not just all about increasing the capital of the institutions. Many other aspects must still be taken care of if we want to ensure a transparent, trustworthy and efficient financial system.

References

Brunnermeier, M., G. Gorton and A, Krishnamurthy (eds.) (2014), *Risk Topography: Systemic Risk and Macro Modeling* (Chicago: University of Chicago Press).

Gorton, G. (2012), *Misunderstanding Financial Crises: Why We Don't See Them Coming* (Oxford: Oxford University Press).

Rajan, R. (2005), "Has Financial Development Made the World Riskier?" *Proceedings — Economic Policy Symposium*, Jackson Hole, Federal Reserve Bank of Kansas City, August, pp. 313–369. Available at: http://www.kansascityfed.org/Publicat/sympos/2005/PDF/Rajan2005.pdf.

Where To From Here?
Financial Regulation 2.0
— Chapter 27

■ Andrew W. Lo
MIT

I would like to start by thanking the Federal Reserve Bank of Chicago and the Bank of England for inviting me to participate in this conference, and am particularly grateful to Doug Evanoff for asking me to join this distinguished panel.

Unlike my fellow panelists, I may be uniquely *unqualified* to share the stage with them because I don't have any regulatory experience to speak of, nor have I been part of any government agency, so I have to admit I was a little reluctant to accept the invitation. But then I realized that my role might be to provide the perspective of private-sector finance, and I do have some experience in this respect: a few years ago I started an asset management company with which I'm still affiliated (Alpha Simplex Group). From this perspective, I would like to propose a slight change in the narrative that has been part of the current regulatory conversation.

Andrew Lo is the Charles E. and Susan T. Harris Professor at the MIT Sloan School of Management, and Director of MIT's Laboratory for Financial Engineering. He is also a principal investigator at MIT's Computer Science and Artificial Intelligence Lab, and an affiliated faculty member of the MIT Department of Electrical Engineering and Computer Science.

That narrative was reflected in comments of earlier speakers, including Alan Blinder's wonderful talk at lunch[1] about his Financial Entropy Theorem. As an erstwhile hedge fund manager, I guess I'm an example of the mouse in Alan's cat-and-mouse game that regulators engage in with the regulated. And while there may, indeed, be certain adversarial aspects of regulatory oversight, more often than not, and despite 'cognitive capture', I believe there exists a broader framework in which all stakeholders have an incentive to maintain financial stability.

So let me begin with a somewhat controversial set of graphs. These graphs will undoubtedly be interpreted differently depending on your opinion of financial innovation. They show that finance is becoming more and more important over time. Figure 1 illustrates this fact through several metrics: percentage of GDP, the number of people employed in the financial sector, the value added per capita of this sector, and the starting salaries of financiers vs. engineers. Now I'm not arguing that this is a good thing or a bad thing — it is simply a true thing, an empirical fact.

This trend is very much in keeping with the comments that Alan made in his talk, and I would like to provide what must surely be the fastest follow-up to an author's paper and presentation in our profession, despite the fact that I have not yet seen Alan's paper. I would like to frame my remarks by proposing a few corollaries to Alan's Financial Entropy Theorem, his idea that financial regulations are weakened over time except during and after financial crises and scandals, which suggests the need for periodic over-regulation.

Now when I first started listening to his talk, I was actually expecting to disagree with much of it. But as is often the case with Alan, the more I listened to him, the more I agreed with what he had to say. There's a great deal of wisdom in his Financial Entropy Theorem.

But in the spirit of encouraging open debate, let me propose a few slight modifications to some of his assumptions and then derive a few corollaries. The first modification is to emphasize that regulatory objectives are multi-dimensional. Alan acknowledged as much at the start of his talk — he listed four different objectives of regulation (protecting borrowers and lenders; protecting taxpayers; limiting financial instability; and

---

[1] *Editor's note*: Blinder's talk is Chapter 1 of this book.

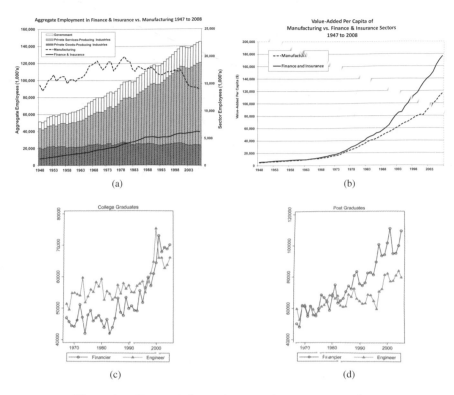

Figure 1. Finance is becoming more important over time.

Note: (a) aggregate US employment in manufacturing vs. finance and insurance sectors; (b) value-added per capita in manufacturing vs. finance and insurance; (c) and (d) Annual income of college-graduate and post-graduate engineers and financiers (all wages are in 2000 US dollars and are weighted using sampling weights), from Phillipon (2009, Figure 7).

reducing macroeconomic instability). In a multivariate setting, it isn't obvious that a one-dimensional measure of 'weakening' regulation exists, as the Financial Entropy Theorem assumes.

Moreover, when we attempt to optimize a multivariate function, things get complicated very quickly. In particular, it becomes difficult to tell whether or not we are actually maximizing the objective function as we vary one or more variables, and we can't always tell how to trade off one variable against another. For example, what if protecting today's borrowers and lenders via government guarantees hurts taxpayers 10 years from now? Or what if reducing financial instability means triggering a recession and deflation? Regulators may be making these trade-offs implicitly and intuitively, but we should be doing so explicitly and systematically.

My second modification to Alan's framework is to acknowledge that there are significant adjustment costs to formulating, implementing, changing, complying with, and skirting or 'arbitraging' regulation. In fact, the so-called '(S,s)' policies that Alan referred to — first derived by the mathematical economist Herb Scarf (1960) as the solution to a dynamic inventory control problem — are the optimal policies for dealing with transaction costs, i.e., the cost of holding an inventory of goods versus the cost of a 'stock out'. Such costs have to be factored into the Financial Entropy Theorem as we consider over-regulating markets to compensate for anticipated regulatory arbitrage. Regulatory overshooting imposes tremendous costs on society, including taxpayers, yet little research has been devoted to quantifying these costs and developing a genuine (S,s) policy to determine the appropriate amount of 'overshoot', if any.

My third modification to the Financial Entropy Theorem is to acknowledge that there is considerable risk and uncertainty in predicting the general equilibrium implications of any policy decision. This is simply a version of the well-known Lucas Critique combined with parameter uncertainty and estimation risk. We know that regulation provokes responses from the regulated, but we have not yet developed the tools to predict those responses — and the responses to the responses, and so on — with any degree of accuracy.

These three modifications are not especially controversial, but they lead to some very important corollaries of the Financial Entropy Theorem.

Corollary 1 is that over-regulating is not well defined because of the multiple dimensions of the objective function. In certain dimensions we have over-regulated, and there may well be good reason to do so, as Alan pointed out. For example, in the banking industry we definitely have added many more layers of regulation. However, we have not done so in the hedge fund industry, an industry I'm particularly familiar with, and I can attest to the fact that hedge funds have more flexibility today than they did a decade ago.

Also, as we over-emphasize macroprudential policies, we may end up short-changing other objectives such as investor protection. For example, the low-interest-rate environment facilitated by the Fed's quantitative easing program has encouraged investors to seek out higher-yielding investments, some of which offer higher yields by taking on additional and subtle risk exposures that the typical retail investor may not fully appreciate.

As a result, Corollary 2 of the Financial Entropy Theorem is that the chances of unintended consequences increase with over-regulation as regulated entities adapt to these changes in complex and unpredictable ways.

Corollary 3 is that there will be even more brain power drawn to the financial industry to deal with these complexities. We can argue whether this is good or bad, but the fact is that it is already happening. Given the large frictions in the labor market, this artificially induced incentive to choose a career in financial services can impose tremendous adjustment costs on society, not to mention the opportunity cost of forgone careers in cancer research and other social priorities.

Corollary 4 is perhaps the most important: over-regulation increases the complexity of the financial system, which can reduce financial stability and be a source of systemic risk in and of itself.

So let me get to the point of this panel: *where to from here?* The short answer for me is "I have no idea"; I'll let my fellow panelists answer this question. But I do want to propose a different narrative. Rather than blaming the adversarial relationship between regulators and the regulated for threats to financial stability, we should turn to the fact that financial technology has become more important and more complex today than ever before. As a result, financial crises can be easily explained by the combination of powerful financial technologies coupled with age-old human behavior. Therefore, what is needed most may not be over-regulation or under-regulation but smarter, more effective regulation — in engineering terms, more 'robust' regulatory technology, or Financial Regulation version 2.0.

Developing such robust regulations is not a simple task. However, it is easy to identify the starting point: more data and better measures of systemic risk. We all know that the shadow banking system is a problem and that we need to bring more institutions out of the shadows. But we're also familiar with the unavoidable trade-off between transparency and privacy — the regulator's need for data balanced against the private sector's need for privacy to protect trade secrets and client confidentiality.

And so I want to start wrapping up by presenting one example of new regulatory technology that allows us to balance these two competing objectives in an elegant fashion using results from a completely different field: computer science. By applying well-known methods from the field of secure multi-party computation, it turns out that we can have our cake and eat it too, sharing certain kinds of information while keeping private other information. Let me give you a simple example of how this works.

What do you think the average salary is of all the attendees in this room? We've got central bankers that aren't paid very well, but we also have a few investment bankers who are paid considerably more. To get us started, can I get a volunteer to tell me what his or her annual salary is? Nobody? Well, this isn't surprising because salaries are very private — unless you happen to be from a Chinese family and your mother asks you what your salary is, you generally keep this information to yourself!

So let me start by telling you what my salary is, and then showing you how we can calculate the average salary in this room. Now I'm not going to tell you what my salary is by itself. I'm going to give you my salary plus a random number of my choice, a random number that only I know and which I intend to keep strictly private. And so that sum — my annual salary plus that random number — is US$15 (presumably, I've added a negative number to my salary!). I'm going to reveal that sum to David and I'm going ask David to add to this number his salary and his random number that only he knows. And after he does that, he'll pass the sum to Vitor, who adds his salary and his random number before passing the new sum to Svein, and so on. This process continues throughout the rest of the room until the very last person then gets the sum of salaries and random numbers, say Charlie, and then he adds his salary and his random number to it. Suppose that number is US$28 billion. That sum gets passed back to me, and then I subtract my random number and then pass it to David, who subtracts his random number and passes it to Vitor, and this process continues until Charlie gets the number and subtracts his random number, at which point he has the sum of everybody's salary which, when divided by the number of people in the room, is the average salary. At no point during this entire process did any one of us have to reveal our annual salaries, yet we are able to compute the average salary of everyone in the room.

Now this very simple and beautiful algorithm can easily be gamed. For example, if David and I colluded we could probably figure out what Vitor's salary is by comparing our individual pieces of information. But there are very easy ways to make this algorithm cheat-proof, to the point where the security of this algorithm is as cryptographically secure as the Amazon transactions you engage in when you submit your credit card number online.

In Abbe *et al.* (2012), we show how this technique — known in the computer science literature as "secure multi-party computation" — can be used to encrypt highly propriety data from banks, broker/dealers, and other financial institutions while still allowing regulators to compute aggregate risk measures such as sums, averages, value-at-risk, loss probabilities, and Herfindahl indexes. Figure 2 provides a concrete illustration of this technology applied to the sizes of the real-estate loan portfolios of Bank of America, JP Morgan, and Wells Fargo. Figure 2(a) contains the individual time series for these three institutions (the line graphs), which are the proprietary information of each institution and only publicly disclosed with a lag. From a systemic-risk perspective, the individual values are of less importance than the aggregate sum, depicted by the bar graph in Figure 2(a). Using a particular algorithm designed just for this purpose, Abbe *et al.* (2012) show that the individual time series can be encrypted, as in the line graphs in Figure 2(b), yet the sum of the encrypted time series yields the very same bar graph as in Figure 2(a). Aggregate sums can be shared by financial institutions while maintaining the privacy of each institution.

Of course, techniques like secure multi-party computation certainly do not eliminate the need for regulations or regulators — for example, there is no way to ensure that institutions report truthfully other than through periodic examination — but they can lower the cost of sharing certain types of information and provide incentives for the private sector to do so voluntarily. If financial institutions can maintain the privacy of their trade secrets while simultaneously sharing information that leads

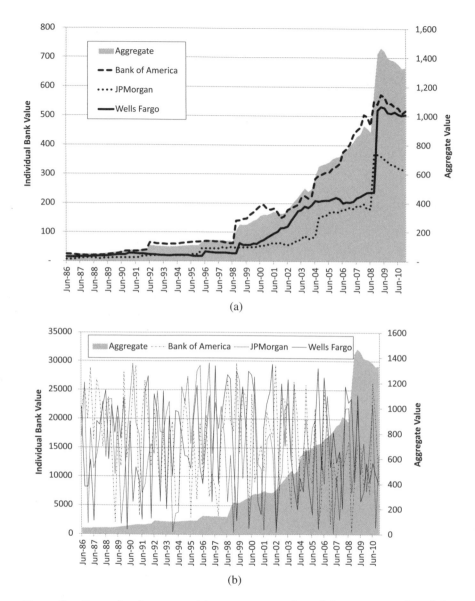

Figure 2. Example of secure multi-party computation of the aggregate size of the real-estate loan portfolios of Bank of America, JP Morgan, and Wells Fargo.

Source: Abbe *et al.* (2012).

to more accurate measures of threats to financial stability, they stand to benefit as much as the regulators and the public.

So let me conclude by pointing out that there are many examples where Blinder's Financial Entropy Theorem can be addressed by better technology. We know that the financial system is getting much more complicated and there's not much we can (or should) do to fight that trend. However, the one thing we *can* do to reduce potential threats to financial stability is to provide more data and better measures to create the necessary feedback loops to increase financial stability, and to simplify regulatory oversight as Haldane and Madouros (2012) called for in their insightful 'dog and frisbee' article.

The financial system is too complicated for any one individual to understand, but if we have the necessary data to compute more accurate measures of systemic risk, we have a chance of being able to deal with that complexity in a more efficient manner.

We cannot easily measure the quantity of regulation we have, so we may not be able to determine whether we need more regulation or less regulation. But I'm fairly certain that we need better regulation — Financial Regulation 2.0 — and technology can help us get there.

References

Abbe, E., A. Khandani and A. Lo (2012), "Privacy-Preserving Methods for Sharing Financial Risk Exposures," *American Economic Review: Papers and Proceedings*, 102: 65–70.

Haldane, A. and V. Madouros (2012), "The Dog and the Frisbee," speech at the Federal Reserve Bank of Kansas City's 366th economic policy symposium, *The Changing Policy Landscape*, Jackson Hole, Wyoming, August 31.

Philippon, T. and A. Reshef (2009), "Wages and Human Capital in the U.S. Financial Industry: 1996-2006," NBER Working Paper 14644. Available at: http://www.nber.org/papers/w14644.

Scarf, H. (1960), "The Optimality of (S,s) Policies in the Dynamic Inventory Problem", In K. Arrow, S. Karlin, P. Suppes (eds.), *Mathematical Models in the Social Sciences, 1959: Proceedings of the First Stanford Symposium* (California: Stanford University Press), pp. 196–202.

Key Fragilities of the Financial System

— CHAPTER 28

■ Randall S. Kroszner
University of Chicago

To determine 'where to from here', we first have to determine exactly where we are. I very much agree with Vitor Constâncio that we are not quite sure where 'here' is yet, that is, we have not fully assessed the impact of the dramatic changes in regulation and supervision of the financial system since 2008.

In order to understand where we are and where we should go, it is important to identify the key fragilities of the financial system and assess the extent of the progress we have made on addressing them. Such an exercise will then allow us to highlight where further reform would be most beneficial.

From my perspective, the key fragilities fall into three categories: *leverage, liquidity,* and *interconnections* (see Kroszner and Melick 2011; Kroszner and Shiller 2011; and, Kroszner 2012). Svein Andresen has explained many of specifics of what international regulators have done and are doing to address these, including: increases in the quantity and quality of capital, introduction of liquidity requirements and more careful liquidity monitoring, and a variety of changes — from encouraging the migration of over-the-counter (OTC) derivatives onto centrally

---

Randall S. Kroszner is the Norman R. Bobins Professor of Economics at the University of Chicago's Booth School of Business.

cleared platforms to improvements in the resolution regimes for large financial institutions — to begin to address the interconnectedness issue. Also, risk-management and market practices have evolved in response to the crisis.

The first fundamental question is: How far have we gotten in fact in addressing the fragilities? Since many of the reforms are in process of being phased in or are relatively new, this is not a straightforward task. One simple, and by no means perfect, summary measure would be the movements in large US bank credit default swap (CDS) spreads over time. These CDS provide a window into how risks associated with holding the debt of key players in the financial system have been perceived over time.

As illustrated in Kroszner (forthcoming), in the years prior to the financial crisis, the CDS spreads for these institutions was extremely low and showed little variation across institutions or over time. That suggests that the markets were pricing in either virtually no risk of default or the expectation of complete bailout. (It is difficult to distinguish between these two explanations from these data.) During the crisis, the spreads explode and vary significantly over time and across institutions. Since 2009, the CDS spreads have come down but remain substantially above where they were pre-crisis and continue to vary across firms and over time. These data suggest then that the market perceives more risk to bond holders despite significantly higher equity capital (that is, lower leverage) greater liquidity, and fewer risky activities being undertaken by these institutions. Importantly, these risk perceptions are now differentiated across institutions and vary over time with overall changes in market and economic risks, e.g., they rose during the initial phases of the Euro-crisis and came down subsequently.

Now these data alone do not necessarily mean that 'too big to fail' has gone away, but it is worth noting that there does seem to be now more market monitoring or market awareness of risk and more differentiation among institutions. These movements would suggest that at least some progress has been made since the financial crisis to address some aspects of the underlying fragilities. Obviously, this doesn't give us a specific measure but gives some information about 'where we are'.

Parsing out exactly what reforms are driving the change in risk perceptions is not straightforward. Certainly changes like significant increases in equity capital and liquidity from pre-crisis levels must be part of this. Greater awareness of the interconnection issues for risk management and supervision are helpful, but as Vitor said, we have made not as much formal progress as we would like in, for example, actually migrating OTC derivatives onto centrally-cleared platforms. We have the structures that we're getting in place but we're not where we would like to be on this issue yet. We need to assess the cumulative effects of private changes as well as government changes in regulation, to fully understand 'where we are', but it is clear some progress has been made.

The second fundamental question is: What are the highest priority areas for reform going forward? To think about the next steps in policy, as well as to evaluate in more detail the steps that we have taken, we need to have a framework for analyzing risks and rewards. Some earlier speakers including Luc Laeven [Chapter 16] and Alan Blinder [Chapter 1] have mentioned this. Introducing into the policy discussion an explicit framework for considering trade-offs between costs and benefits of reform has been a hobby horse of mine for quite some time (see, e.g., Kroszner 2011; 2012; 2014; and, Kroszner and Strahan 2011; 2014). The notion of trade-offs is often lost in the policy discuss.

Consider capital requirements. In principle, we should be weighing the benefits of increases in stability that come from increasing banks' loss absorbing cushion against potential costs in terms of higher costs and/or lower supply of credit. Moving from a common equity requirement of 2% pre-crisis to 4.5% or 8% under Basel III, including various add-ons, the costs have likely been relatively low. Post-crisis, markets would have demanded significantly higher common equity cushions for banks. The question moving forward concerns the potential costs of increasing capital requirements from here. The 2014 Total Loss Absorbing Capital (TLAC) proposal from the G-20 could drive capital minimum significantly higher than where we are. We are still in comment phase of that proposal so we don't know the levels or the instruments that will be considered 'loss absorbing', but it is in the ranges being contemplated that it would be valuable to consider seriously the possible trade-offs between lower leverage and higher borrowing costs or lower credit availability.

There's a large empirical literature, most of it pre-crisis, on banking and finance as an important contributor to economic growth (e.g., Levine 2005; 2011; Arcand *et al.* 2012; Cecchetti and Kharroubi, 2012; Dell'Ariccia *et al.* 2012; Kroszner 2007; 2013, Kroszner *et al.* 2007; Kroszner and Strahan 2014). The results of this work suggested that deeper, larger, and more developed banking and financial systems were drivers of growth. These results seem to have largely been absent in the policy debates over the last few years but, as Vitor mentioned, they are starting to come back in.

Unfortunately, there have been very few studies updating the earlier work to take into account the financial crisis. I think that would be a very valuable for researchers at the many of academic and policy institutions represented here to delve into this issue. Ultimately, the policy makers should be calibrating their choices of capital minima to the costs and benefits. It is thus valuable to have some rough estimates of how much an additional unit of capital reduces the likelihood of the failure of a large institution and of shocks ramifying through the system versus the potential for reduction in credit and, possibly, growth.

That's the ideal of where we want to go. We're very far from there. That doesn't mean that we shouldn't be doing anything and I don't want to suggest that we should succumb to 'analysis, paralysis', that is, we have to have everything completely worked out before we act. It is important, however, to try as best as possible to assess the costs and benefits, particularly where we have already made significant changes, like increases in capital requirements.

The notion of a trade-off is starting to come back into the discussion, more in Europe than in the U.S. Vitor and many of his colleagues, for example, have mentioned their concerns about the real impact on the economy of insufficient lending and about transmission mechanism of monetary policy. Part of the motivation in Europe for buying asset-backed securities is to try to help get some of these assets off of the banks' balance sheets to give them a little more capacity to be able to lend.

Given the uncertainties, we should avoid having a false sense of security by focusing, perhaps excessively, on capital as the cure for all ills.

I've suggested before that the focus on capital requirements could have a potential parallel to the Maginot Line (see Kroszner 2012). Policy makers have placed so much emphasis on capital in the beginning that they can lose sight on other important regulatory reforms. Also, as you keep focusing on one particular mechanism, you give very strong incentives to find ways around that particular mechanism.

That's exactly what the Germans did in World War I. The French built a well-fortified concrete bunker along the border, and some of the Maginot Line still survives today. This structure, however, gave the Germans incentives to find ways to undermine its effectiveness. They did this in two ways. First, they looked for the weak spot. The French did not build the fortification through the Ardennes forest because they assumed it was too dense for a rapid invasion. Second, they innovated the concept of the "blitzkrieg" and the Panzer tank that would allow them to roll a large force through a forest like the Ardennes quickly.

The Maginot Line gave the French a false sense of confidence that the Germans could not invade quickly so they didn't invest in other technologies or maintain a large standing army. The technological and conceptual innovations by the Germans then allowed a rapid invasion, and France fell within weeks. The lesson is that we should not take too much comfort in any one type of regulatory protection.

Stress tests and scenario analyses are crucial tools for exploring the potential weak points and vulnerabilities of capital requirements. As such, they are also crucial for trying to assess 'where we are' and where we need to be going. There has been a revulsion against the use of models in capital calculations and stress tests but I think that's gone too far. Certainly, supervisors should avoid a false sense of confidence from risk modeling, but it would be foolish to ignore the systematic assessment of data and risks that models can provide. Til Schuermann captured this idea when earlier today he said, "You don't want models on and brain off." I very much agree that makes no sense at all.

The data we have, even if stretching back a few decades, may not be sufficient to model and estimate the 'once in every 25 years or 50 years or hundred years' shocks. That's not to say that the data sets or the estimation exercises are worthless. I think they're very valuable in trying to be systematic and thinking about the risks; however, they are necessary but not sufficient. To try to mitigate the 'models on, brain off' phenomenon, when I was at the Fed I tried to link an experienced senior supervisor, who may not have had deep technical skills, with the modeler, so that they as a team would be more likely to be asking the right questions and doing the right analysis. In addition, my hope was that each would appreciate what the other brings to the table so that each would realize that neither alone has the complete answer. Trying to do this in practice, never easy, I believe has high value.

In some sense, the best of the stress tests do exactly that. They are models-based, but the questions that they're asking are ones that try to explore the gaps in the data or the models. Martin Hellwig mentioned yesterday the problems of non-stationarity, changing risks, and limits of historical data. Surely, there are fundamental problems but that doesn't mean models are worthless. They can provide benchmarks. The key is not to have a false sense of confidence in them and to realize that supervisors need to do scenario analyses to explore the limits and vulnerabilities of the models themselves. I think that can be very valuable.

Improvements in risk measurement, monitoring, and management also need to be instilled in the culture of the supervised institutions. In 2008, the Fed and other supervisors undertook a 'senior supervisors group survey' of risk management practices within major financial services firms. It revealed that practices varied widely regardless of the formal structure of risk management and monitoring within the firm, and that often senior executives were not actively engaged in understanding and monitoring enterprise-wide risks. Risk management had to go beyond PowerPoint presentations. Often, in practice, risk managers had a difficult time really making a difference in the operations of firms.

It would be valuable to consider having senior executives, in consultation with the risk committee of the board, report to the supervisors about what risks they see and how they are mitigating those risks. Rather than using the supervisors as, in some sense, a consulting firm, to advise the board and the senior management on where the risks are, it would be valuable to consider having the financial institution be proactive in this. Obviously the supervisors need to be doing their own assessment, but we can perhaps change the conversation a bit to have more active engagement on the financial institution side, which may help to empower the chief risk officer and her staff. The stress tests involve some of this, e.g., effectively grading subjectively the internal risk modeling, measurement, and mitigation, but it may be helpful to make this more explicit.

In conclusion, I come back to the three fundamental fragilities of *liquidity, leverage, and interconnections.* Supervisors and institutions always should be thinking about the sources of the fragility in evaluating the risks of the system and of individual institutions in that context. We should be clear about what we know and not shy about what we don't know about 'where we are' in order to determine what data and analysis we need to figure out 'where to from here'. We have made progress on leverage and liquidity, but I'm more skeptical about how much progress we have made in practice on interconnectedness, particularly on the robustness of the market and legal infrastructure (Kroszner and Shiller 2011). That's where I would like to see more emphasis going forward, in particular on OTC derivatives, tri-party repos, and on cross-border resolution. Ultimately, we would want to integrate our framework for analyzing regulatory and supervisory reforms on financial stability with a monetary policy framework for central banks that encompasses financial stability considerations (e.g., Borio and Lowe 2003; Stein 2014; Bean *et al.* 2015).

References

Arcand, J.-L., E. Berkes and U. Panizza (2012), "Too much Finance?" IMF Working Paper No. 12/161, Table 2.

Bean, C., C. Broda, T. Ito and R. Kroszner (2015), "Low for Long? Causes and Consequences of Persistently Low Interest Rates," International Center for Money and Banking, Geneva Report 17.

Borio, C. and P. Lowe (2003), "Imbalances or 'Bubbles?' Implications for monetary and financial stability," In W. C. Hunter, G. G. Kaufman and M. Pomerleano (eds.) *Asset Price Bubbles,* (Cambridge, MA: MIT Press), pp. 247–270.

Cecchetti, S. and E. Kharroubi (2012), "Reassessing the Impact of Finance on Growth," Bank for International Settlements Working Paper 381, July.

Dell'Ariccia, G., D. Igan, L. Laeven, H. Tong, B. Bakker and J. Vandenbussche (2012), "Policies for Macrofinancial Stability: How to deal with credit booms," IMF Staff Discussion Note 12/06 (Washington: International Monetary Fund).

Kroszner, R. S. (2007), "Analyzing and Assessing Banking Crises," speech at Federal Reserve Bank of San Francisco, Conference on the Asian Financial Crisis Revisited, September 6.

Kroszner, R. S. (2011), "Challenges for MacroPrudential Supervision," In S. Claessens, D. Evanoff, G. Kaufman and L. Kodres. (eds.) *Macroprudential Regulatory Policies: The New Road to Financial Stability?* Hackensack, NJ: World Scientific Publishing, pp. 379–86.

Kroszner, R. S. (2012), "Stability, Growth, and Regulatory Reform," In *Financial Stability Review: Public Debt, Monetary Policy, and Financial Stability*, Banque de France, Paris, April, pp. 87–93.

Kroszner, R. S. (2014), "Fire Extinguishers and Smoke Detectors: Macroprudential policy and financial resiliency," *Banking Perspectives*, Quarter 4, 2014: 16–20.

Kroszner, R. S. (forthcoming), "A Review of Bank Funding Cost Differentials," *Journal of Financial Services Research*.

Kroszner, R. S., L. Laeven and D. Klingebiel (2007), "Banking Crises, Financial Dependence, and Growth," *Journal of Financial Economics*, 84(1): 187–228.

Kroszner, R. S. and W. Melick, (2011), "The Response of the Federal Reserve to the Recent Banking and Financial Crisis" In J. Pisani-Ferry, A. Posen and F. Saccomanni (eds.) *An Ocean Apart? Comparing Transatlantic Responses to the Financial Crisis*, Brussels: Bruegel Institute and Peterson Institution for International Economics, pp. 148–182.

Kroszner, R. S. and P. E. Strahan (2011), "Financial Regulatory Reform: Challenges ahead," *American Economic Review, Papers and Proceedings*, 101(3): 242–46.

Kroszner, R. S. and P. E. Strahan (2014), "Regulation and Deregulation of the U.S. Banking Industry: Causes, consequences, and implications for the future," In N. Rose (ed.) *Studies in Regulation*, Chicago: NBER and University of Chicago, pp. 485–543.

Kroszner, R. S. and R. Shiller (2011), *Reforming US Financial Regulation: Before and beyond Dodd–Frank* (Cambridge, MA: MIT Press).

Levine, R. (2005), "Finance and Growth: Theory and evidence," In P. Aghion and S. N. Durlauf (eds.) *Handbook of Economic Growth*, Amsterdam: North-holland Publishing, pp. 865–934.

Levine, R. (2011), "Regulating Finance and Regulators to Promote Growth," In Federal Reserve Bank of Kansas City, *Symposium on Achieving Maximum Long-Run Growth*, Jackson Hole, pp. 271–312.

Stein, J. C. (2014), "Incorporating Financial Stability Considerations into a Monetary Policy Framework," speech at the International Research Forum on Monetary Policy, Washington, DC, March 21.

Where to From Here for Financial Regulatory Policy?

Analyzing Housing Finance

— CHAPTER 29

■ David Scharfstein
Harvard University

The financial crisis of 2007–2009 revealed major deficiencies in financial regulation. Since then, policymakers around the world have undertaken a major overhaul of financial regulation, particularly in the realm of bank regulation. These reforms include:

- An increase in the quantity and quality of capital that banks are required to hold, particularly for the largest, most systemically important banks.
- The greater use of stress tests for the largest, most systemically important banks to ensure that they have enough capital to withstand a stress scenario.
- Increase in liquid asset holdings for banks with less stable short-term funding (combined with a proposal that such banks also hold more capital).

David Scharfstein is the Edmund Cogswell Converse Professor of Finance and Banking at the Harvard Business School.

- Enhanced authority to restructure liabilities of banks and affiliated non-bank subsidiaries, and agreement to require banks to issue debt that can be written down in times of a crisis (i.e., 'bailed-in').
- Requirements that many derivatives be traded through clearing-houses rather than in over-the-counter markets.

This panel was asked to address the question: 'Where to from here?' I could answer with any number of suggestions about how to improve on capital and liquidity requirements, design better resolution regimes and bail-in bonds, and enhance the oversight of clearinghouses. But instead, let me discuss an aspect of regulation and financial intermediation that has received somewhat less attention, or where policymakers have made less progress. I will focus on housing finance, but there are a number of other areas that deserve greater scrutiny including asset management, the structure of the bond market, credit ratings, compensation, and the size and scope of banking institutions.

It is, of course, well understood that the proximate cause of the financial crisis was the housing boom and bust in the United States. While there are a number of views about what caused the boom and bust, it is well documented that the increase in household leverage on the way up, and the difficulty households and lenders faced in dealing with this leverage on the way down, were key elements of the financial crisis and the resulting deep recession. The US experience is hardly unique; Jorda *et al.* (2014) document that since World War II increases in mortgage credit were predictive of financial crises around the world. This period is one in which banks around the world took a much greater role in housing finance.

And while the system has arguably been made more resilient to real estate shocks through the measures listed above (capital, liquidity, resolution etc.), little progress has been made in addressing the underlying risks in the housing finance system that could generate financial system shocks. This is a major shortcoming of reform efforts. Indeed, if we had a more stable system of housing finance, we would not need to be as aggressive in enhancing the capital and liquidity of financial institutions. For example, if homebuyers were required to put down 20% to purchase a home and cash-out refinancing was limited, then mortgage defaults would be significantly reduced both because leverage-induced housing booms would be less likely and house price declines would be less likely to wipe out homeowner equity. This, in turn, would limit losses on financial institutions and negative spillovers to the rest of the economy of the sort documented by Mian *et al.* (2013) and Chodorow-Reich (2014). Whether such a housing policy is desirable is open to debate, but an implication of allowing a less stable housing finance system is that we need a more resilient banking system.

The US housing finance system is currently dominated by the government entities — Fannie Mae and Freddie Mac (now under the government conservatorship) and the Federal Housing Administration (a government agency). These entities now guarantee over 80% of all new mortgages that were issued in 2013. These government guaranteed loans account for an overwhelming share of mortgage securitization. Private label securitization exists only for the highest quality mortgages that do not qualify for government guarantees. Private subprime lending is essentially non-existent. The risk to the financial system is modest in the current environment in which most mortgages are government guaranteed and the others are of very high quality.

But there will come a time when the private sector will take on more mortgage risk. The leading housing finance reform proposals — such as the proposal by Senators Johnson and Crapo, which was approved by the Senate Banking Committee but failed to advance to the floor of the US Senate — envision private entities, possibly affiliated with banks, offering mortgage guarantees and buying reinsurance from a government entity. The down payments required for such guarantees could end up being quite low, which will put private financial intermediaries at considerable risk. There will also come a time when private subprime mortgages will again be issued in larger numbers. Financial institutions will need more loss absorbing capacity and liquidity to protect themselves from these mortgage risks. As far as I know, the current regulatory capital regime does not require banks to hold more capital against riskier mortgages. Indeed, historically there appears to be a *positive* relationship between the leverage of the household sector and the leverage of the banking sector. That is, just when the household sector levers up and poses more risk to the banking sector, the banking sector also

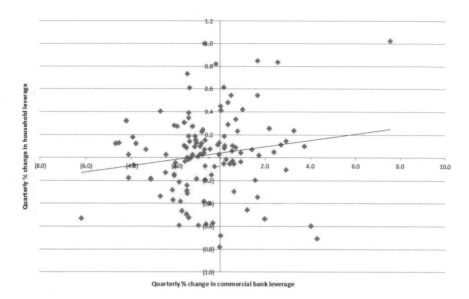

Figure 1. Commercial bank vs. household leverage (quarterly % changes).

Data Source: Financial Accounts of the United States, Board of Governors of the Federal Reserve System. Data period is 1984Q1–2014Q2.

appears to increase its leverage. This is evident in the Figure below, which shows a modest positive relationship between the quarterly change in household leverage and the quarterly change in commercial bank leverage during the period 1984–2014. While the underlying forces that drive this relationship are unclear (and worthy of more investigation), it seems clear that this is not good from a financial stability perspective. What we would like to see is just the opposite: the banking sector should reduce its leverage when the household sector increases its leverage.

Going forward, regulators need to think more carefully about the tradeoff between household leverage and banking leverage. The tendency will always be for the political system to facilitate greater household leverage, partly in an attempt to increase affordability and encourage homeownership. Regardless of what one thinks of these objectives and the ability of government to meet these objectives, regulators need to make sure there is adequate capital and liquidity — both for individual financial institutions and the financial system as a whole — to absorb the losses arising from high levels of household leverage. Our bank regulatory regime needs to adapt to whatever emerges as the new housing finance system, but in designing a new housing finance system we also need to be mindful of its implications for financial stability.

References

Chodorow-Reich, G. (2014), "The Employment Effects of Credit Market Disruptions: Firm-level evidence from the 2008–2009 financial crisis," *Quarterly Journal of Economics*, 129(1): 1–59.

Jorda, O., M. Schularick and A. Taylor (2014), "The Great Mortgage: Housing Finance, Crises, and Business Cycles," National Bureau of Economic Research, Working Paper No. 20501.

Mian, A., K. Rao and A. Sufi (2013), "Household Balance Sheets, Consumption and the Economic Slump," *Quarterly Journal of Economics*, 128(4): 1687–1726.

Index